ALSO BY JACKIE WULLSCHLAGER

Inventing Wonderland

H. C. Andersen.

Jackie Wullschlager

Hans Christian Andersen

The Life of a Storyteller

ALFRED A. KNOPF · NEW YORK
2001

THIS IS A BORZOI BOOK
PUBLISHED BY ALFRED A. KNOPF

Copyright © 2000 by Jackie Wullschlager
All rights reserved under International and Pan-American Copyright Conventions. Published in the United States by Alfred A.
Knopf, a division of Random House, Inc., New York. Distributed
by Random House, Inc., New York.

www.aaknopf.com

Originally published in Great Britain by Allen Lane
The Penguin Press, London, in 2000.

Knopf, Borzoi Books and the colophon are registered trademarks
of Random House, Inc.

Library of Congress Cataloging-in-Publication Data
Wullschlager, Jackie.
  Hans Christian Andersen : the life of a storyteller / Jackie
Wullschlager. — 1st American ed.
    p.   cm.
  Includes bibliographical references and index.
  ISBN 0-679-45508-6 (alk. paper)
  1. Andersen, H. C. (Hans Christian), 1805–1875. 2. Authors,
Danish—19th century—Biography. I. Title.
PT8119.W85 2001
839.8'136—dc21
[B]   00-062003

Manufactured in the United States of America
First American Edition

Frontispiece:
Andersen in Copenhagen, aged sixty-seven;
photograph by Budtz Müller, 1872.

FOR WILLIAM

CONTENTS

(Photographic acknowledgements in parentheses)

The endpapers show a papercut made by Andersen at Frijsenborg Manor, July 1865, in a private collection

Frontispiece: Budtz Müller, photograph of H. C. Andersen, 15th October 1872 (photo: The Royal Library, Copenhagen, Department of Maps, Prints and Photographs)

Page 15: Søren Læssøe Lange, *Odense*, 1805 (photo: © Odense City Museums/ The Hans Christian Andersen Museum)

Pages 18, 31: Johan Henrik Trytzschler Hanck, *Munke Mølle*, 1836 and 1831 (photos: © Odense City Museums/The Hans Christian Andersen Museum)

Page 37: Heinrich Hansen, *View from Gammelstrand, Copenhagen*, 1836–1868 (photo: DOWIC Fotografi/Statens Museum for Kunst, Copenhagen)

Page 40: Peter Christian Klæstrup, *Høkerloge*, c. 1870 (photo: Copenhagen City Museum)

Page 61: Jens-Christian Deichmann, *Caricature of Professor Meisling*, c. 1840–1856 (photo: © Odense City Museums/The Hans Christian Andersen Museum)

Page 82: Johan-Vilhelm Gertner, *Portrait of Jonas Collin*, 1839 (photo: © Odense City Museums/The Hans Christian Andersen Museum)

Page 96: Photograph of Riborg Voigt, c. 1840 (photo: © Odense City Museums/The Hans Christian Andersen Museum)

Page 101: Hans Christian Andersen, *Self-portrait Confined in a Bottle*, c. 1830 (photo: © Odense City Museums/The Hans Christian Andersen Museum); Hans Christian Andersen, *The Poet's Grave*, 1831 (photo: © Odense City Museums/The Hans Christian Andersen Museum)

Page 112: Adam Müller, *Portrait of Ludvig Müller*, 1836 (photo: The Royal Library, Copenhagen, Department of Maps, Prints and Photographs)

Page 117: Wilhelm Marstrand, *Louise Collin*, 1833 (photo: © Odense City Museums/The Hans Christian Andersen Museum)

Page 125: Portrait of Hans Christian Andersen, 1833, by Adam Müller © Odense City Museums/The Hans Christian Andersen Museum;

ACKNOWLEDGEMENTS

Anyone writing on Andersen owes an incalculable debt to the Danish scholars whose outstanding critical editions of his works, letters and diaries are the bedrock of all subsequent study. This book would have been impossible without the authoritative work begun in the 1930s and continued throughout the twentieth century by Helge Topsøe-Jensen, Svend Larsen, Erik Dal and Elias Bredsdorff, and I am deeply grateful to them.

I had the good fortune to receive the direct help and encouragement of Professor Dal and Professor Bredsdorff in Copenhagen, and I thank them and their wives, Astrid Dal and Anne Lise Bredsdorff, for the warmth and hospitality with which they received me into their homes. I benefited inestimably from their wisdom and generosity, and hope that when they disagree with my interpretations and conclusions here, they will be indulgent.

It was a pleasure, too, to discuss Andersen with the next generation of scholars in Denmark. In Copenhagen, another most generous host, Professor Klaus Mortensen, shaped my thinking on Andersen's youth, and kindly took time off from his busy schedule to read my manuscript and to make many valuable suggestions. Dr. Niels Kofoed shared with me his fascinating insights into Andersen's early works, Professor Hans Hertel gave me essential historical background and my friend Professor Sten Engelstoft was the perfect guide to his country's geography. In Odense, I learnt much from Professor Johan de Mylius of the Hans Christian Andersen Centre and Niels Oxenvad, former director of the Hans Christian Andersen Hus.

The staff of many Danish institutions were unfailingly helpful and patient in tracing books and pictures, giving me information or showing me round: in Copenhagen at Det Kongelige Bibliotek, Københavns Bymuseum, Den Hirschsprungske Samling, Tivoli, the Lokalhistorisk Cafe in Østerbro, Teatermuseet, Frederiksborg Museet and the Thorvaldsen Museum; in Odense at the Hans Christian Andersen Centre and the Hans Christian Andersen Hus, and elsewhere in Denmark at Gisselfeldt Slot, Helsingør Kommunes Museer and Den Voigtske Gaard in Faaborg. I thank too the staff of the British Library in London for much assistance and attentiveness.

As I retraced Andersen's life in Denmark and his travels across Europe, I had the pleasure of incurring many debts. I began and finished my research as the guest in Copenhagen of Sten Engelstoft and Rosemarie Boeck, who repeatedly and lavishly opened their home to me and my family. The Hotel Angleterre in Copenhagen and Brøndums Hotel in Skagen—both places where Andersen stayed—invited me as their guest, and the Danish Tourist Board in London arranged one of my visits. In Germany, I enjoyed the hospitality of the Berlin Intercontinental and of Marion Andert and Jürgen Wengel, in Italy of Holly Snapp, and in Sevenoaks of Martin and Catherine Rodger.

My heartfelt gratitude goes to my two wonderfully sympathetic editors, Stuart Proffitt at Penguin and Charles Elliot at Knopf, and to my agent and friend Carol Heaton for her enthusiasm and support of all sorts. I am under obligation also to the people at Penguin who worked on my behalf: Pernilla Pearce, Karen Whitlock, Cecilia Mackay, Daniel Hind, Juliet Mitchell, and to a series of literary and arts editors at the *Financial Times*, J. D. F. Jones, Annalena McAfee, Peter Aspden and Jan Dalley, for their interest and understanding.

I should particularly like to thank Dinah Cannell, Peder Holtermann, Dorte Larsen and Alice Thomson for help with points of translation and Danish history, and Alastair Macaulay and Ann Geneva, who made the writing of this book easier and more enjoyable by indulging me in many long afternoons of discussions about Andersen and biography.

The Winston Churchill Trust generously awarded me a Fellowship which allowed me to spend a summer of research in Denmark. I am grateful to the trustees, to the Society of Authors for grants from the Authors' Foundation and the K Blundell Trust, and to the Arts Council for a Literature Award which enabled me to finish the book.

Lastly, my greatest thanks are to my family. My mother, Maria Wullschläger, was the best of companions on my travels, and indefatigably generous in help of all kinds at home, from finding obscure texts to looking after my children. For Naomi, Zoë and Raphaël, Andersen has been a presence in their lives for as long as they can remember; they have never tired of reading his tales with me and giving their own eclectic interpretations, and have happily followed me round Europe. Most of all, I thank my husband William Cannell, for his love and ceaseless encouragement; without him, this time as ever, there would have been no book.

H. C. Andersen's Denmark, c. 1850

SKAGERRAK

Skagen

KATTEGAT

Viborg

JYLLAND
(JUTLAND)

Aarhus

D E N M A R K

Elsinore

Copenhagen

SJÆLLAND
(ZEALAND)

Bogense

Odense

Slagelse

Sorø

FYN
(FUNEN)

Korsør

Nyborg

Faaborg

Svendborg

Flensburg

SCHLESWIG

Rendsburg

Kiel

HOLSTEIN

GERMANY

Hamburg

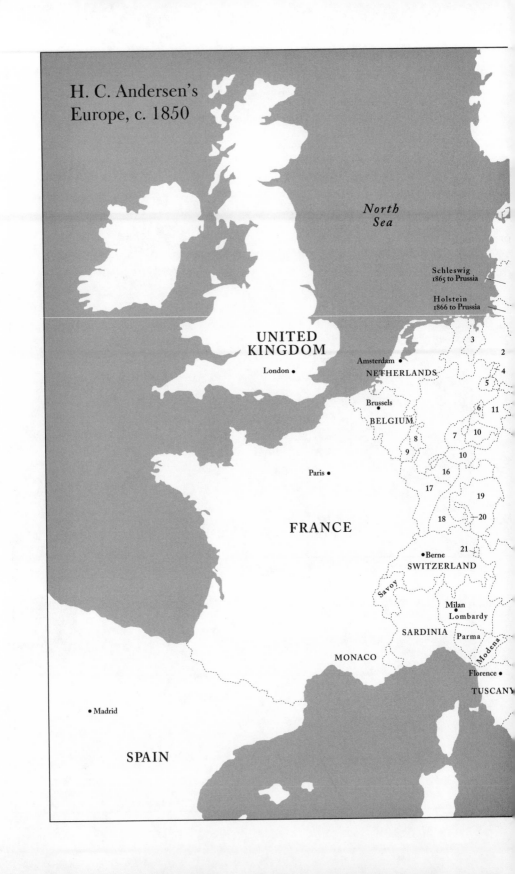

H. C. Andersen's
Europe, c. 1850

*North
Sea*

Schleswig
1865 to Prussia

Holstein
1866 to Prussia

UNITED
KINGDOM

Amsterdam •

London •

NETHERLANDS

3

2

4

5

Brussels
•

BELGIUM

6   11

7   10

8

9

10

10

Paris •

16

17

19

18   20

21

FRANCE

•Berne

SWITZERLAND

Savoy

Milan
•
Lombardy

SARDINIA   Parma

Modena

MONACO

Florence •

• Madrid

TUSCANY

SPAIN

Oslo

Stockholm ·

SWEDEN

ENMARK

· Copenhagen

Hamburg 1

RUSSIAN EMPIRE

PRUSSIA

12 · Magdeburg   · Berlin

13

Leipzig

eimar 15   14

· Dresden

· Prague

BAVARIA

Iunich

AUSTRIAN
EMPIRE

Vienna ·

Budapest ·

Tyrol

Key

1 MECKLENBURG–SCHWERIN
2 HANOVER
3 OLDENBURG
4 SCHAUMBURG–LIPPE
5 LIPPE–DETMOLD
6 WALDECK
7 NASSAU
8 RHINE–PROVINCE
9 LUXEMBOURG
10 HESSE–DARMSTADT
11 HESSE–KASSEL
12 BRUNSWICK
13 ANHALT
14 SAXONY
15 THURINGIAN STATES
16 LICHTENBERG
17 ALSACE–LORRAINE
18 BADEN
19 WÜRTTEMBERG
20 HOHENZOLLERN
21 LIECHTENSTEIN

San Marino

PAPAL
STATES

Patrimony
of St. Peter

ome

KINGDOM OF
THE TWO SICILIES

Naples

OTTOMAN EMPIRE

Constantinople ·

Hans Christian Andersen

Life Stories

Every character is taken from life; every one of them; *not one of them is invented. I know and have known them all.*

—HANS CHRISTIAN ANDERSEN, letter, 1834

Hans Christian Andersen was a compulsive autobiographer. At school, he says, "I told the boys curious stories in which I was always the chief person, but was sometimes ridiculed for that." He wrote his first memoir in 1832, when he was twenty-seven, and published a new autobiography for every decade of his adult life—in 1847, 1855 and 1869. The gulf between his childhood as the son of an illiterate washerwoman, and his career as a writer famous across Europe, the confidant of monarchs and princes, prompted constant self-review. Throughout his writings about himself you can hear him gasping for breath as his high connections sweep him off his feet. "Twenty-five years ago," he wrote in 1844, "I arrived with my small parcel in Copenhagen, a poor stranger of a boy, and today I have drunk my chocolate with the Queen, sitting opposite her and the King at the table."

His best-known self-portraits, inventive, harsh, spiritually true, are in his fairy tales. He is the triumphant Ugly Duckling and the loyal Little Mermaid, the steadfast Tin Soldier and the king-loving Nightingale, the demonic Shadow, the depressive Fir Tree, the forlorn Little Matchgirl. These are the characters and the stories which made Andersen a household name, and give him a place in literary history as one of the greatest and most original of European writers.

His importance as a creator of fairy tales is immense. While before him a few authors—Charles Perrault in France, the Grimm brothers in Germany—collected folk tales deriving from oral lore, Andersen was the first writer to treat this peasant form as a literary genre and to invent new tales which entered the collective consciousness with the same mythic power as the ancient, anonymous ones. Almost two hundred years after Andersen wrote them, stories such as "The Emperor's New Clothes" and "The Ugly Duckling" remain bywords for aspects of the human condition, while characters epitomizing terror or sacrifice, such as the Snow Queen or the Little Mermaid, are as deeply imbedded in our culture as those from traditional folklore like "Cinderella" or "Sleeping Beauty."

Andersen's miniaturist universe encompasses the full scope of human frailty and grandeur of spirit. His vanity and his egoism, characteristics that infuriated his friends, as well as his generosity and perception, make him extraordinarily good company as a writer. In life he was the archetypal outsider: haunted by the fight to escape his humble origins, sexually uncertain and lonely. He was ugly and gauche, and he described himself to Dickens as "one who seemed to have fallen from the skies." He wrought from the fairy tale his own art, pouring into it his compulsion to understand and mythologize his own life, transforming the emptiness and pain he felt into artistic order. Any random object, it appeared, would do as an alter ego—a soldier or a snowman, but also a spinning top or a darning needle. "I have heaps of material, more than for any other kind of writing; it often seems to me as if every hoarding, every little flower is saying to me, 'Look at me, just for a moment, and then my story will go right into you,' and then, if I feel like it, I have the story," he said. "[Ideas] lay in my thoughts like a seed corn, requiring only a flowing stream, a ray of sunshine, a drop from the cup of bitterness, for them to spring forth and burst into bloom."

"The history of my life will be the best commentary on my work," Andersen wrote. The autobiographical imperative driving his tales, their honesty to experience, consoles, amuses, enlightens us as we try to make sense of our own lives. For Andersen that honesty in his art was especially hard-won, for his social and sexual traumas made him in life a man of secrets, repressions and half-truths. "If you looked down to the bottom of my soul, you would understand fully the source of my longing and—pity me. Even the open, transparent lake has its unknown depths which no divers know," he wrote to his closest friend Edvard Collin in 1835, the year he began writing his stories.

Only when he discovered the literary genre of the fairy tale did he find a medium whose formal distance from reality allowed him to write as he was and felt. As the world's first great fantasy story–teller, he used speaking toys and animals, and he gave them voices, easy, colloquial and funny, with which children could instantly identify. Addressing himself to the child in the adult through a revolutionary shift in perspective, he gave voice through these characters to groups which had traditionally been mute and oppressed—children, the poor, those who did not fit social or sexual stereotypes. Introducing fantasy and comedy as the key veins, he determined the course of children's literature, suffusing his popular domestic settings with the fatalism of legend and with his own modern sense of the absurd.

"I must paint for mankind the vision that stands before my soul in all its vividness and diversity," he said as a young man. In Britain and America he was soon relegated to the nursery, encouraged to stay there initially by poor translations which did no justice to the complexity of his vision or the brilliance of his style. Just before his death in 1875, he saw the design of a statue to commemorate him, which showed him surrounded by children. He fought back at this early example of the Pied Piper myth which was to engulf his reputation: "I said loud and clear that I was dissatisfied," he wrote in his diary, "that I didn't tolerate anyone standing behind me and never had children on my back, on my lap or between my legs, that my tales were just as much for older people as for children, who only understood the outer trappings and did not comprehend and take in the whole work until they were mature—that naivety was only a part of my tales, that humour was really what gave them their flavour."

In the twentieth century, many twee, sentimentalized accounts of his life, and the Hollywood version, in which Danny Kaye depicts Andersen as a sweet-natured, pathetic entertainer, all conspired to maintain the public image of Andersen as a caricature, a divinely inspired fool. Nothing could be more unjust. His much-worked manuscripts show what a painstaking perfectionist he was, and in his tales both the joy and the pain of the creative process is evident: "The Snow Queen," he said, "came out dancing over the paper" in a few days; "The Ugly Duckling" took more than a year to compose. His little-known later stories, such as the terrifying "Auntie Toothache," experiment with form, narrative and representations of the unconscious mind, anticipating modernism. Writers as diverse as Dickens and Oscar Wilde, Strindberg and W. H. Auden, acknowledged his influence and his greatness; Thomas Mann called "The Steadfast Tin Soldier" "fundamentally the story of my life."

Yet two centuries after his birth, Andersen is still not appreciated as the world-class author that he undoubtedly was, as representative a figure of the European romantic spirit as Balzac or Victor Hugo—who were, incidentally, both friends of his. By children his works are among the most widely read in the world, and as an English reviewer wrote in an article celebrating

Andersen's seventieth birthday, "It is only a writer who can write for men that is fit to write for children." In this account of his life and his art I have tried to describe the inner mind of the writer, his concerns, hopes and fears as he wrote, and to place him in the rich cultural context which formed him. I have used letters, diaries and contemporary accounts which have often not been translated from Danish before, and several of which have remained obscure even in Denmark. The picture that emerges from them will be unfamiliar to English-speaking readers, and, largely, to Danish ones too. I hope I have shown how much Andersen has to offer an adult audience, and conveyed some of the struggle against both circumstances and liabilities of temperament—wild imagination, inner rage, tormenting anxieties and hypochondria, insatiable ambition—that formed him. He is a writer of whom one never tires, who grows in depth and maturity with his readers, whose sense of the adventure of life is infinite.

CHAPTER I

The Country

1805–1812

It doesn't matter about being born in a duckyard, as long as you are hatched from a swan's egg.

—HANS CHRISTIAN ANDERSEN, "The Ugly Duckling"

On 3 December 1867, a tall, lean, elderly man in an old-fashioned suit and large coat arrived at Copenhagen Station to travel, by train and steamship, to Odense, Denmark's second city, on the island of Funen. An anxious traveller, he was early for his train and carried a rope in his luggage in case there was a fire in his hotel; he shuffled on board alone and nervously, aware that he always attracted attention. A companion, William Bloch, who made a journey with him a few years later, described him as

> strange and bizarre in his movements and carriage. His arms and legs were long and thin and out of all proportion, his hands were broad and flat, and his feet of such gigantic dimensions that it seemed reasonable that no one would ever have thought of stealing his boots. His nose was in the so-called Roman style, but so disproportionately large that it seemed to dominate his whole face. After one had left him it was definitely his nose that one remembered most clearly, whereas his eyes, which were small and pale and well-hidden in their sockets behind a couple of huge eyelids half covering them, did not leave any impression . . . On the other hand there was both soul and beauty in his tall, open forehead and round his unusually well-shaped mouth.

This was Hans Christian Andersen in his sixties, described by the English writer Edmund Gosse as "one of the most famous men at that time alive in Europe." In the winter of 1867 he was on his way to his native city which, almost half a century after he had left it as a boy to seek fame and riches in Copenhagen, was awarding him the freedom of the city. When he was a child, a fortune-teller had told his mother that Odense would one day be illuminated for him; once he became famous, Andersen mentioned this prophecy frequently, and it satisfied his greed for recognition that it was now to be enacted.

But when the time for the ceremony came, he was in such agony from toothache that he could not enjoy it. He stood at the open window of the medieval Odense Town Hall on 6 December as a choir sang for him, looked on to the blaze of light from the torches and the crowds of people packed into the square below, and suffered silently. "The toothache was intolerable," he wrote later, "the icy air which rushed in at the window made it blaze up into a terrible pain, and in place of fully enjoying the good fortune of these minutes which would never be repeated, I looked at the printed song to see how many verses there were to be sung before I could slip away from the torture which the cold air sent through my teeth. It was the pitch of suffering."

The experience was emblematic of many of the contrasts in his life. Personally he was caught between inner suffering and outward vanity; publicly his honour was a statement by Danish society which, in fêting the rise of an individual from poverty to riches, was announcing its own progress from absolutism to democratization. The illumination, linking the struggle of his childhood with the worldly success to which he later became accustomed, was symbolic too. Andersen saw himself as Aladdin, "who when by his wonderful lamp he had built his grand castle, stepped to the window and said: 'Down there I walked a poor boy.' So has God granted me such a spiritual lamp—Poetry." Despite the toothache, he enjoyed the ritual of the return of the native, revisiting the tiny house, now owned by a tailor, that had been his home: "The yard was quite the same, only the shed in the rear had been placed in the middle of it. A couple of gooseberry bushes were probably still there from my childhood."

As for most men who rise from obscurity to fame, there is a disproportion between the little that is known about his early life and the vast amount of material relating to the later years, lived out in the glare of public scrutiny. For Andersen the disparity is extreme, partly because few writers anywhere have come from such an impoverished and illiterate background, partly because he sought public attention so assiduously afterwards. He told the story of his childhood in all his autobiographies, concentrating on it in his first memoir, *Levnedsbog* (*The Book of My Life*) in 1832, refining it in the German *Das Märchen meines Lebens ohne Dichtung* (1847) and the Danish adaptation of it, *Mit Livs Eventyr* (*The Fairy Tale of My Life*) (1855). None of these is entirely reliable, but in unravelling the man from the legend he wanted to create, one learns to understand the romantic vision that fuelled the writer, and was a part of both his family and his cultural inheritance.

He was born at one o'clock in the morning on 2 April 1805, in a small cottage in the poorest part of Odense. He was christened Hans Christian at home the same day—a common precaution at a time when many babies died in the first weeks of life. The names were used either together, as if they were hyphenated, or abbreviated simply to Christian, but never to Hans (a mistake still made by some English publishers). His parents, Hans Andersen, a 22-year-old shoemaker, and Anne Marie Andersdatter, aged about thirty, had married two months earlier, on 2 February. They had been engaged for just a month before that, and had probably moved only very recently into the cottage, for at their wedding at St. Knud's Church neither gave a fixed address.

In both *The Book of My Life* and *The Fairy Tale of My Life* Andersen wrote that on his first day he lay on his parents' bridal bed, which his father had built from the wooden planks surrounding a nobleman's coffin, and which still had the black cloth fringes draped round the sides. If true, this may have reflected a lack of enthusiasm on Hans Andersen's part for his shotgun wedding to an older bride; alternatively, Andersen may have made up the detail, either to herald his later involvement with kings and princes, or to establish his lifelong sense of death intertwined with life, pain with joy.

A second story in *The Fairy Tale of My Life* sows more forcefully the idea of genius in the making. At the child's blessing two weeks later, on Easter Monday, 15 April, at St. Hans Church, a squat sand-coloured building with a square tower on the northern outskirts of the town, and the least distinguished of Odense's three churches, the vicar complained that the baby screamed like a kitten. The godfather, a French emigrant called Gomar, is supposed to have consoled Anne Marie with the observation that the louder a baby cried, the better he should sing when he grew older; this "prophecy" came true, for Andersen initially attracted public attention as a singer. A third detail about his first days is equally suspect—his father, he says, read to his screaming new son from Ludvig Holberg, Denmark's eighteenth-century comic playwright, saying "Will you go to sleep? Or listen quietly?" This is to establish Hans Andersen's cultured credentials; he had wanted to be a scholar, and wept, said his son, when grammar school boys who came to buy shoes from him showed him their books.

Andersen described his parents romantically: his father as "a man of a richly gifted and truly poetical mind," and his mother as "ignorant of life and of the world," but with "a heart full of love." In fact, theirs was an unlikely match between two very different but well-meaning people; each had come through a hard childhood and wanted something better for their son, but their opposing outlooks quickly put a strain on the marriage. Anne Marie was a practical, robust, energetic woman, who worked hard and kept her home bright and clean: she had a special pride in keeping her linen and curtains snow-white. A typical peasant survivor with a weakness for drink—she liked schnapps—and no intellectual aspirations, she read printed words with difficulty, could not make out handwritten letters and could not write her name. She was pious and superstitious. She stuck pieces of St. John's wort into the clefts between the beams on the ceiling, and from their growth judged whether people would live long or die soon. Her conversation was full of trolls and ghosts; she invited fortune-tellers to the house and sent her son off to consult them in times of crisis. Hans Christian grew up terrified of the dark and of churchyards.

She adored her son, however, and the few stories we know about her all testify to a warm, kind, tolerant nature. She made it a condition of 5-year-old Hans Christian attending his first school that he was never beaten, and removed him instantly the day he was. When at a gathering a drunken woman was being roundly criticized as "no good," Anne Marie spoke up for her—her mild and understanding words stayed in her son's mind and this incident formed the kernel of his story "She Was No Good," in which Anne Marie is portrayed as the alcoholic, hopeless washerwoman that she later became, yet defended as a loving mother. Writing of his mother's childhood in *The Fairy Tale of My Life*, Andersen said, "I continually heard from my mother how very much happier I was than she had been, and that I was brought up like a nobleman's child. She, as a child, had been turned out by her parents to beg, and when she was not able to do it, she had sat for a whole day under a bridge and wept."

If this were true, it must have been Anne Marie's mother who sent her, for she never knew her father. Her mother, Anne Sørensdatter, born around 1745, came from the area around Bogense, a town on the northwest coast of Funen, and had three illegitimate daughters by three different men. Anne Marie, born around 1774 or 1775 near Bogense, was the first; her father disappeared without trace. Her mother moved to Odense and in 1778 had another daughter, Christiane, followed by a third daughter, born in 1781, who died in infancy. In 1783 Anne Sørensdatter spent a week in prison for having produced three children outside wedlock; when released she married an ex-convict and had another child, who did not survive. In 1790 her husband died and, aged about forty-five, she married a 30-year-old glovemaker; in 1804 she returned to live in Bogense.

Poverty, and what seems to have been a family tradition of promiscuity, drove Anne Marie's sister Christiane to run a brothel in Copenhagen. The sisters fell out; Andersen recalled Christiane visiting Odense once, parading her fine clothes and giving him a silver coin. Anne Marie was not impressed, and after that communication between her and Christiane ceased. Anne Marie, less ambitious for riches, went into service, working until 1798 for the Ibsen family at a manor house. She must have been well thought of there, for she was invited to return to visit a married daughter outside Bogense—she made the journey of some fifteen miles with her son, taking two days on foot over rough roads.

While she was in service, Anne Marie met a potter called Rosenvinge, a married man with several illegitimate children, and in 1799 she had a daughter, Karen-Marie, by him. This half-sister haunted Andersen, for whom she was an emblem of degradation, ignorance and promiscuity. He rarely saw her, because she lived with her maternal grandmother, but as he fought his way out of his family's poverty, he always feared that Karen-Marie would emerge to shame him and drag him back down. He gives her name to the wicked, wild heroine of his story "The Red Shoes."

Andersen was also disturbed by the legacy of his father's family. Towards the end of the eighteenth century, many Funen peasants driven out of the countryside by the policy of enclosures had come to settle in Odense, among them Anders Hansen Traes and his wife Anne Catherine Nommensdatter, Andersen's paternal grandparents. Anders Hansen Traes, born around 1751, was a Funen village labourer and smallholder who also worked as a journeyman shoemaker. Traes (tree, wood) suggests connections with woodcutting or carving wood, and this was Andersen's memory of his grandfather; he used to watch him "sit carving strange figures out of wood—men with beasts' heads and beasts with wings; these he packed in a basket and carried them out into the country, where he was everywhere well received by the peasant women because he gave to them and their children the strange toys." By the time Hans Christian was old enough to remember him, Anders Hansen Traes was insane; he was looked after at home, though he sometimes wandered into the woods and came back covered in garlands of flowers and twigs, singing at the top of his voice and pursued through the streets by shrieking children.

This grandfather only spoke to Andersen once in his life, addressing him by the unfamiliar formal pronoun "De," but it was from him, Andersen believed, that he inherited an artistic talent and a strong visual sense. He felt a kinship with him. In old age, when he had lost his teeth, he thought he resembled his grandfather, and he always feared the legacy of madness: "One day, when he was returning to Odense, I heard the boys in the street shouting after him; I hid myself behind a flight of steps in terror for I knew that I was of his flesh and blood." He wrote about him in the patriotic story "Holger the Dane," where a grandfather-woodcarver compares his own work to that of Holberg: "'He knew how to carve, too,' said the old grandfather. 'He hacked away at the follies and oddities of people for all he was worth.'" By implication, this links three generations of the family—Andersen's grandfather, his father, who loved reading Holberg, and himself, another literary satirist.

In 1781 Anders Hansen Traes married Anne Catherine Nommensdatter, born in 1745, and their only child Hans Andersen was born in 1782. The family did not prosper. According to a story Anne Catherine told her grandson, a series of disasters—dead cattle, a farmhouse burned down—turned her husband from well-to-do farmer to madman, and they were forced to go to Odense, apprentice their son in a trade and live in poverty. In fact, they were never wealthy or substantial farmers; hard times drove them into the town, where Hans Andersen became a shoemaker like his father and Anne Catherine worked in the garden of the asylum and old people's home, Graabrødre (Greyfriars) Hospital. Here her husband sometimes spent time and her grandson often played; the harmless lunatics wandered into the garden, and "with curiosity and terror" Hans Christian used to follow them about. Once he ventured into the corridor where the dangerous patients languished in their cells, and a woman with wild hair flew at him: "She stared down upon me and stretched out her long arm towards me. I screamed for terror. I felt the tips of her fingers touching my clothes. I was half dead when the attendant came."

Anne Catherine, a delicate woman with mild blue eyes, was a loving grandmother who visited her son's family daily, often bringing flowers from the garden. The benign, wise grandmother is a recurring figure in Andersen's work—in "The Little Matchgirl," "The Snow Queen," "The Grand-mother." But Anne Catherine was also a fantasist set on glorifying her ancestors. Her father had been a glovemaker who ended his days in the Odense workhouse, but among her fanciful tales was one that described her maternal grandmother as a noblewoman in Kassel, north Germany, who had eloped with an actor and so lost her fortune. There is no evidence for this story; her grandmother, Karen Nielsdatter, was in fact a poor Danish woman from Assens, a town on Funen, who was widowed early and left with eight children. But Andersen liked to believe the tale; he repeated it as fact in *The Fairy Tale of My Life*, and as late as 1857 he mentioned it in a let-ter when passing through Kassel. The story about a family in decline encouraged in the young Hans Christian a reversed fantasy about a social ascent which he saw almost as his right. All his life Andersen was fascinated by the collapse of old dynasties, and made them the subject of some of his tales, such as "The Wind Tells of Valdemar Daae and His Daughters."

Hans Andersen took from his parents a dreamy, unpractical nature that he passed on to his son. Hans Christian remained his father's only child and the two were very close. He was, he says, "extremely spoiled"; "my father gratified me in all my wishes. I possessed his whole heart—he lived for me," he wrote. The two shared a love of literature which gave them a bond and excluded Andersen's mother: "From as early as I can remember, reading was my sole and my most loved pastime . . . my father enjoyed reading very much and so had some books, which I swallowed. I never played with other boys, I was always alone." His father read Hans Christian plays, the fables of Jean de la Fontaine and *The Arabian Nights*, and made him panoramas, the-atres and pop-up pictures. Andersen wrote that "it was only in such moments that I can remember to have seen him really cheerful, for he never felt himself happy in his life and as a handicraftsman." Out of sympathy with his wife and with his place in society, Hans Andersen spent much time wandering in the forest, alone or with his son, who recalled that "he did not talk much, but would sit silently, sunk in deep thought . . . Only twice in the year, in the month of May, when the woods were arrayed in their earliest green, did my mother go with us."

He had few friends, and spent much time reading history and the Bible, on which his freethinking mentality horrified his wife:

> He pondered in silent thought afterward upon that which he had read; but my
> mother did not understand him when he talked with her about it, and there-

fore he grew more and more silent. One day he closed the Bible with the words, "Christ was a man like us, but an extraordinary man!" These words horrified my mother and she burst into tears. In my distress I prayed to God that he would forgive this fearful blasphemy in my father. "There is no other devil than that which we have in our own hearts," I heard my father say one day, and I made myself miserable about him and his soul; I was therefore entirely of the opinion of my mother and the neighbours, when my father, one morning, found three scratches on his arm, probably occasioned by a nail, that the devil had been to visit him in the night, in order to prove to him that he really existed.

One of Andersen's earliest memories is of the arrival of "the great comet of 1811," which his mother told him would destroy the earth. "With my mother and some of the neighbouring women I stood in St. Knud's churchyard and looked at the frightful and mighty fireball with its large, shining tail," he wrote. "All talked about the signs of evil and the day of doom. My father joined us, but he was not of the others' opinion at all, and gave them a correct and sound explanation; then my mother sighed, the women shook their heads, my father laughed and went away."

Another vignette concerning his father suggests pride and impulsiveness. Applying for a position as shoemaker to an aristocratic family, which offered a cottage as well as a salary, Hans Andersen made some dancing shoes to show the lady of the house. She was displeased with them and said he had ruined her silk. The shoemaker immediately slashed the soles, saying that if she had wasted her silk, he would waste his leather. Andersen perhaps invented or embellished this episode, but it is clear that his father's dreams of a brighter future were dashed very early, and that the frustration of an intelligent man denied opportunities, which may have driven Anders Hansen Traes mad, led Hans Andersen to depression and inactivity. Andersen recognized his father as an essential influence, and shoes and feet are repeated symbols in his tales—"The Red Shoes," "The Galoshes of Fortune," the little mermaid who pays for human feet with her tongue. A draft found among his papers after his death eulogizes the shoemakers' guild, naming Hans Sachs and the Wandering Jew as examples of famous cobblers.

In his last work, "Old Johanna's Tale," he was still recapitulating the conflict between his parents in the battle between a poor, defeatist tailor whose motto is "What's the good?" and his earthy, optimistic, pious wife Maren. Their son Rasmus, caught between a drive to make his way in the world and

Odense in 1805, the year Andersen was born there. He wrote that the country town was a hundred years behind Copenhagen: as a child he heard folk tales which were no longer told in the capital.

his father's passivity and pessimism, is ultimately destroyed. Some scenes from this story are identical to those in Andersen's memoirs—when Maren thinks the tailor talks blasphemously, she carries her son to the peat shed and throws her apron over him, as his mother once did to Hans Christian, and says, as Anne Marie did: "Those words you hear over there, little Rasmus, they weren't your father's. It was Satan who went through the room and used your father's voice. Say 'Our Father'—we'll both say it." Andersen sympathized with his mother, but also felt he understood his father. He knew he had inherited from him the depressive, self-destructive streak against which he struggled all his life, and which was perhaps offset in him, although he did not acknowledge it, by his mother's robustness. He was desperate to get away from the world of his childhood, yet more than most writers he made his life's work out of the conflict between his parents' worldviews and temperaments. Until old age he went on reshaping the primitive folk heritage he took from his mother via the scholarship and fantastical imaginings encouraged by his father, which were themselves determined by the social trauma of his upbringing, and the unique opportunities afforded him by his native town.

The Odense that Andersen remembered from his childhood was a vibrant and colourful place barely touched by the industrialization which had transformed it by the time of his triumphal return in 1867. At the start of the nineteenth century, Odense had 8,000 inhabitants, 1,100 houses, "forty big and small streets," according to the *Provincial Lexicon*, and three churches that dominated the flat skyline. The city layout was medieval, with winding streets of one-storey half-timbered cottages, mostly painted yellow, running down to a water mill and the pretty river, lined with willows and elder trees, that flanked the town's southern border. The town hall on Flakhaven, the central square, was built in the fifteenth century; Andersen used to watch a clockmaker, Schmidt, who drew large crowds to his workshop there. The town hall looked down to St. Knud's, a solid brown brick church with a grey spire, and to a market square, Albani Torv, where the shoemakers and tailors had their wash-houses. All around lay the lush pastures of Funen, a rich farming island some eighty miles from Copenhagen. Meadows began at the end of the streets, cows often wandered into town, and when times were hard, poor families like the Andersens walked half a day to relatives in the country to get food. At harvest times, the women earned extra money by going out to glean in the fields.

The town had—and still has—a rural mentality; folklore and superstitious beliefs were strong among its people, and foreign influences minimal. When visitors arrived from southern Europe, they caused consternation. One of Andersen's earliest memories was the arrival of Denmark's Spanish allies on Funen in 1808, when he was three. Denmark, as an ally of Napoleon, declared war on Sweden in March 1808, and French and Spanish troops in support of Denmark landed on Funen on their way to Sweden. Their bright uniforms—red, yellow, white, green—and gold brocade and great black hats, their drums and guns, would have been irresistible to any child: "I remember very well those dark-brown men bustling in the streets, and the cannon that were fired in the market-place and before the bishop's residence; I saw the foreign soldiers stretching themselves on the sidewalks and on bundles of straw in the half-burned St. John's Church—a Spanish soldier one day took me in his arms, and pressed to my lips a silver image, which he carried on his breast."

As in any traditional rural community, differences between the seasons were more marked than today. The island of Funen has mild, pleasant summers and long cold winters, when Odense could lie covered in snow for four months and children would skate down the river and hurl snowballs during the short daylight hours. Feasts and festivals were eagerly anticipated: flautists and drummers leaping through the white streets to bring in the New Year; popinjay shooting on the moors at Whitsun; trips to a holy spring on Midsummer Eve; or the summer celebration of St. Knud, who had founded the city, on 10 July. Andersen wrote in *The Fairy Tale of My Life* that when he was born there, Odense

> was a hundred years behind the times; many customs and manners prevailed which long since disappeared from the capital . . . The guilds . . . went in procession with flying banners and with lemons dressed in ribbons stuck on their swords. A harlequin with bells and a wooden sword ran at the head . . . the first Monday in Lent the butchers used to lead through the streets a fat ox, adorned with wreaths of flowers and ridden by a boy in a white shirt and wearing wings. The sailors also passed through the streets with music and flags and streamers flying; two of the boldest ended by wrestling on a plank placed between two boats, and the one that did not tumble into the water was the hero.

But Odense also provided a culture particularly alive to social nuance, which early on fuelled in Andersen a burning ambition. In 1805 it was a place of pretensions. At first sight it seemed a typical Danish country town, with its winding streets and small squares, but as the second city in Denmark, the capital of Funen and a royal seat, home of the Crown Prince, it was also known as "little Copenhagen," because it had a garrison, a gaol and a castle that served as the royal summer residence. It had exclusive cloisters for unmarried noblewomen, a bishop and a cathedral; the teachers at the cathedral school considered themselves professors. It also had the only theatre in the kingdom outside Copenhagen, an elegant classical building erected in 1795, where actors from the capital's Royal Theatre came on tour during the summer. An élite bourgeoisie of rich merchants, government officials and army officers living in the large courtyard houses on the main streets thus enjoyed the pleasures and privileges of court and culture, while just a stone's throw away in the side streets and alleys artisans, labourers and the unemployed lived in poverty.

The Andersen family moved to their first settled home in one of these poor streets in May 1807, when Hans Christian was two. From a master

Munkemøllestræde 3–5, Odense: Andersen's home from the age of two to fourteen.

shoemaker they rented a cottage divided into three parts near Flakhaven. This was Andersen's home for the next twelve years; to keep the same home for so long showed a rare stability, for early-nineteenth-century poor families tended to move frequently because they could not pay the rent. Asking the painter J. H. T. Hanck to draw it in the 1830s, Andersen remembered a little yellow house with two doors, close to the wing of a baker's shop; this was 3, Munkemøllestræde (Monk's Mill Street), a low, half-timbered cottage with a steep roof and a big chimney, and two stone steps to the front door; inside was an L-shaped room covering about eighteen square metres with windows at each end and a stove in the corner. Outside, a little yard was shared with the neighbours. Next door, at number 4, in an even smaller room, lived Frantz Kocker, a glovemaker, his wife and six children. On the other side of them, at number 5, was hatter Philip Schenk, his wife and four children. A customer could thus buy his shoes, gloves and hat within the same building. In "The Travelling Companion," based on a Funen folk tale, the hero wins the princess by guessing three times what she is thinking about—first her shoe, then her glove, then a sorcerer's head.

"One little room, which was filled with the shoemaker's bench, the bed and my crib," was how Andersen described his childhood home in *The Fairy Tale of My Life*. "The walls, however, were covered with pictures, and over the workbench was a cupboard containing books and songs; the little kitchen was full of shining plates and metal pans." There was also a loft, reached by a ladder, which then led out on to the roof: in the rain gutter stood a large box full of earth, where Andersen's mother grew kitchen herbs, and where children could play. This is the world of Kai and Gerda, painted as a childhood idyll in "The Snow Queen." In his autobiographies and his fairy tales, Andersen romanticizes his childhood, but the tone of his home as a cosy, sheltered place full of interest rings true: he remembered the little room as large and the pictures on the door as interesting to a child as a whole picture gallery.

Across the road was a set of smart houses, "Eilschou's Dwellings," recently built for vicars' and merchants' widows. Leading off on the west side was Pogestræde, home of Andersen's grandparents; then the street turned a gentle bend and wound down to the back-river at Munke Mølle, where the washerwomen worked. On the next street was Odense Tugthus, the large sand-coloured gaol; Schenk became a caretaker here about 1811, and the Andersen family, with Hans Christian in a state of excited terror about the unlocking and locking of the iron gates, was invited to supper and served by prisoners.

Although the Andersens were poor, there was more money to go round in the household than in neighbouring families because they only had one child. Andersen wrote, "I had not the least idea of what it was to be in want. My father lived, as the saying is, from hand to mouth, but what we had was more than enough for me." A story handed on by oral tradition in Odense, however, but not mentioned in Andersen's autobiographies, comes from some cousins who lived in the country and would sometimes spot a woman making her way across the fields to see them, an empty basket at her side, a boy straggling along beside her. "Is that Anne Marie?" the cry would go up. "Has she got her basket? Is her son with her? Then we know why she has come." She would return to Odense with provisions, and her resourcefulness and willingness to beg in hard times was probably what enabled her to keep the home in Munkemøllestræde for so long. She also sometimes fostered other children to make extra money; when Andersen returned to be fêted in Odense in 1867, his visitors included the widow Henrichsen—"little Ane, who boarded with my parents and with whom I wouldn't share a cot. She was now at a charity home for old folks; looked quite well dressed and wept at the thought of how far I had gone in life."

For working-class city children in the early nineteenth century, there were many deprivations—they might be cold, hungry or dressed in rags— but they had one advantage over modern children: they were free to roam around unaccompanied, and the entire town was their playground. Thomas Overskou, Andersen's contemporary, who grew up poor in Copenhagen and became Denmark's eminent theatre historian, remembered that "when I was young, most of the poor people's 'urchins,' as they were commonly known, romped around all day long, left to their own devices, bare-legged, bare-headed and half-dressed in grubby rags, in the streets, the squares and the many gutted ruins, or lay poking around in the gutters for whatever they could find." Hans Christian, though, fed on his grandmother's tales of fallen nobility, felt that he was a class apart, and pursued the lonely, cerebral passions of the only child.

> I very seldom played with other boys; even at school I took little interest in their games, but remained sitting within doors. At home I had playthings enough, which my father made for me. My greatest delight was in making clothes for my dolls, or in stretching out one of my mother's aprons between the wall and two sticks before a currant-bush which I had planted in the yard, and thus to gaze in between the sun-illumined leaves. I was a singularly dreamy child, and so constantly went about with my eyes shut, as at last to give the impression of having weak sight.

Many only children feel that they are unique. Often indulged by parents who lavish huge amounts of time on them, they tend to be more geared to adult company, less inclined to the high-spirited mischief of groups of children. All this was true of Andersen: he was a tall, thin, gauche boy with long flaxen hair who stood out in the town because of his unusual height and his dreamy eccentricity. "He's too big and gawky," says the duck who bites the ugly duckling, "so he's going to get it." Andersen was also effeminate—he recalls running about stringing strawberries on a long stalk, or weaving garlands and playing with dolls, and he also loved dressing up, a passion that lasted into adulthood: "An old woman altered my father's clothes for me; my mother would fasten three or four large pieces of silk with pins on my breast, and that had to do for vests; a large handkerchief was tied around my neck with a mighty bow; my head was washed with soap and my hair curled, and then I was in all my glory." But there are no accounts in his autobiographies of the ordinary pleasures and mishaps of childhood, of skating or playing ball or tree-climbing. Just one such story survives in Odense, handed down from his mother's cousins in the country, of Hans Christian and Anne Marie visiting one winter and the boy going with the other children on his first sledge ride. Of course, he fell off, and into a pond; mortified, he came back, and while his clothes were drying before the fire he had to wear a girl's skirt, which upset and embarrassed him. Clumsy, hopeless at physical activities, over-sensitive and proud—this is a recognizable portrait of Hans Christian in the flawed, everyday setting he rarely gives in his memoirs.

His mother, singling him out as the only boy not to be beaten at his first dame school, emphasized his separate status. When he marched out from this school and ran home to say he had been hit, she sent him instead to a Jewish school—an open-minded move for a woman of her time and class. Jewish ideas about children have generally been enlightened; Hans Christian must have enjoyed this school, for sixty years later he wrote to his old teacher, Fedder Carstens, congratulating him on his golden wedding; the treatment of Jews in his fiction is extremely sympathetic. But a child so fixed in character could not be taught. When Carstens' school closed in 1811, his mother sent him to the Poor School, a ten-minute walk away in an old building painted with religious scenes. He claimed to do his homework on the way to school, and spent his time daydreaming, but he enjoyed theology lessons, when the pictures on the walls seemed to come alive as the teacher told Old Testament stories. He acquired a basic education in reading, writing and arithmetic, but was reproached for not concentrating, and never learned to spell properly. Later, he left spelling and punctuation to proofreaders. He had few friends; he sometimes enjoyed the company of little girls, and one boy, Peder Wich, who lived in a cellar underneath the tailors' laundry in Albani Torv, was a childhood companion. Wich later became a distinguished Odense citizen and was among those responsible for awarding Andersen the freedom of the city—one self-made man acknowledging another.

In his memoirs the friendship he highlighted was that with a Jewish girl, Sara, a little older than him. In *The Book of My Life* he wrote: "I still recall a beautiful little girl of about eight who kissed me and said she wished to marry me; this pleased me and I always let her kiss me, although I never kissed her, and I did not let anyone except her kiss me. I felt a strange loathing for grown-up girls, or for girls of more than about twelve years; they really made me shudder, I even used the term about anything which I did not like touching that it was so 'girlish.' "

Sara's ambition was to be a dairymaid in a manor house, and Hans Christian offered her a post in the castle he would acquire when rich, and drew her a picture of it, explaining that he was a changeling who came from a noble family. "He's mad, just like his grandfather," Sara said to the other boys, and Hans Christian never trusted her again. A manic sense of self— grandiose ideas about fortune and nobility, interleaved with a fear of madness and rejection—was thus established in Andersen by the age of six. This was the essence of the romantic view of genius that he distilled in "The Ugly Duckling"—"It doesn't matter about being born in a duckyard, as long as you are hatched from a swan's egg."

Thus Hans Christian Andersen grew up with two fixed ideas about himself: that he was special and different from everyone around him, and that he must escape from what he called his roots as a "swamp plant." His luck was to grow up just as urbanization and industrialization were allowing a measure of social mobility, and democratic ideas about wider education were taking hold, but to be nevertheless rooted in a more traditional, static world which formed his creative imagination. For in the 1800s these social changes were not yet apparent: Funen was old-fashioned and stood on the fringes of Europe. Steamships had not been invented, a journey from Odense to Copenhagen, over the stretch of the Baltic called the Great Belt, took two days by sailing boat and stagecoach, postal communication was barely developed, and, as Andersen wrote, many customs which had long disappeared in Copenhagen still prevailed in Odense.

For him, the most significant of these were folk tales, told here by old women from the countryside when they were no longer current in Copenhagen. This was the decade when the Grimm brothers were collecting tales from German peasants, aware that an oral tradition was dying out. Andersen heard Danish folk tales in the spinning room of the asylum where his grandmother worked. They included Nordic characters such as ice maidens and trolls and the water-spirit living in the "bell-deep" in the Odense river, as well as the cast of witches and soldiers and princesses that made up his first published collection thirty years later. He was a favourite with the pauper women: he entertained them with chalk drawings on the spinning room door depicting the human anatomy, about which he knew little and they knew nothing. "They rewarded my eloquence," he recalled,

> by telling me tales in return; and thus a world as rich as that of the Thousand and One Nights was revealed to me. The stories told by these old ladies, and the insane figures which I saw around me in the asylum, operated in the mean

time so powerfully upon me, that when it grew dark I scarcely dared to go out of the house. I was therefore permitted, generally at sunset, to lay down in my parents' bed with its long, flowered curtains, because the press-bed in which I slept could not conveniently be put down so early in the evening on account of the room it occupied in our small dwelling; and here, in the paternal bed, lay I in a waking dream, as if the actual world did not concern me.

The theatre, to which he was taken by his parents when he was seven, was also formative. He saw Holberg's *The Political Tinker* in a German vaudeville version, and a German *singspiel*, *Das Donauweibchen* (*The Little Lady of the Danube*). The effect was electric: "From the day I saw the first play my whole soul was on fire with this art. I still recall how I could sit for days all alone before the mirror, an apron round my shoulders instead of a knight's cloak, acting out *Das Donauweibchen*, in German, though I barely knew five German words. I soon learned entire Danish plays by heart." He made friends with the theatre's bill distributor, who let him have a programme every day in exchange for help in giving them out; "with this I seated myself in a corner and imagined an entire play, according to the name of the piece and the characters in it. This was my first unconscious effort towards poetic composition." Odense's unique theatre links with the capital were of vital significance to him, for the theatre suggested the first outlet for his talents. Thus the two dimensions of the city—its old-fashioned folk customs on the one hand, its link with the capital and the sophisticated pleasures of court and theatre on the other—mingled in his mind. His entire life would have been different had he grown up anywhere else in Denmark. Copenhagen lacked the mysterious folk heritage that fed his fantasies; no other provincial town offered the intriguing possibilities of bourgeois culture which shaped his ambition. When, in the following years, his childhood became harder and more troubled, it was literature and drama which sustained him, and which he began to see as his escape route.

CHAPTER 2

Master Comedy-Player

1812–1819

If anyone can become a poet through the events of his childhood, then I will become one.

—HANS CHRISTIAN ANDERSEN, letter, 1823

Over the bright, busy memories of Hans Christian's early years hung a cloud which spread across Europe in the first decade of the nineteenth century, and in 1812 closed in on the Andersen family.

In 1807, Denmark had entered the Napoleonic Wars as an ally of France, and in September a British naval force attacked and spectacularly bombarded Copenhagen, destroying about a thousand houses. When Denmark capitulated, the English towed away the Danish fleet, which was among the largest in the world: a humiliation the Danes took decades to forgive. A major casualty was Danish commerce, for until 1807 Denmark was a substantial trading centre for goods from America, Africa and Asia; after the bombardment she had to reposition herself to exploit trading links within the Baltic and the North Sea. The response of Frederik VI (1808–1839), a frugal and militaristic king, was to pour increasing proportions of the national budget into the army and navy in continuing support of Napoleon. As shipowners and merchants living in the grand colonnaded houses in Copenhagen went bankrupt one after another and young boys made fortunes as privateers seizing the richly laden British merchant ships, Denmark was brought to economic collapse. Between 1807 and 1812 prices rose by nine times, and in 1813 the state was declared bankrupt. In 1814, peace was declared, and under the terms of the Treaty of Vienna, Denmark had to hand over Norway, its major foreign dominion, to Sweden.

Poor families such as the Andersens suffered most from food shortages and rapid inflation in the war years, and this may have led Hans Andersen to brood on what the war offered in terms of social advancement. "My father's rambles in the wood became more frequent—he had no rest," wrote Andersen. "The events of the war in Germany, which he read in the newspapers with eager curiosity, occupied him completely. Napoleon was his hero, his rise from obscurity was the most beautiful example to him . . . nothing but war was talked of." Hans Andersen had been a piper in an Odense regiment since 1806, and in spring 1812 he enlisted as a musketeer. It was a desperate last bid for adventure but also a pragmatic move, for he was offered money to take the place of a wealthy farmer's son who wanted to get out of the army.

Hans Christian, aged seven, was in bed with measles on the morning his father left to march south to Germany. The Odense working class had no time for heroism: when the drums beat, Anne Marie, who hated the army, accompanied her husband weeping to the town gate; the neighbours "shrugged their shoulders, and said it was folly to go out and get shot when there was no occasion for it"; and the old grandmother, wrote Andersen, "looked at me with her mild eyes and said that it would be a good thing if I died . . . this was the first day of real sorrow which I remember."

But soon the shoemaker's romance turned to farce and then to tragedy. He never saw action, for his regiment only got as far as Holstein, then a Danish province, before peace was declared, and in January 1814 he was back at his workbench. Still, the long march and the punishing rigours of early-nineteenth-century army life had taken their toll, and for the next two years he was a sick man. He dreamed of campaigns and of receiving orders from the Emperor, and wanted Hans Christian to follow in his footsteps, but his mother declared that as long as she had any voice in the matter, her son should remain at home and not lose his health as his father had done.

One morning in April 1816, when Hans Christian was eleven, his father became delirious, and Andersen's mother sent her son not for a doctor but to a "so-called wise woman" called Mette Mogensdatter who lived in the country at Ejby, two miles outside the town. She performed some magic tricks, measured the boy's arms, tied a woollen thread round his wrist and placed a twig supposedly from "the same kind of tree upon which the Saviour was crucified" on his chest. Crying, Andersen asked if his father would die; the wise woman told him to return home—"If your father is to die this time, then you will meet his ghost." Frightened, superstitious, excitable, the boy fled home across the field and along the banks of the river and told his mother that he had met nothing, but two days afterwards his father died. He was thirty-three.

His corpse lay on the bed, I therefore slept with my mother. A cricket chirped the whole night through. "He is dead," said my mother, addressing it, "you need not call him, the Ice Maiden has carried him off." I understood what she meant. I recollected that in the winter before, when our window panes were frozen, my father pointed to them and showed us a figure like that of a maiden with outstretched arms. "She is come to fetch me," said he in jest, and now when he lay dead on his bed my mother remembered this.

Twenty years later Andersen still noted the day of his father's death—26 April—in his diary. The fantasy image from that traumatic night was recalled in two great romantic fairy tales, "The Snow Queen," in which love triumphs over death, and "The Ice Maiden," where death triumphs over love, and the elderly Andersen reasserts his parents' fatalism.

Hans Andersen was buried in a pauper's grave; his son followed the coffin, and watched the vicar at St. Knud's Church throw sand on it. At home his mother wailed and his pale old grandmother sat quietly, with wet eyes.

From then on, Hans Christian was left to his own devices, and he stayed at home alone playing with his puppet theatre, making clothes for his dolls and reading plays. In his autobiographies, he paints himself as absorbed and happy, but the depressive streak, in a child traumatized by loss, was clearly there too. Aged eleven, he overheard a conversation about predestination: "all at once I was firmly and resolutely determined to drown myself. I ran to where the water was deepest, and then a new thought passed through my soul. 'It is the devil who wishes to have power over me.' I uttered a loud cry, and running away from the place as if I were pursued, fell weeping into my mother's arms, but neither she nor anyone else could wring from me what was wrong with me."

His mother was now very poor, and worked all day at a variety of jobs: collecting herbs for a chemist, helping in the kitchens at the royal castle, most of all washing clothes from the grand houses down by the river at Munke Mølle. In summer this was hard work but endurable; in autumn and winter, as she stood knee-deep for up to six hours in the icy water, it was appalling, and it was then that she became addicted to gin, which she drank partly to keep herself warm. Andersen describes her work in "She Was No Good," one of the few of his tales which smart with a sense of social indignation:

His mother was standing out in the water at her washing bench and beating the heavy linen with her washing-bat. There was a current running, for the sluices were open; the sheets were caught by the millstream and looked like carrying the bench away; yes, the washerwoman had to hold on tight . . . "Ah, that's what I wanted—how it warms me up! It's as good as a hot meal, and doesn't cost so much. Take a drink . . . Let me have a drop more." . . . Then she climbed on to the little jetty where the boy stood, and stepped ashore. The water was dripping from the rush-matting she had wrapped round her middle and was oozing from her skirt.

At eleven, however, his response to his mother's hardship was to try to escape. His father had been his intellectual stimulus, and he had already realized that he could learn nothing from his mother. He now began to play on his artistic interests in order to cultivate the cultured middle class of Odense. Around this time it was noticed that he had "a remarkably beautiful and high soprano voice" and, he wrote in *The Book of My Life*, "the strange characteristics of my entire nature compared with those of other children of my social class, my love of reading, and my wonderful voice all drew people's attention to me."

He started with Mrs. Bunkeflod, a clergyman's widow who lived with her sister-in-law in Eilschou's Dwellings across the road in Munkemøllestræde: "Hers was the first house belonging to the educated class into which I was kindly received." Soon it was a second home, where Hans Christian could come and go and read books as he pleased. Mrs. Bunkeflod introduced him to poetry and here he first heard the word "poet." The Danish *Digter*, like the German *Dichter*, carries stronger connotations of romantic awe than the English word, and the sense of poetry as a romantic calling was powerful in early-nineteenth-century Europe. Bunkeflod had been a minor poet; Andersen remembered the word spoken "with so much reverence as proved it to be something sacred . . . 'My brother the poet' said Bunkeflod's sister, and her eyes sparkled as she said it. From her I learned it was something glorious, something fortunate, to be a poet."

Mrs. and Miss Bunkeflod also introduced Hans Christian to Shakespeare. Interest in Shakespeare had only recently developed in Denmark, and using an early, poor translation by N. Rosenfeldt from the 1790s, Hans Christian acted out the plays in his puppet theatre: "The bold descriptions, the heroic incidents, witches and ghosts were exactly to my taste . . . I saw Hamlet's ghost, and lived upon the heath with Lear. The more persons died in a play, the more interesting I thought it was." He wrote a play of his own, based on the Pyramus and Thisbe story, called "Abor and Elvira," and read it to his neighbours. *Aborre* means "perch" in Danish, and one of them asked scornfully why he had not called it "Perch and Stockfish." He knew he was being ridiculed, ran home and told his mother, who responded consolingly that "she only said so because her son had not done it," a story which suggests her pride and care even as Hans Christian was moving out of her reach.

He began another play, about a king and a princess; unable to believe that they would speak in ordinary Danish, he used a multi-lingual dictionary and wrote lines for them in a mixture of Danish, German, French and English, such as "Guten Morgen, mon pere! Har De godt sleeping?" This and subsequent fantastical dramas were also declaimed around Odense and, not surprisingly, Hans Christian was taunted by the street boys, who mockingly called him "the playwright" and chased him home, where he hid in a corner, weeping. Gotfred Schenk, his neighbour from 5, Munkemøllestræde, and four years older, used to beat him regularly; Andersen had the pleasure of encountering him again on his return to Odense in 1867, when Schenk was an impoverished fisherman of sixty-six, and giving him one rixdollar. On the other hand, middle-class homes opened up to him; he borrowed books from them, recited Holberg and Shakespeare, and improvised songs for a provincial audience that was by turns amused, intrigued and condescending.

All this meant nothing to his mother, who sent him off to work at a cloth mill, Koch og Hirschfeldts Klædefabrik (Koch and Hirschfeldt's Clothing Factory), which had opened in 1811—one of the first factories in Odense—and employed a neighbour's son. His grandmother took him there, complaining as they went that he was too good for such work, which was done mostly by rough German journeymen. Hans Christian lasted only a short time. On the first day, his beautiful singing voice was discovered—"all the looms stood still, all the journeymen listened to me"—and it was arranged that others should do his work while he entertained them. Days later, however—"when I was in my best singing vein, and everybody spoke of the extraordinary brilliancy of my voice"—one of the journeymen said that he was a girl, and not a boy. They seized him and pulled off his clothes to find out: "I cried and screamed. The other journeymen thought it very amusing, and held me fast by my arms and legs. I screamed aloud, and was as much ashamed as a girl; and then, darting from them, rushed home to my mother, who immediately promised me that I should never go there again."

She arranged for him to work at a tobacco factory instead, which employed only a few boys. "Now I found myself among tobacco plants, watched them make chewing tobacco and snuff, and received quite good treatment myself," Andersen recalled in *The Book of My Life*. "My voice was appreciated here, too, people even came to the factory to hear me sing, and the peculiar thing was that I did not remember a single song, but I improvised both the lyrics and the tune; both were very complex and difficult. 'He should go on stage,' everyone said, and I started to get those sorts of ideas." His mother was persuaded that tobacco was bad for his health, and within weeks he was back with his books and dolls. Encouraged by his fastidiousness in cutting clothes for his puppets, Anne Marie urged him to become a tailor, suggesting Mr. Dickmann, the Odense tailor, as a model, who had a large house with big windows and employed journeymen, but Hans Christian now talked only of acting.

In June 1818, when he was thirteen, a troupe from Copenhagen's Royal Theatre came on tour to Odense, and the bill distributor allowed Andersen to come backstage. He talked to the actors and was given a walk-on part in Charles Guillaume Etienne's operetta *Cendrillon*: "I was always the first there, put on the red silk costume, spoke my line and believed that the whole audience thought only of me." His interest in the theatre turned to frenzy, and he began to dream of going to Copenhagen to make a career at the Royal Theatre.

The next month, July 1818, his desire to leave Odense increased when his mother got married again, to another, much younger journeyman shoemaker called Niels Jørgensen Gundersen. He was thirty-one and, Andersen later recalled, very different from his father and in character and mind more similar to his mother. Andersen claimed that Gundersen's appearance in his life was irrelevant to him, for, fearful of seeming an evil stepfather, he refused to have any part in the boy's upbringing, so everything remained the same for him. But the family lived in one room. Hans Christian had had his mother more or less to himself since he was seven, and Gundersen arrived just as he was entering adolescence. Andersen already associated his mother's family with promiscuity, and was nervous about his illegitimate half-sister Karen-Marie; as he watched his mother grow even poorer with Gundersen—he left her impoverished when he died in 1822—the link between poverty and sexuality that recurs throughout his work may have crystallized in his mind. It is most apparent in his novel *OT*—the initials for Odense Tugthus, the town gaol—where sex is seen as a dark force coming from the criminal underclass; in stories such as "Poultry Meg's Family," where a promiscuous noble lady ends up a poor ferrywoman married to, and beaten by, her former servant, the message is that sex brings you down socially.

Gundersen, however, probably only made more urgent the plan that was already forming in his mind: to make a new life in Copenhagen. He must have felt the family dynamics changing, and the chief casualty was his grandmother, who now became a stranger in their home: Andersen was the only link which kept her there, and she seemed to him to have suddenly turned old with grief and suffering. His mother understood him less and less, and he was confused by his own exalted hopes: "She did not understand my impulses and my endeavours, nor indeed at that time did I myself."

Ambition was the driving force. At thirteen or fourteen, all the Odense children were confirmed: the rich children went to the provost for catechism lessons, the poor children to the chaplain—an unspoken but unbroken rule, though the provost was obliged to accept anyone who presented himself. Andersen did so—"although taking the lowest place, I was still above those who were under the care of the chaplain." The provost made it clear that he was unwelcome, the grammar school boys, whom he watched enviously through the railings of their playground, ignored him; "I had daily the feeling of having thrust myself in where people thought that I did not belong." He stuck it out, and walked down the aisle in a confirmation suit altered from his dead father's coat and new boots. "The boots creaked, and that inwardly pleased me, for thus the congregation would hear that they were new," Andersen recalled—that thought, and damnation as a punishment, is given to Karen as she imagines the portraits in the church admiring her new shoes in "The Red Shoes." Andersen's pushiness paid off, however, for there was one girl in the provost's class, Laura Tønder Lund, from a rich home, who always looked gently and kindly at him, and even once gave him a rose. Andersen, quick to seize his chance, told her of his dreams about going to Copenhagen, and she later became an important contact for him.

In April 1819, just after Andersen's confirmation, his mother and step-father moved to a house at the bottom of Munkemøllestræde by the river, where Anne Marie did her washing. The place, one of Odense's scenic high points, was called Monk's Mill Gate, and the Gundersens' house here had a small garden, which Andersen turned into a stage for his talents:

My habit on summer evenings was to sit in my parents' tiny garden, which ran down to the river; just across from me, water rushed down the mill wheel, between the elder trees I could see as far as Nonnebakken [Nun's Hill], from which the water separated me, and also therefore from the Trolls; over in the mill the journeyman ran up and down and farmers drove across the bridge; in short, it resembled a beautiful painting. Councillor Falbe's garden was next to

The river at Munkemølle where his mother worked as a washerwoman.

that of my parents, and nearby was the old St. Knud's Church. While the church bells rang in the evening I sat there, lost in strange dreams, watching the mill wheel and singing my improvised songs. The strangers in Mr. Falbe's garden often used to listen. (The lady of the house was the famous beauty Miss Beck, who had played Ida in *Hermann von Unna*.) I often sensed the existence of my audience behind the fence and I was flattered. So I became known, and people sent for me to hear "the little Nightingale from Funen" as I was called.

The half-conscious, half-unconscious, presentation of himself as an innocent child set a pattern that lasted a lifetime. In the grand houses of Odense, he established a persona—the naive, talented country boy—which he understood would appeal to a cultured class schooled on romantic ideas of natural genius and the purity of the childish imagination. The soprano voice, emblem of boyhood, was an appropriate vehicle for Andersen: at once by instinct and by calculation, giving free rein to his naturally child-like character yet exploiting it for effect, he played to his audience, and was soon a local celebrity. It assured his rise up the social ladder, but it also marked the start of a process of psychological self-damage, of living a life in which he always felt he had to act a part, until in the end he was no longer certain who he really was. This is a theme of "The Shadow," the frightening tale of *doppelgänger* that he wrote in middle age; at fourteen, he was already turning into his own double.

Andersen's histrionic talents were soon one of the sights of the city. He sang and recited plays at homes ranging from that of Mr. Andersen the chemist to that of Colonel Høegh-Guldberg, who presented him to Crown Prince Christian at Odense Castle. He recited Holberg and improvised a song; asked what he wanted to do, he replied that Høegh-Guldberg had told him to say he wanted to go to grammar school, but he was in fact set on becoming an actor or singer. The Prince considered this inappropriate; he offered to sponsor him through an apprenticeship to a trade, but Andersen rejected the idea without a thought.

Andersen then tried another connection, an eminent printer called Christian Iversen, whom he begged to write a letter of recommendation to Anna Margrethe Schall, the most famous ballerina at Copenhagen's Royal Theatre. It was obvious to Iversen, as it was to the other families for whom Andersen performed, that the boy prodigy was a fantasist whose talent was unlikely to last once his voice had broken; thus Iversen, too, suggested an apprenticeship instead. Andersen claimed to have replied solemnly, "That would actually be a great sin"—the remark accords with his self-righteous faith in his romantic calling. He persuaded Iversen, however, and got his letter to Madame Schall, though the printer protested he did not know her at all.

On 2 September 1819, Andersen called on Mr. Plum, the bishop of Odense, asking for money to help him get to Copenhagen. The bishop's wife asked him to return in the evening to give a performance, and "he accepted at once, bustling out of the door like some dandy," wrote Ottilie Christensen, a dean's daughter from Ollerup who was staying with the bishop. That evening she recorded her impressions—one of the few early, objective records we have of Andersen which were not written with hindsight after he had become famous:

> Master Comedy-Player arrived at dusk . . . At eight o'clock the chandeliers were lit in the drawing room, and all of us . . . were arranged in a circle in the room, and for two whole hours the little gentleman played parts from various comedies and tragedies; as a rule he did well, but we were much amused whether he succeeded or not, the gay parts were the best, but it was most absurd to watch him doing the part of a sentimental lover, kneeling down or

fainting, because just then his large feet did not look their very best; well, perhaps they can improve their style in Copenhagen, perhaps in time he will make his appearance as a great man on the stage. In the evening we had sandwiches and red fruit jelly, our actor joined us, but in hot haste so as not to lose any time parading his talent. At half-past ten the bishop's wife thanked him for coming, and he went home.

Over the past year, Andersen had managed to save thirteen rixdollars from the pocket money wealthy families had given him in thanks for his performances.* This was as much as a journeyman might earn in several months, and he now wept and plagued his mother to let him go to Copenhagen to make his name. "First you go through an awful lot, and then you become famous," he told her. Anne Marie protested but let him go, hoping that his timidity would get the better of him. "He lets me have no peace," she told her neighbours. "I have therefore given my consent, but I am sure he will go no further than Nyborg; when he sees the rough sea, he will be frightened and turn back again."

The rough sea was the Great Belt, the twenty-mile stretch of the Baltic between Funen and Zealand, and to cross it in 1819 you needed a special travel pass. With this and a bundle of clothes, Andersen left Odense on a sunny afternoon on 4 September. His mother bribed the postillion to take him as a cheap passenger on the mailcoach to Copenhagen for three rixdollars. She came with him to the town gate. There his grandmother was waiting to say goodbye: "In the last few years her beautiful hair had turned grey; she fell upon my neck and wept, without being able to speak a word." She never saw him again.

It is hard to imagine the glamour of the farewell for a 14-year-old who had only travelled a few miles before. "The postillion blew his horn," he

---

* Danish currency for most of Andersen's lifetime was denominated in *rigsdaler* (rixdollars), marks and shillings. On 1 January 1870 the kroner, as used in Denmark today, replaced the *rigsdaler*; one *rigsdaler* equalled two kroner. Multiplying *rigsdaler* by about 100 provides an approximate equivalent in kroner today. Multiplying *rigsdaler* by about 10 therefore provides an approximate equivalent in pounds sterling (e.g., 200 *rigsdaler* equals 20,000 kroner, which equals £2,000).

These figures are more easily understood in context, as relative costs and wages were very different from today. Rents, for example, were considerably cheaper; travel, on the other hand, was a luxury item and much more expensive. A well-paid printer in nineteenth-century Denmark earned around 500 *rigsdaler* a year; the headteacher of a grammar school earned about 1,000 *rigsdaler*; there was however no income tax until 1862, when it was introduced at the rate of 2 per cent.

wrote, and "I rolled into the world with ten rixdollars." As they trundled east towards the coast, he rejoiced at every new sight, but when they reached the unfamiliar port of Nyborg and he was borne away by ship from his native island, he recalled, "I then truly felt how alone and forlorn I was." They crossed to Korsør on the island of Zealand. The whole day and the following night they trundled on through cities and villages, stopping occasionally to change horses: "I stood solitarily by the carriage, and ate my bread while it was repacked, and thought I was far away in the wide world." In his own mind, he was at once a fictional hero setting out on an adventure, and a child suddenly and terrifyingly out of his depth in an adult world.

CHAPTER 3

The City

1819–1822

Goodness gracious, what a lot of gold there was! There was enough for him to buy the whole of Copenhagen, all the sugar-pigs that the cake-women sell, and all the tin-soldiers and whips and rocking-horses in the world.

—HANS CHRISTIAN ANDERSEN, "The Tinderbox"

"If a marble city with golden roofs had lain before him he would not have been astonished, his imagination was prepared for anything." Andersen wrote this in the novel *Only a Fiddler*, when his hero Christian first sees Copenhagen. The city lies on the eastern edge of the island of Zealand, and in the early nineteenth century most travellers arriving by land got their first, dramatic view of it when the coach mounted the steep Roskilde Road into the suburb of Frederiksberg. At the top of the hill Frederiksberg Castle, the royal summer residence, stands looking down to the capital. It is a magnificent vantage point: the eighteenth-century castle is surrounded by two great parks, designed in English romantic style with waterfalls and a grotto and a Chinese pavilion. Below range the spires and towers of Copenhagen, which in 1819 still had the layout of a fortress: a small city confined within a shield of moats and high ramparts, some topped by windmills, ringed by a belt of green land. Within, the buildings were forced upwards like asparagus and arranged like flowerpots on a ledge. No dwellings were allowed immediately outside the ramparts, and the city was entered through one of four town gates, which were locked each night. Until 1808 the keys had been deposited with the king, who was said to have slept with them under his pillow.

Frederiksberg was the final staging post before Vesterport, the West Gate, and according to his mother's pact with the coachman, Andersen was to be set down here to walk the last ten miles into town, as he had not paid the full fare. The coach stopped at the top of the hill on Monday morning,

6 September, and Andersen stood quite alone, for the other passengers continued into Copenhagen. He looked down for a moment, enchanted. Then he passed the guards and went into the castle gardens, Frederiksberg Have, which were open to everyone, and where people strolled in the summer to watch Frederik VI being rowed along the canals in a white boat under the arching bridges. Andersen walked across the park, past the octagonal Frederiksberg Church with its odd, pointed roof, and then trudged the length of Frederiksberg Allé, a long straight boulevard fringed with sentinels of lime trees. Next came the suburb of Vesterbro, all low houses and big gardens set in green fields. At its end stood the Liberty Column, an obelisk recently erected to commemorate the liberation of Danish peasants from feudal overlords, and Trommesalen, the livestock market, then the sentries and the Excise Booth, until finally at the West Gate Andersen joined the hordes of carriages, traders with carts, farmers leading their cattle, horses and riders, and pedestrians entering the town. He knew no one in the entire city, but some of his companions in the mailcoach had recommended an inexpensive inn near the gate called Gardergården at 18, Vestergade, and here he went at once, took the cheapest room, put down his bag and rushed out into the streets.

Everywhere was throbbing with unruly crowds, for two nights before the last pogrom against the Jews ever to take place in Denmark had broken out in Copenhagen and in several provincial cities, and unrest was still simmering. Henrik Hertz, a young writer who was to become first an adversary and then a friend of Andersen, was among the many Jews who had fled to Frederiksberg and gone into hiding to protect themselves against the mob. In the city, soldiers were trying to restore order, but gangs of youths were still stirring up disorder, windows were smashed, a few shots were fired. Unaware of its context, however, he revelled in it: "The whole city was in commotion, everybody was in the streets, and the noise and tumult of Copenhagen far exceeded, therefore, any idea which my imagination had formed of this, to me at that time, great city," he wrote in his autobiography. Vestergade, a narrow, undistinguished road of run-down inns and lodging houses, meanders into the city's oldest square, the market place Gammeltorv (Old Market), with its giant fountain at the centre. Regular market days were Wednesdays and Saturdays, but street peddlars, fishwives and people congregating around the public water pumps were out every day, the Town Hall on the square was a natural gathering point, and when Andersen arrived, some of the mob from the previous day were still milling about in

Copenhagen, view from Gammelstrand. Andersen arrived there alone aged fourteen, and wrote that "the noise and tumult of Copenhagen far exceeded . . . any idea which my imagination had formed of this . . . great city."

the side streets. "Everybody appeared to be excited, like the blood of a delirious subject," Andersen wrote when he described the scene in *Only a Fiddler.*

A naive 14-year-old, Andersen noticed only what was grand and bustling in the city. He was oblivious to the sense of menace, and his accounts of his response do not mention those aspects which struck other contemporary commentators—the poverty, the stench, the rubbish floating down the canals. Copenhagen—the name means merchant's harbour—has been an important Baltic trading centre since the eleventh century, and to the country boy its cosmopolitan activity was thrilling. The waters of The Sound, the narrow and strategically vital stretch of the Baltic between Denmark and Sweden, form the city's eastern border, and the busy port, its ships and sailors and merchants, have always dominated the city. The harbour and shallow canals extend inland, and the network of narrow winding streets around the waterways still gives the town a medieval layout. Streets like

Gammelstrand (Old Strand), home of the fish market, and Nyhavn (New Harbour), where Andersen lived for twenty years, are perfect examples of the Northern European mercantile culture: terraces of tall, brightly coloured, gabled merchants' homes and warehouses with steep roofs in the Dutch style flanking a waterway.

These bold, outward-looking façades made Odense seem like a toy town in comparison; so did the fine shops Andersen saw as he left his lodgings, crossed Gammeltorv and walked up Skindergade to the dramatic Runde-tårn (Round Tower) with its arrow-like windows and observation plat-form—one of Copenhagen's landmarks. At the top was the university library; below were flourishing streets of bookshops and newspapers and publishers centred on Købmagergade—1819 was the year Andersen's own subsequent publisher, Carl Reitzel, began his innovative business. Then there were the different sorts of traffic: wagons; the "globe post," gleaming spheres containing mail and newspapers, pulled by two horses; the car-riages of the nobility; between them wandered pigs, cows and chickens. Kierkegaard, who was six years old when Andersen arrived in Copenhagen, lived in a building adjoining the Town Hall, and left this well-known memory of the sounds of the city when he opened his window on a sum-mer's day:

> A wandering musician was playing the minuet from *Don Giovanni* on a kind of piccolo or some such (I could not see because he was in another courtyard), and the apothecary was grinding his medicines and the maid was scrubbing in the courtyard and the stable boy was rubbing down his horse, knocking the currycomb against the cobbles, and far off in another part of town the voice of a shrimp-seller rang out, and they noticed nothing, not even the piccolo player, and I felt so well.

Andersen's first stop was the Royal Theatre, scene of his happiest dreams and wildest longings. A graceful neo-classical building in the western corner of Kongens Nytorv (King's New Square), the best address in town, the Royal Theatre was home to opera, drama and dance, and was a magnet for the Copenhagen middle classes. Playwrights, actors, dancers, singers were the heroes of the day, their performances the gossip of the morning papers. Probably only Vienna, where even today the activities of the Burgtheater regularly make front-page news, was comparable to nineteenth-century Copenhagen in its high-minded devotion to the performing arts. Like Vienna's, Copenhagen's bourgeoisie was a tightly knit, insular community where refinement and civilized living was almost a religion. The singer Jenny Lind, who performed throughout Europe and America, wrote at the end of her life, "I shall never forget the joy with which I sang at Copenhagen, for never since have I found more cultivated artists anywhere."

In his pilgrimage to the Royal Theatre, Andersen was a child of his time; he had sensed by instinct where the spiritual heart of the nation lay, and he was desperate to join it. He walked round the building several times, "looked up to its walls, and regarded them almost as a home." There was already a crowd here, for the cheaper tickets were unnumbered, and there were also ticket touts circling the theatre. In his autobiographies, Andersen exaggerates his naivety, but the story of his encounter with one of these dubious characters on his first night has an authentic ring. Offered a ticket for the evening's performance, Andersen believed he was being given a present, and accepted gratefully; when the tout asked him where he would like to sit, he answered modestly that anywhere would be fine, whereupon the tout thought he was being mocked and flew into a rage. Terrified, Andersen ran away.

It was an inauspicious beginning to a tormented relationship with the Royal Theatre. At fourteen, Andersen was stagestruck. Like generations of histrionic, effeminate, artistically talented boys, he wanted to enter the theatre in any capacity whatsoever—as dancer, singer, actor, dramatist. His youthful romance with the theatre never left him. It was one of the areas where he remained emotionally an adolescent, and thus he was driven, even as an elderly, famous man, to re-enact in his dealings with the Royal Theatre the episodes of insecurity and rejection which marked his early efforts to get on the stage.

He walked back to his lodgings in the medieval quarter, following the route from Gothersgade and Nørreport (North Gate) down to Gammeltorv and Højbro Plads, another market square on the quayside. By early evening in September, the streets were darkening, presenting a slightly sinister aspect to a country boy: the tall houses cast their shadows, people lurked on the corners of alleys. The city was badly lit by oil lamps—gas lighting, common in London by 1820, did not come to Copenhagen until the 1850s—and when it was full moon the streets were not lit at all, lending the economizing Copenhagen authorities the nickname "Corporation Moonshine." In these streets night watchmen, dressed in blue uniforms and carrying maces, were often found drunk or asleep in doorways; a student prank was to swap the shop signs while they slept.

Next morning Andersen began his campaign to join the cultural life of the city. His first attempt was as a dancer, and armed with the Odense printer's letter of recommendation, he presented himself at the home of the leading ballerina, Madame Schall, at 19, Bredgade. Bredgade was part of the long straight sequence of wide streets that lead off from Kongens Nytorv towards Amalienborg, the royal palace on the octagonal square by the harbour, and up to a large formal park called Kongens Have (The King's Garden). On these elegant streets lived civil servants and merchants, fashionable artists and their patrons. Discreet, finely proportioned—the King had decreed a uniform window height in 1749—and finished with decorative sandstone detailing which gave life to their grey façades, these houses spoke of order, cohesion, conformity. To Andersen, their splendour was overwhelming. Dressed in his best clothes—his confirmation suit, his new boots and a large hat which fell half over his eyes—he flung himself on the doorstep to pray for success before ringing the bell, and was horrified to be

Theatregoers at the Royal Theatre, Copenhagen. Andersen's life-long affair with this theatre began in 1819, when he saw the operetta Paul et Virginie. *"When Paul in the second act is torn away from Virginie, I burst into violent crying . . . Those who sat nearby became aware of my intense weeping and gave me apples and comforted me."*

thrown a coin by the maidservant, who took him for a beggar. With Madame Schall herself he fared even worse, for she had never heard of the printer and did not understand why he demanded to dance the *Cendrillon* that he had seen in Odense. In *The Book of My Life* he recalled: "I improvised both text and music, and to be able to execute better the dance scene with the tambourine . . . I placed my shoes in a corner and danced wearing only socks on my feet." Madame Schall thought him a lunatic, and had him instantly removed from her house.

Next he tried a well-known critic, and then the manager of the theatre, who told him he was "too thin for the theatre"—maybe a euphemism for too poor, because when Andersen replied, "O if you will only engage me with one hundred rixdollars salary, then I shall soon get fat," the man sent him away, saying he "only engaged people of education." To console himself, Andersen spent the last of his money on a ticket for the operetta *Paul et Virginie*, at the Royal Theatre. He sat in the gallery, and he interpreted the piece, characteristically, as a variation on his own biography—his separation from the theatre being the equivalent of Paul's from Virginie:

> When Paul in the second act is torn away from Virginie, I burst into violent crying . . . Those who sat nearby became aware of my intense weeping and gave me apples and comforted me. I thought them all such nice people, didn't know the world at all, considered them all kind and excellent, and therefore told them, quite naively, the whole upper circle, who I was, how I had travelled here, and how terrible it was that I could not go to the Theatre, but that my situation was exactly like Paul's down there.

After this, and further fruitless visits to Madame Schall and the theatre director, his savings were gone and he had reached a dead end. He paid his bill at the Vestergade lodging house, and was left, he says in his autobiographies, with one rixdollar. He looked up a friendly passenger with whom he had travelled on the mailcoach to Copenhagen, a Mrs. Hermansen; she was kind but advised him—who would not have done?—to go back to Odense at once. But Andersen was both stubborn and fearful of going home a laughing stock, so he settled on a compromise: he would get apprenticed in Copenhagen, and use the money to fund his attempts to join the theatre.

He bought a newspaper, answered an advertisement for a cabinet-maker's apprentice, and was invited to move into the cabinet-maker's house to try out the work while he waited for his formal papers, an attestation and confirmation of baptism, to arrive from Odense. But next morning the familiar scenario played itself out again. Andersen was teased by the journeymen and the other apprentices: "the rude jests of the young fellows went so far, that, in remembrance of the scene at the manufactory, I took the resolute determination not to remain a single day longer in the workshop." By the afternoon he had fled, and was wandering the unknown streets and considering a return to Odense.

He had now been in the capital twelve days, and had not yet thought to exploit the fine voice that had earned him the nickname "little nightingale of Funen." So he went to the home of the director of the Royal Choir School, an Italian called Giuseppe Siboni. The housekeeper opened the door and listened with sympathy as Andersen told her "the whole history" of his life. She went to report the tale to Siboni, then ushered Andersen into the drawing room. Siboni was giving a large dinner for some of the artistic luminaries of Copenhagen, including the composer Weyse and the poet Jens Baggesen. The assembly was a daunting bunch.

The ageing Baggesen, foppishly dressed, worldly and cavalier, was famous as a poet and as a sophisticated traveller. Siboni, strong-featured and corpulent, with a shock of grey hair, sideburns and thick, curving eyebrows, was a passionate Italian who spoke halting Danish, had a terrible temper and had made enemies by determinedly introducing Italian opera to the Royal Theatre. Weyse, kindly and mild-faced, was nevertheless formidable—his dinner party attire was a blue tail-coat with gilt buttons, a straw-coloured waistcoat, frilled shirt and cuffs and the order of the Knights of the Dannebrog in his buttonhole. His appetite was legendary—an anniversary dinner he recorded consisted of turtle soup, oysters, fricandeau with green peas, halibut with caper sauce and potatoes, chicken with truffles, asparagus, plum pudding, roast venison and grouse, an almond paste basket and two other cakes, fruit and vanilla ice cream, oranges and apples, red wine, port, madeira, hock and champagne—and his eccentricity noted: he had once sat at the piano and drummed out the same five notes repeatedly until his hostess realized that they spelt CAFFE, and that he had had none.

Before this audience, Andersen, in his father's altered coat and his floppy hat, sang, acted some scenes from Holberg, then burst into tears. We have only his own record of this performance, but according to his autobiography, the company applauded and Siboni at once promised to cultivate his voice and train him as a singer at the Royal Theatre. Weyse organized a subscription to fund him. Baggesen, he claimed, said, "I prophesy that one day something will come out of him," and to Andersen, "but do not be vain when some day the whole public applauds you," adding "something about pure true nature, and that this is too often destroyed by years and by intercourse with mankind." Andersen was shown out by the housekeeper, who stroked him and told him to go to Weyse's house the next day.

Whether this support was offered so immediately and readily, or whether Andersen took longer to find it than he later liked people to believe, it is clear that a mixture of luck and those factors which had got him noticed in Odense—talent, persistence, the naive/shrewd play on the romantic idea of innocence—now worked again in his favour. It helped that Weyse himself had risen from relative poverty. In 1789 he had come to study in Copenhagen as a 15-year-old from Holstein, and ever since he had refused to leave Denmark because he had been violently seasick on the ship bringing him there. He had depended on rich merchant families as patrons, and he would have seen immediate parallels with Andersen's situation. It was also significant that this was the beginning of the nineteenth century, the first period in history when musicians were held to be men of artistic genius rather than servants in the households of cathedral functionaries or princes. As late as 1781, Mozart had been placed below the valets in the Archbishop of Salzburg's household; twenty years later Beethoven had pioneered the idea of the artist as touched by the divine, as a sort of intermediary between God and man and a figure beyond social status—in 1812 he told Goethe, as the Empress of Austria and various dukes approached, "they must make way for us, not us for them."

The new romantic notion of an inborn musical genius that deserved cultivating was crucial in inspiring the support that Andersen received. He had the good fortune to arrive in Copenhagen just as Romanticism, with its idealization of childhood innocence, was becoming a dominant strain. At the theatre, the romantic dramatist Adam Oehlenschläger, friend of Goethe, held sway. The Danish poet Bernhard Severin Ingemann was in 1819 making links with German romantic writers like Tieck and Hoffmann, and this was to have far-reaching effects on the country's literature. The physicist Hans Christian Ørsted, in 1819 on the verge of discovering electro-magnetism, was already known as a romantic philosopher through his lectures on cosmology and the spirit of nature. All were to become friends of Andersen; in 1819 they were part of a group of intellectuals whose originality was paving the way for a second generation of outstanding Danish artists to rise from obscurity. In 1819, Christen Købke, great painter of the Danish Golden Age, was nine years old and growing up as the son of a Copenhagen baker, and Johanne Luise Heiberg, leading actress on the Danish nineteenth-century stage, was still a 6-year-old gypsy living with her tinker family on a fairground north of Copenhagen. Like Andersen, they were unconnected, ambitious, and poised to take advantage of the social mobility created by a rising bourgeoisie and its belief in meritocracy.

The morning after his impromptu "audition," Andersen went to see Weyse, who had an apartment on Kronprinsessegade looking out on to Kongens Have. He was told that a subscription at the dinner had raised seventy rixdollars, which he would receive in monthly instalments of ten rixdollars. He had to learn German in order to communicate with Siboni, who would give him all his meals, and the run of his house during the day, although he would have to find his own lodgings. But rents were lower than they are today, and his ten rixdollars a month would cover the price of a cheap room. Thrilled, he wrote home of his success; his overjoyed mother showed his letter to all her friends, although she could not read it herself.

Andersen now began the double life which was at once enthralling to a 14-year-old country boy and devastating to his fragile, unformed ego. By day, he lived at Siboni's house, received singing lessons, sat in on opera rehearsals at the Royal Theatre, and acted as a model for Siboni's niece Marietta, who was drawing the choirmaster as Achilles and sketched Andersen in a tunic or toga. His patrons' idea was that he accommodate to bourgeois life, but he felt more at home with the servants, and spent hours in the kitchen, helping, running errands and listening to stories, until one day he appeared at the dinner table bearing one of the dishes and Siboni marched off to the kitchen to insist that he was not a servant and should spend his time in the parlour. Siboni as a teacher was compelling—in his poor German and hopeless Danish, "he tried with his whole soul to teach his pupils not only to sing, but also to understand and conceive the character they were representing." He was a kind but exacting master and Andersen was terrified of his rages: "I was so frightened that I shivered in all my limbs . . . and sometimes, when he was giving me a lesson, his severe look would make my voice quiver and bring tears into my eyes. 'Hikke banke Du,' (Me no you beat), said he in his broken Danish and let me go; but calling me back again he put some money into my hand, 'to amuse yourself with,' said he, with a kind-hearted smile."

By night, the picture changed entirely. Andersen found lodgings round the corner from Siboni's house with a widow, Mrs. Thorgesen, in Ulkegade, a dark slum street notorious for its brothels, behind Kongens Nytorv. He had a tiny room, not much more than a larder, without a window, which led off the kitchen; later he was joined by another lodger, a Miss Müller, who was visited for a few hours each evening by her "father," so shy that he was muffled up with coats and scarves and a hat pulled over his eyes. Andersen sometimes opened the door to him; many years on, he came across "Mr. Müller" in high society, "a polite old gentleman covered with orders." But despite his naivety, he discovered, while living in Ulkegade, that his aunt Christiane ran a brothel in the capital. He visited her just once: "[she] was very hard on my poor mother, whom . . . she rebuked for being vulgar and uncivilized and without education, and she ended by saying 'And see, after having behaved so badly to me, she now lumps me with her child! And a boy as well—if only it had been a girl!' "

The first thing a provincial newcomer to a slum street like Ulkegade would have noticed was the dreadful stench. There was dung in the streets and dirty water in the canals nearby; there was a shortage of washing facilities, for only half of the city's houses had their own water pumps; from the market squares round the corner there drifted up the mixed odours of unwrapped meat, soured milk being transported in wooden churns and fish, carried into the city in barrels by fishwives from the coastal villages, and either dried up by the sun or soaking in ice and rainwater. A peculiarity of the capital was that most of the aquavit distillers, and some other citizens, kept cows; they were fed on the residue from aquavit, of which their milk tasted unmistakably, and they lived in filthy byres in back yards, cellars, outhouses, even in tenement flats. Distillers might have around twenty-five cows in stalls lined with thick layers of muck, and so densely packed that the cattle could not lie down. There were fines for "the flushing away of cow dung," but it was a frequent practice, and the mess merged with the smelly effluent discharged by the tanners up at the ramparts, with particles of straw, potato peelings and old boot soles which swam in a blackish-grey slime in open gutters. In the early morning, night soil carts clattered through the streets collecting the rubbish, often after the butchers had opened. The wooden butchers' booths around the ruined St. Nicholas Church near Ulkegade were notorious for their smell, the bloody heads and entrails on show, the nearby gutters flowing red. All this in one of the most overcrowded cities in Europe, where large families often lived in one room, every cellar and tiny attic and outhouse was occupied, and a population of

120,000 was crammed into an area which is today occupied by 25,000. In 1825 a Major-General Rasmus Krag returned home from a trip abroad and wrote to tell King Frederik that nothing on his travels could compare with the beauty of Denmark; there was just one exception, he said—nowhere had he seen butchers' shops or fishmarkets as disgusting as those in Copenhagen. The insalubrious food trades made stomach complaints frequent—Andersen always refused to eat pork—and it was a series of cholera epidemics that finally persuaded a subsequent King, Frederik VII, to abandon his vision of the capital as a fortress and allow it to spread beyond the town gates in 1853.

In a city like this, as in most nineteenth-century capitals, the contrast between the sheltered life of the rich and that of the poor was extreme. The gulf between Mrs. Thorgesen's and Siboni's homes was enormous—neither could have imagined the other, while Andersen went back and forth between the two throughout the winter of 1819–1820. He spent the nights in the windowless room in Ulkegade curled up in bed reading by candlelight, writing poems and answering the door to Mr. Müller. At Siboni's, he looked increasingly shabby, as he had no warm winter clothes or shoes, and in the spring of 1820 the gap between his two lives looked unbridgeable when his voice began to break and Siboni dismissed him from his lessons and his house. Weyse's fund for him had run out, and again came the advice he had heard from the Odense nobility, from the Crown Prince, now from his Copenhagen patrons—go home and learn a trade. Impoverished and abandoned, he refused, but instead played for all he was worth on the wealthy Odense contacts that he had made.

He called on Laura Tønder Lund, the girl from his Odense confirmation class, who had recently moved to Copenhagen, and she gave him some of her pocket money and collected more from her friends. He looked up the writer Frederik Guldberg, brother of the Odense colonel who had supported him, and once more the miracle happened—Guldberg offered to give him lessons in Danish and German, and organized a subscription fund for him. The contributors included Weyse, the composer Frederik Kuhlau and the philologist and librarian Just Matthias Thiele, who, inspired by the Grimm brothers, had just begun collecting Danish folk tales—something of the new romantic view of folklore may have encouraged him to be generous to the country boy he had never met. Eighty rixdollars was collected, to be paid to Andersen as before in monthly instalments of ten rixdollars.

He was much worse off, though, for now he had to find his own food, and when he asked Mrs. Thorgesen, she demanded twenty rixdollars a month for full board and lodgings, to include the privilege of sitting in her drawing room whenever he wanted, as his own box-room had no light. His description of this crisis in his first autobiography, written twelve years later, shows how close he remained to the peasant superstitions of his mother:

> What could I do? Crying, I asked her to accept the ten rixdollars I had, and then wait for a fortnight for the next ten, I would somehow get hold of the money. "I want twenty rixdollars," she insisted. "You have eighty rixdollars with Mr. Guldberg, that is your money, and he will not keep you from it. From this you can live for four months, and after that he is bound to find ways. Now I'm going to town, and if you do not get hold of twenty rixdollars before I get back, you can go your way!" She left, and I sat there weeping in her drawing room. A picture of her late husband hung on the wall; while lying sobbing in front of it, it seemed to me that the picture looked at me kindly, and in my child-like innocence I prayed through the picture to the dead man that he would soften his wife's heart for my sake, poor child that I was; indeed I took my tears and smeared them on to the eyes of the portrait to make him feel how unhappily I cried.

When his landlady returned, she was more sympathetic, and accepted the ten rixdollars on condition that Andersen produce another ten in a fortnight; each month he scraped together the extra ten rixdollars from various quarters such as Laura Tønder Lund; from Siboni's maidservants, who offered him a little of their wages; from running errands. When the subscription fund ran out early in 1821, Guldberg dedicated to him, as an underprivileged young scholar, the proceeds of a book of verse and prose. He got help in other ways too—he discovered that the librarian at the university library at the top of the Round Tower also came from Odense, and charmed him into giving him the run of the library and allowing him to take books home: "he only commanded me to put them again in their right place." He read voraciously, and his favourite author was Walter Scott. "When I first arrived in Copenhagen, often walking about poor and forlorn, without sufficient money for a meal," he wrote later, "I spent the few pence I possessed to obtain from a library one of Walter Scott's novels, and felt myself rich and happy."

He may have exaggerated his suffering in his autobiographies, but during the years 1820–1822 he certainly lived on the edge of want, he was often cold and hungry, his feet were soaking from the ice on his worn boots, he grew

out of his clothes and he appeared absurd as he tried to pull down his sleeves
and trousers to make them look as if they fitted or stuffed paper underneath
the coats people gave him as cast-offs, refusing to unbutton them so they
would not seem too big for his lean body. His friend Edvard Collin
glimpsed him for the first time during these years, and recalled that Andersen stood out because of his lanky figure and his yellow trousers, which only
reached halfway down his shins. In 1821 Mrs. Thorgesen moved to the West
Indies with a new husband, and Andersen took a room in the apartment
above, with a sailor's family, with whom he later moved round the corner to
another disreputable street, Dybensgade, and another windowless box-
room. To save money, he took only breakfast here; his landlady believed he
lunched with various families, but in fact he only ate a little bread on one of
the benches in the Royal Garden—"I was, in truth, very forlorn."

What made so many eminent men take an interest in a gauche, overgrown
and ill-educated boy from the provinces? By all accounts he was ridiculous.
In the summer of 1820 he did the rounds of thanking all his benefactors in
person, and in his memoirs Just Matthias Thiele leaves a picture of a classic
ugly duckling:

> I was sitting at my desk, with my back to the door, when there was a knock on
> it. Saying: "Come in" I didn't even turn my head, but as I lifted my eyes from
> my papers, I was surprised to see an upstart boy, with quite peculiar looks
> standing by the door with a deeply theatrical bow towards the floor. His cap he
> had already thrown off by the door, and when that lanky figure in a worn-out
> grey coat whose sleeves did not reach his emaciated wrists rose, I saw a pair of
> small, Chinese eyes, that needed a chirurgical operation, in order to get a clear
> view from behind a large, protruding nose. He wore a colourful calico scarf
> around his neck, knit so tightly that it seemed as if his long neck was straining
> to get away, in short, a surprising character, who became even more surprising
> when he, taking a few steps forwards and repeating his bow, began to speak in
> a pathetic way: "May I have the honour to express my feelings for the theatre
> in a poem I have written myself?"
>
> In my astonishment I did not even start to move before he was in the mid-
> dle of the declamation, and when he ended with another reference, there fol-
> lowed immediately the execution of a scene from *Hagbarth and Signe*
> [Oehlenschläger's tragedy], a scene in which he played all the roles. I sat
> dumbfounded and waited for the entr'acte which might give me an opportu-

nity for a question and an answer. But in vain: the performance brought me from one scene in a tragedy to another in a comedy, and when he finally reached an epilogue that he also had written himself, he ended with several theatrical bows, grasped his cap lying as a gaping spectator by the door, and— off he was down the stairs!

Two years later, he had barely changed: a young girl in Copenhagen wrote to her sister:

> Ask Ottilie if she can remember the little shoemaker's son from Odense, who used to act out plays before them; he is now here in Copenhagen and writes tragedies and stories, which once in a while he comes and reads aloud to us; there are a few nice parts in them, but generally it is the most terrible non-sense. Tomorrow he is coming again to read, and I am quite looking forward to it if only I could stop myself laughing, but it is almost an impossibility, for he behaves so foolishly.

The desperation to perform, the burning ambition, the implacable self-belief—all this stood out from the comedy of Andersen's incongruous exhibitionism and made other people believe in him. He had learned early to convey a sense that he was special; and like many indulged children, he was not afraid to show that he needed looking after, and so he was looked after. Later he saw the absurdity of his performances—he relates in his autobiography how, aged seventeen, he introduced himself to Admiral Wulff, the Danish translator of Shakespeare, with the words "You have translated Shakespeare; I admire him greatly, but I have also written a tragedy; shall I read it to you?" Come again soon, Wulff offered genially when the recital was finished. "Yes, I will, when I have written a new tragedy," replied Andersen. Wulff suggested that they would not then be seeing him for some time. "I think," said Andersen, "that in a fortnight I may have another one ready," and with those words he was out of the door.

As an adolescent, one reason his behaviour was so extreme was that he simply had no idea how to act in the homes of upper-middle-class sophisticates like the Wulffs. He had no role models, no friends of his own age, no proper schooling, and he went home every night to Mrs. Thorgesen's dark larder-room, wondering how he could afford the rent. All his social intercourse, therefore, turned on the desire to impress a class above his own, for his very survival in the city depended on men such as Weyse and Guldberg believing in his genius. This left a terrible legacy, for in adulthood, even after he was famous and secure, his need for constant recognition and praise was pathological, and he craved admiration like a shot of an addictive drug. So much of his energy, moreover, was pouring into self-education and theatrical training, as well as into sheer physical survival—getting himself fed and clothed and lodged—that none was left for emotional or social maturing. He leaves a picture of himself at sixteen, when other boys were peering into brothels and getting drunk, of pressing his face against the windows of Blankensteiner and Son, a shop on Købmagergade selling dolls and puppet theatres: "As a boy of sixteen, I lay on my bed sewing dolls' clothes. To get material for them, I thought of going into the shops on Østergade and asking for silk and velvet samples, which I then stitched together into lovely dresses. I also made my own stereoscope and played away a year of my youth."

After Siboni dismissed him, Andersen tried another route on to the stage, and in May 1820 he was accepted into the Royal Theatre's Ballet School. It was housed in the old Court Theatre and run by the solo dancer, Carl Dahlén, who was deputizing for the director, Antoine Bournonville, then away in Paris. Dahlén opened his home to Andersen and was very kind to him, and there he stood for whole mornings with a long staff and stretched his legs, but he was loose-limbed, awkward, and clearly would not make it as a dancer. In August 1820 the board of the theatre decided that he lacked both the talent and the appearance for a stage career, and advised against employing him in any area. He was allowed to sit backstage in the evenings, however, and the actors at the Royal Theatre soon knew him mockingly as "der kleine Deklamator" (the little clamator). When he was invited in September 1820 to join a crowd scene in the *singspiel Two Little Savoyards*—along with supernumeraries, ballet pupils, even stagehands— one of the actors led him cruelly before the foot-lamps and jeered, "Allow me to introduce you to the Danish public." Another actor, Ferdinand Lindgren, gave him free lessons through the winter of 1820–1821, but when Andersen wanted to play tragic parts, he told him he was too lanky and looked ridiculous, and in the end concluded that he was no good for comedy either.

Out of charity, Dahlén gave him a part as a troll in his ballet *Armida*, which had its première on 12 April 1821: "That was a moment in my life, when my name was printed. I fancied I could see in it a nimbus of immortality. I was continually looking at the printed paper. I carried the programme of the ballet to bed with me at night, lay and read my name by candlelight . . . this was happiness."

By coincidence, 16-year-old Andersen made his debut on the same night as 9-year-old Johanne Luise Heiberg, the tinker child who became Denmark's most famous actress. Auguste Bournonville, also aged sixteen, saw this ballet of cupids and trolls, and remembered:

> Among the former were to be found . . . little Johanne Pätges, whose innate grace even as a child suggested what she was one day to become for the Danish stage as the celebrated wife of Heiberg. Among the latter—that is the trolls—no one was more conspicuous than a young lad who had recently come from Odense and whose ballet debut was to take place in the finale of the last act by tumbling headlong out of a crevice. This was none other than H. C. Andersen, to whom a marvellous destiny had pointed out this entrance on the road to world renown as a writer and to a high rung on the social scale.

This was written in 1845, when Andersen was immensely famous, but the hint of condescension is palpable.

The next month, recognition came for his singing, the one performing art for which he had genuine ability, when he was taken on by the Royal Theatre's singing master. He joined the choir and appeared on stage in various minor roles—footman, pageboy, shepherd, warrior. Around this time too he began to make certain connections among the Danish aristocracy and in the artistic world. Laura Tønder Lund introduced him to Madame Colbjørnsen, widow of a distinguished Danish statesman, and her daughter Olivia, who was lady-in-waiting to Crown Princess Caroline. Andersen was invited to perform at Frederiksberg Castle; the Princess praised his voice and gave him ten rixdollars and presents of sweets, grapes and peaches, which he saved to share with his landlady—a sign of how lonely he still was. Madame Colbjørnsen spent her summers in an apartment at Bakkehuset ("The house on the hill") at Frederiksberg, where the liberal poet Knud Rahbek and his wife Kamma played host to the city's intellectuals and writers in a sort of permanent salon/house-party. In this Danish version of the early-nineteenth-century Hampstead of Keats and Leigh Hunt, Andersen played the part of precocious pet to the leisured classes.

The writer Thomasine Gyllembourg, socialite and beauty of Golden Age Copenhagen, left a picture of Bakkehuset as a version of heaven:

> In this house of hospitality people were measured by rules quite different from those in the rest of the world. Events followed their course as in Paradise, where rank and wealth count for nothing. How many did not gather there, of

all that two generations of the nation had to offer of the delightful and the distinguished! In this circle, under this low roof, what meeting arranged that has not borne fruit, just like the trees and flowers of the garden, tended by Kamma's hand.

In fact, Bakkehuset had its tensions and jealousies, but its influence on Andersen was entirely positive. Rahbek never spoke to him, but kind-hearted Kamma Rahbek "often amused herself with me," he wrote, and an old lady who had known the dramatist Holberg predicted that he would become as great as Oehlenschläger. At Bakkehuset, the atmosphere, wrote the historian Troels Lund, was the incarnation of the romantic view of life, in which "Poetry was the light of everyone's life, everybody's darling," and here Andersen imbibed ideas about poetry as a romantic calling which reshaped his ambition:

> One day, when I was going from [Mrs. Rahbek] to Madame Colbjørnsen, she gave me a handful of roses, and said "Will you take them up to her? It will certainly give her pleasure to receive them from the hand of a poet."
>
> These words were said half in jest; but it was the first time anybody had connected my name with that of a poet. It went through me, body and soul, and tears filled my eyes. I know that, from this very moment, my mind was awake to writing and poetry. Formerly it had been merely an amusement by way of variety from my puppet theatre.

Andersen was quick to realize that socially, poetry was a winning card. This was a time when art and literature stood at the intellectual core of the nation, because political life was barely allowed to exist. Denmark in the 1820s was a shell-shocked country, still reeling from a series of disasters: defeat in the war and the loss of Norway in 1814; national bankruptcy in 1813; the English bombardment of the city in 1807; Britain's victory in the Battle of Copenhagen in 1801. Throughout the 1820s, the standard of living remained poor and the mood was frugal—King Frederik VI used to appear in public dressed in a threadbare military greatcoat and an old oilcloth cap—but there was no question of dissent: Denmark until 1848 was an absolute monarchy, presided over by benign but autocratic kings who, in the shadow of the French Revolution, reacted swiftly to the slightest radical tremors. In 1799 King Frederik had banished two liberal writers, Peter Andreas Heiberg and Malthe Conrad Bruun, from the country, and in 1821 another, Dr. J. J. Dampe, was sentenced to twenty years' solitary confinement on an island for arguing in favour of a free parliament. The liberal politician Orla Lehmann later recalled this as a period when complaining to the magazine *The Policeman's Friend* about a missing gutter plank was the legal limit of free speech. Artistic life in the years to 1848 consumed the energy that other nations were pouring into politics, and the result was a Golden Age of culture, a flowering of painting, music, literature and philosophy, unprecedented in Danish history.

Within two generations between 1770 and 1813, Denmark saw the births of Bertel Thorvaldsen, one of the most famous sculptors in nineteenth-century Europe, and of Hans Christian Ørsted; of painters Christoffer W. Eckersberg, Martinus Rørbye, Wilhelm Marstrand, Christen Købke and Wilhelm Bendz; of choreographer Auguste Bournonville, born the same year as Andersen; of poet and theologian Nicolai Frederik Severin Grundtvig, whose ideas have had an immense impact on Danish culture; writer of popular vaudevilles and Hegelian critic Johan Ludvig Heiberg and his wife, actress Johanne Luise Heiberg; and philosopher Søren Kierkegaard. It was an extraordinary concentration of talent; it shaped the Copenhagen in which Andersen launched himself in the 1820s, and it had a pervasive effect in colouring his creative imagination.

There was nothing grandiose about the Danish Golden Age. Rooted in the austerity and restricted horizons which the impoverished Danes saw as their lot, Golden Age art takes its themes from everyday life, and reflects the sober northern European interiors, characterized by restraint, conventionality and utilitarianism, known as "Biedermeier"—the name comes from a fictitious provincial German schoolteacher, and conjures up both bourgeois cosiness and a narrow outlook. "This Biedermeier style crops up again and again during the period of rebuilding which followed . . . the Napoleonic wars," write Hans Hertel and Bente Scavenius in their history of the age, "with people pragmatically retreating into those values closest to home, and the man of the house at the head of the table representing the father of the country in miniature . . . There was also something very Danish about this vaudeville and vicarage culture, this peace-at-any-price harmonization of the holiday cottage mentality, gingham-print idylls, champagne polkas and the monarch in his admiral's uniform on the canals of Frederiksberg Have." "From the dread abyss I turn my gaze," wrote the poet Christian Winther. Yet in art and literature, the Golden Age artists transformed ordinary street scenes or domestic dramas of smoking parties or musical soirées by their ability to see them anew and to look beyond their apparent serenity.

"Fresh as a glass of water is the morning air," wrote another Golden Age poet, Ludvig Bødtcher. Golden Age paintings, characterized by an acutely sensed rendering of light and delicately controlled colour harmonies, express this mood most immediately. Købke's famous *View of a Street in a Copenhagen Suburb, Morning Light*, for example, shows with startling clarity the traffic at the eastern gate to the city where he lived. The monumental effect comes from a contrast between the sun's rays falling across the broad street, striking the water pump and the poplars between the houses, and the variously toned grey clouds and sky which take up most of the picture, offsetting its familiarity with a sense of looming fate. In *Interior at Amaliegade in Copenhagen with the Artist's Brothers*, Wilhelm Bendz catches the gradual transitions from brightness to shadow as light falls through the windows of a classical interior; the cool colours of the room, and the eerie stillness of the two men absorbed in their work, their backs to the light, cast an air of inexplicable uneasiness over the scene. Most emblematic of the Golden Age spirit of smooth harmonies shot through with a hint of danger is Martinus Rørbye's *A View From the Artist's Window*, where sun-lit flowers on a window sill give on to a harbour with ships and cranes fading into a mist. The contrast suggests the serenity of home versus the dangers/temptations of the wider world; a birdcage hanging outside the open window embodies early-nineteenth-century Copenhagen as a claustrophobic, gilded cage.

"The great innovation of the Golden Age," write Hans Hertel and Bente Scavenius, "was an intimate, subtle and evocative style of art—distilled impressionism, discovering the poetry of life in humdrum spots . . . discerning great truths in tiny details." This was the culture of an apolitical nation turned in on itself. It not only influenced the nature of Andersen's creative vision, but made it possible for him to become a writer at all, for in an apolitical climate, patronage of the arts was a way for the upper and bourgeois classes to buy influence and status, and for young ambitious people from backgrounds like Andersen's, there were greater opportunities than at any period before.

But in 1821 his position was still precarious, as he thrashed about trying to enlist support. At this time he wrote a speculative letter to the romantic poet Bernhard Severin Ingemann, which shows both his boldness and his sense of his own obscurity and loneliness:

Mr. Ingemann

Trusting your goodness I am daring to write to you to request of you to read the enclosed paper. I feel greatly having to address myself to strangers, but I realize there is no other way I can reach the goal I consider to bring me my greatest happiness. Without anything I dared come to the capital hoping that by the help of noble people and with the talent many people have judged me to possess I would prosper (if you do not wish to grant my request as I am a total stranger to you, I do hope you will forgive me)—if it would please you I would like to read some scenes and poems to you. I have also dared to write some verses and tragedies, if you were to look at these as I know one has to be overbearing with an unscholared beginner.

In the autumn his prospects went downhill again. Professor Guldberg had arranged free Latin lessons for him—"Latin—the most expensive language in the world," said the first teacher who was approached—but sustained study was impossible for a boy of Andersen's restless, dreamy temperament. He came instantly into conflict with the idea of learning the classics, which were then the emblem of a good education valued by the bureaucratic, academic class who were coming to dominate Danish society. "The theatre was my world . . . and thus it fared ill with my Latin," he wrote; it is likely that he also had particular problems with Latin as the hallmark of the educated bourgeois class of his patrons. Men like Guldberg were trying to shape him into their image; he wanted to join this class yet felt instinctively outside it. Guldberg saw his neglect of Latin as ingratitude and rejection, and broke with him over it. His reprimand "almost crushed me to the earth," wrote Andersen, and made him realize how he floated on the fringe of polite society:

I was heart-broken, begging him to forgive me and not let me become utterly miserable. "Oh! You're just acting for me," he said. "If you abandon me I shall have no one left! I have done wrong, but by God I will work harder" . . . "You unhappy!" he repeated. "What a farce! I've read that before. I will do no more for you . . ." and he slammed the door in my face . . . I walked home in despair. He had told me that I was "bad" and that had a dreadful effect on me. For a long time I stood by the Peblinge Lake and watched the moon shining into the water. There was a cold wind and the terrible thought struck me: "Nothing good can come of you now! You're no good any more! God is angry, you must die!" I looked into the water, then thought of my old grandmother, who would

certainly not have thought that my life would end like this. This made me
weep bitterly . . .

This was written ten years later, and echoes the tone of Andersen's first
diaries, written in 1825 when he was suffering from depression as a grammar
school boy unable to learn Latin. At sixteen, the depressive streak was
already there; the account shows how fragile was Andersen's sense of himself
and his future, and how tenaciously he was holding on to emotional ties that
belonged to the old world of his grandmother and mother, in spite of his
new patrons and connections.

Through the winter of 1821–1822 he continued singing and dancing. He
also wrote, in a fortnight, a tragedy, *The Robbers of Wissenberg*, inspired by
Schiller's *The Robbers* and by Danish legend. It was full of spelling mistakes
and grammatical errors; Laura Tønder Lund had it copied out for him so
that he could submit it anonymously to the Royal Theatre. His hopes of the
theatre were high—on New Year's Day, when the building was closed, he
slipped past a blind porter to get on to the stage and recite a prayer, because
he held the superstitious belief that what happened on this day would condition the rest of the year, and that once he had spoken on the stage on 1
January, his future in the theatre was assured. But in May 1822 he received a
crushing blow—he was dismissed from the singing and dancing schools of
the theatre, and told that his career there was over. A month later his play
came back "accompanied by a letter which said that people did not frequently wish to retain works which betrayed, in so great a degree, a want of
elementary knowledge," though one scene was printed in a journal, *The
Harp*, in August—Andersen's first published work.

He was now seventeen, he had tried three routes on to the stage—
singing, dancing and writing—and it was clear to all who took an interest in
him that although he had some talent, his lack of formal education was
standing in the way of real advancement. "I heard it said every day, what a
good thing it would be for me if I could study," he recalled, but "it was
labour enough for me to keep body and soul together." He could not give up
hope of the theatre, so he wrote a second tragedy, *Alfsol*. This won some supporters, including a preacher called Gutfeldt, who presented it to the theatre
and sent Andersen off to see one of the most powerful men in Copenhagen,
Jonas Collin.

Collin (pronounced "colleen") held the purse strings of both the Royal
Theatre, of which he was director, and the king's fund which provided

money for worthy cases like Andersen's. He was a court official, senior civil servant and well-known philanthropist: he was wealthy but lived frugally and was known for his hard work, business acumen and down-to-earth manner. Everyone told Andersen that if he were lucky enough to capture Collin's interest, then things might start to happen for him. But when he was ushered into the large, bare house in Bredgade, where Collin sat at a low-back painted wooden chair and worked at a simple card table, Andersen found a cool, calm man of few words who promised nothing, and he left "without expecting any sympathy from this man." Collin, however, was a man of actions, not words. When *Alfsol* was returned as "useless for the stage," it was accompanied by a recommendation that Andersen be sent to a grammar school to acquire a basic education. This was Collin's work, and in September 1822 Andersen appeared before a board meeting of the Royal Theatre, and it was arranged that Collin would apply for funds to the King. Within weeks, Andersen was awarded a grant for several years to attend grammar school in Slagelse, a provincial town in west Zealand, after which he was expected to matriculate as a student at Copenhagen University. Collin was to be his patron and give him his quarterly allowance, and he became his hero:

> I was to apply to him in all cases, and he it was who was to ascertain my industry and progress . . . Mildly and kindly he said to me, "Write to me without restraint about everything you require, and tell me how it goes with you." From this hour I struck root in his heart . . . His beneficence was conferred without his making me feel it painful either by word or look . . . in Collin's words was expressed the warm-heartedness of a father, and to him it was that properly I was indebted for everything.

Andersen was, he says, "almost dumb with astonishment" at this turn in his life. It was not the stroke of the magic wand that he had dreamed about, for although he had looked longingly at the grammar school boys in Odense, he had never had academic interests and he had spent three years fixated on the theatre. To return to the classroom aged seventeen, an overgrown schoolboy in a junior class, and banished from Copenhagen to the provinces, was hardly a glamorous outcome. Yet to have won so influential a patron, to have his life mapped out and his finances looked after, was a triumph, and he was always devotedly grateful to Collin. At some level he seems finally to have given in to the reasoned adult voices of his benefactors chorusing in favour of education and discipline. It was clear to him, too, that the theatre doors were now firmly shut—it is likely that Collin chose Slagelse, a safe fifty-seven miles away, to keep the troublesome and fantastical Andersen at bay until, he hoped, the boy had been moulded into a conventional member of society by his years at the grammar school.

Andersen gave his vanity a final swing. He had his tragedy *Alfsol* published, along with a story called "The Ghost at Palnatoke's Grave," written in imitation of Walter Scott, by a Copenhagen printer whom he had met through the theatre. The work, full of elementary mistakes and extremely immature, was called *Youthful Attempts*, and Andersen used a pseudonym: "I loved William Shakespeare and Walter Scott, and of course I loved also myself. I therefore took my name Christian, and so I assumed the fictitious name William Christian Walter." Professor Guldberg replied furiously to Andersen's suggestion that he dedicate the work to him—nothing could annoy him more, he said—and the book was, Andersen admitted later, "a very miserable production throughout." Virtually no copies were sold; in 1827 they were all taken over by a bookseller, who brought the volume out with a new title page, but again none sold. Eventually some copies were used as wrapping paper and the rest pulped—the fate of the manuscript of Andersen's alter-ego, the student in his late tale "Auntie Toothache," written half a century later: "Well, that's where the manuscript stopped. My young friend, the future grocer's apprentice, couldn't lay his hands on the part that was missing: it had gone out into the world as paper to wrap up bloaters, butter and green soap. It had fulfilled its destiny."

And so he went off to Slagelse, with a string of artistic failures behind him, but a new school, a new father-figure and a new undreamed-of future. After three years in the adult jungle of the city, his childhood was reinstated at precisely the time when he was growing out of it.

CHAPTER 4

Aladdin at School

1822–1827

"That's the last kiss you'll get!" she said. "Or I'll kiss you to death!"

Kai looked at her; she was very beautiful. A wiser, lovelier face he could not imag-ine; now she no longer seemed made of ice as she had done when she sat outside the window and beckoned to him—in his eyes she was perfect. He felt no fear at all: he told her he could do mental arithmetic, even with fractions, and work out how many square miles there were in the country and how many people lived there. She smiled all the time. Then he realized that he knew very little indeed . . .

—HANS CHRISTIAN ANDERSEN, "The Snow Queen"

After three years in Copenhagen, arriving in Slagelse felt like going back in time. When Andersen first saw the town on a mellow Saturday evening in October, his hopes for his new existence were tempered by the sense of being sent into exile at a provincial backwater. His new lodgings were comfort-able—with another boarder, he shared a bedroom and sitting room looking out on to the garden at the home of a respectable widow, Mrs. Henneberg; the rooms were luxurious compared to his box-room in Copenhagen. But Slagelse, a dreary, old-fashioned town in the southwest corner of Zealand, was dispiriting. Here, "everybody knew what was done in everybody's house," Andersen wrote in his autobiography, "whether a scholar was ele-vated or degraded in his class," because almost nothing else was going on.

The school, a long, squat block consisting of four classrooms, a library and a schoolmaster's residence, stood on the main road; it had a distin-guished reputation, its alumni including the Golden Age writers Adam Oehlenschläger and B. S. Ingemann, but it was none the less an uninspir-ing place. Slagelse's main road was also the thoroughfare for traffic running from Copenhagen to the port of Korsør on the Great Belt, and passing coaches were the most interesting distractions of the school day. From the capital, fifty-seven miles away, the journey took eighteen hours; the mail-coach came through every weekday, but few people got on or off, for Slagelse with its 2,000 inhabitants was not a town to attract visitors. On his first evening, Andersen asked the landlady of the inn if there were any remarkable sights—"Yes," she said, "a new English fire-engine and Pastor Bastholm's library." There were a few officers of the Lancers stationed there, who made up most of the gentry class; the town had one carriage for hire, and a private theatre converted from a stable, with wooden boxes for seats, coloured paper stuck on the timber-work, an iron chandelier and two arm-chairs for the mayor and his wife. An English equivalent of Slagelse at that time would be the Meryton of Jane Austen's *Pride and Prejudice*, with its officers enlivening a dull local scene, or the Highbury of *Emma*. Beyond the small country town were rolling fields dotted with farmsteads; to the west lay the Great Belt, the stretch of sea separating Zealand from the island of Funen. Andersen used to climb a small hill just outside the town, from where he could watch the sea and glimpse his native island on the other side.

On the first Monday morning, Andersen entered the Grammar School, walked into the classroom of the second form, where the other pupils were eleven years old, and was at once aware that he was an object of astonishment and mockery. The boys sat in rows at wooden desks, with the top boy nearest the teacher at the front. Learning was almost entirely by rote, boys were called to answer out loud in class, and humiliated or beaten if they made mistakes. Long and lanky, with his blond hair flapping over an angular, nervous face, Andersen was so tall, joked one of the teachers, that he could be cut in half and two puppies made of him. Six years older than his classmates, he knew much less than any of them—almost no Latin, no geometry, and in a geography lesson he was unable to point out Copenhagen on a map of Denmark. "I knew indeed nothing at all," he wrote. "I had the greatest desire to learn, but for the moment I floundered about, as if I had been thrown into the sea; one wave followed another; grammar, geography, mathematics; I felt myself overpowered by them, and feared that I should never be able to acquire all these."

In 1822 the school had just acquired an ambitious new principal, Simon Meisling, who was determined to make his mark in Slagelse and quickly came to dominate Andersen's life. At thirty-five, Meisling was a renowned classicist and an acclaimed translator of Virgil's *Aeneid*; he was also a frustrated, unfulfilled man who worked out his rage on his pupils and staff.

A contemporary caricature of Simon Meisling, the headmaster who made Andersen's school years the unhappiest time of his life.

Short, stout and bald, he had a round face with little eyes framed by horn-rimmed spectacles; his appearance was a gift to caricaturists, and he was mocked mercilessly in the press as a strutting buffoon with big hat and umbrella, the embodiment of the charmless pedant. He was unpopular in the school, where he played tricks on the other teachers, and in the town. He was dirty and unkempt, his fingernails were black with ink and filth, and cleaned only when he squeezed a lemon into his nightly bowl of punch: people wondered how a man whose translations of Virgil were so refined could be personally so unappealing. In the classroom he was brilliant but terrifying. His world was classical Rome and Athens; he was sarcastic and vindictive to anyone who did not share his passion; he considered contemporary life a distraction and modern literature unnecessary.

"To me he stood there as a divinity," Andersen wrote of his early days at school, "I believed unconditionally every word which he spoke." Eager to please, naturally docile, still overawed, as his mother had taught him to be, by the educated class, in the right hands Andersen could have been a model pupil. But as a poor Latin student, he was soon the butt of Meisling's scorn. Within days of starting school, he became paralysed with anxiety every time

Meisling entered the room, and quite unable to make progress in the classics. In Danish, history and religion he did well, but he never mastered Latin, never learned to spell properly and never became comfortable with the methods of formal grammar education to which he was introduced so late. Jonas Collin's well-educated son Edvard recalled of him at this time that he worked hard, read a lot and learned much, but that he never learned to learn properly.

Meisling made no allowances for him. A typical early-nineteenth-century meritocrat, his job was to mould young boys through a classical education into conventional citizens who would matriculate at the university and join the civil service. In Andersen he saw an already formed character whose outlook—his romanticism, his self-pity, his glory in the idea of genius—challenged his entire *métier*, and he unleashed on him a battery of ridicule and contempt, calling him nicknames such as "Shakespeare with the vamp's eye." He forbade Andersen to write creatively, and on this issue, Andersen's sympathetic benefactors, Jonas Collin, Guldberg and others, all agreed with the teacher: Andersen's writing was ungrammatical and ill-disciplined, and could not improve unless he concentrated on his education. In term-time, Andersen observed the ban, though with his frank manner and open ambition he let everyone at the school know he wanted to be an author; in the holidays he felt free to write as he pleased. "You're a stupid boy, who'll never be any good," Meisling told him. "When you start to stand on your own two feet you can write a lot of nonsense, but no one will read what you write, and it will be sold as pulp . . . Don't start crying, you overgrown boy!"

This suggests that part of Meisling's reaction to Andersen was the dislike of a strict, stern man for any sign of effeminacy and weakness. Their quarrel, however, went deeper than this: it was a battle not only of wills but of worldviews. Meisling was a classicist, an eighteenth-century rationalist, for whom childhood was the period of waiting before an individual turned into a useful citizen. Andersen on the other hand was a romantic through and through; he would have said with Shelley that imagination, not academic learning, was the great instrument of moral good, and he was already beginning to perceive his childhood imagination as the fulcrum of his life. There was little meeting ground between the two visions.

But at seventeen, Andersen had poor resistance to Meisling's methods. "My character is quite good-natured, but I am bewildered and dreamy. Without God and the kindness of others I would amount to nothing," he wrote to Jonas Collin. He was barely educated, cut off from his family, emotionally and physically alone. He may have responded with undue sensitivity to sarcasm from Meisling which was in fact not especially directed at him, but meted out to all the boys; but even if his autobiographies falsely give the impression that Meisling singled him out for ill-treatment, there is no doubt—later diary entries and even dreams confirm it—that this is how Meisling made him feel, and that as an over-grown adolescent, he anyway felt uniquely ill-positioned at school. He was soon discouraged, and entered a vicious circle of lost confidence, academic failure, boredom and depression. "Am beginning to get bored . . . I'm bored, bored! Tired of it all . . . I am fuzzy-headed and tired of studying," his schoolboy diaries run. He was not by nature especially diligent, he wanted praise rather than challenges, and for years he struggled against himself: he would throw cold water over his head to keep awake, or run around the garden to stop himself falling asleep over his books.

Yet Meisling could not help acknowledging that there was something worthwhile about his royally sponsored pupil. "Now and then I discovered in him a gleam of kindness," Andersen wrote. He was one of the pupils always invited to Meisling's house on Sundays; he was chosen to babysit for Meisling's children and Meisling wrote well of him to Jonas Collin. Repeatedly, between periods of mockery, Meisling showed quixotic flashes of interest in him which usually ended in disappointment on both sides.

In one such bout of enthusiasm, he invited Andersen to join him, his wife and children in a hired carriage for the journey to Copenhagen at the end of the first term, with teacher and pupil eating sweets, playing cards and singing arias from *Don Giovanni* throughout the day-long trip. There, at Christmas 1822, Andersen had dinner for the first time with his patron Jonas Collin, and was invited to other cultured homes. The next holiday, Easter 1823, he returned to Odense for a week—Meisling forbade him to be away longer, for he was now regularly using him to look after his children and Andersen felt unable to refuse. Andersen walked to the port of Korsør, crossed the Great Belt to Funen, then walked from Nyborg twenty miles along uneven roads. After four years away, his first sight of Odense was the tower of St. Knud's Church, rising up over the flat countryside; he fell on his knees, he says, and burst into tears of joy when he saw it.

The return of the native, more sophisticated and socially successful than when he had left, was an irresistible myth for Andersen to capitalize on in his autobiographical writings, but of course his visit to Odense did make the gap between his family and his new status as grammar school boy clear. In the first street he met his mother. "In the little streets I saw the people open their windows to look at me, for everybody knew how remarkably well things had fared for me." His old grandmother had died the year before, too soon to know that Andersen had become a grammar school pupil; she was buried in a pauper's grave. His mad grandfather lived alone, hoarding coins which had not been valid since the national bankruptcy of 1813. His half-sister Karen-Marie had gone to Copenhagen, where she was believed to be searching for a lover who had abandoned her; his mother did not know her address. Anne Marie Andersen had been widowed again and was poorer than ever. She was thrilled that her son was a royally sponsored pupil; as Andersen sailed in a boat on the river with the Bishop and the Høegh-Guldberg family, he watched his mother weep with pride.

At this point he began to tell his life story compulsively in letters to Collin and to teachers at the school; it was as though he could not believe that he had progressed so far. Yet, as he tried to mould himself into a good grammar school boy and dreamed of a great future, he had to hold on to the memories of his childhood as a talisman. "If anyone can become a *Digter* through the events of his childhood, then I will become one," he wrote in spring 1823. "But not a little poet, there are enough of them, if I can't become a great one, I'll strive to become a useful member of the town." He returned to Odense again in the summer of 1825 as the guest of Høegh-Guldberg; by this time his mother had been taken into Doctors Boder, a charitable old people's home, and was declining into alcoholism, and his grandfather was an inmate of the Greyfriars lunatic asylum where his grandmother had tended the garden.

Back at Slagelse, he was the gawky big boy, too old for camaraderie with his peers, exploited as a babysitter and teased by Meisling, too ill at ease with himself to grasp at more adult relationships. As he had done in Odense, he made himself known to the middle-class families in Slagelse— the pastor Fuglsang; the distiller Pedersen, whose son was at the school; a widow in her eighties, Madame Dall—recited and read to them; when Meisling found out, he threatened to expel him. Nevertheless, Andersen began to dine at these houses. "I was in fine fettle, picked walnuts for them on a shaky ladder and ate cherries," he wrote of one visit to the pastor's house, enjoying what was more or less an extension of his role as performing child. In the autumn of 1823 he was promoted to the third form and given a good report, but the work was now harder, and his clashes with Meisling were so bad that he considered withdrawing from school. He plucked up the courage to write Meisling a letter, begging him to be patient and promising to leave the school if he made no progress within three months. The following autumn, 1824, he failed his exams, and had to stay in the third form for another year. He was a young man of nearly twenty, clinging to social respectability, the approval of Jonas Collin and his royal grant by getting his sums and his spelling right, taking his place alongside boys just into their teens.

Meanwhile, Slagelse became more and more tedious to him. In his four years there, the most dramatic event was a public execution a few miles away, outside the port of Skælskør. The boys were given the day off to watch it, and travelled overnight in open carriages to be there by sunrise. The pregnant daughter of a rich farmer had persuaded her lover to kill her father, who opposed their marriage; a manservant, hoping to marry the widow, was his accessory, and all three were hanged. Hanging, in 1820s England still a common punishment for theft, was already in Denmark reserved only for murderers, so executions were rare. The event made an indelible impression on the young Andersen:

> I shall never forget seeing the criminals driven to the place of execution: the young girl, deadly pale, leaning her head against the breast of her robust sweetheart; behind them the manservant, livid, his black hair in disorder, and nodding with a squinting look at a few acquaintances, who shouted out to him "Farewell!" Standing at the side of their coffins, they sang a hymn together with the minister; the girl's voice was heard above all the others. My limbs could scarcely carry me; these moments were more horrible for me than the very moment of death.

An epileptic, escorted by his parents, was waiting to drink the blood of the executed, believing this would cure him; a songster was chanting a ballad about the event and making a fortune from selling the broadsheet. The whole episode—the drive by open coach, the public nature of the ghastly event, the peasant superstitions surrounding it—shows how close Andersen was in his youth to the pre-industrial society which remained unchanged for centuries and then suddenly vanished, in the modern world of railways and industry, within his lifespan.

Just one bright ray shone over these years—Andersen's growing friendship with the poet Bernhard Severin Ingemann, one of very few people to encourage his literary interests. Ingemann, then thirty-three, was a romantic figure with curly hair and chiselled white skin; ten years earlier he had travelled to Germany and forged links with Romantic writers such as Schlegel, Tieck and Hoffmann, and now he wrote Danish historical novels modelled on those of Walter Scott. He had a calm and gentle temperament and is best remembered today for his children's hymns. In 1822 he had just married a doe-eyed young painter called Lucie and begun teaching at the academy, originally for noblemen, in the lakeside town of Sorø not far from Slagelse. Lucie drew delicate sketches of skinny figures, which, when the sculptor Thorvaldsen saw them, he distorted by adding heavy breasts and thighs in chalk, so exasperated was he with the Ingemanns' effete, childless ménage. To the adolescent Andersen, however, the reassuringly sexless Ingemann home was a domestic idyll; on many Sundays, he walked eight miles through the woods to talk to Ingemann about those subjects forbidden in Slagelse—romantic poetry, novels, his own literary hopes. "Flowers and vines twined round his window; the rooms were adorned with the portraits of distinguished poets . . . We sailed upon the lake with an Aeolian harp made fast to the mast," he wrote. He spent many of his holidays with them, and later called Sorø the place where "that which is bitter passes away, and the whole world appears in sunlight."

He also got to know some of the students at the academy, and an informal reading circle developed. Reading was one of Andersen's most intense pleasures; his range was broad and up to date. He knew the classical canon in Danish and German, he read Shakespeare and Walter Scott in translation, and through magazines such as *Miscellany* and *Monthly Roses*, as well as books, he followed developments in modern literature avidly. When one of the students in Sorø offered him the loan of anything in his library, he noted that there was Byron, Schiller, Walter Scott, Shakespeare, Goethe, Heine, Oehlenschläger, but that he took nothing, for he had read them all. He began to set himself tentatively in the context of Romanticism. "Read Byron's biography," he noted in his diary in 1825. "Oh! he was just like me, right down to his love of gossip, my soul is ambitious like his, contented only when admired by everybody, even the most insignificant person who will not do so can make me miserable."

His greatest passion was for Scott. "In my youth," he recalled in his auto-biography, "there were only three authors who, as it were, infused them-selves into my blood—Walter Scott, Hoffmann and Heine." Scott and Hoffmann, born in the 1770s, were at the peak of their fame when Andersen was an adolescent; Heine, born in 1797, was almost Andersen's contempo-rary but was influential in the late 1820s and early 1830s, when Andersen was still an impressionable young writer. All three were objects of popular crazes across Europe in the first part of the nineteenth century, and each answered particular needs of Andersen's at different times. Scott, his first great love in literature, was always held in special affection, and in his schooldays was his literary model.

Between 1821 and 1828 thirty-three translations of Scott were published in Danish. At this time Scott's colourful historical novels with their rural themes, peasant characters and lively regional speech were transforming the idea of fiction at home and abroad, and Andersen instinctively grasped that here was someone whose ideals, with the revolutionary concept of giving voice to an outback, dispossessed class, he could share. He read his first Scott novel, *The Heart of Midlothian*, in an 1822 translation before he arrived at Slagelse and, as we have seen, he had taken Scott's Christian name as part of the pseudonym for his book *Youthful Attempts*. In July 1823 Crown Princess Caroline, the royal patron he had met through the Colbjørnsen family, gave him a Danish translation of Scott's novels as a present—among the first books Andersen owned.

Fuelled by Ingemann's imitations of Scott, in Sorø Andersen confided plans for his own historical novel, *Christian II's Dwarf*, about a dwarf who is really only a head and has no body. He worked on the book in the holidays; he never finished it, but the fragments he wrote give a clue to his psychological state during his school years. He was aware that, like the dwarf at court, he was something of a freak in the classroom; with his mind stuffed full of Latin and algebra, he lived mostly in his head, while repressing the demands of his body.

In September 1825, Andersen also started on another form of creative writing: he began to keep a diary. He was a compulsive writer and for three years he had chafed under Meisling's ban. The diary was an emotional breakthrough: a legitimate vehicle for self-expression, which has from the start an air of self-consciousness about it, suggesting that Andersen hoped to become well-known enough for it to be published. He loved recounting his life story, and he may have been encouraged to begin a diary by an erotic short story, Steen Blicher's "Fragments from the Diary of a Parish Clerk," which had caused a sensation when it appeared in 1824.

Using the form of a young man's diary so convincingly that many readers refused to believe it was fiction, the story tells of the affair between a grand lady and a servant over the years, during which the diarist-narrator turns from the high-spirited hope of youth to tragic stoicism as he watches the liaison's cruel denouement. The story is a sort of Danish *Wuthering Heights*, set on the Jutland moors, the wild western and traditionally uncivilized part of rural Denmark; the diarist, a poor boy given the opportunity of an education by a clergyman, has something in common with Andersen's dependent position as a schoolboy. Andersen was haunted by the tale—half a century later, in 1869, he wrote his own version of it, "Poultry Meg's Family"—and he remained always an admirer of Blicher. Blicher was a devotee of Walter Scott and within his Jutland setting followed Scott's peasant themes. A rural pastor rather than an urban intellectual, he was the sort of modern writer, romantic and fatalistic, with whom the schoolboy Andersen naturally allied himself.

In the autumn of 1825, Andersen's need to express himself was especially keen. For two years he had been languishing in the third form at school, and he was about to sit the exams which would determine whether or not he went up to the top class. Everything that Meisling had tried to repress— ambition and fantasy, self-indulgence and childishness—tumbled out in the first few days of his diary, much of it addressed to God, who emerges as Andersen's only friend, a being not entirely believed in, but clung to with all the lonely fatalism of the schoolboy writer's heart. The sense of vocation, unshakeable since childhood, has survived too. "Forgive me, Almighty Father, these audacious thoughts which are in my soul, but they alone buoy up my courage; otherwise I would sink in despair. I must carry out my work! I must paint for mankind the vision that stands before my soul in all its vividness and diversity; my soul knows that it can and will do this, and so You must not forsake me, for I wish to become Your priest," Andersen writes on the first Sunday—he did not work on that day, keeping the traditional Sabbath. But the next day he is in the classroom: "Unlucky me! Did miserably in Latin. You won't be advanced into the fourth form! Out of school! To become an artisan or a corpse is your fate! God! God, are you really near! . . . Why did the principal have to examine me in precisely what I had trouble with?"

Throughout the diary for 1825–1826, Andersen speaks with the double voice of a split personality, by turns the aspiring artist and the dependent schoolboy. "Being, whose proper name I do not know, give my soul courage to tear itself lose . . . I could become an angel; either an angel or a devil is what I'll become—it is hanging in the balance!" he wrote. As a child, he had feared inheriting his grandfather's madness; now, hovering on the verge of depression, he linked it to the creative energy that Meisling was keeping back. "My powerful fantasy will drive me into the insane asylum, my violent temperament will make a suicide of me! Before, the two of these together would have made a great writer." But the same day, he tries the bargaining power of the small child: "God, I swear by my eternal salvation never again within my heart to mistrust Your fatherly hand, if only I might this time be promoted to the fourth form." For two weeks he worked and worried; "depression, a nasty downpour, grey and autumn-like outside, foggy and raw, as in my soul; God, I wish I were dead!" Then on 1 October Mrs. Meisling whispered to him that he had passed his exams and would move up a class.

The promotion marked a new relationship with the Meislings. That autumn, Dr. Meisling was appointed rector of Elsinore Grammar School, a more prestigious establishment than Slagelse in one of Denmark's most beautiful small towns. The date of his move was uncertain, but with Andersen now in sight of the end of his schooling, Meisling invited him to accompany him and to live in the school house at Elsinore, promising to give him extra tuition with his Latin for the university matriculation exam. Andersen did not want to go to university, but this exam was the goal Jonas Collin had set him, the justification for his royal grant, and Collin approved the plan. To Andersen, an enemy seemed to be turning into a friend, though in fact Meisling's motives were mixed: he may have wanted to help Andersen at this final stage, but he was also going to profit from Andersen's rent, to have someone close at hand to help with his children and, in his frustration, he may also have relished the opportunity for torment and confrontation. Andersen, though, was naively flattered at Meisling's interest in him, and had really no choice but to accept. In order to be ready to leave at short notice with the family, he moved at once into the school house at Slagelse as a lodger, full of hope that he could now win Meisling's support and do well at school.

But he soon found that the school house was a home of horror. The house was as dirty as the man; food was stored in drawers and filthy hardware cupboards; a pig lived in the larder (it died while Andersen was staying there and was given a funeral in the garden). Mrs. Meisling was fat, frumpy and flirtatious; she detested her husband and spent her time tossing her wig of red curls at army officers. When Andersen was new in the house he reported innocently to Meisling that an officer was tapping at the window, and Mrs. Meisling turned on him furiously the next morning. The couple had separate bedrooms; Meisling went to bed early and read the classics; Mrs. Meisling sometimes slipped out disguised as a peasant girl for her rendezvous with the officers. Husband and wife hid food and drink from one another, and accused the maids of stealing it, and Mrs. Meisling tried to seduce the new lodger:

> One evening she came into my room, told me that she was starting to lose weight and that her dress was hanging rather loosely on her body, asked me to feel it. I bowed to my headmaster's wife many times; she gave me some fine punch, was very kind and good—but, I don't know, I was on edge, she was acting incorrectly towards me, or so I thought, she made me think badly of her, and I rushed away as soon as I could, my body trembling all over.

At twenty, Andersen was effeminate and innocent. Mrs. Meisling taunted him that he was not really a man; when an acquaintance told lewd stories, Andersen wrote prudishly in his diary, "We are all of us carnal. Oh God, keep me from suffering temptation myself." It was not difficult for him to resist: since he had left home at fourteen, his energy had poured into self-promotion, literature and education, and he was still emotionally and sexually immature; his prudishness may also have been a reaction to the promiscuity in his mother's family, which he associated with social deprivation. In his diaries from this time, he used a code of Greek letters, sometimes slipped into the middle of a word, to signify masturbation, which was his only sexual activity. He was narcissistic and too uncertain of himself to become absorbed in anyone else. "I certainly feel that I am child-like," he wrote to Collin in 1825, "for just a smile or sympathetic word makes me overjoyed instantly, while a cold face can cause profound unhappiness in my soul."

Living with the Meislings, he soon realized he had no escape from sarcastic comments on the one hand and Mrs. Meisling's indiscretions on the other. As the unhappy couple's lodger, he was plied with inappropriate rebukes—when he had been there two weeks, for example, Meisling ordered that he must no longer greet anyone from the town on his walks. Day by day Andersen agonized over Meisling: "The principal gave me an apple, but was so cold that I was somewhat dejected . . . The principal was quite friendly, gave me a toddy and some morning papers to go downstairs with . . ." Part of what pained him was Meisling's exposure of what he did not like about himself. "My nasty vanity sneaks in," he told Collin. "Meisling has forced me to see that there is a kind of unpleasant dreaminess in me, something restless and impulsive in my soul which makes it twice as hard for me to get a hold on languages." Gradually, in his eighteen months as Meisling's lodger, his already fragile sense of himself began to collapse.

In his desperation, he clung to his Copenhagen connections with a passion. For Christmas 1825, his first holiday as Meisling's lodger, he received an invitation to Copenhagen from Mrs. Wulff, wife of Admiral Wulff, the translator of Shakespeare to whom he had introduced himself as a 17-year-old playwright. He left in the middle of the night, at 3:30 a.m.: "We drove off enveloped in the most wonderful fog imaginable; we rolled onward . . . You might almost think we were travelling through the air, but the road reminded us that we were on the ground because we encountered pothole after pothole, so that I was afraid of breaking both arms and legs, or at least my neck . . ." Wulff was head of the naval academy, and lived with his family in a spacious apartment at Amalienborg Palace, the neo-classical residence, now the Royal Residence, next to the harbour, which looked out on to Copenhagen's famous octagonal Amalienborg Square. Here Andersen arrived just after 9 o'clock in the evening, rang the bell at the gateway, was shown up and welcomed by Mrs. Wulff and her daughters. "What a change it was," Andersen wrote in his autobiography, "to get for a few days out of the Rector's rooms into a house in Copenhagen where all was elegance, cleanliness and full of the comforts of refined life!" He immediately sang the Wulffs a song before going to bed; when he saw where he was sleeping, an elegant square room with four windows on the *bel étage* of the southern pavilion, he was ecstatic.

> I have been given two rooms out toward the square, one to sleep in and the other, which is heated, where I'll read in the morning; the ceiling arches high above me, so I can really imagine that I am in a knight's castle. I was given as a gift from Wulff the three volumes of Shakespeare's plays that he has translated. They are printed on fine paper and beautifully bound, as any work by Shakespeare deserves. I am alone in my room now; a thousand feelings are flowing through me—oh what hasn't God done for me! It is going for me as it did for Aladdin, who says at the close of the work as he is looking out of a window of the palace:
>
>> Down there I walked when just a lad
>> Each Sunday, if I was but allowed,
>> And gazed with wonder at the sultan's palace.

Five or six years ago, I, too, was walking around on the streets down there, didn't know a soul here in town, and now I am gloating over my Shakespeare in the home of a kind and respected family. O Lord, I could kiss you!

Oehlenschläger's five-act *Aladdin* was the most popular play of the day. Through it the Aladdin tale from *The Arabian Nights* became the country's national drama, with the obscure and ill-connected hero seen as an emblem of poor, honourable, defeated Denmark, which would eventually triumph, as Aladdin does, over adversity.

For Andersen, in that king's-eye moment when he looked down on to the vast Amalienborg Square, with a palace on each corner, Aladdin was crystallized as his own story. He spent years retelling it—as a folk tale in his first story "The Tinderbox," as an animal fable in "The Ugly Duckling." In mythologizing his life even as it was happening, Andersen accorded symbolic status to this Christmas visit to the Wulffs. Here he got his first taste of elegant living in the capital, and was able to make the inevitable gauche mistakes of the newcomer—getting up to find the servant who was to bring him tea, and taking a wrong turn that landed him in his stockinged feet in the maids' room, for example—without losing face.

The Wulffs were typical products of early-nineteenth-century bourgeois Copenhagen: a close, cultured, sea-faring family. Both sons became naval officers like their father. Admiral Wulff was a mixture of sailor, *bel esprit* and courtier; a dignified, grey-haired figure who enjoyed the pomp and ceremony and dressing-up of his position, and also had poetic ambitions—he translated Shakespeare and Byron, but his own poems were not well regarded. He treated Andersen with a certain superciliousness, which was compensated for by his wife and children, who were warm and sympathetic. Mrs. Wulff wrote Andersen motherly, sensible letters encouraging him in his troubles at school, though she never stopped hectoring him. Of the children, Andersen struck up an immediate bond with the eldest, 21-year-old Henriette, who was clever, witty, ugly and hunchbacked; like Andersen, she felt herself an outsider and an observer in life, though she was quite without self-pity. Andersen read her his poems and in his autobiography singles her out as one of his earliest friends in Copenhagen: "a very clever and lively girl . . . she possessed my entire confidence; she protected me like a good sister, and had great influence over me, while she awoke in me a feeling for the comic." She became a lifelong friend, and the recipient of the most honest of Andersen's letters.

As the guest of this eminent family, Andersen spent the week in a social whirl. Christmas in Copenhagen was cosy, domestic, small-scale. He was given theatre tickets, he visited Jonas Collin, he read his poems to Oehlenschläger and had dinner with his old ballet teacher Carl Dahlén. He spent Christmas Eve helping Hans Christian Ørsted and his family put up their Christmas tree; he paid visits to various aristocrats and members of the royal family and was rewarded with Christmas gifts: "was at Mrs. von der Maase's (one rixdollar), splendid, lovely rooms . . . visited Countess Frijs (two rixdollars). At Mrs. Buchwald's, from the Princess (five rixdollars)." Danish high society at this time consisted of no more than about a thousand people, and Andersen sought them out, looking for an audience, for patrons.

Only once did the glamour of the occasion defeat him, at the Wulffs' annual ball for the naval cadets, where he felt himself the shabby poor boy, Cinderella in her rags again on the stroke of midnight. "The carriages are rumbling outside; now the King is arriving . . . oh if only I were dressed better!" he wrote.

> I was just upstairs in the magnificent hall. People all dressed up there, in particular the military men, the King and the princes . . . the cadets performed marvellously—I was especially impressed by the sword dance. Oh, what figures, what grace! Oh God, who am I that I thought about dancing among them this evening!—the princes are in the parlour, but I've retreated to my room: I feel embarrassed. Then the guests arrived; the gilded halls shone with the sun-bright light from the chandeliers. I went down in my jacket, but when I saw Wulff speaking to his wife, I suspected that I shouldn't put in an appearance looking like that. I put the question directly to Mrs. Wulff: "Well, if you have a dress coat it would be better." I put on my grey—yes, that was much better. Now the guests were streaming into the house, but all of them were in black. I was the only one in grey and didn't know whether to stand on my head or my heels. Only Oehlenschläger spoke to me. I felt very embarrassed; they probably take me for one of the servers . . . Oh, what torment! I rushed right back to my room, went to bed cursing my fate that I didn't have any dress clothes. The carriages were rumbling outside, and thoughts rumbled inside my head, and that is how I fell asleep.

"From such a house as this," Andersen wrote, "I, after a few days, returned to the Rector, and felt the difference deeply." Meisling had also spent Christmas in Copenhagen, and had heard about Andersen's glittering time. He was an ambitious man, and it was obvious to him that his peculiar pupil's social connections were outstripping his own. On Boxing Day, he left Andersen a note which ran:

> I have nothing to communicate to you upon your departure, only the sternest admonition that you not use your time for writing stories and poems—which you have served up here to this party's great amusement—after your arrival in Slagelse, but for your studies. I shall certainly speak face to face to you about how much you have disappointed me by wasting time in that way, when I trust you to read your assignments, and I will furnish you with various data that might possibly deflate you. I do not wish you to take part in any decoration of the children's Christmas tree, crèches, masquerades or God knows what has been planned, since I can see that you put your time to bad enough use anyway. Meisling.

Andersen spent his last day at the Wulffs' in a fit of misery; in the evening he was given a copy of Boye's new play *William Shakespeare*, which he read aloud to the Wulffs. As he did with many dramas, he identified with it so closely that he burst into tears: "In the first act, William's lines echoed exactly my feelings; he has an intuitive feeling he will become a writer; he decides not to compose poetry. Oh, tears came into my eyes; in bed all my disconsolation was reawakened, but I fell asleep with faith in God." Always a nervous and unsettled traveller, Andersen then returned to Slagelse, sharing his coach with a lieutenant and a drunken journeyman, who showed off his scars to prove that he had served under Napoleon. "'He's probably a scoundrel,' I thought to myself, 'maybe he'll stab the lieutenant in the chest!' The horses were unruly, so I was sitting between the devil and the deep blue sea. At last I screwed up my courage and asked if he didn't want to get off and have his mark refunded . . . He went along with this right away and then walked over to the ditch and lay down to sleep." As they entered Slagelse it began to tip down with rain—"it was the heavens lamenting my arrival"—and on 31 December, he wrote, "we ate our New Year's dinner already at 6 o'clock. I can tell that Meisling has forbidden her [Mrs. Meisling] to allow me to play with the children, because we just sat and looked at each other; and at 8 o'clock we all went to our separate rooms."

In the spring of 1826, the much-anticipated move to Elsinore finally took place, and Andersen rejoiced to see the back of Slagelse, which he always associated with the rhyming word *plagelse*, meaning nuisance in Danish.

Elsinore, a town of quite different calibre, looked by contrast full of hope and promise.

Elsinore in 1826 still had much in common with the pretty market town visited in the late sixteenth century by English theatrical players who may have included Shakespeare. Founded in 1426, it stands twenty miles out of Copenhagen at the end of the coastal road going north through the beech forests, and its centre remains a network of winding lanes of well-preserved half-timbered houses, each brightly painted rather than lime-washed, many decorated with ornamental panels and crenellated gables in the Dutch Renaissance style. "Both in its entirety and in its details, the town is clearly characterized by the work of superior hands," says its tourist brochure. There is a cathedral, a monastery, the Latin school—a long, squat two-storey building just off the main road—and a sprinkling of grand houses with battlements, Gothic bricked-up ogee arches and gargoyles in the gable triangles. Most streets lead down to the sea, where a busy port derives its activity from trade with Sweden, two miles across the water.

Above the town looms Hamlet's castle, Kronborg, a massive, copper-roofed fortress situated on the wind-swept neck of land which reaches distinctively out into the Øresund Channel at its narrowest point. *Hamlet* had already been performed here for the first time in 1816, and for Andersen the Shakespearean connection was a good omen. But Kronborg is anyway an imposing sight, and a Danish national symbol—"with Kronborg on the starboard side again," meaning homeward bound, is a common colloquialism. In Andersen's day the castle's function, as guardian of the Channel, was to ensure that the Sound dues, paid by every ship passing through this key stretch of the Baltic, were collected, as a result of which Elsinore was enormously wealthy.

It was a bright and vibrant town, open and airy, its coastline dramatic, its seascape ever-changing with the arrival of big sailing ships and the sun and clouds hanging over the low hills of North Zealand. In every way it was the antithesis of stagnant Slagelse, and Andersen, writing to Jonas Collin the day after he arrived, was exultant:

> It looks to me like a little Copenhagen . . . What traffic! What liveliness on the ship's bridge, here some fat Dutchmen speak their hollow language, there I hear mellifluous Italian, further down coal is being unloaded from an English brig so that I think I can almost smell London . . . and I felt inexpressibly happy; oh! seeing this beautiful landscape must make one a poet or a painter.

Oh! My benefactor! Thank you! Thank you! for every happy moment. After all, life is marvellous!

For the first couple of months in Elsinore, the new environment invigorated everyone. Meisling was preoccupied with the school, the new teachers and scholars were friendly and Mrs. Meisling was busy smoothing over her bad reputation with the grand ladies of the town who came to call on the headmaster's wife and his lodger.

> "I can't tell you how delighted I am," she said, "to have come here. Slagelse is such a dreadful town, with lots of evil and unpleasant gossip, no decent woman escapes it. You should know what people said about me." And then she told them all the scandalous things people did in fact say of her. The poor ladies would blush and curtsey while I went off into a dream hearing these confessions. As soon as they had gone I asked her why she wished to tell them such things. "It is better," she said, "that I tell them than that they hear it from strangers. Coming from me, they won't believe it."

At the end of the term Meisling sent a glowing report to Collin, painting Andersen as a model student: "endowed with a lively imagination and warm feelings . . . three qualities which a preceptor wishes for, but rarely finds combined in the same pupil, namely, ability, diligence and excellent conduct, are assuredly to be found in H. C. Andersen," he wrote.

But Andersen was never shown this report, and in the summer Meisling again turned sour, Mrs. Meisling fell out with her servants and was widely disliked in the town, there was squabbling over food and complaints that Andersen's rent was insufficient and that he ate too much. Meisling said he regretted ever bringing Andersen with him from Slagelse, while making him a virtual prisoner. "The scenery here made a lively impression on me, but I dared only to cast stolen glances at it," Andersen wrote in his autobiography. "When the school hours were over, the house door was commonly locked; I was obliged to remain in the heated school room and learn my Latin, or else play with the children, or sit in my little room; I never went out to visit anybody. My life in this family furnishes the most evil dreams to my remembrance . . . I suffered so severely in my mind that I was very near sinking under it."

To Collin he wrote of Meisling, "every day he shows his dislike of me and when I take him my Latin composition on Sunday mornings every error makes him destroy my soul with the most awful truths . . . I do not dare question that he means well, but everything arouses his ill will, and I am living under the most horrible stress . . . Please don't cast me over! I have only got you! You must give me life or death!" Collin the utilitarian rationalist told him not to lose heart; Meisling meant well, he said, and even if his methods were unusual, they would achieve the desired goal of Andersen passing his exams.

For the rest of the year, Andersen bombarded Collin, Mrs. Wulff, Høegh-Guldberg and others with melodramatic, despairing letters. He advised a school friend from Slagelse never to read the poets, writing that he wished his father had burned all his books and forced him to be a shoe-maker, for then he would not have become mad, as he now believed himself to be. His was the desperation of the adolescent—intense, self-pitying, unable to see beyond the short-term, certain that he was misunderstood. Mrs. Wulff wrote:

> You certainly do your best to wear out your friends and I can't believe it can bring you any amusement yourself—and all because of the ceaseless concern with YOURSELF—YOUR OWN EGO—THE GREAT POET YOU THINK YOU WILL BE. My dear Andersen! You do realize that you aren't going to be suc-cessful with all these ideas and that you are on the wrong track. Supposing I had the notion that I wanted to be Empress of Brazil and I found that all my efforts went wrong, that no one took any interest in them, would I not then have to do my best to get together sufficient reason and thought to see: I am Mrs. Wulff—do your duty being her! and don't be a fool!

Alone and hopeless, Andersen turned back to the forbidden world of poetry, and wrote a poem in which he imagined himself as a dying child:

> Mother, I'm so tired, I want to sleep now;
>   let me fall asleep and feel you near.
> Please don't cry—there now, you'll promise, won't you?
>   On my face I felt your burning tear.
> Here's so cold, and winds outside are frightening
>   but in dreams—ah, that's what I like best:
> I can see the darling angel children,
>   when I shut my sleepy eyes and rest.
>
> Mother, look, the Angel's here beside me!
>   Listen, too, how sweet the music grows.
> See, his wings are both so white and lovely:
>   surely it was God who gave him those.
> Green and red and yellow floating round me,

they are flowers the Angel came and spread.
Shall I, too, have wings while I'm alive, or —
    Mother, is it only when I'm dead?

Why do you take hold of me so tightly,
    put your cheek to mine the way you do?
And your cheek is wet, but yet it's burning —
    Mother, I shall always be with you . . .
Yes, but then you mustn't go on sighing;
    when you cry I cry as well, you see.
I'm so tired—my eyes they won't stay open —
    Mother—look—the Angel's kissing me!

Andersen was twenty-one when he wrote this, and it is hardly the work of a mature mind. But in his search for his own mode of expression "The Dying Child" is a landmark. Today, it is unfashionably sentimental, but in 1826 it was not only poignant but also original, the first of many nineteenth-century literary and visual depictions of dying children—Dickens's Little Nell, Charlotte Brontë's Helen Burns; the prints of child deathbeds such as Luke Fildes's *The Doctor*, which sold over a million copies—to achieve cult status. This was a time when children dying was part of family life in all classes; by 1826 King Frederik VI and his queen had lost six of their eight children, and of every thousand babies born in mid-Victorian England, only 522 reached the age of five. Andersen was among the earliest writers to focus on this subject and the first to speak as the child itself.

He wrote the poem for his own comfort and showed it to a few people in Copenhagen. So immediate was its appeal that a German publisher had it translated, and it appeared in a German newspaper. Some months later, in September 1827, the Danish original was published in the *Copenhagen Post*. It was a sensational success, the most popular poem Andersen wrote—ten years later, after the fairy tales had appeared, this was the work that made Andersen's name in France. It remained well-loved throughout the nineteenth century and is still powerful today. As for most great writers, important themes of Andersen's work are already present in his debut: first, a child's perspective, which never really left him, and second, the battle between life and death, which, as he struggled with pessimism and a search for meaning, was part of his day-to-day existence. But the humour of his mature work is quite absent.

At a subconscious level, the vision of the dying child probably had two meanings for him in 1826. He was aware that Meisling was trying to destroy in him what was his own, childhood property—native genius, talent, imagination—with layers of bourgeois education; and death is a metaphor for his own despair as an overgrown child crushed in the school room. Later, the image came to have more complex implications, and it never left him—he wrote many fairy tales about dying children, and holding fast to an infant as it died was one of the recurring dreams of his old age.

Indirectly, the poem brought about his release. Meisling heard about it, demanded to see it and pronounced it "sentimentality and idle trash"; "from this day forward my situation was more unfortunate than ever," recorded Andersen. But a young teacher at Elsinore, Christian Werliin, befriended Andersen at this time, and was shocked to see Meisling's treatment of him. Andersen and Werliin travelled together to Copenhagen for the Easter holiday in 1827, and Werliin urged Andersen to talk to Collin. When this failed, Werliin went to Collin himself, and painted Meisling in so disturbing a light that Collin allowed Andersen to leave the grammar school at once, and finish his studies with a private tutor in Copenhagen. Within a few days, after his pleas had been ignored for so long, his school years abruptly ended.

He returned to Elsinore by steamer to bid Meisling farewell, and got an icy reception; when he thanked him for his help, Meisling cursed him in reply: "[he] ended by saying . . . that my verses would grow mouldy on the floor of the bookseller's shop, and that I myself should end my days in a madhouse." But Andersen was free and barely cared. He called his year at Elsinore "the darkest, the most unhappy time of my life," and until he died he dreamed about Meisling, associating him for ever with the social humiliation of his early years. The recurring dreams suggest how deep the social scars went, and how vital a role they played in his psychological make-up. Through the 1860s, more than thirty years after he had left school, his diary includes entries such as "nasty dreams with Meisling in them." In June 1870 he noted, "yesterday my dream was again about being dependent; I fled from Meisling, was frightened of Old Collin because everyone was displeased with me at the new school." And in July 1874, aged sixty-nine, he recorded, "an embarrassing dream about Meisling, before whom I stood unhappy and awkward." His feelings about Meisling were too intensely negative to be transformed directly into his works, but Meisling's example crystallized Andersen's dislike of a reliance on reason and of the arid, intellectual life, which is a theme in many of his fairy tales, most famously "The Snow Queen," and a driving force behind his entire *œuvre*.

CHAPTER 5

Fantasies

1827–1831

The goblin peeped through the keyhole and saw the student reading the tattered book . . . But how bright it was in there! From the book came a ray of light which grew into the stem of a great tree that raised itself aloft and spread its branches over the student's head. Every leaf was so very fresh and every flower the head of a lovely girl . . . the little goblin had never dreamt of splendour such as this.
—HANS CHRISTIAN ANDERSEN, "The Goblin at the Grocer's"

To move in the spring of 1827 from the windswept white school house in Elsinore to a tiny attic room with sloping walls and bare floors in Copenhagen was for Andersen a giant leap to happiness. He was by nature a city dweller: restless, easily bored, in need of constant drama, he loved the theatre, gossip, the rituals of social life. From his window at 6, Vingårdsstræde, there was an open view over the red-tiled roofs towards the tower of St. Nicholas Church: in the summer evenings he used to daydream as he listened to the organ grinder and watched the sun set and the clouds take on the appearance of mountains. He lodged with a widow in one of the oldest houses in the capital, a medieval building with a vaulted cellar that had been a tavern, the King Hans, since the Middle Ages. Round the corner was the Royal Theatre and a few minutes away across Kongens Nytorv were the homes of the Collin and the Wulff families. It was a short walk to the harbour and the sea, where in "The Little Mermaid," one of the mermaid sisters loves to swim to the surface of the water simply to watch city life: "Loveliest of all, she said, was to lie in the moonlight on a sand-bank in the calm sea, watching from close inshore the big city where the lights twinkled like a hundred stars, listening to the music and the sounds and the noises of carriages and people, seeing all the church towers and spires and hearing the ringing of the bells."

Andersen enjoyed living as a student. In some subjects, such as mathematics, he was confident enough to prepare himself for the university matriculation exam, but in Latin and Greek especially he needed help. His new teacher, a linguist and historian called Ludvig Christian Müller, was a kind, religious young man to whom Andersen warmed at once. He lived on the island of Amager, across the harbour from central Copenhagen, and through 1827 and 1828, Andersen walked there and back twice a day, from Kongens Nytorv along a busy thoroughfare called Holmen's Canal, then over the bridge to Amager. In the evenings he studied or wrote creatively, as he pleased. The image of the scholar in his garret was always a luminous one for Andersen: in his volume of stories *Picture Book Without Pictures,* the moon peers through the attic window of a young man to tell him stories, and in the tale "The Goblin at the Grocer's," a goblin is seduced away from the grocer downstairs, who offers him butter and porridge, by a light burning at the top of the house, where "a proper student, who lived in an attic and owned nothing" is reading books.

As Andersen, like the student in the story, was poor, he took his meals every evening of the week with a leading Copenhagen family—the Wulffs on Mondays, the Collins on Tuesdays, the Ørsteds on Fridays and so on. This was common practice for students who came from the provinces; it was one of the ways in which they became absorbed into the bourgeois and intellectual life of the capital. At Ørsted's, for example, Andersen developed an interest in science and met as a social equal the professor, Von Schmidten, who later examined him in mathematics; at the viva voce exam Von Schmidten chatted to him about his literary works. In such circles, Andersen soon found himself on easy terms with the theatrical lions of the day, the playwrights Oehlenschläger and Johan Ludvig Heiberg. He also had the ability to engage with a family on all levels. To amuse children he had an exceptional talent for making paper cut-outs, dancers, palaces with doors that opened, figures from *commedia dell'arte* such as Pierrot, and a favourite image, the stealer of hearts, in which men hung from a gibbet with a heart at its base, and he became a popular guest.

But one home soon took on an emotional significance for him more intense than the others. At first, dinner at the Collins' dark, austere house in Bredgade, furnished with uncomfortable hard chairs, no carpets or cushions or flowers, an old piano in the corner and a pair of bloodhounds lying at Jonas's feet, was intimidating. Collin's five children—Ingeborg (born 1804), Gottlieb (1806), Edvard (1808), Louise (1813) and Theodor (1815)—were

A portrait of Jonas Collin, patron and father-figure.

around the same age as Andersen but formed a unit so tightly knit, sharing their own jokes and allusions in what was almost a private family language, that he felt quite excluded. Edvard later admitted that "our family was somewhat preoccupied with itself; in our little world we kept to the tone which expressed the character of the house." All members of the family resembled each other—solid, well-built, square-faced, poised, dark-haired and conventional in features; in a photograph with them, lean, long, beaky Andersen looks an extraordinarily awkward and different creature, the ugly duckling in the nest.

Over everyone hovered the benign but autocratic Jonas, most energetic and best-connected man in Copenhagen: Minister of Finance; founder of the Copenhagen Savings Bank; theatre director; schools and prisons inspector; secretary of the fund *ad usus publicos*, which assisted artists like Andersen; founder of the Danish Society for the Prevention of Cruelty to Children. Business and philanthropy ran in his blood. Collin was a self-made man whose family had come from Kolding in Jutland and changed their name to Collin. As the family historian wrote, "any touch of provincialism has been washed away, its cultural standing has been nudged up a notch or two, and authority shines through clearly." "I really was kind of frightened of the father," Andersen wrote in *The Book of My Life,* "although I loved him with all my heart; the fear was because I believed my life's happiness, indeed my whole existence, to depend upon him." In his diaries, it is not always clear whether Andersen is referring to God or to Jonas, and indeed he often seemed himself unable to distinguish between the two. In 1839, when he was already a successful author, he wrote that he looked up to Jonas "as someone infallible . . . I suppose he is right when judging as a severe god must judge. I feel my own powerlessness, feel how useless I am in this world, how hollow all my efforts are—and yet one does not dare die." This was how Jonas often made him feel; as with Meisling, fear of Jonas filled his dreams until he died.

Among the children, the boys were in 1827 finishing a classical education and were academic stars set on the road to professional success. Edvard became a civil servant and banker, Gottlieb head of the Pension Fund and a judge, Theodor a ship's doctor and physician at the Royal Theatre, and later Andersen's doctor. The girls both married judges. It was natural for all of them to follow their father's example and be kind but somewhat patronizing to Andersen. Edvard helped him with Latin lessons; Ingeborg, who was married and had left home, teased him to put him at his ease, and he used to squeal with pleasure at her jokes. "The eldest daughter was married and had gone away, she was the one who had talked to me most, the other children did not do so at all," Andersen wrote in *The Book of My Life.* "In fact, Edvard appeared to me so cold, so inaccessible, that I really thought that he could not stand me, that he was haughty and even my enemy. That is what I believed of the man who later became infinitely dear to me, and whom I now know to be my best, my most trustworthy friend."

Slowly he became friends with them, and the more he visited them, the more he wanted to become part of them. They represented the ideal bourgeois family: successful, secure, civilized, benign—the antithesis of his own loneliness and uncertainty. He began to call the house in Bredgade his "Home of Homes," and dreamed of it as a haven that would always welcome him. After Andersen died, Edvard wrote that he had been happy to be treated like a Collin son, but sad not to be one; Ingeborg's granddaughter Rigmor Stampe went further, saying that Andersen always felt a stranger among the Collins, however nice they were to him. In 1827 Andersen was gripped by the first stirrings of an obsession with this family which lasted a lifetime.

The Collins, on the other hand, were at this time only the most attractive part of a world of culture and learning that opened up suddenly before him. He had eighteen months in which to prepare himself for his matriculation exam, and he made a pact with himself that on his twice-daily walk to his teacher on Amager he would concentrate on his lessons on the way there, but on his return breathed more freely, and allowed "bright poetical ideas" to pass through his brain. These were worlds away from the melancholy "The Dying Child": they were comic, fantastic, satirical, and once Andersen had passed the exam (despite low marks in Latin) in September 1828, he gave them free rein—"the ideas and thoughts, by which I was pursued on the way to my teacher, flew like a swarm of bees out into the world, and indeed, into my first work, *A Walking Tour from the Holmen Canal to the Eastern Point of Amager.*"

He wrote it in the winter of 1828 in his attic, where it opens. "On New Year's Eve I sat quite alone in my little room and looked out across the snow-covered roofs of the neighbouring houses; then came the evil spirit, whom people call Satan, who encouraged my sinful thoughts about becoming a writer." The title traces the walk to his teacher; a subtitle announces the journey's dates as "in the years 1828 and 1829"; the joke is that the "walk" is a young poet's midnight stroll as he wanders around the city in the last hours of 31 December 1828 and the first hours of 1 January 1829. It was published on 2 January 1829.

A Walking Tour is a comic fantasy in the style of E. T. A. Hoffmann, whose literary fairy tales were famous in Germany and in north and eastern Europe in the early nineteenth century—Carlyle translated them into English, but they never caught on in the Anglophone world, and today only Hoffmann's *Nutcracker and Mouse King,* the inspiration for Tchaikovsky's ballet, is widely known. Hoffmann had died in 1821, but continued to be immensely popular in Europe in the following decades. In 1828 Andersen named the reading group he had founded with two friends The Serapion Brotherhood, the title of Hoffmann's final volume of short stories. Hoffmann had also belonged to a Berlin club of the same name, and the three young Danish writers met, papers sticking out of their pockets, read each other their latest works and paid homage to Hoffmann.

Hoffmann, the German comedian of the grotesque, now supplanted Walter Scott as the writer "infused" into Andersen's blood. Of the three writers whom Andersen names as his influences—Scott, Hoffmann and

Heine—Hoffmann's influence was unsurpassed and long-lasting, for without his model Andersen would not have been able to harness the fantasies and tales that had filled his thoughts since childhood, and form them into a disciplined art.

Like Andersen's, Hoffmann's personality was shaped by childhood traumas which, in a talented boy, encouraged an absurdist view of the world and produced a man beset by fears and obsessions that no professional success could alleviate. E. T. A. Hoffmann—he was christened Ernst Theodor Wilhelm, but later replaced Wilhelm with Amadeus, in honour of Mozart—was born in 1776 in Königsberg, a Baltic port of the Hanseatic League in East Prussia, across the sea from Scandinavia; today Königsberg is Kaliningrad in Russia. His parents were first cousins, the father a respectable, charming but unstable lawyer, the mother hysterical and rigid. Hoffmann called their marriage "a comedy of domestic dissension"; it ended in divorce when he was four and his father disappeared, taking an older son with him to another East Prussian town and leaving Ernst at his grandmother's home, which was virtually a madhouse.

Grandmother Doerffler, "a woman of Amazonian proportions who had spawned a race of pygmies," was obsessed with the decline of her family's status and rarely left her quarters. In another room Hoffmann's mother lived on her sickbed, frail and nervous, taking her meals alone, seeing no one. A third room was shared between Uncle Otto Wilhelm Doerffler, a forty-year-old bachelor who had trained as a lawyer but botched his only case, and little Ernst. The grandmother treated them both as small children, and Otto was known in the family by his tragic initials O. W., pronounced in German "O Weh" (O woe!). There was an indulgent maiden aunt and, upstairs, a lodger called Frau Werner who thought she was the Virgin Mary and her son the Messiah. Guests were forbidden apart from a schoolboy called Hippel who came on Wednesday and Sunday afternoons to play and to read Goethe; after lunch on these days O. W. went on long walks to give the boys the privacy of the room.

Hoffmann was short and ugly as a caricature: a huge head, a shock of black curls, a big nose, thin lips pressed tight together, tiny hands and feet; but he was intellectual, witty and a brilliant pianist. He became a law student, and spent his time giving music lessons. After an affair with a married pupil, he was bustled off to a government post in Glogau, a dreary Silesian town, where he lodged with cousins who tried to engage him to their daughter. He fled to Posen, in Prussian Poland, but drank too much, upset the governor with malicious cartoons and was exiled to another ghastly eastern town, Plock. In despair, he married a young, uneducated Polish Catholic, Misha, whom he ignored throughout their marriage. Eventually his friend Hippel got him a good civil service job in Warsaw, where he flourished for a year until Napoleon arrived in 1806, the Prussian government was dissolved and Hoffmann, at thirty, was unemployed, penniless and bordering on madness.

His diaries are full of references to doubles and to a "divided self"; "I imagine that I see myself through a multiplying glass—all the forms which move round me are myselfs." Soon, first in the provincial haven of a musician's job in the south German town of Bamberg, then as a civil servant in Berlin's Ministry of Justice, he was writing fantastical stories about *doppelgänger* and puppeteers and automata coming to life—Godfather Drosselmeier in *The Nutcracker* is a self-portrait. Hoffmann revolutionized the development of psychological fiction. In 1814, his volume of eerie tales *Fantasy Pieces in the Style of Callot* launched the split personality in European literature. Later came novels like *The Devil's Elixir*, where the hero kills his double and is haunted by him, *Tomcat Murr*, a double biography of a bourgeois cat and a struggling Kapellmeister, and his story *Doppelgänger*.

His *doppelgänger* images embodied Romanticism's self-conscious agony; out of his own harrowing experiences of isolation, failure and madness, he started a new genre, the supernatural short story in which sanity and insanity, dream and reality, are indistinguishable, and where man's greatest struggle takes place not against the external world but within his own mind—Hoffmann points straight to Freud. He wrote by night, and was sometimes so terrified by his bizarre creations, such as Coppelius and the life-size doll in "The Sandman"—the inspiration for Delibes's ballet *Coppélia*—that he woke his wife for reassurance. By forty-six he was dead from drink, disappointment and poor nerves, and something of an icon among literary young men. Many nineteenth-century authors—Gogol, Pushkin, Dostoevsky—acknowledged their debt to him.

A Walking Tour was particularly indebted to Hoffmann's *New Year's Eve Adventure* and to *The Devil's Elixir*. Andersen called the work "a peculiar, humorous book, a kind of fantastic arabesque,* but one which fully exhib-

---

*An arabesque is an ornamental design of interlocking flowing lines, often resembling flowers or foliage, originally found in Islamic decorations. In literary terms, it means a short piece of prose in which a single episode is elaborated by flights of fancy. The term was in use by 1798, when the German romantic critic Schlegel described Tieck's *Märchen* as poetic arabesques.

ited my own individual character at that time, my disposition to sport with everything, and to jest in tears over my own feelings—a fantastic, gaily coloured tapestry work was this poetical improvisation." It relates a young poet's night-time adventures in the city, his meetings with mythical figures including Faust, St. Peter, who offers him the keys to Amager island, and "long, lean Death," driving across the island on the front seat of "Death's express mailcoach . . . grinning nastily with his wide mouth in the moonlight."

In Andersen's day, the flat island of Amager was Copenhagen's vegetable garden, from where the market stallholders came in every day with their produce; in the book everyday characters such as the Amager Woman, a street vendor selling cabbages and potatoes, and Louise, a girl from the morgue who turns out to be the muse of Romanticism, take on a ghoulish significance. The poet travels forward in time to the Pantheon of Poetry, where Aristophanes, Shakespeare, Cervantes and Hoffmann sit in the four corners; Oberon, Titania, Puck, Queen Mab and "Canibal" (Caliban) appear; a boy with butterfly wings soars aloft; and he hears Hoffmann's book *The Devil's Elixir* telling its own story. But world literature is also represented as a defeated army of tired and worn-out volumes marching to Amager, followed by ambulances, stretchers and hearses, with Amager a mock Pantheon or poetic recycling ground, delivering fresh cabbage heads, or transitory works of literature, for instant consumption in the capital: thus Andersen satirized the deluge of letters in a mass society.

A Walking Tour is a typical young man's book: inventive and ornate, flickering and unstable in form, heady with the discovery of literature, choking on its mass of metaphors. You can see in it how the restlessness and dreaminess that Meisling so disliked in Andersen is on the verge of maturing into brilliant fantasy, but is not quite there. There is something artificial about the tone, for Andersen was still struggling to find his own voice. Yet there is much which indicates his lifelong concerns: fairy tale motifs, a sense of the absurd and the grotesque, the play between life and death, and, underlying it all, doubt about his own work and about the value of poetry in general. This is a theme which recurs in Andersen's later fairy tales and in his diaries; in his twenties, he was still too urgently carving out his career to admit to such anxieties, but they found unconscious, symbolic, expression here.

It was an ambitious first book, and Andersen approached the university publisher Reitzel with a demand for an advance of a hundred rixdollars.

Reitzel offered seventy rixdollars; Andersen turned him down and brought out the book himself. It cost one rixdollar and within a month the first edition of 500 copies had sold out (this was at a time when sales of 1,000 copies were considered excellent in a country with a population of one million, most of whom were illiterate peasants). Reitzel offered a hundred rixdollars for the second edition, which came out in April 1829, followed by a third edition and a Swedish translation. It did so well partly because Andersen had courted so many benefactors, critics, writers, in advance, and all were waiting for his debut, which met their expectations of something precocious and slightly bizarre, and partly because it was fashionably Hoffmannesque. In a flattering review in the journal *Maanedsskriftet for Litteratur*, the playwright and critic Heiberg praised the book as a musical fantasy of originality and grace and compared Andersen as a precocious writer to a young painter who, before daring to take up stronger compositions, practises with the arabesque.

Heiberg was a powerful ally to have won; no literary figure at that time so clearly embodied the Danish literary establishment. Born in 1791, Johan Ludvig Heiberg was the son of the exiled intellectual Peter Andreas Heiberg and his glamorous wife Thomasine. His father had treated his mother with cold disdain, and after he was exiled she wrote him a letter asking for a divorce so that she could marry a Swedish nobleman, C. F. Gyllembourg, with whom she had fallen in love. This letter, considered by Danish historians to be one of the most beautiful in the language, caused a sensation at a time when divorce was almost unknown. Thomasine married Gyllembourg, and from 1827 wrote a series of very popular romantic novels, under a pseudonym never to be lifted in her lifetime. But as a price of the settlement, Johan Ludvig was taken away from her and fostered, for a long time by the literary socialites Knud and Kamma Rahbek at Bakkehuset, where he was very unhappy. Eventually he ran away, but the damage was done. His childhood had made Heiberg Andersen's opposite in every way: emotionally icy, socially and intellectually unassailable, supremely well-connected. He wrote popular vaudevilles and his romance *Elverhøj (Hills of the Elves)* was considered a Danish national drama. By 1829 he had become the arbiter of literary taste in Copenhagen and, suavely handsome, was courting the 17-year-old actress Johanne Luise Pätges, who as his wife was soon to dominate the stage of the Royal Theatre. This was for much of Andersen's life the only theatre in Copenhagen, and the place he most wanted to conquer, too; to keep this couple on his side was to be as crucial as it was difficult.

Andersen immediately followed the success of *A Walking Tour* with a work for the stage, a vaudeville in Heiberg's style called *Love on St. Nicholas Tower*, which opened in April 1829. Subtitled "What does the Pit say?," it tells of a night watchman who tries to marry his daughter to another watchman although she is in love with a tailor. The audience must vote on who is to be the successful suitor; if they applaud, she will marry the tailor, but if they boo or hiss, the watchman wins. The playful interaction with his audience, and the jokey self-referential treatment of art, were noteworthy; they are features of his later work. Part of the vaudeville satirized an already outdated form of chivalric tragedy, but the piece was nevertheless acclaimed at the Royal Theatre.

Since his arrival in Copenhagen ten years earlier, success here had been Andersen's goal. Now,

> My fellow-students received the piece with acclamation and shouted "Long live the author!" I was overwhelmed with joy . . . I could not contain myself. I rushed out from the theatre into the street, and then to Collin's house, where his wife was alone at home. I threw myself down into a chair almost exhausted and wept in convulsion. The sympathizing lady did not know what to think, and trying to console me, said—"Don't let it grieve you so much. Oehlenschläger has also been hissed, and many other great poets."—"They have not hissed at all," exclaimed I sobbing: "they have applauded and cried *Vivat!*"

He was full of his triumphs when he went in June to see his mother in Odense and to spend the summer with the Funen gentry at the country estates of Maryhill and Tolderlund. In October 1829 he passed the second university exam in philology and philosophy, *examen philologicum et philosophicum*, for which he had prepared alone. After this, he considered himself a free man. He abandoned all academic study, and brought out instead his first collection of poems, *Digte (Poems)*, for Christmas 1829 (it bears the date 1830, as was the practice of the times). It included some humorous, some elegiac, verses and a comic self-portrait in which Andersen painted himself as a gawky, unprepossessing youth:

> Look, yonder on the hill a lanky person,
> His face as pale as that of Werther,
> His nose as mighty as a cannon,
> His eyes are tiny, like green peas.
> He sings a German song with a "*woher?*"

And longingly stares at the sunset.
I wonder why he's standing there so long.
Well, bless my soul! I'm not omniscient;
Yet one thing is certain, if I'm not mistaken:
He's either mad, a lover, or a poet.

The volume is unremarkable except for its final item, "The Ghost: A Fairy Tale from Funen." This was an adaptation of a Danish folk tale called "The Dead Man's Help," which Andersen turned to again five years later as the model for his story "The Travelling Companion." In 1830, his version of the story was unshaped and the arch style and clichéd language bears no resemblance to the easy, colloquial mode of his later fairy tales. But "The Ghost" encapsulates many of the themes—the supernatural, the idea of an immutable Fate, the absurdity of existence—which came to dominate his tales, and it is a significant first choice. "As a child," he wrote in his introduction to it, "it was my greatest pleasure to listen to fairy tales, and some of these are either very little or not at all known. I have retold one of these here, and if it wins approval, I mean to retell several, and one day to publish a cycle of 'Danish Folk Tales.' "

This was not a new idea. For twenty years, Jakob and Wilhelm Grimm had been collecting German stories, and their first volumes of *Kinder- und Hausmärchen* (1812–1815) had by the 1820s awakened interest in folk tales across Europe. In England a translation, *German Popular Tales,* illustrated by Cruikshank, appeared in 1823. In Odense, the regimental surgeon, Matthias Winther, had become obsessed by Danish folk tales and travelled up and down Zealand and the islands to the south persuading old country people to tell him stories; in 1823 he published a collection, *Danish Folk Tales.* In Copenhagen, Just Matthias Thiele, assistant at the Royal Library, who had been one of Andersen's sponsors, started collecting Danish legends in 1817. His prized possessions included signed copies of the Grimms' tales and of Walter Scott's folk songs, and between 1818 and 1823 he published his own collections, with an introduction describing the legends as rosy-cheeked farmers' boys running round the village pond in clogs. In 1829 Andersen was announcing his allegiance to this romantic folk tradition. After seven years as a schoolboy and student, he was flirting with various forms in his search for his own artistic voice. "The Ghost" was a small landmark.

· · ·

"I liked to listen to the sounding bell of praise. I had such an overflow of youth and happiness. Life lay bright with sunshine before me," Andersen wrote of the beginning of the new decade, 1830. But there were ripples on the calm surface which were soon to turn to storms. Restless and ambitious, Andersen was sure he was capable of something more than *A Walking Tour* and his poems, and he knew he had to produce a substantial work soon to continue to be taken seriously. Yet the right form eluded him. At the same time he was struggling financially, and still haunted by his escape from his mother's world of poverty and ignorance.

"If you will forget circumstances of birth and always be to me what I am to you, you will find in me the most honest and sympathetic friend," he told Edvard Collin at this time. For Andersen's twenty-fifth birthday on 2 April 1830, his mother dictated a letter thanking him for the money he had sent her, saying that she would have died without his kindness, for she could not live on twenty-four shillings a week. He stood at an astonishing distance from the milieu in which he had grown up, but the future still looked insecure, and to compensate he showed off to his friends and his patrons, boasting about his success, declaiming his works: "Doesn't every youth want to please? I shall have no success with my appearance, so I make use of whatever is available." Beneath it all was the continuing loneliness of the rootless young man in the city, uncertain how to make emotional connections and aware of an attraction to certain male friends which none reciprocated with equal intensity.

Of these, Edvard Collin was the constant; around him circled other young men who now and then glittered more dazzlingly for Andersen, then receded into the background. In 1830, Edvard was a 21-year-old law student with shining prospects. As the son of Jonas Collin, his social position was impeccable. He was a fine scholar and had a cool, disciplined, rational temperament which was to make him an excellent civil servant. In appearance he was nondescript—he had a square face and ordered features, and an expression which was always confident and rather unimaginative. "Brought up under fortunate circumstances of life," Andersen wrote of him,

> he was possessed of that courage and determination which I wanted. I felt that he sincerely loved me and I, full of affection, threw myself upon him with my whole soul; he passed on calmly and practically through the business of life. I often mistook him at the very moment when he felt for me most deeply, and when he would gladly have infused into me a portion of his own character—to me, who was as a reed shaken by the wind.

Part of Andersen longed to be like Edvard, to share his certainties and rectitude and practical competence, and by 1830 Edvard had become his mentor, warning him about his vanity and his ludicrous behaviour in public—the eagerness with which he read his poems aloud at social gatherings, for instance—and Andersen was driven in his efforts to please him. "Something in you drew me early on, many things I respected and found attractive; you expressed an interest in me, and I wanted this interest to increase, I wanted to gain you as a friend, of a sort of which only a few exist," he wrote in 1833. But each time he wanted to establish landmarks of intimacy, Andersen lost his nerve. He found that he had to leave Copenhagen to try to conquer Edvard by written rather than spoken words.

And so on 31 May he boarded the steamboat *Dania* with the painter Martinus Rørbye for the twenty-hour trip across the Kattegat, the choppy stretch of the Baltic which separates Zealand and Jutland. In 1830, steam navigation was just being developed, and to go on a steamboat was an adventure. Before he left, an old sailor, a relative of Ørsted, berated him for considering this new method of transport: " 'From the creation of the world,' said he, 'till this time, we have been satisfied with reasonable ships driven by wind, but now they are trying to make something better; as often as one of those smoke-caps is passing, I cannot forbear taking my speaking-trumpet and scolding it as long as it can hear me.' " But Andersen loved the thrill of new ways of travelling. Writer and artist disembarked at the port of Aarhus, a wretched, tasteless market town, according to Kierkegaard ten years later, and were soon exploring the remote heather-covered moorland and sand dunes of Jutland.

"No keen traveller is ever tempted to visit such an unforgiving patch of earth," proclaimed a parish account of Jutland in 1819. This western rural province of Denmark, known as "the black desert," was still little known in the 1830s and considered backward, the home of dim-witted bumpkins. Blicher's story, "Fragments from the Diary of a Parish Clerk," had just begun to launch the idea of Jutland as a suitable object of romantic pilgrimage: a colourful place of primitive passion and rural enchantment, Denmark's equivalent to Walter Scott's windswept heaths and brooding skies. Andersen was drawn to it as the setting for his *Christian II's Dwarf,* with which he still hoped to make his name as a historical novelist; his attraction to Jutland now also marked an awareness of the romantic in his own nature for the first time. "Jutland really is the most romantic part of Denmark! . . . I think it must have much in common with the Scottish Lowlands!" he wrote in his novel *OT.* By 1840, when Kierkegaard, another admirer of Blicher, made the journey of homage, Jutland was fashionable. The moors where everything lay bare and exposed to God, Kierkegaard said, seemed to have been created in order to generate powerful minds.

Jutland stretches from the flat plains around the German border in the south—then the Danish duchies of Schleswig and Holstein—along the rocky fjorded coast of the Kattegat up to the far northern tip of Skagen, a sand-swept wilderness where even churches are submerged by dunes, and the Kattegat meets the thundering Skagerrak sea. By the end of the century, artists were flocking here to paint the summer sun falling on the overlapping waves from the two seas; in 1830 Rørbye was a romantic pioneer who painted both the harsh landscapes and everyday scenes. He embraced folk motifs— Jutlanders in local costume at the market places of Thisted and Viborg, fishermen, farmhands in their Sunday best, an inspector of a wreck with his dog—which were the pictorial equivalent of Andersen's interest in folk tales.

Rørbye encouraged Andersen, whose imagination was in any case a strongly visual one, to see with the eye of a painter; he even persuaded him to do some sketches, and he was the first person to develop Andersen's power of evoking landscape. In turn, Rørbye took inspiration for some of his paintings from Andersen's Jutland poems, particularly one about a black wreck on a white, sandy beach. From 1830 on, when Andersen wanted to depict the rhythm of nature and the sea, he turned most often to Jutland. He began writing the poem sequence "Pictures of Jutland," which appeared in his volume *Fantasies and Sketches* in 1831, and he returned to images of a Jutland wilderness as a symbol of the grim fatalism of nature in stories such as "A Story of the Sand Dunes" and "Bishop Børglum" in the 1850s and 1860s:

> The brown heath now also extends for miles, with its Huns' graves, its aerial spectacles and its crossing, sandy, uneven roads; westward, where large rivulets run into bays, extend marshes and meadow land, girdled with lofty sand-hills, which, like a row of Alps, raise their peaked summits towards the ocean, only broken by the high clayey ridges, from which the waves year by year bite out huge mouthfuls, so that the impending shores fall down as if by the shock of an earthquake.

As they toured the province, the romantic landscapes of Scott and Blicher were Andersen and Rørbye's mental Baedeker. They visited the Thiele manor house, setting for "Fragments from the Diary of a Parish Clerk," and met friends of Blicher. At the manor of Rosenholm Rørbye they saw an old manservant, who reminded them of a character from Scott's novels. Andersen's dream of seeing Gypsies, romantic icons of freedom, was also fulfilled:

I was approaching Viborg in a heavy downpour when, along a bumpy lane, I came across a tinker family; the woman carried an infant on her back and had another child by the hand, the man had knapsacks slung over his shoulders, they wished me good day in a friendly fashion and went on their way, for there was nowhere for them to find shelter. When my man told me who they were I grew quite blissful; this truly poetic people live in our Denmark; they have their own language, own customs, live the life of nomads and wed their own kind with their own ceremonies, without the interference of the clergy.

As important was his own reception. The local paper in Aarhus reported his visit and the municipal authorities in the town of Lemvig promised to subscribe to *Christian II's Dwarf*. Everywhere Andersen was known as the author of *A Walking Tour* and the poem "The Dying Child," and he enjoyed showing himself off. But by the time they reached the cathedral town of Viborg in the middle of the moors, he had had enough of the keen, damp sea fog, and was complaining that his travelling clothes were too light for the cold weather. While Rørbye went north to paint the stark seascapes around Skagen, he went south through the lush countryside of eastern Jutland to Funen, staying in Odense at Maryhøi (Maryhill), the home of Mrs. Iversen, widow of his old printer-patron, and her granddaughters, the Hanck sisters.

There, a letter from Edvard signed "your sincere friend" was waiting for him. His reply—the convoluted, clumsy attempt of someone grappling to express emotions he cannot control—shows how desperate he was to seize this sign and to urge Edvard to greater commitment:

It was the first time you signed as "friend." This small event was endlessly dear to me for the very reason that I feel attracted to you, not only through gratitude but from the bottom of my heart, and it is my deepest wish that I must never give you any reason for our friendship, if I am allowed to use that term, to be loosened. I shall always come to you with the most sincere trust, and I am confident enough to believe that you will not, even when in low spirits, push me away, without my feeling that it is not due to your friendship for me being smaller, but is caused by the actual circumstances. From now on it will give me double pleasure to write to you quite often, as I see that, although I do not want to say that you value my writing, it gives you some amusement, and that you in response send even more heartfelt letters than mine were, because when you show me sympathy, I ought to show you confidence. Once a week I will therefore write to you, and do I dare hope for a response from you every fortnight at least?

From Funen he wrote several times more to Edvard, sending him love poems, telling him how he clung to him with all his heart. "Do not be surprised, therefore, that I repeat what I told you before that you are the only person I consider as my true friend, and my heart is closely attached to you," he wrote in August 1830. "This is something I may never be able to say to you in person, but you may be sure that I place the greatest significance on your every word, so please never thrust me away—but I am growing sentimental: you will understand what I mean. God give that I may confide in you with my entire heart!"

But another friendship suddenly came to preoccupy him in the summer of 1830. Christian Voigt was a student friend in Copenhagen who came from Faaborg, a port on the southwest coast of Funen, some twenty miles from Odense. In summer, Faaborg is idyllic: a pretty market town and fishing port facing south on to a sheltered bay, with colourful houses, squares and courtyards; it is warm and breezy, and gentler in tone than Odense and the towns of the north. The Voigts were wealthy merchants, conventional and respected, and the leading family in the town; their home, a cluster of yellow-painted gabled houses around a courtyard minutes from the harbour, is still the most impressive building in Faaborg. Christian, a few years younger than Andersen, was kindly, pragmatic, modest: every inch the merchant's son. Andersen had already formed something of a sentimental attachment to him, and on 6 August, in the middle of a tour of Funen, he arrived at Faaborg, took a room at an inn and sent his visiting card to Christian, who immediately invited him to his parents' house. But Christian was still in bed when Andersen appeared next morning, and his elder sister Riborg received him.

In portraits the 24-year-old Riborg, with dark hair and wide brown eyes, thoughtful and demure in her white cap and collar, her features composed yet lively and bright, appears beautiful. Both she and her brother look as if they have stepped out of the pages of *Buddenbrooks*—they shared the Hanseatic mercantile culture Thomas Mann evokes, for Faaborg was not far up the Baltic coast from Mann's Lübeck, and Faaborg merchants had traded with Germans for centuries. In this mellow atmosphere, his mind still full of the romance of Jutland, Andersen became intoxicated with Christian and Riborg. She had read his poems and *A Walking Tour,* and she made much of him. To Edvard he wrote, just after his arrival in Faaborg, "the ladies in this town are the most attractive I have so far met, even including Jutland, and

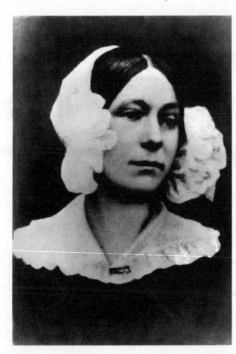

*Riborg Voigt,
Andersen's first love.*

one of Agent Voigt's daughters is even beautiful and, what I especially like, very natural."

Two years later, writing *The Book of My Life,* Andersen remembered how

the eldest daughter . . . received me with great kindness, blushing every instant when she talked to me; this apart, she appeared bright and lively. She had a lovely, pious face, quite child-like, but her eyes looked clever and thoughtful, they were brown and very vivid. She wore a simple, grey morning dress which was very attractive; indeed, her whole simplicity and her face captivated me at once. Her interest in my poems, indeed the fact that she appeared to hold me in some sort of respect, appealed to my vanity and at once made me interested in her. She joked about her brother's sluggish ways, showed so much spirit and humour that I, too, wanted to make myself interesting—I don't know why, but it was almost immediately as if we two had known each other a long time, and all day I took great joy in pleasing the young girl.

He stayed a few days in Faaborg, went boating and walking with the family, chatted to Riborg, and attended a party where, although usually an enthusiastic dancer, she sat out and talked to him all evening on hearing that he did not dance at social events. He told her he would name the heroine of his next novel after her, and when she asked for a copy of one of his poems, he gave her the comic *"Avis aux lectrices,"* which says that if a poet's fiancée does not praise all his poems, he will break off their engagement.

At the inn, he learnt that Riborg had a sweetheart, the local chemist's son, to whom she was secretly engaged, but that her parents disapproved of the match: this made her safely unreachable, but not so unattainable that he could not dream of her. When he returned to Odense on 10 August, the Hanck girls noted a change in him and told him mockingly that he must be in love. "When I first heard this," he recalled in *The Book of My Life*, "it was as if a flame rushed through my body, and I dismissed it as a joke but could not help thinking about it. I was impressed myself by how I had behaved during the few days I had spent with her. I began to long for her; the others joked about me; I did not like it and wanted to get these thoughts completely out of my head."

Back in Copenhagen, Christian engrossed him equally deeply. "Most of my time belongs to the heart and to friendship," he wrote. "I visit my dear Christian Voigt daily, the one I feel most attached to of all; I do not even notice time pass, although I nearly always feel so sad, so mournful. It is as if he has cast a spell over me, I do not know how I can be so fond of him." This was the first hint at a pattern in Andersen's love affairs that was to establish itself forcefully over the years—that to fall in love with a woman, he needed two emotional objects, one male and one female. Part of his pleasure at being in love with Riborg and playing the mournful lover that autumn came from the *frisson* of talking to Christian about her. Two years later, he was to pay court to Louise Collin at a time when his infatuation with her brother Edvard was at its height, and his subsequent grand passion, for the singer Jenny Lind, was also played out against erotic entanglements with men.

At twenty-five, Andersen was confused and inexperienced. In his baroque sentimental fluctuations of the 1830s, there is little of raw sexual hunger and much of a need for close companionship and understanding. "I miss you all so very much," he wrote to Mrs. Iversen when he got back to Copenhagen.

> I was so much at home with you, and, after all, I feel to want a real home. It will take a long time before I shall settle down to my room . . . Please let all read this letter if it will amuse them, because while I am writing it, I fancy that I am sitting in the midst of you, chatting away to my heart's content . . . Remember me kindly to all, and if you have nothing else to think about, then think of me.

He was ready to pour emotion towards any likely, sympathetic object. Physical passion was not a dominant feature of any of his relationships, but artistic sensibility was. The triangular dynamic he set up in his love affairs gave him the chance to verbalize and discuss, rather than indulge, sexual ardour; it was as if he unconsciously perceived that the bisexual nature of such engagements made them universal, and thus useful to him as an artist. There was nothing premeditated in his heterosexual flirtations, they were never simply a mask or a route to homosexual encounters; but these encounters did establish a pattern of male-to-male intimacy within a non-threatening framework which paved the way later for Andersen's more intense erotic relationships with men.

There is no reason to doubt, however, that Riborg was at the fore of Andersen's mind in 1830, as he says she was. She came to the capital in October, staying at the Royal Hotel for three weeks to visit a sick friend, and she told Christian she hoped to see Andersen again. Opening his door to her when she called, he asked straightaway after the ill woman, a *faux pas* as he did not know her at all; Riborg blushed for him, and the pair were thrown into embarrassed confusion. He read her the lovers' dialogue from the libretto of Walter Scott's novel *The Bride of Lammermoor* on which he was working, and he copied for her some of the love poems about to be published as "Melodies of the Heart." Two, "The Thought of My Thought" and "Two Brown Eyes," were later set to music by Grieg:

> Two brown eyes I did lately see—
> A home and a world lay there for me.
> With goodness and child-like peace they shone;
> I'll never forget them while life goes on.

As this suggests, part of Andersen's attraction to Riborg was the need for a home, for the stability epitomized by her close, wealthy family.

One evening, he pressed her hand to his lips and was sure that he was in love with her. Trembling and weeping, he told Christian, who assured him that Riborg liked him. But Andersen could not bring himself to arrange a tête-à-tête. In *The Book of My Life* he claims that he had decided to give up writing in order to earn a living which would support a family and allow him to marry Riborg, but that on his way home after revealing his plans to Christian he had an attack of fainting and dizziness which forced him to return to his room, where he fell asleep and woke up too late for the rendezvous. Whether this is true in fact or only metaphorically true—an invented tale which shows the poet, the inner man, fighting back against bourgeois circumscription—it is clear from the letter proposing marriage which he then sent, appealing to her "sisterly heart" to listen "the first time I really open mine to someone else," that he anticipated and indeed courted rejection. For three months, he says, he has been obsessed with her, but is aware that she is practically engaged to another. He continues:

> I should retreat and be resigned but—I think you have perceived my feelings already, I am not so worldly that I can keep my heart's secret, and I dream of a hope; without it my life is lost. *Do you truly love the other man?* I do not know him at all, cannot hold anything against him, and I expect he has his merits, since you have chosen him, but do you really love each other? . . . If you do not love him as dearly as God and your eternal salvation, if you are not quite sure—? Then do not make me unhappy! I can become anything through you . . . anything you and your parents might wish . . . You are my single and only thought, my all, and a poet's heart beats more strongly than any other heart . . . If you really love the other person, then forgive me! . . . I wish you both happiness and please forget someone who can never, never forget you . . . I shall read my fate in each of your expressions . . . Bless you! Perhaps goodbye for ever!

So many of the contradictions within the young Andersen are caught in this wildly unrealistic yet sober letter: the bashfulness mixed with confidence in his talents, the absolutism ("as dearly as God and your eternal salvation") which made him incapable of compromise, the courtesy which came at the cost of real sexual passion, the pessimism that hangs over the whole proposal. None of it, particularly from a young man who showed no sign of being able to earn a living, was going to persuade a conventional, middle-class girl to break off a long-term alliance. He gave the letter to Christian to pass on to Riborg, and that evening he watched her, looking pale and beautiful, across the auditorium of the Royal Theatre. The following night, her last in the city, he said goodbye to her outside the theatre, and the next morning received a note:

> Goodbye, goodbye! I hope Christian can soon tell me that you are as calm and contented as before.
>   With sincere friendship,
>   Riborg

There is no doubt that Andersen suffered, but also that he enjoyed the posturing of the hopeless lover. "Yes, my poems are no imagination, something terribly real is at the root of them," he wrote to Ingemann.

My soul and thoughts cling to but one being . . . but I feel how hideous it sounds. She is engaged and is going to be married next month . . . I had only been three days in their house, and as I felt what I never before had felt, and heard that she was engaged, I went away at once, but here in Copenhagen we met again . . . I don't know, but God is too hard on me. Oh that I were dead! Here I shall never be happy.

He painted a Riborg ravaged by love versus duty:

She is so beautiful, so gentle, and good, you would love her, so would all the world, and I know she has got the same feeling for me as I have for her, and still I shall never see her again . . . Next month she will be a wife, and then she will and *must* forget me. Oh it is killing me to think of it! Dear, dear Ingemann, I wish I were dead!—dead!—even if death were annihilation; but it cannot be.

To his peers he was more measured. A letter to Henriette Hanck, written in November 1830, just after Riborg had turned him down, runs cheerfully, "People are stunned at my last poems, just think, they believe I'm in love. Everybody thinks so, I have already heard several names among which people are guessing . . . Oh, it is a silly world." He offers various girls as candidates, including "Miss Voigt," but "that is quite foolish, since she is engaged, and I am almost ready to swear that she doesn't mean more to me than I to her."

Riborg married the chemist's son, Poul Bøving, in April 1831. At a dinner with friends a fortnight later Andersen drew a picture of a lyre, a mask, a laurel wreath, a book of poems and two engagement rings lying at the foot of a memorial cross inscribed "Poet." Around the same time he drew an angry self-portrait in which he is imprisoned in a flask, his limbs stretching to its edges and its neck in a desperate attempt to get out and reach Riborg, who, depicted as a winged angel, floats beyond him, an image which implies Andersen's sense of being constricted—in his emotions, in his art—and unable to relate to women, as well as recalling Hoffmann's story "The Golden Pot," whose hero is shut in a glass bottle sealing him from Paradise. Andersen was an unquenchable romantic, and never lost the desire to dramatize himself as a suffering lover: when he died, a leather pouch containing a letter from Riborg was found round his neck. It is unlikely that he had worn it all his life—as his biographer Hans Brix pointed out in 1907, it would have fallen to pieces. But the fact that he wanted to be found wearing it speaks of his pride in loyalty, romanticism's fidelity to all that is lost.

Hans Christian Andersen, Self-portrait Confined in a Bottle, *c. 1830—the angel resembles Riborg, who was beyond his reach—and* The Poet's Grave, *drawn two weeks after Riborg's wedding. The inscription reads "Our dear poet is no more / But we know what he created / He wrote and wrote—as others do / We know what we have lost! The house on Peblinge Lake, 11 May 1831."*

Riborg held an iconic status in his imagination. He met her again, with her husband and children, at a concert in Faaborg in 1840, and subsequently on holidays in Funen in 1842 and 1843, by which time he was famous, and he wrote a vengeful nursery tale, "The Top and the Ball," about their encounter. A ball is too haughty to have a top as her sweetheart; the top goes on "spinning and humming, while all the time his thoughts were of the ball, who grew more and more beautiful in his imagination." Years later, when the top is painted gold and is very grand, he meets the ball in a gutter and ignores her. "The top never spoke of his old love again. That dies when your sweetheart has lain for five years in a gutter; and you never know her again if you meet her in the dustbin." The friendship with Christian cooled too after 1831, but endured until Andersen died. Christian married late; in 1864 Andersen noted in his diary, "Yesterday Christian Voigt came to see me and asked me with an incredible embarrassment and humility—as if he believed that I wouldn't—to be godfather for his first son. Riborg's brother hasn't forgotten his old feeling for me."

At the beginning of 1831, Andersen began to be engulfed by a depression and creative frustration. Riborg was at its centre. Her rejection underlined his social unease—was he inferior to the chemist's son?—and his sexual uncertainty. He was anguished by his feelings for Edvard. He did not know where his writing was going. In his autobiography he wrote of this time that "I betrayed more and more in my writings an unhealthy turn of mind, and was often ready wholly to despair of my abilities, and had, as in the darkest days of my school-life, a feeling as if my whole talents were a self-deception."

An anonymous volume of rhymes called *Letters of a Ghost*, published in December 1830, described him as "a Slagelse nag with paralysed sides . . . intoxicated by the ale of fantasy," and was wounding because it contained a truth about his need to discipline the fantastical in his writing. Andersen was morbidly sensitive to criticism; the attack caused general amusement and left him embittered towards Copenhagen society. "My health is good, but still I don't feel happy. I am not as I used to be; I feel I am getting older, I begin to recognize in life something far deeper than I ever dreamt of, and feel that I shall never, never be really happy here," he wrote to Ingemann. He needed to get away again, and he began to plan a trip to Germany: his first foreign journey.

CHAPTER 6

My Time Belongs to the Heart

1831–1833

If you looked down to the bottom of my soul, you would understand fully the source of my longing and—pity me. Even the open, transparent lake has its unknown depths which no divers know.

—HANS CHRISTIAN ANDERSEN, letter to Edvard Collin, 1835

"Last year I was a gay, wandering minstrel who ridiculed Werther, and this year I am almost the same fool," Andersen wrote in February 1831 to his friend Christian Lorenzen. "Life has already shown me its darkest sides; how I wish it was all over. Yes, how peculiarly romantic it sounds . . . I do wish that I were dead!" Like countless young men in the early nineteenth century, he dignified an adolescent sense of being ill at ease with himself and with society by evoking Goethe's Werther, the hero of the cult novel *Die Leiden des jungen Werthers* (*The Sorrows of Young Werther*) of 1774. Werther, an unhappy, sensitive artist, suffers from both *Weltschmerz* (dissatisfaction with the world) and *Ichschmerz* (dissatisfaction with himself); hopelessly in love with a girl who is engaged to someone else, he eventually commits suicide.

Even in his schooldays Andersen had set himself in the context of European romantic writers. Now, in the aftermath of his failed love for Riborg, German Romanticism coloured his life, and suggested the way forward for his work. He turned especially to the melancholy lyrics of Heinrich Heine, "a poet who, as it seemed to me, sang out from the soul," he wrote. Heine at this point displaced Hoffmann as his literary model, and his Heine-esque volume of love poems, *Phantasier og Skizzer* (*Fantasies and Sketches*), appeared in January 1831, four years after Heine's popular *Das Buch der Lieder* (*Book of Songs*).

In 1831 Heine had already left Germany for Paris; Goethe was still living in Weimar and finishing the second part of *Faust*, but Andersen did not dream of approaching the grand old man of German letters. The next generation of German writers, including Ludwig Tieck (born in 1773) and Adelbert von Chamisso (born 1781), were however within his reach. Denmark at this time looked to Germany, rather than to the rest of Scandinavia, for cultural impetus, and the leading Danish writers modelled themselves on Germans—Oehlenschläger on Goethe, Ingemann on Tieck and von Chamisso, whom he had met during his European journey of education. Ingemann offered Andersen letters of introduction, and increased his ambition to be connected to the European mainstream.

Andersen sensed that these writers were pioneering a modern literature, and he wanted to be part of it. During the decades following the French Revolution of 1789, writes James Sheehan in his history of Germany, "a sense of political possibility quickened the blood of ambitious men throughout Europe, men eager to take advantage of apparently unprecedented opportunities for power, wealth and glory." In a seminal article in 1795, the playwright Friedrich Schiller linked the romantic beliefs in a new freedom of personal lives and in the primacy of culture with the eighteenth-century tradition of moral reform. "If man is ever to solve the problem of politics in practice, he will have to approach it through the problem of the aesthetic, because it is only through Beauty that man makes his way in freedom," he wrote.

The inner life, mysticism, the dark tones of introspection and loneliness, the importance of the emotions, the nature of the artist himself, were the themes of romantic art. "Life is a disease of the spirit," wrote the poet Novalis, "the most mysterious path leads inward [*nach innen*]." In the famous picture *The Wanderer Above the Mists* the artist Caspar David Friedrich painted a single, wintry figure confronting the scenery beneath him—an emblem of Romanticism's loneliness and self-conscious agony; Friedrich wrote that "the only true source of art is our own heart."

Andersen, self-obsessed since childhood, was instinctively drawn towards this view of art. As a social outsider, moreover, he naturally identified with what was new and radical, rather than, as the establishment Collin family did, with the classical formalities found in work such as Heiberg's. He wanted to meet a writer such as Tieck, who, like Hoffmann, wrote complex literary fairy tales—*Kunstmärchen*, or "art fairy tales." Tieck's writings typified the new interest in folk tales and folk culture, which in the eyes of the Romantics embodied mystic nationalism, the democratic voice of the people. Tieck emphasized traditional forest settings and fairy tale visions. In the 1790s he wrote dramatic versions of "Puss in Boots" and "Bluebeard."

Among his own tales from the 1800s are the horror story "The Rune Mountain" and "Eckbert the Fair." In the former, the hero is lured by a strange woman into the secret world of Nature which, once it has his mind in its thrall, will never release him back to the everyday world, and so he goes mad. In the latter, reality and dream world merge in the vision of the sick hero:

> He no longer knew whether he was living a dream or whether it was really a woman called Bertha who had been the dream; the supernatural became confused with the everyday, the world around him was bewitched and he was incapable of summoning up a thought or a memory.
>
> "Oh my God," muttered Eckbert. "So this is the terrible loneliness in which I have been living all my life."

No one was writing like this in Copenhagen. At a time when Andersen felt beleaguered at home, Tieck was the sort of artistic ally he was seeking.

In May 1831 Andersen set out for Germany, full of hope but also anxious about travel, shipwrecks and seasickness. "In the morning when I awoke, I listened every time a carriage drove by because I thought it might be a storm. A swallow was chirping outside my window as if it wished to tell me something or another about my journey, but what it was really saying, I don't know," begins the diary of his first foreign trip on 16 May 1831. That evening he boarded the steamer in Copenhagen, had dinner in his cabin, and watched the sun set over the chalky white cliffs of the promontory of Møn as the boat sailed on a flat sea along the south coast of Denmark. He stayed on deck to watch it rise again next day as they approached Germany, arriving in Travemünde at 11:30 in the morning. "I was so exhausted when I went ashore that I hardly noticed that the tiny children could speak German," he wrote.

His first hours out of Denmark were marred by toothache: "the nerves are in fact delicate tangents that imperceptible movements of air play upon, and that's why those teeth are playing the devil with me—first piano, then crescendo, all the melodies of pain at every shift in the weather ... I didn't go anywhere because of my toothache and went to bed at 9 o'clock." Toothache, which caused him real pain throughout his life, was also a symbol for what he felt was his suffering as an artist. In the story "Auntie Toothache" the two are explicitly conflated: "the throes of writing and the throes of toothache. You see I have attacks of both."

The next day he went on to Hamburg and Altona and symbolically dismissed Riborg from his mind. Visiting the grave of the German poet Friedrich Klopstock, he crawled through a hole in the fence and wrote on the monument his own name, Riborg's and that of Mrs. Læssøe, an elderly, motherly friend from Copenhagen. "It was an impulse. Since Riborg is dead, her name belongs on a tombstone," he wrote. That evening, sitting in a hotel room with a lovely view—"drinking a toddy and writing, as I think about home; and every so often [looking] out of the window over the Alster, where round about lamps have been lit"—he began the letter to Edvard that he had needed to come abroad to write.

"Of all human beings you are the one I consider my true friend in every way," he wrote, continuing:

> But my friend, the person I can love, must also have a spirit, I must be able to esteem him in that sense, and that is really absent in the few others I like, you are the only one of my own age to whom I feel closely attached. I have an important request, maybe you will laugh at me, but if sometime you really want to make me happy, to let me truly have proof of your respect—when I am worthy of it, then, Oh! please do not be cross with me, say "Du" to me!* Face to face, I will never be able to ask you such a thing, it must happen now that I am away. If you have any objections, then please never mention this subject to me and I shall never ask you again, of course. I will see, from the first letter I receive from you, whether you have wanted to make me happy, and I shall drink your health, very genuinely. Are you annoyed with me? You cannot imagine how my heart is pounding while I write this, although you are not here.

Two days later, he set off to forget himself in a pilgrimage to the heart of German Romanticism. For thirty-three hours, "in dust and heat, six people in a close carriage, and shaken on the dreadful road," he travelled over the Luneburg Heath to Brunswick and the Harz mountains. Here he began a walking tour from Goslar to Eisleben over the highest peak, Brocken, famous for the legends which Goethe had drawn on for *Faust*, and full of scenes reflecting his own mournfulness. "We proceeded further into the forest; the way began to wind upward toward the Brocken; the declining sun could not shine in between the thick pines; round about lay the huts of charcoal burners, enveloped in a bluish smoke, so that the whole had a still, strange and romantic character. It was a picture that attuned the soul to sadness," he wrote in *Shadow Pictures*, the account of his travels which he published on his return.

*"Du" is the familiar pronoun in Danish, the equivalent of German "Du" and French "tu." The formal pronoun is "De."

This was quintessential romantic territory: thirty years earlier Wordsworth had stayed at Goslar, and Coleridge and some friends had taken a walking tour in the same forest hills and valleys, observing waterfalls, caves, "woods crowding upon woods" and talking of witches and enchantment. One of Coleridge's group, a 22-year-old future doctor called Clement Carlyon, recalled, "When we were ascending the Brocken, and ever and anon stopping to take breath, as well as survey the magnificent scene, a long discussion took place on the sublime and beautiful . . . Many were the fruitless attempts made to define sublimity satisfactorily, when Coleridge, at length, pronounced it to consist in a suspension of the powers of comparison."

In Andersen's diary from this trip, his intense sensibility to scenic space is first apparent. The Danish topography is flat, pleasant, tranquil; here he was introduced to the drama of landscape, mountains and valleys, precipices and waterfalls. "I felt it to be so impressive, so great, that I was hardly aware of it before the pencil was moving in my hand and sketching the tremendous scene in my diary. I became a draughtsman without ever having had an hour's teaching," he wrote in *Shadow Pictures*.

The experience of the Harz mountains was important, for after it landscape became like a drug for him, his craving for new, powerful visions of it urging him to travel further and further, and making him eventually one of the best-travelled men in Europe. "Oh, to travel, to travel . . . I feel as if the world is my home, and I shall, I must, frolic in this home!" he wrote in his diary—the romantic cry, restless and excitable.

He continued to Leipzig, where he made himself known to the influential publisher Heinrich Brockhaus, who invited him to dinner, and then moved on to Dresden—both leading cities of German high culture in the nineteenth century, and usual first ports of call for Danes going south on their European journey of education. In Dresden he visited Tieck, who wrote a few lines in his album, wished him a poet's success and embraced and kissed him, which, Andersen wrote, "made the deepest impression on me. The expression of his eyes I shall never forget." Andersen regarded this as the kiss of consecration, a romantic gesture which inaugurated him as a poet. In his story "The Ice Maiden," the hero Rudy is kissed by the Ice Maiden, the Glacier Queen, and so marked out both as special and destined for an early death—Andersen may have meant this as an analogy to the kiss of the muse which he received from Tieck. Certainly, Tieck raised Andersen's interest in German Romanticism to a pitch. Andersen loved the kissing and clasping and lofty German sentiments—"I left him with tears, and prayed for strength . . . to express that which I felt in my soul," he wrote about their farewell—and Tieck's disturbing tales answered his unsettled spirit in the early 1830s, and influenced his ideas about his own writing.

In Dresden Andersen was the typical young man on a voyage of experience, alert to each new sensation. "I did a lot of running around," he wrote in his diary. He lapped up the beauty of the city at night, when the air was scented with jasmine, music played on the terraces, the bridges were "mirrored in the water, and Dresden lay with its steeples and domes in the clear air." He ate his first strawberries of the year and gave his stomach a chill with ice cream. Everywhere, he noted male and female beauty and ugliness: "One of [Tieck's] daughters is reasonably pretty; the other had a strange chicken-face"; "The postal employees were handsome fellows; had bright yellow uniforms with a blue collar and a trumpet on the back, with a long braid and a blue and white tassel."

With the Norwegian painter Johan Dahl as his guide, he discovered at the Picture Gallery his sensual responsiveness to art, seeing Italian masterpieces which were then unknown in Denmark. Raphael's *Sistine Madonna* became a favourite work—"it is a child-like, ethereal face; it is to be worshipped, not loved! Now I find it quite natural that Catholics can kneel before a picture"— though he was also struck by the down-to-earth, intimate details in a painting. "*Noah Leading the Animals into the Ark*, painted by Bassano da Ponte, was funny," he noted, "it showed a swine as the first animal to be led in, and it got the best place. *Mary Magdalene* by Batoni was lovely, but somewhat worldly; she seemed to be flirting with her sanctity, and an old colonel remarked about her 'She was probably good for a few more years of service!'"

But beneath the flurry of aesthetic excitement was emotional torment. The day before he left Dresden for Berlin, he wrote to Christian Voigt about Riborg: "Every time I think of her I feel a pain so unspeakably deep, but I cannot cry, and I don't love her any longer, *that is sure*, but now I am suffering *more* at her memory, I feel an emptiness—O God! Christian, may you never feel what I am now feeling." And in Berlin, Edvard's reply to the letter from Hamburg arrived.

He had written back immediately, a polite, patronizing letter, which made clear once and for all the difference in sensibility between him and Andersen. "How shall I make myself understood to you, my dear friend?" he asked:

What I am trying to explain are my feelings on the question of saying "Du" to each other, and this is something I would like to make clear to you . . . Andersen, you must accept that I am being honest with you. If at a cheerful student gathering someone proposes a toast that we should be on "Du" terms then I agree, partly for lack of consideration at the moment, partly not to insult the person . . . I remember just one time when, having drunk "Dus" with a young man at his pressing, I later, after careful consideration, went on addressing him as "De," and however sad I was to insult this person I never afterwards regretted it. Why did I do it? It was someone I had known a long time and liked a lot! There was something certain inside me which I cannot explain, that made me do it. There are many trivial things against which people have what I think is an innate dislike; I knew a woman who disliked wrapping paper so much that she was sick whenever she saw it—how does one explain such things? But when someone whom I respect and like and have known a long time, asks me to say "Du," then this nasty and inexplicable feeling surfaces within me . . .

And why this change in our relationship? Is it to give others an external sign of our friendly relationship? But that would be unnecessary and of no significance to either of us; and is our relationship not very pleasant and useful to us as it is? Why then restart it in a new way, a way which, I suppose, is not in itself important but for which I have, as I have said, a feeling of dislike; I admit to being a peculiar person in this matter. But as much as it has saddened me that this issue should come up at all, so I am sure that our relationship must be how you wish it, provided this is no more than a haphazard idea, for by God! I do not want to insult you. But once again, Andersen, why should we make a change like this? Let us speak no more about it. I hope we shall both forget this mutual exchange. When you come back I shall be in Jutland, so we shall not see each other till the winter. There could never be any question of my being angry at your request. I do not misunderstand you, and I hope you will not misunderstand me either.

It was a devastating blow. Andersen had attempted a closer *rapprochement* with a man for the first time, and he had been rejected. At a vulnerable time when his social and sexual identity were still being formed, this crushing letter had a crucial impact. A detached observer can hear that Edvard, feeling hunted, is embarrassed and evasive, but his tone is so measured and logical— the refuge of the civil servant—that it made Andersen, caught up in an emotional maelstrom, fear that he was mad. He felt lonelier than ever, and he flailed around in his answer. Too fearful to show his disappointment, he tried damage limitation:

Yes indeed I love you as a brother, thank you for every line!—No, I do not misunderstand you, I am unable even to become sad, for you open your heart in so
honest a way to me. If only I had your character, your whole personality! Oh! I
certainly feel how far beneath you I am in many ways, but please always be
what you are now, my true, perhaps my most honest friend, I really need it.

He fell back on the Riborg story to explain his misery, recounting an
idealized version of it to Edvard—"last summer I met a rich, lovely, spirited
girl who feels the same for me as I do for her . . . certain circumstances made
her marry a man who took her for her fortune . . . That was why I wanted to
go away, had to go away, oh! I have been weeping like a child." He concluded lamely, "It is true she had sufficient fortune for us both, but then
people would have said that it was speculation on my side, and that would
have hurt me deeply." But this was an excuse: Edvard's rejection was the
point, Riborg's merely underlining that he was not only loveless but maybe
unlovable: "I now feel an emptiness in my entire soul, it makes me cold and
careless, oh, dear, dear Edvard, I really wish I would die! What will there be
for me to do in the world, large or small?—but no more! no, you are going to
write to me once more, no?"

He never completely recovered from Edvard's letter. Despite Edvard's
strictures, for the next five years, he could not keep the "Du"/"De" issue out
of his letters to him, and he was still mentioning it in the 1860s. It plays an
important part in his second novel *OT* (1836), and it lies at the core of his
demonic fairy tale "The Shadow," written in 1846.

"The Shadow" owes something to Adelbert von Chamisso's *Peter
Schlemihl's Strange Story* (1813), the tale of a man who lost his shadow, and
Andersen connected it with Edvard's rejection because in Berlin it was
Chamisso who lifted his sunken spirits. Chamisso, a friend of Hans Christian Ørsted's, was a dashing figure of fifty with long curly hair and an aristocratic face. Born in France, he had fled the Revolution, joined the Prussian
army, become a German author and biologist, and was now keeper of the
botanical gardens in Berlin. Andersen described the moment when he
called with his letter of recommendation from Ørsted: "that grave man, with
his long locks and honest eyes, opened the door to me himself, read the letter, and I know not how it was, but we understood each other immediately."
This rapport was his comfort against Edvard's coldness, and it is intriguing
that Chamisso's story and Edvard's letter were still bound together in
Andersen's mind so much later. Chamisso thought Andersen an eccentric

novelty—he referred to him as "*der baumlange Däne*" ("the tree-long Dane")—but, as he spoke Danish, he undertook to translate Andersen's poems and was responsible for introducing him to a German audience.

Andersen travelled home in June, with another work suggested by the idea of a shadow, *Skyggebilleder* (*Shadow Pictures*), forming in his mind; he finished it in three months and it was published in September 1831. "The towers of Copenhagen rose before us: they appeared to me pointed and satirical, as if they were a type of that pen which, perhaps, would scratch out my sketches," he wrote. He expected a critical mauling, but in fact his new book was well received. Following the model of Heine's famous *Reisebilder* (*Travel Pictures*, 1826–1831), he mixed travel-writing with short fiction and satire in a polished and inventive account of his German journey; the title of the English translation, *Rambles in the Romantic Regions of the Hartz Mountains* (1848), captures its brooding tone.

The benefits of his first trip abroad were clear: *Shadow Pictures* is permeated by Andersen's excited encounter with German culture, and there are several pointers to a growing interest in literary fairy tales which was the result of his friendships with Tieck and Chamisso. The Little Mermaid makes a first appearance here—"the legend says, that the mermaid alone can receive an immortal soul from man's true love and Christian baptism"—along with tales of elves, myths about beautiful women living in the rocks and the ironic fragment "Three Days in the Life of a Looking-Glass," the first example of Andersen's revolutionary idea of endowing everyday objects with human characteristics and making them central players in a story. The fairy tale drawings he made on his return from Berlin also show the influence of German myths and tales—in one, a fabulous hunting scene, a huntsman kills a small monster, which is also attacked by the claws of a huge beetle and watched by a diabolical double bass, a ghostly horse and a doleful cow standing on its hind legs; in another Andersen draws a witches' dance on the Brocken mountain.

Shadow Pictures also contains a fantasy about Riborg, seen in a vision at Brunswick Cathedral as a bride walking down the aisle, looking around for the man who truly loves her, who, in a cheap novel, "would probably have been standing, pale as death, behind a pillar watching the wedding, but here it was real. He was not there but where—?" To include himself like this, in code for those who knew about Riborg, was an irresistible self-indulgence. But he revealed more than he may have intended, for his crisis of the 1830s was one of self-definition. His sense of himself ended with a blank: the empty soul he had described to Edvard. Travel was one palliative to that emptiness, an answer to his boredom, and in *Shadow Pictures* he recognized his own discontent in his relentless pursuit of the new:

> To be in a strange haste with everything is, in reality, my chief characteristic . . . even in my travels it is not that which is present that pleases me; I hasten after something new, in order to come to something else. Every night when I lie down to rest, I hanker after the next day, wish that it was here, and when it comes, it is still a distant future that occupies me. Death itself has in it something interesting for me—something glorious, because a new world will then be opened to me. What can it in reality be that my uneasy self hastens after?

The most pressing thing Andersen hastened after, in the next few years, was the chance to lose himself in love. From 1831 to 1832, as he worked on a crowd of small projects mainly to earn money—a book of poems, libretti, translations for the Danish stage—his emotional longings poured into increasingly daring letters to men. Despite the rebuff that he had received, it was on Edvard that he remained fixated in 1831. "How I long for you, my dear Collin, long to speak to you from the heart and in friendship, alone, up

Ludvig Müller, with whom Andersen fell in love in 1831.

in that poetical little room," he told him in August; in November he wrote, "I will even tell you, that I am so dearly fond of you, perhaps more so than you think; with all my soul I cling to you," adding, "Fear not, I have a loose tongue, but not concerning my own affairs . . . If only I could truly tell you everything."

In the summer of 1832, Andersen visited his mother, now dying of alcoholism, in Odense for the last time, and his sense of rootlessness was exacerbated; he wrote again to Edvard that he felt a stranger everywhere, and asked if he could consider the Collin home as his own. To his older friend, Mrs. Læssøe, he wrote at this time:

> I am a peculiar being! In Copenhagen I was longing for Funen, and here I have been longing for Copenhagen, or rather the people there. I can never enjoy the present, my life is in the past and in the future, and there is in reality too little for a *real* man. I have been in bad, very bad spirits here; the weather has been dull, and the sunshine from within and without has been almost alike. I have been about a lot from one mansion to another; still I have not been well, although I am not ill.

He moved on from Funen to the Zealand estate of Nørager, where he was the guest of a businessman, C. C. Bang. Bang had two daughters in their early twenties, Emma and Ida, and two other young guests, Mimi Thyberg, whose sister was about to become engaged to Edvard, and a theology student, 23-year-old Ludvig Müller, with whom Andersen promptly fell in love.

Ludvig, one of the three gifted sons of a Danish philologist and historian, Peter Erasmus Müller, was a handsome, sober young man with a passion for numismatics and museums—he later became the first director of Copenhagen's Thorvaldsen Museum. In a portrait by his brother, the painter Adam Müller, he is a fleshy youth with wavy hair, large, wide brown eyes and a full mouth, and a sensitive, eager expression. He was responsive to all things artistic, and in what was effectively a country house party of five young people, much of it taking place on languid summer days in the beautiful parklands of Bang's estate, a romantic friendship developed between the two men. Müller left first, at the end of August, to visit relatives elsewhere, and Andersen wrote him a letter beginning "You dear, dear man":

> You will probably laugh at me, but I miss you so dreadfully . . . I am as fond of you, as if you were my brother, remain always the same person to me as I now imagine you to be. Have no fear that I would let out a friend's confidence, in

this case I am not at all like myself . . . I am a strange being, my feelings run off with me too quickly and I only make myself unhappy. How empty it was at home in my little room last night! I went in to look at your bed, walked around alone, fell into a miserable mood and hardly slept at all—Oh, do come, come my dear, dear Ludvig, and I will—I will not be loving to you at all, that is what you like best! then you will come, won't you . . . Of all people I know I am most fond of Edvard and you, if you find this strange, then remember, as you say, I am an original.

In reply, Andersen received a love letter from Ludvig thanking his "truly dear friend" for lines "which were really born to bring forth the best, the purest feelings in my soul." The letter continued:

How dear you are to my heart . . . I think of you so often and look forward as a child to our meeting soon in the bustling capital, where we would nurse, nourish and protect the flower which sprouted in God's free nature and which shall grow in strength and beauty . . . I miss you but I know how to fight this pain and is it not true you too want to and are able to? Remember also *Qui nescit dissimulare, nescit regnare* [he who cannot pretend, cannot reign].

Reading the letter in front of Emma, Ida and Mimi, Andersen burst into tears of joy. He had had a bet with them, on the lines of "win either way," that Ludvig would not reply, and now paid with two locks of his hair, "but I gladly give them my whole head of hair, because I won." No one before had returned his affection like this. He sent back an extremely unguarded letter, signing himself, most unusually, Christian—even to Edvard and other long-lasting friends, he remained only Andersen to the end of his days. "Oh Ludvig, how I adore you!" he wrote,

How could I believe and hope that you would understand me so, return my love so! . . . You have just now created a happy hour in my life. How true friendship has great effect. You do not know how much you can change my character. I have many, many faults, but through you, through you, you dear, dear man, it will be possible to change much. At this moment I love the whole world, even Hertz.* You have filled my soul with trust and confidence. Oh how can I tell you how much, how unutterably much I care for you . . . you are so

*Henrik Hertz (1798–1870), Danish playwright and poet and a critic of Andersen. His publications included the anonymous *Letters of a Ghost* (1830), which caricatured Andersen as a drunken, worn-out horse from Slagelse; in 1832 he acknowledged authorship of the book.

close to me, so unutterably close . . . If there was a chance, which there isn't, I would come to you for a couple of hours, I long for you so much. For God's sake stay forever what you are to me now . . . Your Christian.

But the bet, and Ludvig's florid style, should have alerted him. The letter that had sent him into ecstasies was a forgery, a joke by Mimi which she could not bring herself to admit to when she saw Andersen's joy at receiving it and realized how seriously in love he was. Only when Andersen was about to send his response did she feel she had to tell him the truth. "From the profoundest joy I have sunk to the deepest misery," Andersen wrote, but his powers of wish-fulfilment were so strong that he could not let the dream go. He sent his letter to Ludvig anyway, enclosed with Mimi's and another one of his own, asking "Would you have written it? I wonder if she has not written out of your heart? . . . I cannot write any more, their joke was too hard. Now as I read Mimi's letter I cannot comprehend that I believed you had used such expressions . . . but in my childish joy I dreamed about and saw only you. You cannot care for me like that."

Even across two centuries, most people will recognize something of themselves in their teens or twenties in this vortex of five young people playing emotional games on a summer holiday. Andersen bounced back fairly quickly, but the episode is of interest for the light it sheds on his persona as a lover. He was unabashed about showing Mimi and the others a homo-erotic attachment, and Mimi understood such romances well enough to be able to mimic their tone convincingly, though she also assumed that were the relationship to proceed, dissembling would be essential. In the first part of the nineteenth century, sentimental friendships between men who wrote lovingly to each other were common, the natural result of a society which tended to separate the sexes in the formative teenage years—school and university for boys, the parlour and the drawing room for girls.

Andersen probably saw his feelings for Ludvig and Edvard in this context. He matured late, and in some ways remained emotionally always an adolescent. Neither did he really draw a borderline between friendship and sexuality.* With women, such as Henriette Wulff and Henriette Hanck, his

---

*The term "homosexual" was not invented until 1869, and reflected increasing medical and philosophical anxiety, as well as moral censure, about the nature of sexual desire in the second half of the nineteenth century. In the 1820s and 1830s, the mood was more relaxed; affectionate letters and gestures between men were not considered unnatural, and taboos were not so

friendships were warm, intellectual and straightforward. With men he was more ambivalent. He looked and had always been effeminate—in his letters he talks of his softness and semi-femininity, and of being "womanly-soft" in his feelings—and he could not help responding to his inherent attraction to Christian Voigt, Ludvig, Edvard. Most men grew out of such friendships and married, but for Andersen they were the beginning of homo-erotic longings and obsessions with individual men which lasted a lifetime.

As his desires intensified, a darker vein of half-expressed longing, promises of discretion, private confessions, crept into his letters which went beyond the extravagant fashion of the period and stands in stark contrast to the public, open manner with which he conducted his courtships of women. At times his interest receded or was temporarily supplanted by sexual longing for women, but it never disappeared. In his writing he developed a pattern of allusion and sexual hints which gives his work a rich, tense undercurrent; in life the loneliness of unexpressed desire often drove him to despair. After his failure with Müller he wrote to Ingemann, "What will become of me? I don't look forward to anything, hope for anything, only write, because I have to, I can't help it. The world would be so beautiful, if only everyone would let their heart play a greater part than it is allowed to do."

In the autumn of 1832, Andersen was back in Copenhagen, but after the hot summer of longing, he could not rest without an object to love. "It is easy for *you* to recount," he wrote to Otto Müller, Ludvig's elder brother, who was travelling in Germany. "It is all new to you, one thing follows another, but *I* sit within the narrow ramparts, in the same old narrow circumstances, talk and listen and talk and so on and so forth, the familiar life da capo and always da capo." Within days of returning to the capital, he turned to Louise Collin, the bright-eyed, dark-haired, 18-year-old cosseted younger daughter of Jonas. She had talked to Andersen sympathetically about Riborg, and now he sent her a poem, "The Brown and the Blue Eyes," in which a pair of

strong as to lead to public scandals such as that surrounding Oscar Wilde in the 1890s. Still, open declarations of homo-erotic love were unacceptable: the Danish writer Laurids Kruse, who translated Andersen's first novel into German, had to leave Denmark because of rumours of his love for men, and Heinrich Heine publicly attacked the writer August von Platen for his feelings for young men. In 1843 Heine told Andersen in Paris that when Kruse died "at the end he was so sick of everything that he didn't even have any appetite for men any more!"

Louise Collin, by Wilhelm Marstrand, 1833. Andersen turned his attentions to her after Riborg and Ludvig rejected him; their friendship lasted until he died.

brown eyes pull the poet downwards, making him dizzy, but a pair of blue eyes open up the heaven of love. Brown-eyed Riborg, he meant, was giving way in his affections to blue-eyed Louise. In September, he told Louise that he was a stranger, alone in the world: "Thank you for all your kindness, for the sisterly spirit of mind you have lately shown me, by God, I do value it, I think of you more than you believe—or can believe, but one scarcely dares say such a thing to a young lady."

As with Riborg, Andersen fell in love with Louise in the certain knowledge that he would not win her. The Collins, noticing his attentions, arranged for the older sister Ingeborg to read all his letters to Louise, but it made little difference, for Andersen liked an audience for his love affairs, and it was anyway the whole family that obsessed him: Louise was simply the latest focus, and his fantasy of a legitimate entrée into it through marriage. Her resemblance to Edvard probably excited him; she was the closest female approximation to him.*

---

*A fictional parallel is Evelyn Waugh's *Brideshead Revisited*—Charles Ryder in his young homosexual phase falls in love first with the brother Sebastian, then with the sister Julia, whose physical likeness to Sebastian "each time pierced me anew," and lastingly with the entire Flyte family, whose aristocratic lives bring glamour into his banal, middle-class background. Andersen romanticized the patrician Collins in a similar way.

In October he gave Louise an oblique but extended proposal in the form of a short memoir of his life. It may have been inspired by Oehlenschläger's recent memoir of his youth, which had appeared in 1830, but it was not intended for publication—it was not published until 1926, under the title *Levnedsbog* (*The Book of My Life*), and Andersen meant it to be seen by only a few close friends. It is a frank, urgently written account, at times sentimental but the most reliable of Andersen's autobiographies—the story of the man written before he saw himself in terms of a character from a fairy tale.

He was only twenty-seven when he wrote it, but he managed to capture two powerful but conflicting aspects of his personality: on the one hand his sense of a fixed character and destiny, from which his hardships in childhood, at school and in the early days in Copenhagen could not deflect him, and on the other his feelings of emptiness, of a hollow self-identity. His letters from the 1830s touch on this but *The Book of My Life* expresses it forcefully, in an image as ghoulish as in his story "The Shadow": "Anyone I have seen and spoken to once, I can later remember their faces clearly, I have their mirror image within me; however, I cannot recall my own features, although God knows I look at myself in the mirror often enough."

The Book of My Life documents the painful process of his accommodation to bourgeois culture, and the obsession with his own biography that was the result. As he had watched his mother dying in the summer of 1832, Andersen repeatedly rehearsed his life story; he never got over his amazement that he had come so far. But the price was a loss of self, because he had had to adapt so much, so young, so quickly—thus the faceless image in his autobiography, and the problems he had meeting others in a relationship, because his idea of himself was so uncertain.

Part of Louise's attraction for Andersen was that she sympathized with the trials of his life—he liked to think that, as Desdemona for Othello, "she loved me for the dangers I had passed / And I loved her that she did pity them." He gave her the manuscript of *The Book of My Life* to encourage her to understand him better, and came up against the implacable Collin spirit—a barrier that went up as soon as he became too emotional. Louise received the book, and simply did not respond at all. A sheltered, conventional 18-year-old, she did not know how to.

As an attempt at seduction, the book was woeful—pages about Riborg and only a single mention of Louise as a child whom Andersen had not initially noticed. But Andersen expected a dramatic response, and between October and Christmas 1832 he wrote her a series of overwrought letters:

Now you have read the history of my childhood, full of trust I have shown you everything, but you seem to me more a stranger than before. I thought of you while I was writing it, oh! up to now you have not given me a sympathetic word about it. This has made me very miserable; many nights when you are fast asleep I am very sad, very unhappy. They say this is being hysterical, I know!—Why have you not said anything at all to me since I showed you my whole youth, not one word about it? Is there something in me which makes me so repulsive, so unworthy of your—friendship?—*You* and Edvard are the two people I most trust in your home, you do not mind me saying that, do you? There is nothing wrong in that. O God! I have become so anxious about any expression of my feelings, I am always frightened it will land me into trouble . . . O God! my dear Miss Collin, I feel so miserable—indeed, I must go away, far away. If only it could happen in the spring . . . If you can then let me feel that I have not judged you wrongly.

[27 October 1832]

Now I am alone with your spiritual self I would like to chat, you have let me do so . . . dear Miss Collin! I have so much confidence in you, I trust you as I trust Edvard . . . It seems to me as if there are eternities between each time I see you, and then when I come I feel awkward realizing that it was the previous day I was there.

[1 November 1832]

Andersen is always the one who is in the wrong; this makes him suffer too the most in his loneliness, that can be his punishment! In another world, where all will be clearer to us, I am sure he will be more humble, though he may need his friends there less than he does here. Please accept his apology for having from time to time considered you as a sister and for having forgotten that he himself is only

H. C. Andersen
[undated, probably end of 1832]

On New Year's Day 1833 came the final blow: the Collin family, possibly hastened by Andersen's unwelcome attentions, announced Louise's engagement to a young civil servant, W. Lind. They were married in 1840.

Andersen's interest in the idea of a simultaneous love for a sister and brother continued. In his novel *OT* in 1836, he casts himself as the student hero Otto and Edvard as Baron Wilhelm, his social superior who will not say "Du" to him. The men are in love with each other's sisters, and the sisters' resemblance to their brothers is emphasized. At a student party, some of the men dress up as girls:

> A young lady, one of the beauties, in a white dress, and with a thin handker-chief over her shoulders, approached and threw herself into [Otto's] arms. It was Wilhelm! but Otto found his likeness to Sophie stronger than he had ever before noticed it to be; and therefore the blood rushed to his cheeks when the fair one threw her arms around him, and laid her cheek upon his: he perceived more of Sophie than of Wilhelm in this form . . . When Wilhelm seated him-self on his knee, and pressed his cheek to his, Otto felt his heart beat as in a fever; it sent a stream of fire through his blood: he thrust him away, but the fair one continued to overwhelm him with caresses.

Andersen ends the scene: "Of the kisses which Wilhelm had given him, of course, they did not speak; but Otto thought of them, thought of them quite differently to what he had done before, and—the ways of Cupid are strange!"

By the beginning of 1833, Andersen had returned to his most enduring passion, for Edvard. His new volume of poems, *Twelve Months of the Year*, was published; and both Edvard and Ludvig Müller received copies with emotional dedications. Edvard's read: "Our friendship, Edvard, is itself poetry in the form, but with genuine contents. We know deeply each other's soul and thoughts, we share with each other pleasure and pain, and faithful heart knocks against heart. But the lips express the formal 'De.'" The book was not well received by the critics—accusations that it was superficial and undisciplined were fair—and Andersen was particularly wounded by a cri-tique from his old supporter Ingemann, who wrote

> What up to now has most prevented your development as a poet, has undoubt-edly been the misfortune that with far too much confidence and an almost child-like affection you have thrown yourself into the arms of this large, many-tongued and fickle audience and into the millpond of empty social intercourse before knowing what you really wanted and were capable of doing . . . You should care a little less about the poet and his laurels and more about poetry! Don't cut the songbird open to collect the golden eggs (all) at once.

At this low point in Andersen's life, Edvard was by contrast on the verge of a brilliant career. In early 1833 he was appointed his father's successor as secretary of the royal foundation *ad usus publicos*, a powerful position, and in the spring he became engaged to the gentle, sympathetic Henriette (Jette) Thyberg. He was visibly withdrawing from Andersen, who wrote him an emotional farewell:

I am, as you know, very overwrought, and this is because I have been able to deceive myself into believing that intimate friendship can exist in this world . . . Every day you distance yourself more and more from me—just now that so much stirs my life and has an upsetting effect on my soul . . . you scarcely talk to me . . . I feel there is something beggarly, something grim in this paining for sympathy, but my pride gives in to my love for you! I do care for you so much, and despair that you cannot, do not want to, be the friend I would be to you, if our positions were reversed . . . What is there in my character that you dislike? . . . Yes, my doubts about you are so strong that I think that I have ruined your last scrap of sympathy for me by these outbursts of my heart . . . I wish you well! In your new position you will acquire many friends but none who will love you as I do.

The Collins were now as keen as Andersen that he should leave Denmark. Jonas drafted an application for a travel grant to the Royal Fund; Ørsted, Oehlenschläger and others wrote recommendations. Interviewed by the King, Andersen burst into tears, but got his stipend—600 rixdollars a year for 1833 and 1834.

He was twenty-eight, and two years in Europe lay before him. This time he felt he must travel to survive, to recapture a youth he had never had, to find romance, to grow as an artist. "I have remained a child ever since I was young. I have never known what it is to be a youth! . . . I have this abiding idea that only by being torn away from my immediate surroundings will I ever come to anything; if I have to stay here, I will be destroyed," he wrote to Henriette Wulff.

On 22 April 1833, he boarded the ship in Copenhagen, watched the steeples of the city dissolving from his view, and began his tour of cultural formation in Germany, France and Italy. Many people came to see him off, including the Collin family, Emma and Ida Bang and Ludvig Müller. Ludvig and Edvard accompanied him on board—"I walked with my arm round Edvard's shoulder, he consoled me in a brotherly way. I saw tears in Louise's eyes as I left, Ingeborg was sad too. They do like me after all! Those dear, very dear people!" Andersen wrote in his diary. As they sailed along the south coast, the captain brought him a letter—it came down "through the air" he said. It was Edvard's farewell:

Believe me, I am saddened by your leaving, I shall miss you dreadfully, I shall miss no longer seeing you coming up to talk to me in my rooms as usual; I shall miss you at your place at the table on Tuesdays, and yet, you will miss us even more, I know, because you are alone.

CHAPTER 7

Italy

1833–1835

Oh, to travel, to travel! If one could only spend one's life fluttering from one place to another!

—HANS CHRISTIAN ANDERSEN, Diary, 31 May 1831

"I am very much changed, all say so; the actors think I am rather paler, but more of a gentleman," Andersen wrote of the Danish community's response to him in Paris, when he had been away two months. Before he left, he had his portrait drawn by Adam Müller, and when he arrived in Rome a year later, he sat for a painting by the Danish artist Albert Küchler. These two pictures (see page 125) were the first professional portraits of Andersen, and the difference between them suggests that as he travelled south Andersen did become both more confident and more urbane.

In Müller's drawing, he is a young, uncertain, feminine-looking man with large anxious eyes, sensual lips and a broad intelligent forehead; Müller captures a fluidity, the expression of a character waiting to be moulded, which does not recur in later portraits. Küchler gives Andersen a sterner, more fixed appearance, emphasizing the long, lean puritanical face and pressing the lips tightly together under a moustache. His Andersen is more mature and a fervent intellectual: beneath the high brow is a taut, defensive look which may have owed something to Küchler's own sensitivities—he later converted to Catholicism and wandered barefoot through Germany as a mendicant friar—or to Andersen's demand that he make the portrait appear more manly.

In Paris, Andersen was the naive provincial, thrilled and overawed by the scale of a great European capital. "Paris is the place! Berlin, Hamburg and Copenhagen, all of them are nothing," he wrote to Ludvig Müller. About the Opéra he wrote, "now for the first time I have a conception of how these things *can* be! . . . Oh if only everybody could have been here to see it! . . . I counted thirty chandeliers and twenty candelabras," while the playhouses made Copenhagen's Royal Theatre look "like a spiritually well-endowed individual who is shabbily dressed and doesn't know how to behave himself."

This might well be taken as a description of Andersen himself, too, who was keen to make links with the European writers in Paris, but not sure how to go about it. He called on Victor Hugo, who was only three years older than him but already famous as the author of *Notre-Dame de Paris* (1830), and asked for his autograph, and was mortified when Hugo inscribed his name as requested, but wrote it at the top of the page, presumably to ensure that a text could not be entered under which his name would appear as a signature. He had better luck when Heinrich Heine, the poet of what he called "my recent young erotic period of life," tried to befriend him, but he was frightened off and wrote home prudishly, "Heine has visited me, or rather the porter, I have not got his card; I will not have anything to do with him. He is indeed a man one should beware of."

At heart Andersen was still the gawping northern puritan, alarmed by the relaxed ways of Latin Europe. "The most sensuous pictures, often very piquant, are to be seen in the streets. What really offends me most is that even holy subjects are made vulgar. I am far from being prudish: I can stand and look at a frivolous picture, but even in the sensuous there ought to be some decorum," he told Ludvig Müller in May. To Christian Voigt he wrote, "Paris is the most lascivious city under the sun. I don't believe there is an innocent person there, incredible things happen, in daytime in the most respectable streets I have been offered 'a beautiful girl of sixteen' . . . everywhere lechery is remarked on as something required by nature etc., so one's sense of decorum is almost made blunt. All the same I dare say frankly that I am still innocent, though hardly anyone who knows Paris will believe it."

He stuck with the Danish community, fretted about communications from home—in two months he received only one piece of mail, a newspaper, postage unpaid, containing a lampoon against him—and could not get Edvard out of his mind. "Oh Edvard (and Ludvig!)! If only you were here!" he wrote in his diary, but during his first two months away Edvard had not even sent him a letter. In June he wrote to him:

Your silence has awakened in me a strange emotion I have not expressed before. It is a kind of anger which spills over into love and sadness . . . Oh,

God, Edvard, I feel so lonely, you have your Jette, your siblings and all of them at home. I have no one, absolutely no one here, and for a full month you have let me feel my loneliness.

A reply from Edvard arrived in July with a casual explanation (he had unexpectedly gone on a journey), followed by one of his fondest declarations of friendship, which suggests that when Andersen was safely distant, and so less pressing in his demands, Edvard was more ready to indulge their sentimental friendship. He had been jealous of Ludvig Müller, he said, but now knew himself to be Andersen's first friend:

> I have known you as the poetic caricature whom we used to call "the clamator" . . . I have known you as the schoolboy who suffered an ordeal . . . I have followed you through your education and at last, I have come to know you in your true poetic talent, the pure natural heart, I have learned to esteem the former and love the latter. During your career as a writer I have loyally shared your happiness and griefs, though many times I may not have seemed to do so clearly because with my less fiery character I could not always share your opinions on how other people treated you. Here is my hand, Andersen, we are old friends.

Andersen sent back a love letter—"How I long for you, Edvard! I think the separation has turned my friendship into love"—followed by another in August: "You can have no idea how much I long for you. Yes, Edvard, you are eternally dear to me. Your Jette cannot in her way be more fond of you than I am."

How much in Paris he remained in the thrall of Denmark was clear from the work he began there, a dramatic poem called *Agnete and the Merman*. The poem is based on a Danish ballad about a girl who is mysteriously attracted to the sea, marries a merman called Hemming, lives on the seabed with him and has seven sons, then is called back to land by the sound of church bells, and refuses to return, leaving Hemming heartbroken. Andersen's poem was a precursor to his tale "The Little Mermaid"—the theme of the outsider versus the insider, merged with images of dangerous, even unnatural, sexuality suggested by the coupling of human and water-sprite, drew him, and he saw himself as the merman abandoned by cold Agnete who was a mix of Louise and Edvard.

Variations of the story were popular across nineteenth-century Europe— Matthew Arnold's *The Forsaken Merman*, for example—and Andersen may also have been inspired by the German legends of water-maidens which he

Portraits of Andersen: aged twenty-seven, by Adam Müller, 1833; and in Rome, by Albert Küchler, 1834.

encountered on his journey south along the Rhine. In his autobiography he mentions the appeal of Lorelei, the rock associated with the legend of the *femme fatale* combing her golden hair and distracting the sailors, who drown because of her, and writes that "the traditions are the chief attractions of the Rhine. Tales and songs—those charming songs, which the German poets have sung to the honour of that mighty sea-green stream—are its highest beauty."

Andersen wanted to finish *Agnete* before he crossed the Alps, for he had already fixed on Italy as the place which would change his artistic consciousness, enabling him to leave Denmark behind. *Agnete* is suffused with a typically Danish landscape—beech forests, flat countryside, the sound of waves. "Oh how I am longing to hear how people at home like her! But she will, she must be appreciated," he wrote to Mrs. Læssøe. Oehlenschläger had sent work home from his European journeys; Andersen believed that this poem, which he referred to as his northern Aphrodite, would make his name. That he longed for renown at this time is suggested also by a comment in Edvard Collin's account of him, published after his death: "Andersen wrote in 1833, 'If I die abroad, then remember, Edvard, to write my memoirs,'" adding—the comment showed the unbridgeable gulf between their outlooks—"he himself wanted that the public at large should be informed about his life's peculiarities, large and small, his thoughts and feelings from cradle to grave. But he was too much of a poet for his rendition and views of his surroundings to be completely correct, and had too strong an imagination for his observations on himself to be reliable."

He completed the first part of *Agnete* in Paris, mailed it to Edvard on 14 August, and then began the long, slow journey to Italy. His first stop was the picturesque Jura town Le Locle, where he was the guest of a watchmaker, Jules Houriet, whose sister was the widow of the Danish royal watchmaker. Houriet lived with a family of indulgent maiden aunts who clucked and fussed over their guest's every whim, gave him flowers and jam, embroidered his stockings and darned the holes in his clothes from Paris.

Between their attentions Andersen worked on the second part of the poem. Its driving force was the drama of the relationships which he had not managed to solve back home. The merman's pathetic cry to Agnete echoes precisely Andersen's valedictory letter to Edvard written earlier in the year:

> Tell me, Agnete, are there flaws in me,
> Tell me, does anything displease you?
> I will change! Oh, tell me all!
> I so wish for you to like me.

And the poem is laced with Hemming's admission of femininity and with the couching of sexual love in brother/sister terms:

> I am too soft as a man,
> I know it well, but I cannot help it!
> You are as dear to me, as if you were my sister,
> And for a sister, a brother may cry.

> Can I help,
> Mine is the soft, weak, female disposition.

Andersen finished this self-indulgent, formless piece in a kind of frenzy, overcome by the Swiss scenery and his memories of Edvard and Louise. "A mountain with ice and snow stood out dazzling white in the clear air," he told Mrs. Læssøe.

Grand and gloomy pine forests surround me—a dead solitude, which I have never known. It is like midnight, although the sun is shining. It has had a strange effect on me: I have been in a sort of ecstasy for some days, and I have now finished *Agnete* . . . I am satisfied . . . I don't know whether it is this ecstasy or the cold weather which has influenced me; but I am strongly excited; there is fever in my blood, and I cannot sleep.

He sent the manuscript to Edvard on 12 September with an admission of how desperate he was for fame—"Oh Edvard! My soul yearns to be recognized like a thirsty man for water!"—and a few days later, he set out to cross the Alps.

The usual travelling worries—baggage, passport, the amount of room in the coach—absorbed him, but he was also investing this journey with symbolic significance. "It is with a sickening feeling that I leave this side of the Alps—I almost said Europe," he wrote in his diary for 19 September 1833. "Well, in the name of God, now begins my journey out into the world. May the Lord let it go for me as best it can!"

In his autobiography, he altered the date on which he first crossed the Alps to 5 September, the anniversary he already celebrated as the day of his arrival in Copenhagen fourteen years earlier. The alteration was one of many small adjustments by which he later built up the image of his life as a perfectly syncopated fairy tale, but it is also telling that he wanted to replace his "Copenhagen" birthday by an Italian one. Before he even reached Italy, he was under the sway of its myth, the promise of rebirth and revitalization of the spirit which many northern Europeans had found there before him. A generation earlier, in 1786, Goethe had travelled to Italy and returned with his view of art radically changed in favour of the classical. The Danish sculptor Bertel Thorvaldsen was twenty-seven when he arrived in Rome on 8 March 1797, stayed for most of his life, and celebrated his "Roman" birthday each year: in Rome, he said, it was as if the snow of the north had melted from his eyes, allowing him to become a classical artist.

Andersen was dreaming about this kind of inspiration as he approached the Alps, sketched the perilous Simplon Road hewn into the cliffs and was awed by the mountain terrain:

Right in front of us was a massive glacier, looking as if it were made of green glass with snow on top . . . The landscape got more and more desolate. At the gallery . . . the huge masses of stone gripped me; on one side a mighty waterfall plunged down. Everything was granite—it was like driving through the earth's backbone. The weather cleared; then we arrived at the Italian border post,

Isselle, and were inspected . . . The Alps looked like the glass mountains of the fairy tale, and now I had crossed them.

The heightened sensibility, always a feature of his arrival in new countries, began at once. "Here at last there are beautiful women to be found," he wrote as he drew near the border; soon there were attractive men, too—he noted particularly a 20-year-old monk in a brown cowl with bare feet. In his autobiographical tale "Under the Willow Tree," he describes how "a longing . . . to go away, far, far into the world" seized the hero, Knud, who "saying farewell to the lands of the North . . . passed on under the shade of blooming chestnut trees, and through vineyards and fields of maize. The mountains were a wall between him and all his recollections; and he wished it to be so." Andersen, like Knud, felt liberated by Italy and quickly came to think of it as his spiritual home—"This is the home of fantasy, the north that of reason, but as I am a visionary, I feel most at home in my real country." A new confidence and independence flooded over him as soon as he crossed the Alps, and when four days later he received a letter from Edvard which cast doubt on *Agnete*, he wrote in his diary, "I don't want any more to be the one who is forever and always accommodating others, to be treated like a child by someone younger, even a friend!—Such a tone as the one Edvard uses is asking for opposition, even though I love him dearly."

Even today, tourists from northern Europe fly in and revel in what is old-fashioned and quaint in Italy; in the 1830s the country seemed to the Danes and Germans, travelling for days and watching landscape and customs change gradually over the miles, to belong to another era. "The mode of travelling," wrote Andersen

> was so entirely different from what we had ever known: the eternal cheatings at the inns; they were continually asking for our passports, which were signed more than fifteen times in a few days; our *vetturino* did not know the way, we got lost . . . we drove through the dark streets, which were without lanterns; the only light we had was a big burning candle which our driver had bought at the city gate, and which he now held before him . . .

Thus Andersen passed through Milan, Genoa, Pisa, Florence, exultant, ravished by the landscape: "If France is the country of reason, then Italy is the country of the imagination. (Germany and Denmark, of the heart.) Here is all you could wish for in a landscape—the oranges hanging so yellow between the lush greenery; big, grass-green lemons greeted us with their fragrance. Everything was like a painting."

In his autobiography, Andersen wrote, "I felt, what since then has become an acknowledged fact, that travelling would be the best school for me." More than his other trips abroad, Italy in 1833–1834 was the sentimental journey of education and self-discovery that changed his life and his work. As he travelled south, landscape merged with the aesthetic in his mind and from Florence, where the splendour of flaming sunsets and shining mountains gave way to "the magnificence of art," he dated a new responsiveness to both:

> I had never had an eye for sculpture; I had seen almost nothing at home; in Paris I had certainly seen many statues, but my eyes were closed to them; but here when visiting the magnificent galleries, the rich churches with their mountains and magnificence, I learned to understand the beauty of form—the spirit which reveals itself in form. Before the *Venus de Medici* it was as if the marble eye had acquired the power of sight; a new world of art revealed itself to me, and I could not escape from it.

In October Andersen arrived in Rome: "the city of cities, where I soon was to feel as if I had been born and was in my own house." For Scandinavians especially, it was the promised city—Oehlenschläger, Thorvaldsen, the Norwegian violinist Ole Bull and later Ibsen, all recorded the significance of the city to their artistic development. Its scale and its classical heritage, its busy atmosphere and its bright colours, all set against a cloudless blue sky and winter sun, were so different from anything they had known at home. Edward Lear, who arrived in Rome in the winter of 1837, four years after Andersen, and spent his first weeks drawing the ruins of palaces and temples in the warm winter sun, wrote that "the melancholy and grandeur of these huge remains are very awful . . . no one who does not see them, can form an idea: the palaces and baths of the Emperors—some filled up into convents—some covering acres of ground with masses of ancient walls—the long line of aqueducts and tombs on the desolate and beautiful Campagna—and (in the enormous palaces of the modern Capitol and Vatican) the thousands of busts and statues!"

Mid-nineteenth-century Rome had, according to the Englishman Sir Rennell Rodd who grew up there, changed little from the Rome of the eighteenth century; it was still lit at night by oil-lamps, the streets mostly had no pavements, but were lively places, brightened by the coloured hoods of the wine-carts and by the coaches of cardinals with their big black horses and red trappings. Lear described the vibrant colours of city life: cattle decked out with ribbons and bells, brightly dressed shoppers, priests everywhere, "white—black—piebald—scarlet—cinnamon—purple: round hats—shovel hats—cocked hats—hoods and caps—cardinals with their three footmen (for cardinals *never* walk)—white friars with masks, bishops and Monsignori with lilac and red stockings—and indeed thousands on thousands of every description of religious orders."

The foreign communities were centred on the Café Greco near the Academy, the English church and the Spanish Steps, round the corner from the Pincian Gardens. Goethe and Thorvaldsen had stayed at the Café Greco when they first came to Rome, and this area had been a foreign quarter for centuries. Andersen was welcomed by the Scandinavian artists, and introduced to their particular haunt, the Trattoria Lepre, as well as to the Café Greco, where he picked up his mail. Ludvig Bødtcher, a Danish poet and

Constantin Hansen, Self-portrait with Danish Artists in Rome, *1837. Andersen was part of the Danish artistic colony in Rome in the 1830s which included Hansen, far left, Martinus Rørbye, third from left, and, centre on balcony, Albert Küchler.*

resident of Rome, "devoted to art, nature and an intellectual *dolce far niente*," was his guide as he explored churches and galleries and went on expeditions to the Campagna, the endless plain that seemed to Keats to resemble an inland sea and to Chateaubriand to be made up of the dust of the antique dead.

The painter Albert Küchler, long-faced and serious, and the writer Henrik Hertz, an old enemy, a cramped little man with a round face and tiny spectacles, were fellow tourists. Thorvaldsen, in his sixties still a mesmerizing figure with curling chestnut locks, shining cornflower-blue eyes and a conviction that art alone was worth living for, took Andersen under his wing. Thorvaldsen's Bohemian colony was based at his studio by day, and revolved round drinking and playing lotto—Thorvaldsen's obsession—by night. A group portrait from 1837 shows half a dozen of the Danish artists in Rome, including Martinus Rørbye, Andersen's friend from the Jutland excursion, and Albert Küchler; tall, blond, pale, mostly wearing top hats and waistcoats, though one has a fez and several smoke hookahs, they stand on a studio balcony looking out over the terracotta rooftops and in at their own sketches.

Away from his familiar surroundings, Andersen felt able to think and see independently of his critics. Reading an old copy of the *Copenhagen Post*, he commented, "It was as if I was looking down from another world on all that childish nonsense and bickering. Everything seemed so trivial, so out of kilter." In Rome, he luxuriated in his own impressions of paintings and sculptures, street life and country scenes, and for the first time tapped into the sensuous in his nature. At Küchler's studio, where he was being painted, he noted prudishly in his diary "saw a model who worked as a prostitute—she was beautiful *once*." But two days later he was there again, and was undermined:

> Went, like yesterday, to Küchler's for a sitting, and while I was there a young model of about sixteen came in with her mother. Küchler said he wanted to see what her breasts were like; the girl seemed to be a little bashful because I was there, but the mother said "Fiddle-faddle" and loosened her dress and pulled it and her shift all the way down to her waist. There she stood then half-naked, with somewhat dark skin, arms a bit too skinny, but beautiful round breasts. As the mother exposed her, I could feel my whole body tremble. Küchler saw that I went pale and asked if there was anything wrong with me.

The artists in Rome picked up on Andersen's erotic fervour and talked to Thorvaldsen about his innocence, about seducing him. They planned to

take him to a brothel, they teased him mercilessly, and, in the sultry intimacy of café life, he was urged on by the confidences of others—"Hertz
quite the confidant this evening! Gossiped about . . . lechery!" he noted in
December 1833. His diary suggests constant sensual/artistic excitement. He
spent New Year's Eve at a Jesuit church lost in a peal of church bells and
organs and a *Te Deum* being sung by candlelight, then dreamed about struggling with a bat: "the wings kept getting bigger and bigger; the moment I
was about to get the best of it, I woke up." Visiting Tasso's grave in the
monastery of Sant' Onofrio in January, he sketched the monument and
scratched his own inscription, that love was the poet's only fault, on to the
wall. Grabbing at each experience, he wanted to be personally engaged with
everything, even the relics—"went to the Lateran, where we saw in the
cloister yard how tall Christ was—approximately my height."

His diary for the Italian journey is dotted with fluent, powerful drawings,
dashed off in moments as an image; Monte Testacio near Rome, Thorvaldsen's house in the Via Sistina, Michelangelo's house in Florence, the temples
at Paestum, absorbed him: the sketches are witnesses to the sincerity and
open, enthusiastic mind with which he travelled. In a few concentrated
months, he honed his perceptions and refined his vision. His encounters
with the masterpieces of the Renaissance and of Roman antiquity, then little
known in northern Europe, thrilled him and affirmed his faith in his vocation as an artist.

This was his heightened mood when on 16 December he received a letter
from Jonas telling him of the death of his mother. He writes in his diary for
that day:

> There was a letter from Collin senior; it reported my mother's death. My first
> reaction was: Thanks be to God! Now there is an end to her sufferings, which
> I haven't been able to allay. But even so, I cannot get used to the thought that I
> am so utterly alone without a single person who *must* love me because of the
> bond of blood. I also received some critical commentary from Heiberg about
> my two singspiels—I am just an improvisator!

He barely refers to his mother's death again, but on 27 December he
noted, "Began this evening on my novel *The Improvisatore*," his novel of
Italian life which opens with a tender evocation of a mother and son based
on Anne Marie and himself. The next day, 28 December, he sketched from
his window a long funeral procession of sixty mourners that was passing by,
as if this was his equivalent of laying his mother to rest. Within ten days, he
had taken Heiberg's criticism to define Antonio, the hero of his new novel,

as a singer with a gift for improvisation who is an Italian version of himself, and used it to explore the role of the artist in society.

The work was to be his breakthrough; the fact that its origins are woven into the news about his mother suggests that in some unconscious way her death, and with it the end of his link with the old Odense world, went hand in hand with Italy in freeing his creative energies. Throughout Christmas his spirits were high. The Danish artists decked a table with garlands and wreaths ("mine was the most attractive") on Christmas Eve and decorated a laurel tree with oranges and a lucky dip of presents, of which Andersen "got the best and most expensive present" (an inscribed silver cup worth six and a half *scudi*). Twenty years later Andersen commented that Christmas "has never since been so joyous, so fresh and bright as it was in 1833."

But at the beginning of the New Year 1834 his happiness collapsed when a furore of opposition to *Agnete* reached him. In December, Jonas had complained about the work's formlessness, and Andersen's publisher Reitzel had

Hans Christian Andersen, A Funeral Procession before My Windows in Rome, 28 December 1833. *Andersen sketched this days after he heard that his mother had died in Odense.*

refused to risk the work, forcing Andersen to publish it himself. But now Edvard, too, who had already written crossly that the merman, "in his conversation with Agnete, talks in the same way, I assure you, with expressions which I have often heard from you addressed to me," condemned the piece.

Edvard was supposed to have gone through the proofs for Andersen and arranged publication. Instead, incensed both at the work's pedestrian dullness and its emotional subtext, he sent off an insensitive letter to Rome, saying that while reading the proofs he had been on the verge of crying because *Agnete* regurgitated Andersen's old themes and ideas so shapelessly; usually, though, irritation had squashed his tears. There was wide hostility to Andersen's work in Denmark, he said, and he advised him to stop writing altogether for six months.

To Andersen, this was a double rejection—both as artist and as lover. For a month, he was as depressed as he had ever been, and longing for letters of support from home. "If only there's a letter today!" began his diary for 6 January 1834, then

> indeed, there was a letter from Father and Edvard, the latter with admonitions and in such a harsh, didactic tone, full of anger. He pronounced for me the death of my reputation. *Agnete* was a desperately ill-conceived, mongrelized, pedestrian work. It shook me profoundly to the core of my being; I was so overwhelmed that I was left numb, my belief in God and my fellow man destroyed. The letter drove me to despair. Bødtcher tried to comfort me. How could he!

The diary continues:

> *7 January:* What a night I've spent! I had a fever; I tossed and turned in my bed. How close I was to ending this cursed life!

> *8 January:* Last night I got a little more sleep, but my feelings have yet to regain their balance. I am ill. All the Danes think so too. I have just written a serious letter to Edvard; he must adjust his tone to that of a friend; I cannot tolerate his hectoring any longer if we are to remain friends. I don't want to distress Father, though, to whom I owe so much. Have therefore sent him the letter; then he can give it to Edvard if he wants ... Maybe I'll lose both of them. But Father is an intelligent man; he won't get angry with me.

> *9 January:* It is difficult to tear oneself away from old relationships that have become oppressive, but better late than never! I won't let Edvard dominate me any longer!

31 January: Well, today is the end of the month. Not since my time with the Meislings have I each morning been in the grip of such demoralizing emotions as I am at this time. Then I was crushed; now I am infuriated and hurt. My God, Edvard, what kind of people are you and the others? You are destroying me.

Thorvaldsen supported him—"Feel your own strength; don't let yourself be led by the judgement of the masses; and go calmly on"—but in the end it was Andersen's standard palliative of travelling further south that broke the mould of his depression by forcing on him the interest of something new and unfamiliar.

Rome, identified now with the cruelty of his critics and with creative frustration, had become a disappointment. In February he left it and with pedantic, squinting Hertz, travelled to Naples, "the sky . . . so infinitely blue, not a cloud . . . a paradise." Of all Italian cities, this was the one closest to his heart. Its languid beauty overcame him: "I strolled in the warm air under the large lemon and orange trees, and threw the yellow, shining fruits into the charming blue sea, which gleamed and broke in gentle waves." By the second day his mood was transformed: "tired, but so inexpressibly happy, thankful to God. Slept." Accommodating letters arrived from Jonas and from Edvard (jovially asking if Andersen's character was still so soft), and at the end of his first week in Naples Andersen was ecstatic. He wrote to Henriette Wulff:

> I am sitting in my room, it is nearly midnight, my waiter has brought me a bottle of Lacrymae Christi . . . there's a smell of Vesuvius in it . . . Listen, now they're singing serenades in the street, the guitar is being played. Oh, this is really too good! My soul is so full of love, I have not been as happy as at this moment for a long time. My pain is crushing when I suffer, but my joy when I'm happy is also inexpressible. The warmth of the South is in my blood, and yet I must—die in the North. It says in the Bible that one who has tasted heavenly bread can never be satisfied with anything earthly, and so I shall never be satisfied in the cold land where I have to belong. But thanks be to God that at least I have seen and felt heaven; I shall dream of it, I shall sing of it.

Many other northern Europeans, for whom Rome had not lived up to its promise, were similarly captivated and changed by nineteenth-century Naples. For Goethe, the memory of Naples would "give savour to a whole life." Two years before Andersen made the journey, Berlioz in October 1831 had left Rome for Naples and wrote home that nothing equals the great bay that unfurls before me, Vesuvius smoking, the sea covered with boats … all this motley, striding people thronging the streets, the crowds of soldiers in their red and gold uniform … the peasant women of the islands in their green bodices with brass stripes, a red kerchief on their heads, the armies of fishermen pulling up their nets, the naked children who leap from the cockleshell craft and hare through the water along the sand. What life! What animation! What dazzling bustle! How different it all is from Rome and its sleepy inhabitants and untilled, desolate, denuded soil! The austerely melancholy Roman countryside is to the plain of Naples as the past is to the present, death to life, silence to vivid, harmonious noise.

With Hertz, Andersen climbed Vesuvius as the volcano was erupting, the lava pouring out of the crater and down the mountain, and visited the recently discovered Blue Grotto at Capri. Writing *The Improvisatore*, his novel about Italy, he dreamed of transferring the effects of colour in painting to literature. "You will find a description of the blue cave in my novel," he told Henriette Wulff. "Professor Kruse, who is working on the [German] translation of the book, says that I am a very great painter; Ørsted says that I should use the brush as I use the pen."

Goethe's response to Naples had been similar: "When I want to put down words it is always pictures that come before my eyes, of the fertile land, the open sea, the shimmering islands, the smoking mountains, and I lack the organs to represent it all." Naples was overwhelming for self-conscious artists such as Goethe and Andersen because it took them out of themselves. "Naples is a Paradise: everyone lives in a kind of intoxicated obliviousness of self. It is the same for me: I scarcely recognize myself; I seem to be a quite different person," Goethe wrote. At Vesuvius, Andersen felt the eruption as a symbol of the hidden powers of nature and interpreted it as his initiation into the mystery of being an artist. In the novel, his hero Antonio has the same experience:

The lava lay in the distance like colossal, falling stars; the moon shone like day. We travelled along the edge of the beautiful bay, and saw the reflection of the moon and the lava in two long stretches of light, the one red, the other blue, trembling on the mirror of the waters. I felt a strength in my soul, a clearness in my comprehension; yes, if I may compare the small with the great, I was so far related to Boccaccio, that the impression of a place, and its momentary inspiration, determined the whole operation of the spirit.

This was Andersen's summing up of the effect of Italy on his art: emotion recollected in tranquillity. In his diaries, he recorded a raw reaction to Italian painting and landscape as reflections of his own erotic desires, which intensified as he went south, and in Naples he expressed for the first time sexual hunger for women:

19 February: The sea was like glass. Capri, which I'd thought was Ischia, lay like a floating cloud . . . In the dusk of the evening I was surrounded by a bunch of pimps, who wished to recommend to me a *bella donna.* I've noticed that the climate is affecting my blood—I felt a raging passion, but resisted. God only knows what Hertz was up to when I got home! The room was locked, and when I knocked on the door he came out and, speaking to me outside the door, apologized for the fact that I couldn't come in . . . I left and was pursued in the street where I live by somebody who asked if I wanted to have a *ragazza* or a *ragazzo.*

21 February: At dusk I walked down to the sea. Vesuvius spewed great streams of lava; it blazed into the air; it was like tongues of fire flaring up. This is the most violent I have seen it. But I had no peace from the pimps—a boy ten or twelve years old pursued me down the length of the street, speaking of this *donna multa bella, excellenza!* I got really randy, but still resisted the temptation anyway. If I'm still innocent when I get back home, I'll stay that way.

23 February: Took a walk round the Villa Reale and watched the frothing of the waves far out . . . My blood is churning. Huge sensuality and struggle with myself. If it really is a sin to satisfy this powerful urge, then let me fight it. I am still innocent, but my blood is burning. In my dreams, I am boiling inside. The south will have its way! I am half sick. Happy is the man who is married, engaged to be married! Oh if only I were bound by strong bonds!

26 February: The boy with the white hat, who keeps trying to seduce me, couldn't praise his *donna* enough: "*O, multa bella!*" he said. She was only thirteen years old and had just this month given herself over to carnal pleasure. Finally I got tired of him and turned into a side street; suddenly he darted ahead of me because it happened to be precisely the street where she lived. He showed me the house, begged me to just take a look at her and said I wouldn't be able to resist. "Exactly," I thought and said "No! No! No!" as I walked to the next street. "Strada Nardona, numero trenta due" he shouted, and I escaped. Then went and had a good supper with a glass of Malaga. Thought about Louise and the others at home. If they had seen me this evening they would certainly be worried about me. Naples is more perilous than Paris, because you freeze there, but here your blood boils. God lead me to what is best and most sensible. I don't regard this gratification as a sin, but I find it disgusting and dangerous to do it with such creatures, and an unforgiveable sin, with an innocent.

28 February: Experienced people will laugh at my innocence, but it isn't really innocence, it is an abhorrence of this thing which I dislike so much.

Timid, gauche, hypochondriac, conscious of his ugliness, Andersen was held back by an instinct stronger in him than sexual desire: fear. "Hertz says I resemble a big giraffe, but begs me not to take offence! He says, as well, that it is a nice animal," he wrote in Naples. In retrospect, he loved the city as the first place that had allowed him to admit his desires; his account of it in *The Improvisatore* bursts with sexual frustration:

She was greatly excited. I saw her bosom heave violently: she loosened a scarf to breathe more freely. "You are deserving of love!" said she. "Soul and beauty are deserving of any woman's love!" . . . She drew me towards her: her lips were like fire, that flowed into my very soul!

Eternal Mother of God! Thy holy image, at that moment, fell down from the wall . . . It was not a mere accident . . . you seized me, as I was about to sink in the whirlpool of passion!

"No, no!" exclaimed I, starting up: my blood was like seething lava.

"Antonio," cried she, "kill me! kill me! but do not leave me!" Her cheeks, her eyes, her glance and expression, was passion; and yet she was beautiful . . . I felt a tremor in all my nerves; and, without replying, I left the apartment; and rushed down the steps, as if a dark spirit had pursued me.

When I reached the street, all seemed in flame, like my blood! The current of the air wafted forward the heat. Vesuvius stood in glowing fire—eruptions in rapid succession lit up everything around. Air! Air! demanded my heart . . . I cooled my brow with the salt water; tore open my coat, that every breath of air might cool me; but all was flame—the sea even shone like the fire of the red lava, which rolled down the mountain. Whichever way I looked, I saw her standing, as if painted in flame . . .

A Danish critic has written of the years 1833–1834 that both literally and emotionally, Andersen trod "on a thin crust over glowing lava." To do so was one of the triumphs of his journey abroad—it enabled him to realize himself, to find his own freedom of expression away from the expectations and repressions that hemmed him in at home. "Let me follow my nature!—Why do I have to trot with the fashion?" he asked in his diary in March 1834. "If my gait is slouching, well, that is the natural way I walk."

But his travel grant was running out, and in April 1834 Andersen left Italy with a sinking heart. In his luggage he carried his diary, his drawings and the first few chapters of *The Improvisatore*. On the coach from Rome to Florence, there were rumours of brigands on the roads, and Andersen wrote melodramatically, "perhaps they may stab me to death, but then I shall die in Italy, and not return home, where much sorrow, much mischief . . . are awaiting me." He sat on the front seat and, he noted, had for a neighbour a very stupid priest, who had never heard of Germany: "So I was obliged to speak some sort of Italian, and as he remarked it was not like his, and heard I came from the North, he asked me if I was not a Milanese."

This was the sort of peasant ignorance that Andersen loved about Italy— "the people here are blessed children who still believe in the devil, in life, in the dead pictures." The young, disaffected Berlioz had similarly envied the undemanding Italian peasants in 1831, asking them, "What are your dreams of wealth? The handful of piastres necessary to buy a donkey and get married: three years' savings will achieve it. What is a wife for you? Someone of a different sex . . . For you, painting means the Virgin coloured in red and green, drama means puppets and Punch and Judy, music means the bagpipe and the tambourine." For Andersen, to romanticize peasant life was rare— usually he was, like many self-made men, modern in outlook and dismissive of past times which had been harder for the poor. But the peasant traditions in Italy struck a chord with memories of his own childhood at precisely the time when he was trying to shake off the bourgeois layers of education that Collin and others expected of him, and this made him love Italy the more.

On his journey home, his diary records how drawn he was to the folk fatalism which was antithetical to the Collin rationalism—next to the war cry "I won't let Edvard dominate me any longer," for example, he writes:

Today, when I was taking a walk, I saw one of the farmers driving the little carts with two wheels climb on board—it looked tricky. He put his foot on the lowest spoke of the wheel as it was turning and let it raise him upwards; when he was as high as he could go, he made a quick move and jumped on board. That is just the way you have to climb on Fortune's carriage, but most fall under the wheel before they make it up.

In Florence he was full of self-pity and dreams of peasant simplicity. He wrote to Mrs. Læssøe that

> God knows if it would not be a happier existence to be a simple man—a good tailor or shoemaker, who sits in his workshop, eats his meals, takes a holiday once a year, and at last retires to the graveyard . . . You talk about me falling in love again when I arrive home etc. God in Heaven! You know well how ugly I am, and how poor I shall always be, and these are things everybody considers, whomsoever the heart may choose, and quite properly too.

Yet he was as restless as ever. "I have a few memories that really characterize me," he told Ingemann:

> Together with a young Scotsman I travelled through the north of Italy and the Tyrol to Munich. He was a wonderful young man, whom I grew very fond of. In Munich we parted ways: but before he travelled on, we wanted to talk more together. One day when I was at the police station to report my new lodgings, I met the young Scot. "I'm collecting my passport," he said, "wait for me here outside, I'll be there in a minute: tonight I'm going to Paris." He enters, I wait a little, he doesn't appear, and—then I leave, God knows how I could! I never see the man again. The next day I finished crying because of my strange behaviour, and it is still saddening to me . . . I have a restlessness in me, as if life was too short, and when I look back, hours and days have passed during which I have done nothing, not even done what my heart desires: to chat with my friends.

Italy had awakened him to a real sexual desire for a woman rather than the remote ideal of Riborg Voigt or Louise Collin, yet as he drew nearer Copenhagen his erotic interest in men came alive again too. "We shall soon meet again. I wonder if you will look older? I wonder if—well, please excuse me!— whether you will delight me even more than before?" he wrote to Edvard, and "I don't think I am as passionate and soft as before . . . I wonder if you will like me more?" He was rekindling other sentimental friendships too, including one with Ludvig's and Adam's brother Otto Müller, whose letter to him in Vienna gives an idea of how he was perceived back home. Müller hoped Andersen's journey had made him change "just a little; principally the old, splendid, tender-hearted Andersen (I quite ignore the writer here), but just a little less egotistic—in so far as that expression can be applied to a disposition that draws nourishment from, and is aflame with, sheer love—and a little less obstinate when given well-meant friendly advice."

Andersen's overwhelming emotion about his home-coming was dread. "I fear greatly going to Copenhagen," he wrote. "Northward, northward, there, where my dear ones live in snow and fog, lies the iron ring to be fastened to my foot. Yes, yes. Denmark is a poor country! Italy's cornucopia is filled with fruit and flowers, while we have only grass and a sloe-hedge." Italy taught him to see himself as an international writer, and it was this, as well as the idea of life as a journey of learning, that he poured into *The Improvisatore* when he stopped for a month in May in Munich and continued the manuscript.

A longing for the south shaped the work as he sketched prose-pictures of Italian life, and read books about Italy, including Goethe's *Italienische Reise* (*Italian Journey*, 1786–1787) and Heine's *Reisebilder* (*Travel Pictures*, 1826–1831). In his mind's eye he could picture exactly the vision of Italy, its excitement and emotional impact on a young traveller from the north, that he wanted to convey; he was consumed with the desire to get it on the page. He wondered to Henriette Wulff: "I have read many books about Italy—how empty they all are. Heine's little leap down to Lucca he might just as well have written in Hamburg, there is no sign of Italian landscape in it. *Corinne* [by Madame de Staël, 1807] is a boring guide full of noveltalk and criticism. Goethe alone gives something true, but it is so fragmentary. Is it impossible to express this superb impression?"

But he was emotionally exhausted, aching for letters from Denmark— "No letter. Feverish. Spent the whole afternoon and evening lying on the sofa. Oh, I wish I were dead! Life holds no joy for me. Her, the joys of youth, Italy! Everything is gone!—Oh, I'm sick in mind and body!" He cheered up when he happened to see in the London *Fortnightly Review* a description of himself as a "youthful poet of great promise . . . evincing much originality of genius"—"Childishly pleased and grateful, I felt myself to be a better person."

Then he proceeded north, falling victim to the usual anxieties and gullibilities—toothache ("a whole *Miserere* that the pain was playing on my nerve pipes"), passport trouble—the Austrians refused to accept "Jean Chrétien" as a French version of Hans Christian, and would not at first let him into the country ("I assured them . . . I hated revolutions, and was a tiptop kind of subject")—and being made a fool of in Bohemia: he stayed an extra two days in Prague to visit a couple he had met on the stagecoach, who had boasted of their fine library, only to find a garret with an old man dressed in a dirty night-gown and a pile of books in a laundry basket.

Approaching Denmark, his resolve strengthened: he would not allow people to educate him any longer. "I won't stand for it! Now I will and must break old habits, otherwise these will persist for the rest of my life," he told Ludvig Müller. Leaving Vienna, he wrote to Henriette Wulff: "The poet is dead, killed in Italy! If there is any life left in him when he gets to Scandinavia, I am sure they will finish him off. I know my people!" In fact, he was warmly welcomed by the Collins (he even saw tears in Jonas's eyes, he wrote) when he arrived on 3 August 1834, and there was a perceptible shift in his friendships, for within two months he wrote to Henriette again that

> I haven't been in such a good mood as I am now for a long time; I feel the point at which I stand myself, see more clearly than before the value of those around me, and if a patronizing preacher appears, one of the sort who were once so keen to educate me, then first I hear him out to see if it is nonsense, and if I find that it is, then I rebuff him . . . Nobody is going to treat me as a boy any longer.

Nevertheless, he left the capital almost immediately to spend the summer with Ingemann in Sorø. There, "in a little chamber in the roof, among fragrant lime trees," he read Dante, Virgil and many books about art and Italy, and wrote much of *The Improvisatore*, which he finished in Copenhagen in the autumn.

The Improvisatore is the first of many fictional autobiographies which occupied Andersen over the next forty years. Its hero, Antonio, is a poor Roman boy from the slums with no father, an indulgent mother and an eccentric, terrifying uncle Peppo. Antonio is a promising singer with a special gift for improvisation, and his talent attracts the interest of the eminent Borghese family, who become his patrons. He is educated at a Jesuit college run by the tyrannical Habbas Dahdah, and eventually, after much suffering and loneliness, and enduring the lectures and criticisms of his benefactors, he achieves social success and romantic happiness in Naples.

Copenhagen readers would have detected the Danish originals of Andersen's Italian cast easily—members of the Collin and Wulff families were the models for the Borgheses, Meisling for Habbas Dahdah. Andersen also put much of his own childhood in the book, from his fear of his mad grandfather—here Uncle Peppo—to the gift for singing which first got him noticed in Odense, to a shrewd account of the way he used, and so tainted, his own child-like innocence in order to climb the social ladder:

I heard her repeat to a neighbour what an innocent angel I was, and it pleased me greatly, but it lessened my innocence—the mustard-seed of vanity drank in there from the first sunbeams. Nature had given me a gentle pious character, but my good mother made me aware of it; she showed me my real and imaginary endowments, and never thought that it is with the innocence of the child as with the basilisk, which dies when it sees itself.

The adult Antonio is also a perceptive self-portrait. "You are not in love!" Antonio's friend Bernardo tells him. "You are one of these intellectually amphibious creatures that one cannot tell whether they rightly belong to the living or the dream world." At one point Antonio almost becomes a monk, because, he says, "I am . . . only a poetical being, not a man, like the rest of you." His patrons try to take charge of him, and he finds it hard to resist: "a bashfulness, a fear, which my poverty and gratitude had instilled into me through all the years of my life, permitted me to do no more than stammer forth." Yet it was said "that I was spoiled, because people made so much of me."

The novel was a wish-fulfilment version of Andersen's own life, transposed to the Italy he fantasized about as his natural home. It is suffused with busy, colourful pictures of Italian landscape, art and society at all levels: peasants, priests, painters, patricians. Andersen was proud of the synthesis of emotion and sense of place. He wrote to Henriette Hanck that she would experience in the novel Rome and Naples as he had done, and that as Scott had described the Highlands and its people, so he had drawn Italy.

The depictions of Rome and Naples are the most passionate part of the book: Rome, city of learning, history and the Church, is set against Naples, sensuous capital of art, nature and love, where Antonio discovers himself as an artist, is tempted by lust and finds romance. The cities represented what Andersen saw as the difference between northern and southern Europe, and reflected the battle between education and "feeling," for which Antonio's singing is constantly praised, in his own art. His accounts come alive partly because they are steeped in his own memories of sexual and spiritual crisis. The importance of Naples to him is shown by the fact that he used the city as a backcloth to a spiritual crisis again, a decade later, in "The Shadow."

The Improvisatore was published on 9 April 1835 at a price of two rixdollars and eight shillings. Andersen was in an optimistic mood when he wrote to his clever and courteous publisher Reitzel a fortnight before publication:

Dear Reitzel,

The printer is almost finished with my novel . . . I hope you will succeed with it! I have given it a year of my life, perhaps the best one! . . . Believe me, dear Reitzel, if I were rich, I would make you a gift of everything I write, but that is not how things go in this world. In that other world, where everything will change for the better, maybe you will be the writer and I the publisher, and then you can do for me what I would have done down here.

Yours affectionately, H. C. Andersen

The book was dedicated to the Collin family—it was both Andersen's tribute and answer to them: "To the Conference-Councillor Collin and His Excellent Wife, in whom I found parents; and to their children, in whom I found brothers and sisters; in whose home, a home; I bring, with a filial and fraternal heart, this the best which I possess."

It was an immediate success, soon went into a second edition and won Andersen a new audience. Andersen had been talked of as a worn-out talent, said the poet Carl Bagger in the first review, "but that he is not exhausted, and that he now, on the contrary, has swung himself into a position altogether unknown to him before, he has by his *Improvisatore* shown in a most brilliant way." To Henriette Wulff, Andersen wrote on 29 April:

Never until now has a work of mine gripped the people so intensely. Hertz came to see me to thank me for the pleasure, telling me, in quite a beautiful way, that many people here who did not care about me, were now devoted to me. Ingemann says that it marks the transition from youth to manhood in my writing . . . Everyone is so kind, so nice to me, many even say that they had not anticipated anything like that from me. I am on the crest of a wave.

His visions of Italy had a significant influence in Denmark. *The Improvisatore* stands, for example, behind the Danish choreographer Auguste Bournonville's famous ballet *Napoli* (1842), and Bournonville's response to Naples in 1841 reads like an extract from the novel: "The morning breeze carried a balmy fragrance from the shore; it was the scent of orange. The harbour was alive with activity . . . I jumped in the air and clapped my hands, and the beggar boys, perceiving my joy, shrieked to the skies and turned cartwheels around me by the hundred . . . In Naples everything is intensified."

The novel was translated into many northern European languages. With the title *Jugendleben und Träume eines italienischen Dichters* (*Youth and Dreams of an Italian Poet*), which acknowledged its debt to Goethe's drama of the growth of an Italian poet, *Torquato Tasso* (1790), it made Andersen's name in Germany in 1835. It was popular in England (1845), Sweden (1838), Russia (1844), Holland (1846) and France (1847). It did not make Andersen rich—Denmark was too small a country to support any writer by royalties alone, and since there was no international copyright in the nineteenth century, foreign earnings were minimal. Unscrupulous foreign publishers brought out pirate editions to rival those produced by the honourable houses who had paid the author an advance. In his autobiography, Andersen quotes a conversation with Charles Dickens about his earnings for *The Improvisatore* which shows the difference between writing in English and in Danish in the nineteenth century:

> "What did you get?" asked he. I answered, "Nineteen pounds." "For the sheet?" he inquired. "No," said I, "for the whole book." "We must be misunderstanding each other," continued he; "you don't mean to say that for the whole work, *The Improvisatore*, you have only nineteen pounds; you must mean for each sheet!" I was sorry to tell him it was not the case, and that I had only got about half a pound a sheet.
>
> "I should really not believe it," exclaimed he, "if you had not said it yourself."

The Improvisatore is a bright, airy, optimistic book, sentimental and melodramatic as was the taste of the time, but with a structural shape and discipline new to Andersen's work that showed how influenced he had been by the classical art of Italy. It mixes the picturesque drama of Italian travel literature—Goethe's *Italian Journey*, Madame de Staël's *Corinne*—which had been popular since the 1800s, with the new realism which was sweeping across the European novel in the 1830s. In narrative form, social detail and psychological observation *The Improvisatore* belongs with the novels of Stendhal, Balzac and Dickens: *Le Rouge et Le Noir* (1830), *Eugénie Grandet* (1833), *Oliver Twist* (1837). Andersen was nothing if not modern. But he added his own twist. In the history of literature, *The Improvisatore* is remarkable as one of the first novels to concentrate on its hero's childhood, and to trace his adult development as a result of it—Charlotte Brontë and Dickens were to do the same in *Jane Eyre* (1847) and *David Copperfield* (1849–1850). This was one of the legacies of Romanticism, with its fixation on childhood as a special state, to the nineteenth-century novel. With Andersen, the focus pointed to a new interest in writing for children, which began to preoccupy him in the autumn of 1834.

The Improvisatore concludes with Antonio and his wife, almost magically rescued from death, visiting the recently discovered Blue Grotto in Capri: "a fairy world . . . now was every supernatural appearance cleared up in reality, or reality had passed over into the spiritual world . . . and yet man will not believe in miracles!" Unconsciously, Andersen here put his finger on the book's central flaw: in trying to work out his own sexual, artistic and social problems through the story, he has a vein of realistic defeat—Antonio's weakness and uncertainty and sexual fear—underpinning what becomes a dream fulfilment. And so the novel lacks conviction, it is too patently about Andersen's own unresolved difficulties, it cannot work on the level of myth and symbol as *Oliver Twist* and *Eugénie Grandet* do. Andersen realized some of this himself; in 1834 he wrote to Mrs. Læssøe: "What a peculiar being I am! Ørsted says that his and my aesthetic religion are widely different: I seek all the discords of the world, while he insists upon it that the poet must seek harmonies; but I believe I am myself the discord in this world. Too many bitter tears have fallen on the chords of my love to produce harmony, neither shall I attain that at which I aimed." Only when he turned to a genre where fantasy and images of desire become real, and sudden turns of fate are essential to story-telling, did his own dilemmas cease to undermine his art. As soon as *The Improvisatore* was finished, he began writing fairy tales.

CHAPTER 8

First Fairy Tales

1835

*"What nonsense is this to stuff into the child's head?" said the tiresome old council-
lor ... He didn't like the student and always used to grumble when he saw him cutting those comical pictures ... The councillor didn't like it, and so he would say as he
said now, "What nonsense is this to stuff into the child's head? What a lot of silly
rubbish!"*

—HANS CHRISTIAN ANDERSEN, "Little Ida's Flowers"

"For five months I believe we have not seen a clear atmosphere . . . how empty and cold it is here in our north," Andersen wrote in March 1835. Through "rain, slush and fog" in the winter of 1834–1835, he sat at his window in 20, Nyhavn, watching the dark sea and listening to the clinking masts in the harbour. His new rooms, which he had taken on his return from Italy, were his most cheerful yet: a furnished bedroom and study in the red gabled house of a skipper's widow, Karen Larsen, on the quayside. Here the tall narrow houses were brightly painted, sailing ships were moored at the quay, boats scurried across the water. In the depths of winter, the canal leading down to the open sea froze over, snow settled on the ships and the street was quieter; in summer, activity went on all evening.

Andersen's house was half-way down on the west side, and his rooms were on the second floor, with his name on the door. His bedroom looked on to the Charlottenborg Palace, home of the Academy of Fine Arts, and the botanical gardens, where in moonlight the black poplars looked like cypress trees from Italy. His study had a clear view of the harbour and if he put his head out of the window, of the Sound on one side and Kongens Nytorv on the other. A minute's walk away was the Royal Theatre and within five minutes he could be across the road at Bredgade for his daily visit to the Collins.

View of Nyhavn, *by Wilhelm Benz. Andersen lived on this street for over twenty years, and wrote his first fairy tales here.*

Now you enter my study. The fire burns in the fireplace . . . over the sofa hangs a painting by Miss Stub, an angel carrying writing materials and a laurel wreath . . . On a little table my cups and beakers and an Italian crucifix that in true Catholic manner I have decorated with silk ribbons this Christmas. Now come my bookshelf and other furniture, and through the window can be seen three-masted sailing ships, and boats darting past each other . . . My mirror is full of visiting cards. Everything is very tidy, except the table, which is littered with magazines, manuscripts, etchings and books, and sometimes even a glove or a cuff.

When he returned from Italy, Andersen settled into a comfortable working pattern which continued unchanged for several years. "I shall give you a plan of my week," he told his friend Henriette Hanck in Odense,

but first the daily routine. At 8 o'clock: coffee; then I read and write until 11 or 12 o'clock, when I go to the society [the Students' Union] to read the papers, then I have a bath, take a walk and make visits until 3 o'clock; then I have a rest. At 4 to 6 dinner, and the rest of the time I am at home working or reading. If something new is on at the theatre in the evening then I'll be there, and nowhere else. My dinners go like this: Mondays at Mrs. Bügel's, where dinner is always on the scale of a large party; Tuesdays at the Collins', where the eldest son and his wife also dine then, so we get something special; Wednesdays at the Ørsteds', who always ask their guests then; Thursdays again at Mrs. Bügel's; Fridays at the Wulffs', where Weyse always comes on that day and after dinner plays his fantasies on the piano; Saturday is my free day, when I eat wherever I might be asked, or at Ferrini's [a restaurant]; Sundays at Mrs. Læssøe's, or in the Students' Union if I don't feel up to the long walk. There you are, that's my week!

From this cosseted existence, dashed with an occasional luxury when the elderly widowed Mrs. Bügel, who had a crush on him, sent presents—Italian wine, fruit, a yellow Parisian dressing gown with red roses on it—Andersen watched the wintry sea and lamented the south. "You cannot imagine how I am longing for Italy," he wrote to Henriette Wulff. "The fresh air, the rich colours, the whole luxuriant nature, the picture galleries, the songs of the beautiful people." Yet at his desk, still sustained by the creative burst with which he had finished *The Improvisatore*, he turned to stories from his childhood.

On New Year's Day 1835 he wrote to Henriette Hanck, "I am now starting on some 'fairy tales for children.' I am going to win over future generations, you may want to know." In February, he told Ingemann, "I have started some 'Fairy Tales Told for Children' and believe I have succeeded. I have told a couple of tales which as a child I was happy about, and which I do not believe are known, and have written them exactly the way I would tell them to a *child*." By 16 March, Andersen had finished four tales and told Henriette Wulff, "I have also written some fairy tales for children; Ørsted says about them that if *The Improvisatore* makes me famous, these tales will make me immortal, for they are the most perfect things I have ever written; but I myself do not think so." On 26 March he reported to Henriette Hanck with a mixture of pride and irony that "they [the tales] will be published in April, and people will say: the work of my immortality! Of course I shan't enjoy the experience in this world."

On 8 May 1835, weeks after the success of *The Improvisatore*, Reitzel brought out a thin, unbound pamphlet entitled *Eventyr, fortalte for Børn* (*Tales, Told for Children*), and subtitled *Første Hefte* (*First Book*). It was sixty-

one pages long and contained four tales. The first three, "The Tinderbox,"
"Little Claus and Big Claus" and "The Princess and the Pea," were folk stories which Andersen had heard from his grandmother in the spinning room
at the Odense asylum and during hop-picking. The fourth, "Little Ida's
Flowers," about a girl's toys and flowers coming alive, he had made up him-
self to tell Ida Thiele, daughter of the folklore collector Just Matthias
Thiele, who had been one of his benefactors. The book was priced at
twenty-four shillings, and Reitzel paid Andersen thirty rixdollars for it.
Seven months later, on 16 December 1835, in time for Christmas, a second
instalment was published. This consisted of "Thumbelina," inspired by
"Tom Thumb," which Andersen would have read in the Grimms' version;
"The Naughty Boy," based on Anacreon's poem about Cupid; and "The
Travelling Companion," Andersen's reworking of the Funen tale about a
ghost with which he had experimented unsuccessfully in 1830.

Almost two centuries on, it is hard to imagine the impact on a child in the
1830s who opened an obscure little volume and read the following first lines:

> A soldier was marching along the high road: Left, right! Left, right! He had
> his knapsack on his back and a sword at his side, for he had been to the wars
> and was going home. And on the way he met an old witch. Oh, she was hor-
> rid: her bottom lip came right down to her chest.

Today, we accept imaginative, anarchic stories as the basis of all good children's books, from *Alice's Adventures in Wonderland* and *The Tale of Peter
Rabbit* to *Charlie and the Chocolate Factory* and the *Harry Potter* stories. But
when Andersen wrote his first fairy tales, children's books were not expected
to be about enjoyment: they were usually formal, improving texts which
highlighted a moral and were meant to educate, not amuse, young readers.
Nor were fairy tales the stuff of literary creativity. Though folk tales had
been collected and published since the end of the seventeenth century—
Charles Perrault's courtly *Histoires ou contes du temps passé*, or *Contes de ma
Mère l'Oye* (1697) and *Tales from the Arabian Nights*, which Andersen's father
had read to him—they were disapproved of by the rationalist educators of
the Enlightenment, and not generally welcomed in the nursery until the
early nineteenth century.* They circulated in cheap, popular chapbooks and

* "Why should the mind be filled with fantastic visions, instead of useful knowledge? Why
should so much valuable time be lost? Why should we vitiate their taste, and spoil their
appetite, by suffering them to feed upon sweetmeats?" asked Maria Edgeworth in the Preface
to *The Parent's Assistant* (1796), a volume of worthy stories which was a mainstay of English

by oral transmission among the poorer classes—Samuel Johnson, born in 1709, for example, recalled the family maid telling him the story of St. George and the Dragon. But in northern Europe, the major influence towards their acceptance in educated circles was the collections of Jakob and Wilhelm Grimm, *Kinder- und Hausmärchen* (1812–1815).* Translated into English and Danish in the 1820s, these brought, under the guise of the folk romanticism then becoming popular, a bright new world of witches and fairy godmothers, beasts and frogs and princesses, to a wide audience of children, and without their influence Andersen could never have written his tales.

But the Grimms' fairy stories are not creative works: they are collections of folk tales which the brothers gathered from oral traditions all over Germany. What made Andersen revolutionary was that he was the first person to take the fairy tale as a literary form and to invent new ones of his own. He had read widely in the genre—Danish folklore; the Grimms' tales; the elaborate, supernatural short stories of Tieck and Hoffmann—and he synthesized all these elements and mixed them with two essential ingredients of his own: humour and the colloquial, vivid style that seemed to speak itself, and which children found instantly accessible and entertaining.

He brought to the genre, too, a purity of form that owed something to his intoxication with Italian classicism—a purity which is a defining feature of folk tales, refined to their basics and stylized through generations of oral retelling, but which had never been matched by the long-winded literary stories of the early nineteenth century, such as Hoffmann's *Nutcracker and Mouse King* (1816). In 1835 Andersen was a breath of fresh air, an authentic

---

middle-class nurseries in the 1800s. Samuel Johnson spoke out against the eighteenth-century orthodoxy in claiming that parents might buy worthy books about "Goody Two Shoes" but children did not read them, for they liked instead "to be told about giants and castles, and of somewhat which can stretch and stimulate their little minds." Reviewing Perrault in 1803, however, the educationalist Mrs. Sarah Trimmer wrote that "the terrific images, which tales of this nature present to the imagination, usually make deep impressions, and injure the tender minds of children . . . Neither do the generality of tales of this kind supply any moral instruction to the infantine capacity."

*In France, the history of fairy tales was different, with a craze for long, over-elaborate fairy tales written in a highly artificial style developing among salon ladies such as Madame d'Aulnoy in the late seventeenth and early eighteenth centuries. Several folk tales were introduced into England from these sources, including "Beauty and the Beast," published in English in 1757 by Madame de Beaumont and based on "La Belle et la Bête," a story of 362 pages published in Madame de Villeneuve's *Contes marins* in 1740.

storytelling voice which carried conviction and truth in language that was simple without being banal, and that everyone could understand. The slim pamphlet called *Eventyr* was the first great creative work of children's litera-ture, and one of the earliest of all books specifically written for children that is still widely read today.

To open with "The Tinderbox" was a masterstroke. The story is based on a Danish folk tale called "The Spirit of the Candle," which has links with "Aladdin" and so had special emotional resonance for Andersen, who saw himself as the poor boy destined to be famous. It recounts the successes of a poor, feckless soldier who is invited by a witch to find bronze, silver and gold in the hollow of a tree if he will scoop out a magic tinderbox for her. He must brave three dogs—one with eyes as big as teacups, the next with eyes as big as mill-wheels and the last with eyes as big as the Round Tower in Copen-hagen. When he strikes the tinderbox, the equivalent of Aladdin's magic lamp, these dogs come to help him, first making him rich, then bringing a princess imprisoned in a tower to visit him at night. Her parents, the King and Queen, follow her, and place a cross on the soldier's house, so that he can be arrested in the morning. The clever dog baffles them by putting a cross on every house, but the next night a trail of grain attached to the princess's clothes leads straight to the soldier's door, he is thrown into jail and condemned to death. At the last minute he retrieves the tinderbox and summons the animals:

> "Now save me from being hanged!" cried the soldier. And the dogs flew at the judges and all the councillors, and seizing some by the leg and others by the nose, tossed them high up into the air, so they all fell down and were dashed to pieces.
>
> "I'm not going!" cried the king. But the biggest dog seized both him and the queen and tossed them after all the others. At this . . . the people all shouted "Good soldier, you shall be our king, and marry the lovely princess!" . . . The wedding feast lasted a week, and the dogs sat at the table with the rest and were all eyes.

It is a confident, young man's tale—jaunty, brisk, exhilarating. It cele-brates youth over age and it has the energy and hope and satisfaction of the traditional folk tale—"Aladdin," "Puss in Boots," "Jack and the Beanstalk"— whose young hero overcomes adversity and ends a contented, successful adult. Yet Andersen personalizes it with humour and detail: when the sol-dier finds the gold, he realizes he "could buy all Copenhagen with it, along with the cake-woman's sugar-pigs and all the tin-soldiers and whips and rocking-horses in the world"; when he loses his money and has to live in an attic, "none of his friends came to see him, because there were so many stairs to climb"—Andersen's characteristic social satire, which marks the double child/adult readership he intended from the start.

"In style," Andersen wrote in the preface to the collected edition, "one ought to hear the narrator; these stories were made to suggest oral delivery; they were told for children but their elders should also enjoy listening to them." The style is the greatest liberation: it draws the teller and the listener together, sharing jokes against the pompous and powerful, enjoying the cunning tricks that allow the poor and weak to triumph, and providing an outlet for Andersen's rage against the bourgeois society that tried to make him conform:

> "Now give me the tinderbox!"
>
> "Fiddle faddle!" said the soldier. "Tell me straight away what you want it for—or I'll draw my sword and cut your head off!"
>
> "Shan't!" cried the witch.
>
> So the soldier cut her head off. So much for her!

Thirty years later, Lewis Carroll used a similar random, nursery rhyme–style violence ("Off with her head!") in *Alice's Adventures in Wonderland* as his fantasy rebellion against the constraints of middle-class Victorian Oxford. Although Andersen did not seek out children for friendship in the way that Carroll did, and was never a Pied Piper figure who defined himself as a magnet for children, there is no doubt that, like Carroll, he had a special affinity with them,* and that this derived in some sense from his feelings of exclusion from the adult world around him. For Andersen, the fairy tale was a form in which he could express forbidden emotions and thoughts without, as it were, being caught. It is no accident that of the first three folk tales he chose to adapt, two are fantasies of social revenge—"The Tinderbox" and "Little Claus and Big Claus," originally a landlord-and-tenant folk tale, where the little shrewd guy outwits the big lordly one through a variety of farcical and grotesque devices (a dead grandmother propped up in a cart as if alive, a parish clerk locked in a trunk), in the Boccaccio-Chaucer tradition.

---

*Rigmor Stampe, Jonas Collin's great-granddaughter, for example, recalled in her memoir of Andersen how he read his tales to many families in different homes, brought children presents and took them to the theatre; she compared his kindness, generosity and tact favourably with the over-sentimental behaviour towards children by other adults in the Collin circle.

With this volume, Andersen challenged the Danish literary establishment. Borrowing indiscriminately from all sorts of sources—the princess in the tower recalls "Rapunzel," the cross on the soldier's door which the dog duplicates all along the street comes from "Ali Baba and the Forty Thieves," the trail of grain from "Hansel and Gretel"—he invented in "The Tinderbox" his own plebian, Danish version of the Aladdin story (the Round Tower is his equivalent of the Arabian minarets). He chose the story deliberately as an answer to Oehlenschläger's five-act drama *Aladdin*, the most esteemed play of the day. In fairy tales he sensed his route to artistic independence, and his ambition when he was writing the first three books was at its zenith. To Mrs. Iversen he wrote at this time:

> My life is really a poetic story, surely I am a poet. The son of the poor washerwoman running around in the streets of Odense in his wooden shoes has already come so far that he is treated like a son in the home of one of Denmark's most esteemed men and has friends among honourable and wonderful people. One *has* to mention me as one of the *good* writers of my time, but I want even more! God grant in me sufficient strength, I want to be mentioned among Denmark's best writers, together with Holberg and Oehlenschläger! But there is one more leap to take, a great leap upwards. I really sense it, although I don't like to talk about it. The good Lord must take me by the arm; it's no use my just lifting my legs. But cheer up! A great writer here and a greater one still in the next world, that is the image of my hopes, and it is a bad soldier who doesn't think of becoming a general, as the proverb says.

Of the early tales, none reveals more clearly the driving force of his ambiguous social position than "Little Ida's Flowers," the one he made up himself. Ida was the pretty, chubby-faced four-year-old daughter of an eminent intellectual—Thiele was now secretary at the Academy of Fine Arts. She lived in a grand apartment in the Charlottenborg Palace which, like Andersen's rooms in Nyhavn, overlooked the botanical gardens—the setting for part of the story. Like Alice Liddell to Lewis Carroll, she was Andersen's neighbour, the daughter of a colleague, a social superior yet a child whom he saw frequently and with whom he felt relaxed. Like Alice too, Ida was an icon for several nineteenth-century artists—her image is fixed in Christen Købke's portrait of her as a rosy-cheeked toddler in a red velvet dress, painted in 1832, a work which particularly captured the love affair of the Danish nineteenth-century middle classes with childhood.

Andersen placed Ida at the centre of a bourgeois dream-fantasy of talking flowers and dolls coming to life, inspired by Hoffmann's *Nutcracker and*

Mouse King and also by the Viennese children's ballet which he had seen in 1834 on his way back from Italy. His ability to catch the child's voice and vision, in the questions she asks and the way she plays with her offended doll, turned out of its bed for the flowers, is immediately apparent and was radical at the time: while telling the story to Ida, Andersen remembered, "I retained some of the child's comments and repeated them when I afterwards wrote the story."

He included himself as a student with a gift for making paper cut-outs, "now a man hanging from a gibbet and holding his heart in his hand, because he was a stealer of hearts; now an old witch riding a broomstick and carrying her husband on her nose": such paper cut-outs were Andersen's party piece, so everyone who knew him would have recognized the self-portrait. As his adversary he set up "a tiresome old councillor" and Professor of Botany, based on Edvard Collin's uncle, Jens Willem Hornemann, Copenhagen's actual Professor of Botany and a crusty, snobbish man who once told Andersen that someone from his low background had no right to accept an invitation from the King. In the tale the Professor objects to the student's stories, and to a nettle courting a red carnation: "He at once rapped it over the leaves, for those are the nettle's knuckles. But of course he got stung." Then Andersen has his vengeance in a surreal, Hoffmannesque sequence:

> And then all at once a wax doll grew big and long; and, whirling round above the paper ribbons, it cried out in a loud voice: "What nonsense is this to stuff into the child's head? What a lot of silly rubbish!" And at that moment it was the very image of the councillor in the broad-brimmed hat, and looked just as grey and grumpy. But the paper ribbons beat him about his lanky legs and he shrank and became a tiny little wax doll again. That was such fun to see!

The story is slight, but seminal in Andersen's *œuvre*, for here for the first time he merged the fairy tale with images of the everyday bourgeois world. This was his starting point for the tales of toys and inanimate objects coming to life in a domestic setting—"The Steadfast Tin Soldier," "The Top and the Ball," "The Fir Tree," "The Shepherdess and the Chimney Sweep"— which made him hugely popular across Europe as the artist of the idealized world of middle-class childhood.

No one but Andersen could have done this. He had the luck to be born during the last period of history when, in the country town of Odense at least, primitive folk culture was still vividly alive, yet in a wider society which afforded for the first time a real chance of social mobility. On the one hand, his first tales are perfect miniatures: products of cultivated, inward-looking Golden Age Denmark, with its smooth harmonies and exclusion of danger. But Andersen's stories betray this serenity: they are shot through with violence, death and the folk tale's inexorable sense of fate. Death plays a central role in three out of the four stories in his first volume, and is present in the majority of his tales. The stories are so powerful because Andersen retained the primitive folk elements and vernacular style of his childhood memories, and fused them with the social climber's private romance about the bourgeoisie, who both accepted and did not quite accept him. He mythologized his own humiliations and nervousness—he is the morbidly sensitive heroine of "The Princess and the Pea," able to feel a pea through twenty mattresses—and made of the folk tale his own art.

This is where his work differs from that of the Grimm brothers and from other traditional folk tales, which are characterized by oral transmission, anonymous tone, formulaic structure and a general lack of style. Although the Grimm brothers shaped their folk material more than they and their critics have often acknowledged, bringing to them a unique artistry, their aim was to chronicle old tales in as anonymous a manner as possible, whereas with Andersen, even in his early adaptations, everything is personal, for his ambition was always literary creativity. An individual, colloquial manner, the light irony of his social satire, exuberant amounts of detail and a fantastical imagination are the elements which define his genius and which bind together his double audience of parents and children. "I seize an idea for the grown-ups," he wrote, "and then tell the story to the little ones while always remembering that Father and Mother often listen, and you must also give them something for their minds."

As with all great writers, language and style are his essential, individual hallmarks: you cannot open a page of an Andersen fairy tale and mistake him for anyone else. The raw and unpolished Danish of these first stories was so radical as to be considered vulgar at a time when literary convention demanded rigorous, high-flown sentiment of the sort practised by the playwright Heiberg. Andersen, by contrast, was deliberately direct and informal. "This was the novelty. Never before had the Danish language been recorded as candidly and ingeniously as in these tales," writes Erik Dal, co-editor of the complete Danish critical edition of the tales.

This was not only how children in particular spoke and thought, but also the way ordinary, non-academic people used the language. The whimsical traditions of speech, the small words that are so alive, the unmisunderstandable breaches in logic—all these were ingredients in what was in addition poetic prose of great breadth of expression. Surprise, even indignation, were the immediate reactions—what a step backward after *The Improvisatore*! Nevertheless, the Danish language was to be influenced by these tales for all time . . . We find ourselves listening to the most intimate shades of meaning our language has to offer, shades so fine that even the best translators often have given up trying to grasp, or at all events reproduce, the full combination of overtones in the unmistakable soughing of the conch-shell.

One of the best English translators, R. P. Keigwin, wrote the following in 1935:

He sprinkled his narrative with every kind of conversational touch—crisp, lively openings, to catch the listener's attention at a swoop; frequent asides or parentheses; little bits of Copenhagen slang; much grammatical licence; and above all a free use of particles—those nods and nudges of speech, with which Danish (like Greek) is so richly endowed. So completely did Andersen maintain the conversational tone in his *Tales* that you are quite shocked when you occasionally come across some really literary turn . . . The language is . . . not limited to children's language, but to language which children can understand and enjoy . . . It is extraordinary, by the way, how far removed Andersen's language is from that found in Grimm—to say nothing of his humour, which is for Danes his best-loved feature.

As Andersen wrote, he heard the tales as they would be read aloud. Not for nothing had he been known as "the little clamator" who read his work to anyone who would listen; for the rest of his life, he refined and worked on his manuscripts by reading them aloud to his friends. The actor *manqué*, as well as the Odense slum child, stood behind the tales, and Andersen's readings were famous and sought after. Those who had heard both Andersen and Dickens, another consummate performer of his own work, thought Andersen had the edge: the American diplomat George Griffin recalled:

He is a remarkably fine reader, and has often been compared in this respect to Dickens—Dickens was in truth a superb reader, but I am inclined to think that Andersen's manner is far more impressive and eloquent. Both of these men have always read to crowded houses. Dickens's voice was, perhaps, better suited for the stage than the reading desk. It was stronger and louder than Andersen's, but nothing like as mellow and musical. I heard Dickens read the death-bed scene of Little Nell in New York, and I was moved to tears, but I knew that the author himself was reading the story; but when I heard Andersen read the story of the Little Girl with the Matches, I did not think of the author at all, but wept like a child, unconscious of everything around me.

Andersen's diaries are full of recollections of reading after dinner to groups of friends: "Most of them said it was only now that you could really understand my tales . . . it was only when you heard me read that my tales could be seen in the proper light." According to Edvard Collin, his dramatic talent was never better deployed than before children, when he worked out exactly how to win their attention on the page with tiny comic details and asides:

Whether the tale was his own or someone else's, the way of telling it was completely his own, and so lively that the children were thrilled. He, too, enjoyed giving his humour free rein, his speaking was without stop, richly adorned with the figures of speech well known to children, and with gestures to match the situation. Even the driest sentence came to life. He did not say, "The children got into the carriage and then drove away," but "They got into the carriage—'goodbye, Dad! goodbye, Mum!'—the whip cracked smack! smack! and away they went, come on! gee up!" People who later heard him reading his tales will be able to form only a dim idea of the exceptional liveliness with which he told them to children.

On the other hand, an adult could perceive in the performance the full range of emotions which Andersen poured into the fairy tale. "Andersen's voice was deep, clear and smooth, could easily be strengthened or weakened," recalled the critic Edvard Brandes.

His reading aloud was not quite dramatic, not like that of an actor. Enthusiastic listeners frequently asked him to read "The Ugly Duckling"—to listen to it . . . was a partial insight into that which this rare and *abused* soul of a human being had felt and suffered in order to be able to create this immortal little work of art . . . He had led his war against everyone and he seemed to be a significant and exceptional spirit, sitting there in his chair and bending his splendid head over the book whose words he knew by heart.

Andersen was the first to perceive the possibilities of a double articulation for children and adults. While revolutionary, he was also a product of his times—of Romanticism, of the revival of the imaginative spirit and of the growth of democratic ideas—in addressing himself to the child in the adult through a shift in perspective, by allowing the child, or toy, or later farmyard animal, to speak with his or her own voice and feelings. In doing so, he

joined the wider movement of cultural decentralization which was begin-
ning to dominate in Europe and America in the early nineteenth century.
In Denmark, Blicher gave voice to Jutland peasants for the first time; in
Britain, the rural themes and regional speech and images of peasant life in
Walter Scott's novels shaped the Victorian novel; across the Atlantic, James
Fenimore Cooper painted pictures of pioneer and American Indian life on
the prairies. Suddenly the dispossessed and the poor were acceptable literary
subjects. The crucial contribution of Andersen and Dickens in the 1830s and
1840s was to focus on children, another traditionally mute and oppressed
group. The urge to speak out, to claim equality of talent and emotional
need—"it is my spirit which addresses your spirit; just as if both had passed
through the grave, and we stood at God's feet, equal—as we are!" the governess Jane Eyre says to her rich employer, Mr. Rochester—was a driving
force for the new nineteenth-century writers who did not come from the
genteel urban classes, and none came from so deprived and uneducated a
background as Andersen.

For most of the 1830s, he still felt his insecure and dependent position
acutely. In the autumn of 1834, he had been financially desperate enough to
apply for a job at the Royal Library, for which he was turned down on the
grounds that he was too talented. In May 1835, just after the success of *The
Improvisatore* and the publication of the first fairy tales, he wrote to Jonas
Collin:

> I am poor and feel my poverty more constricting than that of the most desti-
> tute beggar, and it daunts my spirit and courage . . . There will come a time
> when I will be forced to seek out a sad teaching job in the country or some-
> where on the coast of Guinea. If you die I shall really have no one left to care
> about me, and talent is nothing, except in fortunate circumstances.

And while he was writing the second volume of fairy tales, for publication at
Christmas 1835, he told Henriette Hanck:

> I do have this *idée fixe* that the writer whom *Maanedsskriftet* [*The Monthly
> Review*] described as once showing great promise but that this hope had gone,
> the boy whom one of our leading men told to remember that he was only a
> poor boy, and to whom Bishop Mynster twelve years ago said it was a blessing
> that he be allowed to study—that one day his name will be as famous as theirs.
> This is what I want! If it doesn't happen now, something must be done differ-
> ently, in the other world where we are all to be considered as children of the
> same father, that is, as equals.

Andersen's closest friends, Henriette and Edvard Collin, by Wilhelm Marstrand, 1842. To Edvard, Andersen wrote: "No one have I been so angry at as you! No one have I wanted to thrash as much, no one has brought more tears to my eyes, but neither has anyone been loved so much by me as you."

In the shadows of social unease, too, was his uncertain sexuality, for which he had been trying to find a language for years. In July 1835 he was staying as he did most summers at the estate of Lykkesholm, a lively Funen manor house full of entertainment and dancing, and from here he wrote to Edvard, "If you looked down to the bottom of my soul, you would understand fully the source of my longing and—pity me. Even the open, transparent lake has its unknown depths which no divers know." His emotional drive at this time was the search for a way of expressing what he was not allowed to speak out, socially and sexually, and from the safe distance of Funen he composed a letter addressing Edvard in the intimate form which he had been forbidden to use, as "Du." "My dear faithful Edvard," he began,

> How often do I not think about you. How open does your soul not lie before me. I wonder if you understand me, understand my love as I have perceived you. At this moment I see you as I suppose blessed spirits see each other, I could press you to my heart! Is it infatuation? No it is a pure noble feeling. There must also be moments when you feel something like it. All good people must feel like that. At this moment no "De" icy cold comes between us, I say "Du," and your lips greet me with the same sound as you shall utter first in the next world. Oh, if only I were rich, we would then both fly to Italy, the wonderful Italy which I have not enjoyed at all. Oh, if only we were there together, if only for a month! Edvard, I have many young friends, yet I love no one like you, I disregard them. Am I vain? I feel a power of spirit the world has not seen samples of, but I, the poor child, feel like amongst the best and first of the age and you are near me in spirit and thought. At moments I look up to you and then I love you as I could love the one whom I shall tell you about when with God.

He never sent this letter, yet to write it was emotional relief. Just after leaving Lykkesholm, he sent instead a version of it in which Edvard's fiancée was invited to speak for him; he asked him to tell Jette to say "I love you" from him, because she was free to say "Du." But at the end of August, as he was planning his new novel *OT*, he could not resist writing Edvard a love letter which he did send, and which shows how he still saw the novel as a route to expressing his intertwined social and sexual desires:

> I long for you, yes, this moment I long for you as if you were a lovely girl from Calabria, with her dark eyes and stirring glance. I never had a brother, but if I did, I could not have loved him as I love you, and yet—you do not return my feelings! This pains me—or perhaps this is in fact what ties me even more strongly to you. My soul is proud . . . I have clung to you; you have I . . . *bastare!*; this is a good Italian verb, which in Nyhavn might be translated as "Shut up!"
>
> There is a character in my new novel which borrows heavily from your personality. You will see how dear you are to me, with what care I treat the character; but you do have faults and the character will get even more than you have. He will get faults that you have—can you forgive me? He hurts the hero of the book once in the same way that I was . . . Our friendship is a strange creation. No one have I been so angry at as you! No one have I wanted to thrash

as much as you, no one has brought more tears to my eyes, but neither has anyone been loved so much by me as you . . .

God give that you become very poor and I very rich, distinguished, a nobleman. Then I would properly initiate you into the mystery, you would learn to
appreciate me more than now. Oh, is there an eternal life . . . there we shall
learn to understand and appreciate each other. There I shall no longer be the
destitute one, needing friends and appreciation, there we shall be equal.

This was among the last love letters he sent Edvard. It is significant that his
discovery of the fairy tale in 1835–1836 coincided with the peak of his obsession with Edvard, as he waited for Edvard's marriage in 1836, knowing that it
would put a permanent distance between them. In his account of their
friendship, Edvard recorded Andersen's emotional frustration: "He would
often threaten to use this or that expression about me, but it most often ended
with him saying, 'It is really annoying that one cannot anger you.' " Over the
next year, however, unconsciously at first, but with greater awareness by
the time he wrote "The Little Mermaid" in 1836, Andersen began to perceive
the fairy tale as a medium whose formal distance from reality would allow him
to write as he was and felt—not only as the social outsider but as the forbidden lover. During that Funen summer, he began two further tales, "Thumbelina" and "The Travelling Companion," where the small and downtrodden
pursue their own happiness and triumph through their fantasies of greatness.

By the second volume of *Eventyr*, he was more consciously a literary author,
developing his own material rather than refining folk tales. "Thumbelina,"
the story of a thumb-sized young girl, owes its inspiration not only to "Tom
Thumb" but also to Hoffmann's hallucinatory, erotic *Meister Floh*, where a
tiny lady a span in length torments the hero. But Andersen makes of it an
original tale.

Thumbelina is snatched from her walnut shell bed by a toad who intends
her to marry her son. She flees from the stream to live with the birds and the
butterflies, but when winter comes she nearly freezes to death: "every
snowflake that fell on her was like a whole scoopful on us, for we are big and
she was no bigger than your thumb"—Andersen's playfulness with perspec-
tives is assured. She goes to live with a field mouse, but escapes again when
velvet-coated Mr. Mole courts her and wants to keep her underground. On
the back of a swallow whom she has rescued from death, she flies "to the

warm countries" of orange and lemon trees and grape vines, and is married to the King of the Flowers.

> "Goodbye! Goodbye!" said the swallow; and off it flew from the warm countries, far away back to Denmark. There it had a little nest over the window of the man who can tell fairy tales; to him it sang "T-weet! T-weet!" and it's from there that we have the whole story.

This is Andersen's signature, and also the first of many identifications he makes with the swallow, the migratory bird whose pattern of life his own travelling days were coming to resemble. The story is also the first of many to dramatize the sufferings of the outsider who is different and therefore an object of mockery. Thumbelina is derided by the cockchafers, left to freeze in winter when the animals hibernate, forced to flee her native land and finds a home in the south—Andersen's interpretation of his Italian journey. Her persecutors are small comic masterpieces: the bourgeois Field Mouse, kind-hearted, house-proud and conventional, who loses patience when Thumbelina turns down a sensible match ("Now don't you be stubborn, or I'll bite you with my white tooth. You're getting a nice husband there. And as for his black velvet coat—why, the queen herself hasn't got one like it"), and the scholarly Mole, a rodent Casaubon who insists she "live with him deep down under the earth and never come out into the warm sunshine, as that was nothing in his line . . . he was such a thinking man."

Children love the cast of animals here; though animals had appeared in fables and folk tales before—Aesop, Perrault's "Puss in Boots," the Grimms' tales—Andersen was the first to play on the details of their human/animal duality, and so initiated a popular strain in children's books (from *The Tale of Peter Rabbit* and *The Wind in the Willows*, to *A Bear Called Paddington* and beyond). Oscar Wilde picked up the image of the swallow as a symbol of romance and the freedom of nature in "The Happy Prince," and for Andersen too the underlying theme is nature and the emotions versus the dark burrows of academic and social constraint.

"Thumbelina," like "Little Ida's Flowers," is a fantasy; with "The Travelling Companion" Andersen returned to the folk tale, but injected more of himself into it than he had done in the first volume. It is the story of John, an orphaned, pious boy who protects a corpse from hooligans, and then finds himself accompanied on his wanderings by a "travelling companion" who carries a pair of swan's wings. They come to a town where a princess is choosing a husband by asking her suitors three questions: she will marry the one who answers correctly, but anyone who fails is beheaded, and the city is in mourning because so many youths have lost their heads.

John determines to venture to court, and while he sleeps the night before, the travelling companion dons the swan's wings and flies to the princess's window. Just before midnight, amid the roll of thunder and storms, she flies out with a pair of black wings to a mountain to visit an ugly sorcerer. The travelling companion follows and hears the sorcerer tell her to ask her new suitor what she is thinking of, and that the answer is one of her shoes. His price is the suitor's eyes, which she must bring him to eat the next day, when his head is cut off.

But, primed by the travelling companion, John answers correctly, the princess "went as white as a sheet and trembled all over," and the king turned somersaults of joy. The next day the same scenario, and another correct answer—the princess's glove. The third night, the sorcerer advises the princess to think of his head, whereupon the travelling companion chops it off, wraps it in a handkerchief and tells John to show it to the princess as his answer. He is victorious and they are married, "but of course the princess was still a witch and she didn't love John a bit." So the travelling companion gives him three swan feathers and some magic lotion, in which he must bathe the princess. He ducks her three times, and she surfaces first "a big jet-black swan with glittering eyes," squirming in his hands, then a white swan, and finally a loving princess. Her spell is broken; the travelling companion, the ghost of the corpse, goes to rest in peace; and "John was the king of the whole country."

If Andersen had pushed the erotic out of his mind in writing his first volume of tales, it resurfaced in this gruesome story with a vengeance. John is a self-portrait—there are echoes of Andersen in his reverence for his dead father, in his intimate relationship with God ("Our dear Lord, I could kiss you," he says, as Andersen himself had written in his diary in 1825), in his sexual innocence/desire ("On seeing her, John went as red as a fire and could scarcely speak a word"). But the frigid princess, who recalls the heroine in the ancient story of *Turandot* and in her black- and white-winged transformations anticipates Odette and Odile in *Swan Lake*, is also Andersen: protective of her virginity, terrified of the opposite sex, living in a world of fantasy at the sorcerer's palace. Andersen always luxuriated in the ghoulish, which he mixed here with the human touch of social satire:

> The cushions for sitting on were little black mice biting one another in the tail.
> Up above this was a roof of rose-coloured cobwebs, studded with the prettiest

little greenflies that shone like jewels . . . Big black grasshoppers played Jews' harps and the owl beat its own stomach, as it hadn't got a drum . . . Tiny little goblins with jack-o'lanterns on their caps danced round the hall. The courtiers, who now came in as well, were so grand and genteel; though to anyone with eyes it was plain to see what they were. They were no more than broomsticks with cabbages for heads . . . they were only for show.

The sexual malaise, Andersen's own frustrations, are palpable in this tale. Together, "The Travelling Companion" and "Thumbelina" delineate the essential subjects of Andersen's tales—love, death, fate, survival—and put in place much of the private mythology that dominates them: swallows and swans as birds of travel and good fortune, the symbolic significance of shoes ("The Red Shoes," "The Galoshes of Fortune"), which hark back to his father's workshop. Between them, Andersen included "The Naughty Boy," which stakes out an adult audience with a whimsical account of a poet slain by Cupid. The first volume of *Eventyr* marked a new poetic voice; the second showed the development of artist and personality.

"What nonsense is this to stuff into the child's head?" asks the councillor in "Little Ida's Flowers." The first reviews of the fairy tales, which appeared in 1836, were hostile. The critics, Andersen complained in *The Fairy Tale of My Life*, could not get away from their old preconceived notions: "The *Monthly Review* never deigned to mention [the tales] at all, and in *Dannora*, another critical journal, I was advised not to waste my time in writing wonder stories. I lacked the usual form of that kind of poetry; I would not study models . . ." There was outrage at the chatty, laughing style which flew in the face of traditional literary diction and much harping on the lack of morals. *Dansk Litteraturtidende* (*The Danish Literary Times*) wrote: "It is not meaningless convention that one does not put words together in print in the same disordered manner as one may do quite acceptably in oral speech . . . What is delivered to them [the children] must always be above them, and it is also such things they rather want to hear."

The reviewer objected that "The Naughty Boy" lacked "poetry," that "Little Ida's Flowers" imitated Hoffmann—"whether it is written for children or adults, we are of the opinion that it will satisfy neither"—but acknowledged "Thumbelina" to be "the most delightful fairy tale you could wish for." Even favourable comments, though, illustrated the conventions that Andersen was working against: his friend the critic Carsten Hauch wrote to him that he objected to the moral indifference of "The Tinderbox," but that he admired the delicate nobility of the Queen in "The Princess and the Pea." The disapproving critics show just how radical Andersen was in overturning the expectation of stilted, educational writing for children.

Offering something so different from staple fare, his stories were soon immensely popular with children. Henriette Hanck wrote to Andersen of a child who had told her the *Eventyr* was the most wonderful book in the world, and Andersen wrote the following to Henriette Wulff in 1836: "Wherever I go and children are there they have read my fairy tales, and bring me the most beautiful roses and kiss me, but the girls are so very little, and I have asked several of them if I may be allowed to draw the interest on the capital in about six or seven years."

The response among Andersen's friends was mixed. Several saw, as Ørsted had done when reading the manuscript, that the fairy tales were an achievement beyond anything else he had written. Henriette Hanck wrote after the second volume that Andersen would certainly win posterity for himself, and Heiberg rated the tales higher than Andersen's novels. Others were less sure. Sending Ingemann the second volume, Andersen wrote: "I hope you will be more pleased with these than with the earlier ones. Oddly, many people put these even higher than *The Improvisatore*; others, however, wish, like you, that I had not written them. What shall I believe?"

CHAPTER 9

Walking on Knives

1836–1837

*The latest tale, "The Little Mermaid," you will like; it is . . . except for The Little
Abbess's Story in* The Improvisatore *the only one of my works that has affected me
while I was writing it. You smile, perhaps? Well now, I don't know how other writers feel!* I *suffer with my characters, I share their moods, whether good or bad, and I
can be nice or nasty according to the scene on which I happen to be working.*
—HANS CHRISTIAN ANDERSEN, letter to Ingemann, 11 February 1837

By the beginning of 1836, Andersen was beginning to luxuriate in both the
public image and the private world of the successful writer. He was thirty, he
had an acclaimed novel and two volumes of tales behind him; he was writing
a second novel, *OT*, to be published in April, and he already had the idea for
his most ambitious fairy story so far, "The Daughters of the Air," which later
became "The Little Mermaid." The artist C. A. Jensen painted him in 1836,
and the portrait, the most brilliant one ever painted of the writer, marks a
turning point in the way Andersen presented himself. Jensen's Andersen has
a tender, girlish face, with cheeks more fleshed out than in the portraits from
1833 and 1834, eyes shining with intelligence and pleasure, and an expression
that is confident, even vain. Andersen is basking in the attention of painter
and viewer; sitting with his arm resting on the back of a chair, a large ring
glistening on his left hand, wearing a big black bow-tie and jacket, he looks
almost foppish. Jensen's portrait shows a man aware of his public role, and
happy with it. "The ladies sat on chairs round about," Andersen wrote when
this picture was shown, "looking through opera glasses at the author who, in
the portrait, is of extremely genial demeanour. I find it delightful!"

He still lived modestly in his rented rooms in Nyhavn, but the success of
The Improvisatore made him less worried about his finances, and more confident about a receptive audience. He felt he was at the height of his powers.

"My writing years began when I returned from abroad," he told Henriette Wulff, continuing:

> I may have four or six years more when I can still write well, and I must use them. I am making it comfortable at home, the fire is crackling, and then my Muse visits me; she tells me strange fairy tales, shows me odd characters from everyday life—noblemen as well as commoners—and says "See those people, you know them; draw them and—they will live!" This is asking a great deal, I know, but that is what she says.

To Henriette Hanck he wrote of the winter of 1835–1836:

> No other winter has gone by as quietly and happily as this one. *The Improvisatore* has won me respect among the noblest and best people, even the general public have begun to show more respect for me; luckily I have no financial worries, and lately I have been able to make my life comfortable. The publishers send me magazines, Reitzel sends me books and prints, and then I sit in my dressing gown with my brightly coloured slippers, my legs up on the sofa; the stove purring, the tea urn singing on the table, and the incense is enjoyable. Then I think of the poor boy in Odense wearing wooden shoes, and then my heart melts, and I bless the Good Lord. Now I have reached my peak, I feel. Later it will go downhill.

How much he was still occupied with the poor boy in Odense was shown in his novel *OT*. The title refers both to the hero's name, Otto Thostrup, and to Odense Tugthus, Odense Gaol, where he was born and whose initials are branded on his shoulder. Andersen had high hopes of the novel—"I want to be Denmark's best novelist," he told Henriette Hanck—but from his first references to it there is something flat and schematic that meant it never took off as fiction. "It is a description of our own time from 1829 to 1835 and is set in Denmark only," he wrote. "I think the fact that the writer describes what he knows, the environment where he lives, will be valuable and will give the work a particular interest. In future years people will have a true picture of our time, and if I have been successful in giving that, well, then the book will gain in interest with age." He subtitled it *Life in Denmark* and, to the annoyance of his Danish readers, explained many details about national life with an eye on the German market where *The Improvisatore* had done so well.

The novel combines a realistic portrayal of Denmark with elements of romance and melodrama, such as the appearance of long-lost relatives and a

Andersen in Copenhagen, aged thirty-one, by C. A. Jensen, 1836.

noble mother who was mistaken for a convict. It tells of Otto's flight from his secret past, his terror that an evil girl called Sidsel is his sister and his friendship with Baron Wilhelm, who resembles Edvard and will not say "Du" to him. It is a haunted, frightened work, in which sexuality is identified with proletarian depravity, and the hero is a melancholy Byronic figure who reflects the depressive side of Andersen. Otto is driven by terror of exposure; when his stigma of the letters branded on his skin—emblem of an internalized sense of shame—seems about to be discovered, he tries to commit suicide. Certain elements are autobiographical—Andersen feared that his own half-sister Karen-Marie, who may have been a prostitute, would one day appear to drag him down, while, as we have seen, the episode where Otto/Andersen and Wilhelm/Edvard, dressed as a girl, smother one another with kisses, is a wish-fulfilment version of a friendship without limits.

Andersen commented in the novel that "Our tale is no creation of fancy; it is the reality in which we live; bone of our bone and flesh of our flesh," and his anxiety about his origins, his own flesh and blood, and about forbidden erotic desires, fuel *OT*. He worked on it between writing "The Travelling Companion" and "The Little Mermaid," two fairy tales which deal with fear of sexuality. They transcend his immediate dilemmas by a use of symbolism and fantasy, and take on a breadth of meaning which Andersen was unable to achieve in the genre of the realistic novel.

OT was not well-received by the critics, while many readers who had been stirred by the bright pictures of Italy in *The Improvisatore* found the new novel disappointingly grey and dull. By the time it appeared, Andersen had anyway turned back to fairy tales. On 13 May 1836 he wrote that " 'The Daughters of the Sea' is going to be written either in Tolderlund [the Iversens' home on the canal outside Odense] or at Lykkesholm; it will soon be finished." Andersen was always productive when being pampered at the manor houses of the nobility, and he worked on "The Little Mermaid" through the summer of 1836, staying on Funen to avoid Edvard's wedding on 10 August. A few days before the wedding, he visited St. Nicholas Church in Svendborg, a small port on the south coast of Funen, and noting down details of the family portraits as he wandered past the vaults, he wrote desolately in his diary, "On either side, old tombstones, and on the left, a black one which looks like the plate of an iron stove. Almighty God! I have got only you, you steer my fate, I must give myself to you. Please give me a living! Please give me a bride! My blood wants love, as my heart does."

To Edvard, he wrote a letter of congratulations which, in discussing his own bleak feelings about his love affairs with women, was also a valediction to the sentimental aspect of their friendship. "My dear, dear Edvard—God bless and go with you! Indeed you will be happy, and you deserve it," he wrote, then, "Like Moses I stand on the mountain gazing into the promised land which I shall never reach . . . But my feelings are strong as yours, as you love your Jette, I have also loved! Twice have I loved, but it was just self-deception, though I expect the self-deceived suffers the most. I shall never forget it, but even you and I never talk about it. This is one of the sufferings one cannot speak of even with one's closest friend."

Both knew the friendship was about to enter a new phase. Edvard admitted after Andersen's death that he had not played the part of a sentimental friend, and that this must have pained Andersen. Edvard's lack of sympathy, not only with Andersen, but also with any sense of human nature as richly complex, disturbed or divided within itself—the artist's essential viewpoint—is shown by a comment he made in his memoir of the friendship: "I cannot deviate from the opinion that the best service to Andersen is done by showing the world how diseased a mind he had, so that it is clear to everyone, that everything repulsive, everything that the world was scandalized by, was caused by this mind." There was nevertheless something beyond duty which drew him to Andersen, and he expressed his affection by offering throughout his life untiring practical help—he dealt with all Andersen's finances, publishers' contracts, proofs, he corrected his spelling and grammar and sometimes copied out his manuscripts for him. In death he accepted Andersen's dream of the last leveller: Edvard, his wife and Andersen were buried in the same grave.

Meanwhile, Andersen concluded in his letter that Italy, rather than a woman, was his bride. As he identified Italy with art and with his creative breakthrough, he may already have thought himself wedded to his writing. In his first days in Copenhagen, aged fourteen, he had identified the theatre as his love, his equivalent of Paul's desire for Virginie. Now, in the autumn and winter of 1836, he threw himself into finishing the story in which he drew himself as the "intellectually amphibious creature" he had painted in *The Improvisatore*, and which explicitly suggests immortality as a consolation for the loss of love and sex.

The much-altered manuscript of "The Little Mermaid" shows how persistently Andersen worked at it. It was completed on 23 January 1837 and on 11 February Andersen wrote to Ingemann, whom he had never forgiven for not liking the first volume of *Eventyr*, about how deeply involved he was with it:

> The latest tale, "The Little Mermaid," you *will* like; it is better than "Thumbelina" and is, except for The Little Abbess's Story in *The Improvisatore*, the only one of my works that has affected me while I was writing it. You smile, perhaps? Well now, I don't know how other writers feel! *I* suffer with my characters, I share their moods, whether good or bad, and I can be nice or nasty according to the scene on which I happen to be working. This latest, third instalment of tales for children is probably the best, and you're going to like it! Yes, your wife will like it very much! I have not, like de la Motte Fouqué in *Undine*, allowed the mermaid's acquiring of an immortal soul to depend upon an alien creature, upon the love of a human being. I'm sure that's wrong! It would depend rather much on chance, wouldn't it? I *won't* accept that sort of thing in this world. I have permitted my mermaid to follow a more natural,

more divine path. No other writer, I believe, has indicated it yet, and that's why I am glad to have it in my tale. You'll see for yourself!

On 9 March he wrote to Henriette Hanck about his confidence in the work: "My tales are going to be published at the same time. They comprise 'The Little Mermaid,' which is definitely good, and 'The Emperor's New Clothes.' My love to little Bertha [a pupil of Miss Hanck's], and tell her mermaids can't be called Bertha, otherwise I would have given the little mermaid that name."

"The Little Mermaid" is bold and original. It opens in a kingdom at the bottom of the sea, where "the water is as blue as the petals on the fairest cornflower, and as clear as the purest glass." Here live six mermaid sisters, enchanting sirens who sing during storms and lure sailors to the depths: "They had lovely voices, more beautiful than human beings," and whenever a storm was blowing up and they thought vessels might be wrecked, they swam along in front of the ships and sang beautifully about how lovely it was at the bottom of the sea."

With exquisite detail and some wit—the grandmother mermaid was "proud of her ancestry, and therefore went about with twelve oysters on her tail" instead of the usual six—Andersen returned to the colours of Italy, the blues and reds of Vesuvius and the Bay of Naples, to paint the mermaid's world as an erotic invitation:

> Outside the Palace was a large garden with trees of deep blue and fiery red; the fruits all shone like gold, and the flowers like a blazing fire with stalks and leaves that were never still. The soil itself was the finest sand, but blue like a sulphur flame. Over everything down there lay a strange blue gleam; you really might have thought you were standing high up in the air with nothing to see but sky above and below you, rather than you were at the bottom of the sea. When there was a dead calm you caught a glimpse of the sun, which looked like a purple flower pouring out all light from its cup.

But the mermaids are also fascinated by life on land, and when each is fifteen, she is allowed to swim up to the surface of the sea to glimpse the towns and countryside and people. The youngest, loveliest mermaid falls in love with a prince and saves him from shipwreck, and then "fonder and fonder did she grow of human beings, and more and more did she wish she might go and live among them." Learning that human beings have immortal souls, whereas mermaids live three hundred years, then die "just like the green reeds: once they have been cut they never grow green again," her aspiration

Work by one of Andersen's favourite illustrators:
The Little Mermaid *by Vilhelm Pedersen.*

divides itself into two—a desire to marry the prince and a desire to become immortal.

In folklore, a mermaid can acquire a soul by winning a man's love, so the Little Mermaid goes to consult the hideous Sea Witch. For the price of the Mermaid's voice, the witch says, she will turn her fish's tail into legs, and the Mermaid can try to win the prince and immortality, but she can never return to the sea, and if the prince marries another, she adds, "you shall never have your immortal soul . . . your heart will break, and you will become foam on the water."

Without her voice, the Mermaid charms the prince by her grace and beauty. She becomes his companion, but he thinks of her as a sexless creature, a sort of mute page, and he takes a lovely conventional princess as his bride instead. At the betrothal party, the Little Mermaid "knew that this was the last evening she would see him, the person for whom she had left her family and her home, given away her lovely voice, and daily suffered endless torments without his having realized any of it." As she waits for death, her five sisters rise up out of the sea, their luscious hair no longer billowing, for they have cut it off and given it to the Sea Witch in exchange for a knife with which the Mermaid can kill the prince: when his blood spatters over her feet, they will grow together into a fishtail and she can return to the sea. She refuses, throws the knife into the sea, and her body melts into the foam.

She is transformed into one of the "daughters of the air," transparent, ethereal figures who "do not have an eternal soul . . . but they are able to create one for themselves by doing good deeds," and so after three hundred years "share in man's eternal happiness." In a coda, the young reader is invited to help: the daughters of the air explain that "every time we find a good child . . . God will shorten our period of trial . . . but if we see a naughty child, then we must weep tears of sorrow, and each tear will add a day to our period of trial."

This disturbing, brilliant story made Andersen's name as an international writer and is one of the most famous fairy tales in the world; the bronze statue of the Little Mermaid in Copenhagen is the country's national monument and attracts millions of visitors. But to modern readers, the tale is distasteful as well as moving: sentimental, misogynistic and moralizing, it shows Andersen enjoying the Mermaid's suffering and offering an oppressive mix of self-sacrifice, silence and expiation as ideals of female behaviour. This was among the first of Andersen's tales to be translated into English, in 1846, and it is clear why the Victorians loved it: primitive folklore is layered over with a Christian message. Yet the rich symbolism of "The Little Mermaid" bears many meanings, and it is a tale one returns to at different periods in life. As a tragic account of the permanency of female love encountering male inconstancy, it is timeless. As the drama of the suffering of a social outsider and an unrequited lover who cannot express his or her passion, it is still poignant.* This is surely how Andersen identified with the tale, allying himself in his bisexuality to the mermaid's sense of being a different species from humankind,† and in his position with Edvard—held in affection but never considered as an erotic possibility, and unable to proclaim his feelings—relating to her hopeless love for the prince.

For Andersen, emotional invisibility was the result of the denied realization of sensuality. In the manuscript, there is a deleted, extended ending, in which the mermaid says, "I myself shall strive to win an immortal soul . . .

---

*Andersen's biographer Hans Brix in 1907 interpreted the Little Mermaid's unrequited love for the prince as Andersen's love for Louise Collin, and all that the Collin connection meant for him. The bottom of the sea is the Odense "swamp" from which he came and the dry land above the cultivated Copenhagen class to which he sought to belong, so that this tale is a fantasy version of the social struggle in the novel *OT* which preceded it.

†Andersen's Little Mermaid has often been considered as a homo-erotic character—in Thomas Mann's *Doktor Faustus*, for example, she is one of the novel's leitmotifs, of special importance to the hero Adrian Leverkuhn, who is an artist with homosexual desires.

that in the world beyond I may be reunited with him to whom I gave my whole heart," and it is possible to see this deletion as a fictional parallel to the letters of 1835 imagining Edvard and himself united "before God." He finally deleted it because he could not bear, as he wrote to Ingemann, for individual salvation to depend on another's love. Deliberately, and unique among all versions of the mermaid myth, he separated the Mermaid's double goal of love and an eternal soul, and awarded her immortality as a consolation for sexual disappointment. In human terms, the conventional version of the legend, followed by de la Motte Fouqué and others, is "true"—most of us seek immortality through sexuality and children. But Andersen's version of "The Little Mermaid" was true for him—his bid for immortality in art. Erotically disappointed, he was by 1837 beginning to transform his longing for sex and love into a longing for immortality.

In his letters to Edvard he had dreamed of "the next world"; an eternal soul was for him an essential component of the human condition. Andersen saw immortality as a recompense for earthly suffering, and like the Little Mermaid, who turns down three hundred years of life for the chance to strive for it, he believed life was meaningless without it. His writings are dotted with a casual but absolute acceptance of the difference between "this world" and "that other world" to come. His desperation for fame and his concern with his reputation should be seen in this context; from 1837 until his death he clung to the idea that his muse was his substitute for human love, and it recurs throughout his writings. At the end of his life, for example, he congratulated a young correspondent on his recent marriage, saying, "You have got yourself a home, a loving wife, and you are happy! God bless you and her! At one time I too dreamed of such happiness, but it was not to be granted to me. Happiness came to me in another form, came as my muse that gave me a wealth of adventure and songs."

Symbolically, "The Little Mermaid" expresses psychological truths in the same way as folk tales. Like "Sleeping Beauty," "Snow White" and "Rapunzel," it is a coming-of-age fairy tale in which a young girl at fifteen or sixteen is suddenly forced to cope with her own sexuality and the responses her beauty arouses. Like "Sleeping Beauty," it has images of blood which may symbolize the onset of menstruation, and it is imbued with an adolescent fear of sex which the 32-year-old Andersen shared—when the mermaid's tail becomes two separated legs, she is told:

> It will hurt, it will feel as if a sword is going through your body . . . You will walk more gracefully than any dancer, but every time your foot touches the

ground it will feel as though you were walking on knives so sharp your blood must flow.

But its erotic charge is also rooted in the ancient myths of mermaids and selkies, melusines and sea-brides, who marry mortals on certain conditions and whose silence is often part of the bargain. Nineteenth-century Romanticism, drawn to the mermaid as both representative of a dangerous pagan eroticism and as a being striving for human redemption through love, seized the legend with enthusiasm. Andersen had toyed with it in his poem *Agnete*, and he was familiar with Ingemann's *Creatures of the Sea*, with Tieck's *Sehr Wunderbare Historie von der Melusina* and with Oehlenschläger's *Vaulundurs Saga*, where a mermaid consoles the hero, as well as with Bournonville's ballet about a woman in fairy form, *La Sylphide*, which opened in Copenhagen in 1836. But the biggest influence on "The Little Mermaid," as Andersen's references to him imply, was de la Motte Fouqué's *Undine* (1811), a German medieval-style romance about a knight torn between a woman and a childishly captivating water-sprite, who when she is rejected vanishes over the side of the boat—"only little waves were yet whispering and sobbing around the boat, and they seemed almost distinctly to say 'Oh woe, woe! Ah remain true!'" Later, *Undine* also inspired Tchaikovsky's *Swan Lake*, Dvořák's *Rusalka* and Maeterlinck's *Pelléas et Mélisande*, to which Debussy wrote the music for his opera: all are romantic works fixated on the frozen beauty of the *femme fatale* who is either wholly silent or will not speak about her underwater past. Andersen's story quickly became the most popular literary telling; Oscar Wilde's "The Fisherman and his Soul" (1891) and H. G. Wells's *The Sea Lady* (1902) are among many works which are indebted to it.

The third *Eventyr* pamphlet, containing "The Little Mermaid" and "The Emperor's New Clothes," was published in April 1837. The stories were a good match, a rich tragedy complemented by a punchy social satire which Andersen altered at the last minute and so made into a classic. He took the outline of "The Emperor's New Clothes" from a medieval Spanish collection of stories based on Arab and Jewish sources called *Libro de Patronio*, by Infante don Juan Manuel. In the Spanish version, the Moorish king is conned by fraudulent weavers who claim to make a suit which will be invisible to any man who is not the son of his presumed father. Andersen, who avoided anything *risqué* from his sources, ridiculed instead courtly pride and intellectual vanity: his cheating tailors offer a clothes-mad emperor material which "had the peculiarity of being invisible to anyone who wasn't fit for his post or was hopelessly stupid." In this story, with its simple neo-classical lines, Andersen is the comic virtuoso:

> "What on earth!" thought the emperor. "I don't see a thing! Why, this is terrible! Am I stupid? Am I unfit to be emperor? This is the most dreadful thing that could have befallen me!" ... "Oh, it's beautiful," said the emperor, "it has my most gracious approval!" And he nodded with satisfaction as he looked at the empty loom; he wasn't going to say he couldn't see anything ...
>
> Before the morning of the procession the imposters sat up all night with over sixteen candles burning ... They pretended to take the cloth off the loom, they clipped at the air with their great scissors, they sewed with needles that weren't threaded ...

In the original draft, Andersen ended with everyone simply admiring the clothes:

> "I must put on that suit whenever I walk in a procession or appear before a gathering of people," said the emperor, and the whole town talked about his wonderful new clothes.

This was the version he mentioned to Henriette Hanck in March, and about which he was uncertain. But when the manuscript was already at the printers, he hit upon a new ending, and wrote on 25 March to Edvard, who was proof-reading the book for him:

> The tale "The Emperor's New Clothes" ends with the following sentence: "I must put on that suit etc." I want this to be deleted entirely and the following inserted instead, as it will give everything a more satirical appearance:
> "But he hasn't got anything on!" cried a little child.
> "Dear me! Listen to what the pretty innocent says!" cried its father. And it was whispered from man to man what the child had said.
> "He hasn't got anything on!" says a little child. "He hasn't got anything on!"
> "Why, but he hasn't got anything on!" they all shouted at last. And the emperor winced, and felt that they were right. But he thought to himself: "I must go through with the procession now." And he drew himself up more proudly than ever, while the chamberlains walked behind him, bearing the train that wasn't there.

Thus the romantic image of the child as uniquely wise and pure, which inspired Andersen's entire *œuvre*, here shaped his comic masterpiece at the last minute. For years, he had himself been the precocious naive child admitted into the grown-up parlour, observing the hypocrisy and snobbery of Copenhagen society; here was his exposé. "The Emperor's New Clothes" is a byword for human vanity, and with "The Ugly Duckling" is Andersen's most famous story. Both are known by people who have never heard of Hans Christian Andersen; we regard them, as we do folk tales, as part of our common heritage.

"The Little Mermaid" and "The Emperor's New Clothes" marked a new maturing of talent in Andersen's work. There was nothing tentative or unworked out, as in the first two volumes of tales: here was a confident writer who knew exactly the effects he wanted and achieved them with masterly assurance. He collected these two stories together with the earlier pamphlets and had them bound in one volume, which sold at seventy-two shillings. A title page and a table of contents were supplied and Andersen wrote a preface in which he dared his audience to underestimate his tales:

> None of my writings has been so differently appraised as *Tales, Told for Children*. While some people whose judgement I value very highly think they are the best I have written, others have found these Fairy Tales to be highly unimportant, and have advised me not to continue them. Such different opinions, together with the unmistakable silence public criticism has passed upon them, have dampened my desire to continue this type of fiction. Therefore a year has passed before the third pamphlet has followed the two preceding . . .
>
> With this third pamphlet the Fairy Tales are now gathered in one little volume. It will depend on the impression it makes on the public if this is to be the only one. A poet is always a poor man in his own little country. Fame is therefore the golden bird he has to catch! Time will tell if I catch it by telling Fairy Tales.

CHAPTER 10

Le Poète, C'est Moi!

1837–1840

I covet honour in the same way as a miser covets gold; both are said to be empty, but one has to have something to get excited about in this world, otherwise one would collapse and rot.

—HANS CHRISTIAN ANDERSEN,
letter to Henriette Hanck, 20 September 1837

"My name is gradually starting to shine," Andersen wrote in September 1837, "and that is the only thing I live for." Throughout the year, he chased fame tirelessly. When a French journalist, Xavier Marmier, arrived in Copenhagen to explore Scandinavian culture, Andersen sought him out and told him his life story. Marmier was mesmerized. " 'But may all of Europe know about it?' he asked, and I was—would you call it sufficiently vain?—to add 'I belong to the world! Just let them all know, what I'm thinking and feeling!,'" Andersen reported to Henriette Hanck. The result was Marmier's biographical sketch *"La vie d'un poète,"* which appeared in the *Revue de Paris* of October 1837 and was one of the first reviews to spread Andersen's name beyond Denmark. Marmier also translated Andersen's poem "The Dying Child"; he rated him highly as a poet able to depict childhood pleasures and emotions, though he did not like the fairy tales—Andersen, he said, had attempted something comic, but his muse had not smiled on him, and the mask of fairy tale writer did not suit him.* Marmier's article was widely read; after it was published Andersen wrote to Henriette Hanck that Lady Byron had sent him a greeting after reading *"La vie d'un poète,"* adding, "and you know, le poète, c'est moi!"

---

*France, with a courtly fairy tale tradition going back to Perrault and Madame d'Aulnoy in the late seventeenth century, was much slower than Germany, England and the countries of eastern Europe to appreciate Andersen's mix of humour, earthiness and sentimentality.

Andersen set out, too, to win a broader Scandinavian public. He travelled to Sweden for the summer of 1837, and wrote: "I reckon this journey among the happiest I ever made." A Swedish poet composed a song in his honour; a voyage to Trollhättan was "like a fairy tale . . . the steamboat goes up across the lakes over the mountains, from whence may be seen the outstretched pine and beech woods below. Immense sluices heave up and lower the vessel again, while the travellers ramble through the woods"; and on the boat to Stockholm, he made the acquaintance of the Swedish novelist Fredrika Bremer. He gave her a copy of *The Improvisatore*, which she read overnight in her cabin, and later translated into Swedish; of its author she noted, "A Mr. Andersen is here, of strange appearance, but straightforward, sensitive and warm-hearted, good, with a child-like piety, and the author of fine books!"

Back home, he finished his third novel, *Only a Fiddler* (*Kun en Spillemand*), which came out in November. As with "The Little Mermaid," it was among the writings with which he felt most involved—he called it "a spiritual blossom sprung out of the terrible struggle that went on in me between my poet nature and my hard surroundings." It is a sentimental story of two children, a poor boy called Christian and rich, Jewish Naomi, who are young playmates but grow up into different worlds. This was a favourite Andersen motif, to recur in "The Snow Queen," whose roof garden setting is anticipated in *Only a Fiddler*, and in several later stories—"Ib and Little Christine," "Under the Willow Tree" and "What Johanne Told."

Each time the boy is an Andersen alter ego; in *Only a Fiddler* he even shares Andersen's name. Christian is a talented violinist who lacks confidence, can find no patrons to support him and pursues Naomi in vain. She is described as "the mannish lady"; proud and ruthless in taking charge of her destiny, she too is an outsider because of her Jewishness—there is a compelling description of the last pogrom in Denmark, whose aftermath Andersen had witnessed on his arrival in Copenhagen in 1819. Naomi makes a disastrous marriage but remains haughty and spoiled: the novel concludes with her riding through Funen in a grand carriage and happening to come across Christian's funeral:

> The peasants stepped into the ditch with the coffin, to give the great gentlefolks room to pass; they uncovered their heads respectfully; and the noble lady, with the proud look and the charming smile, looked from the window and bowed.
>
> He was only a poor man whom they bore to the grave—only a fiddler!

Only a Fiddler smarts with a personal sense of social injustice which cramps it as fiction, but its theme is modern—like *OT,* and like "The Little Mermaid" in fantasy, it deals with characters trying to escape their background and finding themselves rootless in an alien, fast-changing world. Most lost is Naomi, whose sexual identity is consistently confused. In one episode she dresses up "in her male attire, which was so becoming to her, and with the little moustache on her beautiful upper lip." There is also a love scene on a ship between a circus rider called Ladislaf and a young Danish boy which reads:

> He had delicate, flexible limbs, the eye shewed power and good will, and upon the fresh lip curled the moustache. He was called Mr. Christian; according to his passport he was from Funen. He rested his arm on Ladislaf's shoulder; they stood arm-in-arm as they approached the coast of Mechlenburg ... The Danish boy pressed a kiss upon Ladislaf's lips. "I am thine," said he. "Only thine!" And Ladislaf answered, smiling, "Mine!—thou wast mine upon the sea!"

Only one page on does Andersen reveal that the boy is Naomi in disguise, travelling on Christian's passport—a scene of cross-dressed intimacy even more daring than the one in *OT.* For the rest of the novel Naomi, like the branded Otto in *OT,* lives in fear of being found out: "she was a lady, and her passport was drawn in the name of a man."

Only a Fiddler has none of the vengeful, working-class triumph of fairy tales such as "The Tinderbox" or "The Travelling Companion." Instead, hanging over it is the fatalistic, depressive worldview which made Andersen a natural writer of fairy tales—where fate governs all—but which is problematic in a novel attempting psychological and social realism. In Denmark the response was lacklustre, but in its German translation, *Nur ein Geiger,* the novel met rapturous acclaim, with many German readers in the 1830s and 1840s referring to it as "their Bible."

The work's most intriguing commentator was an unknown 25-year-old theology student called Søren Kierkegaard, who dedicated his entire first book to a critique of it. It was called *From the Papers of a Person Still Alive, Published Against his Will* and subtitled "On Andersen as a Novelist, with constant regard to his most recent work, *Only a Fiddler.*" Christian, said Kierkegaard, shared with his creator the lack of a coherent worldview and was a complainer who is pronounced a genius but whose only sign of special talent is that he suffers hardship and succumbs to it. Academic, dull, stilted—it was joked in Copenhagen that Kierkegaard and Andersen were the only readers who had actually finished it—the critique nevertheless contains extraordinary shots of perception. "The joyless struggle that is Andersen's in real life now repeats itself in his writing," wrote Kierkegaard, and he went on to define the struggle: Andersen's work "should rather be compared with those flowers which have male and female placed on the same stalk." Andersen had spent the 1830s trying to formulate ways of describing sexual ambivalence, and was one of very few writers who tried to find a language for homo-erotic desire before the term "homosexuality" was coined in 1869; Kierkegaard's response shows that perceptive readers were able to pick up his hints, and understand him.*

Only a Fiddler is the last work in which Andersen explores the role of the sexual amphibian. After Edvard's marriage, his interest in the theme simply faded. His letters to Edvard took on a new, business-like tone, and his overriding concern was his work and his fame. "I do really know that you all love me as a personality, indeed in the Home I am like a brother to you. Sometime you will also have to acknowledge my value as a poet, which in your family and in some others has no high place, and ranks below that of Hertz and Heiberg," he told Edvard. It was several years before he found a man to whom he was as drawn; in the meantime he pursued, mostly in his imagination, a few flirtations with women, while becoming increasingly certain that he would remain alone.

He wrote to Henriette Hanck:

I shall die alone like poor Christian in my novel. There is a girl who is lovely, spirited, kind and charming, she belongs to one of the most distinguished

---

*Despite his criticism, Kierkegaard, whose name means "cemetery" in Danish, may have been drawn to *Only a Fiddler* because he recognized in Andersen someone who struggled through fantasy with the same existential anxieties as himself. He noted in his diary, "You see, Andersen can tell a tale about the 'Galoshes of Fortune'—but I can tell a tale about shoes that pinch." In certain respects Andersen and Kierkegaard are similar. Both reacted against the bourgeois pretensions of Copenhagen's harmonious Golden Age; both were driven by what Kierkegaard called "the most agonizing isolation" in their own lives to describe the loneliness of modern man; both were consumed by their work and convinced of their own genius; both chose sexual abstinence and linked sex with fear and dread. Andersen forgave Kierkegaard's assault, and in 1848 answered it with some wit by sending him a volume of new tales with the note, "Dear Mr. Kirkegaard [*sic*], *Either* [i.e., whether] you like my little ones *Or* you do not like them, they come without *Fear and Trembling*, and that in itself is something. Sincerely, the Author." (Kierkegaard's books *Either/Or* and *Fear and Trembling* were published in 1843.)

families in Copenhagen, that is, distinguished in spirit; but I have no money and—I cannot even fall in love. Moreover, she is precisely half my age!—Thank God she has no idea that I more than like her, and she treats me like an elderly man whom she has known for many years. She trusts me completely and may well say to me one day "Andersen, you must congratulate me, I am engaged."

This was Sophie Ørsted, 16-year-old daughter of Andersen's friend and mentor Hans Christian Ørsted, and a few days later Andersen noted on 11 December:

Today Sophie got engaged. The last time I had dinner there with Marmier he said, "You are in love with her, I know. I can see it. Why don't you propose to her?" I thought all evening what a mistake it would be because I am poor. Last Saturday when I was there she was very kind, but in the evening I felt that it would be quite possible for me to live alone! . . . I shall never be engaged, and it would be a great misfortune if it were ever to take place. God, make the best happen! . . . I took her hand for the first time. I pressed it twice, and I was in excellent spirits, I was sure of that, for I didn't suffer and was infinitely relaxed. Now I'm at home, alone—alone as I shall always be. I might have told her this Christmas, but it would never have been good for her.

He referred to Sophie as a minor infatuation, but the episode teased out his sexual fears, for the same day some of the Collin family mocked him for not behaving like all other young men. Virginity, almost universally prized in women in the nineteenth century, was in many circles derided in men, and a number of doctors, including Theodor Collin, Edvard's younger brother, disapproved of abstinence on medical grounds. Andersen was unnerved: he made the excuse to himself that it was in order not to upset the Collin family that he had not indulged his desires, and now he felt a change in his behaviour: "I want to be like other men, I thought." But when Sophie became engaged, he was relieved not to have to enter the fray, and almost embraced the prospect of the celibate life. "Now I shall never be married, no young woman grows up for me any more, day by day I'm getting to be more and more a bachelor! Oh, just yesterday I could be counted among the young—this evening I am old!," he wrote. His sexual outlet continued to be masturbation, marked by a + in his diaries and his almanac, the diary-notebook, consisting mostly of a few words or a single sentence per entry, which he began to keep from 1833.

Publicly, his excuse for not marrying was poverty. Although he had been less worried about his finances since the success of *The Improvisatore* in 1835, he wrote to a young friend, Frederik Læssøe, soon after *Only a Fiddler* was published:

> No one can loathe talking about money and livelihood more than I do, but here and for this once let me tell you: there is a Goddess of Nuisance called Need who is to blame for most of my wants. You have no idea what a battle I have fought! My childhood went by without my learning anything. I have grown up in an environment of poverty and inanity; no one led me, no one gave any direction to my spiritual power: it burned like a will-o'-the-wisp. When at last I went to school I was treated so roughly and mechanically that it was a miracle I was not defeated. In public, before the audience, I have taken each step of my career as a poet; it has been a play by which the plate has been passed round to get food for the artist.

In December 1837 he sent the plate round again, writing to an aristocratic admirer, Count Rantzau-Breitenburg, whom he hoped would intercede on his behalf with King Frederik for an annual grant, without which, he said, "my work would be at an end, . . . my life's happiness is at stake."

While he was waiting for the outcome of the application, he sold a light-hearted tale, "The Galoshes of Fortune," to Reitzel for forty rixdollars—more than he had received for the whole first volume three years earlier, and a sign of his tales' popularity. He was still refining the colloquial style which was a key feature of the tales, and which appeared so effortless: in the first draft the story opens with a host giving a party "in order, as many will do, to obtain subscription tickets to the others' reciprocal invitations"; in the final version this is changed to the simple "then it's done and you can be invited back again."

By the time the tale appeared he was in high spirits. "Do you know what my most urbane friends are saying?" he wrote to Henriette Hanck on 27 April,

> That Andersen has become magnificently foppish, the biggest dandy! He wears a coat worth sixty rixdollars, with a velvet lining, a hat like an umbrella, and his figure—well, he grows more and more handsome every day. Jette Wulff says, "Previously, you were marvellously original, now you look like a groom-in-waiting or a lieutenant, ugh! a gracious, courtly gentleman!" Mrs. Drewsen [Ingeborg, Jonas's elder daughter] says, "Our friend is getting hand-

some in his old age, but he is still the same silly old fool as before. Is he supposed to be a *célèbre poète*? Well, if only you knew him as we know him."

This gives a fine picture of Andersen at his happiest in Copenhagen, shrieking with laughter at the benign mockery of those maternal women friends with whom he felt most relaxed and unthreatened. In his memoir of Andersen, Edvard Collin recounted how Andersen used deliberately to tell innocuous lies to the Collin family, and then scream with pleasure at being found out. Edvard also emphasized the generosity of his humour, which was often forgotten by those who criticized Andersen's self-pity and vanity: "In conversation, when irony came in and his sense of humour was in evidence, he could be exceptionally funny. I have never known anyone who could in such a way pick out a particular feature, though it might be insignificant in itself, and let his sense of humour work on it. Nearly every day he had an amusing story to relate about something or other which had happened to him . . ."

The next month, Andersen heard the outcome of his application to the King: the award of an annual grant of 400 rixdollars. He told Ingemann that he now had a bread tree in his garden and would no longer have to sing for his crumbs of bread at everybody's door. It was a turning point: "A new chapter of my life began. From this day forward, it was as if a more constant sunshine had entered my heart. I felt within myself more repose, more certainty."

Now he could have married—Oehlenschläger, Ingemann and Heiberg all supported wives on similar grants. But the money set him free in a different way. He had no need to write another novel, and he did not do so for ten years. Instead, basking in financial security for the first time, he immersed himself in writing fairy tales. In the summer he took up an invitation to an aristocratic estate at the Stampe family's home of Nysø, on the west coast of Zealand, and then went on to Funen. On 23 June, he began "The Steadfast Tin Soldier." It is the first tale he wrote which has neither a folk tale source nor a literary model, but comes straight out of his own imagination, and it signalled a new approach to fairy tales which changed the genre for all time.

"The Steadfast Tin Soldier" is one of many sad works which Andersen wrote over the next few years, at the same time as worldly success was falling into his lap, as he was enjoying an active social and travelling life, and as the practicalities of his everyday existence were coming to suit him more and more. Its hero is an ironic self-portrait, the odd man out in a box of tin soldiers where "each soldier was the living image of the next, except for one who was a little bit different. He had only one leg, as he was the last to be made and there hadn't been enough tin to go round. But he stood just as firmly on his one leg as the others did on two, and he was the one that was to stand out from the rest." He falls in love with a paper dancer with a muslin dress and a glistening spangle who stands at the door of a toy castle:

> She had raised one of her legs so high in the air that the tin soldier couldn't make out where it was and so thought that she had only one leg, like himself.
>
> "She'd make a wife for me!" he thought. "But she's a very fine lady, she lives in a castle. I only have a box, and there are twenty-five of us to that—it's no place for her! Still, I must see about getting to know her!

In eyeing her, he makes an enemy of the jack-in-the-box, and the next morning "whether it was the jack-in-the-box or only a draught that did it, all of a sudden the window sprang open and the soldier fell head first from the third floor." He is picked up by street boys, sailed down the gutter in a paper boat, dashed into a drain and pursued by a water-rat in a grotesque version of Andersen's own travel nightmares:

> "Have you got a passport?" demanded the rat. "Show your passport!"
>
> But the tin soldier never said a word; only clutched his rifle more tightly than ever. The boat tore along, with the rat after it. Ugh! How it gnashed its teeth and shouted out to sticks and straws: "Stop him! Stop Him! He hasn't paid the toll! He hasn't got a passport!"

The soldier is washed into the sea, eaten by a fish, which is caught, sold, taken home and cut open—this part of the story recalls "Tom Thumb." The soldier finds ("Well now, what a strange world it is") that he is in the same house as before:

> with the pretty little dancer still standing on one leg with the other high up in the air—she too had been steadfast. The tin soldier was so touched that he could have wept tin tears, only that wouldn't have done at all. He looked at her and she looked at him, but neither said a word.

But just as his troubles seem to be over, one of the little boys picks up the soldier and for no reason throws him into the fire. He "felt dreadfully hot, but whether it was with the real flames or with love he couldn't have said." He looks at the dancer as he feels himself melting away, "but still he remained steadfast as he shouldered his rifle." Then suddenly the dancer is blown into the fire by a wind, "she burst into flames and was gone":

> The tin soldier melted away to a lump, and when the maid cleared out the ashes the next day she found him in the shape of a little tin heart. But all that was left of the dancer was the spangle, and that was as black as a cinder.

This is vintage Andersen: the world of toys, evoked with delicacy and humour; the arbitrariness of fate; the high romanticism of love ending in dust and ashes, an infinitely pathetic sort of nursery *Liebestod*; the dignity and integrity which are the soldier's doom—"had he cried out 'Here I am' they would most likely have found him, but he didn't think it proper to shout out when he was in uniform." With his creator the soldier shares his dogged acceptance of fate, his fidelity and his one-legged sense of being apart. More generally, he is an emblem of the nineteenth-century values of stoical endurance and buttoned-up emotions. Sexual repression lies just beneath the surface—Thomas Mann, who like Andersen spent a lifetime tormented by homo-erotic desire, wrote at eighty: "I have always liked Andersen's fairy tale of the Steadfast Tin Soldier. Fundamentally, it is the symbol of my life." In Andersen's time the soldier was seen as both an inspirational and a consoling figure—one of Andersen's royal friends, the Grand Duchess of Weimar, said that when she went into labour she hoped to behave like the tin soldier.

This rich tale has continued to inspire many interpretations: in 1915, for example, G. K. Chesterton saw the story as a patriotic Danish fable applicable to England in the First World War: "The Tin Soldier of the Danish army and the paper boat of the Danish navy, as in the story, were swept away down the great gutter, down that colossal *cloaca* that leads to the vast cesspool of Berlin." Among numerous dramatic and musical versions, including one by Bournonville in Andersen's lifetime, George Balanchine's 1975 ballet, with its *pas de deux* danced against oversized storybook scenery to Bizet's *Jeux d'Enfants*, was particularly evocative of the myriad themes in Andersen's original. Balanchine's soldier and dancer enjoy a bittersweet brief encounter during which they express their love; the ballerina becomes so excited that she goes to the window for some air, and is blown into the fire, the innocent agent of her own destruction. The soldier is left alone and returns steadfastly to his duty with the regiment: an echo of Andersen's, and Balanchine's, dedication to duty and art as a metaphor for staying true to love.

After "The Steadfast Tin Soldier," Andersen wrote "The Daisy," a brief sentimental story about a dying flower and a caged bird who cannot comfort one another. Then on 10 August, "Edvard's second wedding anniversary," he began another substantial tale, "The Wild Swans." This was an adaptation of a folk tale popular across Europe—the Grimms' "The Six Swans" and "The Twelve Brothers" are variations of it. A telling of "The Wild Swans" had been included in Matthias Winther's collection of Danish folk tales in 1823, which Andersen had read and which he now invited friends to compare unfavourably with his own version, showing how keen he was to make the tale his own.

It is easy to see why Andersen was attracted to the swan story. It tells of eleven (or six) princes and their sister, who struggles for years to rescue them from a spell by which their wicked stepmother has turned them into swans. The young girl must weave eleven shirts from nettles which blister her hands; when the shirts are thrown over the swans, they will again become princes. Until the task is finished, she must not speak or laugh or cry. But she attracts the love of a king, who marries her but is eventually persuaded by his mother—or in Andersen's version an archbishop—that she is a witch. She is about to be burned, and cannot speak to defend herself, when her brothers swoop down. She throws the shirts over them and they become princes, though the youngest keeps a swan's wing in place of one arm she had not managed to finish. She declares her innocence and is taken back to the palace in glory.

In its colourful extremes, its horror, its idealized image of female sacrifice, "The Wild Swans" shares with "The Little Mermaid" primitive, violent elements that always drew Andersen. As in "The Little Mermaid," the story equates female goodness and silence in a way which was particularly attractive in the nineteenth century, although the mix is age-old—Cordelia in *King Lear* and Constance in Chaucer's "The Man of Law's Tale" are early versions of it.* Many of Andersen's tales are wish-fulfilment fantasies; he may have identified with the silent, suffering princess, so long mute about her background and then bursting into triumph when she can explain herself.

---

*The story is not necessarily a myth of oppression: in her study *From the Beast to the Blonde*, Marina Warner sees the swan fairy tale as "a story of female heroism, generosity, staunchness" developed at a time when "women's capacity for love and action tragically exceeded the permitted boundaries of their lives."

The swans, too, gave this tale a peculiarly personal resonance. Swans were part of Andersen's private mythology, recurring in his letters as symbols of mystery and grandeur even before he began writing fairy tales. Certain bird images recur throughout his tales, each reflecting aspects of how he saw himself—swallows mirrored his passion for travel and his migratory habits, storks his gaucheness and singularity and love of chatter. Swans were closest to his romantic self-image as wild, pure, lofty and loyal. Swans love once and for ever. They are mighty and powerful in the air and elegantly resigned on water—images, perhaps, of Andersen the artist—but uncomfortable and graceless on solid earth, as Andersen was in everyday life. He had already incorporated them in his tale "The Travelling Companion" and included a reference to them in "The Little Mermaid," and he was to use them most famously in his fairy tale–autobiography "The Ugly Duckling." In 1838, engrossed in fairy tales and ambitious for his reputation, he adopted them as one of his signatures.

He brought to the folk tale two new ingredients. The first is the characteristic love of detail which would appeal to a child—Andersen's princes "wrote on golden slates with diamond pencils"—and he develops a particularly close relationship between the princess and the youngest swan brother. The second is a series of Christian motifs which overlay the essentially pagan story and debrutalize it—there is no mention of the princess's three babies, snatched from her by the wicked Queen Mother, and the Grimms' ending, in which the wicked Queen is burnt at the stake, is transformed into an image of Christian revelation and forgiveness:

> The people bowed before her as to a saint . . . "Yes, she is innocent!" said the eldest brother . . . And while he spoke there arose a fragrance as of a million roses, for every faggot of the bonfire had taken root and grown branches, and there stood a sweet-smelling hedge, so very high and big, of red roses. At the top was a single white bloom, a white and glowing one which shone like a star. Breaking this off, the king placed it on Eliza's breast; and she awoke with peace and happiness in her heart.
>
> And every church bell rang of its own accord and birds came flying up in big flocks.

This is the Andersen who became so beloved by the Victorians: sentimental and didactic. The Grimms, in shaping folklore into literature, did not superimpose Christian morality on a pagan tale. The strong narrative carries "The Wild Swans," but Andersen's version is weaker than the Grimms' story. In

"The Little Mermaid" and "The Emperor's New Clothes," Andersen made myths his own through fundamental and dramatic changes to the story, but in "The Wild Swans" his literary additions and imaginative freewheeling dilute the story and draw it out unnecessarily. By 1838, his artistry was outgrowing the folk tale model, and it was "The Steadfast Tin Soldier" rather than "The Wild Swans" which pointed the way forward: only a handful of his subsequent tales were adaptations from folk sources, and from now on his greatest stories were purely imaginative works. With "The Steadfast Tin Soldier," he had found his own voice, but he still did not acknowledge any special position for fairy tales in his *œuvre*. For a while he let them take a back seat, and filled his life with a crowd of new projects.

On 1 December 1838, Andersen left his rooms in Nyhavn and moved into a suite at the Hotel du Nord, Copenhagen's grandest hotel, which stood on the north side of Kongens Nytorv and looked across to the Royal Theatre. The move was a statement of his success as a writer as well as an answer to his practical needs. For nearly a decade, until May 1847, he would live in the hotel when he was in Copenhagen, leaving himself free to set off at any moment on a foreign trip. This was luxurious, Bohemian living, ideal for the peripatetic life to which he was drawn. He began working on *The Mulatto*, about a black slave, and he wrote to Henriette Hanck that when he rang the bell, "the servants come, one darker than the other, which must surely have a good effect on me as I'm working on *The Mulatto*."

Although he was in the cheapest part of the hotel, under the roof, he had a superb view: from his bedroom he looked down on to a quiet courtyard at the back, from his sitting room on to Kongens Nytorv, illuminated at night, and across the chimney of a smithy he could see the sea. On his desk he placed Thorvaldsen's bust, on the bookcase his own, along with a crucifix and other knick-knacks; there was a green sofa and above it an oval mirror.

"Feel extremely cosy here," he noted in his almanac—the Danish *hyggelig*, like the German *gemütlich*, carries evocations of home and winter snugness which are hard to translate. "Winter life in Denmark," he wrote of this period in his autobiography, had "its attractions and its variety . . . I felt myself at home with the married sons and daughters of Collin, where a number of amiable children were growing up. Every year strengthened the bond between myself and the nobly gifted composer Hartmann: art and freshness of nature prospered in his house. Collin was my counsellor in

Nysø, by H. C. Buntzen, 1843, home of the Stampe family and the first of many aristo-cratic estates where Andersen stayed and worked. The summer house in the garden was the studio of his friend the sculptor Thorvaldsen.

practical life, and Ørsted in my literary affairs. The theatre was . . . my club. I visited it every evening."

In the autumn and winter of 1838, he was calmer and more secure than he had been at any time in the 1830s. At the hotel and at the theatre he was fussed over. His friends lived minutes away and he saw the Collin family daily. Jonas had just moved to Amaliegade, a graceful classical street running down from Amalienborg Square, to a big dark house set back from the road behind iron railings. Andersen had considered moving in too, but held back because there was a bad smell and not a ray of sunshine, and the house, reached across a courtyard full of dandelions which Jonas refused to have weeded, was as uncomfortable as the family's former spartan home in Bredgade.

New friends, too, illuminated this time. The sculptor Bertel Thorvaldsen, who had sustained Andersen in Rome, returned to a ceremonial welcome in Copenhagen in September 1838, and through the autumn and winter Andersen saw him almost daily in company or in his studio. Thorvaldsen had raised himself up from poverty—he was the son of an Icelandic wood-carver—and then fled from Denmark to achieve international fame; now he was sought after as a guest of the Danish nobility, and Andersen felt a bond with him and his story. Soon after his arrival, Thorvaldsen began spending most of his time at Nysø, where Baroness Christine Stampe gave him a summer house in the grounds as his studio and he could work in peace. The Stampes, wealthy artistic patrons, had met Thorvaldsen in Rome; at home their guests included the royal family, but Nysø was famous for its artistic and intellectual gatherings, to which Ingemann, Ørsted, Oehlenschläger, the painter Marstrand, and also the Wulffs were invited. Through these connections Andersen began to be welcomed there too. Nysø, a neo-classical house that was a model of restrained elegance, stood in lush grounds running down to the sea, surrounded by woods. There was a graceful formal garden with an ornamental pond and walkways between the lawns, a lake and several outhouses. Andersen visited often when Thorvaldsen was established there, and Nysø was one of the first aristocratic estates where he felt at home. He could not resist writing of it in his autobiography: "I lived much with the great sculptor, and here I became acquainted with one of my dearest friends, the future possessor of the place." In 1838, Baron Henrik Stampe was seventeen and a mere boy; gradually over the next five years he became a vital part of Andersen's life.

International fame and acclaim at home were also within his grasp in the winter of 1838. Reitzel paid a hundred rixdollars to bring out a new book of fairy tales containing "The Steadfast Tin Soldier," "The Daisy" and "The Wild Swans," which with very different motifs share themes of silence and resignation to fate. In Sweden, five of his fairy tales were published along with five by the Grimm brothers. In Germany, there appeared the first translation of his tales and a translation of *Only a Fiddler* prefaced by a short biography of Andersen. This was an account of the triumph of genius over adversity, ostensibly written by his translator Captain Jenssen but in fact supplied by Andersen himself; pitched at the sentimental romanticism of contemporary German taste, it made Andersen a household name. "Great happiness over my children's stories coming out in German," Andersen noted in his almanac on New Year's Eve 1838. He felt that he had arrived.

He started the new year 1839 busy and optimistic. As he looked out from his new study across to the Royal Theatre, the centre of Copenhagen's social life, he became inflamed again with theatrical ambitions. He worked on *The Mulatto*, an exotic drama set in Martinique in which the Mulatto, a racial outcast, falls in love with a white countess, Cecilie, who returns his love and fights for him against her demonic rival, Eleonora, in a climactic scene at a slave market. As in *The Improvisatore*, Andersen luxuriated in the glowing colours of the south; the play has some of the exotic dash of Hugo's *Hernani* and Mérimée's *Carmen*, while the character of the Mulatto is another self-projection of Andersen the outsider.

In the spring, he wrote a vaudeville called *The Invisible Man on Sprogø*, which had a good run at the Royal Theatre, and then he took up invitations from the Scandinavian aristocracy. He went to Glorup Manor on Funen, home of an aging nobleman, Count Moltke, and on to Sweden to visit Baron Wrangel's manor, where he found himself the darling of the Swedish nobility. He read them *The Mulatto*, which was applauded. "Count Barck's daughters Louise and Mathilda delighted me, the elder sister was a young lady of the world, we talked of Paris, music and poetry, and half way in love we parted after arranging to meet at their uncle's, Count Beckefrie's."

Andersen now enjoyed a public flirtation with Lady Mathilda Barck, a dark-haired young girl of nineteen with a long, pensive face, dark almond-shaped eyes and a hint of melancholy in her expression that struck a chord with him. "One of the Comtesses Barck has been in Paris a long time, is young, lively and beautiful, alas! my old heart—if I had enough money I should fall in love in my old age," Andersen wrote to Henriette Wulff. When he returned, he wrote a whimsical collection of prose sketches, *Picture Book Without Pictures*, which includes a description of a poet in Sweden written as a love letter to Mathilda:

> "Up on the hill stood a man, a poet. He emptied the mead horn with the broad silver rim, and murmured a name. He begged the winds not to betray him, but I heard the name. I knew it. A count's coronet sparkles above it, and therefore he did not speak it out. I smiled, for I knew that a poet's crown adorned his own name. The nobility of Eleonora d'Este is attached to the name of Tasso. And I also know where the Rose of Beauty blooms!"
>
> Thus spoke the Moon, and a cloud came between us. May no cloud separate the poet from the rose!

He saw Mathilda again the following year, when he was honoured at the University of Lund with a banquet and a serenade. It was his first public honour, and so overcame him that he burst into tears. When he left Malmö, Mathilda and Louise Barck came to the port to see him off. From Copenhagen, he sent Mathilda a letter asking her to be only half as fond of him as he was of her, and he wrote again asking her to pass on to his Swedish friends a bouquet of greetings, of which the best was meant for her. But his interest was half-hearted, and by the autumn of 1839 the theatre was absorbing all his energy.

The Mulatto was accepted and scheduled to open in December 1839, but on the night of the première, Frederik VI died and the theatre was promptly shut for two months of mourning. Andersen's hope of glory on stage was postponed. Meanwhile, some fairy tales appeared in time for Christmas 1839. "The Flying Trunk" is an oddly prophetic story, both about the waiting game that Andersen and Mathilda Barck were playing, and about the feud with Mrs. Heiberg that was about to erupt into Andersen's life. The plot involves a story-teller who woos a princess by flying up to her on his magic trunk and telling her stories. He wins her with a tale about a haughty box of matches, a tinderbox and an old iron pot, which is a satire on Copenhagen literary society—the matches are the actress Johanne Luise Heiberg, dazzling but proud, and Andersen is a nightingale, hanging in a cage outside the room, who can sing well but is despised—"it's true it hasn't learned anything, but we won't speak ill of that tonight." The princess agrees to marry the story-teller, but in the firework celebrations of their engagement, the trunk is burnt up and he can no longer fly to her. "She stood waiting on the roof all day. She's waiting still, while he goes round the world telling fairy tales"— another ironic portrait of Andersen as the restless wandering storyteller.

The other stories are more grim. "The Garden of Paradise" ends with Death approaching a young prince and warning him "to expiate his sins and to grow better" because "one day I shall come. When he least expects it, I shall clap him in the black coffin," while in "The Storks" naughty children who make fun of Andersen's favoured bird are punished by the stork bringing a dead baby brother instead of a live one.* Storks, which at that time were common in northern Europe, building their great nests on city rooftops, continued to be a symbolic signature for Andersen in his tales. The Swedish writer Carl Dahlgren always called Andersen the crane, a cousin of the stork: in Dahlgren's description, he had long thin legs, and long arms hanging like strips, a long thin neck topped by a knob-like head and an ugly face with thick lips and teeth like tusks, and his stooping walk resembled that of a tripping crane.

---

*The myth of the stork was vigorously renewed in the nineteenth century, when, writes Marina Warner, "the stork took its place among the fantasy cast—Easter Bunny, Santa Claus, Tooth Fairy—who provided appropriately child-like explanations for events in the adult world as well as encoding a system of rewards and punishments."

The Mulatto opened on 3 February at the Royal Theatre and was a success—Mrs. Heiberg gave an outstanding performance as Cecilie and the new king, Christian VIII, a lover of the arts, bowed to Andersen across the auditorium and received him next day at court. But Andersen's relationship with the theatre was always fraught, and he did not enjoy applause for long. Soon critics accused him of plagiarizing the plot of *The Mulatto* from a short story by Fanny Reybaud, *Les Epaves* (1838)—it did not help that Andersen's acknowledgement to Reybaud had been omitted by the printers. Andersen fought back with an original romantic drama on a similar theme, *The Moorish Maid*, which was much inferior to *The Mulatto*. It was accepted by the directors of the Royal Theatre, but effectively blocked by the powerful playwright and critic Heiberg, who had hated *The Mulatto* and whose wife now refused to play the title part in the new play, which had been written for her.

A temperamental, unhappy prima donna, Johanne Luise Heiberg was one of the idols of Golden Age Copenhagen. Artists loved to paint her; the composer Hans Christian Lumbye dedicated a dance, the Johanne Luise Waltz, to her; Auguste Bournonville said in his memoirs that "on the Danish stage no star has sparkled as strongly or as long as Johanne Luise Heiberg. She rightfully maintained her position as the Danish Theatre prima donna and outshone everyone." Andersen, who could judge by the standards of the best stages in Europe, wrote "Fru Heiberg can well be classed with a Ristori, a Rachel . . . Our stage will not produce her equal for centuries. In tragedy she is, by her spirit and geniality with which she comprehends and fills any part, a most interesting artist; and in comedy she stands unrivalled." But though he admired her professionally, he knew that personally she was a force to be reckoned with. Their relationship was always uneasy. Heiberg, leader of neo-classical taste and a representative of the established order—he was the Collin family's favourite writer—never really saw the point of Andersen; Johanne Luise liked vigorous and unsentimental writing and said Andersen was not masculine enough.

She was also troubled by the affinity between their backgrounds, for she had grown up the daughter of an alcoholic tinker and a Jewish mother at the fairground outside Copenhagen, where she had been noticed singing and dancing, and as a 9-year-old had made her debut at the Royal Theatre the same night that the 16-year-old Andersen had appeared as a troll. Unlike Andersen, she spoke little of her origins, and had been absorbed with apparent effortlessness into literary society as Heiberg's wife. She was in no mood to grant Andersen special favours, and when he turned up to beg her to take the role, she called the play turgid and was implacable.

Andersen did not react wisely. The part was given to a less popular actress, and Andersen wrote a bitter and self-pitying preface which, he admitted later, "betrayed [his] irritated mind far too palpably," turned the Heibergs into lifelong enemies and made Andersen a laughing stock. Resentful, depressed and boiling over with rage, he determined to leave Denmark and go on his longest journey abroad yet. Before he left, he sent a coy, half-love letter to Mathilda Barck—too self-obsessed to carry conviction, yet aching with loneliness. He hoped, he said, to die abroad, unless he could write a work to bring honour to himself and to Denmark; meanwhile, "let me see if Sweden has really cordial feelings towards me; to me *you* represent the entire country. But do not write unless you want to make me infinitely happy!"

Mathilda replied quickly, but unfortunately her letter, which was kind and sympathetic ("the Danish *Digter* is often the subject of our conversation and thoughts"), arrived neither in Germany nor in Italy. One day in Copenhagen in 1843, the lady whom Mathilda had asked to take it to Rome, so that Andersen would receive it as quickly as possible, found it among her belongings, and apologetically called on Andersen to deliver it, admitting that she had forgotten all about it. But both Andersen and Mathilda were by then in love with other people. It is unlikely that even if he had received it in 1840 Andersen would have pursued Mathilda, but it is a bitter irony that the most encouraging letter he received from a woman arrived three years too late.

Meanwhile, on 31 October, after a farewell dinner at Ferrini's restaurant, the Collin family accompanied him to his ship, *Christian the Eighth*. They epitomized everything he was leaving—both the limited vision and the pleasure of familiarity. Why be cold in Rome when one could be cold in Copenhagen? asked Ingeborg Drewsen. "There was a strong wind with heavy seas driving in off the Baltic," Andersen wrote in his diary. "Edvard Collin was the last one out there. I said goodbye; he pressed a kiss on to my mouth! Oh, it was as if my heart would burst!"

CHAPTER 11

I Belong to the World

1840–1843

The Danes are evil, cold, satanic . . . I don't believe in love in the North, but in evil treachery. I can feel it in my own blood, and it's only in that way I know I am Danish!

—HANS CHRISTIAN ANDERSEN,
letter to Henriette Wulff, 29 April 1843

Every great Scandinavian writer—Andersen, Ibsen, Strindberg—has been torn between patriotism and a longing for the wider world, between an awareness, however reluctant, of having been formed by his distinctive northern milieu and a rebellion against its narrow oppressions. Ibsen, for example, said both that "anyone who wishes to understand me fully must know Norway" and that the Norwegian people could be compared to Cain, and their flag ought to be shunned like a plague pennant. At the end of his life Andersen became intrigued by Ibsen as "this Norwegian poet who does not like the Norwegians"; Andersen's own position as the first Scandinavian writer to cut a serious figure on the international stage meant that he felt such a dichotomy acutely. In the end, he could only accept it by living half his life as a wanderer through Europe, seeking interest, inspiration, unqualified fame—all the things which eluded him in Copenhagen—while acknowledging that in order to write, he needed to be in Denmark. He wrote very little while abroad; "I have never been very productive while travelling, but all the more so after my arrival home again," he wrote towards the end of his life.

Yet the close-knit world of bourgeois Copenhagen, centred on the theatre and consisting of no more than a few thousand people, turned easily from being a source of comfort and security in Andersen's mind to a threatening monster hell-bent on destroying him. The literary community, lined up behind Heiberg, was oppressive and insular; the Collins, although they were sympathetic to Andersen, always considered him inferior as a writer to

Heiberg and Oehlenschläger. Edvard later admitted that "the dejection that he suffered almost daily after having made his debut as an author, had a completely different cause, not the manners of the house, but really the one that he did not find his works sufficiently appreciated by us; and that dejection was bound to increase gradually as he was recognized by others." In Copenhagen in the early 1840s, only the physicist Ørsted, himself an internationally acclaimed figure, really understood the nature of Andersen's genius; when Andersen called him "the only man of all my intimate and sympathizing friends who clearly and distinctly expressed his appreciation of my poetical ability and strongly encouraged me, while he predicted that there ought to come and would come a better time for me at home," he was for once not exaggerating.

Foreign visitors have observed for centuries the Danish tendency to follow the pack and suspect anyone who is different or overly ambitious. When Andersen seemed particularly vain or ridiculous, he felt the full force of the social conformism of a small country breathing down his neck, and he found it unbearable. In *An Account of Denmark As It Was In The Year 1692*, the British diplomat Robert Molesworth (admittedly writing in revenge for his expulsion from the country) claimed that at schools and university, Danes were taught "what they call the *Queen of all Vertues, viz. Submission* to Superiors, and an entire *blind Obedience* to Authority . . . thus the Spirits of men are from the beginning inured to Subjection . . . most have the misfortune to carry these slavish Opinions with them to their Graves." The result, he said, was that "a miserable life which jogs on at the same heavy rate, has a mixture of Melancholy Ease with it . . . is preferred . . . especially by a People naturally of an inactive Body and heavy Spirit." A century later, Mary Wollstonecraft suggested in *Letters written during a short residence in Sweden, Norway and Denmark* (1796) that "the Danes, in general, seem extremely averse to innovation, and if happiness only consist in opinion, they are the happiest people in the world, for I never saw any so well satisfied with their own situation."

As the country diminished in wealth and international standing in the nineteenth century, the village spirit became more pronounced—it was as if, says the literary historian Johan de Mylius, "having lost North Germany, southern Sweden and Norway, all that was left was to look at your neighbour and make sure he did not get too big." In the twentieth century the Danish-Norwegian novelist Aksel Sandemose satirized this Danish attitude in his novel *En flygtning krydser sit spor* (*A Refugee Crossing his Track*) as *Jante-loven* (Jante's law). Jante, a man's name, also means a lead button, used for a form of gambling and the lowest means of legal tender; the first two of the ten articles of Jante's law in the novel are: Don't believe that *you* are any-thing; Don't believe you are better than *us*. The derogatory term *Jante-loven* is now widely used in Denmark to describe the mood of provincial con-formism that in some ways still persists.

Travel was Andersen's defence against this spirit, as well as a palliative against depression; like most drugs, it was both addictive and to work depended on a constantly raised prescription. In 1831 he had fled to Ger-many to escape hostile critics and a personal crisis; in 1833 he had gone as far as Italy. Now, richer, more eminent and more desperate, he embarked on his most adventurous journey, to the Balkans, Greece and Constantinople, which in 1840 were little known and rarely visited by western Europeans. "Your trip to Greece will probably come to nothing," Jonas Collin wrote to him, "and I do not regret this, for God knows why you wish to go there."

Andersen was an unusual traveller. As one of the first well-travelled Danes, he exhibited the humility, openness to experience and eagerness to learn which is now recognized as a characteristic of people travelling from small, insular countries to larger ones; by contrast, as the Danish critic Niels Kofoed has remarked, "a Frenchman will be reluctant to learn anything from a Dane." Andersen was not brave but he was manically driven to journey to far-flung places—by restlessness, curiosity, the need to forget himself in new and undiscovered settings, the thrill of being recognized, the desire to spread his name. As a result he overcame a plethora of fears and neuroses which would have kept most people of his temperament rooted to their armchairs.

There were very real dangers in nineteenth-century travel—bandits attacking carriages, shipwreck, cholera—and these occupied Andersen ceaselessly on his journeys. But he also suffered from a crowd of other obses-sions. He always carried a rope in his luggage because he was anxious about fire. He was so fearful of being buried alive that he kept a note on his bedside table which read "I only appear to be dead," suggesting that in some crucial aspects he never lost his child's vision, for a child typically imagines death as lying cold and awake in a wooden box.* He was frightened of dogs, he never ate pork for fear of trichinosis, he suspected many fellow-passengers in a

---

*When his old patron, the composer Weyse, died in 1842, Andersen heard it said on the day of the funeral that the corpse was "not yet quite cold near the heart." He begged the physicians to re-examine the body. "I asked them finally to sever his arteries before they closed the cof-fin; they would not do it. Oehlenschläger heard of it and came up to me, saying, 'What! would you have him dissected!'—'Yes, rather than that he should awaken in the grave, and you too would rather have them do so to you when you die!'—'I!' exclaimed Oehlenschläger, and drew back."

stagecoach or train compartment of being about to murder him, he was usually sure he had picked up some infection from travelling on a ship and he dreaded seasickness. His indecisiveness about how and when to travel was so extreme that it made him ill, and he called the unrest of being unable to decide whether to continue a journey or not a state of mind so horrible that it was a sickness.

In addition, he was forever on edge about the minor hazards of a journey—missing *vetturinos* or trains (he always arrived an hour early at the station); losing his luggage; having the wrong stamp on his passport or losing it altogether; being over-charged or not having left a large enough tip. "Oh, how good I am at finding things to worry about," he wrote on this trip. It may be that travel was so beneficial for him not only as a distraction from his self-obsession but because he exchanged deeper anxieties—social, sexual, artistic—for more mundane and immediate ones. None the less, it was always an emotional and overwrought Andersen who boarded the ship in Copenhagen and bade farewell to his friends, half-convinced that he would not see them again.

"It is just as well I am leaving—my soul is ill! Even to those dearest to one, one dares not speak of what most burdens one's mind," Andersen wrote to Jonas Collin the day after he fled Denmark in the autumn of 1840. He had scarcely kissed the Collins goodbye before seasickness set in as the boat rounded the island of Amager off Copenhagen. Throughout the night, he wrote in his diary, he was ill: "my seasickness got worse, and there were heavy seas—time was heavy too. I was really suffering. Once we caught a wave that hit so hard that we all thought we had run aground." Twenty-four hours later they landed at Kiel, then the capital of the Danish province of Holstein, and Andersen took a rented carriage to Breitenburg Castle, to which he had been invited for the first time by his patron, Count Rantzau-Breitenburg.

Breitenburg, isolated and half hidden in the middle of a golden-brown forest near the River Stor, was magical, and balm for Andersen's soul. "In the manor courtyard His Excellency gave me a warm welcome—I've been given a handsome sitting room and a pleasant bedroom . . . I took a walk in the lovely manor park, which is traversed by a canal . . . The manor chapel looks lovely out in the midst of the high trees." He loved the ritual at the homes of his aristocratic friends—the pampering by servants, the oysters and champagne and lavish dinners after which he read his tales aloud to the assembled company, the fine sitting rooms with views on to the grounds where he could work in the mornings. In Holstein and in north Germany he suffered the usual range of fears—"all the early morning long I can hear the count's eldest, mentally deranged brother pounding on a door" . . . "the nodule on my gum is plaguing me and making me anxious . . . If only I don't get an infection!" . . . "Already a little anxious about money. Sore penis and worried about it"—but he left Breitenburg refreshed and sailed up the Elbe on a steamship to Hamburg, where a stranger approached him to say how happy he was to meet Denmark's greatest writer and a bookseller from Braunschweig, having read his name on his luggage, asked whether he was the "famous Danish author."

In Hamburg he saw Liszt perform at a concert where "the merchants . . . seemed to be hearing in the music the clink of gold pieces, and that's why they were sitting with a smile hovering about their lips." Liszt was to him the essence of the romantic spirit—"there was something so spider-like, so demonic about him! And as he sat there at the piano, pale with his face full of violent passion, he seemed to me like a devil trying to play his soul free! Every tone flowed from his heart and soul—he looked to me to be on the rack." A few days later in Leipzig he met Mendelssohn, who became a friend, and watched a rehearsal of Beethoven's Seventh Symphony.

These were the sort of highlights for which Andersen travelled. Although his worldview was rooted in the folk mythology of his childhood, he thought of himself as a modern writer, he experimented with new forms and he needed to feel connected with the latest in European culture and technology. He wanted to shake off his Danish provincialism and he was vain enough to enjoy being the first to experience what was new and exciting, and to tell everyone at home about it. While his Danish contemporaries were happy to strut about the Copenhagen stage—Andersen's friend the poet Ingemann, for example, wrote that although he discussed literary relations with Germany and talked of the advantages of foreign theatres, this was only for the sake of appearances and he did not really care at all about it—a European context was essential to Andersen's artistic ambition and his greed for recognition. "I am searching for a literature appropriate to my time and instructive for my spirit," he wrote to Henriette Hanck,

an ideal vision comes vaguely to mind, but its outlines are so formless that I cannot make it clear myself. It seems to me that each great poet has contributed a link, but no more than a link, to this vast body. Our era has not yet found its poet. But when will he come? And where? He must depict nature like Washington Irving, understand the age like Walter Scott, sing like Byron, and yet be rooted in our time like Heine. Oh! I wonder where this messiah of poetry will be born? . . . I was born to be a poet, I feel, and I am conscious that everything enters my life as poetry, and still I want more!

Travelling through Europe in 1840, it was impossible not to be aware of standing at the crossroads of an old and a new world. One part of the journey by stagecoach, tedious and exhausting, might cover sixty miles in little under twenty-four hours, with sleepy passengers jolted about over bumpy roads and frequent stops at coaching inns to change the horses. This could suddenly give way to a stretch of route where the railway had opened, and an equivalent distance be covered in three and a half hours by the terrifying new steam rocket. On 9 November, Andersen saw a steam engine for the first time, and the next day he tried it out himself, travelling from Magdeburg to Leipzig. "I felt as if I were surrendering myself to my God," he wrote in his diary.

> I had the feeling that the earth was rotating—close to me the grass and the fields were moving like a whirling spinning wheel . . . Now I can imagine the flight of migratory birds; this is how they must leave the towns behind them. It was as if one town lay close to the next. There is something quite magical about it . . . I was alone with a man in one compartment that accommodates eight people. The thought occurred to me that he might be crazy and have a fit. I got all worked up about it.

In *A Poet's Bazaar*, his account of his 1840–1841 journey, Andersen gives a chapter to the train, "since many of my readers have never seen a railway." Like many self-made men, he always embraced the innovative; he had no time for the nostalgic idea that the railway was destroying precious traditions, and he made a point of equating the fast and modern with the fantastical. "And what a tremendous effect this invention has on the spirit! One feels so powerful, just like the magician of olden days," he wrote. "Mephistopheles could not fly more quickly with Faust in his cloak. By natural means we are, in our day, as powerful as in the Middle Ages man thought only the devil could be."

A few days later, Andersen was introduced to another new invention. He recalled in his autobiography: "In Nürnberg I saw for the first time daguerreotype pictures: they told me that these portraits were taken in ten minutes; that seemed to me a bit of witchcraft; the art was new then, and far from what it is nowadays. Daguerreotypes and the railway were the two new flowers of the age."

As he moved south, Andersen threw himself into every new enthusiasm he could find, yet nothing could quell his discontent. He was homesick for the Collin house and wept when he wrote to Jonas from Munich that, apart from the Collin family, he never wanted to see Denmark again, for he had felt more unhappy than happy there. He wandered disconsolately into bookshops looking for his own works, trying to draw attention to himself. In one, he alighted on the first volume of *The Improvisatore* in German, and told the bookseller that this was only part one. No, said the bookseller, it was the whole thing. Andersen suggested it ended rather abruptly, to which the bookseller answered triumphantly that this was the sophisticated style of the new novels; he had read it. "But," replied Andersen, "I wrote it."

Arriving in Rome on 19 December, he found the city unusually cold, deserted by most of the friends from his first visit and gripped by disease. "The earth quaked, the Tiber rose, flooding the streets where they rowed in boats; fever snatched numbers away." He caught influenza, suffered from recurring toothache and heard from Edvard that, as expected, the première of *The Moorish Maid* in Copenhagen had been a fiasco; the play had come off after three performances. In an attempt to cheer Andersen up, Edvard had written with characteristic tactlessness, "if you, however, think that the poor reviews of *The Moorish Maid* has left any permanent impression against you, you are wrong, for it is already forgotten. For another literary *Erscheinung* has now taken place—that is, Heiberg's new poems, of their kind and by their excellent form a most strange product." Heiberg's *Digte* (1841) included a satire called *A Soul After Death*, in which those sent to Hell are forced to watch *The Mulatto* and *The Moorish Maid* on the same night, and Andersen complained to his diary that Edvard was "icy-cold."

Rome was a disappointment. On Christmas Eve—the most important Christmas festivity for Scandinavians and Germans—he went out to buy grapes, bread, cheese and apples, then spent the evening alone in his room, going to bed at eight-thirty. On New Year's Day 1841 he begged God for immortality as a writer and peace of mind; on 16 January he wrote:

How lonely I am. At home by 5:30 every evening. I am tired of reading and constantly looking at the clock to see if it isn't past 9 o'clock, so that I can go to bed and sleep my way to a new day!—I'm not afraid of being assaulted any more. Every now and then I even think it might be a good thing if I were killed . . . I have nothing to live for any more. Even art is a bit of a problem for me. My need to be noticed is so great that the idea of sudden death intrigues me.

Oh, I recognize my weakness! I can see my faults!—Oh God, give me a great idea soon or great joy or death!

He saw himself as "a gnat struggling in a spider's web . . . entrapped in the memories that my life's Parcae have spun for me," and for the first two months of 1841 he was as desolate as he had been in Rome at the beginning of 1834, and more lonely. "Today seems to be my most meagre day . . . I have faith in nothing but God, but I'm not pinning my hopes on Him! . . . My mind is like a fallen angel sinking into eternal nothingness! . . . I should like to die, there is nothing left to live for," run his diaries for this period. He could not resist hiring a costume for the carnival (a white Pierrot dress, three-cornered white hat with gold and black feathers and a red silk mask), but as before, it was only when he reached Naples that his spirits really lifted. There, he heard that his admirer Christian VIII had awarded him a travel grant of 600 rixdollars to enable him to continue his journey to the Orient, and on 15 March he sailed from Naples for Greece.

The boat was a wonder:

> The first-class lounge for ladies in an armed steamer is round, with a piano. Above deck is a spacious room for the captain; the lieutenants have their quarters next door. In first class, a large room with a dining table, two mirrors more than five feet wide; the walls inlaid and polished, and along these are the doors to the bedrooms—two built-in bunks, one above the other, with nice curtains. By the rudder hangs an hourglass filled with sand, a bell on which the hours are struck and a rather large clock next to it. In the middle of the ship, the machinery; on the sides, rooms for the commissioner, the first mate, etc. In the middle, a kitchen. Second class, a large dining room with bunks at each end and along the sides, small rooms with four or eight bunks. They ring for breakfast at 9:30, dinner at 5:30, a superb, lavish service—fowl, fish, roast, fruit, coffee.

Now, in uncharted territory, Andersen's enthusiasm got the better of him and his morbidity disappeared.

On deck as they neared Athens, he wrote, "the evening so endlessly beautiful—this transparent air, these clear stars, the shape of the mountain; all these things were both a comfort and an inspiration for me. I sat on a cannon . . . prayed to God for strength and good fortune. In my cabin, read through the letters from home; thought especially about Louise."* In his

---

*After a seven-year engagement, Louise Collin had just married Lind.

autobiography he described "the brilliant nights and days" he spent on the calm Mediterranean Sea, whose "long waves sparkled in the night": "The splendour of the stars astonished me . . . the light of Venus was like that of the moon in our North, and made the objects cast a shade; on the surface big dolphins tumbled; on the ship all was gaiety. We frolicked, sung, danced, played at cards, and chatted together—Americans, Italians and Asiatics; bishops and monks, officers and travellers."

At the Hotel de Munich in Athens, Andersen "got a particularly good room out to the street for three francs a day," hired a servant, went to the barber to be shaved, introduced himself to the Danish consul and got himself invited to the court of King Otto of Greece. Apart from a touch of hypochondria—"my penis is giving me trouble, and, heaven knows, it isn't my fault . . . Penis still bad; if only I haven't caught anything in the ship's loo!"—he spent a marvellous month in the city and flung himself into the Easter and Independence Day festivities, which were the sort of public spectacles he loved. He was welcomed by the Danish and German community and sketched by the Danish painter Christian Hansen, who drew a rather tired and sad-looking Andersen with a fez on his head. On 20 April he sailed on "crashing and cracking" seas, thinking of "shipwreck and death," via Smyrna, "with its pointed red roofs" and streets thronging with ostriches, camels, "Turkish women who only showed their eyes and tip of the nose" and "Jews and Armenians, with white and black hats," on through the Dardanelles and the Sea of Marmara to Constantinople, his destination.

He saw it first at dawn from the deck of the ship—"a Venice risen out of the sea. One mosque more splendid than another rose to our view; the Seraglio lay light and swimming before us." On a long gondola, where "you had to lie down in the bottom of the boat on some cushions . . . you didn't dare move for fear of capsizing, and the boatmen shouted to each other as they passed to avoid collisions," he made a trip to Scutari and saw the dancing dervishes, who seemed to whirl themselves to death, groaning and dripping with sweat and sinking down into "obscene positions." They so impressed him that he gave them a chapter in *A Poet's Bazaar*; at their monastery, everyone had to take off their shoes. Unfortunately he had trousers on with foot straps that could not be unfastened, so he cut the straps. "This is a good person," said a Turk to Andersen's servant.

He went to see them again at Pera, where the sultry heat and the throbbing male dancers sent him into ecstasies. Men such as the swiftly darting gondoliers excited him too. "The rowers had powerful, naked arms sticking out of their wide, gauze-like sleeves; it looked like part of a fairy tale. No one rows more beautifully than the Turks," he wrote. "Feeling sensual . . . sensuality is a thrilling tingling through the nerves as you release a drop of your vitality . . . An Asiatic sensuality is torturing me here. Oh, how I'm burning with longing!" reads his diary for April and May. He languished in the highly charged erotic sensibility which was always his response to hot countries. He lost himself in midnight walks by the sea, looking back to the shining minarets and out to dolphins and the warships in the bay, illuminated with lights in the mouths of their cannons, and with the pale moon hanging big and round over the Seraglio.

By the standards of the day, he had made an extraordinarily adventurous trip, and when Edvard Collin received a letter from Turkey, he wrote back with uncharacteristic admiration for Andersen's courage and determination in getting so far. On the return journey, Andersen really was brave, for, intrigued by the prospect of adding yet more countries to his tally, he chose the dangerous route by steamer up the Danube, travelling through Wallachia, Bulgaria and Serbia. There had recently been violent uprisings in the Balkans and rumours that thousands of Christians had been massacred, and Andersen was proud of himself for risking it. Travellers rode in "big carriages of basket-work, drawn by white oxen," over desolate, war-ravaged countryside where wild dogs were strolling about. In some places "only the tumbled down tombstones of two cemeteries showed us that here had been towns."

At Orsova on the Hungarian border they were quarantined for ten days, and Andersen shared two rooms with the British explorer William F. Ainsworth. Andersen spent his time writing and making paper-cuts of whirling dervishes, which he gave to Ainsworth; they were published in Ainsworth's account of his travels. Ainsworth recalled Andersen as

a tall young man, of prepossessing appearance, pale colour, yet somewhat delicate; brown hair and sharp nose and features, with a very very slight slouch in his gait, and the sidling movement of an abstracted man. He was friendly and cheerful in conversation, although restless and *pre-occupé*; but there was an extreme simplicity in his manners and confidence in others that made it impossible not to entertain feelings of regard and interest for him at once . . . Although always cheerful and companionable, there was never anything light or frivolous in his conduct . . . Herr Andersen was naturally of a pious turn of mind, and observed the sabbath strictly, putting by his papers, and doing no work on that day . . . One evening we had a severe thunder-storm: "I have learned to despise the dread of thunder as superstition," he said, in his peculiar

*Andersen in Dresden,
aged thirty-six, by Carl
Christian Vogel von
Vogelstein, 1841.*

nonchalant manner, "since I have learned to feel and appreciate the goodness of God."

A few weeks after this, Andersen sat in Dresden for the court painter Carl Christian Vogel von Vogelstein, who had just drawn Thorvaldsen and wanted Andersen as a companion piece for the Royal Collection. The result is one of the most handsome portraits of him—von Vogelstein has caught Andersen in profile in a relaxed pose, sitting on a *chaise-longue*, his arm draped over the side and his extraordinarily long hand and fingers drooping willow-like before him. He looks every inch the artist in German salon society: soft, still girlish features, confident expression, hair swept back to reveal his high, intelligent brow, mind engrossed, his demeanour confident with just a touch of the languid. "My portrait," he wrote to Ingeborg's husband Adolph Drewsen, "is quite different from all the others made of me, but resembles me very much and is yet so handsome and brilliantly done that I probably will not have quite this appearance until in the other world, where earthly shapes are after all ennobled."

Andersen had dreaded coming within reach of Denmark. Already in Vienna he complained that the German-Danish atmosphere reminded him of the unpleasantness of home, and said that he wished he had died in the Orient. He consoled himself with plans to write the account of his trip, which he thought he would call "My Evenings in the Orient." In Dresden his spirits picked up, for there were two charming letters from the Collin family waiting for him, which made the evening the happiest of his trip. He travelled from Dresden to Leipzig by train and wrote letters home on "Leipzig-Dresdner Eisenbahn Papier," sumptuously illustrated with pictures of the stations in the two cities and of the train careering through the countryside, waved at by peasants in the fields, and of its progress over bridges and aqueducts. He noted in his diary that he was admired and praised a lot, and writing home he boasted that his table was covered with calling cards from many important artists, that his publisher Brockhaus had given a dinner in his honour and that he had shared a box at the theatre with Mrs. von Goethe.

He returned to Copenhagen via Odense, happening to arrive at the time of St. Knud's Fair, which had been one of the annual highlights of his childhood, and he enjoyed telling a story—he may have made it up—about a "respectable lady of Funen" who greeted him with the praise, "I am very glad that you have arranged your great journey so as to come to the fair. I see that you keep to Odense; that I have always said." He got much the same reaction in Copenhagen—when he visited Weyse at the apartment on Kronprinsessegade, where he had gone in his first weeks in the city to learn about the subscription fund for him, Weyse greeted him cheerfully: "See now, you have not been any further than I! You have reached Kronprinsessegade, and looked out on to the royal garden; I do the same, and you have thrown away ever so much money. Would you travel? Go to Roskilde [a town twenty miles from Copenhagen]; that is enough, until we visit the moons and planets!"

Nevertheless, Andersen was uncharacteristically content to be home, calling the moment of return "the bouquet of the whole journey." He stood at the heart of Copenhagen cultural life; he had to some extent redeemed his reputation after the débâcle over *The Moorish Maid* by positioning himself as a Balkan hero, original and exotic. He was in the theatre for every important première, such as Bournonville's ballet hit *Napoli*, which owed something to his *Improvisatore*. He was a central attraction for every celebrity visiting the city. Liszt sought him out in 1841, and Andersen took him to see the composer Hartmann, Thorvaldsen and the Queen. At the Collins' house, he met the pianist Clara Schumann in 1842; he "possesses a poetical, spiritual mind, is still quite young and very ugly," she wrote in her diary, and to Robert, "he is the ugliest that can exist . . . one can only accustom oneself to his character . . . on the whole his is a ghostly appearance." Months later, Schumann dedicated a musical setting of his poems to Andersen. Over the next eighteen months he was mostly calm, though often he noted in his almanac that he was very sad, and absorbed in his writing; for short times he could revel in being a big fish in the small Copenhagen pond, until the pond suddenly seemed a small puddle, its waters muddied by critical feuds or simple lack of appreciation.

In 1841–1842, Andersen's heart was in his travel memoir, now called *A Poet's Bazaar*, though for Christmas 1841 a new volume of tales appeared. Some had been written at the estate of Nysø with Thorvaldsen, Baroness Stampe and the young Baron Henrik as audience: "Often in the twilight, when the family circle sat in the open garden parlour, Thorvaldsen would come softly behind me, and, clapping me on the shoulder, would ask, 'Shall we little ones hear any tales tonight?'" The longest, "The Sandman," takes its inspiration from the figure of myth and nursery rhyme who urges children to bed: the little man with an umbrella in ancient Greece, Wee Willie Winkie in the English rhyme, Ole Lukøie (Ole Shut-Eye) in Denmark, the Sandman in Germany, who sends the children to sleep with happy dreams by putting sand on their eyes in "Hansel and Gretel" and is the wicked, eye-stealing hero of E. T. A. Hoffmann's surreal story "The Sandman." Andersen's version is benign—his Sandman has two umbrellas, "one with pictures on it which he puts up over the good children," giving them lovely dreams, and one blank one, which makes the naughty children have no dreams at all—Andersen's vision of the emptiness of evil. This gives a frame for his inventiveness, as he tells the different dreams of a boy called Hjalmar for every night of the week.

There is something of the hallucinatory world of Hoffmann here—with a magic squirt, the Sandman makes Hjalmar shrink to the size of a tin soldier, borrow his uniform and drive to a mouse wedding in a scene which Lewis Carroll echoes when Alice shrinks and grows in *Alice's Adventures in Wonderland*. But the dreams are also full of satirical portraits of Copenhageners as animals, which the company at Nysø would have loved—it is easy to imagine Andersen reading these aloud nightly to the artists and aristocrats amid the gentle laughter of recognition. Ingeborg Drewsen, for instance, is a hen who has only ventured as far as the cabbage patch, believing "anybody who doesn't think our country's the nicest is a good-for-nothing wretch." Andersen casts himself as a stork who tries to tell the other birds about the pyramids and ostriches he has seen on his travels, but "What a freak!" they all say.

The tale ends with some dark moralizing—death is the nicest dream from the Sandman, but "only see that you have a good report." It shares with all the stories in this volume a concentration on death and punishment. "The Rose Elf," an adaptation of a Boccaccio story, is full of hidden skulls and murderous revenge. "The Buckwheat" is a parable about conceit and retribution. "The Swineherd" is a genteel version of a folk tale in which a princess is turned out of her kingdom for preferring a swineherd with an artificial music-box to a prince who offers the pure gifts of a nightingale and rose—this is the germ of the idea of "The Nightingale," written two years later. Through it runs the refrain of the melancholy German folk song, "Ah my darling Augustin / Everything's lost, lost, lost."

A Poet's Bazaar, which came out in April 1842, is a brighter book, a delicately sustained account of a northern mind meeting the strangeness of the Orient. Inspired in part by Lamartine's *Souvenirs d'un voyage en Orient* (1835), it wanders from straight travel-writing to little stories, to a conversation between Pegasus and two coach horses, to a debate about the existence of "fairy palaces." Andersen had a natural ability to evoke landscape with the eye of a painter, and partly because its subject matter was unusual and unknown, partly because his fantasy rambles were always liked—both *A Walking Tour* and *Picture Book Without Pictures* had done well—*A Poet's Bazaar* sold excellently and was translated into German, Swedish and English.

At home it was a success with the public despite the critics, who took issue with Andersen's vanity in dedicating the different sections to the various luminaries who had helped him on his journey—the section on Breitenburg to Count Rantzau-Breitenburg, that on the Danube to Liszt, and so on. But it is Andersen's best travel memoir, and one of its charms is its intimate, personal tone. Sometimes it reads as if Andersen is dropping his readers clues about his life—the opening scene, for example, is set at Nysø and mentions Henrik Stampe. The most perceptive review came in the satirical weekly *Corsaren*, in which the radical editor Meir Goldschmidt praised

Andersen's landscape painting but complained that he ignored the poverty and suppression of the people he had met on his travels.

Five years earlier, no one in Copenhagen would have written a review like this. Such writing, set against the unrest and dissent that led to the uprisings and war in Germany and Denmark in 1848, marked the beginning of a new interest in politics in Copenhagen which the absolutist but weak Christian VIII could not check. The Biedermeier cosiness of the small capital began to alter; Danes could not fail to look outwards towards political developments in Germany and France, and it was from this time clear that the overwhelming social emphasis on the arts which had characterized Golden Age culture was on the wane. To this Andersen barely responded at all. He answered Goldschmidt in a paragraph in his autobiography: "I felt no necessity to mix myself up in such matters . . . Politics are no affair of mine. God has imparted to me another mission."

It was around this time that he was visited by his half-sister Karen-Marie, a washerwoman from the Copenhagen slums, and he recoiled in horror at any contact with his childhood background. In February 1842 he returned from the theatre to a startling find: "Letter from my mother's daughter. I lived through that which I wrote about in *OT*. Feverish. An appalling night. Sensuality and despair sneeringly filled my thoughts. +" He rushed to see Jonas Collin the next day and the Collin family rapidly set the matter to rest. Ingeborg's husband Adolph Drewsen, a magistrate, looked up details about Karen-Marie's whereabouts and history, her common-law husband (like her mother's and grandmother's husbands, more than ten years younger than her) was sent for and Andersen gave him four rixdollars. Karen-Marie herself appeared later in the year (when, Andersen commented, she looked quite well-dressed and young, and he gave her one rixdollar) and she turned up again at Andersen's hotel in 1843, after which there is no mention of her. She died in 1846, although Andersen probably never knew this. His rise through society had been too individual and meteoric for him to feel much sympathy with Karen-Marie or working-class solidarity, and he inherited from his mother an unswerving respect for the ruling class.

In his fiction, he rebelled, depicting the triumph of the poor and obscure over the conventional establishment. In life, his instincts were at once apolitical and anti-democratic, while by temperament he was a diplomat, anxious not to pick a fight, always keen for reconciliation, solicitous of treating people of all classes with courtesy and respect. He loved the trappings of wealth and power, and never questioned an élitist social system. "In our days everyone wishes to rule," he wrote. "People forget that that which is thought of cannot always be carried out, and that many things look very different when contemplated from the top of the tree, to what they did when seen from its roots." In the 1840s, he became increasingly obsessed with his high connections. Like travel, visiting the aristocracy and collecting dukes and duchesses among his friends was a way to soothe his nerves, flatter his vanity and keep depression at bay.

Danish *Herregårde*, or aristocratic estates, are quite unlike the sumptuous homes of the English nobility. Denmark is a small conservative country and its country houses are mostly modest, trim and uniform, set in well-kept parks with simple gardens and lawns often sweeping down to a lake, usually full of swans. "It is the humour of all this kingdom to build in the midst of lakes," Robert Molesworth wrote of the Danish estates in the seventeenth century. Serenity rather than glamour is the keynote; like all country houses in the nineteenth century, they gave the visitor access to an exclusive, self-contained world where everyday cares could be forgotten and servants were on hand to attend to every need. Andersen had his first taste of this at Nysø in 1838, and at the manor house of Glorup on Funen in 1839, but from the summer of 1842 he became a regular guest at two of the most exclusive estates in the country, Gisselfeldt and Bregentved, situated near each other some thirty miles south of Copenhagen and buried in the wooded countryside of Zealand.

Gisselfeldt, formerly a monastery, is a towering gabled place, forbidding in its solid red brick and narrow windows, but its gently undulating parkland and gorgeous lake are an invitation to peace and repose. It belonged to an old lady, Countess Danneskjold, mother of the Duchess of Augustenborg, to whom Andersen was thrilled to be introduced; he noted in his diary, too, how happy he was when a servant there wished him "a most humble goodnight." He moved on to Count Moltke's Bregentved, a seventeenth-century house built in the French style, elegantly proportioned and surrounded by a moat. Later, after he had visited England, he described the estate as "in the midst of a beautiful and extensive forest, so luxuriant that there is scarcely another to equal it in Denmark. The garden here, with its great verdant lawns, immense avenues of lime trees and cheerful lakes, where swans and shimmering white lotus flowers float up on the water, reminds me of the English parks," and wrote that "the hospitality which I met with in this place, one of the richest and most beautiful of our country, and the happy, social life which surrounded me here, have diffused a sunshine over my life."

These were places where he found it congenial to work, and on his first visit the two estates inspired his most famous tale. "I was dejected, against my will, roamed around in the woods and fields, felt less than well. Had the idea of 'The Story of a Duck,' this helped my sunken spirits," Andersen wrote at Gisselfeldt on 5 July 1842. He went to see the swans again, on 8 July, noting "the swans have cygnets, and are very irritable." Three weeks later at Bregentved, he noted, "Started on 'The Cygnet' yesterday." "The Ugly Duckling," which Andersen took a year to perfect, opens in a flat, hot, calm, Danish landscape like that around Gisselfeldt and Bregentved:

> Summertime! How lovely it was out in the country, with the wheat standing yellow, the oats green and the hay all stacked down in the grassy meadows! . . . Bathed in sunshine stood an old manor-house with a deep moat round it, and growing out of the wall down by the water were huge dock-leaves . . . and here it was that a duck was sitting on her nest.

It closes again in the park of a country estate, "with apple-trees in blossom and sweet-smelling lilac that dangled from long green boughs right over the

The manor house of Bregentved, where Andersen was a guest from the 1840s to the 1870s. He began writing "The Ugly Ducking" there in 1842.

winding stream." As the ugly duckling realizes he is a swan, children throw him bread and cake and clap him, "and now he heard everyone saying that he was the loveliest of all lovely birds." This is the sort of acclaim Andersen heard when he read his tales to his aristocratic friends; like the children to the swan, they fed Andersen the tame genius the bread and cakes of fine dinners and hospitality, and enjoyed watching him perform. The story is a marker of the new phase Andersen entered in the early 1840s.

He spent the autumn in Copenhagen, working on a long poem about the wandering Jew Ahasverus, which he had begun on his trip to the Orient and which occupied him on and off for years; he identified increasingly with the restless hero. For the Christmas holiday he was back in Gisselfeldt and Bregentved for a round of aristocratic entertainment—balls and amateur dramatics, reading his work aloud and going on wintry walks. In January 1843 he went on to Breitenburg Castle as the guest of Count Rantzau, and then spent his savings on a two-month stay in Paris, where he found himself well known thanks to Marmier's *La vie d'un poète*. Heinrich Heine, whom he had met nervously in Paris ten years earlier, now gave him a warm welcome. "You're good at narrating! Goethe could do it, but I can't," said Heine, but still Andersen noted, "I don't trust his face, though." Maybe he worried that Heine saw through him, for Heine wrote:

> Andersen called upon me some years ago. I thought he looked like a tailor. He is a lean man with a hollow lantern-jawed face, and in his outward appearance he betrays a servile lack of self-confidence which is appreciated by dukes and princes. He fulfils exactly a prince's idea of a poet. When he visited me he had decked himself out with a big tie-pin; I asked him what it was that he had put there. He replied very unctuously, "It is a present which the Electress of Hessen has been gracious enough to bestow on me." Otherwise Andersen is a man of some spirit.

For Andersen, Paris was one long party of meeting famous names who knew his and treated him as a figure of international stature. At the Hotel de Paris, Alexandre Dumas, dressed in a blue-striped shirt and baggy trousers, embraced him and entertained him in his bedroom, where the bed was unmade; Dumas worked there, asking Andersen to wait for a few minutes when he had a sudden "visit from my muse." Andersen stayed in a small room on the fifth floor of an obscure hotel in the Rue Richelieu, but with Marmier as his guide he met Victor Hugo and Lamartine, who wrote him a poem, Gautier and Alfred de Vigny, who visited him and gave him his collected works. The sculptor David took one look at him and said, "I have read you yourself before your books. You are a poet." At the Comtesse de Bocarmé's salon, the Countess Pffaffin, dressed in black and glittering with jewels, dragged him on to a velvet sofa, held his hand and pulled Balzac down on her other side, exclaiming how small she seemed when seated between two giants of the times. "I turned my head and met behind her back Balzac's satirical and laughing face, with his mouth half open and pursed up in a queer manner; that was properly our first meeting"; Balzac, "a little ball with square shoulders," paid him compliments.

This acclaim was despite Andersen's poor French; in his diary, Vigny noted that Andersen spoke not a word of French, and that he spoke to him in sign language. Andersen was never any good at learning foreign languages, except German, which is close to Danish; he would rush through his conversations quickly, he wrote to Jonas Collin's granddaughter Jonna, then stop suddenly when he got stuck, ending abruptly with *Voilà, c'est tout!*

All this florid foreign courtesy contrasted sharply with his reputation at home, which plummeted during his absence when his poem *Agnete* was adapted for the stage, booed and ridiculed. "From Denmark are always coming the chill draughts that turn me to stone!" he wrote to Jette Wulff:

> Here, in this big strange city, Europe's most famous and noble personalities fondly surround me, meet with me as a kindred spirit; and at home boys sit spitting at my heart's dearest creation! . . . the Danes are evil, cold, satanic—a people well suited to the wet, mouldy-green islands from where Tycho Brahe was exiled . . . Have never had a fever like now. I am ill; my home has sent me a fever from its cold, wet forests, which the Danes gaze upon and believe they love; but I don't believe in love in the North, but in evil treachery. I can feel it in my own blood, and it's only in that way I know I am Danish!

The Collins did not remember his birthday, he wrote sourly, and no one was much interested in the boastful letters about the impression he was making. Andersen understood that there was now a gulf between the public, cosmopolitan persona he was assiduously creating, and the narrow world back home.

He did not see, though, that it was in part his failure of human understanding that caused it. In early 1843, Edvard Collin's eldest daughter died aged six, the first of a series of family tragedies to haunt Edvard and his wife

William Etty's portrait of the French actress Rachel, a friend of Andersen's in Paris.

Jette, who had up to now gone through life so smoothly.* Andersen's work, from his first poem "The Dying Child" through countless fairy tales, is full of dying children, but he could not sympathize. He felt shut out by Edvard's grief and mortified by the absence of birthday greetings. "Edvard could have sent me one, for even if I am not so lucky as to be among the friends he takes consolation from speaking to when he has a deep grief, he might nevertheless, when this unhappiness is relieved, remember me by writing some words," he told Jonas, who pacified him that "you are always recalled with love here in Amaliegade, even if it is not always expressed in words." But the division was clear: Edvard was absorbed in his family, in domestic happiness and sorrow; Andersen in his art and his fame.

In Paris, however, art and fame led to a new emotional excitement. "The

---

*In 1843 Edvard and Jette had five children—a child a year since their marriage—but after the death of their eldest, they had no more, though Jette was only thirty, and it is possible that they simply refused to risk such loss again. Tragedy, however, haunted this family. Another child died in 1845, aged four, and their youngest child died at thirteen in 1855. Only two children outlived them: Louise (1839–1920) and Jonas (1840–1905), a zoologist who as a young man became a good friend of Andersen's.

best thing I have to communicate to you," he wrote to Henriette Wulff soon after his disappointing birthday, "is that yesterday I was invited by Rachel to one of her exclusive soirées." The actress Rachel Felix, 22-year-old daughter of a Jewish Gypsy, was one of the most revered names on the European stage, a tragedienne of extraordinary intensity and severe passion; she knew, it was said, "how to chisel living statues out of Racine's and Corneille's blocks of marble." Andersen saw her as Phèdre, and concluded "she is herself the French tragic muse, who reveals herself to us and embodies for us what she had the poet sing of"; later he saw her as Mary Queen of Scots ("shattering . . . what a natural serenity and suffering") in Schiller's *Maria Stuart*.

He met Rachel for the first time when Dumas took him backstage at the Théâtre Français; at her home, adorned with busts of Racine and Corneille and bookcases full of Shakespeare, Goethe and Schiller, he was overawed.

> The room displayed splendour and wealth. Plum-coloured walls, carpets of the same hue, costly curtains and tasteful furniture . . . She made room for me on the sofa beside her, close by the fireplace; she was dressed in black and was extremely gracious. I begged her to speak German, and she replied, "Yes, if you were unable to speak French, then I would; but you express yourself better in my language than I in a foreign one. Your pronunciation is good; and with a little practice would be very good indeed." And so I was obliged to speak French . . . As we were sitting there, one guest after another arrived—Scribe, Gautier—I do not remember all the famous names. Rachel, vivacious and charming, was the only lady among us. She poured out the tea herself, and we gossiped of poetry and art. It was 12 o'clock before I could slip away. Today she has returned my album with these words written in it—"*L'art c'est le vrai. J'espère que cet aphorisme ne semblera pas paradoxical à un écrivain aussi distingué que Monsieur Andersen.*"

Dark, sultry and slender, with a deep, powerful voice, Rachel was unconventional and made no concession to the fashion for winsome femininity; she bore an odd resemblance to Andersen's ruthless, androgynous-looking Jewish heroine Naomi in his novel *Only a Fiddler*, and he was mesmerized by her. "You get ice-cold shivers down your back, as if you were watching a sleepwalker who expressed your hidden, deepest feelings." Each time he saw her, he recorded a "sensual. +." "Fire burning hot in my veins; out—+," "Bought wine; at home by 7:30 +," "bought myself some cakes and am now imagining myself sitting at home—Very sensual +," "Sensual mood +," runs his diary for most of April. He was not in love with Rachel, but there was an understanding of shared artistic values between them, underwritten, perhaps, by the struggle upwards from harsh backgrounds that they had both made. Rachel, Swiss by birth, knew about the different contemporary French and German styles of acting, and talked of these different manners with Andersen, whose knowledge of European theatre was unrivalled. Their friendship opened his eyes to the possibility of a response to a woman which was at once sensual, emotional and aesthetic; to the idea of a union between two artists which would not force him to choose, as he had felt with Riborg Voigt, between domesticity and his vocation. In May 1843, he returned to Denmark reawakened to his need for love and burning to prove his worth as an international writer.

CHAPTER 12

Jenny

1843–1844

Oh, what a glorious gift . . . by means of a scrap of paper to make men see so cleverly
how the noblest often lie most hidden and covered over by wretchedness and rags,
until the hour of transformation strikes and shows the figure in a divine light!

—JENNY LIND,
letter to Hans Christian Andersen, 19 March 1844

If Andersen had set out to invent a female equivalent of himself, he could
not have done better than to imagine Jenny Lind. Their paths had first
crossed at the Hotel du Nord in 1840, when the young Swedish singer was
staying in Copenhagen; they had conversed briefly and then parted without
thought of one another. Now, in the summer of 1843, Jenny was back in the
Danish capital for her first professional appearance outside Stockholm, and
Andersen met her at the house of Auguste Bournonville, the Danish ballet-
master. In Sweden, Jenny had been hailed as a great new prima donna after
singing Agathe in Weber's *Der Freischütz* in 1838; Andersen had a growing
reputation in Scandinavia and Germany. They recognized parallels in each
other's lives at once. Both were unusual, uneasy people; both had felt lonely
and different since childhood; both were absolutely dedicated to their art;
both were romantics who spoke to a vast audience through an emphasis on
the simple and mythical—Jenny with Swedish folksongs, Andersen with
fairy tales. And both were in 1843 on the edge of breakthroughs to world
fame which were to transform their futures.

The similarities in their early lives were extraordinary. Jenny was born in
Stockholm in 1820, the illegitimate daughter of a schoolmistress, Anne-
Marie Fellborg, and her live-in companion, Niclas Jonas Lind. Like Andersen's mother, Anne-Marie Fellborg already had a daughter from a previous
relationship; at seventeen she had married an army officer, Captain Rad-

berg, whom she had—unusually for the times—divorced for infidelity. She took up with Lind some years later but, probably for religious reasons, did not marry him until Radberg died in 1835. Like Andersen's parents, they were an oddly matched couple. When Jenny was born, Lind was an aimless young man of twenty-two with a fine singing voice but no clue about making money, and Anne-Marie at twenty-seven was a tough, practical survivor. Her school provided the family with its meagre income—Anne-Marie, Lind, the elder daughter and the pupil-boarders were cramped together in a dingy third-floor flat, and Jenny's arrival was a nuisance and a threat to the school. Within months she was sent out to foster parents in the country, where she stayed for four years. When she returned, her embittered mother, worn down by drudgery and worry, took out her frustrations on her; her father spent his time drinking and singing, or in the debtors' prison.

For consolation—here too was an experience shared with Andersen—Jenny turned to her grandmother, gentle, devout Fru Tengmark. After a few years of living with her mother, she was fostered again, this time by the couple who ran the old people's home where Fru Tengmark lived, and so her grandmother became a principal influence. As Andersen had done, Jenny sang and danced for the old ladies of the home, who made much of her, and like the young Andersen, it was her voice that got her noticed and offered her the chance to break away from her background. By the mid nineteenth century, the story of her discovery was famous:

> Her favourite seat with her cat was in the window of the Steward's rooms, which look out on to the lively street leading up to the church of St. Jakob's, and there she sat and sang to it: and people passing in the street used to hear and wonder; and among others the maid of a Mademoiselle Lundberg, a dancer at the Royal Opera House; and the maid told her mistress that she had never heard such beautiful singing as this little girl sang to her cat. Mademoiselle Lundberg thereupon found out who she was, and sent to ask her mother . . . to bring her to sing to her. And when she heard her sing, she said, "The child is a genius; you must have her educated for the stage."

Jenny was nine, "a small, ugly, broad-nosed, shy, gauche, altogether undergrown girl," as she later described herself. But at her audition for the singing school attached to Stockholm Opera House, the teachers wept to hear her. They made her mother an irresistible offer: she would start immediately, although the usual age for admission was fourteen, and the school would take on responsibility for her maintenance, education and professional training. But Fru Fellborg, who had spent years trying to get Jenny off

her hands, now hesitated. In the 1820s the theatre was still considered a raff-
ish profession; the eighteenth-century view, that women who made a living
on the stage were little more than high-class courtesans, persisted, and no
respectable mother would have allowed her daughter to contemplate such a
career. As a result, the leading European actresses and singers in the first
half of the nineteenth century all came from unconventional backgrounds:
in Denmark, Johanne Luise Heiberg had grown up on a fairground; in
Paris, Rachel was a Jewish tinker's daughter; the Italian Adelaide Ristori
came from a family of travelling players. This was one reason why Andersen
identified so closely with performers such as Rachel and Jenny. Later in the
century, in part due to Jenny Lind's propriety and high-mindedness, the
stage came to be a more acceptable profession for women.

For Fru Fellborg in 1830, the temptation was too much, and though she
felt she was sacrificing her child to the stage, Jenny joined the school. She
was quickly noticed as an outstanding actress and dancer as well as an
exceptional singer. She made her debut in a sentimental dance drama called
The Polish Mine in November 1830, and the Swedish daily *Dagligt Allehanda*
wrote of her performance next morning that "such spirit and theatrical
assurance, such utter lack of shyness in a little girl appearing before an audience of twelve hundred people, is an exception to the normal course of
nature. We hope, however, that it will have no adverse influence on the
moral training of the grown woman." The reviewer need not have worried.
Throughout the 1830s Jenny dazzled in a number of small parts, while growing up into an idealistic and puritanical teenager. Rejecting outright the
loose-living disorder of her parents, who made it clear only how they wished
to exploit her talent for financial gain, at sixteen she moved away from them
and acquired for herself an alternative legal guardian, Judge Munthe. Like
Andersen she was desperately needy of affection and in her twenties
attached herself to a cultured German family, the Wichmanns, whom she
adopted rather as Andersen adopted the Collins.

At eighteen, Jenny made her adult debut as Weber's high-minded, innocent heroine Agathe, and threw the Stockholm audience into ecstasies at
her brilliant, powerful soprano; she also sang Alice, the sister who protects
her devil-haunted foster-brother, in Meyerbeer's *Robert le Diable*. Bournonville, Copenhagen's ballet-master, was in the audience and remembered,
"She was eighteen years old, but even then possessed such an eminent talent
that her performance as Alice . . . was on a par with the finest I had heard
and seen in Paris; and even though her voice was not yet as highly developed
as it later became, it still had the same sympathies, the same electric power,

which now make it so irresistible. She was adored." She went on to train in Paris, which she hated (she was so miserable there, she said, that she envied the fountain because it did not have to sing), and by the time she came to Copenhagen, the essential qualities of her voice were perfected—the famous pianissimo rendering of her high notes, said to reach every corner of the largest auditorium though delivered in a whisper; the unrivalled swelling and diminishing of her voice from softest piano to fullest power; the astonishing renewal of her breath, effected so artfully that even those close to her did not notice it.

When she sang in London a few years later, the *Spectator* published this description of her performance:

> Her voice is a pure soprano—of the fullest compass belonging to voices of this class, and of such evenness of tone that the nicest ear can discover no differ-ence of quality from the bottom to the summit of the scale . . . her tones are never muffled or indistinct, nor do they ever offend the ear by the slightest tinge of shrillness—mellow roundness distinguishes every sound she utters . . . The same clearness was observed in her pianissimo. When, in her beautiful closes, she prolonged a tone, attenuating it by degrees, and falling gently upon the final note, the sound, though as ethereal as the sighing of a breeze, reached (like Mrs. Siddons's whisper in *Lady Macbeth*), every part of the immense theatre.

"There will not in a whole century," said Mendelssohn, "be born another being so gifted as Jenny Lind . . . She is the best artiste with whom I have become acquainted in my life—the most genuine and noble. She is rather shy and retiring, but when you have heard from her either a small song or an air you will know more about her than I can tell you."

It was not just her voice, but the fusion of her own personality with the role she was playing that mesmerized audiences. "I scarcely ever think of the effect I am producing," she said, "and if the thought does sometimes cross my mind, it spoils my acting. It seems to me when I act that I feel fully all the emotions of the character I represent. I fancy myself—indeed believe myself—to be in her situation, and I never think of the audience." She iden-tified passionately with Weber's Agathe, icon of love and purity, and with Meyerbeer's Alice, the role with which she made her London debut. Asked about her interpretation, she replied, "How could I tell how I sang it? I stood at the man's right hand, and the Fiend at his left, and all I could think of was, how to save him."

Believing the gift of her voice to be heaven-sent, she resolved to dedicate it to uplifting mankind; art and religion merged in her imagination and at various phases in her life she bordered on hysterical religious mania. This thrilled her fans. Her friend Fredrika Bremer, the Swedish novelist, wrote to Andersen:

> If you want to see Jenny Lind's eyes flash like lightning, and her whole face and personality enveloped by the beauty of joy and inspiration, then talk to her about her art . . . about its benign influence on the human soul. But if you want to see the deepest and loveliest aspect of her, then talk to her about the most profound teacher of religion, about his appearance in Christ . . . then you will see tears of joy and emotion streaming across the young face, with its child-like expression, and her eyes will shine devoutly and magnificently, then—then she is beautiful!

Religion was her solace, but, says her biographer Joan Bulman, "the Puritan in her recoiled from the success the artist sought and achieved. The very background of her home, the atmosphere she had breathed as a child, had held the seed of this conflict of character. The elements of music and song, a streak of Bohemian recklessness set against a strict and narrow Lutheranism, had played about her from her birth." Jenny was unhappy, nervous, lonely and confused about her great gifts. She scorned the company of the famous singers who had been her predecessors in Sweden, such as Emilie Högqvist, mistress of Crown Prince Oskar, because of their irregular private lives; when she met Emilie on the street, she deliberately looked the other way. Her self-righteousness and devotion, unattractive to modern taste, were a vital part of her appeal: she shared with two other dumpy, ugly, unlikely heroines of the early nineteenth century, Florence Nightingale and Queen Victoria—both born the same year as she was—a mix of passion, religious fervour and inexorable drive that seemed to embody the twin ideals, purity and high achievement, of her age.

"It is her intrinsic worth of heart and delicacy of mind; it is in her pure and intense feelings that abide her potency," ran a typical British review. "A great and noble simplicity, combined with an ardent imagination—a love of nature, refined by poetry of feeling, pervades her whole being . . . In Jenny Lind is typified the great improvement of the morale of the stage." But this intensity and dedication came at a cost. Like Andersen, Jenny was temperamental, easily upset, and had to be handled with exceptional delicacy. "She is reserved and self-contained," wrote one of her closest friends, pure through and through; so strangely tender that she is easily wounded, and thereupon becomes silent and serious, when no reason for it is apparent. A word will often quickly shut her up in herself . . . She is a true sensitive plant, that closes itself at the lightest touch. Do not think, from this, that she is intolerable. She is by nature a truly lovable creature . . . She speaks little and thinks deeply . . . Free from the slightest trace of coquetry, she regards all coquetry with horror.

She was, like Andersen, immature, prudish and uncomfortable with herself; she was also aware already that the emotional engagement she brought to her roles was too overwhelming to sustain for long, and she thought of retirement from opera-singing almost as soon as she took on leading roles. "The strain was too great," wrote an English friend,

Jenny Lind was worn out with fatigue and emotion. She threw herself into every part, and suffered the woes of the heroine—unlike other great actors and actresses, who . . . succeed in making their representations to a certain degree mechanical. But Jenny Lind's essentially truthful spirit did not do this. The tears she wept in *La Sonnambula* came from her heart. We had more than once the stage box, and could see that she was overpowered by her feelings.

This, then, was the uncertain young woman of twenty-two who arrived in Copenhagen in September 1843. She had not come to sing, but she ran into Bournonville as soon as she arrived and he persuaded her at once to stay at his house—his wife was Swedish, and Jenny was comforted by the cheerful presence of his many children, with whom she sang hymns each morning, accompanying herself on the piano. Once she was installed, Bournonville began his campaign to get her on to the stage of the Royal Theatre; *Robert le Diable*, with which she had caused a sensation in Stockholm in 1839, was playing, and she could sing her part in Swedish. But Jenny was terrified of an unfamiliar stage and a foreign audience with which she had no bond, and when she visited the theatre and saw Johanne Luise Heiberg in full sway, her confidence collapsed entirely.

"She became at once so excited and depressed," wrote Bournonville, "that, weeping, she anxiously begged me to allow her to 'escape,' as she called it, from displaying the insignificance of her talent and her person on a stage which possessed such a combination of genius and beauty [as that of Fru Heiberg]." This was the attack of nerves which was to overcome her at every new capital she visited. To help persuade her, Bournonville invited Andersen one Sunday afternoon, 3 September; Jenny had read some of

Jenny Lind, by E. Magnus, 1846.

Andersen's works and they had a mutual friend in Fredrika Bremer, and Andersen's experience of international theatre was well known.

"Dinner at Bournonville's. Mademoiselle Lind from Stockholm sang for me," Andersen noted in his almanac. He was immediately struck by her—he wrote to Ingemann that she was not good-looking at first glance, but her exceptional character became clear as soon as she spoke. Jenny was never beautiful—she had a homely, almost peasant face; her cheek bones were broad, her eyes deep-set and her skin sallow; she had a heavy expression which suddenly burst into animation when she began to talk. She dressed simply, kept her hair in child-like ringlets and wore no make-up, but the magnetism of her forceful personality was overwhelming.

"No one could see Jenny Lind and not fall under the charm of her perfect naturalness, freshness and originality," wrote an English observer. "Although her features were irregular, she was anything but plain; her complexion was fair, she had abundant flaxen hair and the most wonderful grey eyes, a beautiful figure, hands and arms, and graceful movements. Hers was not the slow, sinuous grace which has a charm of its own: her movements were light, decided and expressive. She always seemed to do everything more quickly than anyone else." She had no illusions about her appearance—when asked why she had never sung in Paris, she laughed that it would be impossible with her potato nose—and this in itself suggested a bond to Andersen. There was an accord between them at once, each responding to the other's honesty and lack of pretension, both recognizing in the other something of their own history as they talked.

Andersen said he could not pass judgement on her singing, because he had never heard it, but "such was the disposition at this moment in Copenhagen, that only a moderate voice and some knowledge of acting would be successful . . . she might safely venture." After a week, she was convinced; Andersen wrote in his almanac on 10 September: "Jenny Lind's first performance as Alice; she had curtain calls. In the evening with her at Bournonville's, her toast and mine were drunk. In love." For the next ten days, he was caught up in the sensational acclaim which followed Jenny everywhere she went. In her memoirs, Bournonville's daughter Charlotte wrote that "of all memories from childhood, the greatest impression is of Jenny Lind singing, of her whole personality. To me she looked like someone from another world. And although I was only ten when I first heard her sing, I not only remember all the songs but even the smallest shadings . . . She sang in *Robert*, and the triumphs she celebrated that year and two years later are almost unique in the history of our theatre." The Bournonville children were allowed to go to hear her on stage, and "when we left the theatre after performances, the streets were absolutely black with people, and I remember these thousands of people crying when they simply saw Jenny Lind."

It was the beginning of the Jenny Lind fever that swept across Europe in the 1840s—a phenomenon familiar in recent times, in the hysterical following of celebrities, but unprecedented in the nineteenth century.* The King showered her with gifts; students serenaded her; rumours of her divine pow-

---

*In Vienna in 1847, for example, it was reported that during Jenny's last performances "the stalls, which are habitually sold at two florins, rose to fifty, and still three thousand persons had their names put down for them and were disappointed. The last night, not content with calling her forward innumerable times with plaudits, cheers and deafening shouts, when she returned home the spectators within joined the crowd without and followed her to her home. Thirty times she was called to her window; the crowd kept constantly repeating, 'Jenny Lind, say you will come back again!'"

ers circulated when it was heard that she had taken time out from her busy schedule to visit a rich musical wine merchant, Mozart Waage Petersen, who believed he was dying and was distraught that he could not get out of bed to hear her, but recovered after she had sung to him at home.

Jenny saw Copenhagen as her turning point; Andersen was part of the inner circle who made her at home and fêted her. He in turn loved the high-pitched, theatrical emotion which surrounded her, and revelled in the fuss. He saw her daily:

11 September: Sent Jenny a poem.

12 September: Evening at Bournonville's with Jenny Lind; gave her a briefcase.

13 September: Jenny Lind second time in *Robert*: she had a bouquet and a poem from me; unhappy because she is leaving on Saturday.

14 September: Her journey delayed; every day at her home; sent her my poems; went to Thorvaldsen's exhibition with her.

16 September: Jenny Lind's concert, in the evening at Bournonville's; Jenny and I confidential.

17 September: Dinner at Oehlenschläger's. In the evening Jenny L. came. I hardly talked to her; *jaloux* of Günther.* We went back by omnibus and I followed her home.

18 September: Visited her, read the others' poems, thought about proposing . . .

19 September: Jenny Lind's diamonds, presented by the King; sent her my portrait, wrote a song. In the evening at Nielsen's, where 300 students gave her a serenade; I love her. Came home at 1:30 in the morning, wrote her a letter.

20 September: At the Customs House this morning at 4:30, said goodbye to Jenny, handed her a letter which she must understand. I love! . . . in the evening at the Hotel Angleterre . . . Sensual. +

21 September: In bad spirits!—Passionate. +

---

*Julius Günther was a gifted and handsome Swedish tenor who often played opposite Jenny in Stockholm. Andersen was prescient; at this time there was no understanding between Jenny and Günther, but five years later they did become engaged, in 1848, at a low point in Jenny's life. The engagement was quickly broken off.

As with Riborg Voigt, Andersen fell in love immediately and thought of marriage within days. The letter he gave Jenny when she left Copenhagen— as with Riborg thirteen years earlier, he waited until the last minute, then could not bring himself to address her face to face—was obviously something of a love letter, for Jenny showed it to Fredrika Bremer, who wrote to Andersen that it was clearly pointless to talk to him about anyone except Jenny. But Andersen was also luxuriating publicly in his obsession—he always did so in his love affairs with women. To Henriette Wulff he wrote, "Now do you understand that all my thoughts are about such a pearl? And yet, she won't be mine—can't be mine, but she shall seem to me like a good and kind spirit who—and this I know—appreciates me, likes me—maybe more than I deserve!" At the Bournonville home, he made himself a figure of fun. "We liked him very much, my sister, brother and I, but of course we didn't imagine him as a *primo amoroso*, and we thought it would be fun to tease him," wrote Charlotte Bournonville. "When Jenny Lind came to see us, he never stopped asking 'Has Jenny Lind never talked about me? Has she never said "I like him?"' But we said 'no,' because although Jenny Lind did talk about him and liked him very much and admired his works, she was not in love with him."

Jenny was young, on the threshold of a career which at once dazzled and frightened her, and was longing for a protector and a confidant. She enjoyed Andersen's company; he was warm and witty, the well-travelled cosmopolitan who could hold an audience, but not for a moment did she consider him in this light. It was obvious that they were too similar, a pair of highly strung artists who each needed calm and selfless support from a partner, and it was unlikely that she found him physically attractive—her later attachments showed her taste to run to the dark, curly-haired, brooding type. Even at the height of his fame, there was something about Andersen—it was his tragic fate—that made him ridiculous as a lover: his big hands and feet waving around in exaggerated gestures, his clumsiness and his vanity, his lanky body enclosed in foppish, fashionable clothes that drew attention to his physical unease with himself.

Andersen, on the other hand, was more deeply roused by Jenny than he had been by any other woman, and his excitement was sexual as well as artistic and intellectual. In the weeks after her departure, his almanac is full of crosses and comments such as "sensual," "melancholy," "wrote erotic poems." Since Edvard's marriage in 1836, Andersen had had his emotionally dead years—there had been a couple of flirtations, and a simmering interest in young Baron Stampe, but nothing to stir his soul. Now Jenny's innocent and natural personality—the characteristics that had most drawn him to Riborg, and which were essential to his idealized vision of the feminine—blended with her art, thrilled him as a man and as an artist. No one had ever appealed to both sides of him like this—Rachel had come closest, but she was too much a woman of the world to interest him sexually. Jenny, fresh and unknown on the international stage, seemed perfect, unique, unmatchable.

At one level Andersen was simply swept off his feet by Jenny in the way that thousands of others in her audiences across Europe were to be over the next few years. A passionate lover of the theatre, Andersen was always responsive to dramatic art; Jenny's first appearance as Alice, he wrote, "was like a new revelation in the realms of art; the youthfully fresh voice forced itself into every heart; here reigned truth and nature; everything was full of meaning and intelligence. At one concert Jenny Lind sang her Swedish songs; there was something so peculiar in this, so bewitching; people thought nothing of the concert room; the popular melodies uttered by a being so purely feminine, and bearing the universal stamp of genius, exercised their omnipotent sway."

But unlike most of her audience, he identified acutely with her particular artistry: the way she raised simple Swedish folk songs to a high art form struck a chord with his ambitions as a writer of fairy tales; both of them tapped into the romantic idealization of the child and of child-like simplicity, and in one letter broadcasting his love for her, Andersen wrote to Ingemann that Jenny was the loveliest child he had met, comparing her to a noble version of Cinderella—this was at the time he was finishing "The Ugly Duckling." In his autobiography he devotes several pages to her. "Through Jenny Lind," he says, "I first became sensible of the holiness there is in art; through her I learned that one must forget oneself in the service of the Supreme. No books, no men have had a better or a more ennobling influence on me as a poet than Jenny Lind." In the 1860s he showed the American diplomat George Griffin a marble bust of Jenny which he kept on his mantelpiece, and said, "She was kind to me at a time when I needed kindness. She exerted the noblest influence over me. She made me forget myself, and first made me acquainted with the command which God has given to genius. On the stage she is a great artist; at home, a sensitive child."

This was sentimental, but it contained the kernel of truth about her role for him as a muse, touched with enough sexual energy to intrigue him, but far more important as a fellow artist. Her belief in the God-given nature of genius was of course a lesson he wanted to learn—since "The Little Mermaid" in 1837 he had thought of art as his route to immortality, and it was what he called "her great moral and intellectual importance to me" that most excited him about Jenny, while the *frisson* of being her suitor legitimized the pleasure he got from participating in the festive pomp around her.

The sexual element added another dimension, but was unlikely to have been dominant, for at precisely the time when Andersen was pouring out his heart in letters to his friends about Jenny, he began quietly courting a 22-year-old man. The familiar emotional triangle was sliding into place once more, and while it was establishing itself in the autumn of 1843, Andersen published a brilliant collection of fairy tales. His last major tale had been "The Steadfast Tin Soldier" in 1838; now Jenny had stirred him into action again. In the year after meeting her, he wrote four of his greatest works: "The Ugly Duckling," "The Nightingale," "The Snow Queen" and "The Fir Tree."

On 7 October 1843, three weeks after Jenny left Copenhagen, Andersen noted in his almanac, "finished the tale of the young swan." He had begun "The Ugly Duckling" more than a year earlier; it was one of the tales on which he worked hardest and longest. As soon as it was finished he threw himself into a new tale, which had been playing in his mind since he met Jenny. "In Tivoli, Carstensen's evening. Began the Chinese tale," runs his almanac for 11 October. The Chinese tale was "The Nightingale," inspired by Jenny Lind and given its setting by the Chinese themes, all pagodas and peacocks and coloured lanterns, of Copenhagen's new pleasure garden, Tivoli, which was opened in the summer of 1843 by the entrepreneur Georg Carstensen. It was a magical place, full of crazy architecture and funfair attractions, its lakes and flowers, theatres and restaurants, illuminated at night by gas lights and fireworks, and Andersen loved it.* He worked on the tale in a frenzy, and within twenty-four hours it was complete: "finished the Chinese tale," he notes on 12 October.

A month later, on 10 November, these tales, along with "The Top and the Ball" and "The Angel," were published by Reitzel in time for Christmas.

*Tivoli is still a delightful amusement park. In 1843, Carstensen was granted royal permission to build it because he persuaded Christian VIII that "people engaged in fun do not engage in politics." It was an immediate success, with 10,000 visitors—almost a tenth of the population of Copenhagen—on the first Sunday.

They carried the title *Nye Eventyr* (*New Fairy Tales*), but for the first time the subtitle "told for children" was omitted. This suggests a new confidence on Andersen's part; these were the most mature and perfectly constructed tales he had written, and though some of them at once became and have remained favourites of children, Andersen here melds together the child-like and the profound with exceptional artistry.

All four stories are original and owe no debt to folk tale or myth. Their settings vary, from the farmyard farce of "The Ugly Duckling" and the nursery world of "The Top and the Ball" to the chinoiserie of "The Nightingale" and the sentimental musing of "The Angel," but the theme of them all is transformation. Andersen plays on it in every key—social comedy, religious awakening, artistic revelation. This volume is the most optimistic since his fairy tale debut in 1835; unlike the jaunty early tales, however, these breathe the hope of adult fulfilment, of pain transmuted to pleasure through suffering and understanding. Jenny Lind's idea of art as uplifting is palpable; behind it lies the more urgent obsession of Andersen's need to tell his own story. This is his most autobiographical volume: "The Nightingale" is rooted in his love for Jenny, "The Top and the Ball" in his memory of Riborg Voigt, while "The Ugly Duckling" is the fantasy of how he liked to see his life story, from gawky child and struggling adolescent to beautiful swan applauded by all.

"The Ugly Duckling" opens as satire. In the grounds of an old manor house like Bregentved, where Andersen began the story, a pair of ducks cluck like old wives swapping pregnancy tales as one waits for her final egg to hatch and surveys her brood ("Every one of them takes after its father! The wretch, he never comes near me!"). When the last one tumbles out, "a big ugly fellow," she takes the ducklings to the duckyard, a vignette of village

Work by one of Andersen's favourite illustrators: The Ugly Duckling *by Vilhelm Pedersen.*

society as two families squabble over an eel's head, an old duck holds court ("She's of Spanish blood, and that's why she's so plump") and a turkey cock "fancied himself emperor" since he had "been born with spurs on." The ugly duckling is mocked and pecked because, like Andersen as a child, "he's too big and gawky . . . so he's going to get it!"

His mother chirps in his defence ("He was too long in the egg, and it's affected his figure"), but the teasing gets worse, the ugly duckling runs away from home and, as Andersen was in his early struggles in Copenhagen, is generally reviled. He runs across a spectrum of farmyard characters whom, with one bright detail each, Andersen makes human types: the bumptious ganders, the complacent hen, ridiculing the duckling's desire to go out into the wide world—Andersen based her on stay-at-home Ingeborg Drewsen, who laughed at his ambitions. Like Andersen, the duckling is lonely and endures physical hardship, nearly freezing to death in winter, while dreaming of the grandeur of swans.

Andersen traces the duckling's trial through the seasons, painting the Danish countryside from summer to winter, its sunsets, freshly fallen snow, the warm sun shining among the rushes. In spring comes transformation. So sad that he hopes a flock of swans will peck him to death, the duckling looks at his reflection as he floats on the water and sees that he has become a swan himself. It is a celebration of the romantic view of genius over background and culture—"it doesn't matter being born in a duck-yard, when you have been hatched out of a swan's egg!"—as well as a triumph for the new order over the old, for as the swan is thrown titbits and clapped, "everybody said, 'The new one is the nicest—so young and handsome!' And the old swans curtsied to him." This was Andersen's vision of the homage paid to him by the establishment; he knew he was a wild bird tamed by the bourgeoisie, but, concludes the swan, "I never dreamt of so much happiness, when I was the ugly duckling!"

Of all Andersen's fantasies of transformation, this is the most universally appealing. The Danish language, earthy and mocking, is the ideal vehicle for it, but even in a poor translation its powerful plot and theme shine through. What child has not sometimes felt neglected, or had fantasies that he is the real offspring of a grand family and has somehow ended up by mistake among those who undervalue and misunderstand him? Through the metaphor of the duck-yard, Andersen fused a record of his own suffering with a wish-fulfilment ending which promised hope and consolation. The story bears the hallmarks of his particular genius—the comic detail, the miniature scale, the undercurrent of Romanticism—yet it carries the emotional sustenance of the traditional fairy tale. Thirty years after it was written, the *Spectator* wrote that "'The Ugly Duckling' . . . is like the proverbs of Solomon, in everybody's mouth; one of those happy arrows which hit the bull's-eye."

The child psychoanalyst Bruno Bettelheim has shown how folk tales confront a child's unconscious dilemmas and help resolve them through fantasy—sibling rivalry in "Cinderella," mother–daughter jealousies in "Snow White," fear of desertion in "Hansel and Gretel." "Through the centuries (if not millennia) during which, in their retelling, fairy tales became ever more refined," writes Bettelheim, "they came to convey at the same time overt and covert meanings—came to speak simultaneously to all levels of the human personality, communicating in a manner which reaches the uneducated mind of the child as well as that of the sophisticated adult." Andersen is the only writer whose invented tales match the archetypal quality and double articulation of such traditional stories; encountered in childhood as a source of amusement and comfort, the ugly duckling remains in the adult mind as a mythic creation. That Andersen could invent such a story suggests that his emotional make-up was still that of a child, but he constructed it with the classical elegance and wit of the mature artist.

"The Ugly Duckling" was Jenny Lind's favourite of Andersen's stories; she identified intensely with its rags-to-riches motif, and wrote to Andersen of it, "Oh, what a glorious gift to be able to clothe in words one's most lofty thoughts; by means of a scrap of paper to make men see so cleverly how the noblest often lie most hidden and covered over by wretchedness and rags, until the hour of transformation strikes and shows the figure in a divine light!"

But it is the story's companion piece, "The Nightingale," which was a direct tribute to Jenny and her art and is one of Andersen's aesthetic manifestos, setting out in fairy tale form his ideal of naturalness and simplicity battling the demons of artifice and reason. When Jenny became internationally famous as "the Swedish Nightingale," the story was thought of as an homage to her, but it was written when her future was less certain, and her unaffected style of singing had still to break through the fashion for the Italian manner of formal artifice which held sway in most European opera houses. It was the effect of her simple Swedish folk songs, which moved to tears audiences unable to understand a word of them, that epitomized the nature of her art, and Andersen saw here a parallel to his telling of fairy tales; the story also recalled his own early renown as a singer, when he was referred to as "the little Nightingale from Funen."

"The Nightingale" opens in China, at the Emperor's palace, built of fine porcelain, surrounded by gardens of flowers which tinkle like bells, lit by thousands of gold lamps—an image of night-time Tivoli. In a wood at the end of the garden lives a nightingale, who sings so sweetly that it is known all over the world, but the Emperor in his palace has never heard it. His gentleman-in-waiting is dispatched to bring the bird to him, but in the end only the kitchen maid can find it. The nightingale comes to the palace and enthralls everyone, for "its song went straight to the heart" and the tears rolled down the Emperor's cheeks. As a reward, he offers to hang a pair of golden slippers round its neck—the King had hung a diamond pendant round Jenny's neck—and, as with Jenny in Copenhagen, "the remarkable bird was the talk of the town, and when two people met, one would say nothing but 'Night!' and the other only 'Gale!'—and then they would sigh and understand each other."

But one day a present arrives for the Emperor, "an artificial nightingale made in imitation of the live one, but studded all over with diamonds, rubies and sapphires. When the artificial bird was wound up, it would sing one of the pieces the real one sang, while wagging its tail up and down and glittering with silver and gold." The pair sing a duet, "though it wasn't really a success, for the real nightingale sang in its own way and the artificial bird ran on rollers," but the toy is hugely acclaimed, and "had its place on a silken cushion close to the Emperor's bed." The real bird flies unnoticed out of the window, and soon "every other Chinaman knew by heart every little cluck in the artificial bird's song" and "the music-master wrote twenty-five volumes about the artificial bird." Then it breaks, and when it is mended it is allowed to sing just once a year.

Years later, the Emperor lies ill in bed and sees "Death sitting on his chest, and it was wearing his gold crown and holding his gold sword in one hand and his splendid banner in the other . . . And Death kept on staring the Emperor in the face with its great empty sockets, and there was silence, dreadful silence." Then the real nightingale flies back to "sing hope and comfort" and demands back the sword and the crown, "and Death gave up each of his treasures for a song while the nightingale went on singing, singing of the silent churchyard where the white roses grow, where the elder-tree sweetly smells, and where the fresh grass is wetted by the tears of the mourners; and, growing homesick for his garden, Death floated, like a cold, white mist, out of the window." The next day, "the servants came in to see to their dead Emperor and—well, there they stood, and the Emperor said: 'Good morning!'"

Few of Andersen's tales combine so many facets of his genius as "The Nightingale." He had played with the themes of art and authenticity before, using the images of the rose and the nightingale in "The Swineherd," but now he made them into something much more. Jenny was the catalyst—underlying the tale is Andersen's sense that Jenny had saved his spirit from death by reaffirming his faith in art, as well as possibly the memory of her singing to the ill Copenhagen wine merchant, Mozart Waage Petersen. The story, of a magical palace, the rivalry between the birds, the threat of death, holds listeners of all ages. The message—about the transformative quality of art and the power of the natural over the artificial—is sophisticated, but it works by primitive images which come out of the folk tales Andersen knew as a child: the personification of Death as a skull coming to claim the dying man; the restoration of his crown when Death flees. Humour—the satire against courtly ritual and against crusty academics, the casual one-line punch of the ending, with the Emperor bouncing back to life—and the delicate detail of the Chinese setting keep the tone light, making the tale a typical product of Danish Biedermeier: the extremes of danger and betrayal mediated into a harmonious miniature.

The remaining two stories in the new volume are similarly genre pictures. "The Angel" is a sentimental story about the transformation of a dying child into an angel; the subject had obsessed Andersen since his poem "The Dying Child," and this tale may have been inspired by the death earlier in the year of Edvard and Jette Collin's eldest daughter. The tale, like the earlier poem, was wildly popular; it suited the taste of the times, perhaps offered consolation, and became internationally famous a few years later when the German artist Kaulbach painted an illustration to it which as a print sold millions of copies; Andersen even came across them in Portugal, where his work was barely known, in the 1860s.

"The Top and the Ball," on the other hand, recasts as a nursery comedy Andersen's first love affair, with Riborg Voigt as the haughty ball and himself as the giddy top who wants to marry her, is spurned, then ends up treasured in the house and painted gold while the ball rots unrecognized in a dustbin. This spare, sarcastic little tale was written when Andersen met Riborg and her family on holiday in Funen, and he may have seen it as a complement to "The Nightingale"—a valediction to an old love affair and a celebration of a new one. As in the other tales, its triumphant conclusion is offset by a pathos of tone; unlike traditional fairy tales, which end in the harmony of marriage, Andersen's heroes and heroines are portraits of himself as an eccentric—the gawky duck, the brilliant nightingale, the dizzy top—and each goes through life alone.

New Fairy Tales was Andersen's breakthrough in his home country. Some of his earlier stories had been praised, but no volume had received such a chorus of ecstatic reviews as this one. Just six months earlier, Andersen had been ridiculed throughout Copenhagen for *Agnete*, his reputation declared finished while he fumed at Denmark from Paris. Now, the first glowing review of the tales appeared in *Figaro* two days after publication, followed by reviews in all the other papers. *Ny Portefeuille*, for example, wrote:

> There is in these tales so much beauty and goodness, so much humour and seriousness, so much poetry and depth, that even the most disparate readers will by necessity find something of interest to them . . . In the last fairy tale, "The Ugly Duckling," the little event is thoughtfully and deeply executed, the dialogues in the ducks' pen funny and the ending most poetical . . . We wish with all our hearts that this little book meets all the good will among young and old that it deserves, and we would not refrain from wishing that the author soon would give us some more, and that he will not desist from letting his imagination roam in the sphere of the child, where it rightly belongs.

"These tales have been received with unanimous applause," Andersen wrote to Henriette Wulff. "None of my other books have had such a success here at home, every paper commends them, everyone reads them—and not through having borrowed them from the neighbour's neighbour, no, they are actually bought! I am appreciated as the best fairy-tale teller—in brief, I have good grounds this time to be very pleased with the public." On 18 December, the first edition sold out, and Andersen wrote again to Henriette, "Today Reitzel sent a message to me saying that the new *Eventyr*, of which 850 had been printed, have all been sold, and that therefore we had better print another 850, since it is not yet Christmas! Isn't it wonderful! The book has sold like hot cakes! All the papers praise it, everyone reads it! No books of mine seem to be appreciated as these fairy tales are!"

For himself, Andersen knew that this volume marked a new maturity. Professionally and artistically he was satisfied. To Ingemann he wrote:

> I think—and it would give me great pleasure if I were right—that I have now discovered how to write fairy tales. The first ones I wrote were, as you know,

mostly old ones I had listened to as a child, and which I then usually retold and re-created in my own manner. Those that were my own creations, such as "The Little Mermaid," "The Storks," "The Daisy," were the most popular, and that gave me inspiration. Now I tell stories out of my own breast, I seize an idea for the grown-ups—and then tell the story to the little ones while always remembering that Father and Mother often listen, and you must also give them something for their minds.

Publicly, Andersen celebrated his success and the whiff of romance with Jenny Lind. The most important things to have happened to him recently, he told Henriette Wulff in December, were the appearance of his tales and "the fact that I received a letter from Jenny L. . . . Jenny's letter was very long and extremely courteous and kind, as excellent as I could wish for. She is a great and beautiful soul; may God see to it that her future husband makes her happy. I imagine it will be G. [Günther]—I am not really in a position to have an opinion on it." But this apparent openness, the child-like frankness which he cultivated, hid another, secret, emotional agenda.

On 17 November, a week after the fairy tales came out, he left Copenhagen for Nysø, the country estate where Thorvaldsen had his studio and the home of Henrik Stampe, now a 22-year-old law student. Stampe in a portrait by Marstrand appears a fleshy, complacent young man: broad figure,

Baron Stampe and his sons Henrik and Holger, by Bertel Thorvaldsen, 1840.

Henrik Stampe, "my darling Henrik . . . you whom I believe I could many times feel inclined to sacrifice my life for," in a painting by Wilhelm Marstrand.

square head, weak jaw, lightly curling hair, eyes staring confidently, but with a lofty lack of interest, at the viewer; an expression suggesting pride but little strength of purpose. He looks, as he was, a typical aristocratic estate owner, brought up to the sort of gracious living that Thorvaldsen and Andersen, men of poor backgrounds, now found intoxicating. Thorvaldsen used Stampe and his younger brother Holger as models for his figures, often depicting them as classical youths, handsome and muscular, naked or lightly draped in loin cloths, sometimes on horseback.

In his biography of Thorvaldsen, Just Matthias Thiele described life at Nysø; Andersen was a frequent-enough visitor to be included in his account of the sculptor's day:

> He would rise early in the morning and set to work in the studio, not leaving off till it was near dinner time, when he would take a drive along the wooded beach. After the meal was over, he liked to lean back in an armchair and have a nap, whilst some of the young people played to him his favourite airs on the piano. Then he would get up and walk about the room; and if Andersen happened to be of the party, would go to him and clap him on the shoulder, saying, "Come, are not we children to have our story tonight?" "The Top and the Ball" and "The Ugly Duckling" were his especial favourites, and he was never tired of hearing Andersen repeat them.
>
> When it began to get dusk, and lights were brought in, he would sit down to play his favourite game of lottery. Indeed, if anything occurred to prevent

their playing, he would be a little out of temper. His friends, therefore, always humoured him, though it must be confessed that Thorvaldsen was the only one of the whole party to whom the game did not prove extremely tiresome. When once seated at the card table, with his counters and copper skillings before him, he would throw his whole mind into the game. With him it was no mere pastime, but a downright passion; and although they always played for low stakes, he never could bear losing.

In this climate, Andersen fell in love with Stampe. He stayed at Nysø for over a fortnight, until 5 December, and on 11 December, he noted that he and Henrik were on "Du" terms. He may have loved Jenny as well, and fed each feeling by a reflection from the other; or he may have felt that in pursuing Jenny, he was betraying his real needs, and thus was propelled months after meeting her into the arms of Stampe. It is also possible that the success of his fairy tales gave Andersen a new social confidence which enabled him to approach an aristocratic man for the first time as a lover. What is clear, is that in writing to Stampe he allowed himself the authentic tone of the nervous, anguished lover, laying himself bare for scrutiny, as he had done years ago in his response to Ludvig Müller's "false" love letter and in some of his letters to Edvard, and in a way which was quite distinct from his letters to women.

My darling Henrik [he wrote on 27 December],

It is strange that I write to you, whenever I like I can be with you, speak with you, squeeze your hand, but—at least I express myself better on paper, there I am not tied by thousands of small considerations, as I am face to face even with you! I have often heard it said about Englishmen that they have spleen. All I know about this illness is that it is an eccentricity, but yet a sadness, due to which they often take their lives. I suffer from something similar to this, therefore I was so far from kind to you today, could become impatient over waiting, where I could do you a favour, you whom I believe I could many times feel inclined to sacrifice my life for. "Speak to me," you often say. Yes, that is what I want to, that which this evening, lonely as always, I must do.

During the following months, the relationship with Stampe developed physically, and Andersen's almanac for the beginning of 1844 is full of cryptic references to jealousy, hope, desperation, sensuality and worry over pain in his penis. "My darling Henrik. Was at Henrik's. He later with me. He caressed me," reads the almanac for 4 March 1844. He saw in Stampe the ideal of youth just as he felt himself reaching middle age. He enjoyed the association with the Stampe family, wealthy, glamorous, well-connected both to royalty and to Danish artists. And he believed his affection was returned.

But Stampe, too, had his own agenda. He flirted with Andersen and caressed him, but he had already met the woman he wanted to marry. While Andersen was using Jenny Lind as something of a cover for his love for Henrik, Henrik was using Andersen as a route to 17-year-old Jonna Drewsen, whom Andersen had known since she was a baby. She was Jonas Collin's eldest grandchild, the daughter of Ingeborg and the judge Adolf Drewsen. Of the Collin grandchildren, she was closest to Andersen. He had always thrived in his relaxed relationship with her mother, homely, teasing Ingeborg, and this extended to Jonna as soon as she was old enough; he wrote to her independently from his foreign journeys and was genuinely fond of her. Jonna trusted him; through him she and Henrik came to know one another, and by the end of the spring Andersen had outlived his purpose for Stampe.

For many reasons, the spring of 1844 was a time of dissolution of hope, the passing of old security. On 23 March Andersen received a letter from Jenny making it clear that she thought of him as no more than a friend.

> My Good Brother,
>
> Mr. Bournonville mentioned in his last letter to me that you have been shedding tears because of my silence. This, naturally, I take to be nonsense, but as my conscience does reproach me in regard to you, my good brother, I hasten to recall myself to your memory, and to ask my friend and brother not to be angry with me, but rather to furnish me soon with a proof that I have not forfeited my right to his friendship and goodwill. A hundred thousand thanks for the pretty tales! I find them divinely beautiful to such a degree as to believe them to be the grandest and loveliest that ever flowed from your pen . . . I long now very much for the moment when I shall be allowed to tell my good brother by word of mouth how proud I am of this friendship, and with the help of my *Lieder* to express—if even in a trifling degree—my gratitude! and that you, my brother, are surely better fit than anyone to comprehend our Swedish proverb: "Every bird sings according to his beak" . . . My dear friend! I do feel so happy now. It seems to me I have come from a stormy sea into a peaceful cottage. Many struggles have calmed down, many thoughts have become clearer, many a star is gleaming forth again and I bend my knee before the Throne of Grace and exclaim "Thy will be done." Farewell! God bless and protect my brother is the sincere wish of his affectionate sister, Jenny.

Andersen, who had always courted women by addressing them as sisters, may not have read in this the definitive rejection he was intended to find; his desire for Jenny burned hot and cold for several years to come, though he probably had no serious hope of winning her by now. The next day, 24 March, however, came a worse blow: Thorvaldsen died. Andersen had dined with him and Oehlenschläger and the painter Constantin Hansen at Baroness Stampe's house in Copenhagen on the evening of his death. "He was very expansive and amiable. I sat beside him and never dreamt that in an hour he would be numbered with the dead," Andersen wrote; he was so shocked when Bournonville came to tell him that Thorvaldsen had collapsed and died at the theatre that he could barely believe the news. He ran at once to Thorvaldsen's house, where an inquest was already being held in the drawing room; in the bedroom a few strangers surrounded the bed on which the body lay; the floor was wet with the snow which people had carried in with their boots and outside the clouds were leaden.

Thorvaldsen's death was bound up in Andersen's mind with the winding down of his affair with Henrik. At around this time Stampe began to withdraw from the friendship, and in June Jonna and Henrik were engaged. Andersen heard the news on 4 July in Dresden, and wrote in his diary, "It is a lie." He continued to see Stampe socially, for their circles were now much entwined,* and for at least a year he kept in his imagination the erotic constellation of Henrik and Jenny; in his almanac for 26 April 1845, for example, he notes "excellent mood! Theodor [Collin] kind, Henrik Stampe at my house . . . Thought of Jenny. +" He did not record the pain Stampe caused him at the time—the fact that he had been passed over for a member of the Collin family could not have helped—but years later, in Montreux in 1862, he talked to Edvard's wife Jette, by then his most trusted friend, about Stampe, and wrote in his diary, "confided to Jette, Stampe's strong love for me, which changed when he had used me as a stepladder up to Jonna."

In May, Andersen set out to find comfort at Breitenburg with his old patron Count Rantzau, but found a dying man: walking in the grounds with Andersen, Rantzau pointed out his grave next to the chapel, and the following year he was buried in it. Andersen went on to tour Germany through the summer. As usual his response to crises at home was to flee; this time, however, he embarked on a journey which was to catapult him into a new, royal, world.

---

*Henrik and Jonna's eldest daughter, Rigmor Stampe, born in 1850, became one of Andersen's most fervent supporters. Her book *H. C. Andersen and his Immediate Circle* (*H. C. Andersen og hans nærmeste omgang*), in which she took Andersen's side against the Collin family and alleged that they had treated him shabbily, caused a furore in Copenhagen when it was published in 1918.

CHAPTER 13

Winter's Tales

1844–1845

He would lay out his patterns to form written words, but he could never hit upon the word he wanted, the word "eternity." The Snow Queen had said, "If you can work out that pattern for me, you shall be your own master, and I will present you with the whole world—and a new pair of skates." But he could not do it.

—HANS CHRISTIAN ANDERSEN, "The Snow Queen"

When Andersen left the safe haven of Breitenburg in June 1844, he set out for a place whose sense of myth and history was for him second only to that of Rome. Since he was a young man he had dreamt of Weimar, the small town in the middle of the Thuringian hills that was known to the world as the "German Athens." For generations, artists had been drawn to Weimar. The painters Lucas Cranach and his son had lived there and Cranach's masterpiece, *The Cruxifixion*, hung in the town church of Saints Peter and Paul. Bach had been choirmaster at the court chapel. A series of Grand Dukes and Duchesses, rulers of the province of Saxe-Weimar-Eisenach, had been enlightened patrons, establishing a "court of the Muses" which had at the end of the eighteenth century drawn Goethe, Schiller and other writers to make the town their home. Shortly after Andersen's first visit, Liszt was to move there and direct operas and concerts, compose and teach, making Weimar the musical centre of Germany. In the years before unification, when Germany was a group of small nation states, each top-heavy with a large-scale court and its own kings and princes, civilized, urbane Weimar evolved into the German cultural capital.

"Everything pointed to a briskly active literary and artistic life," Goethe wrote of Weimar. Since Goethe's time, the town had become a place of pilgrimage for any young man in the German-speaking world with literary ambitions. Andersen had passed nearby on his first journey to Germany in

1831, when Goethe was still alive, but was too timid to approach either the man or the place. That he now felt able to go there was a sign of his new confidence in his position on the world literary stage. "An extraordinary desire impelled me to see this city where Goethe, Schiller, Wieland and Herder had lived," he wrote, "and from which so much light had streamed forth over the world. I approached that land which had been rendered sacred by Luther, by the strife of the Minnesingers on the Wartburg and by the memory of many noble and great events."

He arrived in Weimar on 24 June, which happened to be the birthday of the heir to the throne, the Hereditary Grand Duke. There were celebrations in the streets, at the theatre the young prince was fêted as he arrived to watch a new opera, and Andersen was absorbed by the festivities. "I did not think," he wrote in his autobiography two years later, "how firmly the most glorious and the best of all those whom I here saw around me would grow in my heart; how many of my future friends sat around me here—how dear this city would become to me—in Germany, my second home." He always talked of Weimar as of a love affair.

First impressions, however, often disappointed foreign visitors, who were astonished by the minute scale of this town with so lofty a reputation. In 1803, Madame de Staël reckoned it not a town at all but simply a large château with houses dotted round about. Thackeray visited in 1830 and satirized Weimar in *Vanity Fair* as "the little comfortable Ducal town of Pumpernickel," preposterously provincial. George Eliot, arriving there in 1854, ten years after Andersen, asked, "How could Goethe live here in this dull, lifeless village?" and G. H. Lewes on the same trip described Weimar to his son as "a very queer little place although called the 'Athens of Germany' . . . Fancy a little quiet town without cabs, omnibuses, very few carts and scarcely a carriage—with no gas lights for the streets, which are lighted (in winter only) by oil lamps, slung across the streets on a cord."

There were some gabled houses on the largest square, the Pottery Market, an impressive theatre and a grand library, the Green Palace, overlooking the flat meadows bordering the narrow River Ilm, which ran along the town's eastern side and on into the Saale and the Elbe. There were two hotels, the Elephant and the Erbprinz; the Esplanade, a promenade shaded by trees, with a goldfish pond and a Chinese pavilion; and the famous White Swan Inn, where Goethe had had his *Stammtisch* (regular table). Goethe's summerhouse was across a park by the river; a royal residence, the rococo Belvedere Castle, with park and orangery, was just outside the town,

Weimar, "the Athens of Germany," which Andersen considered his second home.

while a few miles away another country seat, Ettersburg Palace, towered out of the beech forest hills.

It was, says Goethe's biographer Nicholas Boyle, "a simple place with but a single function: well over a quarter of its 6,000 inhabitants was made up by the court, by the court's families, employees and pensioners. The remainder, the tailors and shoemakers, the bakers and blacksmiths and apothecaries, were all directly or indirectly meeting the needs of the court or of each other." There was an army of a few hundred men, but no trade, commerce or industry, and virtually no middle class. "The court expressed its existence principally by eating," with a daily formal dinner when "men were expected to wear court uniform of green stuff with epaulettes, or something more splendid in silk or satin with gold and silver embroidery." In 1830, Thackeray wrote from Weimar begging his mother for a cornetcy, because "the men here are all in some yeomanry uniform"; he went to court in leather breeches decorated with pink rosettes.

In *Vanity Fair*, Weimar's royalty is cast as "his Transparency the Duke and Transparent family," possibly echoing "The Emperor's New Clothes," for

Thackeray was a devotee of Andersen. A gentleman-in-waiting is decorated with "the star and the grand yellow cordon of the Order of St. Michael of Pumpernickel"; the duke "bowed serenely to everybody," then "amid the saluting of the guards, and the flaring of the torches of the running footmen, clad in scarlet, the Transparent carriages drove away to the old Ducal Schloss, with its towers and pinnacles standing on the Schlossberg. Everybody in Pumpernickel knew everybody. No sooner was a foreigner seen there, than the Minister of Foreign Affairs, or some other great or small officer of state, went round to the Erbprinz, and found out the name of the new arrival."

This was more or less what happened to Andersen. On his first day he ran into an acquaintance from Oldenburg in north Germany, Kammerherr Carl Olivier von Beaulieu-Marconnay, who at once invited him to stay at his house. The next day Beaulieu-Marconnay, who was Lord Chamberlain to Grand Duke Carl Friedrich, introduced Andersen to the royal family. He had tea and dinner with the Grand Duke and Duchess, and was invited the following day to Ettersburg where he met their son, Carl Alexander, the Hereditary Grand Duke.

Ettersburg, known as a hunting castle (*Jagdschloss*), stood high in the hills and close to a deep forest, and Andersen perceived something of the fairy tale about it as soon as he saw it. "The old-fashioned furniture within the house, and the distant views from the park into the Harz mountains, produced immediately a peculiar impression," he wrote. "All the young peasants had assembled at the castle to celebrate the birthday of their beloved young Duke; climbing poles, from which fluttered handkerchiefs and ribbons, were erected; fiddles sounded, and people danced merrily under the branches of the large and flowering lime trees. Sabbath splendour, contentment and happiness were diffused over the whole."

Carl Alexander was then twenty-six, a lean, handsome youth of aristocratic bearing but unassuming manner. He had dark hair and piercing, intense dark eyes, bushy eyebrows and a curling moustache, but a tender, almost girlish face. Andersen, fresh from rejection in love, found in him a more perfect and elevated version of Henrik Stampe: another charming young nobleman, a patron of the arts, a sympathetic, gentle man. He was immediately drawn to him, and wrote in his diary on 26 June, "The young duke was extremely amiable. I could have chosen him as a friend had he not been a duke . . . Inside the palace itself I recited some fairy tales and was admired . . . I quite love the young duke, he is the first of all princes that I find really attractive, and that I wish was not a prince, or that I was one myself."

Carl Alexander, who had recently married a Dutch princess, Sophie, was also drawn to Andersen, and for his week-long stay he was affectionately welcomed into the royal circle. Carl Alexander showed him the garden at Ettersburg, and the romantic old tree, split through by lightning, on whose trunk Goethe, Schiller and Wieland had carved their names. Carl Alexander's grandfather, Grand Duke Carl August, had been Goethe's patron, and Goethe and Schiller were buried close to him—"In life, the prince and the poet walked side by side; in death they slumber under the same vault," Andersen wrote. The idea of re-enacting the emotional bond between patron and writer two generations later worked on him like a charm; he could not help imagining the grandson of Goethe's patron as his own protector, with himself in Goethe's role as Europe's first author.

Carl Alexander's friends were mainly artists and writers, and he was keen to add Andersen to his entourage; his court was international and culturally outward-looking—his mother was the daughter of the Russian Czar Paul I, and the primary language at court was French, in which Carl Alexander wrote his diaries. In Weimar, Andersen wrote, "the evenings passed like a spiritual dream; alternately someone read aloud; even I ventured, for the first time in a language foreign to me, to read one of my own tales—'The Steadfast Tin Soldier.'" Of all the royal families who were to befriend and reward Andersen over the next decade, none rivalled the special relationship created at Weimar. Just before he left, Andersen recorded, "The Grand Duchess told me how dear I was to her son, asked me to return to Weimar, the Grand Duke too . . . I read 'The Princess and the Pea,' 'The Emperor's New Clothes' and 'Little Ida's Flowers'; but was quite ill. The Hereditary Grand Duke wanted me to stay longer in Weimar, held my hand firmly and for a long time, said he was my friend and that he hoped to show me that some time in the future. His consort also asked me to return to Weimar and not to forget them; also the Duchess . . . I was really soft-hearted."

Andersen left in a frenzy of emotion.

> It seemed to me as if I had formerly lived in this city; as if it were a beloved home which I must now leave. As I drove out of the city, over the bridge and past the mill, and for the last time looked back to the city and the castle, a deep melancholy took hold on my soul, and it was as if a beautiful portion of my life here had its close; I thought that the journey, after I had left Weimar, could afford no more pleasure. How often since that time has the carrier-pigeon, and

still more frequently, the mind, flown over to this place! Sunshine has streamed forth from Weimar upon my poet-life.

When Carl Alexander wrote to him, Andersen replied that "your letter now lies among my most sacred treasures." In their taste for sentimentality and high-flown passion, the two men were well-matched. At an important time, Carl Alexander filled an emotional gap in Andersen's life, and their passionate friendship over the next few years gave Andersen both stability and excitement. It was one of the first friendships, moreover, really to begin to heal the social wounds which still smarted for Andersen in Denmark; Weimar's simple social structure, where status depended on court patronage and there was no independent middle class, suited him.

In Germany, moreover, the story of his rise from poverty to fame was told as a romance, as popular as his fairy tales, and Andersen was seen as coming almost from another world, remote from class and social status. For years travel had been essential to his mental balance, an antidote to his conflicted and claustrophobic feelings about Denmark as well as a stimulus to someone who was always on the edge of boredom. But with the trip to Germany in 1844, he felt he had defined for himself an international role. At home, the response to his fame was mocking. Edvard laughed at the fuss that was made of him, joking that he should try to bring home a decoration.

After Weimar, Andersen swept on, to Dresden, Leipzig, Berlin. In Leipzig he visited Carl Maria von Weber and Robert Schumann, at whose home the singer Livia von Frege "sang lovely versions of 'The Sweet Violets,' 'The Soldier' and particularly 'The Fiddler' [Andersen poems which Schumann had set to music]. Clara Schumann playing, it was hard to judge whom of the three deserved the highest praise; we dined luxuriously in the evening and drank Rhine wine and Champagne." Schumann wrote to Andersen afterwards, "I have constantly thought of you . . . May we hope to soon welcome you again in Germany? Such a meeting as on that evening when you were with us—a meeting of poet, songstress, actress and composer! That evening will never be forgotten by me."

Outside Dresden, Andersen stayed for the first of many visits with Major Serre and his wife on the estate of Maxen, where the house parties of artists and intellectuals were legendary. "It is not possible for anyone to exercise greater hospitality than is shown by these two kind-hearted people," Andersen wrote. He began to meet some of society's glamorous notorieties, such as the novelist Countess Ida Hahn-Hahn, who had divorced her wealthy husband and converted publicly and dramatically to Catholicism, and now toured Europe with her lover, Baron Bystram; he was fascinated by the "writing nun," as he called her, while she liked the "dark glass" of *Only a Fiddler* and some of Andersen's tales. In these circles, Andersen was, as at Weimar, in some ways more relaxed and natural than he was with the Danish bourgeoisie. Unlike Jenny Lind, he had no prudish sensibilities about other people's behaviour, and had a child-like acceptance of whatever ménage he found himself in—later in Weimar he was a regular guest of Liszt and his lover, Princess Carolyne zu Sayn-Wittgenstein, and in London in 1847 he frequented the home of Lady Blessington, who had outraged society by living with the husband of her step-daughter. And so he moved on across north Germany, everywhere invited by writers, publishers, society hostesses: "I found myself unspeakably happy on this little journey in Germany, and became convinced that I was there no stranger."

Oddly, only a visit to the Grimm brothers on this trip disappointed him. He turned up without a letter of introduction:

People had told me, and I myself believed it, that if I were known by anybody in Berlin, it must be the brothers Grimm. I therefore sought out their residence. The maidservant asked me with which of the brothers I wished to speak.

"With the one who has written the most," said I, because I did not know, at that time, which of them had most interested himself in the *Märchen*.

"Jakob is the most learned," said the maid-servant.

"Well, then, take me to him."

I entered the room, and Jakob Grimm, with his knowing and strongly marked countenance, stood before me.

"I come to you," said I, "without letters of introduction, because I hope that my name is not wholly unknown to you."

"Who are you?" asked he.

I told him; and Jakob Grimm said, in a half-embarrassed voice, "I do not remember to have heard this name: what have you written?"

It was now my turn to be embarrassed in a high degree; but I now mentioned my little stories.

"I do not know them," said he; "but mention to me some other of your writings, because I certainly must have heard them spoken of."

I named the titles of several; but he shook his head. I felt myself quite unlucky.

"But what must you think of me," said I, "that I come to you as a total stranger, and enumerate myself what I have written: You must know me!

There has been published in Denmark a collection of the *Märchen* of all nations, which is dedicated to you, and in it there is at least one story of mine."

"No," said he good-humouredly, but as much embarrassed as myself; "I have not read even that, but it delights me to make your acquaintance. Allow me to conduct you to my brother Wilhelm?"

"No, I thank you," said I, only wishing now to get away; I had fared badly enough with one brother. I pressed his hand, and hurried from the house.

It was extraordinary that Jakob did not know him—Wilhelm Grimm insisted the following year that he would have done, and Jakob himself visited Andersen to apologize when he was in Copenhagen a few months later. German culture of the time was intoxicated with romantic fantasy, while social values were beginning to be fixated on the family, childhood, the *gemütlich* and sentimental ideals of parents reading stories in the nursery, of children clustered beneath a candle-lit Christmas tree, a nineteenth-century German invention. Andersen's fairy tales met both these moods. In the years before the 1848 wars, when what Goethe's biographer Nicholas Boyle calls "the new Germany of the mind . . . that existed wherever the German language was spoken" was being defined by the cultured, domestic middle class, and centred on "the world of the German book, created and sustained by the capitalist publisher-booksellers," Andersen was the man for the moment.

He returned home to spend the rest of the summer with Count Moltke at Glorup on Funen, but as he was settling in an invitation arrived from King Christian and Queen Caroline to visit them at a spa on the island of Föhr, one of the Frisian islands in the North Sea. Andersen did not really have enough money for the journey, but he started out at once anyway, travelling across Funen over to Jutland, and south to Flensburg, by which time his expenses were so high that he feared the trip would end up costing over fifty rixdollars, an eighth of his annual grant. But the lure of royalty was irresistible. He had inherited an unquestioning reverence for kings and princes from his mother, never shed it, and now fuelled it with his raging ambition to be acclaimed. As word spread of his success with one royal family, so another took him up; his artistic persona, the child-like romantic genius who was tamely obsequious rather than threateningly radical, fulfilled, as Heine had pointed out, "exactly a prince's idea of a poet." Christian VIII, who ignored politics in favour of culture, was one of Denmark's most enthusiastic patrons of the arts, and did not want to lag behind Weimar in playing host to Andersen.

And so Andersen found himself getting up at one o'clock in the morning in Flensburg to drive in an open carriage by moonlight through marshy roads and watch the sun rise over flowering heather. This far western corner of the province of Schleswig (now Germany) has a unique half-sunken landscape, with the shore covered, in Andersen's day, with plaited straw so that it would not be lapped away by the waves. "The road was liquefied earth; the horses sank deep with each step, and so we had to drive up on the dykes which provided lee for the houses and which we expected to fall off." The Frisian villages were impoverished, the people unfriendly and the sea stormy, but after a long wait, Andersen boarded the ferry and had barely disembarked on the island before two young ladies called out "Andersen! Mr. Andersen! Mother, there's Andersen"—"A lady looked out of the garret. It was the Duchess of Augustenborg and her daughters. It was embarrassing for me that I was still in my travelling suit."

The journey was worth it. Monarchs and dukes were packed on to the exclusive island spa for the summer and Andersen was invited to dinner with the King and Queen at once. The rituals of Weimar were re-enacted; on the first evening another guest, Danish cellist Christian Kellermann, played to the party and Andersen read "The Top and the Ball" and "The Ugly Duckling"; the King laughed a lot and it was intimated that he would have his trip paid for. There were dinners in the resort salon, walks on the promenade with the Duchess and the princesses, boating trips with the Queen and frequent readings of the King's two favourite tales, "The Swineherd" and "The Nightingale"—both have royal themes. Bathing, "infinitely refreshing and salty," was a complicated affair: "You undress, while the hired hand, on horseback with large boots on, pulls the bathhouse out into the water. If the tide rises too high, he comes back and hauls it up a bit. You are drawn up on the beach, and during the trip you get yourself dressed." All around the coast were whale tusks looking like large gateposts, green and weathered; every day brought "matchless summer weather."

The spa town, Wyck, Dutch in style, its one-storey houses with sloping roofs and gables turned to the street, was much enlivened by the presence of the court. In the evenings, "the moon rose so wrapped in haze and clouds, so red, so stormy-looking. The lighthouse could be seen below it; the waves were striking high up on the shore, and the water was spraying like champagne, like foaming sharks." Sometimes Andersen dined on board the royal steamer, sailing by sunset through the archipelago of low islets covered with dark turf as the deck of the ship was changed to a dancing room; sometimes when the tide was low they drove by carriage across the white sand between the islands, watching as the ships lay like dead fishes upon the sand, waiting for the returning tide, and the wet sand became inscribed with strange hieroglyphics left by the receding sea. To Carl Alexander, Andersen wrote that "Life here is like a fairy tale of the sea, dreamed in an open boat on the waves of the German Ocean."

Here he celebrated the twenty-fifth anniversary of his arrival in Copenhagen—the anniversary he kept as assiduously as his actual birthday. Everyone fussed over him; the German visitors to the baths drank his health in the pump room. "Thanks be to God for these twenty-five years!" he wrote in his diary. "Spoke about the meaning this day had for me . . . Strangely, forlornly happy . . . The evening, with the king; it was the 5th of September. The king came over to me, congratulated me about what I had gotten through and overcome; came over again later and asked about my first efforts, spoke of my recognition in Germany." The King invited him to ask for a rise in his annual grant, but he was too proud to do so; the following year, however, his stipend was increased by 200 rixdollars. "King Christian," he wrote, "is enlightened, clear-sighted, with a mind enlarged by science . . . the gracious sympathy he has felt in my fate . . . is doubly cheering and ennobling."

Before he left, the Duke and Duchess of Augustenborg wooed him to follow them home for another holiday, at Augustenborg Castle on the Baltic island of Als, where he stayed for three weeks until the end of September. He became friendly with the Duke and with Prince Frederik of Nør, Governor of Schleswig-Holstein; he closed his ears to the rumbles of anti-Danish sentiment that were already sounding, four years before the Schleswig-Holstein insurrection of 1848 in which these two noblemen played a leading part, and he idealized the easy atmosphere of Als, whose "happy domestic life is like a beautiful summer's evening."

Als, with the Baltic Sea on one side and the Little Belt, the narrow stretch of sea between Jutland and Funen, on the other, was a lush mix of orchards and cornfields enclosed in hedges of hazels and wild roses, running down to serpentine bays. From one ducal home to another, he wrote to Carl Alexander in Weimar that "this island is a garden of fruit; the castle lies in the midst of a wood. The Baltic ripples against the borders of the flower-beds, and an arm of the sea stretches far into the gardens and wood." Andersen luxuriated in the opulent settings of his princes' retreats. A contemporary drawing has him as the dandy, effete in flowing cape and striped trousers, hastening obsequiously to the Duke; in another, he is lean, bony and animated, reading his tales aloud to the Duke and his fashionable wife and daughters as they recline in a semi-circle, mesmerized by the story-teller.

On the crest of a wave, Andersen returned to the Hotel du Nord in Copenhagen, buoyed up by a year of unparalleled attention, emotionally alive in two safely long-distant relationships, with Jenny Lind and Carl Alexander. Confident that in the invented fairy tale he had found both his own voice and his ideal genre, and that an enthusiastic audience was waiting for his work, he now wrote the two winter tales which are among his masterpieces, "The Snow Queen" and "The Fir Tree."

He began "The Snow Queen" on 5 December and on 10 December he told Ingemann that "It has been sheer joy for me to put on paper my most recent fairy tale, 'The Snow Queen'; it permeated my mind in such a way that it came out dancing over the paper"; the tale was published on 21 December. Many of his greatest tales were laboriously worked on—"The Little Mermaid," "The Ugly Duckling"—but the speed with which he finished "The Snow Queen" shows, as the critic Naomi Lewis says, "the pace of inspiration rather than worked-out thought." The conviction of the story-telling is clear from the opening:

> Now then, here's where we begin! When we get to the end of the story, we shall know more than we know now. It's about a wicked imp. He was one of the wickedest of them all, the very Devil himself.

The long, seven-part narrative tumbles out, a rush of events and impressions which hold the reader in thrall. Yet the poetic construction is unsurpassed in Andersen's *œuvre*, and the symbolism complex and profound.

Andersen begins with the Manichaean, fatalistic vision which is the essence of the folk tale, and which was central to his own outlook, but he gives it a sophisticated twist. A devil has created a magic mirror, which has the power of making anything good and beautiful shrink to nothing, while magnifying and making even worse everything bad or ugly. Shrieking with laughter, the devil and his imps fly heavenward with the glass, which shatters and falls to earth,

> causing even more mischief than before; for some of the bits were scarcely as big as a grain of sand, and these went flying round the world, and if they got

into anyone's eyes they would stick there, the people then seeing everything wrong or having an eye only for what was bad in anything . . . Some people even got a little bit in their hearts, and this was really dreadful, for then their hearts would be like a lump of ice.

The second scene is nineteenth-century picturebook sentimentality: two children living in adjacent attics, Kai and Gerda, play in their roofbox garden (as Andersen had played at home in Odense) and listen to a grandmother telling them stories. Rose trees grow in the garden, which is an urban, poor man's re-creation of Eden before the Fall; the image is emphasized by lines from a hymn, "In the valley grew roses wild / And there we spoke with the Holy Child," which trill through the narrative. In the winter, the garden freezes, and the children play inside, watching snowflakes form patterns on the window panes. Flitting across this idyll comes the seductive, malevolent figure of the Snow Queen, a northern *femme fatale*, "a woman, dressed in the finest white gauze, which seemed to be made up of millions of starry flakes. She herself was so pretty and delicate, and yet was made of ice—glittering, dazzling ice—although she was alive." This image went back to Andersen's childhood, when his father traced the outline of a woman with outstretched arms on their frozen panes, saying "She must have come to fetch me"; after his death, Andersen's mother told a chirping cricket, "He is dead, you need not call him, the Ice Maiden has carried him off."

Subtly, Andersen introduces unease into the narrative: the first sight of the Snow Queen; the splinters of glass pricking Kai in the heart and eyes; the changes in his behaviour—sneering, mimicry and moodiness, observations on the switch from childhood to adolescence. The portrait of Kai maturing is magically compressed: one wintry day, he joins the big boys, who play at tying their sledges to farmers' carts and speeding around the main square. Kai ties his sledge to a big white sleigh which drives round and round the square, but when he reaches to untie himself, the sleigh takes off in a snowstorm and races out of town. The driver, in fur cloak and cap of snow, is a lady, "tall and straight and all gleaming white. It was the Snow Queen." She squeezes him next to her on the sleigh, then kisses him:

> Ugh! It was colder than ice and went straight to his heart, which was already half ice. He had a feeling that he was going to die . . .
>
> The Snow Queen kissed Kai once more, and by this time he had forgotten little Gerda and Granny and everyone else at home.

"That's the last kiss you'll get!" she said. "Or I'll kiss you to death!"

Kai looked at her; she was very beautiful. A wiser, lovelier face he could not imagine; now she no longer seemed made of ice as she had done when she sat outside the window and beckoned to him—in his eyes she was perfect. He felt no fear at all: he told her he could do mental arithmetic, even with fractions, and work out how many square miles there were in the country and how many people lived there. She smiled all the time. Then he realized that he knew very little indeed . . .

The psychology is flawless—the adolescent mix of thrill and terror as the adult world opens up, the realization that academic study barely counts in the whirl of life.

That Kai grows up, and Gerda doesn't, so saving him by her innocence, is central to the story—this is Andersen's version of a favourite nineteenth-century theme, woman's redemption of man. The tale has eight strong women characters and only one male, a victim, the boy who must be saved. Gerda, the innocent, wise child, propels the narrative by her loyal search for Kai. "The Snow Queen" is a classic quest story, a tale of dangerous journeys through many seasons and strange landscapes. This was a natural genre for Andersen, and the sweep of his snowscapes, wolves howling and ravens squawking in the forest, blue Northern Lights gleaming and blood-red sky, is unforgettable. In the midst of each scene stands Gerda, alone, frightened, too cold to speak; without shoes, gloves or muff, all of which she has lost or bartered in her search for Kai.

Around her Andersen paints a succession of bizarre worlds, each carrying an absurd detail of human weakness. There are the self-absorbed flowers ("'I can see myself! I can see myself!' said the narcissus. 'Oh, oh, how I smell!'") in the witch's garden, where the roses—symbol of truth—are buried to try to make Gerda forget Kai. There is the cautious crow asking for a permanent appointment at court instead of freedom, because he wants a pension. At the robbers' castle, there is the rough bandit girl with a heart of gold; later come the practical, wise Lapp and Finn women, who live miles apart over bleak terrain and communicate by messages scrawled on pieces of dried cod. And on the last freezing lap of the trip, there is the emotional reindeer who romps through snowfields, and kisses Gerda goodbye "while big glistening tears rolled down the creature's cheeks."

The details are so rich, the twists in the story so exciting, that it is only in the final part that the overarching structure becomes clear, as Andersen returns to the battle of good and evil. The reindeer begs the Finn woman to help Gerda, but she replies, "I can't give her any greater power than she already has. Don't you see how great she is? Don't you see how human beings and animals are forced to serve her, and how well she has got on in the world, in her bare feet? She hasn't to learn of her power from us; it's in her heart, in her heart! She's a sweet and innocent child."

In the Snow Queen's palace, empty rooms enclosed by walls of drifting snow and windows of cutting winds, Gerda's love overcomes the Snow Queen's might in the battle for Kai:

> Little Kai was quite blue with cold—nearly black in fact—but he did not notice it, for she had kissed his shivers away, and his heart was nothing but a lump of ice. He spent his time dragging sharp flat pieces of ice about, arranging them in all sorts of ways, and trying to make something out of them . . . a sort of intellectual ice-puzzle. In his own eyes the patterns were quite remarkable and of the utmost importance—that was what the grain of glass that was stuck in his eye did for him! He would lay out his patterns to form written words, but he could never hit upon the word he wanted, the word "eternity." The Snow Queen had said, "If you can work out that pattern for me, you shall be your own master, and I will present you with the whole world—and a new pair of skates." But he could not do it.*

Gerda's tears fall on Kai's breast and melt his heart; he bursts out crying, washing out the glass from his eye; the ice splinters dance in joy and form the word "eternity" by themselves, and Kai and Gerda are free. This is an image which could stand for the essence of Andersen's *œuvre*—that love conquers all; that a reliance on reason and the intellect leads to barren misery (Andersen never forgot his schoolmaster Meisling, and his diary is littered with satirical comments against academic life, such as meeting a professor "who said nothing in seven languages"); that truth lies within— that it is how we see the world, in Gerda's terms or in the Snow Queen's, with a splinter of glass in our eyes like Kai or comically like the robber girl, that shapes our existence.

---

*This is the passage which W. H. Auden chose as the best illustration of Andersen's genius, and of the difference between his tales and folk tales. It could never occur in a folk tale, wrote Auden, "firstly because the human situation with which it is concerned is an historical one, created by Descartes, Newton and their successors, and secondly, because no folk tale would analyse its own symbol and explain that the game with the ice-splinters was the game of reason. Further, the promised reward, 'the whole world and a new pair of skates,' has not only a surprise and a subtlety of which the folk tale is incapable, but also a uniqueness by which one can identify its author."

In the last scene, Kai and Gerda trek through the snow, and suddenly it is spring. Bathos ("You're a fine one for roaming around," says the little robber girl to Kai, "I wonder whether you deserve to have people running to the ends of the earth for your sake") is interleaved with sadness (the crow is dead, so will not draw his court pension), and with the longing for spiritual meaning. Then the roses are in bloom, the children are home:

> They had forgotten like a heavy dream the cold empty splendour of the Snow Queen's palace. Grandmother was sitting there in God's bright sunshine and reading aloud from the Bible, "Except ye become as little children, ye shall not enter into the kingdom of heaven!" And Kai and Gerda looked into each other's eyes, and all at once they understood the old hymn, "In the valley grew roses wild /And there we spoke with the Holy Child!" There they sat together, grown up, yet children still, children at heart—and it was summer, warm and beautiful summer.

Graham Greene once defined his artistic consciousness with an image from "The Snow Queen"; it was the splinter of ice in his heart, he said, that gave him his novelist's detachment. Andersen had no such glacial quality, and generally could not separate himself from his work at all. But "The Snow Queen" is, apart from its few shades of childhood memories, among his least autobiographical works. On the other hand "The Fir Tree," the tale with which it was published as the second instalment of *Nye Eventyr* (*New Fairy Tales*) in December 1844, is as precise a fantasy self-portrait as he ever composed, tragic and self-pitying in its witty self-recognition. It is as if the intense involvement with his own autobiography in the one tale released him from the need to pour himself into the other, and allowed him in "The Snow Queen" to compose a work of pure symbolism.

Anyone who, like Andersen in 1844, has reached mid life and has lived intensely in his imagination, will recognize himself in the biography of the Fir Tree. The tale portrays a certain psychological type who, as Andersen was, is unable to be happy in the moment because he is always hoping for greater glory, then being wracked by regret. Growing up in the forest, the fir tree is oblivious to the pleasures of youth and health, sun and fresh air, and the joys of landscape—the hare bounding through the glistening snow, the crimson clouds above. The tree thinks impatiently of more glamorous destinies, the swallows and storks tell it of life beyond the forest. Will it be cut down as a trunk and shipped across the sea? Taken to town and decorated as a Christmas tree? It "knew neither peace nor rest but was forever wanting to push on . . . 'There must be something greater, even grander! But what? I'm yearning! I'm pining! I can't think what's come over me!'"

Eventually it is felled and rolls away on a wagon, but is at once in pain and homesick, "unable to think of anything happy." It is installed as the centre of a gracious drawing room, one of Andersen's hallmark settings: "there were portraits hanging on the walls, and standing by the fireplace were big Chinese vases with lions on the lids. There were rocking-chairs, silk sofas and big tables piled with picture-books and toys." The trembling tree is decked out with candles, sweets and tinsel, but all it can think is "If only it was tonight! If only the lights would soon go on! And I wonder what will happen then? Will trees come from the wood to look at me, I wonder?" It gets "bark-ache" from "sheer longing"; then at last it is lit, but of course, "the tree was too frightened even to tremble now. It was really horrid! It was so afraid of losing some of its finery, and was quite bewildered by all the glory." Then the children strip it, open presents and listen to stories, and the tree, no longer the centre of attention, wonders, "Don't I come in here! Don't I have a part?"

It spends the next day waiting for the finery again. It never comes—the wilting tree is banished to the attic, where it whines to the mice about "the happiest evening of my life; only then I never realized how happy I was!" Months later it is thrown out into the yard—"'Now for a new life!' thought the tree." But in contrast to the blossoming roses and lime trees, it is withered and yellow, and it is soon nostalgic even for the attic:

> It thought of the freshness of youth in the wood, of the merry Christmas Eve and of the little mice that had listened so delighted to the story . . .
>
> "All, all over!" said the poor little tree. "If only I'd been happy when I could have been. All, all over!"
>
> And the servant came and chopped the tree into little bits; a whole bundle of them. It made a lovely blaze under the scullery copper . . . while at each crackle, which was a deep sigh, the tree thought of a summer's day in the wood, or a winter's night when the stars were shining . . .
>
> The boys played in the yard, the smallest wearing on his breast the gold star which the tree had borne on its happiest evening. Now that was all over, and it was all over with the tree, and the story's over as well. All, all over! And so it is with every story!

All Andersen's friends would have smiled in recognition at this bittersweet self-portrait. Like its creator, the fir tree is a fantasist, vain, fearful, restless, afflicted with the trembling sensitivity of the neurotic, manically swinging from hope to misery. By placing this tragic portrait within the miniaturist frame of an unthreatening domestic setting, however, Andersen broadened its appeal to all those members of the bourgeoisie who at times suffered despair within their silk-draped and gilt-hung interiors. Fantasy comforts as well as liberates: you can afford to see yourself in an Andersen character as you would not wish to do in one from, say, Ibsen. Andersen is gentle, too fatalistic to be really aggressive, and this surely contributed to the popularity of tales like "The Fir Tree" among adult readers.

"The Fir Tree" sounded new notes in his art. He had written tales with unhappy endings before—"The Little Mermaid," "The Steadfast Tin Soldier"—but they had been about love fought for and lost. "The Fir Tree" has a more deeply ingrained pessimism, suggesting not only the mercilessness of fate but the pointlessness of life itself, that only the moment is worthwhile. The existential doubt which haunted Andersen, and which his efforts at religious belief could not lay to rest, is expressed here for the first time in a fairy tale; it recurs in late works such as "Auntie Toothache" and "Old Johanna's Tale," but by then Andersen had moved on to a different kind of story.

Andersen spent Christmas 1844 at the manor house of Bregentved and New Year with the Collin family, both times a welcome guest who was nevertheless an outsider. This was the Andersen—the joker, the melancholic—who took a perverse pleasure in presenting his bleak vision in the guise of a cosy Christmas story to be unwrapped beneath the candle-lit branches. "The Fir Tree" reiterated his suffering self to the princes and aristocrats keen to absorb him into their circles. Andersen was flattered, but a kernel of artistic self-preservation—his memories of hardship, his sexual apartness—would not let him wholly belong to them. While fame and fortune consoled him, they also threatened to isolate him further, as he climbed the social ladder and left behind the world which had created him. His fairy tales were a way of keeping faith with his past.

Through the first part of 1845, he continued to reap successes. His novel *The Improvisatore* appeared in Russian and in English, translated by Mary Howitt, who sent him a copy of the work with a letter saying "Your name is now an honoured one in England." A pirate edition came out shortly afterwards in New York. In February his fairy tale opera *The Flower of Fortune*

(*Lykkens Blomst*), with music by Henrik Rung, opened at the Royal Theatre; one of the characters was based on Jenny Lind. In March his comedy *The New Lying-In Room* was also premièred. Andersen submitted it anonymously to avoid Heiberg's prejudice, Johanne Luise Heiberg took the leading role, and the play did well, running to sixty-one performances. Hans Christian Ørsted and the Collins were let in on the secret; otherwise Andersen kept his counsel and enjoyed accusing other writers of being the author. (Amid the speculation, he was enraged that when his name was suggested, the general reply was no, "Andersen could not have kept still after such a success!")

In April the King increased his annual grant by 200 rixdollars to 600 rixdollars and the third volume of *New Fairy Tales* (*Nye Eventyr*) appeared; in June came "The Bell," the story inspired by Ørsted's romantic philosophy of truth in nature; in August *Only a Fiddler* and *OT* were published in English, again translated by Mary Howitt, and in September *Picture Book Without Pictures* went into its sixth German edition. Andersen had his portrait painted twice that spring; celebrating his fortieth birthday on 2 April, he felt reasonably content within his Copenhagen circle. The following month his position as an adopted son in the Collin family was confirmed when he was summoned to the midnight deathbed of Henriette Collin, Jonas's wife. He wanted to show his sympathy, yet when he wrote to the bereaved Jonas he was incapable of expressing anything but his own longings. "I wish I could say it, show it, that I love you, love you with the entire soul of a son," he wrote, explaining how moved he had been to be allowed into the family circle, and that if Jonas died before him, he would despair.

In his new tales, Andersen played with a range of styles. "The Shepherdess and the Chimney Sweep" is another story from the Biedermeier drawing room, delicate and whimsical as its silly porcelain heroine, who ends up united with her china sweep, loving one another "till they broke."

"The Red Shoes," which associates feet and the human soul as in "The Little Mermaid," tells of a young girl who goes to her confirmation in bright red shoes, "and all her thoughts were of these when the clergyman laid his hands on her head and spoke of holy baptism." The idea has innocuous origins in Andersen's memories of his own confirmation, when he could think only of his squeaky new boots, but he makes of it a gruesome morality tale in which Karen—the name of his half-sister—is punished for going to a ball in her red shoes instead of caring for her ill guardian. She has to dance forever, through woods and fields, day and night, in the shoes, which take on a life of their own; an angel tells her, "Dance you shall! . . . Dance in your red shoes till you grow pale and cold, till your skin shrinks up like a skeleton!" Only when her feet are cut off and the red shoes dance off with them into the forest, leaving her on crutches—recalling the queen dancing herself to death in red hot shoes in the Grimms' folk tale "Snow White"—does she "repent" and return to church, where her heart breaks and her soul flies "on sunshine up to God."

"The Red Shoes" is Andersen's most vindictive tale. By contrast "The Bell" idealizes the harmony of nature and philosophy. In this mystical tale, a prince and a poor boy each take their own way through the woods seeking a bell, and arrive at the same moment under a diamond-studded sky: "they ran forward to meet each other, and clasped each other by the hand in the great temple of Nature and poetry, and over their heads pealed the invisible holy bell, while blessed spirits danced airily around them." The story is a parable about the search for wisdom, in which the prince represents science and the physicist Ørsted, and may also suggest Carl Alexander of Weimar, while the poor boy is an emblem of poetry and of Andersen himself. Andersen, in his drive to be modern, had always been attracted to science and in Ørsted had seen how a scientist could be also a philosopher and a perceptive literary adviser. In "The Bell" scientist and artist, rich and poor, reach the truth their own way.

The benign influence of Ørsted shines through "The Bell." Ørsted had been the first to recognize the importance of the fairy tales, and remained Andersen's kindest friend in Copenhagen. One evening Andersen took him a harsh review of his work. Ørsted listened to it, then reflected that it was severe, adding "yet it seems to me that there is something in it, some arguments which are really striking and give us an insight into you!" Andersen shrieked with laughter that this was true, because he had written the critique himself. It was the sort of self-centred practical joke that he loved. Ørsted indulged him ("He is a true humourist," he said soothingly), but many were alienated by the shrill exuberance with which Andersen claimed attention, by his affectations and his panics.

This, as well as jealousy of his international fame, made him enemies at home. In his memoir of working at Reitzel's bookshop in the 1840s, the bookseller Otto Wroblewski tells how one day the shop doorbell rang and in came an elegant, balding man, Professor Heiberg, who demanded to see Reitzel. The assistant stuttered that Reitzel was out, though he was flustered by the sound of voices coming from Mr. Reitzel's office. Heiberg asked ironically whether Reitzel was at the Leipzig book fair, then took a seat to wait for him, whereupon the office door opened and out stepped Reitzel with his guest, Hans Christian Andersen. Reitzel, glaring at his assistant, shook hands affably with Heiberg, who greeted both him and Andersen cordially. But Andersen, visibly dismayed, dashed out on to Købmagergade, horrified at meeting his adversary. Reitzel, shrewd and perceptive, tried to protect his prickly author; one of the reasons for the success of his publishing house, according to its historian, was that "it gave house room to both hawks and doves; to cool ironic characters—style personified, like Heiberg—who had to be handled with studied care—and fragile souls, like Hans Christian Andersen, who would shrivel up under the derision of the ironists, and whose tremendous sensitivity had to be taken into account."

This was the contemporary view of Andersen, and it surfaced most maliciously in print in 1845, when Carsten Hauch portrayed Andersen as an egotistical, affected poet, Eginhard, in his novel *Slottet ved Rhinen* (*The Castle on the Rhine*). The novel caused a new buzz of Andersen-ridicule in Copenhagen; Andersen accepted it with forbearance, showing his characteristic forgiveness to Hauch, who, he suggested, had not realized how widely the fictional character would be identified with its model. Privately he was mortified. To Ingemann he wrote:

> Yes indeed, they are right when they say "That is Andersen!" Here are all my faults collected together! I hope and think that I have lived through that time; but all this poet says and does I could have said and done. I felt strangely moved by this raw portrait showing me in my wretched state . . . My own grandfather was insane, my father went insane just before he died. You will therefore understand how the disintegration of the unlucky [poet] in Hauch's art moves me—the disintegration of him who is my mirror image.

Ripples of his old fears returned easily even in the midst of success and productivity. He spent a quiet summer in Jutland and at the aristocratic manors of Funen, and then suddenly he was back in an emotional vortex.

CHAPTER 14

The Princes' Poet

1845–1846

I love your heart better than your crown, and yet there's something holy about your crown.
—HANS CHRISTIAN ANDERSEN, "The Nightingale"

In September 1845, Jenny Lind returned to Copenhagen. In the two years since her last visit, she too had had her successes, she too had launched an international career in Germany and had been persuaded by the adulation she received there to think of the country as her second home. Her Germany, the high-romantic musical world of Mendelssohn and Meyerbeer, Schumann and Liszt, bordered on Andersen's cultured circles in Weimar and Leipzig. Andersen counted Schumann as a friend, and it was Andersen who had first mentioned Jenny to Meyerbeer, "First Court Composer" to Frederick William of Prussia. As a result she had triumphed in Berlin, at the new Royal Opera House, and been invited to sing at court, where Lady Westmorland, wife of the British ambassador, remembered as the most extraordinary experience of her life the transfiguration of Jenny's face and figure as she sang, "lighting them up with the whole fire and dignity of her genius," and her daughter wrote that in Berlin Jenny was spoken of "with reverence, like no one else, as you would speak of a particularly beautiful religious painting or poem."

Full of confidence, she sang better than ever; after her final performance in Berlin in 1844 she wrote:

It was the loveliest day of my life! And that is saying much! But then who could have guessed that in so short a time I could have so grown into the hearts of the Berliners. To express . . . the emotion that ran through the audience each time I was called back at the end of the performance is impossible, I can only say that a more wonderful moment I can never experience, have never experienced . . . And how I have risen at every performance!

She had gone on to tour in north Germany and had sung privately to Queen Victoria, Prince Albert and Leopold, King of Belgium, at royal castles on the Rhine. Here the fastidious Berlioz had heard her, and wrote "her talent is really high above anything one ever hears in the French and German theatre." Vienna, Hamburg, Paris, were crying out for her, but she was exhausted, uncertain, fluctuating between amazement at her triumph and a desire to give it all up.

To Madame Birch-Pfeiffer, a mother-figure who had taught her German, she wrote at this time that "this life does not suit me at all. If you could only see me and my despair each time I have to go to the theatre to sing! It is altogether too much for me. I sing far worse than I should were it not for this enemy." For the money she was offered, she said, musical directors could "get singers anywhere who are not so difficult to satisfy as I am, and who at least wish for something, whereas I wish for nothing at all." She was never materialistic, and gave much of her money away to charity, feeling most at ease about her singing when she was giving a benefit performance for one or other of her good causes. She resolved to leave the stage in a year, and in this mood travelled for a valedictory season in Copenhagen. The Royal Theatre there was a half-way house for her between the comfort of singing in Stockholm and the strain of international performances, when she had to sing in German: in Copenhagen she sang in Swedish while the other singers sang in Danish and "the two kindred languages," says Andersen, "mingled very beautifully together, there was no jarring."

By the time Jenny arrived, Andersen was whipped up to a frenzy. She fuelled his sexual fantasies all over again. He wrote a song to welcome her, and on 21 September went down to the quayside to meet her off the boat, finding over a thousand people there. They were disappointed; Jenny did not show up, and Andersen returned to the Hotel du Nord and drew another frustrated cross in his almanac. Four days later she arrived—still the same fresh, pale, innocent-looking girl of Andersen's imagination, wearing the same simple clothes, unadorned by jewellery, seeming just a little older because she had exchanged her childish ringlets for the style in which she wore her hair for the rest of her life, parted in the centre and drawn down in loops over her ears.

Andersen followed her home from the theatre, and for the next four weeks he danced attendance on her daily. He loved the excitement that whirled about her, which was even more tumultuous than during her last visit. Ticket prices at the Royal Theatre quadrupled and still crowds queued for them all night, from eleven in the evening until ten next morning, through biting winds and sheets of rain. After the performances, the audience rushed to Bournonville's house, where Jenny was staying, to greet her again when she returned from the opera. There were parties nightly at the Bournonvilles'; the King once more overwhelmed her with gifts. Her *La Figlia del Reggimento*, which had never been heard in Denmark, and her *Norma* were rapturously received; the role of Norma had become her signature, and she mesmerized audiences with her unorthodox interpretation. Instead of the traditional "raving Italian"—the part had been composed for the singer Giuditta Pasta, and was a favourite of Malibran and Grisi—who lunges forward to stab her children, seething with jealousy and hatred, Jenny was, Andersen wrote, "the suffering, sorrowing woman . . . who is immediately disarmed when she gazes into the eyes of the innocent ones."

Andersen was spellbound. He thrilled to pure theatricality, and Jenny was now a sensational performer. One observer wrote how he nearly cried with delight at her coloratura singing; there was something of the conjuror about the way she held on to a note—people counted the length of time (sixty seconds was her reported record). "She could hold on until the audience believed she must be at the very end of her resources," her biographer wrote, "but then, instead of breaking off, it would gradually swell out in an unbelievable crescendo of sound. Her breathing control was the secret of her wonderful pianissimo, that incomparable achievement that filled everyone with amazement and that Chopin loved so."

For Andersen, as for Jenny herself, it was divinely inspired art. "People laugh, people cry; it does them as much good as going to church; they become better for it. People feel that God is in art; and where God stands before us face to face there is a holy church," he wrote of her stay in Copenhagen. Of all those who wrote about her, he comes closest to her own descriptions of her art. Singing masters were useless, she wrote, because "to such a degree had God written within me what I had to study, my ideal was (and is) so high, that no human being existed who could in the least satisfy my demands. Therefore I sing after no one's *méthode*—only after that of the birds (so far as I am able); for their Teacher was the only one who responded to my requirements of truth, clearness and expression."

While Andersen was with her or hearing her sing, she squashed his own doubts about the meaning of art; at a time when he felt middle-aged, she invigorated him with her youth and her religious faith. For a month, he hung suspended in the present, neither working nor thinking of the future, concentrating only on the next hour when he would see Jenny, or letters he was writing to her. "Jenny in *Norma*; at home loving towards me; happy and hopeful—yet I know," he noted one evening in his almanac, ending on a pessimistic note.

She stayed longer in Copenhagen than expected; the weather was too bad to make the crossing to Germany and several ships had been lost in the Sound. On her last evening she gave a dinner party for her closest friends at the Royal Hotel. Andersen was there from five o'clock until midnight, when Jenny toasted Bournonville as a second father to her in Denmark. Bournonville responded that if this were so, every man in Denmark would want to be his son and so Jenny's brother. That would be too many, Jenny thought; she must therefore choose one to represent them all, and she asked Andersen if he would be her brother. Thus his attentions were publicly repudiated. Jenny took him no more seriously as a suitor than she had done two years earlier, though at twenty-five she was by now longing for love and marriage. The next day, 22 October, he went to say goodbye to her, and the memory of her was as sexually exciting as the prospect had been, for the almanac for the days after her departure is as full of crosses as it was before she arrived. Jenny's visit disturbed his equilibrium so violently that he found it impossible to stay in Copenhagen. He had long wanted to make another major European journey; nine days after she left for Berlin, he followed her.

Two temperamental Nordic geniuses now made a triumphal progress south through Germany, their lives and careers intersecting repeatedly. Jenny went straight to Berlin, opening in *Norma* on 9 November; Andersen took his usual meandering route, crossing via the Great Belt to Funen rather than the treacherous Sound to Kiel, as he always preferred to do in winter, and aiming to be in Berlin for a Christmas reunion with Jenny. On his last day in Copenhagen he had an audience with the King, and a large gathering of Collins said goodbye to him, with Edvard, Jonna and Henrik Stampe waving him off at the posthouse. He was nervous and fatalistic as he left Copenhagen, superstitiously changing seats because he did not like facing backwards in the coach. "I didn't get to give my beloved Father Collin a kiss," he wrote in his diary, "Oh, I'm so worried I won't ever see him again!—God, as I roll out of the city this evening, how many hearses in the coming year will drive along this road with the names of dear ones shining from the coffins."

His first stop was Glorup Manor on Funen, home of Count Moltke, where he was restless, and felt old. He took solitary walks around the gardens and through the forest in clear, freezing weather; the leaves had fallen, there was frost on the ground and ice on the water, and the withered leaves crackled with each gust of wind, but everything was bathed in golden autumn sun: "You might almost think it was a spring day. The older man has moments like this in the autumn, when his heart is dreaming about spring," he wrote. The stillness of the country days and the leisurely routine in the quiet old manor seemed almost ghostly after the flurry of his month with Jenny in Copenhagen, and he was bored to distraction, though at other times it was just such luxurious calm which he found most conducive to work.

His day went thus:

> Up at 8 o'clock and drink coffee; potter around and write until 10 o'clock; then walk up along the long, tree-lined drive and out the gate to the path through the field . . . look at the strait and wander back; read, sew, put things in order; and lunch at 12 o'clock with a glass of port. Then a short rest and after that, as before, an hour's walk. It is the same route, and I take it a little farther out in the other direction. Read and write until around 4 o'clock, get dressed; and dinner is from 4:00 to 5:00. Now comes the most boring period, until 8 o'clock. I sit in my room; don't want to do anything, not to sleep either. One of the servants is playing the flute badly, practising a piece . . . The wind is whistling outside; the fire in the tilestove is rumbling; the moon is shining in . . . Downstairs I conduct the entire conversation from 8 until 10 o'clock. Miss Lise's stomach growls. The only respite is when the servant calls His Excellency out, for the foreman is here now to talk with him. I look at the clock; it doesn't seem to be running at all; and when it does finally strike, each stroke falls as if marking time to a funeral march. At 10 o'clock, upstairs; and a half hour later, in bed.

His mood barely picked up as he moved on to Gravensteen, home of the Duke of Augustenborg, where he stayed for most of November. He read his tales aloud, strolled out to Flensborg fjord, sat for a watercolour portrait and complained in his almanac that he was unhappy, ill and that his penis was sore. He makes no record of it in his diary, but he almost certainly suffered from the tense political atmosphere at Augustenborg, for just three years later the Duke rose up against the Danish king and demanded independence from Denmark in the Schleswig-Holstein wars, and anti-Danish sentiment must have been rife—it would have left Andersen, whose loyalty to his king was never in question, embarrassed and uneasy.

As at Glorup, Andersen took lonely walks; after one of them, on 18 November, he came home to write "The Little Matchgirl," like "The Fir Tree" another bitter Christmas story. Inspired by a drawing by the Danish artist Johan Thomas Lundbye, it is his best-known rendering of a subject which continued to haunt him, the death of a child. It was written when he was cocooned and dissatisfied in dull, aristocratic luxury, and is, on a social level, his most fiercely indignant tale. With this story he returned to his childhood as the impoverished outsider; the tale echoes not only his own memories of his caring, storytelling grandmother, but an account his mother had told him of her childhood in the 1770s, when like the little matchgirl she was sent to beg on the streets and stayed out, cold and hungry, because she was too frightened to return home penniless.

Nowhere was Andersen closer in tone to his contemporary Dickens than in his story of a beggar child freezing to death as she looks through the window at the lavishly decorated Christmas tree and steaming roast goose in the dining room of a rich family. As in Dickens, the palpable human sympathy which pervades the story is somehow enhanced by the living, breathing quality of inanimate objects, as if everything was calling out for our engagement. This also gives the tale an anarchic flavour: the goose stuffed with prunes and apples, which "jumped off the dish, and waddled along the floor with a knife and fork in its back. Right up to the poor little girl it came," anticipates Lewis Carroll's scene in *Through the Looking Glass*, where "the leg of mutton got up in the dish and made a little bow to Alice" and the pudding began to talk. "The Little Matchgirl" has the surreal quality of a dream—the world the beggar girl imagines each time she lights a match trails into the real world around her, which in turn is symbolic:

> She struck a fresh one. And now she was sitting under the loveliest of Christmas trees. It was even bigger and more prettily decorated than the one she had seen through the glass door of the rich merchant . . . Thousands of candles were alight on the green branches . . . The little girl stretched both her hands into the air—and then the match went out, the Christmas candles all went higher and higher, and she saw that they were the bright stars. One of them fell, leaving a long fiery strip in the sky.
>
> "Someone's dying!" said the little girl; for old Granny . . . had said that when a star falls a soul rises up to God.

Of course, it is she herself who is freezing to death, but "with rosy cheeks and a smile on her lips" because of her hallucinatory imaginings, first of bourgeois comfort, then of love and warmth with her grandmother, finally of heaven. When she is found next morning, all her matches burnt, "she had wanted to warm herself, they said. No one knew what beauty she had seen, or in what radiance she had gone with her old granny into the glad New Year." This sentimental, condensed tragedy is Andersen's double answer to the establishment "they" with whom he could not feel at peace. The matches are a metaphor for the creative imagination, illuminating another world which "they" cannot dream of; the matchgirl is the victim of a harsh, divided society where outsiders are left to die.

Andersen finished the tale in a day, edited it the next morning, and a few days later set off for Berlin via Hamburg and Oldenburg, home of his old friends the Eisendeckers, who always made him feel welcome. It was a journey suspended between two worlds, the graceful aristocratic milieu where Andersen was now practised at promoting himself, and the restless anxiety of his inner life. Everywhere he stopped, he was invited to court. "Yesterday it said in the *Frankfurt Times* and *The Correspondent* that I was spending my second week in Oldenburg and giving pleasure with my costly tales at the Court and in private circles," he noted. Grand Duke August of Oldenburg gave him as a parting gift a ring, which, he was subsequently told, was worth 200 Prussian thaler.* He sped on to Berlin watching autumn change to winter around him, meadows lying under lakes which now froze over, skaters darting across them as his train steamed into the Prussian capital. "Rather used to the railroad," he mused in his diary, for "what are distances in our days?—the steam-carriage goes from Hanover to Berlin in one day!"

He reached Berlin at lunchtime on 19 December. He knew the city well, and took a good room at the British Hotel facing out over Unter den Linden, the grand avenue lined with lime trees where the Berlin *beau monde* liked to promenade and be seen. He sent a hired servant at once to Jenny Lind to announce that he had arrived and to ask for a ticket. But by evening none had come; Andersen walked out in the rain, bought himself a cheap seat—it was all that was available—at the Opera House, and in "crude company—soldiers and a drunken Frenchman," stood against a door, listening to Jenny.

> Was actually inclined to be angry with her, but she melted me. She sings German the way I suppose I read my tales—where I come from shows through;

*In 1846 200 Prussian thaler equalled 270 rixdollars—the equivalent of about £2,700 today.

but, as they say about me, this adds something interesting. The theatre is splendidly magnificent, but I haven't looked at it; I was there only for Jenny's sake. I have heard her as if in a dream. I don't love her, I guess, the way everyone does. I am not very happy, and yet it is pleasant here in this room. Today I feel so alone here in Berlin.

The following days were even more disappointing. Early next morning, a Saturday, Andersen took a carriage to Jenny's apartment, but she was at a rehearsal; Louise Johansson, the Swedish companion whom she took on her tours, had stayed at home to receive him. "Not pleased," he tried again on Sunday: " 'She isn't receiving anyone,' said the janitress. 'Yes, me! Give her my card!' and then I didn't have one! 'Tell her my name!'—Then she came to receive me herself; she looked as if she were flourishing even more than when she was in Copenhagen . . . We sat on the sofa and talked . . ." But it was clear that she was distancing herself from Andersen. On 23 December, he wrote, "Not really in a good mood; felt a little lonely!—Jenny still hasn't sent a ticket . . . I was annoyed. Took a numbered seat . . . Jenny sang so beautifully that I wasn't angry with her. No, no! She can't have forgotten me!" On the morning of Christmas Eve, he went to visit her again, certain that he would spend the evening with her, but: "no one at home; left a letter . . . I wonder what she could be thinking about, since she is taking so little notice of me, I who came to Berlin mostly for her sake, I who could have spent a much more joyous Christmas Eve."

On Christmas Eve he began to understand her message, and he let himself go in an orgy of self-pity:

> Haven't heard anything from Jenny. I'm feeling badly treated and sad!—She's not acting toward me like a sister here in Berlin; if I'd been a stranger to her here, then she could have told me what was wrong; and I would have done something about it! She once filled my heart—I don't love her any more! In Berlin she has cut out the diseased flesh with a cold knife! . . . In Copenhagen I lived for her—what good did it do me? I have given a lot, and to someone the world calls the noblest and finest! Now it is Christmas Eve! How happy it must be in a home where a man has a hearth!—Now the Christmas tree is being lit.* The wife is standing with the smallest child on her arm; it is stretch-

---

*By tradition, the Christmas tree is lit for the first time in the early evening of Christmas Eve in Germany and Denmark, and it is then that children receive their presents. In German Christmas Eve is called *Heiligabend*—holy evening.

ing its hands out towards the many candles and is jumping up and down with joy on its mother's arm; the other children are clamouring and looking for what they might have got, and a circle of friends is sitting there. The stranger abroad—his Christmas trees are the starry skies; his pictures, new cities, new faces!—He rushes along!—Under God's Christmas tree I raise my head and ask, "Father, what have I been granted?"—and maybe it'll be a coffin.

This was the Andersen who saw himself as the little matchgirl, looking through the window at other families' Christmas trees, emotionally frozen out by Jenny, alone and with only the pictures of his imagination for sustenance. "There is a veil over my thoughts, but they fly toward Jenny," he wrote on Christmas Day. "What have I done to her!—Is it out of caution for her reputation that she is taking so little notice of me? 'I don't hate you, because I have never loved you,' she once said. I didn't understand it; now I do."

But this was only half the story. Andersen did not sit in all night on Christmas Eve, as he says he did in his autobiography. At 8 o'clock he went to a party where the guests included aristocrats from the Prussian court and a number of artists; he read his tales and the ladies sang, and underneath the tree two angels handed him his presents, a beautifully bound writing book and a lampshade. And between Christmas and New Year he was sucked into a vortex of high society engagements, invited by princesses and counts, professors and authoresses, to read his tales as part of the festivities.

For both Jenny and Andersen, the Berlin winter of 1845–1846 was a highwater mark of German acclaim and welcome. If she did not take much notice of him, it was because her world had expanded beyond anything she could have imagined in the two months since she had left Copenhagen, and Andersen no longer had much significance in it. This season, in which she had sung two operas, *Don Giovanni* and *Der Freischütz*, each in a controversial interpretation which had won over the Berliners, was her most dazzling yet. Her pre-eminence on the European stage was now so obvious that she began to enjoy her triumphs, rather than be surprised by them, and for the first time to throw herself into theatre life. "I am splendidly well. I am enjoying myself very much," she wrote from Berlin to a Swedish singer. "My voice has grown twice as strong as it was . . . My acting has become something quite different; it has much more vivacity and passion; it is solid and stout, quite first-rate! If my success was great last year, it is now overwhelming."

Like almost every Scandinavian artist who has achieved acclaim in western Europe, she exulted at her new international status while cursing the pettiness at home which had held her back. "How changed is everything now!," she wrote home. "What a position I have attained! All the musical talent of Europe . . . is at my feet . . . What a pity that we Swedes cannot get on in our own country! No Fame! nothing! nothing! In only seven months I have succeeded in making my reputation here: while after seven years at home not a soul knew of me. At this moment all the most important engagements in the world are offered to me!" These were sentiments Andersen understood well, but they excluded him too, for at twenty-five Jenny was turning herself into a cosmopolitan European. She never went back to live in Stockholm and she needed a fellow Scandinavian in her orbit much less than Andersen did. With her 1845 season, Germany became her musical home, and her intimate circle consisted of Germans.

In Copenhagen, she had valued Andersen as a fellow artist; now she had met Mendelssohn, so close to her in spirit and outlook that, artistically, she felt she had no need of anyone else. She was mesmerized by his dark eyes and handsome, mobile face as he sat at the piano extemporizing—a contemporary once compared him to a centaur, with the piano as the horse. Clara Schumann believed Jenny had fallen in love; certainly the hours she spent talking and making music with Mendelssohn every day at the home of the sculptor Professor Wichmann and his wife Amalia on the Hasenheger Strasse were among the happiest she had known. Almost at once, the Wichmanns became her adopted family. "Amalia, for the first time in my life I have felt as if I had tasted the blessedness of home," Jenny wrote in the spring of 1846. By the time Andersen arrived in Berlin, lonely and eager, Jenny was beyond his reach. She was kind to him when she thought about it, but her emotional centre was elsewhere.

On Christmas Day Jenny did write—"a letter from Jenny; she is very endearing"—and on Boxing Day he celebrated a late Christmas with her under her tree: "she gave me a bar of soap in the shape of a piece of cheese, Eau de Cologne; was so wonderful, patted me, called me a child." Jenny introduced him to her German teacher and mother-substitute, Madame Birch-Pfeiffer; "said I was such a good person and a brother to her. When I got home, I found an invitation from the king for dinner at the palace . . . ," wrote Andersen. As soon as Jenny began to fuss over him as much as everyone else did, his demands on her lessened. His new, grand social circles excited and occupied him too much; what Jenny told him about herself, that she now "felt so at home in Germany," was true of Andersen too, once he allowed himself to enjoy it.

. . .

For Andersen had not, of course, gone to Berlin entirely for her sake. She had been the goal to give his journey a *frisson* of sexual anticipation, but Berlin was only one stop in a long voyage of discovery and self-promotion which occupied him for almost a year from 1845 to 1846. At the back of his almanac for 1845, he lists not only the Danish ambassadors for the countries he thought he might visit, and the consuls in the main towns, but also the rulers of every principality he would cross, together with their dates of birth and the names of their spouses—eighteen of them, from King Ludwig of Bavaria and Duke Wilhelm of Brunswick to King Frederick of Saxony and Grand Duke Leopold II of Tuscany. He expected to be invited by many of them, and he set off prepared; he wanted honours and worldly glory, and he was disappointed that he had had to set off in October without a Danish decoration.

"In the *Prussian Times* it says that I am here and that I belong more to Germany than to my fatherland," he noted on 27 December. At soirée after soirée, he was fussed over. The sculptor Christian Rauch pressed him into his arms, kissed him and said that his tales were immortal, the scientist Alexander von Humboldt said that he didn't need any letters of recommendation, for his writings were his recommendation, and the authoress Bettina von Arnim waddled in, "slovenly, peculiar," to say he was looking better this year than last: "Go to your room," she said to her daughter, "you haven't got any prettier, he has!" On Boxing Day Andersen dined with the King; two days later he was summoned to the Princess of Prussia's residence. She was the sister of his friend Carl Alexander, the Hereditary Grand Duke of Weimar; "she received me extremely graciously; looks like her brother," he noted. "I read 'The Fir Tree' and 'The Ugly Duckling.' She seemed delighted. Her son, who will one day be king, pressed my hand two times and asked me to write my name in a book ... The princess said, 'Indeed we must meet again before you leave.'"

On Christmas Eve he visited Jakob Grimm—"who talked with me about tales"—and on Christmas Day at a party at Count Bismarck-Bohlen's, he read his tales and met Wilhelm Grimm: "[He] listened with evident fellowship of feeling ... his personality appealed to me. He liked 'The Fir Tree' a lot." This was a successful version of the visit he had attempted to make to the Grimm brothers a year earlier. Now he was in the heartland of Berlin intellectual and artistic life, and "saw these two highly gifted and amiable brothers almost daily." The Grimms were then in their sixties, and had both been professors in Berlin since 1841; they had fled there from Göttingen University, where they had been among a group of professors dismissed by the authoritarian Elector of Hanover. Jakob, the elder, was the more scholarly, a shy bachelor, serious and gentle; Wilhelm, who was married with three children, was more vivacious, though he suffered ill health; he had a teasing humour and an engaging warmth which brought out the best in Andersen. "I should have known you very well, if you had come to me the last time you were here," he said.

The brothers had lived together almost all their lives; Andersen liked them and found many points of common experience. The Grimms' father, a lawyer, had died when Jakob was eleven and Wilhelm ten, leaving them as the oldest of six children to fend for the rest of the family, which was not well provided for. They had studied law at Marburg, but were swept up at university by the new Romantic movement's interest in folk culture. From 1806, when they were in their twenties, they began collecting tales, visiting villages and spinning rooms in Germany at exactly the same time that Andersen, as a child in Odense, was listening to the old women's tales in the spinning room where his grandmother worked. Andersen grew up among the sort of storytellers whom the middle-class, scholarly Grimms deliberately sought out: Katharina Viehmann, for example, a tailor's wife who sold eggs and swapped tales, including "The Goose Girl," for cups of coffee on her rounds; an old soldier who was persuaded to tell stories in exchange for pairs of trousers; "Old Marie," the nanny of the children next door, who told them "Little Red Riding Hood" and a version of "Sleeping Beauty." Andersen liked the mythical link between himself as the great creator of new tales and the Grimms as the great collectors of old ones. Among the tales he read them were "The Snow Queen," "The Swineherd" and "The Fir Tree"; "it was," he wrote, "my desire and pleasure that they should listen to my little stories, that they should participate in them—they whose names will be always spoken as long as the German *Volks Märchen* are read." Of his own tales, he wrote to Ørsted that in twenty years' time he did not believe that they would have been forgotten.

In Germany in 1845–1846, he was stunned at his own fame, and made of it myths about his own life which comforted him when he could believe in them, and left him more restless and disoriented than ever when he could not. To Jonas Collin he wrote sourly that while he was ignored at home, Berlin high society gathered round him. Jonas was unimpressed; what an empty life, he didn't care to crawl about on the floor with the children of dukes, wasn't Andersen going to write anything? It was a vicious circle: beneath Andersen's insatiable need for fame was the hollowness of the man still seeking his sense of himself. Perhaps only the ever-yielding, ever-admiring love of a parent could have helped him towards his own identity, and that Jonas could not offer. So Andersen remained the whinging child, searching across Europe for the sort of love and absolute approval that no one accords to adults, catching glimpses of it in an adulatory newspaper article here or a flattering party guest there, as he moved from one social triumph to another.

He spent the first part of New Year's Eve 1845 with Jenny, helping her pick ribbons before she went to the British ambassador's ball and he went to another party. On 6 January, the feast of Epiphany, he was made a Knight of the Red Eagle by Frederick Wilhelm IV, the King of Prussia—his first decoration. The next day he left Berlin for Weimar. He went to say goodbye to Jenny, who was preoccupied and cross. He, too, was exhausted but looking forward to seeing Jenny again in Weimar, where she was expected at the end of the month. Standing on one point of the triangle between her and Carl Alexander, Andersen had the chance to introduce the two current passions of his life to one another.

If in Berlin he had dabbled in royalty-worship, in Weimar he abandoned himself to the tidal wave of his attraction to Carl Alexander. They met again at a ball given by a general on Andersen's first evening: "the Hereditary Grand Duke rushed to me, pressed my hands and said, 'I cannot receive you here as I would have liked to at home, oh! my friend, I have been longing for you!'" Next morning at ten, "I went to the Hereditary Grand Duke, in those magnificent rooms. He came towards me, pressed me to his breast, kissed me several times, thanked me for my love for him; we walked arm in arm to his room, sat talking a long time until he was called to the Council, then he walked, arm in arm with me, to the furthermost door!" Once again, the foppish, weepingly demonstrative side of Andersen found its match in Carl Alexander, young and overwrought, haunted by the ghosts of Weimar's cultural heyday, full of excitement at re-creating that world with Andersen installed as the new Goethe of his court.

Gentle yet emotionally extreme, intellectually curious, unpretentious, the Duke brought out the best in Andersen. In public drawing rooms and in

Carl Alexander von Saxe-Weimar-Eisenach, "the first of all princes that I really find attractive."

private dressing rooms, the pair cuddled up to one another on sofas; they held hands and squeezed each other's palms under the table at ceremonial dinners; they sneaked off to Carl Alexander's little greenhouse and to his son's nursery for intimate chats ("'He knows you are his father's friend,' he said. 'That is why he is so placable'"), and the Duke begged Andersen to regard Weimar as his second home. All this took place behind a spectacle of public formality which Andersen loved: "Banquet at the Grand Duke's, was carried there in a sedan, it is the first time in my life I have been carried . . . Was in my best clothes, with a rapier and three-cornered hat to Court." His vanity was flattered that someone of the rank of Carl Alexander, who was not only heir to a duchy but also a nephew of the Russian czar, should be interested in him. But what excited him more were the small subterfuges by which intimacy could be achieved in the ritualized setting of court life. He liked to watch Carl Alexander in formal mode, and to feel that he had secret access to the inner man. "Before the world I think of you as the Prince . . . before God and ourselves we are friends, but before men I must never forget what a high position you fill," he wrote to the Duke.

For years he had struggled in relationships with men where he was not allowed to express himself. By now he needed some sort of barrier in an intimate tie: it reassured him that he was on familiar ground. He enjoyed boasting of his grand friend—in *The Fairy Tale of My Life* he wrote, "Never, in the presence of the world, will I forget the high position which his birth gives him, but I may say . . . I love him as one who is dearest to my heart." The natural barriers of class and country served an emotional purpose; he did not hope wildly for unconditional love but he could revel in the Duke's attentions as a favourite servant might enjoy those of a gracious sultan. "I sat 'in my seat,' as he called it, on the sofa," he wrote on his third day in Weimar. "He said we must always stay friends, and that one day I should come to live with him for ever in Weimar. I replied that I loved my native country. 'But we Germans appreciate you more than the Danes do. All right, then take turns between us. Give me your hand!' He clasped it so firmly in his, told me he loved me and pressed his cheek to mine." A month later the two were still at fever pitch: on 7 February, "went to see the Hereditary Grand Duke at 8 o'clock in the morning, he received me in his shirt with only a gown around himself; 'I can do that, we know each other.' He pressed me to his breast, we kissed each other. 'Think of this hour,' he said, 'as being yesterday. We are friends for life.' We both wept."

When Jenny arrived towards the end of January, emotions at this self-indulgent court spiralled higher. She sang songs and hymns which made her audience burst out crying. The Hereditary Grand Duchess Sophie hugged and kissed Jenny, and Jenny herself collapsed in tears. At the theatre, she appeared in *Norma* and as Amina in Bellini's *La Sonnambula*, which Andersen thought her greatest part. German audiences had always rather despised *La Sonnambula*, but Weimar was amazed by Jenny's psychologically gripping performance. Her *coup* was to play the sleepwalking scene herself—most *prime donne* left it to a supernumerary, changing places behind a piece of rock planted on the stage. But Jenny's identification with her characters made this impossible for her. She had to cross a ramshackle wooden bridge over a millstream with a millwheel turning below, waiting to crush her to death; one of the rotten planks gives way, the lamp drops from her hand into the torrent, but, eyes fixed ahead in the dark, she reaches the other side. The scene, Jenny said, made her horribly frightened; she imagined the dangers as real, but could not have faced her audience pretending to have crossed the bridge if she had not. Andersen felt that the religious fervour she brought to this role gave the stage an aura of holiness; in *La Sonnambula* she became the quintessential nineteenth-century heroine.

Andersen, Carl Alexander and Sophie were all half in love with her, and Beaulieu, the lord chamberlain, entered the fray with sobs and tears as well.

Jenny, too, was invited to live at Weimar, as the companion of the Heredi-tary Grand Duchess. After her concerts she sat round a quiet tea table with the inner circle—Andersen, Carl Alexander, Beaulieu—and Andersen read tales; they drove together in the royal park; at Goethe's house in Frauenplan Andersen read "The Little Mermaid" and Jenny sang Mendelssohn's songs. The re-creation of times past was crystallized when Andersen and Jenny were taken together to the funeral vault of the Grand Dukes of Saxe-Weimar-Eisenach, to see the coffins of Goethe and Schiller. All of them were playing their parts, but all of them felt their parts to be real. "Beaulieu said I was falling in love with Jenny; I told him it would not happen. He told me his love story, I thought of my own and cried," Andersen wrote. After she had gone, "at home we talked a lot about her; I was in pain; B. told me to cry unreservedly, kissed me lovingly." Jenny became a sort of erotic secret between Carl Alexander and Andersen: "at the Hereditary Grand Duke's this evening. He had written asking me to come half an hour early to talk about Jenny. I arrived at 7:30, sat on the sofa with him, he was quite moved, asked me always to write about her, without mentioning names, just 'our friend.' He pressed my hands in his."

Andersen felt his stock rise with Jenny as a result of his exalted position at so civilized a court; he also liked to impress the ducal family with his love for her. But his sexual obsession with her was waning; being fêted and cele-brated was a good substitute for sex, and there are no crosses in his almanac during the two months he spent with Jenny in Berlin and Weimar. Some months after they parted Andersen wrote to Louise Lind (née Collin):

> You ask me about Jenny. I hear from her regularly; they would like to keep her in Weimar, in that case I would like to be there; it won't happen. I have a sister in Jenny, a faithful soul, no more, do you understand me? She is unlikely to marry, if I have gathered and understood everything; I know to a certain extent her determination, but I have no right to talk about it. Concerning myself, it is clear that I may give up, I am not building any castles in the air, but accept what God makes happen to me, I am tranquil in my soul as never before. God only knows if I would be happier as a married man, whether I could make another person happy.

Jenny was more relaxed and friendly with Andersen as a result; she too felt that there was something magical about the frosty, sunlit winter days at Weimar, writing to him that they had spent their most delightful time together there.

Yes, yes, Germany is a glorious country. I certainly long for no other, except, of course, the best of all, the last one . . . Oh, how I wept at your story of the Grand Duchess and her little sweep! . . . Dear Andersen, if you should write to our high-born friends, tell them, if you should mention me, that I shall remember those few days at Weimar as long as I live. And it is only truth that I have never found such peace of mind and utter happiness, although I have everywhere and always been kindly received. I like these high-born personages, and that, as you say, brother, not for the jewels and decorations they wear, but for their genuine and honest hearts and souls. I get quite carried away when I think of these people! God's peace over them and theirs!

There is just a hint of mournfulness here, and there was something poignant about Weimar's attraction for Andersen, too. Weimar so epitomized the old order, the triumph of civilized values, the cosy Biedermeier culture, that it seemed almost unreal, and the dukes and aristocrats and artists whirled around in a frenzy of exaggerated feelings as if they knew its days were numbered. The emotional decadence, the posturing energy, of the court suggests a comparison with the Edwardian culture of privileged grace before the storms of war. Over the next year, the elegiac notes sounded more clearly. When Andersen returned to Weimar in the summer of 1846, his mood was even more enchanted, but also more sombre:

> The Hereditary Grand Duke crossed the courtyard arm in arm with me to my room in the evening, kissed me affectionately, begged me always to love him although he was only an ordinary person, asked me to stay with him this winter. Unhappy me, *I* have the feeling in all this that this great love can't last. Went to sleep with wistful happy feelings that I was a guest of this strange prince at his castle and he loved me; the footmen call me: *gnädiger Herr*! [Honoured Sir.] It is like a fairy tale.

After this visit, Andersen's sense of himself and Carl Alexander as figures on a doomed world stage intensified. "I will do everything in my power to be worthy of you," he wrote on 14 September 1846,

> for I know that the soul that lives and moves in you will cast new rays of sunshine over the country that I love as a second fatherland. I will also do everything to inspire love and interest for the place where I have been received as if I were a child of that country by its Princes and leading men: I want so much that everyone should love what I love. You, my noble, beloved Grand Duke, are new proof to me of the nobility of man, which I love more and more and in

which I must always believe! Through *you* I love and understand what is noble in princes, who are much too strongly criticized these days.

His letters grew increasingly passionate; following a bad sea voyage in which he had feared death, he told how "sorrow burdened my soul, and I wished so fervently to see you once again," and a few months later he wrote, "I am, as a poet, as fine as if I were in a fairy tale, perhaps it would be happy for me to die now! But I love life, I love people—oh! I am so longing to come to Weimar once more; to you, my most intimate, beloved noble Lord! Oh, if only you weren't a prince!—Clouds go through my soul!" After another visit to Weimar in 1847, he wrote, "I love you as a man can only love the noblest and best. This time I felt that you were still more ardent, more affectionate to me. Every little trait is preserved in my heart. On that cool evening, when you took your cloak and threw it round me, it warmed not only my body, but made my heart glow still more ardently." Months later, Prussia and Denmark were at war, and the Weimar Andersen loved vanished for ever.

CHAPTER 15

The Shadow

1846–1847

I looked where no one could see, and I saw what no one else saw; what no one was meant to see! When all's said and done, it's a mean world. I'd never want to be human, but for the fact that it's the thing to be.
—HANS CHRISTIAN ANDERSEN, "The Shadow"

When Andersen left Weimar in February 1846, nothing could halt his triumphal march through German-speaking Europe. Beaulieu accompanied him to the university town of Jena; Andersen then moved on to Leipzig, "city of bookselling." There word had spread of his acclaim in Berlin and Weimar and, having never had a foreign contract before, he found four publishers competing to sign him up. Previous German editions of his work had been pirate translations, but Andersen was now famous enough for a complete edition of his writings, endorsed by himself with the inclusion of a new work, to be lucrative for a publisher. Andersen was torn between Brockhaus, Leipzig's most esteemed publisher and a man who stood at the heart of German literary life, and the Danish-born Carl Lorck, for whom he eventually plumped. On 19 February he signed a contract for a collected edition of his works in German, receiving 300 Prussian thaler together with an additional 200 thaler for an autobiography which Lorck commissioned to introduce the edition. Apart from writing the short tale "The Little Matchgirl," Andersen had done no work since he left Copenhagen in October; the autobiography now became his project as he travelled, and suited the review of his life which new triumphs always prompted.

He immediately sat for a portrait by the German painter August Grahl, who produced the best picture of Andersen since C. A. Jensen's portrait of 1836. Jensen had caught the young Andersen on the brink of fame, fashionable, genial, charmed by the attention of the viewer. Ten years on, Grahl depicts the established writer in middle age. The face has filled out and the hair has thinned; the broad, high, intellectual brow is still pronounced, and the lips full; the eyes gleam with clarity and depth, but Grahl has also captured in them a well of melancholy, and the cheeks are marked by strong, shadowy lines. This portrait reflects Andersen's public persona in mid-century Germany: at ease with his fame, gazing confidently at his audience, foppish as before, with a high white collar and a swirling black tie, he appears none the less unsettled, a little too eager, perhaps obsequious, in his desire to please. The twin poles of vanity and dissatisfaction are combined in this sensitive painting; reproduced as the frontispiece to Lorck's collected edition of Andersen's works, it embodied for a generation the image of Andersen as the romantic, troubled, prince's poet.

In Leipzig he was fussed over by Mendelssohn, who teased him about the frequent appearance of storks in his stories and, when he heard Andersen read his tales, "bounded up joyfully . . . and said, 'But you read marvellously, no one reads fairy tales like you!'" In Dresden he read to King Friedrich August at the Saxon court; in Vienna to Archduchess Sophia and her son, the future Emperor Franz Joseph. But as soon as he was alone for a few hours, restlessness and resentment surfaced. To Edvard, detailing his successes, the newspaper reports about him, the valuable ring he had been given and the decoration from the Prussian king, he complained that at home no one was proud of him and everyone laughed at his vanity.

Edvard, who had real griefs—he had recently lost a second child, aged four—wrote back with equanimity that the Danes loved his fairy tales probably with more honesty than the Germans, and that Andersen was simply miserable because after all the fuss in Weimar he was now sitting alone in a hotel room in Dresden, using his vivid imagination to construct a story that he was despised in Denmark. Edvard understood Andersen well, and knew how to handle him. He kept the depths of his own sorrows from Andersen, and engaged with him on the banal, jollying-along level that a mother would use to a child. It was the tragedy of Andersen's egotism that in mid-life he could evoke only two types of relationship: the teasingly consolatory, as Edvard's was, or the velvet adulation of princes and kings. He tended to get the former from Denmark, where his gaucheness and vanity over many years could not be forgotten, and the latter from Germany, where he had launched himself fully fledged. He needed both, but he felt sharply the division between the two, and neither took away his loneliness. As he travelled on to southern Europe, musing on the autobiography he would write in

Danish for a German readership, he pondered the different images of himself, and the one he wanted to fix upon his public began to take shape.

The German trip had healed and soothed him. The hospitality he received was so generous that in five months, from October to March, he spent in total less than 500 imperial thaler, including the high expenses of travel by train and coach. "Oh, you do not know how amiable they have been to me in Germany—princes, artists—yes, I have seen and felt all there that is noble in man," he wrote to an English correspondent. "As in the middle ages the troubadour wandered from court to court, so wandered I, and wherever I went smiles met me. Home after home was opened to me, and in most I was nearly at home." In Germany, he could construct a legitimate persona out of the restless, solitary artist that he had always been; he merged this with a saccharin version of his fatalism in which he depicted his life as a fairy tale, and so he came up with the unreliable self-portrait of *Das Märchen meines Lebens ohne Dichtung.*

He began to write it in March, and from this time his letters rehearsed

Andersen in Dresden, aged forty, by August Grahl, 1846.

the idea of a benign fate which had ordered everything for his good. To the Danish King Christian VIII he wrote from Vienna on 12 March, "Life is so delightful, and everyone is really good at heart. I have confidence in all men, and in truth I have never yet been deceived . . . I could not have ordered everything more delightfully than the dear God has done to me, even if I had had the great power to do it"—words which were repeated almost verbatim in his autobiography. He reached Rome at the end of the month, in time for his birthday on 2 April, and told Jonas Collin, "Today I am 41! How old, and yet inside I am barely more than twenty. What a life full of happiness and sunshine I have behind me . . . I celebrate my birthday being in Rome for the third time, how few can achieve this!"—a sentiment also repeated in *The Fairy Tale of My Life*.

But in fact Rome, for the third time, was a disappointment. By the time he arrived Andersen was exhausted from his long trip, noting in his diary "how greatly I have tortured myself this time with luggage, anxiety and efforts at figuring out my finances." He enjoyed the attentions of the Scandinavian community, but Rome, he wrote to a friend, was not the Rome of thirteen years ago when he was first there: "It is as if everything was modernized, the ruins even, grass and bushes are cleared away. Everything is made so neat . . . I no longer hear the tambourines in the streets, no longer see the young girls dancing the Saltarella; even in the Campagna intelligence has entered by invisible railroads; the peasant no longer believes as he used to do." Andersen suffered from the heat and from abdominal and digestive pains; he was bored and listless and had plenty of time to work up his resentments. "One day when I am made *Etatsraad* [Councillor of State] and have a son, he shall refuse to say 'Du' to your son Jonas if you are still only a *Justitsraad* [Councillor of Justice]," he wrote to Edvard on 26 April. "Time drags and I don't feel like doing anything . . . I felt weak, we wanted to get a carriage but there weren't any, I had an even stronger attack . . . I am getting no benefit out of Rome—Let me fly off, I will probably never come back to this splendid city," he wrote on 30 April, and the next day he left for Naples.

Twice before, in 1834 and 1841, Naples had rescued him from depression. He associated it with creativity and sensuality; *The Improvisatore* had beautifully captured its colours and sultry heat for a northern audience. Now the city worked its magic on him again. It was oppressively hot: "the heat was some eighty degrees in the shade; the sun hung in the sky like a vampire that sucks blood and marrow from the limbs. I have never experienced anything like it before," he wrote. He was still physically ill—"stomach upset, my body limp, the heat intolerable"; he slept in front of the open balcony door of his hotel room with only a sheet over him, "but it was no better than just bearable." Once he fainted and was carried into a coffee house, where they piled ice on to his head, and after that he hardly dared venture outside. But the purging heat seemed to liberate his energy for writing. Day after day he sat indoors, listening to the "grabbing, roaring, screaming, rending maelstrom" of blacksmiths hammering, wagons rolling, people arguing on the street below, and, his head spinning, his mind cleared of the distractions of socializing and sightseeing, he worked continuously on two opposing yet crucially linked projects—his autobiography, which was fantasy dressed up as fact, and the tale "The Shadow," in which a far more revealing self-portrait is cast as fantasy.

The autobiography, at first, was uppermost in his thoughts. Fresh from his triumphs in Berlin, Weimar and Leipzig, Andersen dreamed of himself as the new Goethe, the most famous author in Germany, and he modelled his autobiography on Goethe's. His German title, *Das Märchen meines Lebens ohne Dichtung*, is an echo of Goethe's *Aus meinem Leben. Dichtung und Wahrheit (From My Life—Fiction and Truth)*. Yet where Goethe allows his inner turmoil to surface in spite of the artistry that to some extent must eliminate truth from autobiography, Andersen promises honesty but delivers only the public persona he offered up in life to kings and princes. Even allowing for the discretion of the genre in the nineteenth century, Andersen's autobiography is a masterwork of self-concealment. With his opening lines he sets his history in a deliberately false context: "my life is a lovely story, happy and full of incident. If when I was a boy . . . a good fairy had met me and said 'Choose now your own course in life' . . . my fate could not, even then, have been directed more happily . . . The history of my life will say to the world what it says to me—there is a loving God, who directs all things for the best." Over three hundred pages, this tone of sunny self-congratulation never lifts.

The early chapters, on growing up in Odense and his struggles in Copenhagen, are the most convincing. The child's-eye view came naturally to Andersen, and his descriptions of a boy's delight in the small town excitements of festivals and feast-days, in the folklore and magic tales he heard from his grandmother, and his fear of his mad grandfather, are vibrantly authentic, as is his account of how his parents indulged him. But his real subject even here is to provide a setting for himself as a genius-in-waiting, and the first pages are littered with details which underline the romantic idea of an alliance between childhood innocence and artistic genius. So, as we have seen, on page two, when the vicar complains that the baby Hans Christian screams like a kitten, there is a dose of folk wisdom from a "poor emigrant": "the louder I cried as a child, all the more beautifully should I sing when I grew older"—a prophecy proved true when Andersen's singing voice becomes his passport to social acceptance and success in Odense.

Comparisons between the more artless *The Book of My Life* and the later autobiography illustrate how Andersen embellished events in order to fix himself as the golden child of romantic myth. Timing is subtly altered for dramatic effect; the fortune-teller's prophecy of greatness for the boy, for example, which in *The Book of My Life* clearly occurs before 1816, is shifted to 1819, as the decisive factor in persuading Andersen's superstitious mother to let him go to Copenhagen. More revealing are the childhood incidents which appear in *The Fairy Tale of My Life* for the first time: an account, for example, of going gleaning with his mother in the fields outside Odense and coming across a notoriously violent bailiff, from whom all the women and children ran away:

> I had wooden shoes on my bare feet, and in my haste I lost these, and then the thorns pricked me so that I could not run, and thus I was left behind and alone. The man came up to me and lifted his whip to strike me, when I looked him in the face and involuntarily exclaimed, "How dare you strike me, when God can see it?"
>
> The strong, stern man looked at me, and at once became mild; he patted me on my cheeks, asked me my name and gave me money.
>
> When I brought this to my mother and showed it her, she said to the others, "He is a strange child, my Hans Christian; everybody is kind to him: this bad fellow even has given him money."

This is Hans Christian as the fairy tale child who brings virtue and enlightenment—like the boy muttering "But he hasn't got anything on" at the end of "The Emperor's New Clothes," or Gerda melting icy evil with her tears in "The Snow Queen." It was a crucial tenet of the romantic vision that had formed Andersen intellectually but he also makes so much of it because from his earliest memories it was the persona of the unworldly innocent that had got him noticed and rewarded. At forty-one, he was still playing it; another version recurs when he describes a clergyman, criticizing every word of his writings, who is caught short by a six-year-old girl who heard with amazement that he discovered everything to be wrong, took the book, and pointing out the conjunction *and*, said, "There is yet a little word about which you have not scolded." He felt what a reproof lay in the remark of the child; he looked ashamed and kissed the little one.

Again, child-like innocence is marked out as on the side of Andersen's genius, and it is the mood of sickly piety and false humility about the adult man which is so irritating throughout the rest of the autobiography. Andersen follows the broad flow of his life, journey by journey, achievement by achievement, and while the factual details of his travels mostly correspond to those in his diary, the inner man simply is not there.

Instead, there is the stage show and the applause. Acclaimed in Sweden: "there is but one manner for me; at once, in the midst of joy, I fly with thanks to God." In Germany: "estimation or over-estimation from a man of genius erases many a dark shadow from the mind. I received from Rauch my first welcome in Berlin: he told me what a large circle of friends I had in the capital of Prussia. I must acknowledge it was so. They were of the noblest in mind as well as the first in rank." In Rome: "I felt so happy, so penetrated with thankfulness and joy; how much more God had given to me than a thousand others—nay, than to many thousands . . . where joy is very great . . . there is only God on whom one can lean!"

By excluding, understandably, anything that might shock the prudish sensibility of his middle- and upper-class audience, Andersen sanitized even his childhood. He conceals his mother's illegitimacy, the existence of his illegitimate half-sister, the fact that his parents married two months before his birth; he glosses over hardships and ignorance and paints instead a glowing picture of love in poverty, hinting that an unwise, romantic match had led his father's family to fall from aristocratic splendour, and playing up the glamour of his folk roots for a bourgeois audience in the throes of the nineteenth-century love affair with country values. Understandably too he makes no allusion to his longings for young men, though he describes with warmth his friendships with Edvard and with Jenny Lind. But the omissions silence Andersen on many of the forces which governed his emotional life: the unhappiness that stemmed from his early social exclusion, the loneliness that came from feeling unloved, unlovable and unable to love freely. What is left are the petty vanities which seem, in this context, to have no cause: the insatiable hunger for praise, the resentment of criticism. Although Andersen writes that "I have refused to show the full cup of bitterness: I have only let fall some drops from it!," on page after page he carps about the hostility to his work in the theatre, the initial dismissal of his fairy tales, about how he received little attention from his countrymen yet "found it in a high degree among foreigners."

As a result *Das Märchen meines Lebens* descends into a patchwork of Andersen's social triumphs and minor grievances which is not so different from the celebrity autobiography of today. Repeatedly, he meets strangers and brings the conversation around to a writer named Andersen, listening with gratification as his companion says, "I should like to know that man"; then he reveals himself, basking in his fame—you can almost hear him yelling inwardly with pleasure, as he had screamed in amusement when the Collin family used to unmask little lies he had told. The royal name-dropping is absurd:

> I had the happiness of visiting the Princess of Prussia many times . . . on taking leave, she honoured me with a richly bound album. I shall guard the volume as a treasure of the soul . . . I was astonished to the highest degree, on taking leave of the Grand Duke [of Oldenburg], to receive from him as a mark of his favour and as a keepsake, a valuable ring . . . It is good to see a noble human nature reveal itself where one might expect to find only the king's crown and the purple mantle. Few people could be more amiable in private life than the reigning Majesties of Denmark . . .

Advertising himself as both a household name and the intimate of monarchs, Andersen sentimentalizes his role as the child of Romanticism who sees through the glitter to the truth, the urbane cosmopolitan who on the final page ends up sitting beneath the Christmas tree in provincial Denmark. He finishes the book a prince's puppet, waving to an imagined, adulatory crowd:

> From the prince to the poorest peasant I have felt the noble human heart beat. It is a joy to live and to believe in God and man. Openly and full of confidence, as if I sat among dear friends, I have here related the story of my life . . . as I might even express it before God himself . . . In a few days I shall . . . return . . . to dear, kind Germany, where so much joy has flowed into my life . . . When the Christmas tree is lighted—when, as people say, the white bees swarm—I shall be, God willing, again in Denmark with my dear ones . . . A star of good fortune shines upon me . . . To God and men my thanks, my love!

Though contemporary reviewers were polite, the more perceptive among them, particularly in England, where the book appeared in 1847 as *The True Story of My Life*, failed to be persuaded by this assiduously cultivated persona. The *Examiner* admired the chapter about Andersen's childhood, commented on the book's "revelation of restless vanity," and concluded "We have had much of this true story already told in Andersen's fictitious stories, and we doubt if the rest had not better have remained untold . . . One is moved to say of the book, that the childish portion seems written by a man, and the man's experience by a child." In *The Times*, Manley Hopkins (father of the poet), saw the whole book as a pretence: in his stories, Andersen had drawn pictures or shadows of himself, he wrote, but

> in his *True Story of My Life*, the shadow falls on a flat surface, and is of natural size . . . if we were to disbelieve any part of what he says, it would be the opening sentence . . . where he calls his career a happy one, and those subsequent passages in which, against the detailed evidence of much mental suffering, he would make the world and himself think that his life had been almost cloudless . . . Of all influences that produce peculiarities in the mind, that of loneliness may rank highest. Genius is egotistic. When her bright flame burns within, it is great shadows of self that are projected all round.

And in an unguarded letter to Andersen's translator Charles Boner, the popular dramatist and novelist Mary Russell Mitford wrote:

> Between the vanity of the writer, and the baldness and poverty of the translation [by Mary Howitt], I was completely disgusted. I did not think it possible to so entirely do away with the interest of the rise of a poor boy into intellectual eminence. But he has no sympathy with his own order—he is essentially a toad-eater, a hanger-on in great houses, like the led captains of former days, a man who values his acquaintances for their rank and their riches and their importance in the world . . . who uses fame merely as a key to open drawing-room doors, a ladder to climb to high places.

What purpose did this piece of self-invention serve for Andersen? Since his schooldays, he had obsessively recounted versions of his life; by 1846 he had filled his tales with self-portraits—some harshly perceptive, as in "The Steadfast Tin Soldier" and "The Fir Tree," others wishful fantasies, such as "The Ugly Duckling." Indeed, it is the autobiographical leaning which characterizes his work as romantic and modern, and made it so impenetrable to classically minded men such as Heiberg and the Collins. But in *The Fairy Tale of My Life* he fictionalized himself almost out of existence. In the relentless false sunshine of his autobiography, he sent himself into the shadows. Yet no one who had suffered a lifetime of his anxieties and depressions could write this and not be aware that it was a wish-fulfilment account which shut out much of his deeper personality, and while he was engrossed in it, his real, creative self began to take revenge. On 9 June, when he was still finishing the autobiography, he noted in his diary, "in the evening began writing the story of my Shadow"—a demonic tale of self-annihilation, and one of Andersen's most mesmerizing.

"The Shadow," the tale of a man without a shadow, and a shadow who becomes a man without a soul, is a psychological horror story which works on many levels. A scholar, a good but ineffective man from the north, loses his shadow in a Naples heatwave. In the dizzy, bright setting, anticipating the madness of the tale, "the scholar from the cold countries . . . felt as if he were sitting in a red-hot oven," as Andersen did while writing the story. He grows a new shadow and returns home, but years later the original Shadow turns up, a spookily thin figure which has done well for itself and is at pains to conceal that it ever was a shadow. "Dressed all in black, it had the finest of black coats, patent leather boots, and a hat that could be let down flat, leaving only the crown and the brim . . . Yes, the Shadow was immensely well-dressed; and it was just that which made it so very human." The Shadow boasts to the scholar of all he has seen, of how he has grown rich by hiding himself, playing the observer, and exposing the vices of the world:

> "I have been at the Court of Poetry . . . I also got to know my inner self . . . I looked where no one could see, and I saw what no one else saw . . . When all's said and done, it's a mean world. I'd never want to be human, but for the fact that it's the thing to be . . . I saw . . . what no one was supposed to know, but what everyone was eager to know—ill of their neighbour. Had I been writing a newspaper, it would have been read! But I wrote direct to the person himself, and there was great alarm in every town I visited. They were so afraid of me that they grew very fond of me. The professors made me a professor, the tailors gave me new clothes (I'm well rigged out), the mint-master minted money for me, and the women said I was so handsome! And so I became the man I am. And now I'll say goodbye. Here's my card; I live on the sunny side of the street and am always at home when it's wet."

The mood darkens; as the Shadow prospers, the scholar is dogged by grief, no one reads his books, he becomes ill. "'You look just like a shadow!' people said to him; and the very thought of it made the scholar shudder." The Shadow offers to be his companion at a health resort ("my whiskers aren't growing as they should"), and the scholar mildly suggests that they are now intimate enough to be on "Du" terms. The Shadow, in terms almost identical to those used by Edvard Collin in the letter turning Andersen down in 1831, refuses. As Edvard had done, he insists on how frank and honest he is being; like Edvard, he compares his dislike of using "Du" to the irrational revulsion of someone who cannot touch wrapping paper without being ill:

> "What's that you say?" said the Shadow, now, of course, the real master. "That was very frank and well-meant of you; I'll be equally frank and well-meaning with you. You who are a scholar must know the strangeness of human nature. Some people cannot touch grey paper without feeling ill; others shudder if a nail is rubbed against a window-pane. It gives me the same sort of feeling when you're familiar with me: I feel flattened out as in my first job with you. It's only a feeling, you understand; it isn't pride. I can't allow you to use my Christian name, but I'm quite willing to use yours. That'll be something!"

At the resort, a clever princess, there to be cured because she "saw only too well," perceives that the Shadow's complaint is not a lack of whiskers but an inability to cast a shadow. The Shadow replies smartly that the scholar is his shadow, and that the princess is now cured—she no longer sees too well. She is a cousin of the emperor in "The Emperor's New Clothes," vain and gullible, and she falls for the Shadow. When they dance, "she was light, but he was even lighter; such a dancer she had never seen . . . she fell in love, as the Shadow could tell, because she pretty well looked straight through him." She tests him out as a ruler of her kingdom by asking him questions, which he gets his shadow—the scholar—to answer. The lifeless scholar suddenly rebels—"I'll tell everything: that I'm human and you're the shadow, that you're only dressed up"—but "No one will believe it," says the Shadow, and the scholar is thrown in jail. "Poor shadow!" says the princess. "How wretched he is. It would be a happy release to rid him of what little life he had." That evening, the Shadow marries the princess to the sounds of cannons booming, but "the scholar heard nothing of all this; for they had done away with him . . ."

Elements of this tale had been in Andersen's mind for over a decade, since he had met the German author von Chamisso in Berlin in 1831 at the time that Edvard had refused to say "Du" to him. He implies a reference to Chamisso's *Peter Schlemihl's Strange Story* (1813), about a man who lost his shadow, when, after the scholar loses his shadow, Andersen writes "he was annoyed at this, not so much because the shadow was missing as because he knew of another story about a man who hadn't a shadow. It was known to everybody at home in the cold countries, and if the scholar were to go home and tell his, they would say he was copying, and there was no need for him to do that." But Chamisso's famous story was only one of many recent German ghost stories of *doppelgänger*. The double was a favourite romantic theme because of the possibilities it afforded for delving into the unconscious and the unknown powers of the imagination; Hoffmann, for example, used it in his dream-like long stories *Doppelgänger* and *New Year's Eve Adventure*.

Andersen, however, treated the subject in a new way, and his seamless mix of comedy and nihilism is surprisingly modern. The decent, well-meaning hero out of control of his fate, locked up by forces he does not understand; the stylistic masterstroke by which the scholar dies off-stage and in a subordinate clause, by now too limp and colourless to merit a sentence of his own; the final words of the story trailing off as an unfinished sentence; the mockery of the fairy tale tradition, with the villain ending up married to the princess and ruling the kingdom—all this has more in common with the black-humoured modernism of the 1920s and 1930s, the stories of Kafka or Saki or Evelyn Waugh, than with the work of Andersen's contemporaries. "The Shadow" marks a turning point for him; after it, his stories become increasingly self-referential and stylistically sophisticated.

Georg Brandes, Andersen's first serious critic, interpreted "The Shadow" as showing Andersen's bleak perception of the triumph of the second-rate, and certainly it is the depressive streak in Andersen that makes him kill off the good and innocent with sudden relish in "The Shadow," as he does elsewhere (the tin soldier suddenly being blown into the fire, for instance). The story also clearly refers to Edvard. By 1846, Andersen's feelings for Edvard had settled down into a warm friendship which occasionally flared into resentment—he had moaned at Edvard about the "Du"/"De" business in a letter just two months before he wrote "The Shadow." He was sufficiently distanced from it to put it into his tale with humour rather than rancour; some of the balance in their youthful relationship is none the less echoed in the story—the worldly, successful shadow (Edvard) triumphs over the anaemic, depressive scholar (Andersen).

But Andersen's interest in *doppelgänger* in 1846 had more to do with the divisions within himself than with any external relationship. Symbolically, "The Shadow" is about how we accommodate, or fail to accommodate, the darker side of our souls—the selfishness and thwarted desires which get suppressed in the process of becoming a decent and civilized citizen like the scholar. Jung wrote that everyone carries a shadow, and the less it is embodied in the individual's conscious life, the blacker and denser it is. The scholar refuses to face his dark side, so it defeats him. While he was writing the tale, Andersen was posturing, shadow-like, to the world, holding back much of the truth about himself in his autobiography. There are parallels between the scholar, who grows weaker and less of a flesh-and-blood character as "The Shadow" progresses, and the figure of Andersen, vivid enough in the opening pages of *Das Märchen meines Lebens*, but ending up little more than a puppet shaking hands with the high and mighty.

But of course Andersen is not only the scholar but the shadow as well, a shifty dark figure watching behind the scenes—the artist as a man without identity of his own but finely tuned to all experiences. Keats's idea of the poet's negative capability—the passive receptivity necessary for artistic creation—is echoed in a letter Andersen wrote in 1855: "I am like water, everything moves me, everything is reflected in me, I suppose this is part of my nature as a poet, and often I enjoy this and receive blessings from it, but often it also torments me." In Andersen's first memoir he had written: "Anyone I have seen and spoken to once, I can later remember their faces clearly, I have their mirror image within me; however, I cannot recall my own features, although God knows I look at myself in the mirror often enough." "The Shadow" is a terrifying story of the loss of self-identity. It recalls the hollow feelings Andersen complained about in letters written in his twenties, and it suggests that, as he pandered to kings, princes and an international audience, he knew that he remained lonely and loveless. He feared the void in himself while acknowledging that it was a crucial part of his creativity.

But he could not resist seeking out wider acclaim. On 23 June he sailed by steamer from Naples to Marseilles, where he met the Norwegian violinist Ole Bull, just returned from America. Andersen was on the verge of completing his autobiography, and immediately reported their conversation in its closing pages: "he told me . . . that my works also had many friends in America, that people had inquired from him about me with the greatest interest, and that the English translations of my romances had been reprinted, and spread through the country in cheap editions. My name flown over the great ocean!"

For the moment he put aside the excitement of gaining English-speaking readers, for he was set to continue to Spain, which, he wrote, was "to be the bouquet of my journey"; he was always enticed by the prospect of visiting countries little known to Danes, and Spain was not at that time on the itinerary of many northern European travellers. He now began a hellish journey through Languedoc where the heat was as blistering as it had been in Naples. He nearly suffocated on a barge along the Canal du Midi and at Béziers he was forced into the back part of a diligence with "an ugly woman in slippers" and "a couple of dirty fellows" while "thick clouds of dust whirled into the vehicle, and the sun burnt and blinded" him. From Narbonne to the Pyrenees he was plagued by the obsession that his passport would be out of order, and by other travel neuroses. Passports were demanded repeatedly—"they gave you as a reason, the nearness to the Spanish frontiers, the number of fugitives from thence, and several murders which had taken place . . . all conduced to make the journey in my then state of health a real torment."

By Perpignan he gave up the idea of Spain and fled to Vernet, a spa in the Pyrenees, where he finished *Das Märchen meines Lebens*. He was sending it home to Edvard chapter by chapter. Edvard corrected the spelling and grammar, and, though he was a busy civil servant and family man, he offered to make a fair copy for the German translator—a real labour of love. It was almost as if Edvard had fleetingly become his double. "You do not know how this has affected me, filled me with shame . . . that you are copying out my biography! . . . I shall never forget this proof of your fraternal soul, it is an embrace, a kiss—a toast to our becoming Dus, you know what I mean," Andersen wrote.

In August Andersen began the long journey home, staying again with great joy at Weimar *en route*; in north Germany in September he heard that he had at last received a Danish honour, the Order of the Dannebrog, and on 14 October he arrived by steamer from Kiel in Copenhagen. He had been away a year, and had had undreamed-of triumphs, but even before he arrived home he began to think of new lands and cities to conquer, among them London. "I will fly there in rather less than a year, but my spiritual self [*mein geistiges ich*], my writings, come earlier," Andersen wrote in German to his translator Mary Howitt in September 1846. Other literary figures encouraged him: in the autumn of 1846, William Jerdan, editor of the *Literary Gazette* and a friend of Dickens, invited him to London, and Richard Bentley, who had just brought out a translation of *A Poet's Bazaar*, wrote to him that "among the most pleasant passages in my career as a publisher I beg to consider my connexion with your works."

So Andersen settled back into the Hotel du Nord for the winter of 1846–1847, and planned his trip to England. On 10 December he wrote in

Danish to Bentley but added an English postscript (translated for him) to thank him for *A Poet's Bazaar*, saying:

> It is a singular feeling to see the children of my soul and spirit in such a richly garb, though in a language I don't understand. I have a sensation very like the hen going to brood swans and afterwards not able to follow them; but I *will* and must! In a few days I begin to learn english [*sic*] and when I next year visit England, I hope my dear Sir to express to you in english my thanks and affections.

The English lessons started on 16 December; his teacher was another English translator, Charles Beckwith Lohmeyer, but Andersen made poor progress, and in March 1847 he wrote in German to Charles Boner that he had "so little time and no great talent for languages."

Meanwhile in December his collected poems appeared in Denmark; in January and February 1847 came the first volumes of Lorck's collected German edition of his works, including *Das Märchen meines Lebens*; in April a French translation of *The Improvisatore* and a new volume of tales including "The Shadow." Foreign publishers, including Bentley, sent copies of the translations to Christian VIII, and Andersen began to be particularly noticed by the King. He was invited to dine at court and the King, seeing his potential as an ambassador for Danish culture, offered to help fund his trip to England. Andersen refused, but the opening of royal circles, as well as the increasing number of foreign editions of his works, made him eager to travel again.

He told Jerdan that he longed to see Britain: "I have often felt a longing to see that country, the literature of which has so remarkably enriched my fancy and filled my heart." In his autobiography he named Walter Scott along with Hoffmann and Heine as formative influences; now he recalled how he had read Scott's novels when he was young and poor in Copenhagen. As he had done in Germany, he wanted to make connections with British writers; like many travellers from small countries, he visited larger ones with a mind not just open but keen to engage with a foreign culture. In May he left Copenhagen and travelled through Holland to take the steamer from Rotterdam to London.

CHAPTER 16

Lion of London

1847

"Farewell, farewell!" said the litle swallow and flew again fort from the warm coun-
tries, far, far away, to Denmark, ther it had litle nest above the window of a room in
wich dwelt a poet, who can tell tales; for him it sang: "Quivit, quivit! all is good and
beautiful in England!"—"I know that," answered the poet.

—HANS CHRISTIAN ANDERSEN, adaptation of the
last lines of "Thumbelina," written in dedication
to an unknown Englishman, London, 1847

A year earlier, Andersen had been unknown in England; now his "spiritual
self" had already arrived, for in 1846 four different translators produced versions of his fairy tales. Lady Duff-Gordon's translation of "The Little Mermaid" appeared in the popular periodical *Bentley's Miscellany*, assuring
Andersen a large readership. Mary Howitt's *Wonderful Stories for Children*
came in February, followed by Charles Boner's *A Danish Story Book*, by Caroline Peachey's *Danish Fairy Tales and Legends* and by further volumes from
Boner. They were immediately and enthusiastically reviewed—the first recommendation came in the *Athenaeum* of February 1846 for "John Andersen's
Wonderful Stories for Children: a book after our own hearts—full of life and
fancy; a book for grandfathers no less than grandchildren, not a word of
which will be skipped by those who have it once in hand."

The timing of the English editions of the fairy tales was no accident.
When Andersen's first pamphlets appeared in Denmark between 1835 and
1837, they fell on stony ground, and had they arrived in England at that time,
they would probably have met a similar response there. But they were not
translated, because few people then thought them important. In the decade
since 1835, however, the cultural climate had changed in England. Dickens
had become the first great Victorian novelist and was revolutionizing liter-

ary expectations with his emphasis on the emotional and the sentimental. Since 1837 he had published a series of novels and stories—*Oliver Twist, Nicholas Nickleby, The Old Curiosity Shop, A Christmas Carol*—which focused on children in a way which changed for all time perceptions of childhood and of its importance. Reading of Little Nell's death in the serialization of *The Old Curiosity Shop* in 1841, for example, grown men wept openly and Dickens received so many bereft letters that he felt he had committed a murder. The MP Daniel O'Connell, reading the novel on a train, burst into tears, exclaimed "He should not have killed her!" and threw the book out of the window. Andersen's tales met this new mood. "In a utilitarian age, of all other times, it is a matter of grave importance that Fairy Tales should be respected," Dickens was to write in an article called "Frauds on the Fairies" in 1853. "Everyone who has considered the subject knows full well that a nation without fancy, without some romance, never did, never can, never will, hold a great place under the sun."

Across Europe, Dickens and Andersen recognized one another as anti-utilitarian allies at a time when the popular imagination was undergoing a sea-change. Both had been formed by struggle and hardship; neither came from the gentlemen class which had more or less held a monopoly on the literary establishment before 1800; each was among the first to portray an underclass with sensitivity and understanding, which had a profound effect on wider social attitudes. "How I should like to shake the hand of 'Boz.' When I read his books I often think I have seen such things, and feel I could write like that. Do not misunderstand me; and if you are a friend of 'Boz,' and he sees these lines, he will not consider it presumptuous; but I do not know how better to express myself, than to say, that what completely captivates me, seems to become part of myself," Andersen wrote to Jerdan. Jerdan replied with a critique of English society: "At present our literary world is very dull. Irish Famine, like Pharaoh's lean kine, seems to eat up all that is worth anything, physically, morally or intellectually. The failure of potatoes has led to the failure of mental culture . . . The mechanical Sciences alone continue in full activity: for they bring money, direct as cause and effect, and Money is the mighty Idol to which all bow the knee in a Commercial Country."

It was against the ruthless mercantile values of industrializing Victorian England that Dickens was writing; men like Jerdan and Dickens were ready to welcome Andersen as one of themselves, and it was this intellectual inclusion that Andersen cherished about his journeys abroad and that allowed him to see himself as a genuinely European author. Dickens was intrigued by Andersen; when he learnt in July 1847 that Andersen was in London, he wrote to Jerdan in the midst of a hectic schedule that whatever else he did, he "*must* see Andersen." Dickens's son wrote later of Andersen that "my father thought very highly of his literary work," and there was by the beginning of 1847 a *frisson* of excitement surrounding Andersen's name in literary circles. Thackeray, for example, wrote to a friend in January: "And Hans Christian Andersen, have you read him? I am wild about him, having only just discovered that delightful fanciful creature."

"Enlarged sympathy with children was one of the chief contributions made by the Victorian English to real civilization," wrote G. M. Trevelyan in *English Social History*. "Children's books of which the pleasure was intended to be shared with grown-ups was a characteristic invention of the time." In 1846, however, the new style of children's book, which emphasized fantasy and enjoyment rather than moral instruction, was only beginning to be published. The Grimms' collections had been read since the 1820s; James Halliwell's *Nursery Rhymes of England* (1842) was becoming a standard work; Edward Lear had just emerged into print with his limericks in *A Book of Nonsense*, though this was barely noticed, and Browning's poem "The Pied Piper of Hamelin" had appeared in 1842. A few collections of imaginative if rather tame stories, such as Sara Coleridge's *Phantasmion* (1837) and Catherine Sinclair's *Holiday House* (1839), were available, but there were not many exciting new children's books. Andersen began to be translated just as interest in a new genre of children's literature was developing in England, but before the golden age of Victorian fantasy took off in the 1860s, with Lewis Carroll, Charles Kingsley and George MacDonald. He was a fresh voice which chimed with the changing Victorian taste, and he met an immediate demand.

It was no surprise, therefore, that he was suddenly a magnet for translators, who competed with one another to claim him as their own. "We cannot consider you as a stranger. Pray think of us as your friends," Mary Howitt wrote in her first letter. "It is impossible for me to address you as a stranger, but rather as a friend whom I have long known, and towards whom I am drawn by those feelings of sympathy which similar struggles and similar pursuits are ever sure to call forth," wrote Charles Boner. Andersen responded with warmth to these sentiments, without realizing either that he was a lucrative asset to his translators, or that they were fixing his image in a particular and lop-sided way.

In their eagerness to tumble after each other into print to exploit a new market, none of his translators had taken the time even to learn Danish properly, let alone to construct translations whose style had any literary merit. Although some could read Danish, they all worked from German translations, picking up errors that were already there, adding new ones of their own and altering as they went any points of sensibility which happened to disturb their conventional imaginations.

Mary Howitt, the most intelligent and ambitious of them, made basic mistakes such as translating *Sommerfuglene* as "summer birds" instead of "butterflies" and *Svalen* as "the breeze" instead of "the swallow"; among her alterations was the prudish change to the opening of "Thumbelina," which risked questions about where babies come from. A literal translation of Andersen's version reads:

> Once upon a time, there was a woman who longed for a little child of her own, but she had no idea where she could get one. So off she went to see an old witch, and she said to her, "I'd so much like to have a little child! Won't you please tell me where I can get one from?"
>
> "Why yes, that's no trouble at all!" said the witch. "You must take this grain of barley—it's not the kind that grows in the farmer's field or that hens eat, either—put it in a flower-pot, and then wait and see what happens!"

but Mary Howitt opens:

> Once upon a time a beggar woman went to the house of a poor peasant and asked for something to eat. The peasant's wife gave her some bread and milk. When she had eaten it, she took a barley-corn out of her pocket and said— "This will I give to thee; set it in a flower-pot and see what will come out of it."

Mary Howitt could not capture Andersen's genius as a storyteller—his colloquialisms and chatty manner, his abruptness and humorous asides, his mix of warmth and satire—but this was a failure of style rather than wilful misreading. Subsequent translators, though, had a more disastrous effect. Both Charles Boner and Caroline Peachey misunderstood what was revolutionary in Andersen's earthy, joking language and its play on a double adult/child readership, and returned to the embellished literary diction that he had deliberately rejected. For "see" Boner used "behold," for "sweetheart," "the affianced one"; Andersen's "little mermaid" became a "dainty little mermaid" and the king's exclamation, as he is about to be killed, of "I will not . . ." in "The Tinderbox" was changed to "We are not graciously pleased."

Unable to grasp the satire of "The Princess and the Pea," Boner and Peachey followed a German translation which tried to make the story credible by having three peas instead of one placed under the mattress, ending not on the joke of the pea(s) going to a museum, but with a rhetorical flourish: "Now was that not a lady of exquisite feeling?" In "The Ugly Duckling" Andersen describes the moment when the eggs hatch:

> "How big the world is!" said all the young ones, for they undoubtedly had much more room to move about in now than they had had inside their eggs.

which Miss Peachey translates as:

> "How large the world is!" said the little ones, for they found their present situation very different to their former confined one, while yet in the egg-shells.

In "The Emperor's New Clothes," the minister goes to see the cloth and:

> "Yes," he told the Emperor, "it's quite the finest thing I've ever seen!"

but Miss Peachey writes:

> "Indeed, please your Imperial Majesty," said he to his sovereign, when he returned, "the cloth which the weavers are preparing is extraordinarily magnificent."

Miss Peachey embellishes many details in "Little Claus and Big Claus" to take the story further from its *risqué* folk source. Her dog in "The Tinderbox" is "the monstrous guardian of the golden treasure." Her soldier does not kiss the princess but kneels down to kiss her hand. The queen, satirized by Andersen as "a very clever woman, who could do other things besides riding in a coach," is not regal enough for Miss Peachey, who adds that she could "look very grand and condescending."

Boner and Peachey set the tone, and for almost a century English translations continued to range from the inadequate to the abysmal. One rendered "The Ugly Duckling"—*den grimme Ælling* in Danish—as "The Green Duck," presumably following a German mistranslation of *grimme* into *grün* (green) and so missing the point of the tale. Negatives were ignored so that the reverse of Andersen's intended meaning was conveyed; stories were changed to give happy endings or avoid brutal passages, such as Karen's feet being chopped off in "The Red Shoes." Repeatedly comments crept in which showed that the translator failed to grasp Andersen's humour, and was therefore floundering in an attempt to explain the tale to his readers. In

"The Nightingale," for example, the real and the artificial bird sing together without success, the music-master defends the mechanical one and the court prefers it. In his translation of 1861, Alfred Wehnert cannot believe this and loses the satire by adding "the practised ear of a musician might easily have detected a grating sound of the machinery. But the reader must recollect that they were only Chinese."

Yet so powerful is the structure of Andersen's tales, and so emotively simple the message, that not even a poor translation can entirely ruin them. The fabular quality of "The Ugly Duckling" or "The Emperor's New Clothes" shines through; so does the heartbreak of "The Little Mermaid" and the aesthetic idealism of "The Nightingale," and also the originality of talking toys, then unknown in England, which characterizes "Little Ida's Flowers" and "The Streadfast Tin Soldier." English readers responded to this bright new world, but they did so in a context dictated by the nature of the translations: the simple, clear-cut aspects of the stories were appreciated, with the sentimental emphasized out of all proportion to the humour and irony. As a result, Andersen was perceived as wholly a children's author, whereas in Denmark and Germany he was seen as a writer for both adults and children. The more complex tales were not initially translated into English—in 1847 Andersen lamented to Boner that in his volumes "my best tales, 'The Fir Tree,' 'The Snow Queen' and 'The Shadow' are unfortunately not included"—and thus Andersen's *œuvre* appeared more child-centred than by the 1840s it really was.

In even the best translations, certain aspects of an original are lost; emotional subtlety, humour, the nuances of fine language, are almost impossible to reproduce. But the effect of Andersen's translators on the way he was interpreted was particularly unfortunate, and it is clear from the earliest reviews. The *Athenaeum* of June 1846, for example, wrote that "The most fitting review of this volume would be a strain of Elfin music . . . Common Cheapside paragraphs are too square, and sharp, are ungraceful to invite gentle readers to pages so full of enchantment." *Fraser's Magazine* of January 1847 praised Andersen's "angelical spirit," continuing, "Heaven bless Hans Christian! Here *are* fairies! Here *is* fancy . . . may we not be charmed by the play and prattle of a child? And Hans Christian Andersen so affects me. Every page . . . sparkles with delightful grace and genial fancy. Hans and you are friends for life after an hour's talk with him. I shake thy hands, Hans Christian, thou kindly prattler and warbler."

Even more highbrow commentators, by marking out those tales which in simplicity of structure and immediate meaning translated best, followed a trend which relegated Andersen to the nursery. In a long analysis of Andersen's *œuvre* in October 1846, the *Spectator* wrote:

> The genius of Andersen is above all cordial and kindly . . . He has many superiors in intellectual strength, in depth and range of thought . . . but who can refuse to sympathize with his warm, ingenuous nature, his delicate but healthful sensibility, his quiet happy humour? Who that remembers his own boyish days can resist the sway of Andersen's creative fancy . . . It is highly characteristic of the man, that among his most successful efforts are his "Tales and Stories," written for children. Some of them are exquisitely beautiful: one in particular, "The Ugly Little Duck," is not surpassed by anything of its kind we have ever seen.

Several perceptive reviewers, however, linked Andersen to the anti-rationalist school. The *Athenaeum* of July 1846 wrote that "The more such beautiful and delicate poetry can be diffused among our children and grandchildren the better. When we think of the *calculation-morality* books which were in vogue twenty years ago, and turn to these, it seems as if the world were growing young again." *Chambers's Edinburgh Journal* of October 1846 said that Andersen's stories should "assist in the good cause—lately too much neglected—of cultivating the feelings" and in a further review in January 1847 the *Athenaeum* wrote that "no faery tales surpass those by Hans Christian Andersen . . . those who have moaned over Poetry as driven out of the world, and Fancy as planed to death by machines of utilitarian inventions, may be sorry to lose their grievance; but this they must do, as long as Hans Christian tells his capital faery tales." The *Spectator* called Andersen "the Cockney of Denmark" and the *Examiner* of July 1846 published a sensitive interpretation of Andersen's "rare and surprising art," highlighting his revolutionary idea of giving human individuality to the animal and the inanimate ("his vegetables have as much conversational character as his ducks and geese") and commenting that "some of his descriptive touches recall the wonderful observation and exquisitely graphic felicity of Mr. Dickens." The review quoted "The Emperor's New Clothes" in its entirety, and ended "Apply this, O ye conventionalists, quacks and pretenders of all kinds! to your everyday proceedings, and endeavour to be little children in the school of Mr. Hans Christian Andersen."

Other reviewers, though they appreciated the imaginative vision, persisted in seeing the tales through the prism of children's morality books.

Douglas Jerrold's Weekly Newspaper in December 1846 commented that "The moral hidden in every story is, we fear, too closely veiled to allow the youthful mind any glimpse of it. Children will be delighted with the book because of the fairy-tale witchery that works out each tale; and older readers, who can see the wisdom enshrined in the fiction, will like the stories for their excellent purpose." Two years later, when Andersen was better known, this remained a prominent strain among reviewers; "if . . . healthfulness of tone and kindliness of feeling can render fairy tales pleasing," wrote the *English Review* in 1848, "these are so in the highest degree; and beyond and above all things, there is a deep moral running through almost every tale, and a reverential cast of thought throughout the volume, which greatly increases its value."

Andersen's influence was quickly apparent in English children's writing. Whereas the robust fatalism and gruesome violence of the Grimms' folk tales had not inspired English authors to write their own stories, the perceived virtues of Andersen tapped into the Victorian taste for sentimental moralism and awakened more interest in fairy tales. The first imitators of Andersen's specific nursery world came rapidly: *The Enchanted Doll* (1849) by Mark Lemon, editor of *Punch*, and Frances Browne's *Granny's Wonderful Chair* (1856), where a chair tells fairy tales and takes its child owner to far-off lands. By the late 1860s and 1870s collections of invented fairy stories such as Anne Isabella Ritchie's *Five Old Friends and a Young Prince* (1868) and Juliana Ewing's *The Brownies and Other Tales* (1870) were common, though nothing with the lasting appeal or the literary quality of Andersen appeared until Oscar Wilde's *The Happy Prince and Other Stories* (1888), which owes a clear debt to Andersen; the *Athenaeum* compared the two writers. But while adults appreciated Wilde's tales, Andersen remained a children's author, absorbed into the Victorian cult of childhood. Looking back to that period in 1915, G. K. Chesterton wrote:

> When the English romantics wanted to find the folk-tale spirit still alive . . . they found a whole fairyland in one head and under one nineteenth-century top hat. Those of the English who were then children owe to Hans Andersen more than to any of their own writers, that essential educational emotion which feels that domesticity is not dull but rather fantastic; that sense of the fairyland of the furniture, and the travel and adventure of the farmyard.

The benefits Andersen brought to English children's literature were inestimable. He gave the fairy tale a key place in nineteenth-century culture. He showed that writing for children and literary and imaginative talent could go together. He introduced the idea of fantasy in children's stories, preparing the climate for Lewis Carroll in the 1860s. And in creating a separate children's world of talking toys and animals, he had a profound effect on later classics of childhood such as *The Wind in the Willows* and *Winnie the Pooh*. This legacy continues in contemporary Anglo-Saxon children's culture, from Disney remakes of fairy tales to films such as *Toy Story*. But in the process, much of Andersen the mature and complex artist, familiar to Danish, German and eastern European audiences, was lost to the Anglo-Saxon world.*

In part, the spiritual climate of Victorian England made the nature of his reception inevitable. But it was also Andersen's eagerness, when he arrived in London in 1847, to play the role already consigned to him by readers and reviewers in the mid 1840s that sealed his reputation as a twee, naive children's writer which the first translations of his works had already built up. Although Andersen never understood how bad the English translations were,† he grasped instinctively the image the Victorians had formed of him, he acted it out to perfection and he was rewarded with the applause and acclaim he wanted. But by delivering to the Victorians the persona they had imagined, he helped ensure that the full dimension and scope of his work remained misunderstood and underrated in Britain and America. Had he never visited England, the general perception of him today would be very different.

"The Thames surely bears witness to the fact that England rules the ocean," Andersen wrote as he sailed up the river into London on a cloudy morning

---

*In the twentieth century, a few good translators emerged—R. P. Keigwin, L. W. Kingsland, Reginald Spink, Naomi Lewis and, most recently, Neil Philip, but even today Andersen's work continues to be read in poor translations or bowdlerized versions. There is still no scholarly English edition of the stories, nor a well-translated volume of the complete tales. Even well-edited selections continue to surprise by their omissions: "The Nightingale" is missing from Oxford's "World Classics" edition, and "The Snow Queen" from a selection of eighty stories published in English by Reitzel. Many of Andersen's later great works, written for an adult audience, remain unknown.

†This was partly because he spoke little English, but also because he had no faith in any translations, and so took little interest in their quality. He knew German well and understood how much was lost in the German translations; his letters to his German friends are full of hopes, for example, that they "will soon be able to read the Danish edition, for the peculiarities of these works cannot be repeated in another language."

in June 1847 after a thirty-one-hour crossing from Rotterdam. "The ships come running under full sail, pluming themselves like swans. Thousands of fishboats, like a teeming marketplace, like a brood of chicks, like confetti. Steamer after steamer, like rockets in a great firework display." Passing Gravesend, he saw streaks of lightning flashing overhead and there was "a splendid thunderstorm"; while running alongside the river "a railroad train raced along with its blue smoke against the black clouds." "They know you're here and bid you welcome," an Englishman on board told him flatteringly, and the next morning, when he ventured out from his room at the Sablonière Hotel in Leicester Square, "plodded around the streets" and attempted to orientate himself, the first thing he saw was his picture staring out from *Howitt's Journal* in a shop window. He bought a copy and found that he was already famous. Nothing could have been calculated to make him feel more instantly at home. "I am strangely happy! I cannot realize it. I am actually famous, so much so as neither myself nor Denmark is aware of," he wrote to Henriette Collin that day. "It is delightful, it makes one happy, the Lord is wonderfully good to me, it is really curious that he, too, can have his favourites, if this happiness is not an alarming prepayment."

He loved London, its size and bustle and relentless commerce, at once.

> Went out for a bit and looked at the illuminated shops. How many gas flames are burning? Well, ask about the number of stars in the sky! . . . Everything rushes busily by . . . Omnibus follows omnibus; cab after cab, equipages—with a speed as if an important event had taken place in one or another part of the city, and everyone had to get there. Musicians, a whole chorus of them, are standing on the sidewalk performing . . . London is the city of cities, with all due respect to Rome. These two cities fascinate me—London is the busy day; Rome, the great, silent night.

To Henriette Wulff he wrote: "Victor Hugo, or whoever it is, who calls Paris 'the city of cities,' shows that he does not know the cities of Europe; of all the cities I know there are only two that would deserve that name, and they are Rome and London. But London is the living city. What a bustle, what traffic!" Yet, coming from his background, he could not help but be struck and moved also by the dire poverty that he saw all round him. London, so much bigger than Copenhagen, had greater extremes of wealth and deprivation, which Andersen did not forget. "That strange staring gaze of the poor," he noted. "They don't dare to beg but their hunger can be seen on their faces. They stand outside of a pastry shop and stare fixedly at the stranger inside. Often they wear a sign on their chest: 'Have not eaten in two days.'" Another day, "a neatly dressed man was standing with some children—five of them, each one smaller than the next—all of them in mourning and holding bunches of matchsticks. Was it planned to attract attention? I don't think so. People looked at them and went on."

As it happened, the stars of his favourite constellation had regrouped that summer in the capital: both Carl Alexander and Jenny Lind were in town. An invitation was waiting at his hotel from Carl Alexander, who was staying at Marlborough House; Andersen went to him immediately and afterwards wrote, "[he] fell on my neck, embraced me heartily," adding, "he said to me that he felt restricted here. It wasn't possible for him to meet with literary figures . . . everything was cliques . . . 'This is the land of freedom, where you die from etiquette.'" Carl Alexander also told him that "Lovely Lind is here; she sings more beautifully than ever and has remained true to herself and to us," and waiting for Andersen on his first day was an invitation from her. "At this very moment, while they are acclaiming her, I am sitting here with a letter from her; she bids 'her dear brother' welcome! Tomorrow we shall meet—Oh, if you knew my thoughts. No one knows them," Andersen told Henriette Collin.

Jenny, living "infinitely far out" in Old Brompton, was enjoying in London still greater triumphs even than in Germany the previous year. At that time, a friend recalled, Jenny "lived in a little house, called Clairville Cottage, it was covered with roses and creepers, had a pretty garden and was thoroughly rural. She . . . often accompanied us in our country rides; in those happy days the country began at Haymore Lane, now Gloucester Road, and continued right into Surrey." Andersen drove out there in a hired carriage on his second day; he found an unassuming, double-fronted, two-storey house off Gloucester Road, and Jenny playing with a little dog she had bought in "a lovely little garden with mown grass, flowers and shady paths." She welcomed Andersen, invited him to visit whenever he pleased and offered him free tickets to hear her at the opera, where prices had become absurdly inflated for her performances.

She was the talk of the London season. Queen Victoria made a point of expressing her admiration for "the exquisite shake, the wonderful clear, sweet *piano* way of singing the very highest notes without losing any of their fulness and freshness"; Arthur Coleridge, taken as a boy by his tutor to see Jenny in *I Puritani*, remembered nearly crying with delight to hear her "showering her trills and roulades like sparkling diamonds all over the place." In the spring of 1847, *Jerrold's Journal* reported that three times the House of Commons was unable to vote because so many MPs were at the opera hearing Jenny Lind; on the streets her portrait was everywhere; boxes of chocolates, matchboxes, handkerchiefs depicting her were selling like hot cakes. Jenny hated the crowds, though she had fallen in love with everything that was old-fashioned and prudish in Victorian England. Andersen was received as a familiar face and a fellow Scandinavian, a comfort from the madding crowd.

But the crowd was rushing in on him too, and he had little time to visit her that summer, for the next day he made his debut into London society. "Felt indisposed and anxious about the big world I shall now venture into," he noted as the Danish ambassador Count Reventlow drove him to Lord Palmerston's. But he need not have worried—here was a soirée after his own heart:

> The highest of the nobility were here ... I was presented to one lady after the other. Each one knew almost all of my writings. The hereditary grand duchess introduced me to the duchess of Suffolk ... The hereditary grand duke shook my hand. It was so hot there; I could hardly manage standing on my feet and had to go out for some air ... They say that Dickens and D'Israeli are excluded from these circles; they acknowledged me, they accepted me ... English ladies overwhelmed me with enthusiasm for "The Ugly Duckling," "The Top and the Ball," *The Improvisatore*. Their toilettes expensive and tasteful ... Diamonds glittered and huge bouquets in people's hands caught the eye. We were standing crowded against each other and I was dragged through the most densely packed groups.

Andersen's success at Lord Palmerston's was the beginning of a love affair with the British aristocracy, for whom he became the craze of the season. At lunches, teas and dinners over the next month, the scene of adulation was repeated at the homes of Lady Morgan, Lord and Lady Stanley, Lord Castlereagh, Lady Duff-Gordon and other leading lights of Victorian society. On his fifth day, Andersen drove to Lady Poulett's:

> Terribly hot, packed with people on the steps, in the rooms; the dancers had something like a table top to move around on. Spoke with Lady Palmerston, Lady Stanley, etc. Lots of beautiful roses, baskets on the walls filled with roses and periwinkle, a table looking as if entirely covered with roses. I was about to faint a couple of times from heat and exhaustion. This is supposed to be a pleasure! I couldn't get away until 2:30.

Lady Morgan vowed to "invite all of London's famous authors" in his honour. After visiting Lady Montgomery, he wrote, "it was remarkable how she was able to understand my English, indeed, almost better than I did myself. How polite the English are, and how nice their compliments sound." At one gathering, "a middle-aged lady in velvet and with a gold chain . . . sat looking at me, lost in adoration; and once she grabbed my hand and wanted to kiss it . . . 'I must kiss that precious hand,' she said . . . at my departure she again wanted to kiss my hand, looked at me with adoring eyes." At another, "I was fussed over a lot. The young ladies fanned me. I was allowed to leave the table with the ladies. They were clinging to me, plaguing me; I was peered at like a strange animal."

Rapidly, Andersen's self-presentation as quaint and child-like—an image enhanced by his extremely poor English, which forced him to say everything very simply—charmed English society while confirming him as a nursery writer. Charles Boner told the writer Miss Mitford that Andersen was "perfectly unspoilt, as simple as a child, and with as much poetry in his every-day doings as in his prose"; Miss Mitford in turn wrote to "The Queen's Miss Skerrett, who has so much to do in recommending books all through the palace . . . begging that if the Danish stories were not in the royal nursery that she would place them there, which she says she will do."

Elizabeth Rigby, a writer-friend of Lady Stanley, remembered Andersen as "a long, thin, fleshless, boneless man, wriggling and bending like a lizard with a lantern-jawed, cadaverous visage. Simple and child-like, and simpletonish in his manner . . . His whole address and manner are irresistibly ludicrous." Later he came to dinner, where he chatted in halting English about Rachel and Jenny Lind and the King of Denmark. "He had one stream of interesting talk perhaps rather too much of himself, but to me that was novel and entertaining . . . Altogether he left a most agreeable impression both on mind and heart, especially on the latter, for his own seemed so affectionate. No wonder he finds people kind; all stiffness is useless with him, as he is evidently a simple child himself." Leigh Hunt, who met Andersen at Lord Stanley's house, recalled that "he looks like a large child, a sort of half-angel. There were many people of rank present, yet no one in the room looked more *distingué* than Andersen, the shoemaker's son." Lady Blessington told Jerdan, "I have seldom felt so strong an interest in a person of whom I saw so little, for he interested me as being quite as good as he is clever, and of how few authors can we say this!"

It is also likely that some of his glory that season came from the linking of his name with Jenny Lind's; the English public, already riveted by one Scandinavian star famed for her child-like simplicity and impeccable morals, was eager to welcome another. William Jerdan, writing in the *Literary Gazette* when Andersen had been in England a few weeks, compared the two:

> Everyone who has met [Andersen] is delighted with his character, in which is united to acknowledged originality of genius and poetic imagination, a simplicity most captivating, and a candour and truth of that rare nature which lays the individual soul . . . open . . . in his sphere Hans Christian Andersen is the counterpart of Jenny Lind, that pure and noble representative of the other sex, and bright ornament of a profession beset with difficulties and temptations.

In turn, Andersen, like Jenny, admired the demonstrative religiosity and self-conscious respectability of the early Victorians. England, he wrote in his diary, "[is] a big nation, and in our times perhaps the only truly religious one. There is respect for proper behaviour, there is morality."

Andersen, wrote Miss Mitford, "is the lion of London this year—dukes, princes and ministers are all disputing for an hour of his company." Fans began calling at Andersen's hotel, although Reventlow had warned him that Leicester Square was an unfashionable address and he must give out that he was staying at the embassy. Reventlow and the rich, elderly Danish banker Joseph Hambro, who had set up the London branch of Hambro & Son in Old Broad Street, danced in attendance on him; invitations from English aristocrats flowed in, and Andersen never ceased to be impressed. At Anthony Rothschild's, for example, "there was a princely splendour to everything there—marble stairs, flowers and a fountain in the room, a magnificent fireplace in the dining room, carved wooden panelling, rococo silver on display, a really exquisite dinner. The young Rothschild, an authentic, simple Jewish face, round and fat. The baroness quite lovely." Though worn out by the round of partying, Andersen felt healed and content; resentment for past ills smouldered but did not spoil his satisfaction. He complained that the Danish press was not recording his success, but concentrating instead on Oehlenschläger's visit to Sweden; to Edvard he wrote, "It says in the newspaper where my portrait is that I am 'one of the most remarkable and interesting men of his day,' but you were too proud to say Du to me—phew! I might almost be sufficiently vain to say again: Edvard, let us be on Du terms, and you would answer as I make my Shadow reply. Well, I expect you have understood that the malice is aimed against you."

. . .

The literary world, however, was also lying in wait for Andersen, and here the adulation was not so innocent. Andersen was hot property. In the absence of international copyright, publishers and translators sought to establish a monopoly on English versions of his work by procuring from him stories which could be translated into English before Danish or German publication—the only way of preventing piracy. Rival translators, moreover, were busy promoting their own reworkings in high places— Boner, for example, used Miss Mitford's influence at court to ensure that his would "be the first English translation of Andersen that Her Majesty and the Government will see."

Among the translators, publishers and writers trying to curry favour, there was the inept Beckwith ("he digs in and is so piteous"), uncritical Anne Bushby ("has translated several of my poems; precisely the ones I've rejected"), fawning Charles Boner, forceful, difficult Mary Howitt, dignified Richard Bentley and the young Irish writer William Allingham. At first, Andersen naively lapped up the attentions of the entire pack. Boner, who often appeared early in the morning to escort him anywhere he wanted to go, was "a charming man." Mary Howitt, who turned up at his hotel after a week with a copy of her new translation of *The True Story of My Life*, was "exceedingly selfless and friendly." Only the genial Allingham, too shy to make himself understood, was turned out by a nervous Andersen as a beggar; Allingham wrote the next day that in "the farthest corner of Ireland, nearly 500 miles from London—a place where there are few books and no booksellers—yet . . . even there *your* books are well known and loved . . . if you should visit us—and if I should *in any way* be able to assist you—I would consider it the greatest honour of my life." Allingham published his diary some years later, writing of the encounter at the Sablonière Hotel that Andersen "had not English enough to allow of our conversing, asked me to write to him; but I have nothing to say save that I love him, and many people tell him that. He is tall and lanky, with a queer long face, but friendliness and intelligence shining through."

It is always harder to be discriminating in a foreign culture, and this was especially true for someone of Andersen's anxious, eager temperament. Soon he had to acknowledge that he had made mistakes. Boner paled when set against more illustrious company, and his subsequent correspondence with Andersen is a ceaseless whine about being ignored, while Mary Howitt had shot herself in the foot before Andersen even arrived. Cashing in on a double craze, she had taken it upon herself to dedicate *The True Story of My Life* to Jenny Lind; she also tried to buy Andersen by announcing in the preface that he was to be paid "a certain sum" for each edition of the auto-biography. This turned out to be £10, and upset everyone: Andersen, who found it and the reference to Jenny in poor taste; Hambro, who thought it a derisory sum; and readers and reviewers such as Jerdan, who complained that "an uncongenial preface talks of pecuniary interests . . . it is a harsh dis-cord, a crash, to prelude a beautiful harmony." To Edvard, Andersen wrote that "There is a muddle and a cackling which confuses me in this situation." Hambro offered to take over negotiations and Andersen accepted gratefully, but Howitt persisted, besieging him with first invitations and then insis-tences that he come out to visit her.

Howitt and her husband had lived some years in Germany and made a living translating Scandinavian authors, via German editions of their works, into English. Hambro called her a "translation factory"; now living in Clap-ton, east of London, she was, under a genteel surface, a shrewd woman des-perate to maintain her tenuous links to literary society. As Andersen's first translator, she was especially proprietorial; she had written a flattering piece about him in her journal, which was prominently displayed in bookshops, but within days she saw him slipping from her grasp. "I only wish I could make you feel that in truth we are your oldest friends in London, for we knew and loved you through your books, in which you have so beautifully developed yourself, long before anybody else in London," she wrote petu-lantly after he had become the talk of the town and still not bothered to make the trip to Clapton. Eventually and reluctantly he went, "hot and bothered" in an omnibus, for Sunday lunch, which was a fiasco: "listless from the heat and the conversation . . . The husband distant, despite his cor-diality. I was very listless; wasn't happy about driving that long way home . . . the heat oppressive; the omnibus was constantly stopping. I felt very nerv-ous, about to faint, so alone. I was about to leap out of the carriage and into a house, saying I was sick. Sweat was pouring out of all my pores; it was awful—never!"

A second visit, after an acrimonious exchange of letters, was little better: "I got very nervous and had to lie down on the sofa. Was fearful and profoundly exhausted. Our carriage was the last to come—those were ago-nizing, painful hours." Mrs. Howitt was dumped as Andersen's translator and had her revenge in a memoir of 1852, which pierced through the

English image of Andersen bitterly. "Andersen is a singular mixture of simplicity and worldliness," she wrote. "The child-like heart which animates his best compositions appears to your astonished vision in real life, in the shape of a *petit-maître* sighing after the notice of princes. The poet is lost to you in the egotist." Later, in her autobiography, she wrote maliciously that Andersen was financially greedy and that "unfortunately, the over-sensitive and egotistical nature of this great Danish author much marred our intercourse."

In contrast to this débâcle, Richard Bentley, Andersen wrote, "was very charming, [his] personality appealed to me a great deal." Bentley was then in his fifties, white-haired, courteous and serious, and with an impeccable pedigree—he had started his publishing business in 1819, the same year as Andersen's Danish publisher Reitzel, and he had published Dickens and Disraeli; *Oliver Twist* had first appeared in his magazine *Bentley's Miscellany*, whose later contributors included Longfellow and Thackeray, as well as Andersen. He was cautious and unpushy, was happy to deal with Hambro, and Andersen trusted him. When after two weeks in England he allowed himself to be on his own for the first time "with three people who could only speak English," it was at Bentley's country home in Sevenoaks. He loved the grandeur and peace here; the beautiful garden bordered the aristocratic estate of Knole, and he wrote to Henriette Wulff of the extraordinary elegance—"footmen in silk stockings wait on you—there's a bookseller." A dinner was given in Andersen's honour, with toasts proposed, he recorded, "to great acclamation—to my child-like spirit, my religiosity, my fervour etc.—I was moved, saying 'I can not speake Englisch, bat I hope I scal in a neuw Worck give the Sentimens of my Heart! I thank you!' It was so marvellously old-fashioned there. Everything was rococo in the dining room: the mantel of the fireplace of wood, the polished wooden walls, the old cabinets, the porcelain vases."

Bentley became a lifelong friend as well as his English publisher; in 1848 Andersen dedicated his novel *The Two Baronesses* to him. Andersen visited him several times; Bentley's daughter recalled: "Andersen charmed us all by his simplicity and naivety, his quaint and broken English and his graceful pretty stories. Well do I remember . . . when our younger sister, then a mere girl of twelve or thirteen, came in on the bright summer morning, all in white and glowing with health, how Andersen rose from the breakfast table, and hailed her coming with 'Ah! the little standard rose!'" A fellow guest at one of Bentley's breakfasts also caught that foppish, bachelor courtesy which was already making Andersen in his early forties appear something of an old man. Miss Annie Wood wrote:

> I remember on one occasion at a singularly happy breakfast party, when everyone was in a genial, pleasant mood, and the spirit of harmony seemed to have breathed itself into each person present—the coffee was delicious, the bread and fruit and various dishes all that could be desired—Andersen, who had been enjoying himself more than usual, rose from his seat and said quietly, "Friends, I will say grace!" Then raising his hands and bowing his gaunt figure low over the table, he said in a reverential, hushed but audible tone: "I thank Thee, O Lord, that Thou has permitted me to enjoy another breakfast such as I had at Mr. Bentley's! Amen!" For a moment I thought the dear old man had lost his senses or was making fun, but a glance at his earnest face rebuked the idea, and I felt ashamed of my mistake.

This was a very different Andersen from the high-pitched joker and complainer in Copenhagen whom the Collin family teased as "*pauvre pomme de terre*" and whom his publisher Reitzel shielded from any social encounter which might unnerve him. The English version of Andersen—earnest, innocent, sentimental—resembled a caricature: it exaggerated a few crucial features, but missed many other elements in the whole picture—Andersen's insecurity and inner rage as well as his humour. Although this had a long-term effect on the interpretation of his work here, for Andersen as a visitor, it did not much matter. He had long been a self-publicist so skilful that he barely knew where the persona ended and the real self began, and he gave himself up to the excitement and the praise. "At this moment I am probably at the peak of my honour and recognition," he panted to Edvard on 8 July, when he had been in England for two weeks.

> From now on it must go downhill; I cannot achieve more here in this metropolis than I already have . . . It is a fact: I am "a famous man." The aristocracy here, so discouraging to its own poets, has welcomed me as one of its own circle. Today and for the next fourteen days I have been invited out; dinner from eight to eleven, and parties from half-past eleven until late at night. I cannot stand it, I am sinking, am being overwhelmed by invitations, by requests for my autograph. All this is like a dream, and in the pure pleasure it gives me, pleasure that your father and Denmark is honoured by me, I am happy.

A week later came the highlight: his meeting with Dickens at Lady Blessington's salon. As he was writing his name in his autobiography for his hostess, he told Henriette Wulff,

A man came into the room, quite like the portrait we have all seen, someone who had come to town for my sake and had written "I *must* see Andersen!" When he had greeted the company I ran from the writing desk to meet him, we seized both each other's hands, gazed in each other's eyes, laughed and rejoiced. We knew each other so well, though we met for the first time—it was Charles Dickens. He quite answers to the best ideas I had formed of him. Outside the house there is a lovely veranda running the whole breadth of the house, vines and roses hang like a roof over the pillars, here are gaily-coloured birds, and below a green field, green as you only see them in England; out here we stood for a long time talking—talking English, but he understood me, I him.

Dickens had let his London house and was out of town for the summer, and arrangements for a subsequent breakfast had to be cancelled, but he called on Andersen at the Sablonière Hotel and, finding him out, left the collected edition of his works in twelve volumes, beautifully bound and each inscribed "Hans Christian Andersen, From his Friend and Admirer Charles Dickens." "I was ecstatic!" Andersen wrote in his diary; he sent Dickens a thank you letter via Jerdan, with a note which showed how limited his English was: "My dear friend, I know not te direction of Dickens, will you, immediadly giw him this letter. Yesterday I returned from the country I found all his works he haw giwen my! O I am verry heppy!" Andersen sent Henriette Wulff Dickens's calling card, "so that you may also have something," and wrote "as I hear from others and his kindness to me shows, he is not only said to appreciate my books highly, but he likes me so much myself."

Eventually, the strain of social and professional pressures and of speaking English exhausted Andersen, and he lapsed into nervousness and anxiety. "Now I am tired of London!" he wrote on 25 July, "had the feeling in my bones that I would go crazy." His diary for August is full of hypochondriacal mutterings and financial worries: "I am anxious about this lassitude, this buzzing in my spine. I'll probably get spinal consumption or go crazy . . . One of my testicles is sore . . . diarrhoea all day long . . . didn't sleep well . . . Time passes, and it is costing me one pound per day at the hotel . . . Went over to Covent Garden . . . but since it cost a sovereign, I gave it up and walked home; ate oysters and drank stout." He escaped to Hambro's country house, where he could speak Danish all the time and where he felt very at home. "Out here it is green and fresh. London lies at my feet, the railway's train of carriages is puffing along down the fields and highroads; it all looks so genuinely Danish round here, but it is Denmark on a large scale, as everything in this glorious country," he wrote to Henriette Wulff. When Hambro offered to pay his expenses on a trip to Scotland, he accepted, and fled London in relief.

He had met Dickens, and he had conquered London society; there remained a hero to whom he wanted to pay homage: Walter Scott. Now, after a two-day journey by coach and train to Edinburgh—most of the passengers got off at the station before the city, because they feared a tunnel just outside it would collapse—Andersen found himself hailed as "the Danish Walter Scott." He stayed in luxury at the home of Hambro's son: "matchless in his attentiveness to me and in discerning my every wish and fulfilling it"; he saw the monument to Scott; he was fêted as he had been in London; the Hambros took him on a tour of the Scottish countryside to see Scott's landscapes, and Prince Albert invited him to visit the royal family at Loch Laggan. The journey had worn him out further, however, and when he left the Hambros to stay in a hotel he fell into a hysterical panic. "In England and Scotland I have received so much appreciation, or rather overrating, so much amiable kindness, that it turns my head to think of it. It was so excessive that I could bear it no longer, and at last, in Scotland, I became so nervous and exhausted, that I was obliged to return, and did not go to Loch Laggan, where His Royal Highness Prince Albert had graciously invited me," he wrote to Carl Alexander. Andersen turned down royal invitations only reluctantly; in a "bad frame of mind; feverish morning; sensual, sick thoughts; unhappy, really desperate," he travelled south. As soon as he boarded the train, he heard that a Scottish newspaper had wrongly reported that he had visited the Queen, and he became even more overwrought. "I was so desperate I wouldn't have minded if there were a train accident. How detestably egotistical! How our fate hangs suspended from fine threads . . . We go out through the front door and are for a moment uncertain whether we should turn to the right or the left, and whatever we spontaneously choose will lead some of us to our death, others to the great events in our lives. Never before have I travelled with such nonchalance on the railroad." He arrived in London and fell sobbing into the arms of Reventlow.

It was time to go home. Carl Alexander had left England without saying goodbye, writing from on board his ship to Ostend:

The last few moments were so crowded and I was so sad. You wouldn't have had any benefit from seeing me. There is sorrow in my heart and I sit here, lonely, on the sea while my heart is on land, the coast of which is now disappearing. Give my greetings to Lind and come again, as usual. Write to me soon and in detail about everything you do and see. I like to see things through your eyes. Recently you were at the opera when *La Sonnambula* was performed. I observed you carefully, we understood one another. It is wonderful when in a strange world two hearts understand each other so well, that when their eyes meet their hearts understand . . . Adieu, don't forget me, I hold fast to you.

Andersen now left without saying goodbye to Jenny—"despite the fact that I could have. What a mystery I am to myself!" England had opened his eyes to new artistic allies, and, with the little energy he had left, he made instead just two efforts to say farewell: he went to Sevenoaks to see Bentley again, and on 29 August, after juggling the English draft around as best he could, he wrote to Dickens at his home in Broadstairs in Kent:

My dear dear Dickens!
    to morow I shall kome to Ramsgate, I hope you will giw yours Adresse in the Royal Oak Hotel, where I shall remane till the next morning, when I shall go by the stamboat to Ostende. I must see you, and thank you; that is the last flower for me in the dear England! Your Admirer and true Friend for ever,
                                                    Hans Christian Andersen

"Dear delightful Charles Dickens," Andersen's ambivalent host in England in 1857.

Dickens invited him to supper with his family at once, and wrote that "when you come back to England—which you must take an oath today to do soon—I shall hope to see you often in my own house in London, where I have a few little pictures and so forth, that I hope may interest you. But wheresoever you are, believe me that I always am Your friend and admirer, Charles Dickens." At the Dickens' family supper, surrounded by children kissing him, Andersen was happy: "so happy there that I only later discovered that we were sitting right by the ocean—the waves were rolling under our windows. Dickens was amiability itself." Next morning, as Andersen went to board his ship, Dickens was standing on the wharf waiting for him.

> He had walked from Broadstairs in order to say goodbye to me, dressed in a green Scottish dress coat and colourful shirt—exceedingly, elegantly English. He was the last to shake my hand in England . . . As the ship was gliding out of the harbour, I could see Dickens on the outermost point. I had thought him long gone. He was waving his hat and finally raised one hand up toward heaven; did it perhaps mean that we won't see each other until up there?"

He returned home via Weimar, where Carl Alexander invited him to recuperate at his hunting lodge at Ettersburg; their reunion was a fleeting moment of calm after the bustle of England and before the storms to come. Back in Copenhagen in the autumn, news of Andersen's status as a foreign celebrity arrived at the same time as he did, the Danish *Jante-loven* spirit reasserted itself, and he was mocked. The magazine *The Corsair* had four cartoons and a satirical account of Andersen's success in high society, called "Andersen, the Lion"; hours after his arrival, Andersen wrote, "I was standing at my window, when two well-dressed gentlemen passed by; they perceived me, laughed, and one of them pointed at me, and said so loud that I could hear every word, 'See, there stands our orang-outang so famous abroad!' "

On the other hand, he glowed inwardly like Cinderella reliving the thrill of the ball. To Carl Alexander he wrote:

> I am home again in the old street, in the old house. The same people are passing to and fro, the carts are rolling along—everything is going on in the old track; I myself am making the usual visits, attending the theatre and sitting alone once more in my own room, as if nothing had happened; and yet my head and heart are so full. It is with me as after a great ball, the music still sounding in my ears, my thoughts like dashing waves. I can find no rest . . . My stay in Holland, England and Scotland floats before me like a phantasy woven

of joy and sunshine, and at the close come the beautiful days at Ettersburg, with our reunion, our life together there, and our parting.

To Henriette Wulff he wrote of England: "I almost think the homage, the value given to my writings in all classes, in short the new position in life in which I felt myself placed, affected me most." Confident in his role as international author, he began work on a new collection of tales and on finishing a dramatic poem, *Ahasverus*, which had occupied him on and off for years.

Ahasverus, published in December, is rambling and undisciplined, and was not a success, though Andersen's obsession with the Jewish wanderer-hero expresses his identification with the rootless, damned figure of legend. But as a writer of fairy tales, he remained versatile, inventive, in command of what he wanted to do. Three of the five tales of autumn 1847 are comic vignettes, buoyant and light-hearted examples of Andersen perfecting the miniaturist's art. They centre on a snail, a shirt collar and a drop of water, and in different ways each bears the stamp of his London trip. "The Happy Family," the story of a family of snails who live in the humble forest but aspire to go to the manor to be cooked black and lie on a silver dish, turns on snobbery and was conceived in London when Reventlow advised Andersen to conceal from his aristocratic admirers that he was staying at the Sablonière Hotel. Andersen wrote it at Glorup Manor on Funen, which is the model for its manor house; it is a happy, witty work in which the snails are saved from their Fir Tree–like wish to go grandly to their doom.

"The Collar" is a punning self-portrait—as a collar is constantly turned down, so Andersen's hero is rejected by all his sweethearts: a garter, an iron, a pair of scissors and a comb. His proposals grow less and less flattering ("It's remarkable the way you keep all your teeth, ma'am," he says to the comb) and he finishes life, "turned down again!," in a box at the paper mill, where he boasts incessantly and falsely about his conquests (the pair of scissors "gave me the gash I still bear, she was so passionate!"). In a neat twist, the collar is turned into white paper, from which Andersen draws a comic moral that mocks the Danes' censorious reports of him boasting his way across England, but is also a bitter-sweet joke at himself as a compulsive autobiographer. The collar becomes:

> the very piece of white paper that we have here, and on which this story was printed. And that was because it boasted so dreadfully about what it had never been. So let us bear this in mind, that we don't go behaving in the same way; for we can never be really sure that if we do that we won't also land in the rag

box and get made into white paper and have our whole history printed on us, every secret bit of it, and have to go about telling it like the collar.

"The Drop of Water," written for Ørsted, ponders the advantages of a scientific perspective; a magician called Creepy-Crawly looks at a drop of dirty water seething with tiny pond creatures through a magnifying lens and asks his friend to guess what it is. The story ends:

> It did indeed look like a town, with all the people running about without any clothes on! It was horrible! But it was even more horrible to see the way one pummelled and pounded another, and how they pinched and nipped and bit and tugged at one another. The ones at the bottom had to get to the top, and the ones on top had to get to the bottom. "Look! Look! His leg's longer than mine! Biff! Off with him! There's somebody with a pimple behind his ear! A harmless little pimple; but it troubles him, and it's going to trouble him more!" And they hacked at him and they heaved at him, and they ate him for the sake of that little pimple. Another was sitting as quietly as any little lady, wanting nothing more than to be left alone in peace. And so they went for her; and they tugged at her and tore at her, and they ate her! . . .
>
> "It's plain enough to see," said the other. "Of course it's Copenhagen, or another city. They're all alike! Anyway, it's a city!"
>
> "It's ditch-water!" said Creepy-Crawly.

This is an early representation of the city as a jungle where the weak are trampled underfoot, the selfish economic ethos wipes out the helpless individual and only the brutish survive. Andersen's diaries show how London, its size and grandeur and its extremes of wealth, had led him to consider the nature of urban life and how people survived it, as he had never done in Copenhagen or Rome or Paris.

"The Drop of Water" shares something of the big city vision that Dickens painted, on a larger canvas, while in the two tragic stories of this new collection, "The Old House" and "The Story of a Mother," the influence of Dickens is clear: in the feel for minute detail, in the life Andersen breathes into inanimate objects, in the mix of the grotesque and the sentimental. "The Old House," a musing on mortality and transience which seems to anticipate, on a microcosmic scale, the ending of the old world order the following year, was one of Dickens's favourite tales; "I read that story over and over again, with the most unspeakable delight," he wrote.

From his window, a little boy watches a Gothic house with gargoyles and verses cut into the beams. An old man lives there alone, and the boy sends

him a tin soldier—a German child had similarly given Andersen a tin soldier to stop him, he said, being lonely. The boy is invited there himself and
the fabric of the neglected house comes alive for his visit. The trumpets
carved into the door boom "Ta-ra-ta-ra-tah! The little boy's coming!" The
furniture shouts "Crack! Crack!" and the pieces fall over each other trying to
see the boy; a high-backed armchair croaks "Sit down! Sit down . . . Ugh,
how my joints crack! I'm in for rheumatics like the old cupboard." The
swords and armour rattle, the walls covered in pigskin and printed with
gilded flowers boast "Gilding's soon gone; / But pigskin lives on!" and a picture of a lady in old-fashioned dress and powdered hair gazes at the little
boy "with gentle eyes." Meanwhile, "the pendulum of the big clock swung to
and fro, and the pointer turned, and everything in the room went on growing older, though none of them noticed it."

The old man says he is content with his memories and his portrait, but
the tin soldier begs bitterly to go home to the noisy, happy family across the
road, where the little boy's sister, based on the composer Hartmann's toddler
daughter Maria, is always singing and laughing. "Oh how lonely the old
man is! Do you think he gets kissed? Do you think he gets nice looks, or a
Christmas tree? He'll get nothing—only a funeral. I can't bear it!" cries the
soldier, and he topples down and is lost under the floorboards. Winter
comes, and "the windows were quite frozen. The little boy had to sit breathing on them to make himself a peep-hole across to the old house. There the
snow had drifted into all the scrolls and inscriptions, and it lay right over the
steps. And there was nobody in: the old man was dead"—an image which,
as often in Andersen's moments of bleak perception, prefigures a scene in
modernist literature: at the end of *The Cherry Orchard*, also an elegy for a
lost world and class, another old man, the servant Firs, dies locked up and
forgotten in an old house.

The house is cleared, the portrait goes back to the second-hand dealer's;
"and there it stayed, for no one knew her any more and no one cared for the
old picture." Later the house is pulled down and a bright new one built,
which is bought by the little boy, now grown up. His wife finds the tin soldier in the garden, and with it a scrap of pigskin wall-covering:

It had lost its gilt and it looked like wet earth. But it had an opinion, and it said:

"Gilding's soon gone;
But pigskin lives on."

Only, the tin soldier didn't believe it.

The companion piece to this is "The Story of a Mother." Like Dickens's account of the death of Little Nell in *The Old Curiosity Shop*, it depicts a dying child in the sort of scene that the Victorians, more preoccupied than us with the death of children, loved to weep over. Yet so emotionally authentic is Andersen's description, so masterly his symbolism, that the story is still very moving today. In it, Andersen returned to the folklore images of his childhood. In an icy winter, a mother sits with her dying child. Death, in the form of an old man shivering with cold, knocks at the door. The mother has not slept for three days and nights; now for a moment she closes her eyes, only to shudder awake and find that the old man has vanished with her child. She embarks on a nightmare hallucinatory pilgrimage through a snow-covered forest to follow them, bartering for directions with the characters of the forest. First, Night, personified by a woman in long black robes sitting in the snow, takes her children's songs. Next a hawthorn bush must be warmed at her heart so that "her blood flowed in big drops," then a lake promises to carry her across its waters if she cries her eyes out so that they "sank to the bottom and became two precious pearls." Finally an old woman guarding Death's glass-house demands her long black hair in exchange for her own snow-white locks. Thus, old and blind, the mother arrives at Death's garden where every human life is represented by a tiny flower or plant, and "among millions of others she recognized her own child's." Death, God's "gardener," arrives, and shows her in his well two mirages, one of happiness and one of sorrow, and suggests she accept fate. The mother cries out, "Which of them was my child? Tell me! Save the innocent one! Take him away instead! . . . Forget my prayers, and everything I have said and done!" Death asks: "Do you wish for your child back again? Or shall I take him with me to the place you do not know?" In the original manuscript Andersen gives the tale a happy ending. The mother bows her head:

> As she did so, her lips touched the child's lips, as it lay there in a sweet, sound sleep, and the sun shone on the cheeks, so they seemed red; and when the mother looked round she found herself sitting in her little room; the lark was sitting in its cage, as though it felt the coming of spring; and death was not in the room. Folding her hands, the mother thought of the house of the dead, and of the child's future, and said again "God's will be done!"

Then at the last moment he changed it, replacing this with one line: "And Death went off with her child into the unknown land." There is no return from the allegorical universe into the cosy living room, because this would have betrayed both Andersen's pessimism and his faith in the world of the imagination over that of the everyday. Few manuscript changes show more clearly how ruthless he could be on matters of artistic integrity; and indeed that ruthlessness was carried over into life where his art was concerned, for when he tried the tale out, as was his habit, by reading it aloud to friends, he chose Edvard's wife Henriette, who had lost two young children in the previous four years, as his audience, and only when she broke down in tears was he persuaded to stop.

He finished the tales in November, and offered them first to Bentley in London as a Christmas book, to be entitled *A Christmas Greeting to my English Friends*. Bentley paid £30 for them on the condition that they would appear in English before the Danish edition came out, but soon discovered that Andersen's unworldliness made him a publisher's horror. The stories arrived late—on 15 December—and none, apart from "The Old House," was more than a few pages long. "The small amount of pages quite alarms me as to the course I must pursue. It is perfectly hopeless to endeavour to make *any* kind of volume out of it," wrote Bentley; he was forced to add some stories which the translator, Charles Beckwith, had written, and to sell the very slim volume which resulted at three and a half shillings instead of the five shillings on which he had relied. Dedicated to Dickens, the book was, however, enthusiastically received; the ingredients the Victorians loved—sentimentality, tenderness, a miniaturist's scale—dominated the volume, and it maintained Andersen's popularity at the peak it had been when he left England in the summer. Thanking Andersen for the dedication, Dickens wrote: "I am very proud of it, and feel deeply honoured by it, and cannot tell you how much I esteem so generous a mark of recollection from a man of such genius as yours."

As a publishing venture, *A Christmas Greeting* was a shrewd practical move, for by defeating English pirate publishers it assured Andersen an advance from Bentley as well as from Reitzel in Denmark. But there was also an emotional impetus: "I feel a desire, a longing, to transplant to England the first produce of my poetic garden," Andersen wrote in the dedication: the decision to publish first outside Denmark marked a turning point in his sense of himself as above all a European writer. What he did not know was that before the stories were even to appear in Denmark in the spring of 1848, Europe would be so altered by war and revolution that he would find such a role barely tenable. The five stories in *A Christmas Greeting* hold a special place in Andersen's *œuvre* as the last he wrote from within the old world order. After them, international events silenced him for almost half a decade, and when at last he felt able to return to fairy tales, a much changed writer emerged. The trip to England remained imprinted on Andersen's memory for similar reasons: it was his last journey across an innocent, peaceful Europe before the political catastrophe of 1848, which cost him dearly both personally and artistically.

CHAPTER 17

Between the Wars

1848–1851

Who would have thought that while Europe is being reshaped I should come to Dale-carlia and revolutionize the shapes of ginger nuts?

—HANS CHRISTIAN ANDERSEN,
letter to Henriette Wulff, 24 June 1849

"The year 1848 rolled up its curtain," Andersen wrote, "a remarkable year, a volcanic year, when the heavy waves of time washed also over our country with the blood of war." The year opened with the death of Christian VIII in Copenhagen; though politically ineffectual, he had been the artists' king, and writers, painters and musicians mourned him. "*One thing is certain,*" wrote the ballet-master Auguste Bournonville, "he knew how to value art, and for this artists ought to be eternally grateful to him. For us, in his mild eye there lay feeling, encouragement and satisfaction, and we had to admit that—even apart from his majesty—we stood before an excellent man." Andersen told Carl Alexander that "King Christian is so good, so cultured, so intellectual that one must love him"; on the day the King was known to be dying, Andersen was so agitated that he walked out several times from the Hotel du Nord to the Amalienborg Palace and stood in the evening snow looking up at the windows. When the news came at 10:15 p.m. that the King had died, he went home, he recalled, "and wept bitterly and tenderly for him, whom I had loved unspeakably."

More than anyone suspected, the death marked the passing of the old order. Under Christian, the last absolutist monarch, there had been censorship of the press and no real political debate; instead the energy of Danish intellectual life had poured into the arts. Now politics came to the fore, events in Europe made Denmark a player on the international stage, journalism became a potent literary force and the gentle harmonious culture under which Andersen had grown up vanished.

On 22 February 1848 revolution broke out in Paris when King Louis-Philippe outraged the people by forbidding a banquet intended to raise money for reforms. Students, workers and the national guard took to the streets calling for an end to political repression, the King was forced to flee and France was declared a republic. News of the victory and similar popular rebellions spread to Italy, Prussia and Vienna; revolution erupted in Berlin on 18 March and for a brief spell it seemed as if the people had been successful. In Copenhagen there was growing demand for a free constitution, which Christian VIII's successor Frederik VII granted within a year, but Denmark was dragged more fiercely into the European turmoil by an uprising in the German-speaking duchies of Schleswig and Holstein. Encouraged by the revolutions elsewhere, Andersen's aristocratic friends Prince Frederik of Nør and Duke Christian August of Augustenborg led an armed uprising in the duchies on 23 March. Prince Frederik attacked the Danish garrison at Rendsburg and the Duke went to Berlin to drum up Prussian support, which was willingly given. After the battle of Schleswig on 23 April, Prussian troops occupied the southern part of Jutland, and Denmark found herself at war.

Andersen's patriotism and defence of the old regime was never in doubt. "We have war!" he wrote to Jerdan, in a letter published in the *Literary Gazette*,

a war where noble-born and peasant, inspired by a righteous cause, place themselves voluntarily in the ranks of battle; an enthusiasm and patriotism fill and elevate the whole Danish nation . . . In all the houses women are picking lint; in the upper classes of the schools boys are occupied in making cartridges . . . young counts and barons place themselves as subalterns in the ranks of the soldiers . . . At the present time the storms of change sweep through the countries, but the one above all of them, the righteous God, does not change! He is for Denmark—the great Will which is right, and which shall and must be acknowledged; truth is the victorious power of all people and nations.

Yet behind the rhetoric, Andersen was more divided than most Danes. His international reputation had been launched in the German states; here he had become a famous author, his audience was bigger and less carping there than in Denmark and he had many close friends among the Germans, including some of their ruling families. In his 1855 autobiography, written in Danish at a time when relations between the two countries were still poor, he exaggerated his military fervour, but what he said about his bitter self-division was true.

I felt more than ever before how firmly I had grown to the native soil and how Danish was my heart. I could have taken my place in the soldiers' ranks, and gladly given my life an offering to victory and peace, but at the same time the thought came vividly over me how much good I had enjoyed in Germany, the great acknowledgement which my talent there had received, and the many single persons whom I there loved and was grateful to. I suffered infinitely!

In February he had been awarded the Order of the White Falcon from Weimar, and he had told Carl Alexander of his joy: "You have made me infinitely happy, what could I give in return?—you have already had my whole heart and my innermost life for a long time, and will have for ever." He saw Weimar as home of a great poetic tradition, and now he felt culturally and personally torn. In May he wrote to Carl Alexander:

The agitations which are passing through the lands I feel to my finger tips. Denmark, my native country, and Germany, where there are many whom I love, are standing opposite to each other in enmity! Your Royal Highness will be able to feel how all that pains me! I believe so firmly in the nobility of all men, and feel certain that if they only understand each other, everything would blossom in peace. Yet I did not wish to speak of politics, it stands far from me like a strange distant cloud, but now it has spread all over Europe, and its sharp mist penetrates every member, and one breathes nothing but politics. Thanks for your noble friendship! When this greeting reaches your hands, may you feel in it the pulsations of my heart.

Carl Alexander replied, asking, "Have our feelings for each other anything to do with the battle of political opinions? Are we friends because of our political views? Certainly not! The sympathy of souls, our minds, our imagination brought us together and will also, I think, God willing, unite us in the future. O, promise me, my dear friend, that the time and the opinions of the moment will never win an influence over our friendship." Over the next month, Carl Alexander persisted in trying to keep politics out of the friendship; when Andersen, writing about the houses on the island of Als which were destroyed by shells, talked of the parent storks who stayed with their young there as a symbol of peace, for example, Carl Alexander moved the reference into the realm of poetry, praising Andersen's image and replying, "what power lies in the imagination!"

But for Andersen there was no clear-cut division. He found it impossible to reconcile the cultured German courts where he had been so graciously received with the machinery of war which the German states were now unleashing on Denmark. In this sense his reaction had much in common with that of the many foreigners a century later who enjoyed the culture of Weimar Germany in the 1920s and 1930s and were dumbfounded to watch the country descend to Nazi barbarity within years. To Richard Bentley, Andersen wrote in May 1848, "These are heavy, unhappy days, a great injustice is being done to little Denmark . . . the Prussians have advanced into the country itself, have occupied Jutland . . . they oppress in the hardest way this poor country . . . the Prussians wish to plunder and set towns on fire. That such things can happen in our times, that such things can happen in civilized nations, that is to me as if I were dreaming a bad dream." And to Henriette Wulff he wrote that war was a terrible monster, living off blood and burning cities.

None the less, a part of him was stirred by the drama of military action. As a child he had loved the bright uniforms of the Spanish soldiers in Odense during the Napoleonic wars; now forty years later he wrote of the glory of putting on the red jacket, of how "ladies in silk and gauze walked with the red-jacketed soldier." Among the first to enlist were his former intimate friend Henrik Stampe and one of Jonas Collin's grandsons, Viggo Drewsen, of whom Andersen was fond. Watching how "almost every day troops of young men were marching off," Andersen was moved, and composed a patriotic poem, "In Denmark I Was Born," which became a rallying wartime song. Like many men, the vision of crowds of youths alongside one another, the flamboyance of their uniforms and their massed courage in the face of death excited him in spite of his horror of war.

It was in part to be closer to the action, and in part because war made it impossible for him to travel abroad, that he spent May and June 1848 on the island of Funen, mostly staying at the manor house of Glorup. This was as close to the heart of things as he wanted to be; all Funen was heavily occupied by Danish troops waiting to fight, and on the train and ship as Andersen travelled there he met soldiers and heard their stories. When he reached Glorup he found forty men stationed there, telling of their marches through the sands of west Jutland, and the grounds given over to military exercises and "shooting . . . with live cartridges, so you hardly know where you can go." On his first morning he noted in his diary, "heard a good deal about the battle: the men shot in the chest or head had lain as if they were asleep; those shot in the abdomen had almost been unrecognizable because their faces were so convulsively distorted with pain. One had lain literally 'biting the dust' with his teeth; his hands had clutched at the turf . . . The wounded in the camp hospitals stink horribly—the ones shot in the abdomen have faeces draining out of their sides."

Andersen also heard first-hand of the most famous Danish accidental killing in the war. One of the volunteers at Glorup had been standing next to Johan Thomas Lundbye, the artist whose picture had inspired Andersen to write "The Little Matchgirl." Thirty-year-old Lundbye was leaning dejectedly on his rifle, when "some farmers were passing by close to where the other rifles were propped up in front of him and happened to knock them over. They heard the shot and saw Lundbye fall to the ground, shot from below upward through the chin, his mouth torn and a piece of flesh with beard on it shot away. He emitted a few weak sighs, was wrapped in the Danish flag and buried."

But Andersen was enjoying himself. "I feel so wonderfully free from the pressures of Copenhagen, feel myself to be a better person and the people around me, as well, feel free to express a greater degree of enthusiasm," he noted in his diary. On 25 May a reinforcement of Swedish troops landed in Nyborg, Funen's major port, and a large contingent was stationed at Glorup. "Their stay here is among the most beautiful and bright images of this summer," Andersen wrote in a newspaper article. The old stewardess of the manor, Miss Ipsen, threw herself into the quartering of the Swedes with patriotic fervour. "'A great bed must be made for them in the barn!' was said. 'To let them lie in the barn upon straw!' said she. 'No, they shall have beds! They are coming to help us and they shall certainly have a bed!' and she had wood procured and bedsteads made for ten or twelve rooms. Feather-beds were also obtained; coarse but white sheets were shining in her 'caserne' as she called it."

For Andersen, to be in the thick of this activity was a romantic dream. He could luxuriate in aristocratic life, feed on asparagus and the first strawberries of the season, work on a new novel, *De to Baronesser* (*The Two Baronesses*), yet at the same time feel in tune with the war effort. "While they were doing drills along the road, I made great progress on my novel . . . Today is a great day for ushering a novel into the world!" he wrote in his diary in May. In these surroundings, he exulted in the righteousness of the Danish cause and to his German friends wrote patriotic letters justifying every aspect of national behaviour. "The prison-ships lie in the shelter of the harbour, looking on to the Sound," he told his old friends the Eisendeckers in Oldenburg, for example. "The steamers pass close by every day, and then there is life and change. I could choose no more beautiful spot for myself.

The prisoners have several hours every day in which they can walk by the sea or bathe." He felt so happy at Glorup that he returned for another two months, in August and September 1848; these were still early days in the war, and at this point Andersen's excitement often outstripped his sense of grief.

Back in Copenhagen for the autumn, he was distracted from war by the publication of his new novel. *The Two Baronesses* appeared first in England, where publication was Andersen's way of reasserting his links with the international community at a time when he could not trust German audiences, and two months later in Denmark. It is set patriotically in three areas of Denmark—Funen, the Frisian islands, where he had spent time with the Danish royal family earlier in the 1840s, and Copenhagen. The two heroines are an eccentric old baroness—based on his former wealthy patron, Mrs. Bügel, the sender of lavish presents in the 1830s—who rises from a peasant background to marry the son of an oppressive and haughty overlord, and a poor orphan girl who marries her grandson. The message is egalitarian— "we are all of one piece—all made from the same clod of earth; one came in a newspaper wrapping, another in gold paper, but the clod should not be proud of that. There is nobility in every class; but it lies in the mind and not in the blood"—though *The Two Baronesses* is a romance rather than a political novel. The critics liked it but it sold poorly; Bentley, who paid Andersen £200 for it, made a loss. Andersen was by now associated in the mind of his public both at home and abroad with fairy tales, and could not win a comparable audience for his novels.

Andersen was not bothered by the money; he had his stipend and various other projects, and he felt settled enough that autumn to move out of the Hotel du Nord where he had lodged between his foreign journeys for a decade. Though an armistice was signed on 1 September, it was clearly not to be trusted, and Andersen could see that with war across Europe, he would travel less, and he wanted a permanent base. On 1 October he took the furnished rooms which were to be his home for the the the next sixteen years—the longest time he lived anywhere. His new address was 67, Nyhavn; this was the busy quayside street where he had lived between 1834 and 1838, and he was still attracted to its colourful houses and the ever-clinking masts of the great ships moored in the harbour. This time he chose a tall, narrow white house on the east side at the bottom of the street, almost on the seafront, with a spectacular view on to the Sound, across the port and towards Christianshavn and the tall spiralled spire of Our Saviour's Church.

He rented three rooms on the second floor from a skipper, Captain Johann

Anholm, whose wife took lodgers to supplement their income; Andersen paid eighteen rixdollars a month. He still had no furniture and few belongings of his own. The Anholm furnishings were primitive—the nicest piece was a mahogany sideboard with two low side cupboards, on one of which Andersen stood a bust of himself and on the other one of Jenny Lind. Mrs. Anholm was attentive with little details that mattered to Andersen, such as putting fresh flowers in the rooms, but he was frequently disturbed by the six Anholm children clattering up and down the stairs past his rooms, and terrified of the family's large shaggy dog. One of the daughters told how early in Andersen's sojourn, the dog began to bark furiously when Andersen appeared; startled and alarmed, Andersen rushed upstairs again and, when he had reached the safety of his own quarters, stood at the door and shouted "Did he bite me? Did he bite me?" Nevertheless, he felt comfortable in the house, and with his top hat and a manuscript under his arm, he became one of the famous sights of Nyhavn over the next twenty years.

When fighting erupted again in the spring of 1849 in what was to become the Three Year War between Denmark and Prussia, the first flush of patriotic fervour was gone and the prevailing mood shifted from excitement to resignation. For Andersen the personal conflict this time was worse. Among the smaller German states which looked to Prussia in matters of foreign policy was Weimar, and Carl Alexander was leading the contingent of Weimar volunteers against the Danes in Schleswig-Holstein. Andersen felt he had to break off all contact with him. The cost of war in human terms was clear by now, too, and Andersen was overwhelmed by depression. "My mind was sick, I suffered in soul and body," he wrote. To Bentley he said in May that "much blood is flowing, men are being maimed, towns burned. I live in ceaseless tension, it is not possible to tear one's thoughts away from the shocking events; I have no peace to settle down to work." A year earlier, he had rushed closer to the scene of action; now he wanted only to distance himself from it, and on 17 May he set off on a three-month summer trip to Sweden. "No sound of roaring cannon was heard in that happy, politically sound Sweden," he wrote to Dickens.

Two familiar tonics, travel and invitations from royalty, revived him. King Oscar of Sweden decorated him with the Order of the North Star; at the Stockholm court he read "The Ugly Duckling," "The Collar" and "The Story of a Mother" to the King and Queen; "on my retiring the Queen stretched out her hand to me, which I pressed to my lips," he boasted in his autobiography, and "a feeling of congeniality, if I may dare use the word, drew me especially to the young amiable Prince Gustavus," with whom he discussed Weimar, music and poetry. By August there was again talk of peace. Andersen wrote joyfully from Trollhättan to Carl Alexander:

> Oh you scarcely know how highly I rate you, how firmly you have grown into my heart! I have only rightly understood that this summer . . . I heard that a contingent of Weimar troops had marched to the north, and finally I read that your Royal Highness had yourself gone to the seat of war. I understood the circumstances, and sorrowed deeply on account of them, but could write no more. But now the proclamations of peace are ringing in my ears I may follow the wishes of my heart and send this letter to my friend.

Meanwhile, wild, rural Sweden in midsummer was a magical place. In the mid nineteenth century there were still no hotels—visitors traditionally put up at the parsonage in each village—and neither train nor stagecoach; one had to travel by private carriage, and at a time when tourists had already become a feature of most European resorts, there was here by contrast a feeling of true remoteness and outback adventure. "The mountain streams of the North have foamed on during thousands of years in unacknowledged beauty. The great high road of the world does not lead this way," Andersen wrote of the Dal valley landscape. "Clear as the waves of the sea, the mighty Dal Elf rolls on in endless windings through silent forests and changing plains, now spreading out in its broad bed, now hemmed in, sometimes reflecting the nodding trees and the red blockhouses of the lonely towns, at others falling in cascades over great boulders of rock . . . We linger in the dark woodland waste, where the Elf seems to be surrounded by all the solemnity of nature." The only famous traveller known to have preceded Andersen here was Schubert. Andersen liked discovering an unknown region; here his spirits soared and he began to feel he could leave the world of war behind.

Out of this trip came *Pictures of Sweden*, a collection of landscape paintings, legends and fantasies, begun at a time when he did not feel psychologically free enough to write fairy tales, but poured out his longings in the literary form that came closest to them. Like the fairy tales, *Pictures of Sweden* shows that Andersen's natural gift was as a miniaturist; the broad canvas of a novel was too large for him, his skills were lost in it. In this book, too, he shifted from western Europe, which had been his stage since the 1830s, back to Scandinavia. His account is full of the romance of the northern lights, of his whimsical motifs of travel and restlessness—it opens with the chatter of a swallow and a stork—and of domestic details about provincial Sweden. It is a conscious turning away from the international arena to everyday cosiness and the inner landscape of the mind played upon by the majesty of the natural world. It celebrates the timelessness and reassuring continuity of small pleasures; these, and Andersen's mood in the late 1840s and early 1850s, are encapsulated in his memory of making paper cut-outs in the small town of Dalecarlia:

> As I sat in my room, the hostess's little granddaughter came in; a nice little child, who was delighted to see my night bag, my Scottish travelling rug and the red morocco in my trunk. I quickly cut out for her from a sheet of paper a Turkish mosque with minarets and open windows, and she ran off delighted. A little later I heard a lot of talking in the yard outside. I had a feeling it was about my paper-cut; stepping quietly on to the wooden balcony, I saw Grandmother down in the yard holding my paper-cut up and beaming. A crowd of Dalecarlians stood around, all in an ecstasy about my work; while the child . . . was crying and holding her hands up for her lawful property which she was not allowed to keep because it was so nice . . . A moment later there was a knock at the door. It was Grandmother; she had brought a whole plateful of ginger biscuits. "I bake the best ginger biscuits in Dalecarlia," she said, "but they have the old shape from my Grandmother's time. You cut out so well; wouldn't you come and cut some new shapes for us?" And I sat there the whole of Midsummer Eve cutting shapes for ginger biscuits: nutcrackers with riding boots; windmills that were both man and mill, but in slippers and with a door in the stomach; and dancing girls pointing one leg at the Pleiades. Grandmother got them, but kept turning the dancers up and down; the legs were too high for her—she thought they were one-legged and wooden-armed. "They're supposed to be new shapes," she said, "but they are difficult." I hope that I live in Dalecarlia in new shapes of ginger biscuits.

"Who would have thought," Andersen asked, "that while Europe is being reshaped I should come to Dalecarlia and revolutionize the shapes of ginger nuts?"

Andersen believed that *Pictures of Sweden*, published in 1851, was among his best books: "it displays better than any other of my writings those points most characteristic in me: pictures of nature, the wonderful, the humorous, and lyric." To Carl Alexander he said that the book "will show you how life and the world are now reflected in me." The final chapter, called "Poetry's California," summed up much of his wartime musings on meaning in life and art. "Indeed, in knowledge and science lie Poetry's California!" he wrote. "The sunlight of science must penetrate the *Digter*, he must perceive truth and harmony in the minute as well as in the immensely great with a clear eye: it must purify and enrich his understanding and imagination, show him new forms, which will make his words even more alive." Inspired by Hans Christian Ørsted's last book, *The Spirit of Nature* (1850), he had reflected long on the role of science and the choice between scientific enquiry and blind faith. He would rather, he told Ørsted, see God with his eyes open than blindfold, and the pleasures of a mind enriched outweighed the contentment of an unquestioning faith.

At a time when he felt able to write little, Ørsted's book engaged his intellectual energy. In December 1850 he told Carl Alexander:

> I am forty-five years old, but I often feel in many ways as if I were twenty. I believe that, as a poet, I have several stages to go through, and that I have reached one of those by means of Ørsted's work. This book has awakened in me a longing for science, and I have latterly read a good deal in this direction which has naturally disturbed my productiveness—and also my correspondence with friends. Ørsted has always been good to me. He has been my faithful friend for many years; but now he is even more to me—he has understood my sincere aspiration.

During the Three Year War, Andersen had a sense of biding time creatively; he was in no rush, and he was so highly strung that a leisurely unpressured life was essential for his work. "My life has been luxuriant and not arduous," he told Carl Alexander; apart from the early years, this was true. He knew he had more to say and new paths to take as a writer of fairy tales; he concluded to Carl Alexander that he could not leave literature for philosophy; "for me the human heart is the fairy-lamp of poetry, which I firmly grasp, and I stand like Aladdin with this lamp glowing in the cavern of science."

And yet, as war dragged on through 1850, he sometimes found it impossible to keep faith. "Melancholy; my progress as a writer is a thing of the past," he said in his diary; to Mathilde Ørsted he wrote, "The feeling that I haven't written anything really clever—and my certainty that I am unable to do so—torments me horribly!" He missed his regular summer journeys south into Europe. He was often crabby and ill-humoured; he accepted invitations and then on a whim failed to turn up, sending no excuse or apology; he was a poor correspondent; then he berated himself for his impoliteness, for by instinct he was gracious and peaceable. Towards the end of the war he tells in his diary how the journalist Goldschmidt chided him in the street for such behaviour, to which he replied:

> I didn't think my not coming was anything to take offence at—I do it so often to my friends! You'll have to take me as I am! But if I have been impolite, then I ask your forgiveness and assure you that it grieves me terribly much; I didn't give it a thought, and you've certainly distressed me greatly, so that if I've offended you, you have now wounded me, and so let the one balance the other out!

Andersen occupied himself with plans for ballets and operas, and wrote many dramas for the new Casino Theatre, the first private playhouse in Copenhagen—a sign of the end of royal censorship, under which the Royal Theatre had been the only one in the capital. His relationship with the Casino was smooth and easygoing from the start, and his successes there healed the wounds dealt out over the decades by the autocratic managers of the Royal Theatre. Andersen's comedy *More Than Pearls and Gold* was an early triumph for the new theatre in 1849—it played 162 times in the next forty years; other successes were the fairy plays *Ole Lukøie* (1850), about a chimney sweep offered three wishes, who gets money but no contentment, and *Hyldemoer* (1851). Danish critics interpreted *Ole Lukøie* approvingly as a vote for the *ancien régime*, and to emphasize his sympathy towards royal families, Andersen quoted one of them in a letter to Weimar: "that riches are not synonymous with happiness, but that real happiness consists of a contented, cheerful spirit and a healthy mind, is the great lesson which the poet has dressed here in a rich poetical garment, a lesson which could hardly find application at a more fitting time than the present, when false notions of a perfect equality in worldly circumstances for all, govern the masses."

In fact, the war years had made it clear to Andersen that he was not a political writer; his sympathies were not clear-cut, for although his impoverished childhood and sense of social exclusion gave him the sympathy for the underdog that is a feature of his tales and novels, this was also the class from which he was desperate to escape. Moreover, his mother's love of kings had given him so powerful a belief in the unalterable hierarchy of the social system that he came close to accepting some sort of divine right of monarchs. He would never be a true friend of democracy; like many writers, he was a mix of the artistically radical and the socially conservative, and his work deliberately avoided political categories. *Ole Lukøie* is a dream play which has much in common with the fairy tale of the same name that he wrote in 1841, and his fairy plays from the 1850s represented further attempts to approach the world of fantasy at a time when he had no inspiration to write new fairy tales.

But Andersen's literary monument from the war years was neither his plays nor his travel book but a new collected edition of fairy tales in five volumes, published between August and December 1849, with 125 drawings by Vilhelm Pedersen, a young artist whom Andersen favoured above all others, and who is now recognized as the best of his illustrators—in Denmark he is felt to be as irreplaceable and as close to the text as Tenniel is to Lewis Carroll's *Alice* books or as E. H. Shepherd is to *The Wind in the Willows* and *Winnie the Pooh*. Pedersen's value is that he barely seems to interpret: unfalteringly, he catches Andersen's lightness of touch, his gentleness and humour, his mix of rigour and sentiment, the precision of his detail and his ability to transport the reader at a word to another world. As with Shepherd, there was something nostalgic about his work even when it was new. Pedersen is an artist of the war years, wistfully looking back to a more comfortable era, which he captured just as it was waning.

For Andersen, a sense of change, of the end of old securities, was powerful in 1850–1851. He spent much of the period at Glorup, but the Danish patriotism that had thrilled him in 1848 was now an irritant. "It's appalling to hear the vacuity of the aristocratic world—to talk confidently and cavalierly about everything! Ignorance! Stupidity!" he wrote in his diary in June 1850. " 'As long as you're truly Danish, Andersen!' says Miss Ipsen. 'Isn't that a handkerchief from Schleswig-Holstein that you have there!' says Countess Sophie Scheel . . . 'You're certainly not writing to the Duke of Weimar, are you?'—It goes on and on like that! Never have I felt myself to be more Danish than during this war." His diary is full of complaints of real and imagined illnesses; at Glorup he becomes effete and nervous: "toothache and an abscess. Diarrhoea. I took a dose of Chinese rhubarb; stayed in my room all day; ate a little capon and some strawberries . . . There was a hideous vagabond standing by the spring; I had the feeling he might know who I was and could say something embarrassing to me—as if I were a pariah mixing with a higher caste." He felt mournful now, seeing the soldiers depart: "I was very sad when they turned on to the road and disappeared behind the hedges. Who knows, I thought, if most of them aren't going to their death; we'll never meet again."

In July 1850 there was an announcement of peace. "Peace! Peace with Germany! so it rings through the country," Andersen told Carl Alexander. He was wandering in the deer park at Glorup and was fetched in by a game-keeper; "he said they had been looking for me to tell me something joyful, namely the authentic news of peace. I hurried to the castle and saw the printed document. Oh my noble friend, if only I could have embraced you that moment! I had to cry for joy and go back into the forest, where I sang German and Danish songs from an overflowing heart." Carl Alexander, more wary and politically sophisticated, once again emphasized the personal in his reply, writing of the peace, "may it bring you joy, may it at last also lead to general peace, which we long for so greatly, yet which, I fear, is still so far off! But I will not disturb your joy with this, and I will especially rejoice with you if your heart draws you again to Germany and Weimar."

Shortly afterwards hostilities resumed and the Danes had a decisive victory at Isted, which brought about the end of the war with Prussia and retained Schleswig-Holstein for Denmark; nationalists in Schleswig-Holstein fought on into 1851, but without Prussian support their cause was hopeless. Isted, however, brought heavy losses to both sides, among them Colonel Frederik Læssøe, the son of Andersen's friend Signe Læssøe, whom Andersen had known since he was a boy. "For the last eight days I have done as good as nothing," Andersen wrote to Ørsted a week after the news. "I am so enthralled. I forget the victory of our brave soldiers when I think of all those young men who have sacrificed their lives; I knew several of those who have fallen. Læssøe, you know, was a friend of mine; I knew him since he was a young cadet, and always felt something would become of him."

His gloom continued through the winter of 1850–1851. In February 1851 his collection of patriotic poems was published in time for the celebrations in Copenhagen in honour of the returning victorious troops, but soon the festivities were blacked out for Andersen by the deaths within a week of one another in March of two of his oldest friends: Hans Christian Ørsted and Emma Hartmann, the wife of his composer friend.

Emma Hartmann, warm and accepting, witty and lively, had always lifted Andersen's spirits; she had teased him gently and made him welcome in her large family circle. The sense of the end of an era which coincided with her death was made worse when a couple of days later her youngest daughter, six-year-old Maria, sickened and died, as if life without her mother was unsustainable. "In the mother's hour of death the little head drooped; it was as if the mother had prayed our Lord: 'Give me one of the children, the smallest one, the one who cannot be without me!' and God had listened to her prayer. The same evening that the mother's coffin was carried to the church, the little girl died, and a few days later was buried in a grave close by her mother." Andersen had based the singing, laughing child in "The Old House," representative of life versus the funereal old building across the road, on Maria, and although the deaths of children were common at the time, he was especially moved by this one.

Four days later, Ørsted, one of his most sympathetic friends and the first lone voice, in the 1830s, to recognize the significance of the fairy tales, died. Andersen, who had run from one sickbed to another hoping against hope for recovery, was bereft. Almost exactly a year earlier, Oehlenschläger had died, and two years before that Andersen's patron King Christian. The fixed points of his life in Copenhagen were vanishing, and at the same time the Europe from which he had gained psychological sustenance was changing beyond recognition.

CHAPTER 18

Weimar Revisited

1851–1856

Tears came into my eyes, I thought that I, the poor shoemaker and washerwoman's son, was being kissed by the Czar of Russia's grandson.

—HANS CHRISTIAN ANDERSEN, diary, 23 June 1856

With the end of the war, Andersen's thoughts turned to Germany, but the spirit of peace was a long way off. His first wish was to see Weimar again, and tentatively in 1851 he wrote to Carl Alexander's diplomat, Beaulieu, to ask if he had anything to fear from the Weimar proletariat if he now made a visit. Beaulieu, who had always been affectionate and welcoming, sent back a hostile, arrogant letter which stunned Andersen. He showed it to Edvard Collin, who advised him "guard yourself from ever going to Weimar" and drafted a cool, well-argued response to Beaulieu, adding, with the fair-mindedness of a civil servant, that if Andersen sent it, "it could only be correct by your pointing out to him my competency to give such an opinion, partly on account of my relation towards yourself, which justifies me in casting back the scorn intended for you, and partly because the writer of it is an official of the *ancien régime*, and no friend of Democracy—least of all 'a product of Democracy.'" It was typical of Edvard to reveal his protectiveness of Andersen so undemonstratively, *en passant*, in a subordinate clause. Andersen, more conciliatory by nature, did not use Edvard's letter, but wrote back generously and forgivingly:

> I truly confess there was something in your letter which surprised and grieved me—words which I did not think you could have written to me. I possess, however, so many dear and pleasant remembrances of your feeling towards me, of your own charming and good-hearted personality, that I soon saw your letter was over-shadowed by the mood you were in when you wrote it.

As far as concerns the cultivated classes, I had no thought or fear of coming
into collision with any of them: we have so many other interests in common
which are dear to us, so much that is good and beautiful as subjects of conversation to mutually entertain us, that I should certainly have flown to my old
friends. Time will clear up much . . . Therefore, no more of politics, only of the
world, of the heart and the intellect.

But he did not visit Weimar that year.

He set off instead in May 1851 for Paris via a leisurely trip through other
parts of Germany and Prague, accompanied by Jonas Collin's grandson
Viggo Drewsen. But it was a depressing journey; through Schleswig-
Holstein every landscape told a story of war—there were burnt-out buildings, bare earth where the rain of cannon balls had ploughed the soil, lines
of graves which made Andersen call a town such as Flensburg a garden of
death. Danish soldiers were everywhere, and Rendsburg, seat of the insurrection, was seething with anti-Danish feeling. "It was as if I drove through
a pit of death," Andersen wrote.

> Ugly memories came in my thoughts; the town had always seemed to me
> mouldy and oppressive, and now it was a smarting, unpleasant feeling for a
> Dane to come here. On the railroad I was seated by the side of an old gentle-
> man, who, taking me for an Austrian, praised them, calling them my country-
> men, and then spoke ill of the Danes. I told him I was a Dane, and our
> conversation stopped; I fancied I saw evil looks round about, and only when all
> Holstein, and Hamburg too, were lying behind me did I breathe freely.

The journey barely improved, however, after they left Germany. "I felt
depressed and full of angst, I was close to feeling pain," Andersen wrote in
his diary in Prague. He suffered persistent toothache, and Viggo was an irritating and graceless companion—the first of many of Jonas Collin's grandsons to accompany Andersen on his foreign travels in the 1850s and 1860s,
each as troublesome and ungrateful as the one before. But Andersen liked to
see Europe as for the first time through the eyes of young men, and, in the
financial security of middle and old age, it was one of his ways of repaying
the Collin family, for the Collin grandsons could not otherwise have
afforded the expenses of foreign travel. The unhappy holiday cost him 200
rixdollars, paid for by the success of the German translation of *Pictures of
Sweden*.

When he returned home in September, he was greeted with a new award—he was made an honorary professor—and he settled down to a mild Danish winter on Nyhavn and wrote a new volume of fairy tales. The first in four years, it appeared in spring 1852, followed by another instalment in November. For the first time the collections are called *Historier* (*Stories*) rather than *Eventyr* (*Tales*), and Andersen now gave up the appearance of writing for children. He abandoned the classical forms and fabular quality which make his early work, with its resonance of myth and archetype, so enduringly popular among all ages and nations, and he attempted instead short stories for adults which mostly contain no magic or supernatural ingredients. It took him a decade to evolve in this genre a new voice which was convincing and powerful; the stories of 1852 were early attempts.

There is no evidence as to why Andersen made so fundamental a change around this time. His tales since "The Shadow" in 1847 had been leaning more and more to an adult audience. Maybe he felt that the changing European order called for a different form, and that the old certainties implied by the classical model were no longer relevant. Maybe he believed he had achieved as much as he could in tales such as "The Ugly Duckling" and "The Snow Queen." Always aesthetically open-minded, innovative and easily bored, in 1852 he wanted new challenges and experiments, and this mood was embodied in the tale "Thousands of Years From Now," an expression of his excitement about science and a prophetic vision, down to accurate details about air travel and the Channel Tunnel, of our own times.

It is not a story but a two-page picture of how "flying on wings of steam through the air and over the ocean" the young inhabitants of America will visit old Europe, "our ancient monuments and our crumbling ruins":

"To Europe!" cry the young people of America. "To the land of our fathers, the splendid land of memory and romance, Europe!"

The airship comes. It is packed with travellers, for the speed is faster than by sea . . . Europe is already in sight; it is the coast of Ireland, but the passengers are still asleep as they are not to be called until they were over England. Here they set foot on the soil of Europe in the land of Shakespeare, as the learned call it: the land of Parliament, the land of machinery, others say . . .

Off they speed under the Channel Tunnel to France, the land of Charlemagne and Napoleon. Molière's name is mentioned; the learned talk of a Classical and Romantic school . . .

The air-steamer flies on . . . through the air and over the sea to Italy . . . to Greece, in order to spend a night at the rich hotel on the top of Mount

Olympus, to say they have been there . . . Remains of mighty cities by the swift-flowing Danube are crossed in flight . . . here and there the aerial caravan alights and once again takes off . . . One day's stop for Germany and one day for Scandinavia . . .

"There's a lot to see in Europe," said the young American, "and we saw it in a week! And it's possible to do it, as the great traveller" (mentioning a contemporary name) "has shown in his celebrated work, *Europe Seen in Eight Days.*"

Written only fifteen years after the first railway was built, this predates *Round the World in Eighty Days* by twenty years, and may have inspired Jules Verne. It is the work of Andersen the reflective, middle-aged man, looking on from the sidelines at the busy world, yet infused with optimism about the scientific developments of the future.

By contrast, many of the other tales from 1852 are sentimental autobiographical sketches. "She Was No Good" is a romantic but indignant picture of Andersen's mother as a hard-working washerwoman with a weakness for gin, whom the bourgeois world paints as a good-for-nothing alcoholic. She dies just before she can be told that she has been left a fortune in reward for her selflessness in giving up a rich lover years ago; her son stands at her grave, asking, "Is it true about her being no good?"

"Under the Willow Tree," based on Andersen's failed courtship of Jenny Lind, is imbued with self-pity and regret. Childhood sweethearts Knud and Joanna (Jenny's real name), the children of poor people, grow up in idyllic countryside. Their tragedy is anticipated in a story they are told by a gingerbread dealer about gingerbread figures of a boy who has a bitter almond on his left side—his heart—and a girl who is "honey-cake all over." They fall in love; she is content, but "his thoughts were far more extravagant, as is always the case with a man. He dreamed he was a real street boy, that he had four pennies of his own, and that he purchased the maiden and ate her up." She cracks in two for love of him, and the dealer ends the story by giving both figures to the children. Soon afterwards they part; Knud is apprenticed to a cobbler, Joanna goes to Copenhagen where she looks to "a brilliant future on the strength of her fine voice." When Knud visits, she sends him a ticket to watch her at the theatre; he cannot believe how talented she is, and he proposes, but she replies, "Knud, do not make yourself and me unhappy. I shall always be a good sister to you, one in whom you may trust, but I shall never be anything more."

She goes on, like Jenny, to international success; he travels across Europe as a journeyman-cobbler, restless and discontent and, "saying farewell to the lands of the North," crosses to Italy: his travels recall Andersen's as a young man. Three years later he sees Joanna at the opera, "dressed in silk and gold and with a crown on her head: she sang as he thought none but angels could sing"; she does not recognize Knud, but "a man with a star glittering on his breast gave her his arm—and it was whispered about that the two were engaged." Knud packs his knapsack to go back to the willow tree under which they had once played; "a whole life is sometimes lived through in a single hour," Andersen writes, "no one would have believed in the sorrow of his heart, the deepest a human heart can feel." On his way home, Knud sleeps under a willow tree and dreams that both he and Joanna and the gingerbread couple are getting married; "towards morning there was a great fall of snow. The wind drifted the snow over him, but he slept on. The villagers came forth to go to church, and by the roadside sat a journeyman. He was dead—frozen to death under the willow tree!"

This morbid story about a man locked into a vision of his own childhood speaks of Andersen's sense of himself in the 1850s. Knud is the first of several bleak self-portraits of the writer as ineffectual and passive which continued through the 1850s and 1860s and culminated in his final story, "Old Joanna's Tale," in 1872. "Under the Willow Tree" was written a few months after Jenny Lind, aged thirty-one, had married a German pianist called Otto Goldschmidt, in a move which surprised all who knew her. Andersen at this time had no romantic entanglements, and saw himself as emotionally freezing to death and creatively in torpor.

By abandoning the elements of fantasy which had been central to his earlier tales, however, Andersen lost the vital ingredient of transformation by which he turned his own psychological dilemmas into myths and symbols which convince at a deep and universal level. He needed to work out a way of writing short stories in which the rigours of form and his excitement at fashioning a new style could overcome his instinct for self-pity and self-dramatization. That was what he was struggling towards as he travelled and sought inspiration over the next decade.

"For five years I had not seen Weimar, not for five sad, troubled years, the billows of which still course through my heart," Andersen wrote in 1852. In May he risked a visit. The night before his reunion with Carl Alexander he was plagued by "horrible dreams"; then "at 11:30 I went to see the Hereditary

Grand Duke; he was at his mother's. I was taken to his room, where there was a fire in the stove. I felt nervous. He arrived, embraced and kissed me fondly. We talked about the war years, and I explained the good cause of the Danes . . . In the evening, read from *Pictures of Sweden* and translated from *Stories*. Don't feel quite at home."

As he had feared, he had trouble from Beaulieu ("not a pleasant man . . . I don't feel comfortable with him"—an extreme expression of dislike in Andersen's mild-mannered vocabulary) and from the hangers-on at court such as the governess ("One of the first things she said was: 'How have you treated those poor Holsteiners!' and I got furious at her."). Throughout the visit, Andersen was on edge and haunted by thoughts of the war; one evening, for example, he noted in his diary, "Lieutenant Beaulieu-Marconnay was seriously disabled—he had his head split open in the war with Denmark. Here at home today he is nearly collapsed in a faint; he had complained about pain. He is lying in the room outside of mine; I'm completely shut in by him, and the thought occurred to me that he might go berserk in the night and come to murder me. I can't lock my door . . ."

But the royal family merely murmured that "difficult days have intervened since we last met" and were all cordiality and charm. He was introduced to the Empress of Russia, who was visiting; he was shown round the newly decorated castle, with its rooms dedicated to Goethe, Schiller, Herder and Wieland, and welcomed by many old friends. Wandering through the palace gardens to Goethe's summerhouse, he "strolled along the river and thought about the great men who have passed away." New Weimar residents since his last visit were Franz Liszt, who was making the town the European capital of the musical avant-garde, and his lover the Princess Carolyne zu Sayn-Wittgenstein. She had left her husband to live with him, and the couple were accepted in Weimar society. Liszt "won't do Mozart—who he says is old-hat—but Wagner and other sensation-mongers," Andersen wrote in his diary.

The Grand Duchess Maria Pavlovna had given Liszt the Villa Altenburg, the large mansion on the hill above the town, to use as a centre for music-making. "There was nowhere in Europe like the Altenburg," writes David Cairns of Weimar at this time, in his biography of Berlioz.*

The house was a world, with its spacious salons, one of them containing the original death-mask of Beethoven, its endless bedrooms, many occupied rent-

*Liszt organized a "Berlioz Week" in Weimar in 1852.

free by resident pupils, its fabulous collection of keyboards, including Beethoven's Broadwood piano and a spinet that had belonged to Mozart, its exuberant music-making, its sense of being the headquarters and nerve-centre of a campaign to change the face of music, its ease and conviviality, and its late-night parties at which the cigar-smoking Princess Carolyne presided and radical ideas in politics and art were the norm.

This was a fresh and stimulating environment for Andersen, who had been shut off from developments in European art during the war years. To be again connected to what was new and contemporary abroad was important for him at a time when he was trying to fashion a modern idiom for fairy tales. He was soon invited to dinner, where he read "The Nightingale"—Liszt's favourite tale—and "The Ugly Duckling." Princess Carolyne accompanied him to the table, Andersen recalled, and "received me especially vivaciously . . . She applauded and was very attentive at each humorous touch. When we had coffee, she smoked a cigar and asked me if I didn't find it strange to see a lady doing that sort of thing . . . They (Liszt and the princess) asked me to think of their house as my home; wanted me to dine there tomorrow."

Andersen could not sympathize with Liszt's admiration for Wagner; of *Tannhäuser*, which played to a full house at Weimar's theatre, he wrote: "The text, good; the performance on the whole better than expected. The music competent with regard to idea but lacking in melody. What Carl Maria von Weber or Mozart couldn't have done with it!" He found Liszt's music difficult too—writing to Henriette Wulff a few years later, he said, "I read [your letter] over again in the theatre, as otherwise the music would have killed me. Everything was Liszt. I could not follow this wildness—this, as I think, thoughtless composition. They played with the cymbals, and I thought a plate had dropped. But the audience was in raptures, and it rained wreaths! It is a strange world." Liszt himself, on the other hand, was an inspiration: "He and the princess seem to me like fiery spirits blazing, burning—they can instantly warm you up, but if you draw close you get burned. It's like looking at a picture portrait to see those fiery beings and know their story."

After Weimar, Andersen moved south to Bavaria, where he enjoyed the company of young King Max. The King loved "The Little Mermaid" and "The Garden of Paradise," invited Andersen to his hunting castle at Starnberg, on the edge of a vast lake which lies in the shadow of the Alps, and took him sailing. Max's court was another royal establishment just after

Andersen's heart, florid, effete, hungry for artistic visitors—the fairy-tale castle of Neuschwanstein and other fantasy buildings and gardens were a product of this court in the mid to late nineteenth century. Andersen wrote to Carl Alexander about how, crossing the lake to "a little flower island," the King picked him some lilac blossom. This, he said, "will be placed in my album beside the lime-tree branch which you gave me once long years ago on my first visit to Ettersburg."

He went on to Switzerland—"a whole poem written by the dear God Himself; this, perhaps, is the reason why the country has produced no poet"—and Milan, where, he wrote, "some days before my arrival the diligence was attacked by twelve banditti, six of whom were arrested and hanged on the day I arrived." He paid a final royal summer visit to the castle at Sorgenfri, the guest of the Danish Dowager Queen Caroline Amalia, then returned home to Copenhagen for a quiet autumn and winter, where he worked on a play, *The Elder-Mother*, which did well at the Casino Theatre and won praise even from Heiberg.

But to Beaulieu, Andersen wrote that "with the fall of the leaves in the autumn my spirits always fall. It seems to me then, as if all the dear ones would also fall away, and as if the most recent meeting would also be the last one," and this was prophetic. The publisher Carl Reitzel died in spring 1853, for Andersen another sign of the passing of the old order. Reitzel had run the business on stern pre-1848 terms: he and his staff worked seven days a week, never took holidays, and his employees ate their meals with the Reitzel family. Andersen got on well with Reitzel's sons, under whom the business became more relaxed; they had a more luxurious lifestyle, travelled abroad and spent their summers in the countryside.

Soon after Reitzel's death, Andersen was mourning Weimar's Carl Friedrich, who died aged seventy; Carl Alexander was now the Grand Duke. That spring, too, cholera broke out in Copenhagen, killing almost five thousand people in under three months; among Andersen's friends, its victims included the poet and pastor Casper Johannes Boye, Oline Thyberg (Edvard's mother-in-law) and another relation of the Collin family. "The angel of death went from house to house; now on the last evening he stopped at my home of homes," Andersen wrote. People fled Copenhagen. Andersen, already at Glorup to join the silver wedding party for Count Moltke-Hvitfeldt, lay weeping in his room listening to the dancing and fireworks at the manor house, to which all the peasants from the estate had been invited: "It could not be endured. New mourning messages came daily." He was advised not to return to Copenhagen, and spent the summer instead at Silkeborg in Jutland with the Drewsen family.

By the autumn of 1853, the cholera was over; "all are well and healthy, the theatres are filled, social life begins, and everything again has the same familiar appearance," Andersen wrote. He settled back into his comfortable winter routine, spending Christmas Eve with Jonas Collin and Christmas Day with Hartmann, his equilibrium only briefly disturbed by two women. One was Clara Heinke, a 28-year-old German painter from Breslau, who in the autumn of 1853 began to pursue Andersen by letter. The second was Mathilde Fibiger, a young Danish author whose semi-pornographic novel about incest, *Minona*, deeply affected him; he wrote to Ingemann how shocked he was that a young woman could write this way, and yet how the book had excited him.

From 1853 to 1855, Andersen was working on a prestigious new collected edition of his works, which was issued in Denmark in twenty-two volumes; the first two appeared in November 1853. He received a generous 1,485 rixdollars for it from Reitzel's sons, and a further 600 rixdollars for a second edition of his tales illustrated by Pedersen. This gave him the means to travel extensively in 1854 and 1855, and once again it was Germany that attracted him.

He set off in May 1854 with another Collin grandson, Einar Drewsen, Ingeborg's son, and stayed with the Serre family in Dresden. Here he was taken to be photographed, and "looked like a peeled nutcracker," he remarked in his diary; his cross and worn expression was probably the fault of Einar, who was bad-tempered and ungrateful throughout the trip. For Andersen this journey was about renewing old friendships: he saw a radiant Jenny Lind, her husband and baby son in Vienna; in Bavaria he was fetched in a royal carriage and taken to visit King Max; he met Liszt again in Weimar and spent two days with Carl Alexander. Back in Denmark, he stayed with Jonna and Henrik Stampe, took his publisher Richard Bentley, over from London, to Tivoli, spent time with another foreign literary visitor, Fredrika Bremer, and occupied himself with works for the theatre and with a Danish version of his autobiography. New volumes of his collected works continued to appear in 1854 and 1855; in 1855 Andersen also had five plays running simultaneously in Copenhagen, as well as some new stories, including another tale of childhood sweethearts torn apart, "Ib and Little Christine," which were incorporated into Pedersen's illustrated edition.

The collected edition marked the beginnings of a new reverence in the

Danish response to Andersen, but it took an Icelandic author, Grimùr Thomsen, to write the first serious critical article on his work: it was twenty pages long and appeared in March 1855. A few years earlier, in 1848, the artist A. M. Petersen had published a lithograph called *Danske Digtere (Danish Poets)* in which fourteen living Danish writers were sketched together, the size and positioning of the portraits revealing the contemporary estimation of each one. Ingemann has a lofty position as a grand old man of letters at the back; Oehlenschläger, at the centre, is the largest figure, flanked by Heiberg and Carsten Hauch (the novelist who had satirized Andersen in *Castle on the Rhine*). Two other former adversaries of Andersen's, Henrik Hertz and Kierkegaard, stare out prominently from the middle row. A depiction of Andersen as a foppish lightweight, by contrast, is one of five small portraits in the front; he is grouped with the poet Frederik Paludan-Müller, who had matriculated at the same time as him, and three now forgotten writers.

This relative insignificance was extraordinary at a time when he was already hailed in Germany and England, and Grimùr Thomsen pointed out that Andersen was now so famous abroad that he must be appreciated seriously at home. Andersen was overjoyed: it was, he told Henriette Wulff on 3 April 1855, the first judgement in Denmark "on me as a poet which is unconditional in its approval—beautifully composed, as well as clever, written with knowledge and with love." This was written the day after his fiftieth birthday; he celebrated with Adolph and Ingeborg Drewsen, returning home in the evening to correct the proofs of his Danish autobiography. It was called *Mit Livs Eventyr (The Fairy Tale of My Life)* and was updated to that day, 2 April 1855; it was published in May, and among those who received copies from Andersen was his old schoolteacher in Odense, Fedder Carstens.

In tone *Mit Livs Eventyr* is no different from the German work, ending with the same myth: "the story of my life up to this hour lies now unrolled before me, a rich and beautiful canvas . . . I feel that I am fortune's child, so many of the noblest and best of my time have met me with affection and sincerity." But in the eight years since *Das Märchen meines Lebens*, the roll-call of kings and princes had grown longer and more tedious. After Andersen's death, the critic Georg Brandes wrote: "His personality is scarcely ever occupied with anything greater than itself, is never absorbed in an idea, is never entirely free from the ego. The revolution of 1848 in this book affects us as though we heard someone sneeze; we are astonished to be reminded by the sound that there is a world outside of the author."

Andersen's obsequiousness was incomprehensible to his oldest friends. The egalitarian, humanist, hunchbacked Henriette Wulff wrote to him:

> To me it is a complete denial of oneself, of one's own person, of the gifts God has graciously given us, such an inexplicable humility that I am surprised when someone like You, Andersen—if you do not recognize that God has given you special spiritual gifts—that You can think yourself happy and honoured to be seated—well, that is what it says—at the table of the King of Prussia or of someone else of high rank—or to get a decoration, of the sort worn by the worst scoundrels, not to mention a crowd of very insignificant people. Do you really put a title, money, nobility, luck in what is nothing but external things, over genius—spirit—the gifts of the soul?

Andersen, too uncertain not to need the approval of the world, could not defend himself. "Just in the brilliancy of the court I am thinking of these people," he told her, "they never enter my thoughts when a Dickens, a Humboldt, Liebig or Carl Alexander presses my hand in loving sympathy. Perhaps I am not thankful enough to God when I let the small things affect me, but I believe it has its reason in my first appearance under such poor circumstances. My life is still the strangest fairy tale." It is possible to sympathize, but not to acquit him from Henriette's charge of snobbery. He enjoyed spectacle and the visible trappings of success; the searching, creative part of his mind that made him sensitive to new ideas and cultures also made him impressionable to worldly achievement, and fame soothed him. And so he moved on, whirling across the courts of Europe almost as if, like Karen dancing ceaselessly in her red shoes, he was propelled to seek fame by a force beyond his control.

In June 1855 he set off again for Germany and Switzerland, this time with nineteen-year-old Edgar Collin, the son of Edvard's older brother Gottlieb. Edgar, who became a journalist and stage historian, was better company than his cousins; he helped Andersen when he was ill, and is referred to in the diary for this trip as "dear Edgar . . . so full of warmth and gratitude." Andersen visited King Max once more, met Richard Wagner in Zurich, stayed in Weimar, and began there to collaborate with Liszt on the staging of a libretto, *Liden Kirsten* (*Little Kirsten*), which he had written in the 1830s; Hartmann had composed music for it in 1846. But the highlight of the journey was at the spa of Wildbad, where Andersen had arranged to meet his two greatest friends and to introduce them to one another: Carl Alexander, now Grand Duke of Weimar, and Edvard, staying there with his wife Jette and son Jonas. The introduction, and the kindness extended to the Collins as a result, made Edvard and Jette understand at last the nature of Andersen's fame; Jette said she now regretted that she had ever been less than respectful to him.

At home, Andersen visited Ingemann in Sorø and spent the winter in Copenhagen, absorbed in Professor D. F. Eschricht's writings on materialism, the first sparks which led him to plan his philosophical novel *At være eller ikke være* (*To Be Or Not To Be*). He wrote much of it in 1856 at two aristocratic estates on the south coast of Zealand, which he visited so frequently and for so long from the mid 1850s until his death that they became virtually his country homes. Basnæs, home of a new noble friend, Henriette Scavenius, was an imposing moated castle with turrets and gables, set in extensive grounds; in summer the woods were green and the blackthorn bloomed, nightingales sang and Andersen strolled with his hostess through the long garden down to the sea in the evening, and gazed at the beech-covered islands off shore. Close by was another estate, the manor house of Holsteinborg, home of Countess Mimi Holstein. Henriette Scavenius, though only in her thirties in 1856, was prim and forbidding, but attentive to Andersen's every need; Mimi Holstein was younger and fun-loving. Between them these aristocratic women calmed and spoiled him as he grew older, making allowances for his moodiness and eccentric demands.

The new railway from Copenhagen via the ancient city of Roskilde to Slagelse, which opened in 1856, made it possible for Andersen to visit these estates easily and quickly. When he set out from Copenhagen in the snow on 30 April 1856, he noted that at the stations "the garlands were still green from last Saturday, when the king made the maiden run." At Slagelse the coachman from Basnæs picked him up, and there was a "friendly reception," he wrote. "Got a room with a view of the water. A fire in the stove. This evening, a dance in the barn, an annual ball the lady of Basnæs holds for her people. The barn was decorated with greenery and there were eight musicians. They were going to dance hand in hand down to the barn from the manor house over the drawbridge." This was worlds away from the pressures of Copenhagen, and a few days later Andersen wrote:

I am dreaming a lot every night here at Basnæs—pleasantly and in great detail. Last night I thought I was in Constantinople; saw and recognized many things that have been as if erased from my memory. Suddenly I was in Japan— strange flowers. A quiet moorish arcade—I knew I was risking my life by walking there, but I was quite safe because also I knew that if they came and killed me I would wake up at Basnæs.

There are many records of a pampered Andersen engrossed in the quiet domestic routines of Holsteinborg and Basnæs, where life seemed untouched by the realities of war and social change in the 1850s and 1860s. Baroness Bodild Donner, who was a little girl when Andersen began visiting Holsteinborg, recalled how "when I was a child I was delighted when [Andersen] cut out chains of little dolls in white paper that I could stand on the table and blow so they moved forward. He cut many silhouettes which Mamma later pasted up partly on lampshades. He always cut with an enormous pair of paper scissors—and it was a mystery to me how he could cut such dainty delicate things with his big hands and those enormous scissors." From 1856, Andersen spent Christmas at Basnæs most years, and occupied himself cutting out complicated patterns—pavilions with bells and steps and turrets, for instance—while the family rushed about preparing for the festivities. "On Christmas Eve I was at Basnæs," he recorded one year, "where the Christmas tree was lit, not only for the guests but also for the poor children of the estate; their tree stood there just as rich and radiant as ours. Mrs. Scavenius had decorated it herself and lit every candle; I had cut out and pasted the figures that hung on the branches. The snow fell, the sleigh bells jingled, the wild swans sang on the seashore; it was charming without, it was snug within."

At Basnæs in 1856, Andersen read philosophy as he worked on his novel. "Finished *Letters in Opposition to Materialism* by F. Fabri. They have enlightened me, but haven't clearly eradicated every materialistic argument. Even with greater experience, I stand none the wiser between the spiritual and the material, but the intangible in me is drawn to the intangible," he noted in May, and the next day, "The entire structure of the new novel revealed itself to me: a struggle for the only comfort human knowledge can attain." *To Be Or Not To Be* is the story of Andersen's own spiritual crises in the war years; "none of my works have demanded so much preparatory study as this one. I have lived in this book, written it, and then rewritten it again and again," he told Carl Alexander. Like many mid- and late-nineteenth-century novels, it is about the battle between belief and scientific rationalism, here told through the life of Niels Bryde, who loses his Christian faith and develops a passionate interest in science, but regains at the end a belief in the immortality of the soul. Niels is Andersen's alter ego, down to comic details such as his "inborn fear of dogs"—"it was a great distress to him that these creatures existed; if a dog so much as sniffed at him a shock went through all his limbs"—and Andersen ends with an image of Niels close to the one he had drawn of himself as an artist for Carl Alexander in a letter in 1850: "Like a new Aladdin he had descended into the cave of science in order to find among its wonderful fruits the lamp of life, and he was holding—his mother's Bible, not its body, but its divine soul."

Andersen visited Germany again in the summer of 1856, staying first with the Serre family in Maxen, where a fellow guest, the German author Karl Gutzkow, criticized his tale "Under the Willow Tree" and, Andersen wrote, "was so tactless as to ask whether I had ever been in love—one couldn't tell from my books, where love came in like a fairy; I was myself a sort of half-man!" Andersen fled to Weimar ("Mrs. Serre was crying, said she'd like to thrash Gutzkow, who was now chasing her dearest friends away") and once again in Carl Alexander's company his high connections consoled him. On 23 June he wrote in his diary: "Tears came into my eyes, I thought that I, the poor shoemaker and washerwoman's son, was being kissed by the Czar of Russia's grandson. How the extremes were meeting."

CHAPTER 19

Dickens

1856–1857

Hans Andersen slept in this room for five weeks—which seemed to the family AGES*!*
—CHARLES DICKENS, note pinned in his house in
Gad's Hill Place, Kent, July 1857

On his way home from Weimar in July 1856, Andersen received at Maxen a letter which threw him into excitement. "Nine years . . . have flown since you were among us. In these nine years you have not faded out of the hearts of the English people, but have become even better known and more beloved," Dickens wrote. "You ought to come to me, for example, and stay in my house. We would all do our best to make you happy . . . I assure you that I love and esteem you more than I could tell you on as much paper as would pave the whole road from here to Copenhagen." Andersen was thrilled with this letter, writing at once to tell Jonas Collin and Henriette Wulff about it. Meanwhile another invitation to England came in December: "let me say how delighted we shall all be to see you again in Old England, where in feeling if not quite in the matter of language you had become an Englishman," wrote Richard Bentley. Bentley was to publish *To Be Or Not To Be*, which was to appear simultaneously in Danish, English and German, thus avoiding piracy. Andersen liked the idea of being in England for publication, but it was primarily to renew the relationship with Dickens, which was for him of both artistic and social significance, that he was eager to take up the invitation.

On 15 December 1856, however, Dickens told the vicar Charles de la Prynne "I have not the slightest reason to suppose that Andersen is coming to England at all, otherwise than that I have seen it stated in some newspapers that he is coming on a visit to me." Characteristically, Andersen was already broadcasting his hopes of visiting his famous friend, but had not bothered to reply to Dickens himself. On 10 January 1857 *Punch* published a caricature of Andersen being mobbed by children, with a "genuine letter from a young lady" asking "Will you put In punch wat everybody is to Do to let Mr. Hans Ansen know how Glad we are He is Coming." Andersen was busy in the winter of 1856–1857 correcting *To Be Or Not To Be*, and he finally replied to Dickens in March 1857, nine months after he had received his invitation. He would make the trip to England if Dickens were there, he wrote, but "if you are not in London, I shall not go to England, my visit is intended for you alone . . . Above all, always leave me a small corner in your heart."

He no longer had the strength for another round of the London season, and accepted with alacrity Dickens's suggestion that he stay at the family's country home in Gad's Hill in Kent, where "we have children of all sizes, and they all love you. You will find yourself in a house full of admiring and affectionate friends, varying from three feet high to five feet nine." He was, he said, finishing *Little Dorrit*, but "you will find me in the summer quite a free man, playing at cricket and all manners of English open-air games."

For Andersen, after a decade in which so many certainties surrounding his life had altered, it was a chance to revisit some of his happiest memories. "Dear delightful Charles Dickens, Your letter has made me infinitely happy," he wrote. "I am quite full of and overcome with joy at the thought of being with you for a short while, being in your house, being one of your circle. You do not know how much I appreciate it, how I thank God, you, and your wife in my heart." He was anxious that he spoke English very badly, he said, but his "longing and desire to see you and talk with you" overcame his fear. He would come in June and stay, he reckoned, a week or a fortnight.

He could hardly have chosen a worse time to visit. Dickens was exhausted from finishing *Little Dorrit*; his marriage was on the verge of breaking up; one of his closest friends, Douglas Jerrold, had just died, leaving a family in poverty, and Dickens was consumed by the rehearsals for a play, Wilkie Collins's *The Frozen Deep*, with which he was raising money for the Douglas Jerrold Family Fund, and through which he was about to meet Ellen Ternan, who signalled the end of his marriage and soon became his long-term mistress. In the midst of all this, Andersen was at best an irrelevance and at worst a nuisance, while innocently and happily believing himself to be at the centre of his host's world.

Dickens was not even sure that he would turn up, writing maliciously to a friend in May that "Hans Christian Andersen (who has been 'coming' for about three years) will come for a fortnight's stay in England." Dickens's son Henry wrote of his father's high estimation of Andersen's literary work, but even before Andersen arrived Dickens was writing patronizingly of the man, telling the wealthy philanthropist Angela Burdett-Coutts: "Hans Christian Andersen may perhaps be with us, but you won't mind *him*— especially as he speaks no language but his own Danish, and is suspected of not even knowing that."

Andersen arrived on 11 June and was warmly received. Dickens embraced him, gave him breakfast and walked with him in the garden; later he met Miss Burdett-Coutts, who was also staying, and the children. Gad's Hill Place was beautiful in a typically English picturesque way: "the whole landscape is like a garden, and from the hills one can follow the winding Thames for many a mile, and looking far over woods and fields, catch a glimpse of the sea. There is a scent of wild roses and ivy here, the air is so fresh too, and inside the house itself happy people live. Dickens is one of the most amiable of men that I know, and possesses as much heart as intellect," Andersen wrote to the Dowager Queen Caroline Amalie.

But trouble started at once. Going to bed that evening Andersen "found it a little cold"; the next morning, no one came to pick up his clothes or to shave him. Henry Dickens, aged eight, recalled: "on the first morning after his arrival . . . he sent for my eldest brother to shave him, to the intense indignation of the boys; and with the result that he was afterwards driven every morning to the barber's at Rochester to get the necessary shave." Worse still, his host took off immediately for London, leaving Mrs. Dickens to show Andersen around Rochester. Dickens returned in the evening. "I was a great success after dinner with my cut-outs," Andersen noted, although Henry Dickens told a different story: "at dinner time on the same day, he greatly embarrassed my father, who was offering his arm to a lady [probably Miss Burdett-Coutts] to take her into dinner, by suddenly seizing his hand, putting it into his own bosom and leading him triumphantly into the dining room."

Nevertheless, there were pleasant afternoons—"the smallest of the children held my hand and danced around and asked about what every little thing was called in Danish"—and cosy evenings when the ladies sang from *Lucia di Lammermoor* and *Don Giovanni*. "Dickens came home, and we talked a lot together about Danish folk legends," he recorded, and the ostentatious pieties that had drawn him to England in 1847 continued to reassure him: "the good old fashion of saying grace before meals is still observed in Dickens's home." After a week, he sent back to Henriette Wulff a rosy picture of family life which entirely missed what were by then almost unbearable tensions between Dickens, his wife Catherine and her sister Georgina Hogarth, who took Dickens's part: "The family seems very closely knit together, and a young Miss Hogarth, who has been a member of the household for many years, pours tea and coffee, teaches the young Misses Dickens music, and seems to be a very amiable, cultivated lady. Dickens himself is like the best part in his books: cordial, lively, cheerful and fervent."

In his diary, however, Andersen admitted that "it was difficult for me to express myself." Dickens's daughter Kate later told her own daughter that Andersen's faltering English and broken accent made it extremely hard for him to express himself, or be understood.* He communicated with the children largely through his paper cut-outs. "He had one beautiful accomplishment," wrote Henry Dickens, "which was the cutting out in paper, with an ordinary pair of scissors, of lovely little figures of sprites and elves, gnomes, fairies and animals of all kinds, which might have stepped out of the pages of his books. These figures turned out to be quite delightful in their refinement and delicacy in design and touch."

Dickens himself was an exemplary host, rashly asking Andersen to stay until he could see *The Frozen Deep*; "said he, his wife and daughters were so happy to have me with them. I was moved; he embraced me, I kissed him on the forehead." But the strain on the others soon showed. Henry Dickens recalled Andersen as:

> a lovable and yet a somewhat uncommon and strange personality. His manner was delightfully simple, such as one rather expected from the delicacy of his work. He was necessarily very interesting, but he was certainly something of an "oddity." In person, tall, gaunt, rather ungainly; in manner, thoughtful and agreeable . . . Much as there was in him to like and admire, he was, on the other

---

*"I have been told the following story about him," Edvard Collin wrote in his memoir of Andersen. "In London he was given the advice to write down the name of the street where he lived, so that he could show this to a constable in case he got lost. He heeded the advice, stopped at the corner of the street, and wrote down the following words: 'Stick no bills.' He subsequently got lost, showed the note to a constable, was taken to the police station, and only released when the Danish Consul appeared and explained that he was not crazy." On another occasion Andersen introduced himself to Mark Lemon, editor of *Punch*, with the words "I am so glad to know you, Mr. Lemon—you are so full of comic!"

hand, most decidedly disconcerting in his general manner, for he used constantly to be doing things quite unconsciously, which might almost be called "gauche": so much so that I am afraid the small boys of the family rather laughed at him behind his back.

The others were less tolerant. As the days wore on, Andersen jotted down "Little Kate cutting; the aunt is definitely tired of me . . . young Walter Dickens asinine . . . Charles [the author's son] not exactly pleasant . . . the daughters without a thought for me; the aunt less so." The sons deputed to look after him were neglectful, five-year-old Edward's refrain was "I will put you out of the window" and there was "too little sugar in the tea"—i.e., the family was not sweet enough to him. Worried by his poor English, he was more thin-skinned than usual—"feeling like that, you have eyes and ears to your very fingertips," he wrote, and he picked up every whiff of hostility.

When the reviews of *To Be Or Not To Be*, which was dedicated to Dickens, began to appear in the English press, Andersen became even more prickly. He had drawn his hero Niels Bryde as a self-portrait, he had written from his own need to believe in an immortal soul and he thought that Niels's struggles showed him to be upholding Christian values, but the critics saw the book as subversive. The *Athenaeum* wrote that "Niels Bryde will be perennially wearisome to all men and races . . . his failure is absolute . . . Without his knowledge or consent, M. Andersen may deceive some young intelligence, some susceptible heart. In one word, the book is dangerous." Andersen was disconsolate, and threw himself, sobbing, face down on the lawn, where Mrs. Dickens found him. That evening, Andersen wrote "was heavy in the head, tired, confused, had the feeling that no one had any sympathy for me," and the next day, "I'm not content, cannot be so and feel myself a stranger among strangers. If only Dickens were here!"

Even in his self-centredness Andersen noticed that Catherine Dickens, to whom he was very sympathetic ("so mild, so motherly, quite like Agnes in *David Copperfield*"), was emerging from her sister's room in tears. But every time Dickens returned, sweetness and light flooded back:

> "You should never read anything in the newspapers except what you yourself have written; I haven't read criticism of me in twenty-four years!" . . . Later Dickens put his arms around me, saying "Don't ever let yourself be upset by the newspapers; they're forgotten in a week and your book will live on! God has given you so much . . ." He wrote with his foot in the sand, "That's criticism!" he said and rubbed it out, "and it's gone just like that!"

This was a rare sort of author-to-author sympathy, and although he knew he was outstaying his welcome—when asked by a guest how long he would remain, Andersen replied, "Long for Mr. Dickens, short for me"—Andersen could not tear himself away from Dickens's exuberant charm and boisterous spirits, which picked him up from his own languor and self-doubt. He accompanied Dickens to London, saw the tragedienne Adelaide Ristori, heard *The Messiah* performed for an audience of ten thousand at the new Crystal Palace and enjoyed the lavish hospitality of Miss Burdett-Coutts: "doorman, servants in princely livery, the corridors carpeted. I got the best bedroom I've ever had with a bathroom and a toilet, fire in the fireplace, view out over Piccadilly and the garden in front. Beautiful paintings and statues downstairs." He told Henriette Wulff that he could speak more easily to Miss Burdett-Coutts, "very straightforward, amiable and good-natured in the highest degree," than to her servants, "who are too haughty."

He paid brief visits to his publisher Bentley, where the exceptional courtesy of the entire family showed the Dickenses up in an even worse light. But what really cheered Andersen up was Bentley showing him a poor review of *Little Dorrit*. "We have yet to meet the man or woman, boy or girl, who can honestly say that he or she has read *Little Dorrit* through. It is the *cultus* of the middle classes to purchase Dickens, but an Act of Parliament would fail to enforce the serious reading of his last production," the *Saturday Review* claimed. " 'You see, you're not the only one!' said Bentley. I don't know, but my mood improved. What is criticism—often only born of the passion of friendship or envy; often stupidity, often the product of haste."

Eventually, Andersen saw *The Frozen Deep* on 4 July in the company of the King of Belgium, the Prince of Prussia, the Prince of Wales, Prince Albert and Queen Victoria ("She knew I was there, Dickens said"). Dickens was a mesmerizing actor; *The Times*, reviewing the production the following week, said that "the performance of Mr. Dickens as the vindictive and (afterwards) penitent Richard Wardour is, in the truest sense of the word, a creation. Nay, we may go further and say that it is the creation of a literary man . . ." Andersen burst into tears at Dickens in the death scene, and drank champange with the cast afterwards, but he could not genuinely throw himself into an event where he was not the main participant ("Not really in a good mood the entire evening," his diary for that day concludes).

The next day, Bentley came to Gad's Hill and Andersen felt fussed over again. Bentley recalled the occasion as "this happy meeting of these two most genial and gifted friends," continuing, "I passed a very happy day, which I shall always remember with gratification. It was a bright sunshiny day, and we strolled about Mr. Dickens's pretty garden with positive enjoyment. Mr. Wilkie Collins was there, with Mrs. Dickens and her two daughters and Miss Hogarth. In the evening we had vocal and instrumental music, and it was late before I could tear myself away from his hospitable roof." Andersen noted in his diary: "Big dinner party. In the evening walked with all of them up on the hill—to 'Andersen's monument' as Dickens calls it, because I was the first to take them up there and it is my favourite place."

But even here there was a teasing subtext. Henry Dickens recalled:

Wilkie Collins was at Gad's Hill . . . and the hat which he wore was a very large wide-awake. Andersen . . . quite unknown to Wilkie, surreptitiously crowned this hat with a large garland of daisies, a fact of which full advantage was taken by the mischievous boys in the family. With apparent innocence, they suggested to Wilkie a walk through the village. To this Wilkie, quite unconscious of his garland, willing assented; but he must have been somewhat surprised, I think, at the amount of merriment which his presence seemed to arouse in the minds of the villagers who passed us on our way.

"We are suffering a good deal from Andersen," wrote Dickens to Miss Burdett-Coutts on 10 July, when he had been with them a month. The next day he saw *The Frozen Deep* again, at the benefit performance for the Jerrold Fund, and he finally left in tears on 15 July. "Dickens himself drove me to Maidstone. My heart was so full. I didn't speak much, and at parting I said almost nothing. Tears choked my voice." Dickens kissed him goodbye; "I travelled alone in the steam serpent to Folkestone." He crossed to Calais, where he stared out at the sea and wrote, "I'm on the verge of morbid obsessions."

He had stayed more than twice as long as he had promised. Kate Dickens summed him up with "he was a bony bore, and stayed on and on," while Dickens pinned a note in his room after he had left which read "Hans Andersen slept in this room for five weeks—which seemed to the family AGES!"

To William Jerdan, Dickens painted Andersen as an absurd caricature who might have stepped out of the pages of one of his novels:

Whenever he got to London, he got into wild entanglements of cabs and Sherry, and never seemed to get out of them again until he came back here, and cut out paper into all sorts of patterns, and gathered the strangest little nosegays in the woods. His unintelligible vocabulary was marvellous. In French or Italian, he was Peter the Wild Boy; in English the Deaf and Dumb Asylum. My eldest boy swears that the ear of man cannot recognize his German, and his translatress declares to Bentley that he can't speak Danish!*

One day he came home to Tavistock Square [Dickens's London house], apparently suffering from corns that had ripened in two hours. It turned out that a cab driver had brought him from the City, by way of the new unfinished thoroughfare through Clerkenwell. Satisfied that the cabman was bent on robbery and murder, he had put his watch and money into his boots—together with a Bradshaw, a pocket-book, a pair of scissors, a penknife, a book or two, a few letters of introduction and some other miscellaneous property.

These are all the particulars I am in condition to report. He received a good many letters, lost (I should say) a good many more, and was for the most part utterly conglomerated—with a general impression that everything was going to clear itself up TOMORROW.

Alas, while Andersen dimly suspected that through Dickens's charm this might have been his true feeling, he was unable either to behave differently or to be unselfish enough to drag himself away sooner from the pleasure of Dickens's company. On his way home, he wrote to him:

None of your friends can be more closely attached to you than I. The visit to England, the stay with you, is a bright point in my life; that is why I stayed so long, that is why it was so hard for me to say good-bye. Indeed, when we were driving together from Gad's Hill to Maidstone, my heart was so heavy, it was almost impossible for me to carry on a conversation; I was on the verge of tears . . . I have no terms in which to tell you, even if I could write my letter in Danish, how happy I was with you, how grateful I am . . . I understood every minute that you cared for me, that you were glad to see me, and were my friend . . . I realize that it can by no means have been very agreeable for your whole circle to have for weeks among them one who spoke such bad English as I, one who seemed to have dropped from the skies. And yet how little you made me feel that . . . Kindly forget the unfavourable aspect which our life together may have shown you of me. I wish so much to leave behind a good memory with him whom I love as a friend and brother.

Yet Andersen may already have perceived that it was the end—"sad, very sad, as if I were leaving one of my dear ones whom I should never see again,"

---

*This was probably Mary Howitt, still piqued at being dropped as Andersen's translator.

he wrote four days after the parting at Maidstone. Dickens wrote to him once more, in September 1857, with slight condescension ("Baby says, you shall not be put out of the window, when you come back"), ending "Good by, dear Andersen," as if he had decided this letter to be the last. By now Dickens had met Ellen Ternan and was speaking openly of the misery of his marriage.* As Claire Tomalin has pointed out, *Little Dorrit* "has a bearing on Dickens's state of mind in 1857. The reader senses that Amy has an extra significance for her creator. She is . . . the child-bride of middle-aged fantasy, the unlooked-for reprieve, the new start in life for the hero whose own youth lies behind him." Dickens was about to leave his marriage, and the dying cadence of his letter to Andersen reflected much more than the end of a friendship: "The corn-fields that were golden, when you were here, are ploughed up brown; the hops are being picked; the leaves on the trees are just beginning to turn; and the rain is falling, as I write, very sadly—very steadily."

Dickens never answered another of Andersen's letters, nor received any of the Danish friends for whom Andersen wrote letters of introduction in the late 1850s and early 1860s. Less than a year after his visit, Dickens and Catherine separated, and Andersen was probably a casualty of Dickens's reshaped life as well as a victim of his own gaucheness in having overstayed his welcome. He never fully comprehended Dickens's silence. He did not hear about the separation for some time, which explains why he wrote an account of the harmonious and happy family life he had experienced at Gad's Hill Place in the Copenhagen newspaper *Berlingske Tidende* early in 1860. This was translated into German and reviewed in *Bentley's Miscellany* in August 1860, when Dickens's marital affairs continued to fascinate the British public. "Since you last visited England what changes have taken place! Dickens has greatly lowered himself in public estimation by acts of folly quite unworthy of him," Bentley wrote to Andersen in May 1862, and in December 1862 Mrs. Bushby replied to a query from Andersen with "You ask about Mr. Dickens. It is quite true that he has separated from his wife. Some people blame *him*, some blame *her* . . . I hear that he does not stand so high in public opinion as he used to do."

Bentley's Miscellany hypocritically reprinted the idyllic depiction of the Dickens' ménage while blaming Andersen for "the way in which he has

---

*He wrote in August 1857 to John Forster, his future biographer, that "Poor Catherine and I are not made for each other, and there is no help for it. What is now befalling I have seen steadily coming."

betrayed private confidence," and the Andersen scholar Elias Bredsdorff has suggested that Dickens saw *Bentley's Miscellany* and cut Andersen for what appeared to be the extraordinary tactlessness of publicizing private details about his home life at such a time. In his extended autobiography of 1869, Andersen mentioned that Dickens stopped writing to him, and quoted from the sad end of "The Fir Tree"—"'Done with! Done with!' and that's what happens to all stories!"

He returned home via Paris ("a beehive without honey," "this rumbling hot town where I am sitting all alone in a poky little room") and Dresden, and then made a brief visit to Weimar, seeing Carl Alexander also for the last time in his life at a ceremony unveiling statues of Goethe and Schiller ("Schiller looks like me"). "Like the Nightingale of the fairy tale, which always flies away from the castle but ever returns after long flights abroad, and sings from the heart for its Emperor, so I also return to home-like Weimar, and I know that I shall never be scared away by a disdainful look," he wrote to Carl Alexander, but war loomed again and his letter already had the wistfulness of nostalgia.

His welcome had been undeniably warm, but what should have been two joyous visits, to Carl Alexander and to Dickens, marked the end of an era, and he returned to Copenhagen melancholy and bitter. "I am so little appreciated—am still only a poor schoolboy always in the lowest form! If I am wronged, Denmark, it is your shame!" he wrote to Henriette Wulff in July 1857. "Oh Lord! My heart is warm, my feelings are so strong! You do not know how much I suffer. And yet still I would not be without this 'to be,' no matter how bitter it may be!" It is this existential questioning which now came to the fore in his fairy tales, and determined the innovative and modern nature of his late works.

As in 1847, his visit to England refreshed him and gave him new ideas. Cholera ("a disease which I fear the most of any") was back in Denmark; "it was raging in the little town of Korsør, to which the steamer from Kiel brought me," he told Dickens in September, and in Copenhagen—"even in the street where I live there were a few cases." He spent most of the autumn and winter of 1857 in the country, at Ingemann's in Sorø and at Basnæs, where, "over Christmas," he wrote to Carl Alexander, "I have been very productive, and have written no fewer than three new fairy tales, of which one, 'The Old Oak Tree's Last Dream,' is probably among my best."

CHAPTER 20

Experiments

1858–1859

*"Well, that's a new ending to the story," said Stork-papa. "I had certainly not
expected it. But I like it very well."*
"But what will the young ones say to it?" said Stork-mamma.
——HANS CHRISTIAN ANDERSEN, "The Marsh King's Daughter"

In February 1858 Andersen told Henriette Scavenius that he had been
stopped from writing any letters because he had over the last few months
been more productive than for a very long time. On 2 March, *Nye Eventyr og
Historier* (*New Fairy Tales and Stories*) was published; on 12 March it sold
out. That month Andersen was invited to dine with King Frederik VII and
was decorated with the silver cross of the Order of Dannebrog, but what
really absorbed him was finishing a long story, "The Marsh King's Daughter," on which he had been working for months. He researched extensively into
Viking sagas and legends, he read books about Africa and about the flights
of birds, and he rewrote the tale six times. In April he read it to the poet
Paludan-Müller, and it appeared on 15 May as the central work in the second
volume of *Nye Eventyr og Historier*.

Through the 1850s he had wrestled with issues of faith and immortality;
in the two volumes of 1858 he found at last the poetic images to express both
his fatalism and the affirmative Christian vision which he had fought to
hold on to. One of his favourite tales, "The Old Oak Tree's Last Dream," is
a mystical story comparing the fate of an oak tree, which lives many centuries, with that of an ephemera fly, which lives for one day. The details of
the natural world—the fly gliding down on to the soft grass blade, the sunbeams among the tree's twigs and leaves, the grasshopper cleaning his
wings—are delicately drawn; then at Christmas, dreaming sublime thoughts
of life "in heaven, in the better land" and to the music of a carol celebrating

"the redemption of the soul of man by His blood," the tree falls in a storm, and "his three hundred and sixty-five years were now as the single day of the Ephemera."

"The Marsh King's Daughter" is a more complicated and multi-layered meditation on these themes. Andersen uses a family of chattering storks to recount the adventure of an Egyptian princess in Viking times who flies as a swan in search of a magic flower which will restore her dying father to health. With her fly her two wicked sisters and as they cross a marsh, they strip the princess of her swan's feathers and she sinks. She becomes the property of the terrifying marsh king, to whom she bears a daughter, and she is believed drowned under the bog. The stork-father discovers her child in a flower and takes her to a childless Viking woman, for "people always say, 'the stork has brought a little one,' and I will do so in earnest this time." The girl, Helga, is beautiful but violent by day; at night she becomes a sorrowful, gentle and hideous frog—the legacy of her marsh-father. She is redeemed by a Christian priest, about to be sacrificed by the Vikings, whom in her gentle frog form she rescues. He directs her back to the marsh where she meets her mother; the storks, who on one of their migrations to Egypt have stolen the swan costumes belonging to the two wicked sisters, cloak mother and daughter in feathers and lead them back to the Egyptian king. Through Helga—who symbolizes the magic flower in which she is found, and for which her mother was searching—the king recovers; the line "love gives life" rings as a leitmotif through the tale, binding its complex elements together.

Many elements here are familiar to Andersen readers. There is the comedy of the minor characters in the contrast between the stork-father, who is outward-looking and tries to interact with the story he is telling, and the stay-at-home stork-mamma ("You ought not to tell me anything of the kind at such a time as this, the eggs might suffer by it . . . Think first of yourself, and then of your family, and all the rest does not concern you"). There are the vivid scene paintings of Egypt and of the Vikings' wintry Denmark, and the symbolic use of Andersen's favourite birds, the stork and the swan; the morbid, brooding sexuality in the underground union of princess and marsh king, too, is an Andersen hallmark.

But where this story differs from Andersen's earlier work is that the emphasis is no longer on the plot, but on the complicated, interwoven structure and on the modulation of comedy and tragedy achieved by using the storks as a sort of Greek chorus, commenting on, sometimes contributing to, the action. That love is the meaning of life, and that the soul is immortal, is a theme running through Andersen's *œuvre*, but "The Marsh King's Daughter," along with "The Little Mermaid," "The Snow Queen" and "The Nightingale," is one of a small number of tales whose action turns on this fundamental belief. In this story, one of those closest to his heart, Andersen was seeking a new way to convey these truths, and he found it in a narrative style which allowed him to dovetail the sublime with the bathos of the storks:

> "Love gives life! The highest love gives the highest life. Only through love can his life be preserved."
>
> That is what they all said, and the learned men said it was very cleverly and beautifully spoken.
>
> "That is a beautiful thought!" Stork-papa said immediately.
>
> "I don't quite understand it," Stork-mamma replied, "and that's not my fault, but the fault of the thought."

In a final Christian twist, Helga is swept up to heaven on her wedding day—"the body crumbled to dust, and a faded lotus flower lay on the spot where Helga had stood"—and Andersen saves himself from sentimentality by giving the last lines to the storks:

> "Well, that's a new ending to the story," said Stork-papa. "I had certainly not expected it. But I like it very well."
>
> "But what will the young ones say to it?" said Stork-mamma.
>
> "Yes, certainly, that's the important point," he replied.

Thus, opening his new phase as a writer of fairy tales in 1858, Andersen challenged his readers to ridicule if they classed him as only a children's writer.

The diverse ingredients of "The Marsh King's Daughter" show how broadly Andersen now saw the scope of the fairy tale: it harks back to animal fables of transformation but it also anticipates the modernist novella. "The wonder story holds a merry court of justice over shadow and substance, over the outward shell and the inward kernel. There flows a double stream through it: an ironic over-stream that plays and sports with great and small things, that plays shuttlecock with what is high and low; and then the deep under-stream, that honestly and truly brings all to its right place," he wrote. He had not been so engrossed in fairy tales for over a decade.

Between June and August 1858, he travelled again to Germany and Switzerland, though he avoided Weimar because he feared political tensions with Carl Alexander and the court: the German Confederation was now opposing a joint constitution for Denmark and Holstein, one of the German-speaking duchies which had risen against Danish rule. Harald Drewsen, another Collin grandson as unpleasant as his cousins ("difficult to rouse in

*Henriette Wulff, Andersen's
loyal friend from his early days
in Copenhagen until her tragic
death in 1858.*

the morning and awkward to have around—he won't call on people, won't speak German, very ponderous like Viggo"), was his companion, and they spent much time with the Serre family in Maxen. Here Andersen was visited in July by Clara Heinke, who had been trying unsuccessfully to start a love affair with him by letter; here too he received a letter from Henriette Wulff, who was staying at Eisenach, a few hours away by train, asking him to make an important visit to her.

Henriette came from a seafaring family—her father was Admiral Wulff, the Danish translator of Shakespeare and an early patron of Andersen; "for her," Andersen wrote, "it was a necessity, one may even say a matter of health, to travel, and she loved the sea passionately." She had sailed frequently with her brother, Christian Wulff, a lieutenant in the navy, but on a recent trip to the Danish West Indies he had caught yellow fever and died. She had been restless ever since, and now decided to immigrate to America. She was at Eisenach waiting for her boat to leave Germany, and she longed to see Andersen a final time. Andersen, comfortable at the Serres', hated changing his travelling plans, made excuses and did not go, and Henriette answered his refusal in a generous and perceptive letter:

> That you are what is called a famous man—would you believe it, I often forget
> this, surely much too often just by seeing into my own heart, and the feelings

there, which I have always felt for you . . . Please forget completely my inconsiderate little plan . . . I know your heart, it is a safe harbour, it will not betray me, of that I am totally and firmly convinced, *even though* appearances sometimes might give a different picture.

A few weeks later, Henriette set sail for New York, her ship caught fire and sank, and along with 470 of the 560 passengers, she died. It emerged that she had suffocated to death in her cabin, and Andersen could not get out of his mind the image of Henriette's "little feeble form" (she was a hunchback) struggling in the fire. "Day after day my imagination has been struck by the horrifying vision of it, I was immediately frightened by how feverishly I could see everything, for several weeks I have not been able to work," he wrote to Mrs. Læssøe. "She was one of the few people who really and truly loved me, she appreciated and over-rated me . . . she had a depth of feeling to give, and gave it, I—I reproach myself for it now—did not sufficiently reciprocate . . . It torments me now that I did not on my way home from Germany this summer make a detour, as she wished, so that we could meet once more before she left Europe." From this time on, Andersen always carried a rope in his luggage in case of fire in a hotel, and, knowing that he could never now face the sea voyage, made up his mind to refuse all invitations to America. The loss of Henriette, who had encouraged him since he was an uncertain teenager, stayed with him, and he published a poem about her death.

While he was waiting in October to know whether Henriette was on the list of those saved or those killed, Andersen prepared a speech he had been asked to make to the newly formed Mechanics' Association in Copenhagen. This was far from his usual audience of aristocrats and princes; the crowd of working men who wanted to hear him was so large that when seats and standing places were full, people climbed the outside of the building up to the windows and demanded to have them opened. Andersen read some tales, and then gave one of his rare commentaries on his art.

In England, in the royal navy, through all the rigging, small and great ropes, there runs a red thread, signifying that it belongs to the crown; through all men's lives there runs also a thread, invisible indeed, that shows we belong to God.

To find this thread in small and great, in our own life and in all about us, the poet's art helps us . . . In the earliest times the poet's art dealt most with what are called Wonder Stories; the Bible itself has enclosed truth and wisdom in what we call parables and allegories. Now we all of us know that the allegory is not to be taken literally by the words, but according to the signification that lies in them, by the invisible thread that runs through them.

We know that when we hear the echo from the wall, from the rock, or the heights, it is not the wall, the rock and the heights that speak, but a resounding from ourselves; and so we also should see in the parable, in the allegory, that we find ourselves—find the meaning, the wisdom and the happiness we can get out of them.

So the poet's art places itself by the side of Science, and opens our eyes for the beautiful, the true and the good.

As a writer of tales, he had never been more confident, and as he worked in the winter of 1858 and spring 1859 on a new volume, he experimented still more radically with the form. In March 1859 he told Carl Alexander that he had written six new stories:

> They form some of the best of my work. One of these stories, "The Wind Tells of Valdemar Daae and His Daughters," is, perhaps, regarding the construction, of special significance. I have tried, and I hope I have succeeded, in giving the whole narrative a tone as if one heard the wind itself. Another story, "Anne Lisbeth," I consider the best from a psychological point of view. I have endeavoured to show in it how small a germ of good and of evil is hidden in the heart, and how it springs into life according as it has been touched either by "einem Sonnenstrahl oder von einer bösen Hand" [by a sunbeam or by a wicked hand].

In "The Wind Tells of Valdemar Daae and His Daughters," the decline of the grand house of Borreby, a manor on southern Zealand close to those at Basnæs and Holsteinborg, is told through the voice of a howling wind which sees human life as fleeting and insignificant. Andersen reworked the story many times to capture the sound of the rushing wind, and the narrative style determines the mood of the tale. With the wind, we follow the fortunes of the aristocratic Daae, an alchemist so obsessed with striking gold that he lets his castle crumble around him, and of his daughters—two cold and haughty, the youngest gentle and thoughtful; as in "The Marsh King's Daughter," there are echoes of *King Lear* and other myths of two bad and one good sibling.

> Empty grew the barns and store-rooms, the cellars and magazines. The servants decreased in number, and the mice multiplied. Then a window broke, and then another, and I could get in elsewhere besides at the door [says the wind]. I blew through the courtyard gate like a watchman blowing his

horn . . . the door fell off its hinges, cracks and fissures made their appearance, and I went in and out at pleasure; and that is how I know all about it.

The wind's chorus is the changing seasons, which herald not new life but its ephemeral quality:

> And the winter passed away; winter and summer, both passed away, and they are still passing away, even as I pass away; as the snow whirls along, and the apple blossom whirls along, and the leaves fall—away! away! away!—and men are passing away too!

Eventually, half mad, Daae lets his alchemic glass fall and break into a thousand pieces: "and the last bubble of his happiness had burst! Hu-uh-ush!—rushing away—and I rushed from the gold-maker's house." The family are forced out of Borreby while the wind shrieks around the walls and blows down the trees—"they walked along the road on which they had once driven in their splendid carriage—they walked forth as beggars"—and live in a mud hut. The eldest daughter marries a peasant, the second goes to sea dressed as a man—"I blew her overboard before anybody found out that she was a woman, and, according to my thinking, that was well done"—and the third dies in the hut. The story ends with a sudden leap into the present, then into eternity, and then into the self-referential aside which was to become a feature of Andersen's late work:

> "The stork covered her hut till her death. I sang at her grave!" said the Wind. "I sang at her father's grave; I know where his grave is, and where hers is, and nobody else knows it.
> "New times, changed times! The old high road now runs through cultivated fields; the new road winds among the trim ditches, and soon the railway will come with its train of carriages, and rush over the graves which are forgotten like the names—hu-ush! passed away! passed away!
> "That is the story of Valdemar Daae and his daughters. Tell it better, any of you, if you know how," said the Wind, and turned away—and he was gone.

"Anne Lisbeth," which uses dreams to suggest the haunting nature of guilt, is also about how pride and respectability are brought low by that obsessive part of the mind beyond rational control. Beautiful Anne Lisbeth, her "colour like milk and blood," rejects her ugly son and becomes nurse-maid to a count's child. She lives in the city, is called Madame, and feels her dignity, but in old age her wealthy count-child refuses to acknowledge her and her own unloved son is drowned. In a series of nightmares, black crosses and ravens dance before her eyes, she thinks she is about to be transformed into a croaking black bird, she sees her son dragging her along the ground by her sleeve while hundreds of other mothers cling to her, and she slips out of his grasp as he cries, "The world is passing away! Hold fast to me, for you are my mother after all . . . Hold me fast!" In between the dreams, "in her mind a great space opened for thoughts that had never before been there . . . many things of which she had never liked to speak came into her mind." She spends each night wandering along the seashore, obsessively digging in the sand; "only one thought she had disentangled, namely, that she must carry the spectre of the seashore to the churchyard, and dig a grave for him, that thus she might win back her soul."

Suspended between hallucination and reality, "Anne Lisbeth" delves into the workings of the unconscious mind in ways which anticipated Freud and the writers of the early twentieth century; Anne Lisbeth herself is less a character than a consciousness floating across the story. Like most of the heroes and heroines of the 1858–1859 tales, she dies, but not until a final vision affirms the power of love: she hears her child tell her, "You have dug me only half a grave, but you have now, for a year and a day, buried me altogether in your heart, and it is there that a mother can best hide her child!"

The vision of a dead child was one of Andersen's own most frequently recurring dreams in later life, and it was perhaps for this reason that it appears so often in his late work. In "The Child in the Grave," also written in 1859, a mother who has been cast into "the fathomless abyss of despair" by the death of her child similarly gains comfort through meeting him in a dream: "In her grief she fell away from God and then there came dark thoughts, thoughts of death, of everlasting death—that man was but dust in the dust, and that with this life all was ended. But these thoughts gave her no stay, nothing on which she could take hold." Sleepwalking to her son's grave, she sees and holds him again, her belief in immortality is restored and she returns in peace to care for the rest of her family. This story reflects Andersen's own need to believe in an immortal soul, and the blackness he felt when unable to do so.

In different keys, he played on the themes of mortality, the perspective of eternity, man returned to a handful of dust, throughout the tales of 1859. A witty example is "Ole the Tower Keeper," the random and gruesome musings of a night watchman. It recalls an image from *A Walking Tour* in the depiction of artists and writers riding their paintbrushes and pens like witches on broomsticks: "All indifferent poets and poetesses, musicians, newspaper writers and artistic notabilities, I mean those who are no good, ride in the New Year's night through the air to Amager. They sit backwards on their painting brushes or quill pens, for steel pens won't bear them, they're too stiff," says the tower keeper. That art is demonic is the central idea of two later tales, "The Will o' the Wisps Are in Town" and "Auntie Toothache"; in "Ole the Tower Keeper" the evil powers of chaos triumph on New Year's Eve and Ole from his turret in the clouds asks, "Isn't it a delightful experience to get reset to zero now and then, when you are sitting as high as I am and then remember that we all of us are just shortlived ants on the hill of this earth, even if we are highly decorated ants?"

The collections of 1858 and 1859 mark a new phase in Andersen's composition of fairy tales. Leaving behind the folk models of his youth and the grand classical archetypes of his middle years such as "The Ugly Duckling" and "The Snow Queen," he reinvented the fairy tale as a modern, self-referential, experimental genre. He anticipated some of the ingredients of modernism—the expression of meaning primarily through style, form and poetic image; fluidity of character and an awareness of the irrational workings of the unconscious mind; a diminished importance of plot. The new experimental mode saved him from the boredom that was becoming an increasing problem for him; behind it also lay an agony of self-doubt and questioning about the value of art. This had already been evident in his work as early as *A Walking Tour*, but the war years, and the pessimism about the future of civilized values that came with them, brought these doubts to the forefront of his mind, and his later tales, with their sense of fragmentation and psychological confusion, are his response to the uncertainties of mid-nineteenth-century Europe.

The third instalment of *Nye Eventyr og Historier* (*New Fairy Tales and Stories*) appeared in March 1859, and in May Andersen read "The Wind Tells of Valdemar Daae" to King Frederik. He avoided Germany that summer, writing with the sweet pleasure of nostalgia to Carl Alexander, "how often I live over again in memory the first hours when I saw your Royal Highness and learned to know you. It was your Royal Highness's birthday when I saw you for the first time . . . it was then that I spoke to you for the first time in Ettersburg . . . Many beautiful reminiscences of graciousness and kindness pass through my thoughts again and again, and then my heart always flies to dear Weimar." Instead, from June to September he made a long trip up the coast of Jutland, travelling as far as Skagen, the northernmost tip of Denmark. Here the Kattegat and the thundering Skagerrak seas meet in a wild landscape of sand dunes, and it is possible to stand with one foot in each sea. "From the immense gulf of the sea the rolling and breaking of the ground swell gave a deep roar. The view out over the level sea as it meets the sky makes one dizzy; one unconsciously looks to see out here on the point if there is still solid ground behind him and that he is not out on the expanse of the sea, a worm only for these cloudy swarms of screaming fowl," Andersen wrote.

In the late nineteenth century Skagen became a Mecca for *plein air* artists such as P. S. Krøyer, drawn to the penetrating quality of the light on its long summer evenings, the flat, white sandy shores which seemed to stretch to infinity, the contrasting foaming seas and the tumbledown fishermen's cottages and boats. But in the 1850s Skagen was remote and little known. "We drove over pasture-land, heath and moor-land; we drove on the beach over the hard, burning sand," Andersen recalled.

> We came soon to the sand hills that lay like great snow drifts in winter time. The shore was nearly covered with quivering, reddish-brown medusae, large shells and round, smooth pebbles. Wreck after wreck lay there . . . The streets here are shifting; they are marked also by a cable stretched from pole to pole, just as the quicksands may determine. Here is a house half buried by a pile of sand, there another; here a dark, tarred wooden house with straw thatch, there a few houses with red roofs.

The attractive red-brick gabled lodging house that became Brøndums Hotel, centre of Danish summer artistic life in the 1880s and 1890s, had just opened, and Andersen was one of its first famous guests.

He wrote to Carl Alexander about his strange choice of travelling to a "barren desert land with its sand hills, there to find poetical treasures or the mood for composition." In Skagen in 1859 he found "a rich harvest of poetical material": "The scenery of Jutland has been a great revelation to me. The storms of the North Sea whip up the great sand dunes, the whirling sand cuts the face, the sea dashes and rolls like a seething cataract against the coast, and loosens the clay of the precipices." Jutland, he wrote in his diary, "was material for a whole novel." Occasionally its wildness unsettled him ("A letter, probably from a madman—I had myself convinced that it was from a smallpox patient and washed my hands . . . My room is off the garden—worked out how I could get out in the event of an assault . . . lay feverish, waiting to be attacked") and he attracted another unwelcome female admirer, Anna Bjerring, who besieged him with her attentions to such an extent that he noted in his diary on 23 August, "People will have me engaged to Miss Bjerring." But mostly Jutland was inspiring. He wrote two Jutland tales, "A Story of the Sand Dunes" (1859) and "The Bishop of Børglum and his Warriors" (1861); as in "The Wind Tells of Valdemar Daae," these stories take their incantatory rhythm and motifs from what Andersen called the Wester-wow-wow—the roar of the North Sea breaking against the western coast of Jutland.

"A Story of the Sand Dunes" has a musicality as if an ebbing and flowing storm were recounting the narrative, and Andersen dedicated it to the composer Hartmann. Both stories are tragedies set around particular Jutland landmarks: "The Bishop of Børglum" in a lofty old monastery built on a mountain of sand; "A Story of the Sand Dunes" around a famous Skagen site, *den tilsandede Kirke*, a snow-white church buried, apart from its giant spire, in the sand dunes, which Andersen took as a symbol of the convergence of the natural and the spiritual world. He made it the tomb of his hero, writing to King Max of Bavaria:

> The whole description is the result of a visit I made last summer to the weirdest part of my country, West Jutland to Skagen. Nature is there so strange, from the magnificent beech forests of the eastern coast, which are still the haunts of the eagle and the black stork, one reaches vast moors covered with heather . . . the west coast presents green meadows and mighty sand dunes, which rise in jagged points like a chain of Alps, a bulwark against the rolling sea . . . As in the fairy tale of the enchanted forest, the church, covered with sand and overgrown with thorns and wild roses, presents a peculiar spectacle, only the spire projecting above the sand.

"A Story of the Sand Dunes" was the highlight of the fourth volume of *Nye Eventyr og Historier*, published in December 1859. Andersen was paid 500 rixdollars for the first edition of 5,000, which sold out almost instantly. That autumn, *Mit Livs Eventyr* went into its second edition and Andersen's royal stipend was increased from 600 to 1,000 rixdollars a year. He counted his savings at over 8,000 rixdollars, most of which Edvard was investing for him, and at last felt appreciated at home. In December came the award of the Maximilian Order for Art and Science from King Maximilian of Bavaria: "since your writings have a very German ring about them, and your tales are so popular in Germany," King Max wrote, he had decided to give Andersen a decoration as he strolled one evening by the lake and mountains; "I made a note of my resolve on my tablets by moonlight." Andersen replied that "my dearest wish is that God will let me live to visit Bavaria again . . . The last few years have brought me much joy—great, almost too great, recognition in my fatherland, and my works have been kindly judged in foreign countries, and most cordially received. God has allotted me unspeakable happiness, and I acknowledge it with deep gratitude." The next year he set off for Bavaria, but his calm was disturbed, for he made there a new friend who threw him into the ecstasies and agonies of love.

CHAPTER 21

Kiss of the Muse

1860–1865

You are a lucky man. When you look in the gutters, you find pearls.
> —B. S. INGEMANN, letter to
> Hans Christian Andersen, 10 April 1858

Andersen called Harald Scharff "a butterfly who flits around sympathetically." They first met in Paris in 1857; Andersen was on his way home from his visit to Dickens, and Scharff was staying in the French capital with the Danish actor Lauritz Eckhardt. Scharff was then twenty-one, lean and lithe, a flamboyant dancer at the Royal Theatre in Copenhagen. In his memoirs Auguste Bournonville wrote that Scharff "is full of life and imagination, and is unquestionably the finest leading man [of Danish ballet]." Photographs of him starring in Bournonville's productions, as Gennaro in *Napoli* and as the Norse hero Helge in *The Valkyrie*, show a very handsome young man with dark eyes and long lashes, black curly hair and thick sensuous lips; he sometimes wore a curling moustache. Like Stampe, there is something irresolute and uncertain in his expression and bearing which is apparent even when he is acting out the forceful role of a warrior, but his face has nevertheless a magnetism which suggests why he was so compelling a performer.

In Paris, Scharff and Andersen visited Notre-Dame together, but their paths did not cross again until July 1860, when Andersen was travelling in southern Germany and made a detour to the Bavarian village of Oberammergau to see the famous Passion Play, performed there every ten years. Eckhardt and Scharff, who shared a house in Copenhagen, were there to see it too, and the three Danes teamed up and travelled back to Munich together, where they were in each other's company ceaselessly for the next week.

By 1860, southern Germany was beginning to replace Weimar in Ander-

sen's affections. "Munich has an immense attraction for me," he wrote to
Carl Alexander. "In the *Bazaar* I have compared it to a rose-bush, which is
now in full bloom. The Au-Kirche is a veritable passion-flower, as if sprung
up in a moment; the Basilica a golden pink with exquisite perfume and
organ tones." Tainted less by the war than the northern states, touched by
the warmth and sensuality of Italy across the Alps, spectacular in its landscapes of high mountains plunging down to crystal clear lakes and its
colourful baroque architecture, and presided over by sentimental King Max,
who fussed over Andersen like a favourite pet, Bavaria drew him back continually. By the time he reached Oberammergau and put up with the pastor,
he was excited, and in a receptive mood. Few places could have been more
conducive a setting in which to fall in love than this picturesque Alpine village where the outsides of the chalets were painted with brightly coloured
religious scenes and the villagers, like Andersen's grandfather, made their
living by wood carving.

That such a place should host a theatrical spectacle of rare magnificence
and spiritual grandeur was for Andersen overwhelming. "I had always feared
that the representation of Christ on the stage must have something sacrile-
gious about it, but, as it was given here, it was elevating and noble," he told
Carl Alexander. The open-air theatre, built of beams and boards on the
green plain outside the village, embodied the convergence of nature and religion; the folk elements of the Passion Play's tradition also attracted Andersen. The play lasted from eight in the morning until five in the afternoon;
"we sat under the open sky; the wind sighed above us, the birds came and
flew out again. I thought of the old Indian play in the open air where the
Sakuntala was given; I thought of the Greek theatre . . . There was an ease
and a beauty about it that must impress everyone," Andersen wrote. And
everything was more exhilarating because he was falling in love with Scharff.

The pleasure continued in Munich. "Scharff and Eckhardt came to me,
we talked together until after 11 p.m. . . . went with Eckhardt and Scharff to
the Basilica . . . now I am going with Scharff and Eckhardt to Kaulbach's
studio . . . to the Residenz Theatre with Scharff and Eckhardt . . . came
home at 10 p.m. and had a visit from Scharff and Eckhardt," he jotted down
in his diary over a week in the city; then, on 9 July 1860, "don't feel at all well;
Eckhardt and Scharff travelling to Salzburg at 8 o'clock today." The next
day, Andersen, who had been photographed very little since the early days
of the daguerreotype in the 1840s, went to the studio of the photographer
Franz Hanfstaengel, and came away with a splendid photograph of himself.

Andersen in Munich, aged fifty-five, photograph by Franz Hanfstaengel, 1860.

In a full-length, sitting portrait in profile, with sunlight streaming in behind, Hanfstaengel captured a look which is at once serene, serious and full of movement and excitement; the dignity and humanity of a man on the brink of old age, and the radiance and warmth that lit up Andersen's face as he stood on the verge of a new love affair. Early pictures show that Andersen's eyes were unnaturally small; here they are open, wide, eager, illuminating his powerful, intelligent features. Wrapped up, as he always was, even in midsummer, in layers of long coats and waistcoats, with a thick tie around his neck, there is something self-protective about the elegant pose, yet it is eased out of stiffness by the expressive, big, bony hands, and by a playfulness about the sensual lips, which seem about to burst into talk. Andersen, who was generally convinced that he was ugly, was ebullient about the result. "I've never seen such a lovely and yet life-like portrait of myself. I was completely surprised, astonished, that the sunlight could make such a beautiful figure of my face. I feel unbelievably flattered, yet it is only a photograph. You'll get to see it, it is the only portrait which my vanity allows me to leave to those coming after me. How the young ladies will exclaim 'And he never got married!' " he wrote home to Henriette Collin.

Unlike some more handsome young men, Andersen aged well; at fifty-five a lifetime of thought and concentration was etched into his features, and Scharff's attentions at this time perhaps made him believe in himself more strongly. While early accounts of his appearance all emphasize his gaucheness and peculiarity, after 1860 the accent is always on his distinguished and animated features. "Andersen's personal appearance is prepossessing," wrote the American consul George Griffin, who visited him in the early 1860s.

> He would not however be called a handsome man in the popular acceptance of the term. He is tall and slender. While standing or sitting, he holds his body erect, but when walking he stoops a little. His nose is large but well-proportioned and his hair, which curls around his temples, is sprinkled with gray. His forehead is high, but not broad, still it is a noble-looking forehead, and not altogether unlike that of one of Titian's heads. His eyes are of a dark grey and literally beam with intelligence.

Another admirer, J. R. Brown, visiting around the same time, remembered:

> Before me stood a big bony figure, a man who had his best years behind him, but still wasn't quite old. He had lively eyes in a fine, wrinkled face, which was vivacious, and in the middle of this face a big protruding nose which by some quirk of fate was a bit crooked and was flanked by two protruding cheek bones below which were deep wrinkles. Numerous folds and grooves lay round the corners of a large mouth which was like a deep, irregular opening; one could easily have taken it for the mouth of a monster who ate children—if it were

not for the kind and sunny smile round the corners of his lips and the humanity which shone from every fold and groove.

A liaison with a figure of such gravitas and fame may have been one of Andersen's attractions to the flighty Scharff, who was over thirty years younger and still had his name to make at the Royal Theatre; certainly letters flew between the two for the rest of the year, and Andersen sent Scharff his photograph.

Andersen moved on to Switzerland, but the joy of his foreign trip was extinguished by Scharff's departure and, alone abroad, he soon grew despondent. His diaries from Geneva, where he spent the beginning of September, show how rapidly he descended into depression:

1 September: Want to go home ... my blood in a wild turmoil.

2 September: My spirits are down; want to go home and yet don't want to ... I have a morbid feeling, a strange fear about going crazy.

3 September: It's as if there's a demon riding my spirit. Where does it come from? Why? I'm unusually tired of everything! ... Took a walk by the rushing Rhone; a demonic urge to throw myself in ... I made cut-outs, which were greatly admired, for two nice little boys, Emile and Ernest. People were very attentive to me, and at 9 o'clock I was driven home. If only I could curb the demon riders that oppress my spirit. It reminds me of a dream I had about a bat that was grappling with me and almost choked me.

4 September: Upset. My spirit demon-ridden. Wished for sudden death; a frequent thought.

5 September: Nervous, in a morbid mood and got to feeling worse and worse ... My legs were shaking; I didn't feel well.

6 September: My mood depressed.

7 September: Was in a foul mood ... At home I found a couple of books ... in one I was mentioned in favourable terms. I read aloud in French ... I really am having an incredibly good time; only I myself can ruin my enjoyment ...

But not even flattery satisfied him for long, and although he had intended to spend Christmas in Italy, he turned back at Geneva, and in a black, confused mood began the journey north to Denmark. "I'm drifting like a bird in a storm, a bird that cannot fly but also cannot quite fall. O Lord! My God!

have mercy on me!" he wrote in his diary on 27 October. He reached Copenhagen in November ("went to bed as usual in a bad mood, godless") and fled
to Basnæs for the Christmas holiday.

Here, as often happened, his spirits lifted and his creative energy returned.
His diary is full of close, acerbic observations on those at the Basnæs house
party ("Nelly is a strange, cold person who stands as if her hands were wet
and she were saying: 'Don't touch me!'"), and on New Year's Eve he wrote the
short tale "The Snowman," whose setting recalls the woods on the estate: "all
the trees and bushes were covered with hoar frost. It was like a forest of white
coral, as though all the branches were studded with silvery blossom ... It was
like lace, and as dazzling white as though a brilliant white light streamed
from every branch. The silver birch stirred in the wind and seemed to be as
much alive as trees in the summertime. How lovely it all was!"

Here lives a snowman, who ought to have been in his element but can get
no peace because he falls in love with a stove which he has glimpsed in the
kitchen. "It's the exact opposite of you! It's as black as soot, and has a long
neck with a brass front! It eats wood till the fire comes out of its mouth," a
watchdog tells him, but all day the snowman gazes in:

> "I must get in; I must lean my head against hers, if it means breaking the win-
> dow."
>
> "You'll never get in there," said the watchdog. "And if you did get to the
> stove, you'd be off! Off!"
>
> "I'm as good as off now," said the snowman. "I'm breaking in two, I
> think." . . .
>
> Whenever the stove door was opened the flames would leap out in the way
> they had, shining bright red on the snowman's white face and throwing a red
> glow all over his chest.
>
> "I can't bear it," he said. "How it suits her to put her tongue out!"

The frost crunches and crackles, and like Andersen in the months before he
wrote the story, the snowman "could have felt happy, and he ought to have
felt happy, but he wasn't happy; he was pining for a stove." The weather
changes, as the watchdog has threateningly predicted, and the snowman
melts—at which point the dog sees that he has been built around a stove-
scraper, which explains his lovesickness, but "'it's all over now! Off! Off!'
And soon the winter, too, was over ... And then no one ever thinks of the
snowman any more."

Lyrical and poignant, "The Snowman" is another veiled, self-mocking autobiography which expresses Andersen's view of love as a burning, unreciprocated pain, his bitter acceptance that he would end life alone and a comic awareness that, as he wrote in his diary, "only I myself can ruin my enjoyment." The Snowman is a light-hearted cousin of the tragic Fir Tree; in this story Andersen returns to his earlier, tragi-comic mode of sketching the fleeting autobiography of an everyday object which seems to have caught his eye at random and yet whose life story has an uncanny appropriateness to its physical form. Just after "The Snowman" Andersen wrote "The Silver Penny," after he was cheated by a false coin; with the story, he joked, he got his money back. To tell such tales was almost a compulsion, like relating his own life story. Sometimes such ideas stayed in his mind for years before coalescing with some event or mood in Andersen's own life. Although it is told with the lightest touch, "The Snowman" sprang to life at least partly out of Andersen's discontent and pining over Harald Scharff.

He saw Scharff again during the winter of 1860–1861, and began a long, slow campaign to fix his interest. In January 1861 he had his photograph taken by the Copenhagen photographer Rudolph Striegler; in contrast to the upright, rigid poses he adopts in all other photographs, this one is languid and seductive, and he sent it to Scharff with an inscription, using the familiar "Du" form, "Dear Scharff, here you have again Hans Christian Andersen." On 20 February, Scharff's twenty-fifth birthday, he gave the dancer five volumes of his "Fairy Tales and Stories," and four days later Scharff came to see him; for his birthday in April Scharff gave him a reproduction of the Danish sculptor Herman Bissen's "Minerva." Nevertheless, Copenhagen left him restless and ill-tempered, and on 4 April 1861, just after publication of a new volume of tales including "The Snowman," and only four months after his return from his last foreign trip, he set off again, this time determined to reach Rome.

He was in a febrile and nervous state, which his choice of travelling companion, Edvard's son Jonas, only made worse. By now Andersen felt too old to travel far alone, and the Collin grandsons were becoming a necessity to him, to jolly him along and look after him. Jonas, at twenty-one, was a clever, moody, strong-minded and taciturn young man with a passion for zoology; as Edvard's son, he caused Andersen more agony than any of his cousins, because Andersen was so desperate for the relationship to be successful, while Jonas inevitably picked up something of the manoeuvrings between his father and Andersen, and knew that, although Andersen was his host and was paying his entire expenses, he could treat him badly. Edvard predicted problems, but was extremely grateful: "At this moment I only feel capable of telling you, my dear Andersen, that I more and more appreciate what you are doing for Jonas . . . I hope you will always get pleasure from what you are doing; that Jonas is grateful to you, you can be sure of it, even if he doesn't express it in so many words; this is hardly his skill, as surely as it is not mine."

It took Andersen and Jonas nearly a month to reach Rome, travelling by train to Marseilles, by stagecoach to Nice and Genoa, and then by boat to Civitavecchia. By the time they arrived, suffering from over-exposure to one another in train carriages and closed coaches, from exhaustion and frayed nerves, their relationship was in tatters. Jonas was red-faced with anger and silent; "I asked him if I had done anything to incur his displeasure; he said no, he wanted to go home to do some writing. I became dispirited—I live for him, do everything for him; and he said the other day that I have only 'my egoism'—I'm feeling despondent, unwell. Sat in tears on my bed," Andersen wrote in his diary on 5 May. A few days later: "I explained how ill I felt. He told me to pull myself together and then went off . . . I had the feeling and the hope that he would be concerned enough about me to stay, but he went . . . Jonas had as refrain, 'You must pull yourself together!'" Towards the end of the month, there was little improvement: "Jonas went around always brooding . . . He has no consideration for me, just like Drewsen's sons [his cousins Viggo and Harald]; I was grieved and offended . . . I did . . . without supper, terribly depressed, spiteful and in tears, jumping out of bed and ranting, beside myself . . . Got up early and went out. Came home just as unhappy, brooding, was irritable and upset."

Another evening, after they had quarrelled about Viggo Drewsen, whom Jonas praised over artists and writers because "he worked on his own development and had nothing to do with other people," Andersen wrote his tale "The Snail and the Rosebush" in revenge. Andersen, or the creative artist, is the rose bush, who cannot help giving beautiful, blooming roses to the world; Jonas is the snail—the image is wonderfully apt, because as a budding zoologist he collected snails—locked inside his own house who snarls, "The world doesn't concern me. What have I to do with the world? I have enough of myself, and enough in myself . . . What am I giving? I spit at it! It's of no use. It doesn't concern me." The tale has often been taken as Andersen's view of the creative life versus the intellectual one, with the snail an embodiment of Kierkegaard; it is in fact a shrewd comment on the narrow-minded impetuosity of youth versus the tolerance and generosity towards the wider world that comes with middle age. This was the core of the conflict between Jonas and Andersen. A wise and loving parent would perhaps have accepted Jonas's youth and found him less of an irritant than Andersen did; Andersen remained too much a child, anxious to be indulged and to be in the right himself, to be able to do so.

Once again, Rome had turned sour on Andersen; it also, as usual, made him feel sensual and sexually frustrated, and he was probably no easier to live with than was Jonas. He poured out his discomfort in another Roman tale, "The Psyche," begun in the theatre during a badly danced ballet days after his arrival, and continued on and off throughout the trip. The germ of the story had been in his mind since he began *The Improvisatore* in Rome thirty years earlier. He began it, he said, when he remembered an incident that occurred there in 1833–1834: a young nun was to be buried, and when her grave came to be dug there was found a beautiful statue of Bacchus. The story also owes much to his own early experiences in Rome, to the life of the Danish artist-monk Küchler, who had intrigued him since Küchler painted the first, puritanical portrait of him in 1834, and something, too, to Andersen's continuing obsession with Scharff.

It turns on a gifted sculptor with "warm blood" and "a strong imagination" who is consumed by sexual longing as his friends taunt him to use a prostitute, which he cannot bring himself to do—Andersen had endured similar teasing in Rome in 1833–1834. The sculptor devotes himself to his art, preferring the cold marble of his statues to female flesh and blood, but he is such a perfectionist that he destroys most of what he makes. His best work is a figure of a noble young woman, his "Psyche," and in fashioning it he falls in love with her. When she rejects him, he gives up his resistance and listens to a friend telling him, "Be a man, as all the others are, and don't go on living in ideals, for that is what drives men crazy . . . Come with me: be a man!" They find a pair of girls, but sex is described in terms of repulsion. The sculptor cries:

> "I feel as if the blossom of life were unfolding itself in my veins at this moment!"
>
> Yes, the blossom unfolded itself, and then burst and fell, and an evil vapour arose from it, blinding the sight, leading astray the fancy—the firework of the senses went out, and it became dark.

His decision is to bury his beautiful statue of Psyche, to give up art and, as

Küchler did, become a monk. Andersen visited Küchler at his monastery while he was writing the tale and was much taken by another monk there, Brother Ignatius ("He was a young man, kind and happy in Christ; remarked that there was religious feeling in the North and that each approached God in his own way . . . We all were in search of truth. He found he had so much in common with me"), who appears by name in the story as a model of the spiritual life. But the sculptor finds no peace:

> What flames arose up in him at times! What a source of evil, of that which he would not, welled up continually! He mortified his body, but the evil came from within . . . The more deeply he looked into his own heart the blacker did the darkness seem. "Nothing within, nothing without—this life squandered and cast away!" And this thought rolled and grew like a snowball, until it seemed to crush him.
>
> "I can confide my griefs to none. I may speak to none of the gnawing worm within. My secret is my prisoner; if I let the captive escape, I shall be his!"

Aware that he has wasted his gifts, he dies. Centuries later the white marble statue of Psyche is discovered when a young nun is buried, and although the artist is unknown, his art, as well as "the Psyche—the soul—will still live on!"

How much of Andersen's own sexual uncertainty went into this sultry, guilt-ridden tale? He recognized it as one of his most erotic works, and was furious when Bentley dedicated the English translation without his permission to the Princess of Wales ("I'm not at all pleased to have a story like 'The Psyche' dedicated to a young woman"). It is remarkable how close "The Psyche" is to the pent-up emotional tone and lurid Italian setting of *The Improvisatore*, and to the tales of sexual revulsion or denial, such as "The Travelling Companion" and "The Little Mermaid," which he wrote in the 1830s. Like his other tales of the same period, "The Psyche" questions the value of art, but, though more acrid in mood and contorted in style, its final message is that of "The Little Mermaid"—that immortality can be won through art not sex. "The Little Mermaid" was written twenty-five years earlier at the height of Andersen's obsession with and renunciation of Edvard Collin. Did he feel any bitterness that he was now travelling with Edvard's grown-up son, yet emotionally he had himself barely moved on, and was caught in the throes of a similar fixation on another young man, Harald Scharff? Certainly the tale, followed weeks later by a greater work of brooding eroticism, "The Ice Maiden," suggests that "the gnawing worm" of sexuality gave him no peace.

Publicly, however, a quite different persona was at work in Rome. This was the occasion, for example, when Andersen met Robert Browning at the Palazzo Barberini, the home of the wealthy American sculptor William Wentmore Story; Henry James was there and recalled Andersen as the quintessential Pied Piper, charming a group of children:

> The small people with whom he played enjoyed, under his spell, the luxury of believing that he kept and treasured—in every case and as a rule—the old tin soldiers and broken toys received by him, in acknowledgement of favours, from impulsive infant hands. Beautiful the queer image of the great benefactor moving about Europe with his accumulations of these relics. Wonderful too our echo of a certain occasion—that of a children's party, later on, when, after he had read out to his young friends "The Ugly Duckling," Browning struck up with the "Pied Piper"; which led to the formation of a grand march through the spacious Barberini apartment, with Story doing his best on a flute in default of bagpipes.

The dying Elizabeth Barrett Browning made Andersen the hero of her last poem, "The North and the South," in which the South yearns for a poet to express its beauty. The poem ends:

> The North sent therefore a man of men
> As a grace to the South;
> And thus to Rome came Andersen.
> —*"Alas, but must you take him again?"*
> Said the South to the North.

In a letter, she left another record: "Andersen (the Dane) came to see me yesterday," she wrote, "kissed my hand, and seemed in a general *verve* for embracing. He is very earnest, very simple, very child-like. I like him. Pen [her twelve-year-old son] says of him, 'He is not really pretty. He is rather like his own ugly duck, but his mind has developed into a swan'—That wasn't bad of Pen, was it?" Andersen knew he was perceived as something of a curiosity; in a short comic tale of self-acceptance, "The Butterfly," written just after he left Rome, he painted himself as a butterfly who flits about indecisively between girlfriends only to find he has become too old to be married, ending "a crusty old bachelor . . . stuck on a pin in a box of curios."

Another well-known writer charmed by Andersen in Rome was the Norwegian poet Bjørnstjerne Bjørnson, who soon got the measure of Andersen's crankiness and minor upsets, and unlike Jonas was willing to indulge them. When Andersen complained about the draughts and the crowds, Bjørnson suggested good-humouredly that the moment Andersen entered heaven he would turn round and ask Peter to close the door against the draught—unless of course he demanded to go back the minute he was in the doorway because he was being pushed by the crowds. He was, he said, very fond of Andersen, both for the glories and the weakness of his character.

After Rome, Andersen and Jonas went on to Switzerland, staying at the resort of Montreux on Lake Geneva, with its magnificent Alpine backdrop, where, Andersen wrote, "was wrought my Wonder Story 'The Ice Maiden' . . . in which I would show the Swiss nature as it had lain in my thoughts after many visits to that glorious land." "The Ice Maiden," more a novella than a tale, is the tragic love story of two Swiss peasants, Rudy and Babette, told in fifteen parts. Its emphasis on setting, on letting the story almost emerge by itself through the ice and snow, the use of dreams, the brooding psychological unease, the images of destruction that ring out from the start—all these link it with the recent works of 1858–1859, but with the figure of the Ice Maiden, Andersen returns to the dramatic mythic creations of his middle years.

The story opens with a light touch and with Andersen's reassertion of the romantic belief in the child as visionary, as young Rudy chatters to his pet cats and dogs—"for you see, children who cannot talk yet, can understand the language of fowls and ducks right well, and cats and dogs speak to them quite as plainly as father and mother can do . . . with some children this period ends later than with others, and of such we are accustomed to say that they are very backward, and that they have remained children a long time. People are in the habit of saying many strange things." The cats and dogs remain commentators throughout, telling us of the progression of the love affair ("Rudy and Babette were treading on each other's paws under the table all evening. They trod on me twice, but I would not mew for fear of exciting attention"), but the tragic impulse of the story is overriding, its fatalism hanging heavy and thundering as the glaciers and streams of melted ice that rush down the valleys. Andersen's mountain scenery is spectacularly drawn; here Rudy's mother is killed, and the Ice Maiden, "the Glacier Queen," who rules this "wondrous glass palace," feels cheated that she has not captured Rudy too. She is one of Andersen's *femmes fatales*:

> She, the death-dealing, the crushing one, is partly a child of the air, partly the mighty ruler of the river . . . she sails on the slender fir twig down the rushing

stream, and springs from one block to another, with her long snow-white hair and her blue-green garment fluttering around her and glittering like the water in the deep Swiss lakes.

"To crush and to hold, mine is the power!" she says. "They have stolen a beautiful boy from me, a boy whom I have kissed, but not kissed to death. He is mine, and I will have him!"

Rudy goes to live with his grandfather, a woodcarver like Andersen's, and becomes the embodiment of nature, climbing and hunting in the mountains like an animal, repeatedly depriving the Ice Maiden of her prize. In this cinematic story, she looms in and out of dark icy snowscapes, sometimes as a hallucination, sometimes as a real, terrifying presence. Once Rudy nearly falls, and "below, in the black yawning gulf, on the rushing waters, sat the Ice Maiden herself, with her long whitish-green hair, and stared at him with cold death-like eyes." But his undoing is to fall in love with Babette, who represents culture and worldly sophistication, and to become jealous when a cultivated Englishman gives her a book of Byron's poems. He swaps Babette's betrothal ring for a kiss from a phantom woman on the mountains, and as in "The Psyche," this instant of pure eroticism spells darkness and death:

> In that moment . . . he sank into the deep and deadly ice cleft, lower and lower. He saw the icy walls gleaming like blue-green glass, fathomless abysses yawned around, the water dropped tinkling down like shining bells, clear as pearls, glowing with pale blue flames. The Ice Maiden had kissed him—a kiss which sent a shudder from neck to brow; a cry of pain escaped from him; he tore himself away, staggered, and—it was night before his eyes.

In "The Snow Queen," when Kai is seduced by the icy *femme fatale*, he is rescued by the purity of Gerda's childish love, but here there is no redemption. Rudy is saved, briefly reunited with Babette and then snatched from her on the eve of their wedding day, as they celebrate the flowering of adult love by sailing at sunset under a mountain that "gleamed like red lava"—as in *The Improvisatore* and "The Little Mermaid," the signal colours of "The Ice Maiden" are those Andersen used to symbolize passion, fiery red and deathly blue. Rudy is dragged under the water where he sees crowds of the drowned who have sunk into the crevasses among the glaciers, and

> beneath all the Ice Maiden sat on the clear transparent ground. She raised herself towards Rudy and kissed his feet; then a cold, death-like numbness poured

through his limbs, and an electric shock—ice and fire mingled! . . . "Mine, mine!" sounded around him and within him. "I kissed you when you were little, kissed you on your mouth. Now I kiss your feet, and you are mine altogether!" And he disappeared beneath the clear blue water.

Babette realizes "The Ice Maiden has got him"—the words spoken almost half a century earlier by Andersen's mother when his father died.

Now this deep-seated memory merged with the fatalism of a lifetime, with his idea of sex as death—forbidden, frightening—and with intimations too of the price the artist pays for his gift. In his ballet version of the tale *Le Baiser de la Fée* Stravinsky interpreted the early kiss of the Ice Maiden as the kiss of the muse, marking out the hero Tchaikowsky for suffering brilliance;* Andersen's use of the symbolic kiss may in turn have derived from the fatal kiss planted on the brow of the hero by the fairy-woman in Bournonville's ballet *La Sylphide*, which opened in Copenhagen in 1836. "The Ice Maiden" is one of Andersen's most powerful tales; the heroine is one of the three demonic women in his stories—the others are the Snow Queen and his late creation Auntie Toothache—who are archetypes as memorable as those from myth or legend. Bjørnson, to whom the story was dedicated, thought it exceptionally bold:

> "The Ice Maiden" begins as if it were rejoicing and singing in the free air, by the pine trees, and the blue water, and the Swiss cottages. The thought that fashions the last portion has something divine in it—so it impresses me, the thought that two people should be separated at the very highest point of their happiness; still more that you showed clearly how as when a sudden breeze ruffles the still water, so there dwelt in the souls of both that which could overthrow their happiness; but that you should have the courage to do this with these two of all people!

Bjørnson was one of the earliest critics fully to appreciate Andersen's widening range; he wrote to Jonas Collin junior that all the other forms from which Andersen had been discouraged—the novel, drama, even philosophy—now turned up in his fairy stories, which were no longer traditional tales but freewheeling narratives embracing tragedy, comedy, the epic and the lyric; their lack of restraint made one tremble to think what he might do next.

Andersen was still working on "The Ice Maiden" as he travelled home to

---

*Later commentators have suggested that the kiss also suggests the stigma of homosexuality.

Denmark in August, staying *en route* in Sorø with Ingemann, to whom he read it as he was revising the ending and changing the title from first "The Mountain Hunter" and then "The Eagle's Nest." At the last moment his relations with Jonas improved, and Andersen suggested that Jonas call him "Du": "he was surprised but said Yes in a firm voice, and thanked me. Later, when I was in bed he came in to me before lying down in his own room, took my hand and repeated once more such a heartfelt 'Thank you!' that tears came into my eyes; he gave me a kiss on my forehead and I felt so happy." This was the best compensation he could have had for Edvard's refusal to accept "Du" terms thirty years earlier; its symbolism as a healing of Collin wounds was magnified when Jonas senior, aged seventy-five, died just days after this *rapprochement* with his grandson.

Although the old man had been declining for months, Andersen was shocked at how intensely he felt the loss of his father-figure and first patron. "Toward evening I had a physical reaction . . . felt faint and went to bed," he wrote; he returned to Copenhagen for the funeral, after which he "ate at a restaurant and felt very alone." Heiberg, who had died the year before, had written that as civil servant, patron of the arts and director of the Royal Theatre, Jonas had been "an active participant and often instigator of almost everything produced in this country of any lasting significance." Jonas had always been instinctively more in sympathy with Heiberg's art than with Andersen's, and in his final year he was much cheered by twilight visits from the widowed Johanne Luise Heiberg, his favourite protégée, who described in her memoirs how she tiptoed along to the house standing behind the iron gates and rang the doorbell which had once sounded constantly as "the high and the lowly, the young and the old, all sought out this mighty man." Now the house was silent, a dozy servant peered out curiously from "a half-opened door . . . as though he did not really believe in the unwonted sound of the bell," and the pair sat by the firelight and reminisced about the heyday of the theatre. Jonas Collin haunted Andersen's dreams until his death; in 1865, four years after the old man's death, Andersen had a nightmare in which "mighty Collin" was pitted against "poor Andersen," dependent on him as in adolescence for his survival in the intellectual classes.

It often happens, however, that the death of a parent or parental figure both galvanizes and liberates an individual towards a new sexual relationship, and so it was with Andersen. In the winter of 1861–1862 his friendship with

Andersen's last love: Harald Scharff, as Gennaro in Auguste Bournonville's ballet Napoli *at the Royal Theatre, Copenhagen, 1860.*

Scharff finally turned into a love affair, about which he was too excited to be discreet. Through the autumn he read aloud his erotic tales "The Psyche" and "The Ice Maiden" to Scharff as he was preparing them for publication in November 1861, then on 2 January 1862 he noted in his diary, "Scharff bounded up to me; threw himself round my neck and kissed me! . . . Nervous in the evening." Five days later he received "a visit from Scharff, who was very intimate and nice." In the following weeks, there was "dinner at Scharff's, who was ardent and loving," on 16 January; "a visit from Scharff, who is intimate and deeply devoted to me," on 23 January; and several more visits during the rest of the month. He saw Scharff, now promoted to a solo dancer, perform at the Royal Theatre several times in January and February; on 12 February he recorded a visit to the theatre which simply ends "Scharff," and on 13 February he wrote, "Yesterday Scharff was at my house, talked a lot about himself with the greatest familiarity."

By 17 February the relationship had been noticed and Andersen's doctor, Edvard's brother Theodor Collin, was warning him to be careful. "Theodor put me in a very bad mood," he wrote, "he emphasized how strongly I showed my love for S, which people noticed and found ridiculous." He was so upset by Theodor that he fled home from a lunch at Louise Lind's—his old love Louise Collin, Theodor's sister—but nothing could now stop the flow of the affair. On 20 February Andersen was celebrating his 26-year-old lover's birthday at a dinner at Eckhardt's house; he sent Scharff a bouquet, a teacup and saucer and a book of Paludan-Müller's poems. Next day Scharff was again at Nyhavn, "intimate and communicative," gossiping about Madame Heiberg and the Royal Theatre—their chief shared interest. Through March the two saw each other every few days and Andersen often saw Scharff dance at the theatre; the diary for 6 March records, for example, "visit from Scharff . . . exchanged with him all the little secrets of the heart; I long for him daily," and on 12 March, "Scharff very loving, gave him my picture." Andersen was utterly absorbed in him; he spent an evening at the house of the young banker Einar Drewsen, another Collin grandson (Ingeborg's son), in whom he confided—"I told all about my erotic time"—and on 2 April the highlight of his fifty-seventh birthday was Scharff's present, a silver toothbrush engraved with his name and the date.

The happiest photographs we have of Andersen, taken by Georg Hansen in Copenhagen to be mounted on visiting cards, date from these months. Leaning on the back of a chair, his elbows on a table and his head leaning against his hands, his expression smiling and his face shining with pleasure, they show Andersen in a relaxed and sunny mood. Elizabeth Jerichau-Baumann's portrait of Andersen reading to children was also painted at this time; though sentimental, it catches a luminous grace and contentment about Andersen, absorbed in his imaginative world, that is rare. We can only guess at the physical details of his relationship with Scharff, but there is no doubt that here was an affair which brought him joy, some kind of sexual fulfilment and a temporary end to loneliness. As important, Scharff was Andersen's link to youth at a time he felt himself getting old; his enthusiasms, his flighty, high-pitched personality, his youthful beauty and his lithe dancing were all restorative for the ageing writer.

His new fairy tales sold out rapidly and were well-received, he had 8,200 rixdollars in the bank at New Year 1862 and a few weeks later Theodor Reitzel offered him an astonishing 3,000 rixdollars for a reissue of the illustrated edition of his collected tales and stories—the first payment on which he had to pay income tax, introduced in 1862 at a rate of two per cent, which Andersen considered outrageously high. When the theatre season ended in

Andersen in Bordeaux, aged fifty-seven, with Edvard Collin's son Jonas, "an inso-lent fool on whom I have wasted the kindness of my heart," 1863.

June and Scharff departed with Eckhardt for Vienna, Andersen did not languish long in Copenhagen; he used the money from Reitzel to fund an exotic trip he had long wanted to make, to Spain, and in July 1862 he set out, again taking Jonas Collin with him. The journey was not a success. Andersen was unknown in Spain and received none of the gratifying recognition that usually bolstered him up on foreign trips; indeed the reverse happened, and several times he was laughed at in the street for his long lanky figure. It was the primitive and medieval aspect of Spain that most appealed to him, such as his visit to the Alhambra to see the Moorish halls in the sunlit air, where he was driven in a diligence drawn by ten mules with jingling bells; crossing to Tangier, where he took tea with the Pasha, was, he said, the highlight of the entire journey. These experiences poured into notes for his travel book, *A Visit to Spain*, finished on his return in 1863. But the account has none of the enthusiasm and beneath-the-skin knowledge of the country of his best travel books, such as *Pictures of Sweden*, and the muted tones of his diary too show that this was a lacklustre trip. His heart was not in it, and how much he was still preoccupied with Scharff is suggested from the diary entry for 15 September in which a dramatic description of a flood in Barcelona is interrupted by the underlined sentence "Sent letter to Eckhardt and Scharff" and then continued, with an account of those who had drowned.

The desperation for new experiences and inspiration which had marked his journeys as a young man was gone; he was weary, irritable and often bored. Jonas, who travelled with an increasing collection of small animals such as snails, provided a focus for his complaints and some moments of farce, as when the Spanish customs confiscated his menagerie and its supply of poisonous food, and he and Andersen had to wait for a chemist to inspect it. A photograph of the pair of travellers in Bordeaux *en route* for Denmark in January 1863 shows the strain: Jonas, square-faced, tight-lipped and cold, the very image of his father, stands erect and unhesitating, staring straight ahead; Andersen, sitting at right angles to him, is taken in profile, looking tired, tense and old. By the time they arrived home, Jonas was recorded as "an insolent fool on whom I have wasted the kindness of my heart."

But Copenhagen in 1863 gave Andersen no peace. The clouds of war were gathering, and the relationship with Scharff that had brought such pleasure was clearly on the wane. In June Scharff was still loving, and at a party he boldly proposed a toast "to his two dearest friends, Eckhardt and Hans Christian Andersen," but on 27 August Andersen wrote in his diary: "Scharff's passion for me is now over; he has transferred his attentions completely to someone else fascinating. I am not as upset about it as over earlier, similar disappointments." So the world-weary older man contrasted his resignation with the intense feelings of youth. He may have been remembering his agony at what he considered Henrik Stampe's betrayal back in 1844, or even the blow to his youthful desire for Ludvig Müller in 1832—or there may have been other romances with men in the intervening years, too secret even to be mentioned in the diary.*

But Scharff's attentions had kept him young, and as soon as he realized they were over Andersen felt like an old man. He guessed that he would never have another love affair, although his sexual interest in women would still revive. "I am not satisfied with myself. I cannot live in my loneliness, am weary of life," he wrote on 16 September. "Felt old, downhill, sad," he noted on 5 October; the next day, "visited Scharff, who gave me his photograph and was a good child . . . Poor young love, I can achieve nothing there." Through the autumn of 1863 his spirits fell; "Scharff has not visited me in eight days; with him it is over," he wrote on 13 November; in December he saw Scharff at Eckhardt's house—Eckhardt was by now married—where he

---

*The silence of Danish commentators, from Andersen's own time until the present day, on the subject of his homosexual relationships, is remarkable. Andersen's diaries leave no doubt that he was attracted to both sexes; that at times he longed for a physical relationship with a woman and that at other times he was involved in physical liaisons with men. Danish scholars from Hjalmar Helweg (*H. C. Andersen: En psykiatrisk Studie*) in 1927 to Elias Bredsdorff today have consistently denied Andersen's involvement in homosexual relationships, pinning much on the argument that the Collin family would have known had Andersen had homosexual tendencies, and would not have allowed him to take their young sons and grandsons on foreign holidays. But we know from the diaries that at least two of the Collins, Edvard's brother Theodor and Ingeborg's son Einar Drewsen, discussed Andersen's homosexuality with him at precisely the time when he was travelling abroad with members of the family—not to mention Andersen's confidential relationship with his favourite Collin grandchild, Ingeborg's daughter Jonna, whom Andersen once asked, "do not judge me by ordinary standards," and who was married to Andersen's former lover Henrik Stampe.

Much definitive Andersen scholarship—the editing of the diaries and letters—was completed by the 1960s, when discretion about sexual matters was still considered appropriate in many academic circles, but even recent Danish scholarship has swerved away from it. Patricia L. Conroy and Sven H. Rossel, editors of the English edition of Andersen's diaries (1990), for example, include none of the erotic references to either Stampe or Scharff, leaving only the tantalizing hint that "at Oberammergau he saw two familiar faces from home—the actor Lauritz Eckhardt and the ballet dancer Harald Scharff—which he got to know much better in the coming years." Only two scholarly papers in recent years have discussed Andersen's homo-erotic attachments: Wilhelm von Rosen in "Venskabets Mysterier" in 1980, and the German critic Heinrich Detering in *Intellectual Amphibia* in 1991.

read some fairy tales and noted, with the infallible instinct of the spurned lover, that a dancer called Petersen was there. A few years later Scharff and Camilla Petersen were engaged, though they never married. Andersen now had to recognize that, like all the young men with whom he had toyed, Scharff would move on from homosexual flings to a stable heterosexual relationship; he married another ballet dancer, Elvida Møller, in 1874, when he was thirty-eight.

There was no apparent bitterness; Andersen and Scharff continued to move in overlapping social circles, saw each other from time to time, and Andersen remembered Scharff's birthday almost every year until his death. There was a poignant coda to the relationship in 1871, when Scharff was due to dance the lead in Bournonville's ballet version of "The Steadfast Tin Soldier," one of Andersen's most memorable characterizations of resignation and disappointment in love. Shortly before the ballet opened, Scharff, while performing a dance in a divertissement for *The Troubadour*, ruptured a kneecap, "an accident which," said Bournonville, "in all my years of experience, has not happened to any dancer, either here or abroad." Scharff had given his parts a highly individual stamp, and he was severely missed as the star of the Copenhagen ballet. "This tragedy," Bournonville wrote, "was greeted with universal sympathy, for while there was certainly hope of a cure which would make it possible for him to move about unhindered in private life, and maybe even on the dramatic stage, he had to be considered lost to the Ballet."

The end of Andersen's affair with Scharff combined with two national events, the death of King Frederik VII on 15 November, and the signing of a new constitution for Denmark and just one of the duchies, Schleswig, to make Andersen look towards the new year of 1864 with horror. The new constitution, separating Schleswig and Holstein, provoked Prussia, and by the end of 1863 Danish troops were being called up for war. "The year is over; the outlook is pitchblack, sorrowful, bloody—the New Year," he noted in his diary; in his autobiography he wrote:

> The bloody waves of war were again to wash over our fatherland. A kingdom and an empire stood united against our little country. A poet's way is not by politics ... but when the ground trembles beneath him so that all threatens to fall at once, then he has only thought for this which is a matter of life and

death . . . He is planted in his fatherland as a tree; there he brings forth his flowers and his fruit; and if they are sent widely through the world, the roots of the tree are in the home soil.

During the 1864 war he was much harsher on Germany than in 1848–1851, refusing to speak German: "it was against my heart of hearts to speak that language, found it unpatriotic." Meeting Robert Lytton, he said, "at present there is for me in that language the sound of cannon and of the shouts of enemies. I would rather speak bad English." Two days later he wrote that "Today I've been really tormented by the pressure of political events . . . I feel each kindness people in Germany have shown me, acknowledge friends there but feel that I, as a Dane, must make a complete break with them all. They have been turned out of my heart: never will we meet again . . . My heart is breaking!" New Year's morning 1864 at Basnæs was a tingling, frosty day. Andersen had apple dumplings and spiced red wine, and read aloud to the guests, but the cosiness and luxury could not take his mind off war and the soldiers in their cold barracks, and once again he was unable to write. "Every day soldiers left for the seat of war, young men, singing in their youthful gaiety, going as to a lively feast. For weeks and months I felt myself unfitted to do anything; all my thoughts were with the men."

He returned to Copenhagen on 5 January. "Mrs. Anholm's eldest son was there to welcome me. My room was toasty warm. A cup of tea was my dinner. Walked over to Edvard Collin's." War brought financial problems to Copenhagen, and that year Andersen lent money both to Edvard (2,500 rixdollars) and to Henrik Stampe (1,000 rixdollars); his own savings exceeded 10,000 rixdollars. He tried to absorb himself in the city's social life, visiting the same group of people almost every day, and depending, as he had since his student days, on the weekly rota of dinners with leading Copenhagen families. Though early patrons like Jonas Collin and Ørsted were dead and the children of Andersen's contemporaries had mostly left home, the dramatis personae were remarkably unchanged. On Mondays he dined with Edvard and Henriette Collin; on Tuesdays with Ingeborg Drewsen and her husband; on Wednesdays with Ørsted's widow and his daughter Mathilde; on Thursdays—the evening formerly devoted to Jonas Collin—with the merchant Moritz Melchior; on Fridays with Ida Koch, the widowed daughter of Admiral Wulff and sister of Henriette; on Saturdays with an aristocratic friend, Madame Neergaard; and on Sundays with another merchant family, the Henriques. Andersen was just beginning now to know the Henriques and the Melchiors, wealthy Jewish families related by marriage; they were to be of paramount importance to him in his last decade. In 1864, however, his greatest support was Edvard's sympathetic wife Henriette, whom he now felt closest to within the Collin family. In his extended autobiography, he paid her tribute: "I lost for a moment my hold on God, and felt myself as wretched as a man can be. Days followed in which I cared for nobody, and I believed nobody cared for me. I had no relief in speaking to anyone. One however, more faithful and kind, came to me, Edvard Collin's excellent wife who spoke compassionate words and bade me give thought to my work."

But he could not work. His muse dried up as wholly as it had done during the first Danish–German conflict; as before, he could not dislodge thoughts and nightmares of war from his head. "I feel gloomy and depressed. Can't get anything done. Wish for an end to everything," he noted in January 1864, then a few days later, "overwhelmed and bitterly aware of my forsakenness" and "Now I'm sitting at home all alone. The African cactus gets shifted every evening away from the cold windows, but I'm not expecting any flowers, not even that it will survive." On the eve of his fifty-ninth birthday on 2 April, Andersen looked back: "the past year of my life has been full of trials and tribulations . . . The king died. The war is threatening Denmark with destruction. I've aged. I have false teeth that torment me. I'm not in good health. I'm heading for death and the grave." Andersen signed a petition to the Swiss people to stir up international sympathy for the Danes; after it was published he began to suffer nightmares that the Germans would attack him. "What a night I've spent in self-torture, in rehearsing fixed ideas, in half madness, envisioning myself at the bottom of a ship, cast into a dark cell, tortured and abused—I'm making a fool of myself by recording my fixed idea. I lay bathed in sweat, unsleeping in the early morning hours," he wrote on 18 April. Two hours later came word of a Danish defeat, along with the news that Viggo Drewsen, Ingeborg's dark, curly haired, rebellious son, of whom Andersen was fond despite their difficult travelling days together, was wounded and taken prisoner.

Another Danish defeat followed in June; "Godless and therefore unhappy," Andersen noted on 30 June. A ceasefire was declared on 20 July, and a peace treaty drawn up on 30 October, by which Denmark lost both Schleswig and Holstein. "I am disgruntled and depressed, angry with so many people. Only disaster, violation, oblivion and death are waiting for me," Andersen wrote in his diary the next day. That night, he recorded his recurrent nightmare: "Last night I again dreamed my usual, hideous dream about a living child that I press up against my warm breast—this time, though, it was just in my sleeve; it breathed its last, and I was left with only the wet skin."

The dream, so close to the images of dead children in his tales, may have had many subconscious meanings, but it seems linked to his awareness both of his public image and of his own creativity. At some level, he had been exploiting the child in himself as a persona since his teens—the image he liked to cultivate of innocent but gifted *naïf*. This recurring dream may have been an acknowledgement that by doing so he had in a sense killed it, thus forcing himself always to act a part. Yet childhood memories and echoes of folk tales remained the well-spring of his creativity; this dream was symbolic too at a time when he was mourning the loss of his creative powers. A few weeks after recording it, he was complaining about a tumour in his hand, which he thought he would die from, adding that he believed it was time for him to die as he hadn't enjoyed life, nor accepted the gifts God had given him.

Yet almost as soon as war was behind Denmark, and "the darkest, gloomiest year" of Andersen's life was over, inspiration flooded back. At Basnæs on New Year's Day 1865, he began "The Will o' the Wisps are in Town," which summed up his desperate feelings about the war, his doubts about art as devilish as well as redemptive, his fears about the end of civilized values.

> For more than a year and a day I had written no wonder-story; my soul was so burdened; but now, as soon as I came out into the country to friendly Basnæs, to the fresh woods and the open sea, I wrote "The Will o' the Wisps are in Town" in which was told why it was that the wonder stories had been so long unwritten; because without was war, and within sorrow and want that war brought with it.

Set in a hazy, chiaroscuro world reminiscent of *A Walking Tour*, the story tells of "a man who once knew many stories, but they had slipped away from him—so he said; the Story that used to visit him of its own accord no longer came and knocked at his door." He sets out to seek the story, in the woods, on the seashore, and finds it at the home of the Moor-woman, a grotesque parody of the poet's muse.

> And the man asked about the Story, and inquired if the Moor-woman had met it in her journeyings . . . "I don't care about it either way," cried the woman.

"Let the rest write, those who can, and those who cannot likewise. I'll give you an old bung from my cask that will open the cupboard where poetry is kept in bottles, and you may take from that whatever may be wanting. But you, my good man, seem to have blotted your hands sufficiently with ink, and to have come to that age of satiety, that you need not be running about every year for stories, especially as there are more important things to be done."

But as she mocks him, she tells him a story about the will o' the wisps who live on the marsh and go "dancing like little lights across the moor." Once a year, those born at "that minute of time" when the wind blows a certain way and the moon stands at a certain size, have the power to enter the soul of a mortal for 365 days, during which time they must lead 365 people to destruction; they then "attain to the honour of being a runner before the devil's state coach." But of course these devilish will o' the wisps are as insubstantial and fleeting as the moment when they are born. They are emblems of the insubstantiality of art, yet paradoxically they make up the authenticity and solidity of the story that Andersen is narrating. "One could tell quite a romance about the Will o' the Wisps, in twelve parts," says the man who tells stories, but "I should be thrashed if I were to go to people and say, 'Look, yonder goes a Will o' the Wisp in his best clothes.'" In the end he concludes that it does not matter if he dares to speak the truth, as no one will believe him; "for they will all think I am only telling them a story." Thus, in this satirical story-within-a-story, the value of fairy tales is demolished and Andersen's own worth as a writer rejected—except that through its comedy and the vitality of its characters, wisps and Moor-woman, "The Will o' the Wisps" reaffirms the very power of the art it appears to doubt. Here Andersen returned to the questioning, innovative mode of the late 1850s, as he turned reinvigorated to those aspects of his life he thought he had put behind him.

"Especially cheerful and well," he wrote in his diary in February 1865. Not even three evictions from his Nyhavn apartment of sixteen years—first rain flooded the bedroom, then snow burst into the living room and finally the landlady declared she needed more space—quenched his spirits. At sixty, he still had no furniture; he simply packed his bags, stayed first with Edvard and next at Basnæs, where he wrote more tales, and in the autumn toured Sweden. In between, he stayed at the new, exclusive Hotel d'Angleterre on Kongens Nytorv; in the winter he was briefly given rooms on the King's estate, where Bournonville was a neighbour. A new volume of tales—including "The Will o' the Wisps"—was published in November 1865. Andersen was himself more of a will o' the wisp than ever; at the end of 1865 he was planning another exotic trip, to Portugal. He had a decade to live, and was bursting with energy for new experiences of travel, love, friendship and the continual redefining of the genre he had made his own.

CHAPTER 22

Aladdin's Palace of the Present

1865–1869

Give me human life, human happiness, only a short span, only the one night.
—HANS CHRISTIAN ANDERSEN, "The Dryad"

In the mid 1860s Andersen formed a friendship which helped make his old age exceptionally comfortable and productive. When he met the Melchior and Henriques families, the merchant Moritz Melchior was the richest commoner in Denmark and his brother-in-law Martin Henriques, a stockbroker, was not far behind. Andersen first came across Henriques at Bournonville's house; his wife Thérèse was a gifted musician, several of their children became composers and painters, and Andersen was immediately drawn to the Sunday soirées at their house on Tordenskjoldsgade, on the corner of Kongens Nytorv, where Copenhagen's artists and musicians gathered regularly. Edvard Lehmann's painting of such an evening in 1868, with Thérèse seated at the grand piano surrounded by family, the composer Niels W. Gade and the ballet dancers the Price sisters, the room lit by chandeliers, is an image of the unchanging values of the Copenhagen middle classes as political unrest swept across Europe. The Henriques and the Melchiors re-created the world of Golden Age Copenhagen in which Andersen had grown up, and they made him feel at home.

The two families were cultured, Jewish, cosmopolitan and multilingual; their ancestors had come to Denmark from Holland and north Germany in the seventeenth century, and they maintained extensive links with family members across Europe. Moritz, ten years younger than Andersen, had made his money trading in tea, coffee and sugar with the Danish West Indies; his company thrived until the Second World War, and in the 1860s was in its heyday. Moritz was then head of the Copenhagen Wholesalers' Association, had a seat in parliament, and though indifferent to politics, was respected for his civic and philanthropic work. Edmund Gosse, meeting him in 1872, described him as "a handsome man of about sixty, a little deaf, a little shy"; he was quiet and serious, and sympathy shone out of his expressive, lined face and warm eyes. His wife Dorothea, Henriques's sister, was some twenty years younger than Andersen and became the closest confidante of his last decade; intelligent, lively, affectionate, unstintingly generous and thoughtful, she had through the 1860s a charmed life, full of wealth and happy, healthy children, and she spread benevolence and grace around her.

The family had two homes in Copenhagen: a sumptuous apartment in the centre of town, on Højbro Plads, whose second-floor balcony looked on to the city's most famous market square and the canal, and a villa, "Rolighed" ("Tranquillity"), in the newly fashionable suburb of Østerbro in the north of the city. Gosse walked there "through the vague land of villas then skirting the old lime kilns" along the coast, where the bourgeoisie of the 1860s sought fresh sea air and open spaces, and found a country mansion surrounded by beautiful gardens running down to the sea. Andersen's old friends the Drewsens lived nearby; a little along the coast in woody Klampenborg lay "Petershøi" ("Petershill"), the Henriques' summer retreat, and Andersen spent long periods both here and at Rolighed. "May God protect the happiness you have in your blessed family life . . . If I had a home like yours I would think less of flying away," he wrote to Martin Henriques at the beginning of their friendship at Christmas 1865.

The Melchiors had bought an eighteenth-century house once owned by Ørsted, and rebuilt it as "a miniature of Rosenborg Palace, with a tower, and with high balconies overlooking the Sound." It was an exquisitely proportioned house, painted pink and white, neo-classical in style with Gothic additions of turrets and towers, its interior luxurious and modern, its aspect, until a new harbour was built there in 1895, unrivalled (the suburban Nordhavn station now stands on the site). Andersen called Rolighed his "home of homes," as he had in the past referred to Jonas Collin's austere house on Amaliegade; at Rolighed, however, he was unquestioningly welcomed and accepted at all times. A suite of rooms looking out to sea was put at his disposal; Gosse recalled how Andersen conducted him over the house, "showing off its magnificence with a child-like enthusiasm . . . finally he stopped in his own bright, high rooms open to the east. He took me out on to the balcony and bade me notice the long caravan of ships going by in the Sound below—'they are like a flock of wild swans,' he said—with the white towns of Malmö and Landskrona sparkling on the Swedish coast, and the sunlight falling on Tycho Brahe's island."

Sun-dappled photographs of Andersen *en famille* at Rolighed, taken mostly by Moritz's brother Israel, a gifted amateur who knew Andersen well, show him taking tea in the flower-strewn grounds; lying on the grass on a blanket, wearing his top hat and holding a bouquet as the family cluster round attentively; watching the children play beneath the trees; flanked by protective coachmen as he perches on the steps of the Melchiors' stately carriage, in his last years the only vehicle in which he would travel. Nearby is always Dorothea, reassuring and calm, and some of her daughters. Andersen looks soothed, happy, absorbed. He never tired of being fussed over; on his sixty-third birthday, for example, he noted: "along with some flowers, Mrs. Melchior sent me a comfortable chair for in front of my desk. Louise Melchior [her daughter], an embroidered strap for the plaid blanket I take with me on trips. Sophie Melchior [her sister-in-law], a lovely case for newspapers . . . Several pots full of violets and stocks from Mrs. Melchior . . . A telegram from Moses Melchior in England . . . Telegram from Israel Melchior, who is at the moment in Hobro." In the evening, the Melchiors hosted his birthday party: "the dining room was decorated beautifully—a bust of me with a laurel wreath and greenery and Danish flags all around; beneath a verse written by the editor Bille . . . Moritz Melchior gave the speech . . . What a lavish day!"

There were many reasons why Andersen felt so at peace here. Like him, the Melchiors and the Henriques stood at the heart of Copenhagen society and yet felt themselves to be outsiders. Their Jewishness set them apart; swarthy, dark-haired and dark-eyed, the two families looked different from most Danes; only since 1849, a few years after the Melchiors had married, had Jews enjoyed full constitutional and civil rights in Denmark, and the last pogroms had taken place in Moritz's lifetime. They were assimilating fast—Moritz's brothers, Israel and Moses, born in the 1820s, still bore traditional Jewish names; his sons Carl and Emil, born in the 1850s, have typical Danish names. Andersen had always identified with Jews, who are characterized in his works with sympathy and interest at a time when caricature was the norm—Naomi in *Only a Fiddler*; the rootless Ahasverus; Sarah, the heroine of a fairy tale, "The Jewish Girl." Like him, the Melchiors and the Henriques were cosmopolitan in outlook; Moritz Melchior helped Andersen with his English and American correspondence and on one occasion in 1869 pointed out that a letter from America enclosed a £10 note, which Andersen had not understood; he later found it lying on the floor of his apartment—a lovely symbol of the way the worldly Melchiors looked after the unworldly Andersen's interests.

Andersen, aged sixty-one, with the Melchior family at their estate outside Copenhagen, Rolighed, which in his later years was his "home of homes." Dorothea Melchior is seated at the centre, Moritz Melchior stands next to Andersen. Photograph by Israel Melchior, 1866.

The Melchiors had none of the stubborn Danish provincialism that so infuriated him when he took the Collin grandsons on trips to Europe, nor did they taunt him, as his aristocratic friends did, for not being sufficiently patriotic in wartime. He found no conflict between his own rather unorthodox Christianity and their spiritual beliefs; he rarely went to church, and the only religious tenets which mattered to him were providence, grace and immortality, which he increasingly saw as a compensation for the pain and injustices of mortal life. By contrast, the nit-picking religious squabbles of some of his narrow-minded noble friends incensed him as he got older—at Basnæs with Mrs. Scavenius, for example, he recorded:

> A big unpleasant argument this evening . . . about Christ and religion. I said Christian dogma was from God and it was a blessing, but that although the circumstances of the birth and family were of interest, they were not necessary for me. Then the fur began to fly—if one didn't take His birth and death into account, then His teachings would be meaningless! . . . Since I didn't believe in the Father, the Son and the Holy Ghost, I wasn't a Christian. I answered that I believed in them as concepts but not as people, corporeal beings. They almost gave up on me . . . One must constantly try to keep in mind the exceptionally kind heart of this opinionated woman in order to be able to put up with listening to such things . . . I don't have many years left to live. Why, then, spend my days where I feel so oppressed?

At Rolighed, however, everyone was tolerant and easygoing. At a time when the Collin clan moved increasingly inward—several of the Collin grandchildren intermarried towards the end of Andersen's life, Ingeborg's son Viggo Drewsen to Edvard's daughter Louise, and another Drewsen son, Harald, to Ingeborg, the daughter of Andersen's old love Louise Lind—he welcomed the Melchiors and Henriques as outward-looking and open-minded. It mattered, too, that the new families had not known Andersen through his years of struggle; there was no legacy of ridicule or indebtedness as there was with the Collins. Instead, there was the undiluted admiration of civilized patrons, who made Andersen feel that he could bring something of interest to their lives. This was crucial, for the sense that the Collins did not need to bask in the glory of his fame continued to rankle. Rigmor Stampe, Jonas Collin's great-grandchild, the daughter of Jonna and Henrik Stampe, knew Andersen well in the 1860s and wrote in her memoir,

> When I consider the impression I have of Andersen's place in our family in our childhood and youth, it is remarkable that we never really felt we had "a famous man" among us. He was there as an old friend or uncle we took for granted, we certainly did not think more of him than of any of the other uncles. He had of course written the dearly beloved fairy tales, but that he was "a great man," who by his presence lent a lustre to our circle, never crossed our minds.

But most important of all was probably the affectionate temperament and uncomplicated warmth of the Melchiors and the Henriques, in particular of gentle, balanced Dorothea and the more highly strung, febrile Thérèse, which made Andersen able to confide in them at once as he had never been able to do with the Collins. In one of his first letters to Thérèse, he wrote, "How happy you are! After all, a home, a true home, is the greatest of blessings. I shall never have one on this earth, and that is why I am so restless, and feel a desire to move all the time, which, however—if I am to open my heart entirely to you—does not give me complete happiness." She in turn trusted him; "Mrs. Henriques, who has been so emotional and neurotic since the birth of little Marie, unburdened herself to me today—she's afraid of going crazy. There's a buzzing in her head, and she feels so devoid of feeling," Andersen noted in his diary in 1870. It was inconceivable that these sort of exchanges could have taken place with his first adopted family, the Collins, who had not shared their major griefs with him. At last, in old age, when he had long given up expecting to find it, he came as near as he ever got to a real home with a family who accepted him and his quirks and foibles unquestioningly.

When Andersen set off in the middle of a week of Copenhagen sleet, hail and thunder, for Portugal in January 1866, Moritz Melchior was among the last to come to say goodbye. He appeared with a selection of fur boots, because Dorothea wanted Andersen to be comfortable on the journey; "got an excellent pair that came to up over my knees," Andersen wrote. "Then he told me warmly and in confidence that should I need money he was always at my service. I replied that I hoped I wouldn't and told him about my modest assets. And he added then that should it ever happen that I didn't wish to touch them, if I just would turn to him, he would be so very pleased to be of service to me." Melchior steadied Andersen's nerves at a time when he was in a frenzy of anxiety about what he believed would be his last foreign trip, worrying about the costs, sewing money into his clothes, hiding gold and Prussian bills in his luggage and dashing to his dentist because his false teeth felt as if they were cutting a hole in his mouth. "Felt like an old man! Wrote with the old man's fear of travelling abroad, his pining for this and that from home," he noted.

He was cross at the Collins' "going-away party for me, so-called, but there were people there who couldn't be counted among those who should be invited to such an occasion," and feverish the next day when his coat was not ready from the tailor's and he was given a substitute for a few hours:

"when I went out on to the street, it occurred to me that it belonged to someone else—if he were now to come along and say, 'That is my coat you have on!' I thought people were looking at me." At the last minute, Reitzel announced reissues of *The Improvisatore, The Two Baronesses* and *Picture Book Without Pictures*, and agreed to Andersen arranging a selection of his poems; the royalties from these, Andersen reckoned, would cover an eight-month trip, for which he budgeted 900 rixdollars. Two days before he left, he had an elegant, rather lugubrious portrait taken by the Copenhagen photographer Georg Hansen; with an enormous bow-tie and high white collar, wrapped in his usual layers of coat and waistcoat, he looks something of a fop, pampered, innocent, eager to please, cultivating the impression, as the British diplomat Robert Lytton who met him in Portugal a couple of months later wrote, of "a perfect faun, half child, half God." Then he set off, travelling via Amsterdam and Paris, where he arrived for his sixty-first birthday; Mrs. Melchior sent a bouquet of flowers to the hotel.

He continued via Bordeaux and Madrid; crossing the border from Spain to Portugal in May was "like going from the Middle Ages into modern times." He stayed first with the businessman and consul general in Lisbon, Jorge O'Neill, a friend of the Wulffs, and met the Portuguese King Fernando, then went on to spend a month with Jorge's brother, the Danish vice-consul, Carlos, in Setubal, returning to visit the ancient university town of Coimbra to stay with a third O'Neill brother, José, in Cintra in July. His diary for the trip is full of complaints and minor irritations with his hosts— "wandered all morning in this boring town," "during the entire trip, José was mischievous and disagreeable," "don't feel quite well. Hot heavy air, but the sky full of clouds"—and his final weeks were spoilt by dread of the return journey by steamer from Lisbon to Bordeaux, across the notorious Bay of Biscay. "Every new sound gave me a fright . . . I thought of Jette Wulff on that burning ship, I was lying at night counting the hours, thought of the moment an accident might happen, whether we would crash with another vessel, whether we would sink to the bottom, maybe this would happen within the next ten minutes; a few times I was in mortal fear and thought it probable that we would never reach Bordeaux." It was clear that, as with the trip to Spain four years earlier, Andersen was too old to throw himself into the excited discovery of new places, yet he still needed the stimulation and the enhanced sensuality that he derived from the Latin countries, and over the next two years this drew him abroad repeatedly.

Jorge O'Neill may have been a catalyst for the erotic discovery of Andersen's late years: his fascination with brothels. Jorge remarked casually one day that he needed to *kneppe* (fuck), that Andersen was clearly sexually frustrated, and that he could arrange for him, too, to visit a Lisbon prostitute. Andersen declined, but the thought stayed with him, and as soon as he found himself alone, stopping over in Paris on his way home for one night on 30 August, he went to a brothel. He paid the Madame five francs and was given a choice of four girls; he chose the youngest, an 18-year-old, and watched her strip off for him; he gazed at her, but he did not try to do more than talk to her. It was the most active move he had taken towards sex with a woman, and it intrigued him. His diary at this time shows him still musing on his lack of erotic fulfilment, and attempting to console himself with his artistic achievement; at a dinner party he describes some guests, noting, "they were, by the way, a handsome young couple. Why was I not granted such youthful happiness? But I've been granted it another way." Paris, which he had long disliked as a city of sin, suddenly became a magnet to him in its association with prostitutes and the chance to explore his own sexuality; at the same time it became the source of inspiration for a highly charged tale, "The Dryad," on which he worked obsessively for two years. Sex and creativity came together; as he was writing the tale over the next twenty months, he visited Paris three more times, going to brothels on each visit.

He returned to Copenhagen in September 1866; the Melchiors met him at the station and took him straight to Rolighed, where above the door garlands of flowers were woven into the word "Welcome." In October, he moved into new lodgings at 1, Lille Kongensgade (Little King Street), on the corner of Kongens Nytorv, above a popular café and restaurant. The house was built in the classical style in 1857 for the *pâtissier* Stefan à Porta, but a restaurant had stood on the site since 1788, when a Swiss chef opened the first pâtisserie in Copenhagen. The building continues to house the restaurant A Porta today, hung as a century ago with golden leather tapestry and pictures of its long history; in the summer, tables spill out on to the main square.

For Andersen, it offered a model of urban living. From his two rooms on the third floor he could see straight across to the Royal Theatre, which he still visited every night when he was in town, and the Casino Theatre in Amaliegade was round the corner. The café and the restaurant were sometimes useful to him; on the third floor, along with his apartment, there was also a doctor and a photographer's studio, and Andersen joked that he would therefore not die without medical attention, and that posterity would be assured of his picture. His rooms were cosy and bright, and friends made sure they were always decorated with flowers.

His new lodgings were only partly furnished, and so at sixty-one, encouraged by Henriette Collin, he was forced for the first time to buy his own bed. He told Hartmann,

I have had to invest a hundred rixdollars in a bed, and it will be my death-bed, because if it does not last that long, then it is not worth the money. I wish I were only twenty, then I would put my ink-pot on my back, take two shirts and a pair of socks, place a quill at my side and wander into the wide world. Now I am, as Jette Collin writes so nicely, "an elderly man," so I suppose I must think of my bed, my death-bed.

The lure of the wide world was too strong, however, to keep him in Copenhagen for long. In January 1867 he told Henriette Collin, "I think Death will snatch me away this year; if I knew that, I would at once fly out into the wide world to breathe properly before I'm taken away completely from this sack of worms." He celebrated his sixty-second birthday with the Melchiors and then, as if he felt his time were running out, left immediately for Paris.

"Robert Watt told me many wild, sensual stories, and so I got a deep insight into Paris life," he noted two days after his arrival. Watt, his favourite companion in the city, was a young journalist and editor of the Danish journal *Figaro*, who had published a piece on Portugal by Andersen in the autumn, and they now got to know one another better. Watt, good-looking in a Byronic way, with dark curls, flashing dark eyes and full lips, and an energetic, engaged manner, fascinated Andersen. He was Andersen's opposite by temperament—uncomplicatedly extrovert, confident, highly sexed—but he had shared with him a childhood of deprivation after his family's business had failed and he had become destitute. He was boundlessly ambitious as a result, and had travelled to Australia to make his fortune, working in the gold mines and recounting his experiences of the new world in lively articles in the Danish press. Andersen saw in him something of himself when young, making his own way "with spirit and a fresh youthfulness" in a hostile world.

There was nothing homo-erotic in Andersen's attraction to him or to a handful of other gifted young men—the stage director William Bloch, the writer Nicolai Bøgh, the critic Georg Brandes—with whom he surrounded himself in the 1860s and 1870s; he used these youths to keep in touch with

One of the radical young men who enlivened Andersen's old age: journalist Robert Watt, whom Andersen accompanied to brothels in Paris.

modernity, seeing the changing world through their young eyes, and so to feel that artistically and intellectually, he was keeping old age at bay. If their wild ways and fiery opinions challenged his, so much the better. As he replaced the conservative and truculent Collin grandsons with this artistic young élite, their company became a pleasure of his old age, their mix of reverence for the eminent author and free-thinking liberalism offering him the flattery and inspiration he needed.

In Paris, the boastful ease with which Robert Watt recounted his conquests inflamed the sexual desire which had driven Andersen to the city. "Went out to see Watt, who was with his compatriots yesterday evening at the Mabille, all of them rather drunk. Some of them spent the night with some wenches—a wild life! . . . I have in me the feeling that I'm not a young man any more. Went home and pondered this in my room," he wrote on 3 May. Two days later he again ran into Watt, "who told about new adventures with the ladies."

> I wonder whether they're true. He's youthfully high-spirited, but not so polished that the ladies, as he describes them, would throw themselves at him like that. After eating dinner, I paced back and forth in a sexual frenzy. Then went

suddenly up into a meat market—one of them was covered with powder; a second, common; a third, quite the lady. I talked with her, paid twelve francs and left, without having sinned in deed, though I dare say I did in my thoughts. She asked me to come back, said I was indeed very innocent for a man. I felt so happy and light when I left that house. Many might call me a fool—have I been one here? In the evening, wandered around on the boulevard and saw painted ladies sitting in the cafés and playing cards, drinking beer and chartreuse.

All these impressions dovetailed with another heady experience, the Paris World Exhibition, which caught Andersen's imagination as a living, modern fairy tale. He took as a challenge a comment in a Danish newspaper that only Dickens could weld from this spectacle an artistic picture; as he worked on "The Dryad," he began to merge his response to the exhibition with the romance of sexual liberation in Paris to create a haunting, contemporary tale. This occupied his thoughts so fully during the summer of 1867, spent at Rolighed, Basnæs and Holsteinborg, that Moritz Melchior offered to pay for him to return to Paris in the autumn to work further on the tale. This was luxurious travel for a Dane: a journey which took a week each way, for a fortnight's stay in Paris. Andersen accepted 300 rixdollars from Melchior; how closely the trip was linked in his mind with sexual adventure as well is suggested by his choice of Robert Watt as guide and travelling companion. The pair went together to a brothel almost as soon as they arrived, though again Andersen only talked to the prostitute he chose, describing her as a poor girl.

The contrast between his private life and obsessions and his image as a grand old man of European letters had never been greater. He enjoyed playing off the dual lives, the slightly seamy visits to Paris which helped him write his erotic fantasy versus the ultra-respectable Copenhagen existence, where he was cared for at home by a stable, loving family and laden with honours. Through 1867 and 1868 he combined the two lives as new recognition flooded his way. In the spring of 1867, he was made a titular councillor by the King. A collection of stories illustrated by Lorenz Frølich, regarded as the only Andersen illustrator worthy to succeed Pedersen, was well-received. Then in December he was awarded the freedom of Odense, and his home town was illuminated in his honour.

Schools were closed for the festival, flags waved, townspeople stood in uniform in front of the City Hall and a band played Andersen's song "In Denmark I Was Born" as he was driven in the mayor's carriage to the city council, and then to the town hall, where his bust was draped with a laurel wreath, flowers and the Danish flag; children danced for him, there was a banquet and a torchlight parade saluted him. But toothache—an intimation of mortality for him since the 1830s—spoilt his enjoyment, leaving him sometimes unable to speak because of his loose false upper teeth and the agony of his hurting stumps. Just before the illumination he became tormented too by the idea that someone was about to murder him or ruin the celebrations. The Melchiors, "endlessly happy" for him, Robert Watt, the King and many others sent congratulatory notes or telegrams, but what Andersen wrote bitterly in his diary were the names of those friends—the Collins and the Drewsens—who failed to do so. In some ways the honour closed a circle which had begun in hardship in Odense and now finished in grandeur; in other ways it could only awaken painful memories, and Andersen was so emotional that he was, he wrote, "near to sinking, overcome by the whole scene."

Over the following days in Odense Andersen received visitors grand and obscure. Then, bearing a bouquet of white roses from the mayor's wife, he drove with the bishop to the station, where crowds gathered to see him off. The journey, which when he had left Odense in 1819 had taken two days by stagecoach and sailing ship, now took an evening by train and a "new screw-propelled ship, which is to be used for breaking the ice." "The passengers were friendly and attentive, as if the hurrahs from Odense still filled the air. The sea was calm." Edvard and Jonas were waiting at Copenhagen station to take him home; "the sitting room was warm; letters and books lay there for me." The next day, Andersen wrote "the whole thing is like a dream."

On 31 December, Andersen reflected on a brilliant year: "now ends the year 1867, the most honouring and changeable for me; twice I was in Paris . . . I have been made Councillor of State and in Odense I experienced a homage of the rarest kind this world can offer . . . Lord, my God, my only God, Thank You for the year that has passed, whatever the New Year may, will, shall bring: I pray, Lord, give me strength to carry it, don't let go of me!"

He worked quietly in Copenhagen through the winter of 1868, then left again as soon as spring came, travelling to Paris, Germany and Switzerland. In Paris in May he met Einar Drewsen, and they went to a brothel together; Andersen seems to have enjoyed accompanying young friends and waiting for them while they used the prostitutes to whom he only talked. This time, he wrote, "I however only sat and talked to Fernanda, the little Turkish girl, while E. enjoyed himself. She was the most beautiful of them, we talked of Constantinople, her native city, of the illuminations there on Mahommed's birthday; she was very pressing *pour faire l'amour*, but I said I had come just to talk, no more. 'Come soon,' she said, 'but not tomorrow, because that is my day off.' Poor woman!"

Andersen's sexual frustration poured into his long tale "The Dryad," which, with a travel book about Portugal, occupied him during the summer of 1868. A dryad is a wood nymph who inhabits the hollow of a tree. Andersen's lives in the country, where she hears tales of a girl who goes to Paris and returns a rich but ruined lady. Desperate to follow her, she bargains her soul for one night of pleasure in the venal city. Andersen's evocation of seedy, slightly unreal Paris at the time of the World Exhibition is skilful in its ambiguity— he both loves and hates the temptations posed by this "Aladdin's palace of the present," and depicts by turns the bright boulevards with women drinking chartreuse and dancing the cancan, and the sewers filled with rats which run beneath them. The city/country duality that occupied the nineteenth-century European imagination as the effects of industrialization became marked is essential here. The steamers and carriages and crowds rushing at the exhibition, "a kingdom of Babel, a wonder of the world," "move like a busy swarm of ants"; the dryad's tree is "killed by the fumes of the gas, the steam of kitchens, and the bad air of the city." But the dryad rejects innocence along with the green leaves and the fresh country air; the bargain is that her life will be shortened to one night, during which "your yearning and longing will increase, your desire will grow more stormy . . . and your life-taper will be blown out."

Her expression of desire is a classic female sexual fantasy of subjugation and punishment which Andersen has only slightly shrouded by a sentimental gloss: "Give me human life, human happiness, only a short span, only the one night . . . and then punish me for the wish to live, my longing for life! . . . let my shell, the fresh young tree, wither, or be hewn down, and burnt to ashes," she cries. Virginal and spring-like, her silk dress "green as the freshly opened leaves . . . a child, and yet a grown maiden," she is let loose on the city in a whirling dance of sensuality and death:

> The soaring upwards of rockets, the splashing of the fountains, and the popping of champagne corks accompanied the wild bacchantic dance. Over the whole glided the moon through the air, clear, but with a somewhat crooked face.

A wild joviality seemed to rush through the Dryad, as though she were intoxicated by opium . . . Her partner whispered words to her . . . He stretched out his arms to draw her to him, but he embraced only the empty air.

The Dryad had been carried away, like a rose-leaf on the wind . . .

As in the other erotic stories from the 1860s, "The Ice Maiden" and "The Psyche," Andersen cannot allow his hero or heroine the moment of consummation without the association of death and disintegration. The dryad's tour of Paris includes, significantly, the Church of the Madeleine: she is a fallen woman, and in her last moments Andersen, in strokes of local colour, paints her like the worldly, fallen heroines of the French mid-century novels (Dumas's *La Dame aux Camélias*, Flaubert's *Madame Bovary*, Zola's *Thérèse Raquin*). The dryad hallucinates, seeing the fruit of passion, red pomegranate flowers, as the wind warns that the sun "will kiss the clouds red, then you will be among the dead—blown away, as all the splendour here will be blown away before the year shall have ended . . . All is dust!" She "felt a terror like a woman who has cut asunder her pulse-artery in the bath, but is again filled with the love of life, even while she is bleeding to death." The first rays of the sun fall on her and "her form was irradiated in changing colours, like the soap-bubble when it is bursting and becomes a drop of water; like a tear that falls and passes away like a vapour." As he did with the little mermaid thirty years earlier, Andersen punishes the dryad for sexual love by simply making her disappear. This can be read as misogyny, but his sympathy for both characters suggests that he identified with them, and, finding it easier to express himself through the sexual language of a woman, is subconsciously punishing himself for the sexual desires he cannot indulge.

He was very pleased with "The Dryad," especially with its contemporary themes, its up-to-date setting. "Our time is the time of fairy tales," he says in the story, and as a modern fairy tale its suffusion of erotic imagery, the shifting, suggestive tones and the undertow of sexual malaise anticipate the *fin de siècle* tales of Oscar Wilde and the early novellas of Thomas Mann—both writers who played on sexual ambiguity. "The Dryad" was published in December 1868 in an edition of 3,000, and sold out immediately—its unrivalled portrayal of the World Exhibition was one reason, its *risqué* themes another. A second edition appeared ten days later. Two important new fans who applauded the story were Horace Scudder, the American editor of *Riverside Monthly Magazine for Young People*, and 26-year-old Georg Brandes, a dashing and original Danish critic. Both were important in presenting Andersen as a modern, international author in the last years of his life.

Scudder had been trying to open communications with Andersen since 1862, but Andersen was a poor correspondent with any but his closest friends, and it took until 1868 for him to respond. Scudder had been a devotee of Andersen since childhood. "I remember with what a half-terrified, wholly fascinated sensation I used to steal to the bookshelves and get down a book that had in it your story of 'The Red Shoes,'" he wrote. "I read everything of yours that I could find. What marvellous little life you discovered in the humble objects around me! . . . you gave a voice to the very tongs of the fireplace." Eventually such approaches paid off, and Andersen sent Scudder some stories for publication in the *Riverside Magazine*. He received $500 for the first twelve—the first money he had ever received from America—and a promise of royalties on an authorized collected edition of his stories. Scudder also suggested American publication of an updated version of Andersen's autobiography. In November 1868 Andersen sent Scudder "The Dryad"—"I consider it as one of my best . . . a tale from the Exhibition in Paris in 1867—I fancy that I have given in that tale a lively sketch of the exhibition and have tried to prove that our present time, the time of engines, as many call it, is as poetical and as rich as any age"—and then began work on his last memoirs, updating them in a year-by-year appendix until 1867. This extended version of *Mit Livs Eventyr* was published by Hurd and Houghton, and Andersen's *Collected Writings* in ten volumes appeared in New York in 1870–1871. The additional material was as sentimental and self-congratulatory as the rest, and won reviews full of reverent pathos; in England Edmund Gosse in the *Spectator* hailed a story "written so simply and so tenderly that for the most part we can all sit together, children and grown-up folks, and read the pages that show how wonderfully God has guarded the child-like poet of the children."

He still derived keen pleasure from seeing his name spread far abroad. Among the fan letters which amused him at this time came one from Anna Mary Livingstone, daughter of the explorer Dr. Livingstone, which read, "I *do* like your fairy tales so much that I would like to go and see you but I cannot do that so I thought I would write to you when papa comes home from Africa I will ask him to take me to see you." Andersen could never resist a grand connection; he used to carry Anna's letters in his pocket-book, extract them to show to visitors, and kiss them with a remark such as "Don't you think I am a happy man, to have all the world love me like that?" Her father Livingstone was a great man, he would add, "but he was not loved in the hearts of the world as I am. When I die *everyone* will come and put flowers on my coffin."

This was, however, sentimental self-consolation, and Andersen knew it. What he really wanted in old age was to be *au courant* with the new, modern generation, and it was through writers like Georg Brandes and Robert Watt that he tried to connect himself. Brandes, to whom Andersen had been immediately drawn when they met at the theatre and at Edvard Collin's house earlier in the year, was honoured with a private reading of "The Dryad" in October 1868, and declared himself crazy about it. Brandes, with his blazing eyes, long, intense face, shock of black hair and flamboyant moustache and beard, cultivated the role of a radical, and he represented youth and intellectual excitement for Andersen. "All us older folks were in one dining room. The younger people in the one next to us—that's where all the fun was," he complained about a dinner party in 1872, cheering up when he came across Brandes at the end of it.

Brandes knew how to play Andersen, offering his controversial, liberal opinions with enough of a whiff of danger to excite, but not to threaten, the older man. In February 1869 Brandes's former professor Rasmus Nielsen gave a lecture on Andersen, who wrote: "it was extremely interesting, but I was sort of embarrassed listening to it, since the entire lecture concerned mainly me as a composer of tales . . . I felt myself to be exalted by it all, as if I were dead and now witnessing one of the university's venerable professors holding a lecture about me at the University of Copenhagen."

He spent much of the spring in Petershøi, where another new young artistic friend, 35-year-old Carl Bloch, was painting his portrait: a psychologically penetrating picture, it shows Andersen on the threshold of old age, in reflective, serious mood, his face lined, his expression careworn and self-absorbed. It is one of the few portraits where he does not seem to pose for an audience, and it invites an almost frightening degree of intimacy. Martin Henriques bought it for 200 rixdollars, and Andersen followed Bloch's career with interest and enthusiasm over the next years; he was flattered when Bloch named a son after him.

In July 1869 came more intense interest from his young circle of friends when Brandes began a series of perceptive articles about Andersen in *Illustreret Tidende* (the *Illustrated News*), which are the first serious Andersen scholarship. Knowing Andersen's bitterness towards critics, Brandes preempted him with a charming letter suggesting that if Andersen would read his analysis and "be ready to have a little faith in this aesthetic branch of scholarship," he would find that Brandes had "revenged himself" on him for "his many bad words about literary criticism." He was, he told Andersen, indebted to him "for true spiritual enrichment." "In my humble way I have wished to contribute to an understanding of what you really signify for Denmark."

By the time Brandes wrote, Andersen had been composing fairy tales for over thirty years and his classic status was assured. Nevertheless, it took a critic with exceptional perspective to pinpoint so soon Andersen's unique role as a creator of fairy tales, and to dovetail this with an understanding of his psychology that was daring at the time and is still among the most penetrating written. Brandes, in a modern, unaffected style, opened by praising Andersen as an innovative genius:

> He who possesses talent should also possess courage. He must dare trust his inspiration, he must be convinced that the fancy which flashes through his brain is a healthy one, that the form which comes natural to him, even if it be a new one, has a right to assert its claims; he must have gained the hardihood to expose himself to the charge of being affected, or on the wrong path, before he can yield to his instinct and follow it wherever it may imperiously lead . . . The universal formula of a gifted nature . . . expresses the right of talent, when neither traditional form nor existing material suffice to meet the peculiar requirement of its nature, to choose new material, to create new forms, until it finds a soil of a quality to give nurture to all its forces and gently and freely develop them. Such a soil the poet Hans Christian Andersen has found in the nursery story.

Brandes grasped both the double articulation that lay at the root of the earlier tales—"what author has such a public? . . . His stories are numbered among the books which we have deciphered syllable by syllable and which we still read today"—and that Andersen used the genre as a cover behind which he could reveal himself. It was only a step from here to unravel the sexual ambiguity that lies at the heart of many of the tales, and Brandes took it with delicacy and tact. Andersen's novels failed because he did not have "the cool, calm power of observation of the man of the world . . . his men are not manly enough, his women not sufficiently feminine." In the world of fantasy this did not matter:

> I know no poet whose mind is more devoid of sexual distinctions, whose talent is less of a nature to betray a defined sex, than Andersen's. Therefore his strength lies in portraying children, in whom the conscious sense of sex is not yet prominent. The whole secret lies in the fact that he is exclusively what he

Critic Georg Brandes, "a superb character with his seductive teachings."

is—not a champion, as many of our great writers have been, not a thinker, not a standard-bearer, but simply a poet. A poet is a man who is at the same time a woman.

Reading Brandes, Andersen was astonished by his acuteness. He had always acknowledged the feminine in himself, and comments such as the one to Edvard Collin, "I am like water, everything moves me, everything is reflected in me," suggest that he may have recognized that his attraction to both men and women was part of his floating identity as a writer, sensitive to all experiences. At the time the articles appeared, Andersen was working on "Poultry Meg's Family," another long erotic tale, featuring a mannish heroine, Marie Grubbe, who rejects her rich husband ("I'd rather lie on coarse sacking than lie in his silken beds") for rough lovers who beat her.

Marie Grubbe is a strange figure in Danish history; the story of her uncontrolled sexuality leading to her fallen fortune had lain in Andersen's mind for forty years, since he had read Blicher's account of it, "Fragments from the Diary of a Parish Clerk," as an adolescent. A few years after his own tale, one of Brandes's followers, the impressionist novelist Jens Peter Jacobsen, wrote a popular, psychologically gripping version called *Fru Marie*

Grubbe (1876). The connections suggest how in tune Andersen was with the themes and motifs of Brandes's circle; after Brandes's essays on him, he became a devotee, and enjoyed being shocked by his ideas. "Brandes is a superb character with his seductive teachings," he wrote, "he is working for *free love* and the abolition of marriage, and he does it in lectures mainly for young girls." Andersen, for all his own sexual ambivalence, had the conventional prudishness of his own early-nineteenth-century generation about women's sexuality; it was breaking this taboo that gave stories like "The Dryad" a *frisson*, which he also derived from Brandes's work. "Finished the Brandes book [*The Romantic School in Germany*]. In it is a German poem, it lies between the pages like a flower, an obscene flower," he wrote in his diary in August 1874. "A lustful young girl longs to be embraced by *ein süsser Knabe* [a sweet youth] and is cross with her mother because she is not allowed to display the beauty nature has endowed her with."

What Andersen wrote to Brandes suggests that he saw his art as a way of expressing the inexpressible, and was pleased that someone had understood him. He told Brandes:

> With the cleverness and intense sensitivity of youth you have looked straight into the bottom of the heart of my little spiritual children, and reading your essay I felt a happiness that I wish God may grant you too. No one has, more than me, in days past, been more cruelly and ruthlessly treated by what is called criticism; it did its best to eradicate and destroy me . . . The young generation is now making good the crimes of the older generation, and you, my dear friend, are among the young men whom I appreciate and value highly.

After Andersen's death, Brandes was more critical: he wrote to Bjørnson that Andersen's mind was wholly filled by himself and that he had no spiritual interests—a verdict which contains only a half-truth, and which is more revealing about the gap between Andersen's mid-nineteenth-century vision of religious doubt and spiritual questing, and the confident certainty of late-nineteenth-century atheists like Brandes. Andersen spent his life searching to understand the world, and this quest still drove him in his final years, when Brandes became one of the tools by which he tried to do so. That Brandes was so modern a young man as to miss this aspect of Andersen was one of his attractions; with the ruthless selfishness of the dedicated artist, Andersen took what he needed from people and ignored the rest. With the Melchiors and the Henriques, Robert Watt and Carl Bloch, Brandes joined the protective ring that encircled Andersen in his old age.

CHAPTER 23

So Great a Love of Life

1869–1875

It's over! It's all over! And that's how it is with all stories!
—HANS CHRISTIAN ANDERSEN, "The Fir Tree"

On 6 September 1869 Andersen celebrated the fiftieth anniversary of his arrival in Copenhagen at a banquet for 244 people, after which he left for Basnæs and a trip to Vienna and the south of France. From Basnæs, he wrote that "like an afterglow of my festivities in the city was the lovely welcome which beamed here. I arrived in the evening, and before the bridge of the castle I saw erected a large and beautiful triumphal arch with decorated lights and the Dannebrog waving." But as soon as he was abroad, disappointment set in; he suffered from rheumatism, it was unusually cold, and he realized he was now too frail to travel alone. To Henriette Collin he wrote that he would never go abroad by himself again; to Scudder he described his comfortable rooms in the Pension Suisse in Nice, and the cosy Christmas party there, but ended "in spite of all this, I have nevertheless during the whole of this journey often felt quite lonesome, have not been thrilled with travelling as before, have been mentally depressed, without actual reason."

He was to have joined up with the Melchiors in Nice for Christmas, but their daughter was ill and they had moved on to Algiers in search of better weather. Andersen was lonely enough to invite the troublesome Jonas, Edvard's son, to come to Nice to escort him home; they travelled together via Paris. By March 1870 he was back in Copenhagen, where the ice was still so thick that there was little traffic on the Sound. He moved into the Melchiors' empty apartment on Højbro Plads, from where he wrote to Scudder, "I have felt myself oppressed by the winter, have felt out of sorts, have written *nothing* at all and therefore decided to return to the north, seek the home where it seemed that my muse had remained. For the first time abroad I have been homesick for our cosy winter life."

He busied himself with new tales and with his last novel, *Lucky Peer*, an Aladdin-like story about a poor boy who achieves fame through his musical genius and then dies at the peak of his success and happiness, in the mould of *The Improvisatore*. On his sixty-fifth birthday in April 1870 he wrote, "this is an advanced age, according to the common calculation, but I still have the full spirit of youth, feel most at home with the younger people. But time brings nearer the last journey. I am now in the front rank of those our Lord may summon, but when? And right now I have so great a love of life!" His winter journey had convinced him that he was an old man.

Old age is a great leveller. Much of what Andersen suffered all his life—hypochondria and depression, nervousness and neediness—becomes in old age the norm, and so in his later sixties he found his life surprisingly convergent with those of his friends such as Edvard Collin from whom he had been very different.

As most older people do, he felt the passing of the old order as friends and acquaintances died. Dickens's death, of which he heard in June 1870, was a shock—Dickens was younger than him, and had not reached sixty; "so we'll never see each other again on earth, never tell each other our innermost thoughts. I won't get an explanation from him why he didn't respond to my last letters." A month later, Signe Læssøe, the mother-figure who had cared for him since he first came to Copenhagen, died aged eighty-nine; shortly afterwards Orla Lehmann, the radical politician whom he had known since his earliest days in the capital, died aged sixty.

"Thought, as always, of death in various forms," Andersen wrote one fine summer's day in 1870 at Basnæs. From childhood, he had been obsessed with death; in his diaries since adolescence, he often says he wishes for it; more than five-sixths of his 156 tales include death in some form. In old age he pondered mortality daily: "I'm sitting here like a person sentenced to death, who daily awaits his execution, who is afraid of how embarrassing it would be and who nevertheless would like to see an end to it all." Each time a friend died he asked the same metaphysical questions—after Carsten Hauch's death in 1872, for example, "He's now dust and ashes, dead, extinguished, burned out like a light which is no more! My Lord God, can You let us vanish completely? I'm afraid of that, and I've gotten too clever—and unhappy."

With the Franco-Prussian War of 1870 he reacted as he had during earlier conflicts, although Denmark was not involved: he wrote of "the unhealthy despondency, the unending depression and even the total self-resignation that had engulfed me as a result of the awful, bloody course of the war, the omnipotence of the cannons, which had turned me into a blubbering idiot, turned me from God." By the autumn, he "felt depressed and tired of life"; even meeting Ibsen, a young firebrand of the sort that usually excited him, only made him feel out of touch. He liked Ibsen as a man, but finished *Peer Gynt* with the opinion that "It's as if it were written by a mad poet! You go crazy yourself trying to understand that book. The poetry isn't good either—there is something wild and unwholesome in it all. Regret having read it."

He moved again in September, across Kongens Nytorv to Tordenskjold-gade, on the left-hand side of the Royal Theatre, but his new lodgings, two first-floor rooms at the Hotel Garni Kronprinz Louisa, a boarding house belonging to two sisters, were barely satisfactory and over-priced. The poet Sophus Schandorph, who visited Andersen during his brief stay there, left a record of a clean, pretty room, with blue wallpaper and a few bookshelves, but noted that the overall impression was melancholy and cold. Andersen's rooms were above the gate, and in "Auntie Toothache," which he began in 1871, he described the ceaseless disturbances as part of the poet-hero's hellish vision:

> I'm living with a quiet family. They don't worry about me, even when I ring three times. Otherwise, it's a regular house of din with all the hubbub of wind and weather and people. My room is right over the entrance; every cart that comes out or in sets the pictures swinging on the wall. The banging of the gate shakes the house as if there was an earthquake. If I'm lying in bed, the shocks go right through me . . . If it's windy—and it's always windy in this country— then the long window-catches outside swing to and fro and knock against the wall. The gate bell to the yard next-door peals with every gust of wind.
>
> The lodgers in our house come home in driblets, late at night, well into the small hours. The lodger immediately above me, who by day gives lessons on the trombone, is the last home, and before he gets into bed he has a little midnight walk up and down, with heavy steps and hob-nailed boots.
>
> There are no double windows, but there is a broken pane which the land-lady has stuck paper over; all the same, the wind blows in through the crack and produces a sound like a buzzing hornet. That's my lullaby.

By now he was wealthy and did not need to live like this, but attitudes to money are formed early in life and are hard to change. Although he had substantial savings, he still worried about money. At the end of 1872, his savings were 21,000 rixdollars, for example, but a few months later he noted nevertheless, "One goes on living in constant anxiety about how to make ends meet." He continued to see himself as the rootless, wandering artist of romantic myth; he enjoyed being pampered in other homes, especially those of the very rich. Moreover, his relationship with the Copenhagen bourgeoisie was complex: to buy and fill a house like his neighbours' would have been to announce too close an allegiance to them. But most fundamental was a mix of inertia, practical incompetence and a lack of interest in material things. Andersen's snobbery concerned his recognition as an artist and his acceptance by kings; he was never greedy about money, and he simply could not be bothered with the trappings of domesticity.

The Melchiors and the Henriques rescued him from Tordenskjoldgade. He told Thérèse Henriques that if he had not been able to stay in her quiet, peaceful home, he would never have finished *Lucky Peer*. He was aware of his dependence. "The Collins have gone to Hellebæk. The Henriques and Melchiors at a wedding. Today I'll have to resort to a restaurant," he wrote on 27 November 1870. The evening ended in misery: "In a sensual mood. Wandered around in the moist air; came home and felt tired. No desire to go to the theatre. Stayed at home all evening. Discontented. +" Two days later he was expressing the old man's regrets at not having enjoyed the pleasures of the flesh—"If I were young and rich, I would live to embrace life. 'You've got to have a body!'," he wrote, quoting his tale "The High Jumpers" of 1845, in which a flea, a grasshopper and a drumstick compete by high jumping to marry a princess; the drumstick wins, the flea is killed in the war and the grasshopper, a depressive celibate like Andersen, "settled in the ditch and reflected on the ups and downs of this life, and he, too, said, 'Body's what you want! Body's what you want!'"

Fame had been his compensation; now he was obsessed by how his reputation would last; at the centennial celebration for Thorvaldsen he wrote in his diary:

> I need not hide on these pages—which will never be published but stem from my daily thoughts—that I felt I had so much in common with Thorvaldsen— our low birth and our struggle and our great world recognition. To be sure, I am as well known in the world as he, which our countrymen, however, don't see, but it is certainly true. But I think his name will live longer than mine. Indeed, I do believe my name is now more well known around the world than his, but mine will be forgotten and his will live. Is this vanity? Will I ever know?

Five days later he wrote, "I'll be quickly forgotten and flung to the winds by the coming generation—'It's over! It's all over! And that's how it is with all stories!'"—the bitter epitaph to "The Fir Tree."

In the spring of 1871, his mood was black: "I can feel the old man in me—this is his first year. I'm not really taking good care of myself—too much good food, different wines, not enough peace and quiet." He became intensely fearful of going mad. On 2 March he wrote, "God has given me imagination for my vocation as a poet but not to make me a candidate for the madhouse! What are indeed these crazy ideas that so often upset me?" A week later he learned that a parcel had come for him from Leipzig—"in keeping with my mood I suddenly had the notion that it was something evil, sent to me by enemies, and now my imagination conjured up a variety of wickedness." While waiting for its delivery, he broke out in a feverish sweat, only to open it and discover a beautifully engraved reading desk sent as a gift from a German bookseller. But the next day was no better: as he left the theatre, he wrote, "I happened to push very lightly, almost just tap a man with my walking stick, so lightly indeed that I did not even apologize, but when I came out my imagination got the better of me, once again I had a crazy notion; I feel I am on my way to the madhouse."

In April he made the effort to move out of the boarding house that had become a nightmare, and installed himself at the luxurious Hotel d'Angleterre overlooking Kongens Nytorv, from where he told Scudder "I am living most comfortably." In June he went to Basnæs, beginning there his story "Auntie Toothache," and on to Norway and a happy visit to Bjørnson. He spent the rest of summer 1871 at Rolighed and Petershøi, from where a fellow-guest, a young English girl called Annie Wood, who claimed to have slept with his tales under her pillow since she was six, left recollections of his everyday existence at this time. She remembered

his shabby, ungainly, slouching figure, in its ill-fitting, unbrushed clothes—(he always wore flapping trousers which touched the toes of his gigantic boots, and a shawl, his own or anybody's, it did not matter, wrapped around his shoulders), and his ugly, musing face, abstracted-seeming but keenly observant too with its high, receding forehead, its close-set eyes and the steep incline from the top of the forehead to the nape of the neck, as if the back of the head had been sliced away . . . He stoops much when walking, but his hair is not very grey, nor is the thin slight beard he wears under his smooth-shaven chin. His eyes are small, but bright and good-humoured . . . although he is by no means a handsome man, yet his pleasing winsome manners and genial smile unconsciously prepossess one at first appearance.

Free to come and go as he pleased, Andersen's schedule was relaxed. He spent the mornings writing, but he often joined the other guests on the verandah to read to them as he worked on a new story. In the afternoon,

> he liked to walk in the fields with any of our party who were so inclined. For the first quarter of an hour he would not talk much, but shamble along, poking his stick into every hole and corner, or touching with it every odd thing that lay in his path. Then something would attract his attention—a bit of glass, a faded flower, or a half-eaten insect—no matter what it was, he would stoop and pick it up, touch it tenderly, bend over it caressingly, and then, in a kind of low, half-regretful tone, he would begin and tell the story of its life, its joys, its sorrows, and the sad destiny which brought it to the spot where he had found it . . . He seemed to me to live in a world peculiarly his own, all his ideas, thoughts and actions differing from those around him.

Before dinner, he loved arranging flowers; at the table, however, "he was perfectly regardless of the ordinary forms of social life; his personal habits were exceedingly careless, not to say repulsive; he was not agreeable as a next neighbour, or as observed from over-the-way, at a dinner-table, for he ate voraciously, and was a decidedly dirty feeder." He also insisted, wherever he was, on being served first at the table, and when Miss Wood arrived and took precedence as a new English female guest, "he became silent, sulked, would not eat, and disappeared early in the evening; next morning Mrs. Henriques asked Miss Wood if she would mind not being served first, 'it made And'sen so unhappy; he went to the kitchen, and told the servants he could see they no longer loved him, since they thought more of the English lady than of him.'"

After dinner, Andersen cut paper figures "so absurd in their expression and attitudes that roars of laughter always follow their appearance on the table," or read aloud.

> When the drawing room was full of guests, when the fun and laughter were beginning to decline, or when there was a pause in the exquisite music always to be heard at Madame H[enriques]'s charming soirées [recalled Annie Wood], I have noticed Andersen quietly rise from his corner, take a paper from his pocket, draw near a lamp, and propose to read a story . . . Voices would be hushed in eager expectation . . . then, with a few words explanatory of the story,

he would begin softly, as if to ensure and command the attention of all around, and then gradually grow louder and louder, till his voice, always melodious and full of feeling, had reached the pitch fitted for the room. As he read on and on, and the story unfolded itself, one seemed to forget the society around, and to live in the troubles and sorrows or pleasures of those he was describing. His story done, he would rise from his chair, and with a low, awkward bow, and a light wave of his hand, retire to the corner, and shut his eyes and rest.

Annie Wood's account suggests that by now the performance was the man and vice versa; what made him at home with the Henriques and the Melchiors was their acceptance of this. Like all observers, Annie Wood highlighted his friendliness and charm, his open manner and his kindness to servants. Most prominent, however, was the fuss that attended every aspect of his daily life—when he got a thorn in his finger, for example, he spent the day screaming in pain at everyone until being persuaded "by the united influence of the whole household" first to bathe his hand, then to let someone remove the thorn—and his vanity. "Nothing pleases Andersen so truly as to be made much of, to hear that the world speaks well of him, and to be told that he and his words are appreciated outside his own kingdom," she wrote, noting the eagerness with which he scanned her letters to see if he was mentioned. He was

> a child, according to the ideal of childhood; keenly sensitive, entirely egoistical, innocently vain, the centre of life, interest, concern and meaning to himself, perfectly unconscious that there existed another standard, an outer circle, taking it for granted that everywhere he was to be first and all . . . He had no notion of time, and as pertinaciously required everyone to be at his beck and call as any curled darling in the nursery who is at once the plague and the joy of his household.

For Andersen, being treated like this was a summer idyll.

It ended on 23 October 1871 when he moved into his last home. "At 2 o'clock I drove to my new home, Nyhavn 18. Mrs. Melchior came with me. The new rooms made a good impression." He was back in his favourite street, next door to number 20, where he had lived in the 1830s and written his first fairy tales. One room looked out on to the yard at the back, the other on to Nyhavn and the harbour. Photographs show a comfortable, cluttered living room, the walls stacked with portraits in heavy frames, bookcases and display cabinets full of bric-à-brac lining the walls. Andersen

Andersen reading to the Melchior family, drawing by F. C. Lund, 1867.

sat at the bay window and, as in his other Nyhavn apartments, loved watching the weather and the sea. "We are having a stormy winter, I read every day of shipwrecks on the coast, even great steamships are lost," he wrote to Scudder, explaining that he could not face the journey to America, despite Scudder's offer to pay for him and promises that he could make a fortune from public readings. "While I am writing this, the hail is driving against the window panes, the wind is whistling through the ships' tackles in the canal outside my window." By February 1872 it was still "grey and wet"; "the fog is so thick and heavy that one can taste it. Such winter weather is not to my liking, and so for several months I have been delicate and have found it impossible to get rid of my cold."

Left alone, he lapsed back into depression: "felt decrepit, tired, old, sad about myself and my present life." A volume of tales, many first published in America, appeared in March, for which Andersen received 850 rixdollars from Reitzel, but what really cheered him was the prospect of a foreign trip, and as soon as winter ended he set off for Germany, Vienna and Venice, escorted by William Bloch. Bloch's account makes the trip sound like the stately progress of a hypochondriac across Europe: Andersen's panics included the conviction that he had swallowed a pin in some meat, that a small spot over one of his eyebrows might increase to cover his eye, that he would rupture himself because Bloch had accidentally tapped his stomach with his walking stick and that he had hydrarthrosis of the knee.

Back at Rolighed in June and July Andersen was "feeling old and weary!" "God, give me an idea! Give me something I can do! It's awful to be idle . . . my feeling of youthfulness is evaporating. I look forward to nothing. I'm irritable, discontented and lazy. If I could just lie down and sleep all the time." In fact, he was working hard on "Auntie Toothache," often writing from morning to night. The story was "finished and well-rounded" by 11 July; on 12 July Andersen completed a fair copy and read it aloud to Adolph Drewsen, Ingeborg's husband, who thought it "quite brilliant." A few days later Andersen wrote the short tale "The Flea and the Professor"—"in it I have the professor shoot his wife"—and "The Cripple"; in the autumn he wrote his last work, "Old Johanna's Tale." It is clear from his diaries that Andersen still derived pleasure and excitement from reading his latest tales aloud as he revised them. What he did not know was that for the first time in his life his hypochondriac grumblings were legitimate.

One of the people to whom Andersen read his work that summer was Edmund Gosse, desperate for an introduction to the famous writer who was "old, feeble and shielded by a bodyguard of friends against the incursions of the Philistine." Gosse managed to get an invitation to Rolighed, where after a tour of the house by the Melchiors,

> there appeared in the doorway a very tall, elderly gentleman, dressed in a com-
> plete suit of brown, and in a curly wig of the same shade of snuff-colour. I was
> almost painfully struck, at the first moment, by the grotesque ugliness of his
> face and hands, and by his enormously long and swinging arms; but the
> impression passed away as soon as he began to speak. His eyes, although they
> were small, had great sweetness and vivacity of expression, while gentleness
> and ingenuousness breathed from everything he said.

The face of Hans Andersen was a peasant's face, and a long lifetime of sensibility and culture had not removed from it the stamp of the soil. But it was astonishing how quickly this first impression subsided, while a sense of great inward distinction took its place. He had but to speak, almost but to smile, and the man of genius stood revealed . . .

He read in a low voice, which presently sank almost to a hoarse whisper . . . as he read he sat beside me, with his amazingly long and bony hand—a great brown hand, almost like that of a man of the woods—grasping my shoulder. As he read, the colour of everything, the twinkling sails, the sea, the opposing Swedish coast, the burnished sky above, kindled with sunset. It seemed as if Nature herself was flushing with ecstasy at the sound of Andersen's voice.

After the reading, which took place on Andersen's balcony, his voice faded, a bell was rung, servants summoned the Melchiors and it was "decided that the great man had lost his voice by the imprudence of reading aloud in the evening air, and he was conducted to his bed with infinite precaution," recalled Gosse. "I could not help being amused at the languishing way in which Andersen lent himself to all this fuss, gazing silently at me while they supported him from the room."

Another listener in the summer of 1872 was the artist Lorenz Frølich, who said that "Auntie Toothache" "really fascinated him"; his chiaroscuro drawing for it, with a fearsomely illumined, wild Auntie Toothache pointing her finger at the cowering poet in the shadows of his attic, is one of his best Andersen illustrations. The new stories were published in November 1872, and the first edition of 5,000 sold out at once. Andersen did not know it would be his last, but the sense of the volume as an epitaph to his life and work is strong. The two main stories, "Auntie Toothache" and "Old Johanna's Tale," are self-portraits of the harshest kind. In stark contrast to the rosy appendix detailing sunny years of honours and plaudits which he had recently completed for his American autobiography, they are the work of a man looking back on a lifetime of depression and doubt.

Fear of madness hung over "Old Johanna's Tale." It is the story of Rasmus, a boy growing up in a world resembling Andersen's Odense, who is talented but weak, lacking the gumption to pursue the grand farmer's daughter Elsa who falls in love with him. "He took to having fits of depression: he had more of his father's temperament than his mother's," and he ends up poor and alone—"his health and his spirits went up and down"—and mocked as Andersen's grandfather had been by the streetchildren:

Elsa's grandchild pointed at him—"poor Rasmus!" she called out. The other little girls followed her example: "poor Rasmus!" they shouted and ran screaming after the old man.

In "Auntie Toothache" Andersen transmutes two of the other troubles of his old age—toothache and insomnia—into a hallucinatory modernist tale about the links between pain and art.* In this story within a story, the narrator finds a manuscript written by the hero of the inner tale, a poet who as a child is fed sweets and grandiose ideas about his vocation by his Auntie Millie. She "had the loveliest white teeth. She saved them, too—said Brewer Rasmussen—by not sleeping with them at night!" The brewer, her lover, by contrast, had "no teeth at all, only a few black stumps."

Auntie Millie is a temptress; the sweets are symbolic, for her real seduction is to urge the hero on as an artist, suggesting he will be as good as Dickens, praising him in the terms in which Andersen was praised: "You paint, when you talk. You describe your house so that one sees it, and shudders! Go on writing—about something that's alive—about people; best of all, about unhappy people!"

One evening Auntie Millie arrives in a snowstorm at the poet's lodgings—based on Andersen's bleak sojourn in Tordenskjoldgade—and cannot get home. She settles in to talk of toothache. For Andersen, the progress of his teeth had always been a tangible if comic indicator of the road to mortality, and in 1872 he knew that he was about to lose his last ones. In the story, Auntie Millie remembers the poet's first teeth ("the tooth of innocence, shining like a little white drop of milk: the milk tooth"):

> Yet these were only the advance troops, not the real ones that must last right through life.
>
> Then they too arrived and the wisdom-teeth as well, fuglemen in the ranks, born in pain and great trouble.
>
> They leave you again, every one of them. They go before their period of

---

*Andersen is among the first of many writers to have recorded suffering from acute toothache over a lifetime and to have identified it with artistic agony. "My mouth is full of decayed teeth and my soul of decayed ambitions," James Joyce wrote in 1907, aged twenty-five. When Vladimir Nabokov's teeth were removed he said, "My tongue feels like somebody coming home and finding his furniture gone . . . I am orally a cripple"; the experience was distilled in *Pnin*, where the hero's loss of his teeth is symptomatic of the desolation of his lovelessness. I owe both these allusions to Martin Amis's *Experience*, which describes in detail his own toothache.

service has run out; even the last one goes, and that's no day of rejoicing; it's a day of sadness.

And then you're old, even if your heart is young.

Auntie Millie retires to bed in the next room, but returns to visit the insomniac poet, now afflicted by "a full-dress toothache," in a nightmare where "dream and reality became mingled together":

> The moon shone in across the floor. The glimmer came and went as the clouds came and went in the gale . . . at last the shadow on the floor began to look like something . . . I felt my blood run cold.
>
> On the floor sat a figure, long and thin, just as when a child draws with a pencil on its slate something resembling a person . . . I heard a droning sound. Was it her, or was it the wind humming like a hornet through the window-crack?
>
> No, it was Madame Toothache herself, her infernal Satanic Frightfulness—heaven preserve us from a visit from her!

Gleefully, Auntie Toothache ladles on the suffering. "I felt as if a red-hot gimlet was piercing my cheekbone," because "a big poet must have a big toothache, a little poet a little toothache." A bargain is struck—"Please let me be little. I'm no poet, I only have fits of writing like fits of toothache"—in which Auntie Toothache promises to leave the poet alone if he agrees to

Work by one of Andersen's favourite illustrators: Auntie Toothache *by Lorenz Frølich.*

give up writing; if he lapses, she will play his words torturously on his nerves as toothache. He falls asleep, and Auntie Millie awakes him next morning with an innocuous question:

"Have you written anything, dear child?"
"No, no!" I cried. "You *are* my Auntie Millie, aren't you?"

Here the manuscript ends, for the narrator cannot find the part that is missing:

It had gone out into the world as paper to wrap up bloaters, butter and green soap. It had fulfilled its destiny.
   The brewer is dead; Auntie is dead; the student is dead, the sparks of whose spirit went into the tub. That's the end of my story—the story of Auntie Toothache.

Few nineteenth-century works deal in so bitter-sweet and compressed a way with the artist's preoccupations: the link between suffering and creativity, the terror of an imagination beyond control, the fear that art is as meaningless and transient as grocery wrappers—and that, in the last devastating paragraph, so is life itself (the first edition contained the line "everything in the dustbin" at the end, which Andersen deleted from subsequent editions). "Auntie Toothache" recalls elements from every part of his *œuvre*. In its image of the sensitive poet it picks up a theme from "The Princess and the Pea." In its mockery of the uses of art, it continues where his first book, *A Walking Tour*, left off. As a mature work in which psychological insight is dovetailed with fantasy, it recalls the demonic elements of "The Shadow"; it is also an experimental tale that looks in its self-analysis and self-conscious structure to the novellas of the twentieth century. In his final volume, Andersen was still searching to understand the world, and "Auntie Toothache" combines two essential ingredients that make his work both timeless and ahead of his time: the conviction of being chosen by fate, with its echoes of ancient folk wisdom, and a modern sense of the absurdity of human existence.

The new stories appeared in November 1872 and were, Andersen wrote, "received with extraordinary sympathy and great acknowledgement." But immediately afterwards Andersen became seriously ill with abdominal pains, nausea and alternating constipation and diarrhoea. His doctor,

Theodor Collin, diagnosed bleeding haemorrhoids, but Andersen was soon so weak that he was unable to leave his bed. His symptoms were the beginning of the liver cancer which was to kill him. Collin was unsympathetic, and Andersen sought advice from a second doctor, Emil Hornemann, who was kinder. Leaning on Hornemann and William Bloch, almost unable to walk, Andersen attended the hundredth performance of his comedy *More Than Pearls and Gold* in November. He was otherwise too ill to go out, and relied on friends to visit him; in the evenings he was brought the playbill from the Royal Theatre, and, reading the cast list, followed the play, which he usually knew by heart, in his imagination. A photograph taken in October 1872 just weeks before his illness shows him already looking sick, frail and drawn; his hair has receded and his mouth is sunken and depressed.

Although his condition improved at Christmas, he never really recovered, continuing to suffer similar attacks which left him helpless and bedridden. He suspected that, despite encouragement from doctors, he was not going to get better. His vanity remained: he was most cheered by royal visits and inquiries, and by reports on his condition in the press. Two students who lived in the rooms above him, Matthias Weber and Erik Oksen, were solicitous—both subsequently became pastors—but Andersen was most dependent on the Melchiors. He had good days when he would drive out in the Melchiors' carriage—"the only carriage that's warm and comfortable for me"—and he was sometimes able to dine at his friends' houses; otherwise he lay on a sofa in his study and Mrs. Melchior sent a servant daily with food prepared for him. In January 1873 he lost his last tooth:

> Dr. Voss came at about 3 o'clock and pulled out my last tooth. It was anaesthetized, but I could still clearly feel the wrenching. He stayed with me for a good half hour. I was lighthearted at the thought that I was now rid of all my teeth, but not quite as jubilant as the other day when he extracted the first of the four loose ones. Well, now I am completely toothless . . . when was it I lost the first one? Wasn't it done at school in Slagelse by Dr. Hundrup?

But he had little hope of recovering his strength, commenting after a sleepless night that "it seemed to me that now I was indeed finished, and how little have I then accomplished."

By April he could walk the short distance from Nyhavn to the Melchiors' apartment, and he could not resist a spring trip abroad, hoping that a visit to a spa would help him. He travelled with the young writer Nicolai Bøgh to Glion in Switzerland for a whey-cure, but in May he told Scudder "my recuperation has been tediously slow . . . I have indeed been very ill. For all of six months I have had to stay in my room, except for an occasional drive in a closed carriage. I have not yet recovered my strength, and I find difficulty in walking." He wrote a panic-stricken letter to Edvard, whom he was terrified would die before him, and he returned to Copenhagen at the end of July "in a weak and ruined state."

He went straight to Rolighed. To his oldest friends he could now afford to be graceless. "I am more depressed in my spirits than anyone can imagine," he told Henriette Collin in September 1873. "I have spent deadly long days recently, I am not looking forward to anything, have no future any more, my life and the days are washing over me, and I am really just waiting for the curtain to fall. How very ungrateful, you will say. Well, I know everything there is to say." When he returned to his Nyhavn rooms for the autumn, Mrs. Melchior regularly sent flowers to brighten him, and the carriage was at his disposal, but mostly he had to refuse; on 6 October, for example, the Melchior daughters came with the carriage: "it was a great temptation, and I was in tears having to give it up. Tomorrow I'll probably feel worse—it's all downhill."

He had another attack of abdominal and liver pain at New Year 1873–1874, during which Bøgh cared for him in his rooms. It was clear he was soon going to die; while there was still time, the King made him a Privy Councillor (*Konferensraad*) for his birthday in April 1874, which was celebrated with a dinner party at the Melchiors'. Soon afterwards came a telegram asking about his health from Carl Alexander, with whom he had had no contact since the 1864 Prussian–Danish War: "this moved me deeply." He had often wanted to resume connections but had not dared; in Germany in 1867 he had found himself on the same train as the Grand Duke: "I even knew his escort without remembering his name, it was embarrassing for me not to be able to rush out and shake his hands. I didn't know how he would receive me, didn't know either what I would feel later, had I acted on my feelings; so I drew the curtains closely each time he passed by." Now, he wrote, "he is cordial and kind enough to be the one to make the first move. I sent a telegram at once and also wrote a letter which I asked Collin to turn into better German."

The pain apart, the worst affliction was that his inspiration had dried up. In March 1874 he told Scudder:

> My convalescence has proceeded but slowly. I have a liver ailment, and cannot regain my strength; I cannot, as before, disport myself in social life, visit the theatres, and—what is most disheartening of all—I do not feel like any kind of

literary composition . . . As age lies before me, and not youth, I become despondent . . . Before my illness . . . when I was with young people, I felt like one of them, and now I sit suffering in my small rooms while life is throbbing outside.

If he could not write, Andersen saw no point in life. In the summer of 1874, staying at Bregentved, he wrote to Mrs. Melchior:

No fairy tales occur to me any more. It is as if I had filled out the entire circle with fairy tale radii close to one another. If I walk in the garden among the roses—well, what stories they and the snails have told me! If I see the broad leaf of the water-lily, then Thumbelina has already ended her journey on it. If I listen to the wind, then it has told me the story about Valdemar Daae and has nothing better to tell me. In the wood, underneath the old oak trees, I am reminded that the Old Oak Tree has told me its last dream a long time ago. Thus I do not get any new, fresh impulses, and that is sad.

But the urge to express his vision was still strong, and what saved him now was the minor skill that had entertained his friends—his dexterity with scissors. Annie Wood remembered how in 1871 in Andersen's hands

the scissors move rapidly, and apparently without any forethought or effort, and yet the daintiest young ladies in elaborate dress, the most beautiful foliage to trees, or delicate curves in some graceful, fanciful design, will all, as if by magic, start out of the paper . . . He is rather proud of this unusual talent, and will often sign his name to one of these fragile little picture forms, and present it gravely to a lady, and beg her to keep it for his sake.

Such paper-cuts occupied him increasingly; the last one he cut, in 1874, for Dorothea Melchior, is a complex piece with many of his favourite characters: Pierrot, the Sandman, a court lady with a fan, an angel, a dancing girl, as well as some hinting at death—a raven, a pair of invocatory hands and a death's head.

Another diversion was a large screen of pictures on which he worked in 1874, inspired by a screen Countess Danneskjold from Holsteinborg had sent him. Reitzel gave him engravings and English illustrated magazines, the court photographer Hansen sent photographs of eminent Danes, other people sent issues of the Danish magazine *Illustreret Tidende*. Andersen devised eight panels, the first two devoted to Denmark, then one for Sweden, Germany, Britain, France, the Orient and Childhood. Each showed pictures of buildings and famous people, surrounded by images of fantasy

Andersen famously produced intricate cut-out patterns at great speed. He cut this one for Dorothea Melchior in 1874.

creatures and of everyday life. He included cut-outs of himself, of contemporaries (Jenny Lind, Dickens), of favourite historical and literary figures (Napoleon, Walter Scott, Goethe). The screen revealed the cultural landscape of his life; it was installed in the bedroom of his Nyhavn apartment, and he loved it to be admired, recording in his diary how one visitor, the conductor Holger Paulli, said it was better than much of what one saw at exhibitions. To Mimi Holstein he wrote in the spring of 1874 that his only occupation had been to make the screen, which people were comparing to a colourful fairy tale.

But these were consolations: by 1874 Andersen was very ill and his liver causing him great pain. Edmund Gosse, who visited him again in May 1874, was shocked at his decline. Andersen's landlady insisted Gosse stay no more than two minutes.

> As I entered the bright, pretty sitting-room, Hans Christian Andersen was coming in from an opposite door. He leaned against a chair, and could not proceed. I was infinitely shocked to see how extremely he had changed since I found him so blithe and communicative, only two years before. He was wearing a close-fitting, snuff-coloured coat, down to the heels, such a burnt-sienna coat as I remember to have seen Lord Beaconsfield wear . . . in the later 'sixties. This garment, besides being very old-fashioned, accentuated the extreme thinness of Andersen's tall figure, which was wasted, as people say, to a shadow. He was so afflicted by asthma that he could not utter a word, and between sorrow, embarrassment and helplessness, I wished myself miles away.

A few days later Andersen invited Gosse to come back; he arrived just after a photo session—the famous last photograph of a sallow, helpless, aged Andersen staring out of his study window, his face now totally sunken in, his expression one of struggle and suffering. Andersen was exhausted, "affectionate and pathetic," sitting in the midst of a bustle of packing and carrying as "it was thought that the air of the city was bad for him, and he was being hurried away to the country. He was sad, but not agitated; he said farewell with great tenderness; his last words were 'Remember me in your dear and distant country, for you may never see me again!'"

Andersen was still able to go off for the summer to the estates of Rolighed, Holsteinborg and Bregentved. Here he enjoyed the country air, and for a while he believed he was getting better. "My strength is increasing daily. For eighteen long months I was, as you know, very ill; it was even doubtful whether I could live through it. But now it is very different! The sweetness of nature in the forest, the warm sunshine and all the sympathy and attention which have been bestowed on me have been the best kind of medicine for me," he wrote to Scudder in July. But he remained frail and, as with many old people, those aspects of his character which had always been troublesome—his irritable sensitivity, the ease with which he became bored—were now exacerbated. "Mrs. Melchior is kind and considerate, despite the fact that I'm a cranky and dull guest that can't tolerate open windows and doors," he wrote in August, and a week later, "Boring out here. My task is to eat, drink and sleep . . . Nothing is getting done—just that I'm dying of boredom during the time I have left."

Old wounds had not healed. When Jonna Stampe invited him to stay, he declined; "I don't want to be beholden to her husband [Henrik Stampe] for the stay since it's obvious he doesn't care about me. During my entire illness last year he didn't visit me until the very last days when I joked with Jonna about his 'loyalty.' " Many times, too, he wrote, "I got started on my plaint about how old Collin could often be so harsh and exasperated with me." There was something of a *rapprochement* with Johanne Luise Heiberg, who shared so many memories of literary Copenhagen with Andersen, and he thought of going to read her "Auntie Toothache," but, he recorded, "have been on my way to see her several times now and turned back. I don't really believe what she says. She is so hard on most people—I suspect she isn't kind to me when my back is turned." Meanwhile, he was cross with the servants at Rolighed and unhappy with the other guests—"there is a strange, febrile resentment within me. I'm irritated by almost everything and sort of look right into people's hearts and say to myself: I don't like them."

Outwardly, he made an effort to charm. George Griffin remembered him in his last year as "the politest man I ever saw. As I was leaving the room, he accompanied me to the door, and yet he could scarcely stand. He looked at me until I went down the steps, and waved his hand at me as a last farewell." But "deep down inside I don't feel at all kindly, grateful or patient," Andersen wrote in his diary, and he was tormented by his recurring nightmare about a child who sickened at his breast and turned into a wet rag. He took morphine, and through the winter of 1874–1875 continued to decline.

Small things upset him absurdly. He reacted with indignation to the gift from America of $200, known as "the children's debt" after an American newspaper article had invited young readers to contribute towards a comfortable old age for Andersen, and he spent weeks worrying about wording a reply which was at once gracious and firm in its insistence that he was not indigent. Months later he was again furious when, after a Danish appeal

raised money for a statue of him in Kongens Have, the main park in Copenhagen, the sculptor August Saabye produced a sketch for the statue with a
group of children, including a boy leaning against Andersen's groin, which
he hated "because it reminds me of old Socrates and young Alcibiades. I
couldn't tell him but refused to pose or talk to him altogether today. I was
more and more enraged." The eventual statue showed him without children,
sitting holding a book, reading aloud.

By early 1875 he was longing for warmth and sunlight. "Only country
quiet and summer warmth can help me," he told Carl Alexander. "How
happy I would feel if I could see Weimar's noble Grand Duke, the Grand
Duchess, and the children again this summer." Realizing it would be his
last, his friends made enormous efforts for his seventieth birthday. The day
before, the writer George Browning recalled seeing the royal carriage driving down Nyhavn and stopping outside number 18, where Andersen got
out: "his arms full of bouquets, splendid bouquets, and with difficulty he
kept them from falling—they were the small avant-couriers of the following
day." The King had fetched him to Amalienborg Palace to award him the
Order of Dannebrog, first class, and over the next week acclaim flew in from
all over Europe. One which particularly pleased him was a long, rapturous
article from the English *Daily News* of 5 April, which said:

> *Hans Andersen*, the son of the cobbler of Odense, is a household word, and the
> creations of his fancy have passed into the great Pantheon where *Shakespeare's*
> people, and *Homer's* and *Scott's*, enjoy a life less perishable than that of mortal
> men . . .
>
> It has been given to *Hans Andersen* to fashion beings, it may almost be said,
> of a new kind, to breathe life into the toys of childhood, and the forms of
> antique superstition. The tin soldier, the ugly duckling, the mermaid, the little
> match girl, are no less real and living in their way than *Othello*, or Mr. *Pickwick*,
> or *Helen* of Troy. It seems a very humble field in which to work, this of nursery
> legend and childish fancy. Yet the Danish poet alone, of all who have laboured
> in it, has succeeded in recovering, and reproducing, the kind of imagination
> which constructed the old world fairy tales.

On his birthday Andersen received callers, including the Crown Prince,
other royals and the Mayor of Odense, between noon and three o'clock,
then celebrated with a banquet at the Melchiors'. One of the daughters
devised the twelve-course menu, naming the dishes and wines after fairy
tales—"The Wild Swans," "The Ice Maiden and The Snow Man," "Under
the Willow Tree" (mushrooms), "The Old House" (Château Guiraud),

Andersen in his study, photograph by Frantz Clement Stephan Weller, 1874.

"High Jumpers" (Champagne). The day ended with a visit to the Royal Theatre to see two of Andersen's plays, and among crowds of birthday presents was an edition of "The Story of a Mother" in fifteen languages, presented by his English, Danish and German publishers. Carl Alexander decorated Andersen with the Weimar Order of the Commander; thanking him, he wrote, "My birthday . . . was a noble and magnificent day for me, but I was very ill and it was hard for me to receive the deputations and other visitors. Long afterwards, and still now, I am suffering so much that I can only write with difficulty, and can only express weakly what I feel when I write to you, my exalted patron."

After another bad attack in May, the end came quite quickly. Even in this last phase, Andersen felt the need to record every crisis, his enemas, constipation, shaking limbs. Jonas Collin and a young Danish author, Johann Krohn, sometimes spent the night in his rooms, reassuring him and helping him on with clean clothes after accidents, but Dr. Hornemann thought he should go to hospital. Nineteenth-century hospitals were hardly enticing— at this time anyone who could afford it chose to be nursed at home. Andersen had wanted to go to Bregentved, but when this became clearly impossible, the Melchiors came to the rescue and on 12 June Andersen was moved to Rolighed, where a servant was hired to look after him.

"Lord! Lord! What will become of this miserable invalid?" Andersen asked on 14 June. Days later he was unable to write any more, instead dictating his diary to Mrs. Melchior. He sat on his balcony watching the sea and the boats in "warm, incomparably lovely summer weather," and, still planning to visit Bregentved and commenting on letters from publishers, he seems not to have realized how ill he was. Rolighed had a calming effect; he reported good nights—"a miraculous, lovely sleep—slept actually for fourteen hours"—and he enjoyed brief visits from friends, but by July his mind was confused. The rambling fantasies that emerged remained in character: on 21 July Andersen dictated a diary entry about "a silk-clad young girl with a crooked back" who burst into his rooms in the Hotel du Nord, and whom his friends claimed was in love with him, saying she wandered about Copenhagen "quoting indecently" from his erotic play *The Mulatto*:

> "What exceptionally lovely rooms you have!" she exclaimed. "You are *my* poet; I adore you!" She leapt back over to the sofa and stretched. "Embrace me!" she said. "Good Lord! what is wrong with you?" I exclaimed. She got terribly aggressive. "But don't you have a mother?" I said. "Whatever would she think

and say if she could see and hear you like this? . . . you must leave—you're frightening me! You're asking me to . . . ! Go away!" Then her whole personality changed. "You are a disgusting person!" she said. "I used to love you; now I hate you" . . . "Go!" I said, shaking. She ran off. I hurried to get dressed, ran over to Titular Councillor Collin's. Old Madam Thyberg was there; "But what has happened?" "God, there was a female up in my rooms!"

From 28 July Andersen could no longer dictate, and Mrs. Melchior composed the entries herself. "He felt very tired and wished to stay in bed. This morning as usual I brought him a lovely white rose, which he kissed. He took my hand and kissed it repeatedly, pressed my hand warmly as he gazed at me with a blissful smile. 'Thank you and God bless you,' he said as he again closed his eyes and dozed off again," she wrote on 29 July. "He is growing visibly weaker, and his face is shrunken and looks just like a mummy's. Poor Andersen!" On 31 July, "He says 'Don't ask me how I feel, I don't understand anything now.'"

Andersen was frightened of waking up alive in a coffin, and asked her to cut his veins when he died. She joked that he could do as he had often done, and leave a note saying "I only appear to be dead" beside him, at which "a little smile spread across his sunken features." On 2 August he believed he was better. He died in his sleep at five past eleven in the morning on 4 August.

The funeral took place on 11 August at Copenhagen's cathedral, Vor Frue Kirke. Among the hundreds present, including the King and the Crown Prince, there was not one blood relation of Andersen's. In his will, he left his estate of around 30,000 rixdollars to Edvard Collin, along with the rights to his works, which Reitzel bought for 20,000 rixdollars. He was buried in Assistens Cemetery in Copenhagen in a triple plot which, as he had requested, left spaces for Edvard and his wife Henriette.

Edvard published his memoir of Andersen in 1882. Much of it was cold and critical, but it contained his own highest tribute: "I should like to end by referring to what was really the essence of Andersen and concerns his character. I have looked into the depths of his soul, and I have not let myself be confused by the excesses of his imagination . . . I know that he was good. This simple declaration will not be misunderstood by those who really knew him."

Edvard died in 1886 and Henriette in 1894, and both were buried with him, but several years later their bodies were moved to the Collin family plot at Frederiksberg Cemetery. Andersen was left in the original grave alone.

SOURCES

A NOTE ON QUOTATIONS FROM ANDERSEN'S FAIRY TALES

There is no satisfactory translation of the complete edition of Andersen's fairy tales in English. I have used several different editions of selected tales, as cited below. Each stands out as a fine translation, the more so when compared with the mass of poor and inaccurate Andersen translations which continue to be published or reprinted. None of the editions of selected stories, however, includes all the major tales; I have therefore taken quotations from several editions, choosing for each tale the translation which I believe to be the best.

ANDERSEN'S WORKS, DIARIES, LETTERS

H. C. Andersens Samlede Skrifter 1–15, Copenhagen 1876–1880 (second edition).
Eventyr I–VII, critical edition edited by Erik Dal, with commentary by Erling Nielsen and Flemming Hovmann, Copenhagen 1963–1990.
Romaner og Rejsekildringer I–VII, edited by H. Topsøe-Jensen, Copenhagen 1943–1944.
Samlede Eventyr og Historier, edited by Svend Larsen (Jubileumsudgaven, Hans Reitzels Forlag), Odense 1995.
Fodreise fra Holmens Canal til Østpynten af Amager i aarene 1828 og 1829, edited by Johan de Mylius, Copenhagen 1986.
Hans Christian Andersen Fairy Tales, translated by R. P. Keigwin and edited by Svend Larsen (Flensteds Forlag), Odense 1951.
Hans Christian Andersen 80 Fairy Tales, translated by R. P. Keigwin and introduced by Elias Bredsdorff (Hans Reitzels Forlag), Odense 1976.
Hans Andersen's Fairy Tales: A Selection, translated by L. W. Kingsland and introduced by Naomi Lewis (Oxford World's Classics), Oxford 1984.
Hans Christian Andersen Fairy Tales, translated by Reginald Spink (Everyman's Library), London 1992.
The Little Mermaid, translated by David Hohnen and introduced by Erik Dal, Copenhagen 1994 (second edition).
The Improvisatore, or, Life in Italy, translated by Mary Howitt, London 1845.
Only a Fiddler and *OT*, translated by Mary Howitt, London 1845.
A Poet's Bazaar, translated by Charles Beckwith, London 1846.
A Christmas Greeting to My English Friends, translated by Charles Beckwith, London 1847.
The Two Baronesses, translated by Charles Beckwith, London 1848.
Picture Book Without Pictures, translated by Meta Taylor, London 1848.
Rambles in the Romantic Regions of the Hartz Mountains, Saxon Switzerland etc., translated by Charles Beckwith, London 1848.
Pictures of Sweden, translated by Charles Beckwith, London 1851.
To Be Or Not To Be?, translated by Mrs. Bushby, London 1857.
Lucky Peer, translated by Horace Scudder, New York 1871.
Seven Poems by Hans Christian Andersen, translated by R. P. Keigwin, Odense 1955.
A Visit to Portugal, translated by Grace Thornton, London 1972.
A Visit to Spain, translated by Grace Thornton, London 1975.
Das Märchen meines Lebens ohne Dichtung, Leipzig 1847.
Mit Livs Eventyr, Copenhagen 1855.

H. C. Andersens Levnedsbog, edited by H. Topsøe-Jensen, Copenhagen 1962.

The Fairy Tale of My Life, translated by Horace Scudder, London and New York 1975.

H. C. Andersens Dagbøger 1825–1875, vols I–XII, edited by H. Topsøe-Jensen and Kåre Olsen, Copenhagen 1971–1976.

The Diaries of Hans Christian Andersen, selected and translated by Patricia L. Conroy and Sven H. Rossel, Seattle and London 1990.

H. C. Andersens Almanakker 1833–1873, edited by Helga Vang Lauridsen and Kirsten Weber, Copenhagen 1990.

H. C. Andersens Brevveksling med Jonas Collin den Ældre og andre Medlemmer af det Collinske Hus, volumes I–III, edited by H. Topsøe-Jensen, Copenhagen 1945–1948.

H. C. Andersens Brevveksling med Edvard og Henriette Collin, vols I–VI, edited by H. Topsøe-Jensen, Copenhagen 1933–1937.

H. C. Andersen og Henriette Wulff. En Brevveksling, vols I–III, edited by H. Topsøe-Jensen, Copenhagen 1959–1960.

"H. C. Andersens Brevveksling med Henriette Hanck 1830–46" in *Anderseniana* IX–XIII, edited by Svend Larsen, 1941–1946.

The Andersen–Scudder Letters: Hans Christian Andersen's Correspondence with Horace Elisha Scudder, edited by Jean Hersholt and Waldemar Westergaard, Berkeley and Los Angeles 1949.

Breve fra Hans Christian Andersen, vols I–II, edited by C. S. A. Bille and N. Bøgh, Copenhagen 1878.

"Riborgs Broder. H. C. Andersens Brevveksling med Christian Voigt," edited by Th. A. Müller and H. Topsøe-Jensen in *Anderseniana*, second series, 1, 2, 1948.

H. C. Andersens Breve til Thérèse og Martin R. Henriques, 1860–75, edited by H. Topsøe-Jensen, Copenhagen 1932.

H. C. Andersens Moder. En Brevsamling, edited by Svend Larsen, Odense 1947.

Deres broderligt hengivne. Et udvalg af breve fra H. C. Andersen, edited by N. B. Wamberg, Copenhagen 1975.

Mein edler, theurer Grossherzog! Briefwechsel zwischen Hans Christian Andersen und Grossherzog Carl Alexander von Sachsen-Weimar-Eisenach, edited by Ivy York Möller-Christensen and Ernst Möller-Christensen, Göttingen 1998.

Hans Christian Andersen's Correspondence with the Late Grand-Duke of Saxe-Weimar, Charles Dickens, etc., etc., edited by Frederick Crawford, London 1891.

Hans Christian Andersen's Visits to Charles Dickens, as described in his letters, edited by Ejnar Munksgaard, Copenhagen 1937.

NOTES

The primary sources are Andersen's diaries, almanac, letters and autobiographies. Almost all of this material has been published in Danish and some of it—selected extracts from the diaries, some letters and the later autobiographies—has been translated into English. As an English biographer writing primarily for English-speaking readers, I have given an English source where one exists, and on these occasions I have used the published translations quoted with occasional amendments of my own. Where only a Danish or, sometimes, a German source is given, the translation is my own unless otherwise stated.

SHORT TITLES

Almanakker	*H. C. Andersens Almanakker 1833–1873*, edited by Helga Vang Lauridsen and Kirsten Weber, Copenhagen 1990.
Bredsdorff	*H. C. Andersen og England*, by Elias Bredsdorff, Copenhagen 1954.
Breve II	*Breve til Hans Christian Andersen*, edited by C. S. A. Bille and N. Bøgh, Copenhagen 1877.
Breve II	*Breve fra Hans Christian Andersen*, vols I–II, edited by C. S. A. Bille and N. Bøgh, Copenhagen 1878.
E. Collin	*H. C. Andersens Brevveksling med Edvard og Henriette Collin*, vols I–VI, edited by H. Topsøe-Jensen, Copenhagen 1933–1937.
J. Collin	*H. C. Andersens Brevveksling med Jonas Collin den Ældre og andre Medlemmer af det Collinske Hus*, vols I–III, edited by H. Topsøe-Jensen, Copenhagen 1945–1948.
Crawford	*Hans Christian Andersen's Correspondence with the late Grand-Duke of Saxe-Weimar, Charles Dickens, etc., etc.*, edited by Frederick Crawford, London 1891.
Dagbøger	*H. C. Andersens Dagbøger 1825–1875*, vols I–XII, edited by H. Topsøe-Jensen and Kåre Olsen, Copenhagen 1971–1976.
Diaries	*The Diaries of Hans Christian Andersen*, selected and translated by Patricia L. Conroy and Sven H. Rossel, Seattle and London 1990.
Dickens	*H. C. Andersen og Charles Dickens: Et Venskab og dets Opløsning*, by Elias Bredsdorff, Copenhagen 1951.
Fairy Tale	Hans Christian Andersen, *Mit Livs Eventyr*, Copenhagen 1855; translated by Horace Scudder and updated as *The Story of My Life*, New York 1871, reprinted as *The Fairy Tale of My Life*, London and New York, 1975.
Hanck	"H. C. Andersens Brevveksling med Henriette Hanck 1830–46" in *Anderseniana* IX–XIII, edited by Svend Larsen, 1941–1946.
Levnedsbog	*H. C. Andersens Levnedsbog*, edited by H. Topsøe-Jensen, Copenhagen 1962.
Munksgaard	*Hans Christian Andersen's Visits to Charles Dickens, as described in his letters*, edited by Ejnar Munksgaard, Copenhagen 1937.
Scudder	*The Andersen–Scudder Letters: Hans Christian Andersen's Correspondence with Horace Elisha Scudder*, edited by Jean Hersholt and Waldemar Westergaard, Berkeley and Los Angeles 1949.
Weimar	*Mein edler, theurer Grossherzog! Briefwechsel zwischen Hans Christian Andersen und Grossherzog Carl Alexander von Sachsen-Weimar-Eisenach*, edited by Ivy York Müller-Christensen and Ernst Müller-Christensen, Göttingen 1998.
Wulff	*H. C. Andersen og Henriette Wulff. En Brevveksling*, vols I–III, edited by H. Topsøe-Jensen, Copenhagen 1959–1960.

INTRODUCTION: LIFE STORIES

page 3   "Every character is . . ." HCA to Henriette Hanck, November 1834, *Hanck*, vol. IX, p. 92.
"I told the boys curious stories . . ." *Fairy Tale*, p. 21.
"Twenty-five years ago . . ." HCA to Edvard Collin, 5 September 1844, *E. Collin*, vol. II, p. 13.

4   "one who seemed to have fallen . . ." *Munksgaard*, p. 47.
"I have heaps of material . . ." HCA to Bernhard Ingemann, 20 November 1843, *Breve* II, vol. II, p. 95, quoted by Svend Larsen in introduction to *Hans Christian Andersen Fairy Tales*, Odense 1951, p. 20.
"[Ideas] lay in my thoughts . . ." ibid. pp. 20–21.
"The history of my life . . ." *Fairy Tale*, p. 274.
"If you looked down . . ." HCA to Edvard Collin, 5 July 1835, *E. Collin*, vol. I, p. 226.

5   "I must paint . . ." diary, 18 September 1825, *Diaries*, p. 7.
"I said loud and clear . . ." diary, 4 June 1875, ibid. p. 422.
"The Snow Queen . . ." HCA to Bernhard Ingemann, 10 December 1844, *Breve* II, vol. II, p. 106.
"fundamentally the story . . ." Thomas Mann to Agnes Meyer, 1955, quoted in Anthony Heilbut, *Thomas Mann: Eros and Literature*, London 1996, p. 590.

6   "It is only a writer . . ." *Daily News*, 5 April 1875.

I   THE COUNTRY, 1805–1812

page 7   "strange and bizarre . . ." William Bloch, *Paa Rejse med H. C. Andersen*, Copenhagen 1942, translated by Reginald Spink in Danish Ministry of Foreign Affairs, *Danish Journal*, Copenhagen 1975, p. 13.
"one of the most famous . . ." Edmund Gosse, *Two Visits to Denmark*, London 1911, p. 96.

8   "The toothache . . ." *Fairy Tale*, p. 566.
"who when by his wonderful lamp . . ." ibid. p. 557.
"The yard was quite the same . . ." diary, 11 December 1867, *Diaries*, p. 337.

9   "Will you go to sleep? . . ." *Fairy Tale*, p. 2.

10   "a man of a richly gifted . . ." ibid. p. 1.
"ignorant of life . . . love" ibid.
"I continually heard . . ." ibid. p. 2.

11   "sit carving strange figures . . ." ibid. p. 8.

12   "One day . . ." ibid.
"with curiosity . . ." ibid. p. 7.
"She stared down . . ." ibid.

13   "extremely spoiled . . . my father . . ." ibid. p. 2.
"From as early as . . ." HCA to Jonas Collin, 27 March 1825, *J. Collin*, vol. I, p. 21.
"it was only in such . . ." *Fairy Tale*, p. 2.
"he did not talk . . ." ibid. p. 3.
"He pondered . . ." ibid. p. 11.

14   "the great comet . . . With my mother . . ." ibid. p. 6.

16   "forty big and small . . ." Chr. B. Jensen, *Provincial-Lexikon over Danmark*, Copenhagen 1830, quoted in Niels Oxenvad, *H. C. Andersen Et Liv i Billeder*, Copenhagen 1995, p. 12.
"I remember . . ." *Fairy Tale*, p. 5.

17   "was a hundred years . . ." ibid. pp. 4–5.

19   "One little room . . ." ibid. p. 2.
"I had not . . ." ibid. p. 10.
"little Ane . . ." diary, 8 December 1867, *Diaries*, p. 336.

20   "when I was young . . ." quoted in Bente Scavenius, "The Stage of the Golden Age: A Window on to Reality," in *The Golden Age of Denmark: Art and Culture 1800–1850*, edited by Bente Scavenius, Copenhagen 1994, p. 8.

20 "I very seldom . . ." *Fairy Tale*, p. 8.
 "An old woman . . ." ibid. p. 10.
21 "I still recall . . ." *Levnedsbog*, p. 36.
22 "swamp plant" HCA to Henriette Wulff, 16 February 1833, *Breve* II, vol. 1, p. 114.
 "They rewarded . . ." *Fairy Tale*, p. 8.
23 "From the day . . ." HCA to Jonas Collin, 27 March 1825, *J. Collin*, vol. 1, p. 21.
 "with this I seated myself . . ." *Fairy Tale*, p. 11.

2 MASTER COMEDY-PLAYER, 1812–1819

page 24 "If anyone . . ." HCA to Mrs. Andersen (no relation), 1823, quoted in Edvard Collin, *H. C. Andersen og det Collinske Hus*, Copenhagen 1929 (second edition), p. 2.
25 "My father's rambles . . ." *Fairy Tale*, p. 12.
 "shrugged their shoulders . . ." ibid.
 "looked at me . . ." ibid. p. 13.
 "so-called wise woman" ibid.
 "the same kind of tree . . ." ibid.
 "If your father . . ." ibid.
26 "His corpse . . ." ibid. p. 14.
 "all at once . . ." ibid. pp. 17–18.
27 "a remarkably beautiful . . ." ibid. p. 16.
 "the strange characteristics . . ." *Levnedsbog*, p. 42.
 "Hers was the first . . ." *Fairy Tale*, p. 14.
 "with so much reverence . . ." ibid. p. 15.
 "The bold descriptions . . ." ibid.
28 "she only said so . . ." ibid.
 "all the looms . . ." ibid. p. 16.
 "when I was . . ." ibid.
 "I cried . . ." ibid. pp. 16–17.
 "Now I found myself . . ." *Levnedsbog*, p. 39.
29 "I was always . . ." ibid. p. 44.
30 "She did not understand . . ." *Fairy Tale*, p. 21.
 "although taking the lowest . . ." ibid. p. 21.
 "I had daily . . ." ibid. p. 22.
 "The boots creaked . . ." ibid.
 "My habit . . ." *Levnedsbog*, p. 42.
32 "That would actually . . ." *Fairy Tale*, p. 24.
 "he accepted . . . Master Comedy-Player . . ." Kirsten Grau Nielsen, "Fru Ottilies dagbog, den junge Comediantspiller," in *Anderseniana*, 1991, p. 14.
33 "First you go through . . ." *Fairy Tale*, p. 22
 "He lets me have . . ." ibid. p. 23.
 "In the last few years . . ." ibid. p. 24.
 "The postillion . . ." ibid.
34 "I stood solitarily . . ." ibid.

3 THE CITY, 1819–1822

page 36 "The whole city . . ." *Fairy Tale*, p. 35.
38 "A wandering musician . . ." quoted in Hans Hertel and Bente Scavenius, "Home and Abroad, High and Low: Contrasts of the Golden Age," in *The Golden Age Revisited: Art and Culture in Denmark 1800–1850*, edited by Bente Scavenius, Copenhagen 1996, pp. 20–21.

39   "I shall never . . ." Jenny Lind to Madame Bournonville, 11 June 1877, quoted in Henry Scott Holland and W. S. Rockstro, *Memoir of Madame Jenny Lind Goldschmidt*, London 1891, p. 183.

"looked up to . . ." *Fairy Tale*, p. 25.

41   "I improvised . . ." *Levnedsbog*, p. 55.

"too thin . . . O if you will . . . only engaged . . ." *Fairy Tale*, p. 26.

"When Paul . . ." *Levnedsbog*, p. 58.

42   "the rude jests . . ." *Fairy Tale*, p. 28.

"the whole history" ibid.

"I prophesy . . ." ibid.

44   "he tried . . ." ibid. p. 30.

"I was so frightened . . ." ibid.

45   "a polite old gentleman . . ." ibid. p. 33.

"[she] was very hard . . ." *Levnedsbog*, p. 64.

47   "What could I . . ." ibid. p. 67.

"he only commanded . . ." *Fairy Tale*, p. 33.

"When I first . . ." HCA to William Jerdan, October 1846, *Crawford*, p. 203.

48   "I was, in truth . . ." *Fairy Tale*, p. 35.

"I was sitting . . ." J. M. Thiele, *Af Mit Livs Aarbøger 1795-1826*, Copenhagen 1873, p. 204.

49   "Ask Ottilie . . ." Eline Bredsdorff to Hanna Bredsdorff, 3 October 1822, quoted in Elias Breds-dorff, "Spørg Ottilie om hun kan huske den lille Skomagersøn fra Odense," in *Anderseniana*, 3/4, 1983, p. 164.

"You have translated . . ." *Fairy Tale*, p. 41.

50   "As a boy . . ." *Levnedsbog*, p. 72.

"Allow me . . ." *Fairy Tale*, p. 35.

"That was a moment . . ." ibid.

51   "Among the former . . ." Auguste Bournonville, *My Theatre Life*, translated by Patricia N. McAndrew, London 1979, p. 443.

"In this house . . ." Thomasine Gyllembourg, *Extremerne*, quoted and translated in Mette Winge, "With Greetings from Rosenvænget" in *The Golden Age of Denmark: Art and Culture 1800-1850*, edited by Bente Scavenius, Copenhagen 1994, p. 71.

52   "often amused . . ." *Fairy Tale*, p. 37.

"Poetry was the light . . ." quoted in Hans Hertel and Bente Scavenius, "Home and Abroad, High and Low: Contrasts of the Golden Age," in *The Golden Age Revisited: Art and Culture in Denmark 1800-1850*, edited by Bente Scavenius, Copenhagen 1996, p. 13.

"One day . . ." *Fairy Tale*, pp. 37-8.

53   "This Biedermeier style . . . From the dread abyss . . ." Hans Hertel and Bente Scavenius, "Home and Abroad, High and Low: Contrasts of the Golden Age," in *The Golden Age Revisited: Art and Culture in Denmark 1800-1850*, edited by Bente Scavenius, Copenhagen 1996, pp. 19-20.

54   "Fresh as a . . ." quoted in ibid. p. 21.

"The great innovation . . ." ibid. p. 20.

55   "Trusting your goodness . . ." HCA to Bernhard Ingemann, 1821, *Deres broderligt hengivne. Et udvalg af breve fra H. C. Andersen*, edited by N. B. Wamberg, Copenhagen 1975, p. 27.

"Latin . . ." *Fairy Tale*, p. 34.

"The theatre . . ." *Fairy Tale*, p. 34.

"almost crushed . . ." ibid.

"I was heart-broken . . ." *Levnedsbog*, pp. 85-6.

56   "accompanied by . . ." *Fairy Tale*, p. 40.

"I heard it said . . . it was labour enough . . ." ibid.

57   "without expecting . . ." ibid. p. 42.

"useless for . . ." ibid.

"I was to apply . . ." ibid. p. 43.

"almost dumb . . ." ibid.

58   "I loved . . ." ibid. p. 44.

"a very miserable . . ." ibid.

4 ALADDIN AT SCHOOL, 1822-1827

page 59   "everybody knew . . ." *Fairy Tale*, p. 45.
60   "Yes . . ." ibid.
"I knew . . ." ibid.
61   "To me . . ." ibid.
62   "Shakespeare . . ." *Levnedsbog*, p. 112.
"You're a stupid boy . . ." ibid.
"My character . . ." HCA to Jonas Collin, 27 March 1825, *J. Collin*, vol. 1, p. 23.
63   "Am beginning . . . I'm bored . . . I am fuzzy-headed . . ." diary, 6 October 1825, 11 October 1825 and 11 December 1825, *Diaries*, pp. 10, 11 and 13.
"Now and then . . ." *Fairy Tale*, p. 49.
"In the little streets . . ." ibid. p. 48.
64   "If anyone . . ." HCA to Mrs. Andersen (no relation), 1823, quoted in Edvard Collin, *H. C. Andersen og det Collinske Hus*, Copenhagen 1929 (second edition), p. 2.
"I was in fine . . ." diary, 8 October 1825, *Diaries*, p. 10.
65   "I shall never . . ." *Fairy Tale*, p. 52.
66   "Flowers . . ." *Fairy Tale*, p. 51.
"that which is bitter . . ." ibid.
"Read Byron's biography . . ." diary, 20 November 1825, *Dagbøger*, vol. 1, p. 20.
"In my youth . . ." *Fairy Tale*, p. 70.
68   "Forgive me . . ." diary, 18 September 1825, *Diaries*, pp. 6-7.
"Unlucky me . . ." diary, 19 September 1825, ibid. p. 7.
"Being . . ." diary, 19 September 1825, ibid.
69   "My powerful fantasy . . ." diary, 20 September 1825, ibid. p. 8.
"God, I swear . . ." diary, 20 September 1825, ibid.
"depression . . ." diary, 25 September 1825, ibid.
70   "One evening . . ." *Levnedsbog*, p. 131.
"We are all . . ." diary, 13 October 1825, *Diaries*, p. 11.
"I certainly feel . . ." HCA to Jonas Collin, 19 June 1825, *J. Collin*, vol. 1, p. 24.
"The principal gave me . . . The principal was . . ." diary, 15 and 17 December 1825, *Diaries*, p. 13.
"My nasty vanity . . ." HCA to Jonas Collin, 2 July 1826, *J. Collin*, vol. 1, p. 55.
71   "We drove off . . ." diary, 19 December 1825, *Diaries*, p. 14.
"What a change . . ." *Fairy Tale*, p. 56.
"I have been . . ." diary, 19 December 1825, *Diaries*, p. 15.
72   "a very clever . . ." *Fairy Tale*, p. 60.
73   "was at Mrs. von der Maase's . . . visited . . ." diary, 25 and 27 December 1825, *Diaries*, pp. 20 and 21.
"The carriages . . ." diary, 23 December 1825, *Diaries*, p. 19.
"From such a house . . ." *Fairy Tale*, p. 58.
74   "I have nothing . . ." diary, 26 December 1825, *Diaries*, p. 20.
"In the first act . . ." diary, 26 December 1825, ibid. p. 21.
"He's probably . . ." diary, 28 December 1825, ibid. p. 22.
"it was the heavens . . ." diary, 29 December 1825, ibid. p. 23.
"we ate . . ." diary, 31 December 1825, ibid.
75   "it looks to me . . ." HCA to Jonas Collin, 27 May 1826, *J. Collin*, vol. 1, p. 53.
76   "I can't tell you . . ." *Levnedsbog*, p. 151.
"endowed with . . ." *Fairy Tale*, p. 55.
"The scenery . . . I suffered . . ." ibid. pp. 56 and 58.
"every day . . ." HCA to Jonas Collin, 24 October 1826, vol. 1, p. 70.
77   "You certainly . . ." Mrs. Wulff to HCA, 8 March 1827, *Breve* 1, p. 580.
79   "sentimentality . . . from this day . . ." *Fairy Tale*, p. 58.
"[he] ended . . ." ibid.
"the darkest . . ." ibid.

79 "yesterday . . ." diary, 4 June 1870, *Diaries*, p. 356.
"an embarrassing . . ." diary, 30 July 1874, *Dagbøger*, vol. x, p. 297.

5 FANTASIES, 1827–1831

page 82 "our family . . ." Edvard Collin, *H. C. Andersen og det Collinske Hus*, Copenhagen 1929 (second edition), p. 294.
"any touch . . ." Niels Birger Wamberg, "A Born Achiever: Jonas Collin—Potentate and Philanthropist," in *The Golden Age of Denmark: Art and Culture 1800–1850*, edited by Bente Scavenius, Copenhagen 1994, p. 60.

83 "I really . . ." *Levnedsbog*, p. 173.
"as someone . . ." HCA to Louise Collin, 18 November 1839, in Rigmor Stampe, *H. C. Andersen og hans nærmeste omgang*, Copenhagen 1918, p. 177.
"the eldest . . ." *Levnedsbog*, p. 173.

84 "bright poetical ideas" *Fairy Tale*, p. 61.
"the ideas . . ." ibid.

85 "a comedy . . ." *Selected Writings of E. T. A. Hoffmann*, edited and translated by Leonard J. Kent and Elizabeth C. Knight, Chicago 1969, p. 18.
"a woman . . ." ibid. p. 19.

86 "I imagine . . ." ibid. p. 19.
"a peculiar . . ." *Fairy Tale*, p. 62.

89 "My fellow-students . . ." ibid. pp. 64–5.

91 "I liked . . ." ibid. p. 66.
"If you will . . ." HCA to Edvard Collin, 15 June 1830, *E. Collin*, vol. i, p. 20.
"Doesn't every . . ." HCA to Edvard Collin, 28 July 1830, ibid. p. 50.
"Brought up . . ." *Fairy Tale*, pp. 81–2.

92 "Something . . ." HCA to Edvard Collin, 7 March 1833, *E. Collin*, vol. i, p. 118.
"From the creation . . ." *Fairy Tale*, p. 67.
"No keen . . ." P. N. Frost, *Statistisk-oekonomisk Beskrivelse over Waarbasse og Heinsvig Sogne*, 1819, quoted in Hans Hertel, "Our Very Own Scotland," in *The Golden Age of Denmark: Art and Culture 1800–1850*, edited by Bente Scavenius, Copenhagen 1994, p. 176.

94 "I was approaching . . ." *Levnedsbog*, pp. 203–204.
"It was . . ." HCA to Edvard Collin, 23 June 1830, *E. Collin*, vol. i, p. 25.

95 "Do not be surprised . . ." HCA to Edvard Collin, 18 August 1830, ibid. p. 65.
"The ladies . . ." HCA to Edvard Collin, 9 August 1830, ibid. p. 60.

96 "the eldest . . ." *Levnedsbog*, pp. 209–10.

97 "When I first . . ." ibid. p. 214.
"Most of my time . . ." HCA to Christian Lorenzen, 27 March 1831, *Breve* II, vol. i, p. 71.
"I miss you . . ." HCA to Kristine Marie Iversen, 3 September 1830, *Crawford*, pp. 53–5.

99 "I should retreat . . ." *Levnedsbog*, p. 221.
"Goodbye . . ." ibid. p. 224.
"Yes, my poems . . ." HCA to Bernhard Ingemann, 18 January 1831, *Crawford*, pp. 66–7.

100 "People are . . ." HCA to Henriette Hanck, 25 November 1830, *Hanck*, vol. ix, p. 9.

102 "Yesterday . . ." diary, 16 April 1864, *Diaries*, p. 309.
"I betrayed . . ." *Fairy Tale*, pp. 70–71.
"My health . . ." HCA to Bernhard Ingemann, 31 December 1830, *Crawford*, p. 62.

6 MY TIME BELONGS TO THE HEART, 1831–1833

page 103 "If you looked . . ." HCA to Edvard Collin, 5 July 1835, *E. Collin*, vol. i, p. 226.
"Last year . . ." HCA to Christian Lorenzen, 18 February 1831, *Crawford*, p. 71.
"a poet . . ." *Fairy Tale*, p. 70.

104 "a sense . . ." James Sheehan, *German History 1770–1866*, Oxford 1989, p. 324.
"If man . . ." "Die Horen," 1795, quoted in ibid. p. 329.
"Life is . . . the most mysterious . . ." ibid. pp. 332–4.
"the only . . ." ibid. p. 332.

105 "He no longer . . ." Ludwig Tieck, "Eckbert the Fair," in *Six German Romantic Tales* (Heinrich von Kleist, Ludwig Tieck, E. T. A. Hoffmann), translated by Ronald Taylor, London 1985, p. 10.
"In the morning . . ." diary, 16 May 1831, *Diaries*, p. 24.
"I was . . ." diary, 16 May 1831, ibid.
"the nerves . . ." diary, 18 May 1831, ibid. p. 25.

106 "It was an impulse . . ." diary, 19 May 1831, ibid.
"drinking . . ." diary, 19 May 1831, ibid. p. 26.
"Of all human beings . . ." HCA to Edvard Collin, 19 May 1831, *E. Collin*, vol. 1, p. 69.
"in dust . . ." HCA to Signe Læssøe, May 1831, *Crawford*, p. 80.

107 "When we were ascending . . ." Clement Carlyon, *Early Years and Late Reflections*, vol. 1, 1836, p. 127, quoted in Richard Holmes, *Coleridge: Early Visions*, London 1989, p. 230.
"Oh, to travel . . ." diary, 31 May 1831, *Diaries*, p. 28.
"made the deepest . . ." *Fairy Tale*, p. 72.
"I left him . . ." ibid.

108 "I did . . ." diary, 4 June 1831, *Diaries*, p. 31.
"mirrored . . ." diary, 3 June 1831, ibid.
"One of . . . The postal employees . . ." diary, 2 June 1831, ibid. p. 30.
"it is a child-like . . ." diary, 3 June 1831, ibid.
"*Noah* . . ." diary, 3 June 1831, ibid. p. 31.
"Every time . . ." HCA to Christian Voigt, 9 June 1831, "Riborgs Broder. H. C. Andersens Brevveksling med Christian Voigt," edited by Th. A. Müller and H. Topsøe-Jensen in *Anderseniana*, second series, 1, 2, 1948, p. 99.
"How shall . . ." Edvard Collin to HCA, 28 May 1831, *E. Collin*, vol. 1, pp. 73–5.

110 "Yes indeed . . ." HCA to Edvard Collin, 11 June 1831, ibid. p. 79.
"last summer . . . It is true . . ." HCA to Edvard Collin, 11 June 1831, ibid. p. 80.
"I now feel . . ." HCA to Edvard Collin, 11 June 1831, ibid.
"that grave man . . ." *Fairy Tale*, p. 72.

112 "How I long . . ." HCA to Edvard Collin, 20 August 1831, *E. Collin*, vol. 1, p. 95.

113 "I will even . . ." HCA to Edvard Collin, 2 November 1831, ibid. p. 99.
"I am a peculiar . . ." HCA to Signe Læssøe, 2 August 1832, *Crawford*, pp. 83–4.
"You dear, dear . . ." HCA to Ludvig Müller, 23 August 1832, in Erik Dal, "Omkring tre nyfundne breve til Ludvig Müller," 1832, quoted in *Anderseniana*, 3, 4/5, 1984, pp. 208–209; also quoted in Heinrich Detering, *Intellectual Amphibia*, Odense 1991, pp. 41–2.

114 "truly dear . . . which were really . . . How dear . . ." "Ludvig Müller" to HCA, 25 August 1832, in Erik Dal, "Omkring tre nyfundne breve til Ludvig Müller," 1832, quoted in *Anderseniana*, 3, 4/5, 1984, p. 210.
"but I gladly . . . Oh Ludvig . . ." HCA to Ludvig Müller, 26 August 1832, ibid. p. 212.

115 "From the profoundest . . ." HCA to Ludvig Müller, 26 August 1832, ibid.

116 "What will . . ." HCA to Bernhard Ingemann, 20 December 1832, ibid. p. 111.
"It is easy . . ." HCA to Otto Müller, 1 October 1832, Kirsten Dreyer and Flemming Hovmann, "Et overset venskab: H. C. Andersens og Otto Müllers brevveksling," *Anderseniana*, 1993, p. 55.

117 "Thank you . . ." HCA to Louise Collin, 8 September 1832, in Rigmor Stampe, *H. C. Andersen og hans nærmeste omgang*, Copenhagen 1918, p. 166.

118 "Anyone . . ." *Levnedsbog*, p. 1.

119 "Now you have . . ." HCA to Louise Collin, 27 October 1832, in Rigmor Stampe, *H. C. Andersen og hans nærmeste omgang*, Copenhagen 1918, p. 168.
"Now I am . . ." HCA to Louise Collin, 1 November 1832, in ibid. p. 170.
"Andersen . . ." HCA to Louise Collin, undated, probably December 1832, in ibid. p. 172.

120 "Our friendship . . ." dedication written in *Twelve Months of the Year*, copy now in possession of Professor Erik Dal and seen by the author.

120   "What up to now . . ." quoted in Niels Kofoed, *H. C. Andersen og B. S. Ingemann Et livsvarigt venskab*, Copenhagen 1992, pp. 45–6 and in Niels Kofoed, "Hans Christian Andersen and the European Literary Tradition," in *Hans Christian Andersen: Danish Writer and Citizen of the World*, edited by Sven Hakon Rossel, Amsterdam and Atlanta 1996, p. 224.

121   "I am . . ." HCA to Edvard Collin, 7 March 1833, *E. Collin*, vol. I, p. 119.
       "I have remained . . ." HCA to Henriette Wulff, 16 February 1833, *Breve* II, vol. I, p. 113.
       "I walked . . ." diary, 22 April 1833, *Dagbøger*, vol. I, p. 118.
       "through the air . . ." *Fairy Tale*, p. 82.
       "Believe me . . ." Edvard Collin to HCA, 22 April 1833, *E. Collin*, vol. I, p. 120.

7   ITALY, 1833–1835

page 122   "Oh, to travel . . ." diary, 31 May 1831, *Diaries*, p. 28.
       "I am . . ." HCA to Christian Voigt, 26 June 1833, *Crawford*, p. 105.
       "Paris . . ." HCA to Ludvig Müller, 14 May 1833, ibid. p. 90.
       "now for the first time . . ." diary, 15 May 1833, *Diaries*, pp. 36–7.

123   "like a spiritually . . ." diary, 17 May 1833, ibid. p. 37.
       "my recent . . ." *Fairy Tale*, p. 88.
       "Heine . . ." HCA to Christian Voigt, 26 March 1833, *Crawford*, p. 106.
       "The most sensuous . . ." HCA to Ludvig Müller, 31 May 1833, ibid. pp. 100–101.
       "Paris is . . ." HCA to Christian Voigt, 26 June 1833, "Riborgs Broder. H. C. Andersens Brevveksling med Christian Voigt," edited by Th. A. Müller and H. Topsøe-Jensen in *Anderseniana*, second series, I, 2, 1948, p. 119.
       "Oh Edvard . . ." diary, 7 May 1833, *Dagbøger*, vol. I, p. 143.
       "Your silence . . ." HCA to Edvard Collin, 11 June 1833, *E. Collin*, vol. I, p. 134.

124   "I have known . . ." Edvard Collin to HCA, 8 July 1833, ibid. p. 145.
       "How I long . . ." HCA to Edvard Collin, 19 July 1833, ibid. p. 148.
       "You can . . ." HCA to Edvard Collin, 9 August 1833, ibid. p. 161.

125   "the traditions . . ." *Fairy Tale*, p. 84.
       "Oh how I am . . ." HCA to Signe Læssøe, 3 September 1833, *Crawford*, p. 113.
       "Andersen wrote . . ." Edvard Collin, *H. C. Andersen og det Collinske Hus*, Copenhagen 1929 (second edition), p. 290.

126   "Tell me . . ." For these translations of *Agnete*, I am indebted to Heinrich Detering, *Intellectual Amphibia*, Odense 1991, p. 48.
       "A mountain . . ." HCA to Signe Læssøe, 3 September 1833, *Crawford*, p. 113.

127   "Oh Edvard! My soul . . ." HCA to Edvard Collin, 12 September 1833, *E. Collin*, vol. I, p. 178.
       "It is with . . ." diary, 19 September 1833, *Diaries*, p. 41.
       "Right in front . . . The Alps looked . . ." diary, 19 September 1833 and 20 September 1833, ibid. pp. 42–3 and 45.

128   "Here at last . . ." diary, 17 September 1833, ibid. p. 40.
       "This is the home . . ." HCA to Signe Læssøe, 18 March 1834, *Crawford*, p. 126.
       "I don't want . . ." diary, 23 September 1833, *Diaries*, p. 47.
       "The mode . . ." *Fairy Tale*, p. 103.
       "If France . . ." diary, 2 October 1833, *Diaries*, p. 48.

129   "I felt . . ." *Fairy Tale*, p. 80.
       "the magnificence . . . I had never had . . ." ibid. p. 104.
       "the city . . ." ibid. p. 107.
       "the melancholy . . ." Edward Lear to Ann Lear, 14 December 1837, *Edward Lear: Selected Letters*, edited by Vivien Noakes, Oxford 1988, p. 35.

130   "white—black . . ." ibid. p. 34.

131   "devoted to . . ." *Fairy Tale*, p. 109.
       "It was as if . . ." diary, 27 October 1833, *Diaries*, p. 57.

131   "saw a model . . ." diary, 4 January 1834, ibid. p. 68.
        "Went, like yesterday . . ." diary, 6 January 1834, ibid. p. 69.

132   "Hertz . . ." diary, 21 December 1833, ibid. p. 62.
        "the wings . . ." diary, 31 December 1833, ibid. p. 67.
        "went to the Lateran . . ." diary, 21 October 1833, ibid. pp. 50–51.
        "There was . . ." diary, 16 December 1833, ibid. p. 59.
        "Began this evening . . ." diary, 27 December 1833, ibid. p. 65.

133   "mine was the most . . . got the best . . ." diary, 24 December 1833, ibid. p. 63.
        "has never since . . ." *Fairy Tale*, p. 112.

134   "in his conversation . . ." Edvard Collin to HCA, 3 October 1833, *E. Collin*, vol. 1, p. 169.
        "If only . . ." diary, 6 January 1834, *Diaries*, p. 69.
        "What a night . . ." diary, 7 January 1834, ibid.
        "Last night . . ." diary, 8 January 1834, ibid. p. 70.
        "It is difficult . . ." diary, 9 January 1834, ibid. p. 71.

135   "Well, today . . ." diary, 31 January 1834, ibid. p. 72.
        "Feel your own . . ." diary, 8 January 1834, ibid. p. 71.
        "the sky . . ." diary, 19 February 1834, ibid. p. 76.
        "I strolled . . ." *Fairy Tale*, p. 117.
        "tired . . ." diary, 17 February 1834, *Diaries*, p. 75.
        "I am sitting . . ." HCA to Henriette Wulff, 23 February 1834, *Wulff*, vol. 1, p. 161.

136   "equals the great bay . . ." Berlioz to his family, 2 October 1831, quoted in David Cairns, *Berlioz*, vol. 1: *The Making of an Artist* (second edition), London 1999, pp. 512–13.
        "You will find . . ." HCA to Henriette Wulff, 16 March 1835, *Wulff*, vol. 1, p. 215.
        "When I want . . ." Nicholas Boyle, *Goethe: The Poet and the Age*, vol. 1, Oxford 1991, p. 459.
        "Naples is . . ." ibid p. 464.

137   "The sea . . ." diary, 19 February 1834, *Diaries*, pp. 75–6.
        "At dusk . . ." diary, 21 February 1834, ibid. p. 78.
        "Took a walk . . ." diary, 23 February 1834, ibid. pp. 79–80.
        "The boy . . ." diary, 26 February 1834, ibid. p. 85.

138   "Experienced people . . ." diary, 28 February 1834, *Dagbøger*, vol. 1, p. 331.
        "Hertz says . . ." diary, 25 February 1834, *Diaries*, p. 84.
        "on a thin crust . . ." Johan de Mylius, *H. C. Andersen—liv og værk En tidsval*, Copenhagen 1993, p. 43.

139   "Let me follow . . ." diary, 23 March 1834, *Dagbøger*, vol. 1, p. 366.
        "perhaps they . . . So I was . . ." HCA to Signe Læssøe, letter begun Naples 18 March 1834 and continued Florence 8 April 1834, *Crawford*, p. 126.
        "the people . . ." HCA to Signe Læssøe, ibid. p. 129.
        "What are . . ." quoted in David Cairns, *Berlioz: The Making of an Artist* vol. 1 (second edition), London 1999, p. 476.
        "I won't let . . . Today . . ." diary, 9 January 1834, *Diaries*, p. 71.

140   "God knows . . ." HCA to Signe Læssøe, letter begun Naples 18 March 1834 and continued Florence 8 April 1834, *Crawford*, p. 130.
        "I have a few memories . . ." HCA to Bernhard Ingemann, 10 February 1835, *Breve* II, vol. 1, p. 291.
        "We shall meet . . ." HCA to Edvard Collin, 14 July 1834, *E. Collin*, vol. 1, p. 220.
        "just a little . . ." Otto Müller to HCA, 11–14 June 1834, Kirsten Dreyer and Flemming Hovmann, "Et overset venskab: H. C. Andersens og Otto Müllers brevveksling," *Anderseniana*, 1993, p. 55.

141   "I fear greatly . . ." HCA to Signe Læssøe, letter begun Naples 18 March 1834 and continued Florence 8 April 1834, *Crawford*, p. 125.
        "I have read . . ." HCA to Henriette Wulff, 15 May 1834, *Wulff*, vol. 1, pp. 177–8.
        "No letter . . ." diary, 14 May 1834, *Diaries*, pp. 86–7.
        "youthful . . ." diary, 16 May 1834, ibid. p. 88.

141   "a whole *Miserere* ..." diary, 20 May 1834, ibid. p. 89.

        "I assured ..." *Fairy Tale*, p. 124.

142   "I won't ..." HCA to Ludvig Müller, 18 May 1834, *Breve* II, vol. I, p. 231.

        "The poet ..." HCA to Henriette Wulff, 17 June 1834, *Wulff*, vol. I, p. 185.

        "I haven't been ..." HCA to Henriette Wulff, 26 September 1834, ibid. p. 198.

        "in a little ..." *Fairy Tale*, p. 131.

144   "Dear Reitzel ..." HCA to Carl Reitzel, 28 March 1835, *Breve* II, vol. I, pp. 294–5.

        "but that he is not ..." *Fairy Tale*, p. 131.

        "Never until now ..." HCA to Henriette Wulff, 29 April 1835, *Wulff*, vol. I, p. 217.

        "The morning breeze ..." Auguste Bournonville, *My Theatre Life*, translated by Patricia N. McAndrew, London 1979, pp. 90–91.

145   "What did you get ..." *Fairy Tale*, p. 143.

146   "What a peculiar ..." HCA to Signe Læssøe, letter begun Naples 18 March 1834 and continued Florence 8 April 1834, *Crawford*, p. 130.

8   FIRST FAIRY TALES, 1835

page 147   "For five months ... rain, slush ..." HCA to Henriette Wulff, 16 March 1835, *Crawford*, pp. 135–41.

148   "Now you enter ..." HCA to Henriette Hanck, 1 January 1835, *Hanck*, vol. X, p. 105.

        "I shall give ..." HCA to Henriette Hanck, 27 April 1838, ibid. vol. XI, p. 239.

149   "You cannot ..." HCA to Henriette Wulff, 26 March 1835, *Crawford*, p. 141.

        "I am now ..." HCA to Henriette Hanck, 1 January 1835, *Hanck*, vol. X, p. 104.

        "I have started ..." HCA to Bernhard Ingemann, 10 February 1835, *Breve* II, vol. I, p. 292.

        "I have also written ..." HCA to Henriette Wulff, 16 March 1835, *Crawford*, p. 141.

        "they [the tales] will ..." HCA to Henriette Hanck, 26 March 1835, *Hanck*, vol. X, p. 108.

154   "My life ..." HCA to Kirstine Marie Iversen, 4 January 1837, *Breve* II, vol. I, p. 365, quoted in Niels Kofoed, "Hans Christian Andersen and the European Literary Tradition," in *Hans Christian Andersen: Danish Writer and Citizen of the World*, edited by Sven Hakon Rossel, Amsterdam and Atlanta 1996, p. 233.

155   "I retained ..." HCA, preface to *Samlede Eventyr og Historier*, Copenhagen 1862, translated in *Catalog of the Jean Hersholt Collection of Hans Christian Andersen Manuscripts and First Editions*, Washington 1954, p. 24.

156   "I seize an idea ..." HCA to Bernhard Ingemann, 20 November 1843, *Breve* II, vol. II, p. 94.

        "This was ..." Erik Dal, introduction to *The Little Mermaid*, Copenhagen 1994 (second edition), pp. 8–9.

157   "He sprinkled ..." R. P. Keigwin, introduction to *Fairy Tales from Hans Christian Andersen: A New Version of the First Four*, Cambridge 1935, pp. xi–xii.

        "He is a remarkably ..." G. W. Griffin, *My Danish Days*, Philadelphia 1875, p. 209.

158   "Most of them ... it was only ..." diary, 26 January 1866, *Diaries*, pp. 320–321.

        "Whether the tale ..." Edvard Collin, *H. C. Andersen og det Collinske Hus*, Copenhagen 1929 (second edition), p. 299.

        "Andersen's voice ..." Edvard Brandes, "H. C. Andersen Personlighed og Værk," quoted in *Litterære Tendenser*, edited by C. Bergstroem-Nielsen, Copenhagen 1968, p. 249.

159   "it is my spirit ..." Charlotte Brontë, *Jane Eyre*, London 1933 (reprint), p. 303.

        "I am poor ..." HCA to Jonas Collin, 14 May 1835, *J. Collin*, vol. I, p. 120.

        "I do have ..." HCA to Henriette Hanck, 17 November 1835, *Hanck*, vol. X, p. 117.

160   "If you looked ..." HCA to Edvard Collin, 5 July 1835, *E. Collin*, vol. I, p. 226.

161   "My dear faithful ..." Wilhelm von Rosen, "Venskabets Mysterier," *Anderseniana*, 3, 3, 1980, p. 170.

        "I long ..." HCA to Edvard Collin, 28 August 1835, *E. Collin*, vol. I, p. 238.

162   "He would often . . ." Edvard Collin, *H. C. Andersen og det Collinske Hus*, Copenhagen 1929 (second edition), p. 303.

165   "The *Monthly Review* . . ." *Fairy Tale*, p. 135.
"It is not meaningless . . ." *Dansk Litteraturtidende*, 1836, no. 1, p. 11.
"whether . . . the most delightful . . ." ibid, p. 11.

166   "Wherever . . ." HCA to Henriette Wulff, 19 July 1836, *Wulff*, vol. 1, p. 236.
"I hope . . ." HCA to Bernhard Ingemann, 17 December 1835, *Breve* II, vol. 1, p. 315.

9   WALKING ON KNIVES, 1836–1837

page 167   "The latest . . ." HCA to Bernhard Ingemann, 11 February 1837, quoted in *The Little Mermaid*, introduced by Erik Dal, Copenhagen 1994 (second edition), p. 12.
"The ladies . . ." HCA to Henriette Hanck, 28 October 1836, *Hanck*, vol. x, p. 150.

168   "My writing years . . ." HCA to Henriette Wulff, 3 February 1836, *Wulff*, vol. 1, p. 223.
"No other winter . . ." HCA to Henriette Hanck, 19 January 1836, *Hanck*, vol. x, p. 121.
"I want . . ." HCA to Henriette Hanck, 13 May 1836, ibid. p. 139.
"It is a description . . ." HCA to Henriette Hanck, 17 November 1835, ibid. p. 116.

170   "The Daughters of the Sea . . ." HCA to Henriette Hanck, 13 May 1836, ibid. p. 140.
"On either side . . ." diary, 5–6 August 1836, *Dagbøger*; this fragment was originally dated 1830 and then redated 1836, see Niels Oxenvad, "H. C. Andersen i Svendborg 1830—og i 1836, Omdatering af et dagbogsfragment," *Anderseniana*, 1989, pp. 19–28.
"My dear . . ." HCA to Edvard Collin, 4 August 1836, *E. Collin*, vol. 1, p. 262.
"I cannot deviate . . ." Edvard Collin, *H. C. Andersen og det Collinske Hus*, Copenhagen 1929 (second edition), p. 289.

171   "The latest . . ." HCA to Bernhard Ingemann, 11 February 1837, quoted in *The Little Mermaid*, introduced by Erik Dal, Copenhagen 1994 (second edition), pp. 12–13.

172   "My tales . . ." HCA to Henriette Hanck, 9 March 1837, ibid. p. 11.

175   "You have got . . ." HCA to Horace Scudder, 27 March 1874, *Scudder*, p. 144.

176   "only little waves . . ." Frederich de la Motte Fouqué, *Undine*, New York 1845, p. 91.

177   "The tale . . ." HCA to Edvard Collin, 25 March 1837, *E. Collin*, vol. 1, p. 266.

178   "None of my writings . . ." preface to Hans Christian Andersen, *Eventyr, fortalte for Børn*, Copenhagen 1837, translated in *Catalog of the Jean Hersholt Collection of Hans Christian Andersen Manuscripts and First Editions*, Washington 1954, p. 25.

10   LE POÈTE, C'EST MOI!, 1837–1840

page 179   "I covet . . ." HCA to Henriette Hanck, 20 September 1837, *Hanck*, vol. x, p. 199.
"My name . . ." HCA to Henriette Hanck, 20 September 1837, ibid.
"But may . . ." HCA to Henriette Hanck, 20 September 1837, ibid.
"and you know . . ." HCA to Henriette Hanck, December 1838, *Breve* II, vol. 1, p. 470.

180   "I reckon . . ." *Fairy Tale*, p. 139.
"like a fairy tale . . ." ibid. pp. 139–40.
"A Mr. Andersen . . ." Fredrika Bremer to E. G. Geijer, quoted in *Diaries*, p. 95.
"a spiritual . . ." *Fairy Tale*, p. 136.

182   "The joyless . . . should rather . . ." Søren Kierkegaard, *Af en endnu Levendes Papirer*, Copenhagen 1838, p. 27 and p. 389, quoted in Heinrich Detering, *Intellectual Amphibia*, Odense 1991, p. 59.
"I do really . . ." HCA to Edvard Collin, 11 August 1837, *E. Collin*, vol. 1. p. 267.
"I shall die . . ." HCA to Henriette Hanck, December 1837, *Hanck*, vol. x, p. 210.

183   "Today . . ." diary, 11 December 1837, *Dagbøger*, vol. II, p. 31.
"I want to be . . ." ibid.

183   "Now ..." diary, 11 December 1837, *Diaries*, p. 95.
184   "No one ..." HCA to Frederik Læssøe, 9 March 1838, *Breve* II, vol. I, p. 119.
      "my work ..." HCA to Count Rantzau-Breitenburg, December 1837, *Crawford*, p. 148.
      "Do you ..." HCA to Henriette Hanck, 27 April 1838, *Hanck*, vol. XI, p. 237.
185   "In conversation ..." Edvard Collin, *H. C. Andersen og det Collinske Hus*, Copenhagen 1929 (second edition), p. 271.
      "A new chapter ..." *Fairy Tale*, pp. 145–6.
187   "I have always ..." Thomas Mann to Agnes Meyer, 1955, quoted in Anthony Heilbut, *Thomas Mann: Eros and Literature*, London 1996, p. 590.
      "The Tin Soldier ..." G. K. Chesterton, *The Crimes of England*, London 1915, p. 78.
190   "the servants come ..." HCA to Henriette Hanck, 10 December 1838, *Hanck*, vol. XI, p. 297.
      "Feel extremely ..." almanac, 1 December 1838, *Almanakker*.
      "Winter life ..." *Fairy Tale*, p. 178.
192   "I lived much ..." ibid.
      "Great happiness ..." almanac, 31 December 1838, *Almanakker*.
193   "Count Barck's ..." diary, 24 June 1839, *Dagbøger*, vol. II, p. 35.
      "One of the Comtesses ..." HCA to Henriette Wulff, 3 July 1839, *Wulff*, vol. I, p. 262, and quoted in Elias Bredsdorff, "H. C. Andersen og Mathilda Barck," *Anderseniana*, 3/2, 1975, pp. 157–8.
195   "on the Danish stage . . ." Auguste Bournonville, *My Theatre Life*, translated by Patricia N. McAndrew, London 1979, p. 333.
      "Fru Heiberg ..." *Fairy Tale*, p. 155.
196   "betrayed ..." ibid. p. 156.
      "let me see ..." HCA to Mathilda Barck, 25 October 1840, in Elias Bredsdorff, "H. C. Andersen og Mathilda Barck," *Anderseniana*, 3/2, 1975, p. 158.
      "the Danish *Digter* ..." Mathilda Barck to HCA, 29 January 1841, ibid. p. 158.
      "There was ..." diary, 31 October 1840, *Diaries*, p. 96.

II   I BELONG TO THE WORLD, 1840-1843

page 197   "The Danes ..." HCA to Henriette Wulff, 29 April 1843, letter copied into Andersen's diary, 29 April 1843, *Diaries*, p. 138.
           "anyone who wishes ..." Ibsen in conversation, quoted in *Neue Freie Presse*, Vienna, 27 October 1802, and in Michael Meyer, *Ibsen*, London 1992, p. 17.
           "I have ..." HCA to Horace Scudder, 9 December 1869, *Scudder*, p. 63.
198   "the dejection ..." Edvard Collin, *H. C. Andersen og det Collinske Hus*, Copenhagen 1929 (second edition), p. 295.
           "the only man ..." *Fairy Tale*, p. 172.
           "what they call ..." Robert Molesworth, *An Account of Denmark As It Was In The Year 1692*, London 1694, Preface.
           "a miserable life ..." ibid. p. 267.
           "the Danes, in general ..." Mary Wollstonecraft, *Letters written during a short residence in Sweden, Norway and Denmark*, London 1796, p. 239.
           "having lost ..." Johan de Mylius, in conversation with the author, 1997.
199   "Your trip ..." Jonas Collin to HCA, 29 January 1841, *J. Collin*, vol. I, p. 165.
           "a Frenchman ..." Niels Kofoed in conversation with the author, 1997.
200   "Oh, how good ..." diary, 4 May 1841, *Diaries*, p. 122.
           "It is just ..." HCA to Jonas Collin, 1 November 1840, *J. Collin*, vol. I, p. 142.
           "my seasickness ..." diary, 31 October 1840, *Diaries*, p. 96.
           "In the manor ..." diary, 2 November 1840, ibid. p. 97.
           "I took a walk ..." diary, 3 November 1840, ibid.
201   "all the early morning ..." diary, 4 November 1840, ibid. p. 98.

201   "the nodule . . ." diary, 5 November 1840, ibid. p. 99.

"Already . . ." diary, 8 November 1840, ibid.

"the merchants . . . there was something . . ." diary, 6 November 1840, ibid. p. 100.

"I am searching . . ." HCA to Henriette Hanck, 15 May 1838, *Breve* II, vol. I, pp. 425–6.

202   "I felt as if . . ." diary, 10 November 1840, *Diaries*, p. 101.

"In Nürnberg . . ." *Fairy Tale*, p. 158.

203   "The earth quaked . . ." ibid. p. 160.

"if you . . ." Edvard and Henriette Collin to HCA, 1 January 1841, *E. Collin*, vol. I, p. 301.

"How lonely . . ." diary, 16 January 1841, *Diaries*, p. 103.

204   "a gnat . . ." diary, 16 January 1841, ibid. p. 103.

"Today seems . . ." diary, 22 January 1841, ibid. p. 108.

"The first-class lounge . . ." diary, 21 March 1841, ibid. p. 109.

"the evening . . ." diary, 23 March 1841, ibid. p. 111.

205   "the brilliant . . . long waves . . . The splendour . . ." *Fairy Tale*, pp. 162–3.

"got a particularly . . ." diary, 24 March 1841, *Diaries*, p. 111.

"my penis . . ." diary, 24 March 1841 and 25 March 1841, ibid. pp. 112–13.

"crashing . . . shipwreck . . . with its pointed . . . Turkish women . . . Jews . . ." *Fairy Tale*, p. 165.

"A Venice . . ." ibid. p. 166.

"you had to . . ." diary, 29 April 1841, *Diaries*, p. 114.

"obscene . . . Unfortunately . . . This is . . ." diary, 29 April 1841, ibid. pp. 115–16.

"The rowers . . ." diary, 4 May 1841, *Diaries*, p. 123.

206   "Feeling . . . sensuality . . . An Asiatic . . ." diary, 30 April, 1 May and 2 May 1841, ibid. pp. 119–20.

"big carriages . . . only the tumbled . . ." *Fairy Tale*, p. 167.

"a tall . . ." William F. Ainsworth in the *Literary Gazette*, 10 October 1846, quoted in *Bredsdorff*, pp. 39–40.

207   "My portrait . . ." HCA to Adolph Drewsen, 3 July 1841, *J. Collin*, vol. I, p. 184.

208   "respectable . . . I am very glad . . ." *Fairy Tale*, p. 170.

"See now . . ." ibid. pp. 187–8.

"the bouquet . . ." ibid. p. 170.

209   "possesses a poetical . . . he is the . . ." Berthold Lissmann, *Clara Schumann: Ein Kunstlerleben*, Leipzig 1902, vol. II, p. 49.

"Often . . ." *Fairy Tale*, p. 183.

211   "I felt . . ." ibid. p. 177.

"Letter from my mother's daughter . . ." almanac, 8 February 1842, *Almanakker*.

"In our days . . ." *Fairy Tale*, p. 177.

212   "It is the humour . . ." Robert Molesworth, *An Account of Denmark As It Was In The Year 1692*, London 1694, p. 170.

"in the midst . . ." HCA to Carl Alexander, undated letter from Bregentved, *Crawford*, p. 430.

"the hospitality . . ." *Fairy Tale*, p. 178.

213   "I was . . ." diary, 5 July 1842, *Dagbøger*, vol. II, p. 273.

"the swans . . ." diary, 8 July 1842, ibid. p. 275.

"Started . . ." diary, 26 July 1842, ibid. p. 284.

214   "You're good . . . I don't . . ." diary, 6 April 1843, *Diaries*, p. 133.

"Andersen called . . ." *Adam International Review*, nos. 248–9, 1955, p. 3.

"visit . . ." *Fairy Tale*, p. 192.

215   "I have read . . ." ibid. p. 196.

"I turned . . ." ibid. p. 197.

"a little ball . . ." quoted by Graham Robb, *Balzac*, London 1994, p. 348.

"From Denmark . . ." HCA to Henriette Wulff, 29 April 1843, quoted in diary, 29 April 1843, *Diaries*, pp. 137–8.

216   "Edvard could . . ." HCA to Jonas Collin, 12 April 1843, *J. Collin*, vol. I, p. 205.

"you are . . ." Jonas Collin to HCA, 16 May 1843, ibid. p. 213.

"The best thing . . ." HCA to Henriette Wulff, 28 April 1843, *Crawford*, p. 157.

217 "how to chisel . . ." *Fairy Tale*, p. 193.
"she is herself . . ." diary, 27 March 1843, *Diaries*, p. 132.
"The room . . ." HCA to Henriette Wulff, 28 April 1843, *Crawford*, pp. 157–8.
"shattering . . ." ibid.
"You get . . ." diary, 27 March 1843, *Diaries*, p. 132.
"sensual . . ." diary, 27 March 1843, ibid. p. 133.
"Fire . . ." diary, 4 April 1843, ibid.
"Bought wine . . ." diary, 6 April 1843, ibid. p. 132.
"bought myself . . ." diary, 7 April 1843, ibid. p. 134.
"Sensual mood . . ." diary, 15 April 1843, ibid. p. 137.

12   JENNY, 1843–1844

page 219 "Oh, what a glorious gift . . ." Jenny Lind to HCA, 19 March 1844, in Henry Scott Holland and W. S. Rockstro, *Memoir of Madame Jenny Lind Goldschmidt*, London 1891, p. 180.
220 "Her favourite seat . . ." Joan Bulman, *Jenny Lind: A Biography*, London 1956, pp. 10–11.
"a small . . ." ibid. p. 12.
221 "Such spirit . . ." *Dagligt Allehanda*, 30 November 1830, quoted in ibid. p. 16.
"She was . . ." Auguste Bournonville, *My Theatre Life*, translated by Patricia N. McAndrew, London 1979, p. 105.
222 "Her voice . . ." quoted in *Lindiana: An Interesting Narrative of the Life of Jenny Lind*, London 1847, p. 46.
"There will not . . ." Mendelssohn quoted in *Fairy Tale*, p. 210.
"She is the best . . ." *Memoir of Jenny Lind*, London 1847, p. 20.
"I scarcely . . ." Joan Bulman, *Jenny Lind: A Biography*, London 1956, p. 29.
"How could I . . ." quoted in *The Lost Letters of Jenny Lind*, edited by W. Porter Ware and Thaddeus Lockard Jr., London 1966, p. 49.
223 "If you want . . ." Fredrika Bremer, quoted in HCA to Henriette Wulff, 10 December 1843, *Wulff*, vol. I, p. 346.
"the Puritan . . ." Joan Bulman, *Jenny Lind: A Biography*, London 1956, p. 3.
"It is her intrinsic . . ." *Memoir of Jenny Lind*, London 1847, p. 6.
"She is reserved . . ." Frau Birch-Pfeiffer, quoted in Joan Bulman, *Jenny Lind: A Biography*, London 1956, pp. 129–30.
224 "The strain . . ." M. C. M. Simpson, *Many Memories of Many People*, London 1898, p. 86.
"She became at once . . ." Auguste Bournonville, *My Theatre Life*, translated by Patricia N. McAndrew, London 1979, p. 106.
225 "Dinner . . ." almanac, 3 September 1843, *Almanakker*.
"No one . . ." M. C. M. Simpson, *Many Memories of Many People*, London 1898, p. 86.
226 "such was . . ." *Fairy Tale*, p. 208.
"Jenny Lind's first . . ." almanac, 10 September 1843, *Almanakker*.
"of all memories . . ." Walter Terry, *The King's Ballet Master: A Biography of Denmark's Auguste Bournonville*, New York 1979, pp. 71–2.
"when we left . . ." ibid, p. 72.
227 "Sent Jenny . . ." almanac, 11–21 September 1843, *Almanakker*.
228 "Now do you . . ." HCA to Henriette Wulff, 10 December 1843, *Wulff*, vol. I, p. 347.
"We liked him . . ." Walter Terry, *The King's Ballet Master: A Biography of Denmark's Auguste Bournonville*, New York 1979, pp. 72–4.
229 "was like a . . ." *Fairy Tale*, p. 208.
"Through Jenny . . ." ibid. p. 211.
"She was kind . . ." G. W. Griffin, *My Danish Days*, Philadelphia 1875, p. 191.
230 "her great moral . . ." *Fairy Tale*, p. 207.

230 "finished . . ." almanac, 7 October 1843, *Almanakker*.
   "In Tivoli . . ." almanac, 11 October 1843, ibid.
   "finished the Chinese tale . . ." almanac, 12 October 1843, ibid.

233 "The Ugly Duckling . . ." *Spectator*, 12 August 1871, quoted in *Bredsdorff*, p. 482.
   "Through the centuries . . ." Bruno Bettelheim, *The Uses of Enchantment*, London 1978, pp. 5–6.
   "Oh, what a glorious gift . . ." Jenny Lind to HCA, 19 March 1844, in Henry Scott Holland and
   W. S. Rockstro, *Memoir of Madame Jenny Lind Goldschmidt*, London 1891, p. 180.

236 "There is . . ." *Ny Portefeuille*, 1843, vol. IV, no. 7, p. 217.
   "These tales . . ." HCA to Henriette Wulff, 10 December 1843, *Wulff*, vol. I, p. 346.
   "Today Reitzel . . ." HCA to Henriette Wulff, 18 December 1843, ibid. p. 349.
   "I think . . ." HCA to Bernhard Ingemann, 20 November 1843, *Breve* II, vol. II, p. 94.

237 "the fact . . ." HCA to Henriette Wulff, 10 December 1843, *Wulff*, vol. I, p. 346.

238 "He would rise . . ." J. M. Thiele, *The Life of Thorvaldsen*, translated by M. R. Barnard, London
   1865, p. 206.

239 "My darling Henrik, It is strange . . ." HCA to Henrik Stampe, 27 December 1843, in Collin collection of Andersen's letters at the Royal Library, Copenhagen, XVII, H, 32, no. 588.
   "My darling Henrik. Was at Henrik's . . ." almanac, 4 March 1844, *Almanakker*.

240 "My Good Brother . . ." Jenny Lind to HCA, 19 March 1844, in Henry Scott Holland and W. S.
   Rockstro, *Memoir of Madame Jenny Lind Goldschmidt*, London 1891, p. 179.

241 "He was very expansive . . ." HCA to Wilhelm Lenz, 14 March 1844, *Crawford*, p. 160.
   "It is a lie . . ." diary, 4 July 1844, *Dagbøger*, vol. II, p. 407.
   "excellent mood . . ." almanac, 26 April 1845, *Almanakker*.
   "confided to Jette . . ." diary, 22 August 1862, *Dagbøger*, vol. V, p. 203.

13 WINTER'S TALES, 1844–1845

page 242 "Everything . . ." quoted in Nicholas Boyle, *Goethe: The Poet and the Age*, vol. I, Oxford 1991,
   p. 244.

243 "An extraordinary . . ." *Fairy Tale*, p. 213.
   "I did not think . . ." ibid.
   "the little comfortable . . ." William Thackeray, *Vanity Fair*, London 1968, p. 721.
   "How could . . ." George Eliot, "Recollections of Weimar 1854," quoted in Kathryn Hughes,
   George Eliot: The Last Victorian, London 1998, p. 156.
   "a very queer . . ." G. H. Lewes to Charles and Thornie Lewes, 27 September 1954, *The George
   Eliot Letters*, edited by Gordon S. Haight, New Haven 1954–5, vol. VIII, p. 120, quoted in Rose-
   mary Ashton, *George Eliot: A Life*, London 1996, p. 113.

244 "a simple place . . ." Nicholas Boyle, *Goethe: The Poet and the Age*, vol. I, Oxford 1991, p. 234.
   "The court . . ." ibid, p. 238.
   "the men . . ." William Thackeray to his mother, quoted in D. J. Taylor, *Thackeray*, London 1999,
   p. 73.
   "his Transparency . . . the star . . . bowed serenely . . . amid the saluting . . ." William Thackeray,
   Vanity Fair, London 1968, p. 724.

245 "The old-fashioned . . ." *Fairy Tale*, p. 214.
   "The young duke . . ." diary, 26 June 1844, *Dagbøger*, vol. II, p. 400.

246 "In life . . ." *Fairy Tale*, p. 215.
   "the evenings . . ." ibid. p. 214.
   "The Grand Duchess . . ." diary, 28 June 1844, *Dagbøger*, vol. II, p. 401.
   "It seemed to me . . ." *Fairy Tale*, p. 215.

247 "your letter . . ." HCA to Carl Alexander, 26 October 1844, *Crawford*, p. 176.
   "sang lovely . . . Clara Schumann . . ." diary, 22 July 1844, *Dagbøger*, vol. II, p. 417.
   "I have constantly . . ." Robert Schumann to HCA, 14 April 1845, *Crawford*, p. 161.

247   "It is not possible . . ." *Fairy Tale*, p. 216.
248   "writing nun" . . . "dark glass" ibid. p. 217.
          "I found myself . . ." ibid.
          "People had told me . . ." ibid. p. 241.
249   "the new . . ." Nicholas Boyle, *Goethe: The Poet and the Age*, vol. I, Oxford 1991, p. 245.
          "exactly a prince's idea . . ." Heinrich Heine on Andersen, quoted in *Adam International Review*, nos. 248–9, 1955, p. 3.
250   "The road . . ." diary, 29 August 1844, *Diaries*, p. 141.
          "Andersen! . . ." diary, 29 August 1844, ibid. p. 142.
          "infinitely refreshing . . ." diary, 2 September 1844, ibid. p. 146.
          "You undress . . ." diary, 2 September 1844, ibid.
          "matchless . . ." diary, 2 September 1844, ibid.
          "the moon . . ." diary, 3 September 1844, ibid.
251   "Life here . . ." HCA to Carl Alexander, 26 October 1844, *Crawford*, pp. 178–9.
          "Thanks be . . ." diary, 5 September 1844, *Diaries*, p. 147.
          "King Christian . . ." *Fairy Tale*, p. 226.
          "happy domestic life . . ." ibid. p. 227.
          "this island . . ." HCA to Carl Alexander, 26 October 1844, *Crawford*, p. 181.
252   "It has been . . ." HCA to Bernhard Ingemann, 10 December 1844, *Breve* II, vol. II, p. 106.
          "the pace . . ." Naomi Lewis, introduction to *Hans Andersen's Fairy Tales: A Selection*, Oxford 1984, p. xvii.
253   "He is dead . . ." *Fairy Tale*, p. 14.
258   "Your name . . ." Mary Howitt to HCA, 19 July 1845, *Bredsdorff*, p. 45.
259   "Andersen could not . . ." *Fairy Tale*, p. 231.
          "I wish . . ." HCA to Jonas Collin, 2 June 1845, *J. Collin*, vol. I, p. 261.
260   "yet it seems . . ." *Fairy Tale*, p. 232.
          "He is a true humourist" ibid.
261   "it gave house room . . ." Jørgen Hunosøe and Esther Kielberg, "To Reitzel's Have I Been of Late" in *The Golden Age of Denmark: Art and Culture 1800–1850*, edited by Bente Scavenius, Copenhagen 1994, pp. 110–11.
          "Yes indeed . . ." HCA to Bernhard Ingemann, 16 September 1845, *Breve* II, vol. II, p. 122.

14   THE PRINCES' POET, 1845-1846

page 262   "lighting them up . . ." Joan Bulman, *Jenny Lind: A Biography*, London 1956, p. 81.
          "with reverence . . ." ibid. p. 91.
          "It was the loveliest day . . ." ibid. p. 92.
263   "her talent . . ." ibid. p. 97.
          "this life . . . get singers . . ." Jenny Lind to Madame Birch-Pfeiffer, quoted in ibid. p. 101.
          "the two kindred languages . . ." *Fairy Tale*, p. 210.
264   "the suffering . . ." ibid. p. 209.
          "She could hold on . . ." Joan Bulman, *Jenny Lind: A Biography*, London 1956, pp. 52–3.
          "People laugh . . ." *Fairy Tale*, p. 210.
          "to such a degree . . ." Joan Bulman, *Jenny Lind: A Biography*, London 1956, p. 54.
265   "Jenny in *Norma* . . ." almanac, 3 October 1845, *Almanakker*.
          "I didn't get . . ." diary, 31 October 1845, *Diaries*, p. 148.
266   "You might . . ." diary, 3 November 1845, ibid. p. 149.
          "Up at 8 . . ." diary, 6 November 1845, ibid. pp. 149–50.
268   "Yesterday it said . . ." diary, 22 December 1845, ibid. p. 152.
          "Rather used . . ." diary 19 December 1845, ibid. p. 150.
          "what are distances . . ." *Fairy Tale*, p. 240.

268 "crude company . . . Was actually inclined . . ." diary, 19 December 1845, *Diaries*, pp. 150–51.
269 "Not pleased . . ." diary, 20 December 1845, ibid. p. 151.
"She isn't receiving . . ." diary, 21 December 1845, ibid.
"Not really . . ." diary, 23 December 1845, ibid. p. 152.
"no one . . . I wonder . . ." diary, 24 December 1845, ibid. p. 153.
"Haven't heard . . ." diary, 24 December 1845, ibid. pp. 153–4.
270 "There is a veil . . ." diary, 25 December 1845, ibid. p. 154.
"I am splendidly . . ." Joan Bulman, *Jenny Lind: A Biography*, London 1956, p. 110.
271 "How changed . . ." Jenny Lind to Fru Erikson, November 1845, quoted in ibid. pp. 109–10.
"Amalia . . ." Jenny Lind to Amalia Wichmann, April 1846, quoted in *The Lost Letters of Jenny Lind*, edited by W. Porter Ware and Thaddeus Lockard Jr., London 1966, p. 27.
"a letter . . ." diary, 25 December 1845, *Diaries*, p. 154.
"she gave me . . . said I was . . ." diary, 26 December 1845, ibid.
"felt so at home . . ." diary, 26 December 1845, ibid.
272 "In the *Prussian Times* . . ." diary, 27 December 1845, ibid. p. 155.
"slovenly . . . Go to your . . ." diary, 22 December 1845, ibid. p. 152.
"she received me . . ." diary, 28 December 1845, ibid. p. 155.
"who talked . . ." diary, 24 December 1845, ibid. p. 153.
"[He] listened . . ." *Fairy Tale*, p. 243.
"his personality . . ." diary, 25 December 1845, *Diaries*, p. 154.
"saw these two . . ." *Fairy Tale*, p. 243.
273 "I should have . . ." ibid.
"it was my desire . . ." ibid.
274 "the Hereditary . . ." diary, 8 January 1846, *Dagbøger*, vol. III, p. 42.
"I went . . ." diary, 9 January 1846, ibid.
275 "He knows . . ." diary, 17 January 1846, ibid. p. 46.
"Banquet . . ." diary, 22 January 1846, ibid. p. 48.
"Was in my best . . ." diary, 22 February 1846, ibid. p. 55.
"Before the world . . ." HCA to Carl Alexander, 17 May 1846, *Crawford*, p. 199.
276 "Never . . ." *Fairy Tale*, p. 250.
"I sat . . ." diary, 10 January 1846, *Dagbøger*, vol. III, p. 43.
"went to see . . ." diary, 7 February 1846, ibid. p. 57.
277 "Beaulieu said . . ." diary, 27 January 1846, ibid. p. 51.
"at home . . ." diary, 28 January 1846, ibid. p. 53.
"at the Hereditary Grand Duke's . . ." diary, 30 January 1846, ibid.
"You ask me . . ." HCA to Louise Lind (née Collin), 2 April 1846, Edvard Collin, *H. C. Andersen og det Collinske Hus*, Copenhagen 1929 (second edition), p. 226.
278 "Yes, yes, Germany . . ." Jenny Lind to HCA, February 1846, quoted in Joan Bulman, *Jenny Lind: A Biography*, London 1956, p. 118.
"The Hereditary Grand Duke . . ." diary, 20 August 1846, *Dagbøger*, vol. III, p. 171.
"I will do . . ." HCA to Carl Alexander, 14 September 1846, *Weimar*, p. 67.
279 "sorrow burdened . . ." HCA to Carl Alexander, 7 July 1846, *Crawford*, p. 185.
"I am, as a poet . . ." HCA to Carl Alexander, 15 January 1847, *Weimar*, p. 84.
"I love you . . ." HCA to Carl Alexander, 3 October 1847, *Crawford*, p. 228.

15 THE SHADOW, 1846–1847

page 280 "city of bookselling . . ." *Fairy Tale*, p. 251.
281 "bounded up . . ." HCA to Edvard Collin, 14 February 1846, *E. Collin*, vol. II, p. 63.
282 "Oh, you do not know . . ." HCA to William Jerdan, October 1846, *Crawford*, pp. 204–205.
283 "Life is so delightful . . ." HCA to King Christian VIII, 12 March 1846, ibid. pp. 170–73.

283   "Today I am 41 . . ." HCA to Jonas Collin, 2 April 1846, *J. Collin*, vol. 1, p. 293.
        "how greatly . . ." diary, 20 March 1846, *Dagbøger*, vol. III, p. 79.
        "It is as if . . ." *Fairy Tale*, p. 258.
        "One day when I . . ." HCA to Edvard Collin, 26 April 1846, *E. Collin*, vol. II, p. 93.
        "Time drags . . ." diary, 30 April 1846, *Dagbøger*, vol. III, pp. 99–100.
        "the heat . . ." HCA to Carl Alexander, 7 July 1846, *Crawford*, p. 183.

284   "stomach upset . . ." diary, 17 June 1846, *Diaries*, p. 160.
        "but it was . . ." diary, 18 June 1846, ibid.
        "grabbing, roaring . . ." diary, 16 June 1846, ibid. pp. 159–60.
        "my life is a lovely story . . ." *Fairy Tale*, p. 1.

285   "poor emigrant . . . the louder . . ." ibid. pp. 1–2.
        "I had wooden shoes . . ." ibid. p. 10.

286   "who heard with . . ." ibid. pp. 70–71.
        "there is but one manner . . ." ibid. p. 153.
        "estimation . . ." ibid. p. 241.
        "I felt so happy . . ." ibid. p. 258.
        "I have refused . . ." ibid. p. 175.

287   "found it . . ." ibid.
        "I should like . . ." ibid. p. 265.
        "I had the happiness . . ." ibid. p. 246.
        "I was astonished . . ." ibid. p. 240.
        "It is good . . ." ibid. p. 221.
        "From the prince . . ." ibid. p. 274.

288   "revelation . . . We have had . . ." *Examiner*, 24 July 1847, quoted in *Bredsdorff*, p. 452.
        "in his *True Story* . . ." *The Times*, 26 December 1848, quoted in ibid. pp. 465–6.
        "Between the vanity . . ." Mary Russell Mitford to Charles Boner, 9 April 1848, *Memoirs and Letters of Charles Boner*, London 1871, vol. 1, p. 127, quoted in ibid. p. 135.

289   "in the evening . . ." diary, 9 June 1846, *Dagbøger*, vol. III, p. 127.

292   "I am like water . . ." HCA to Edvard Collin, 8 September 1855, *E. Collin*, vol. II, p. 261.
        "Anyone I have seen . . ." *Levnedsbog*, p. 1.
        "he told me . . ." *Fairy Tale*, p. 266.
        "to be the bouquet . . ." ibid.

293   "an ugly woman . . . couple of dirty fellows . . . thick clouds . . ." ibid. p. 269.
        "they gave you . . ." ibid.
        "You do not know . . ." HCA to Edvard Collin, 25 August 1846, *E. Collin*, vol. II, p. 109.
        "I will fly there . . ." HCA to Mary Howitt, 28 September 1846, *Bredsdorff*, p. 52.
        "among the most . . ." Richard Bentley to HCA, 25 November 1846, ibid. p. 142.

294   "It is a singular . . ." HCA to Richard Bentley, 10 December 1846, ibid. p. 144.
        "so little time . . ." HCA to Charles Boner, 4 March 1847, ibid. p. 116.
        "I have often . . ." HCA to William Jerdan, October 1846, *Crawford*, p. 203.

16   LION OF LONDON, 1847

I am greatly indebted to Elias Bredsdorff's *H. C. Andersen og England*, Copenhagen 1954, for much of the material in this chapter. Quotations from early editions of Andersen's fairy tales are taken from *Wonderful Stories for Children*, translated by Mary Howitt, London 1846; *A Danish Story Book*, translated by Charles Boner, London 1846; *Danish Fairy Tales and Legends*, translated by Caroline Peachey, London 1846; and *Andersen's Tales for Children*, translated by Alfred Wehnert, London 1861.

page 295   "Farewell . . ." HCA to unknown Englishman, reproduced in *Bredsdorff*, p. 5.
        "spiritual self . . ." HCA to Mary Howitt, 28 September 1846, ibid. p. 52.
        "John Andersen's . . ." *Athenaeum*, 21 February 1846, quoted in ibid. p. 440.

296   "In a utilitarian age . . ." Charles Dickens in *Household Words*, 1 October 1853.

296 "How I should . . ." HCA to William Jerdan, October 1846, *Crawford*, p. 204.

"At present . . ." William Jerdan to HCA, 21 March 1847, *Bredsdorff*, p. 85.

297 "*must* see Andersen . . ." Charles Dickens to William Jerdan, quoted by HCA to Henriette Wulff, 22 July 1847, *Breve* II, vol. II, p. 172.

"my father . . ." *The Recollections of Sir Henry Dickens KC*, London 1934, p. 34.

"And Hans Christian Andersen . . ." William Makepeace Thackeray to William Edmonstoune Aytoun, 2 January 1847, *The Letters and Private Papers of William Makepeace Thackeray*, London 1945, vol. II, p. 263.

"Enlarged sympathy . . ." G. M. Trevelyan, *English Social History*, London 1944, p. 545.

"We cannot . . ." Mary Howitt to HCA, 19 July 1845, *Bredsdorff*, p. 45.

"It is impossible . . ." Charles Boner to HCA, early 1847, ibid. p. 114.

300 "my best tales . . ." HCA to Charles Boner, 4 March 1847, ibid. p. 116.

"The most fitting . . ." *Athenaeum*, 6 June 1846, quoted in ibid. p. 440.

"angelical spirit . . . Heaven bless . . ." *Fraser's Magazine*, January 1847, quoted in ibid. p. 446.

301 "The genius . . ." *Spectator*, 10 October 1846, quoted in ibid. p. 448.

"The more such . . ." *Athenaeum*, 25 July 1846, quoted in ibid. pp. 440–41.

"assist in . . ." *Chambers's Edinburgh Journal*, 10 October 1846, quoted in ibid. p. 445.

"no faery tales . . ." *Athenaeum*, 9 January 1847, quoted in *Bredsdorff*, p. 441.

"the Cockney . . ." *Spectator*, 8 January 1848, ibid. p. 445.

"rare and surprising . . . his vegetables . . . etc." *Examiner*, 4 July 1846, quoted in ibid. pp. 443–4.

302 "The moral . . ." *Douglas Jerrold's Weekly Newspaper*, 12 December 1846, quoted in ibid. p. 445.

"if . . . healthfulness . . ." *English Review*, 1848, quoted in ibid. p. 446.

"When the English . . ." G. K. Chesterton, *The Crimes of England*, London 1915, pp. 77–8.

303 "The Thames . . . The ships . . . etc." diary, 23 June 1847, *Diaries*, pp. 164–5.

304 "plodded around . . ." diary, 24 June 1847, ibid. p. 167.

"I am strangely happy . . ." HCA to Henriette Collin, 24 June 1847, *Munksgaard*, p. 13.

"Went out . . ." diary, 2 July 1847, *Diaries*, p. 174.

"Victor Hugo . . ." HCA to Henriette Wulff, 22 July 1847, *Munksgaard*, pp. 17–18.

"That strange staring . . ." diary, 1 August 1847, *Diaries*, p. 190.

305 "a neatly dressed . . ." diary, 25 July 1847, ibid. p. 186.

"[he] fell on my neck . . ." HCA to Henriette Collin, 24 June 1847, *Munksgaard*, p. 14.

"he said to me . . ." diary, 24 June 1847, *Diaries*, p. 165.

"Lovely Lind . . ." Carl Alexander to HCA, 13 June 1847, *Weimar*, p. 97.

"At this very moment . . ." HCA to Henriette Collin, 24 June 1847, *Munksgaard*, p. 14.

"infinitely far out . . ." diary, 25 June 1847, *Diaries*, p. 167.

"lived in a little house . . ." M. C. M. Simpson, *Many Memories of Many People*, London 1898, p. 86.

"a lovely little garden . . ." diary, 25 June 1847, *Diaries*, p. 167.

"The exquisite shake . . ." Joan Bulman, *Jenny Lind: A Biography*, London 1956, p. 167.

"showering her trills . . ." ibid. p. 53.

306 "Felt indisposed . . ." diary, 26 June 1847, *Diaries*, p. 169.

"The highest . . ." diary, 26 June 1847, ibid. pp. 169–70.

"Terribly hot . . ." diary, 28 June 1847, ibid. p. 170.

307 "invite . . ." diary, 28 June 1847, ibid. p. 170.

it was remarkable . . ." diary, 14 July 1847, ibid. p. 181.

"a middle-aged . . ." diary, 8 August 1847, ibid. p. 193.

"I was fussed . . ." diary, 13 July 1847, ibid. p. 181.

"perfectly unspoilt . . ." Charles Boner quoted by Mary Russell Mitford to Mrs. Partridge, 26 July 1847, *Mary Russell Mitford, Correspondence with Charles Boner and John Ruskin*, edited by Elizabeth Lee, London 1914, p. 73, quoted in *Bredsdorff*, p. 139.

"The Queen's . . ." Mary Russell Mitford to Charles Boner, 9 August 1847, *Memoirs and Letters of Charles Boner*, London 1871, vol. I, p. 112, quoted in ibid. p. 121.

307 "a long, thin . . ." *Journals and Correspondence of Lady Eastlake*, vol. I, p. 212, edited by Charles Eastlake Smith, London 1895, quoted in ibid. p. 260.

"He had one stream . . ." *Journals and Correspondence of Lady Eastlake*, vol. I, pp. 212–13, edited by Charles Eastlake Smith, London 1895, quoted in ibid. p. 261.

"he looks . . ." William Allingham, *A Diary*, London 1907, pp. 37–8.

"I have seldom . . ." quoted by William Jerdan in letter to HCA, 4 April 1848, *Bredsdorff*, p. 100.

308 "Everyone who has met . . ." *Literary Gazette*, 17 July 1847, quoted in ibid. pp. 89–90.

"[is] a big nation . . ." diary, 2 July 1847, *Diaries*, p. 173.

"is the lion . . ." Mary Russell Mitford to Mrs. Partridge, 26 July 1847, *Mary Russell Mitford, Correspondence with Charles Boner and John Ruskin*, edited by Elizabeth Lee, London 1914, p. 73, quoted in *Bredsdorff*, p. 139.

"there was a princely . . ." diary, 12 July 1847, *Diaries*, p. 180.

"It says . . ." HCA to Edvard Collin, 27 June 1847, *E. Collin*, vol. II, p. 141.

309 "be the first . . ." Mary Russell Mitford to Charles Boner, 11 October 1847, *Memoirs and Letters of Charles Boner*, London 1871, quoted in *Bredsdorff*, p. 125.

"he digs in . . ." diary, 4 July 1847, *Diaries*, p. 175.

"has translated . . ." diary, 13 July 1847, ibid. p. 180.

"a charming man" diary, 4 July 1847, ibid. p. 175.

"exceedingly selfless . . ." diary, 30 June 1847, ibid. p. 172.

"the farthest corner . . ." William Allingham to HCA, 6 July 1847, *Bredsdorff*, p. 248.

"had not English . . ." William Allingham, *A Diary*, London 1907, p. 38.

310 "an uncongenial . . ." *Literary Gazette*, 17 July 1847, quoted in *Bredsdorff*, p. 57.

"There is a muddle . . ." HCA to Edvard Collin, 8 July 1847, *Munksgaard*, p. 15.

"translation factory" ibid.

"I only wish . . ." Mary Howitt to HCA, 10 July 1847, *Bredsdorff*, p. 60.

"hot and bothered . . . listless . . ." diary, 11 July 1847, *Diaries*, p. 179.

"I got very nervous . . ." diary, 31 July 1847, ibid. p. 189.

311 "Andersen is a singular mixture . . ." Mary and William Howitt, *The Literature and Romance of Northern Europe*, London 1852, vol. II, p. 232.

"unfortunately, the over-sensitive . . ." *Mary Howitt: An Autobiography*, edited by her daughter, Margaret Howitt, London 1889, vol. II, p. 30.

"was very charming . . ." diary, 1 July 1847, *Diaries*, p. 173.

"with three people . . ." diary, 9 July 1847, ibid. p. 177.

"footmen in silk stockings . . ." HCA to Henriette Wulff, 12 August 1847, *Munksgaard*, p. 19.

"to great acclamation . . ." diary, 9 July 1847, p. 178.

"Andersen charmed us . . ." *Bredsdorff*, p. 151.

312 "I remember . . ." Annie Wood in *Temple Bar*, December 1877, quoted in ibid. p. 220.

"At this moment . . ." HCA to Edvard Collin, 6 July 1847, *E. Collin*, vol. II, p. 143.

313 "A man . . ." HCA to Henriette Wulff, 22 July 1847, *Munksgaard*, p. 18.

"I was ecstatic . . ." diary, 1 August 1847, *Diaries*, p. 190.

"My dear friend . . ." HCA to William Jerdan, 2 August 1847, *Bredsdorff*, p. 92.

"so that you . . . as I hear . . ." HCA to Henriette Wulff, 12 August 1844, *Munksgaard*, p. 18.

"Now I am tired . . . had the feeling . . ." diary, 25 July 1847, *Diaries*, p. 185.

"I am anxious . . ." diary, 1 August 1847, ibid. p. 190.

"One of my testicles . . ." diary, 3 August 1847, ibid. p. 191.

"Time passes . . . Went over . . ." diary, 7 August 1847, ibid. p. 193.

"Out here . . ." HCA to Henriette Wulff, 22 July 1847, *Munksgaard*, p. 17.

314 "the Danish . . ." diary, 12 August 1847, ibid. p. 196.

"matchless . . ." diary, 15 August 1847, ibid. p. 197.

"In England . . ." HCA to Carl Alexander, 4 September 1847, *Crawford*, p. 224.

"bad frame . . ." diary, 26 August 1847, *Diaries*, p. 204.

"I was so desperate . . ." diary, 26 August 1847, ibid.

"The last few moments . . ." Carl Alexander to HCA, 16 July 1847, *Weimar*, p. 99.

315 "despite the fact . . ." diary, 8 August 1847, *Diaries*, p. 193.

315   "My dear dear Dickens..." HCA to Charles Dickens, 29 August 1847, *Dickens*, p. 23.
316   "when you come back..." Charles Dickens to HCA, 30 August 1847, ibid. p. 24.
       "so happy..." diary, 30 August 1847, *Diaries*, p. 206.
       "He had walked..." diary, 31 August 1847, ibid. p. 207.
       "I was standing..." *Fairy Tale*, p. 326.
       "I am home..." HCA to Carl Alexander, 3 October 1847, *Crawford*, p. 225.
317   "I almost think..." HCA to Henriette Wulff, 9 September 1847, *Munksgaard*, p. 24.
318   "I read that story..." Charles Dickens to HCA, early January 1848, *Dickens*, p. 28.
321   "The small amount..." Richard Bentley to HCA, 17 December 1847, *Bredsdorff*, p. 155.
       "I am very proud..." Charles Dickens to HCA, early January 1848, *Dickens*, p. 28.

17   BETWEEN THE WARS, 1848-1851

page 323   "Who would have thought..." HCA to Henriette Wulff, 24 June 1849, *Wulff*, vol. II, p. 16.
       "The year 1848..." *Fairy Tale*, p. 332.
       "*One thing*..." Auguste Bournonville, *My Theatre Life*, translated by Patricia N. McAndrew, London 1979, p. 161.
       "King Christian..." HCA to Carl Alexander, 12 May 1847, *Crawford*, p. 210.
       "and wept bitterly..." *Fairy Tale*, pp. 332-3.
324   "We have war..." HCA letter to the *Literary Gazette*, 13 April 1848, published in *Fairy Tale*, pp. 334-6.
325   "I felt more than ever..." *Fairy Tale*, p. 336.
       "You have made..." HCA to Carl Alexander, 6 February 1848, *Weimar*, p. 114.
       "The agitations..." HCA to Carl Alexander, 4 May 1848, *Crawford*, p. 230.
       "Have our feelings..." Carl Alexander to HCA, 2 August 1848, *Weimar*, p. 123.
       "what power..." Carl Alexander to HCA, 27 August 1848, ibid. p. 126.
326   "These are heavy..." HCA to Richard Bentley, 24 May 1848, *Bredsdorff*, p. 161.
       "ladies in silk..." *Fairy Tale*, p. 337.
       "almost every day..." ibid.
       "shooting ... with live cartridges..." diary, 16 May 1848, *Diaries*, p. 211.
       "heard a good deal..." diary, 13 May 1848, *Diaries*, p. 210.
327   "some farmers..." diary, 13 May 1848, ibid.
       "I feel..." diary, 14 May 1848, ibid. p. 211.
       "Their stay here..." *Fairy Tale*, p. 339.
       "A great bed..." ibid. p. 338.
       "While they were..." diary, 22 May 1848, *Diaries*, p. 212.
       "The prison-ships..." HCA to Frau Eisendecker, October 1848, *Crawford*, pp. 232-3.
329   "My mind..." *Fairy Tale*, p. 345.
       "much blood..." HCA to Richard Bentley, 1 May 1849, *Bredsdorff*, p. 169.
       "No sound..." HCA to Charles Dickens, 16 July 1850, *Dickens*, p. 34.
       "on my retiring ... a feeling of congeniality..." *Fairy Tale*, p. 349.
330   "Oh you scarcely..." HCA to Carl Alexander, 18 August 1849, *Crawford*, p. 244.
331   "Who would have thought..." HCA to Henriette Wulff, 24 June 1849, *Wulff*, vol. II, p. 16.
       "it displays..." *Fairy Tale*, p. 365.
       "will show..." HCA to Carl Alexander, December 1850, *Crawford*, p. 266.
332   "I am forty-five..." HCA to Carl Alexander, December 1850, ibid. pp. 265-6.
       "My life..." HCA to Carl Alexander, 2 April 1850, ibid. p. 253.
       "for me..." HCA to Carl Alexander, December 1850, ibid. p. 267.
       "Melancholy..." diary, 1 July 1850, *Diaries*, p. 219.
       "The feeling..." HCA to Mathilde Ørsted, 12 July 1850, *Breve* II, vol. II, p. 242.
333   "I didn't think..." diary, 16 February 1851, *Diaries*, p. 225.
       "that riches..." HCA to Carl Alexander, 2 April 1850, *Crawford*, p. 253.

334 "It's appalling . . ." diary, 20 June 1850, *Diaries*, p. 216.
"toothache . . ." diary, 1 July 1850, ibid. p. 219.
"There was a hideous . . ." diary, 24 June 1850, ibid. p. 218.
"I was very sad . . ." diary, 5 July 1850, ibid. p. 220.

335 "Peace . . ." HCA to Carl Alexander, 12 July 1850, *Weimar*, pp. 155–6.
"may it . . ." Carl Alexander to HCA, 29 July 1850, ibid. pp. 157–8.
"For the last . . ." HCA to Hans Christian Ørsted, 3 August 1850, *Breve* II, vol. II, p. 247.
"In the mother's hour . . ." *Fairy Tale*, p. 379.

18 WEIMAR REVISITED, 1851–1856

page 337 "Tears came . . ." diary, 23 June 1856, *Dagbøger*, vol. IV, p. 213.
"guard yourself . . . it could only be correct . . ." Edvard Collin to HCA, 17 June 1851, *Crawford*, pp. 278–9.
"I truly confess . . ." HCA to Carl Oliver von Beaulieu-Marconnay, June 1851, ibid. pp. 270–74.

338 "It was as if . . ." *Fairy Tale*, p. 387.
"I felt depressed . . ." diary, 1 August 1851, *Dagbøger*, vol. IV, p. 56.

341 "For five years . . ." HCA to Carl Oliver von Beaulieu-Marconnay, autumn 1852, *Crawford*, p. 302.
"horrible dreams . . . at 11:30 . . ." diary, 20 May 1852, *Diaries*, pp. 228–9.

342 "not a pleasant man . . ." diary, 27 May 1852, ibid. p. 233.
"One of the first things . . ." diary, 23 May 1852, ibid. p. 230.
"Lieutenant Beaulieu-Marconnay . . ." diary, 23 May 1852, ibid.
"difficult days . . ." diary, 23 May 1852, ibid.
"strolled along the river . . ." diary, 24 May 1852, ibid.
"won't do Mozart . . ." diary, 21 May 1852, ibid. p. 229.
"There was nowhere . . ." David Cairns, *Berlioz*, vol. II: *Servitude and Greatness*, London 1999, p. 499.

343 "received me . . ." diary, 27 May 1852, *Diaries*, p. 232.
"The text . . ." diary, 29 May 1852, ibid. p. 233.
"I read [your letter] . . ." HCA to Henriette Wulff, 6 September 1857, *Crawford*, p. 368.
"He and the princess . . ." diary, 31 May 1852, *Diaries*, p. 234.

344 "a little flower island . . . will be placed . . ." HCA to Carl Alexander, 23 June 1852, *Crawford*, p. 294.
"a whole poem . . ." HCA to Carl Alexander, 21 August 1852, ibid. p. 297.
"some days . . ." HCA to Carl Alexander, 21 August 1852, ibid. p. 296.
"with the fall . . ." HCA to Carl Oliver von Beaulieu-Marconnay, autumn 1852, ibid. p. 300.
"The angel of death . . ." *Fairy Tale*, p. 398.
"It could not be endured . . ." ibid.

345 "all are well . . ." HCA to Carl Alexander, 22 November 1853, *Crawford*, p. 309.
"looked like a peeled nutcracker . . ." diary, 22 May 1854, *Dagbøger*, vol. IV, p. 135.

346 "on me as a . . ." HCA to Henriette Wulff, 3 April 1855, *Wulff*, vol. II, p. 205.
"the story of my life up to this hour . . ." *Fairy Tale*, p. 408.
"His personality . . ." Georg Brandes, *Eminent Authors of the Nineteenth Century*, New York 1886, p. 107.

347 "To me it is a complete denial . . ." Henriette Wulff to HCA, 7 June 1855, *Wulff*, vol. II, p. 220.
"Just in the brilliancy . . ." HCA to Henriette Wulff, 6 September 1857, *Crawford*, p. 371.
"dear Edgar . . ." diary, 2 September 1855, *Diaries*, p. 237.
"so full of warmth . . ." diary, 11 September 1855, ibid. p. 238.

348 "the garlands . . ." diary, 30 April 1856, ibid. p. 239.
"friendly reception . . . Got a . . ." diary, 30 April 1856, ibid.
"I am dreaming . . ." diary, 5 May 1856, ibid. p. 240.

349 "when I was a child . . ." Bodild Donner in a memoir, 1926, quoted in Kjeld Heltoft, *Hans Christian Andersen as an Artist*, Copenhagen 1977, p. 106.

349   "On Christmas Eve . . ." *Fairy Tale*, p. 451

"Finished *Letters* . . ." diary, 22 May 1856, *Diaries*, p. 243.

"The entire structure . . ." diary, 23 May 1856, ibid.

"none of my works . . ." HCA to Carl Alexander, 9 August 1857, *Crawford*, p. 355.

350   "was so tactless . . ." diary, 17 June 1856, *Diaries*, p. 245.

"Mrs. Serre . . ." diary, 19 June 1856, ibid. p. 246.

"Tears came . . ." diary, 23 June 1856, *Dagbøger*, vol. IV, p. 213.

19   DICKENS, 1856–1857

page 351   "Hans Andersen . . ." Gladys Storey, *Dickens and Daughter*, London 1939, p. 22.

"Nine years . . ." Charles Dickens to HCA, 5 July 1856, *Dickens*, p. 38.

"let me say . . ." Richard Bentley to HCA, 12 December 1856, *Bredsdorff*, p. 193.

"I have not the slightest reason . . ." Charles Dickens to Charles de la Prynne, 15 December 1856, *Dickens*, p. 120.

352   "genuine letter . . ." *Punch*, 10 January 1857, reproduced in ibid. p. 92.

"if you are not in London . . ." HCA to Charles Dickens, 1 March 1857, *Munksgaard*, p. 30.

"we have children . . ." Charles Dickens to HCA, 3 April 1857, *Bredsdorff*, p. 42.

"Dear delightful Charles Dickens . . ." HCA to Charles Dickens, 14 April 1857, *Munksgaard*, p. 36.

353   "Hans Christian Andersen (who has been 'coming' . . ." Charles Dickens to James White, 22 May 1857, *Bredsdorff*, p. 120.

"Hans Christian Andersen may perhaps . . ." Charles Dickens to Angela Burdett-Coutts, 3 June 1857, ibid.

"the whole landscape . . ." HCA to Queen Dowager Caroline Amalia, 14 July 1857, *Crawford*, pp. 330–31.

"found it a little cold . . ." diary, 11 June 1857, *Diaries*, p. 247.

"on the first morning . . ." *The Recollections of Sir Henry Dickens KC*, London 1934, p. 35.

"I was a great success . . ." diary, 12 June 1857, *Diaries*, p. 247.

"at dinner time . . ." *The Recollections of Sir Henry Dickens KC*, London 1934, p. 35.

"the smallest of the children . . ." diary, 13 June 1857, *Diaries*, p. 248.

"Dickens came home . . ." diary, 19 June 1857, ibid. p. 251.

354   "the good old fashion . . ." HCA to Queen Dowager Caroline Amalia, 14 July 1857, *Crawford*, p. 337.

"The family . . ." HCA to Henriette Wulff, undated (June 1857), *Munksgaard*, p. 42.

"it was difficult . . ." diary, 19 June 1857, *Diaries*, p. 251.

"He had one beautiful accomplishment . . ." *The Recollections of Sir Henry Dickens KC*, London 1934, p. 35.

"said he, his wife . . ." diary, 21 June 1857, *Diaries*, p. 251.

"a lovable . . ." *The Recollections of Sir Henry Dickens KC*, London 1934, pp. 34–5.

355   "Little Kate cutting . . ." diary, 2 July 1857, *Diaries*, p. 257.

"young Walter Dickens asinine . . ." diary, 12 July 1857, ibid. p. 262.

"the daughters . . ." diary, 30 June 1857, ibid. p. 256.

"too little sugar . . ." diary, 1 July 1857, ibid.

"feeling like that . . ." HCA to Charles Dickens, September 1857, *Munksgaard*, p. 48.

"Niels Bryde . . ." *Athenaeum*, 27 June 1857, no. 1548, pp. 815–16, quoted in *Dickens*, p. 88.

"was heavy in the head . . ." diary, 27 June 1857, *Diaries*, p. 254.

"I'm not content . . ." diary, 28 June 1857, ibid.

"so mild . . ." HCA to Henriette Wulff, undated (June 1857), *Crawford*, p. 345.

"You should never read . . ." diary, 28 June 1857, *Diaries*, pp. 254–5.

356   "Long for Mr. Dickens . . ." diary, 28 June 1857, ibid. p. 255.

"doorman, servants . . . very straightforward . . ." HCA to Henriette Wulff, undated (June 1857), *Crawford*, p. 344.

356   "We have yet to meet . . ." *Saturday Review*, 4 July 1857, quoted in *Dickens*, p. 99.

"You see . . ." diary, 4 July 1857, *Diaries*, p. 258.

"She knew I was there . . ." diary, 4 July 1857, ibid.

"the performance of Mr. Dickens . . ." *The Times*, 13 July 1857, quoted in *Dickens*, p. 113.

"Not really in a good mood . . ." diary, 4 July 1857, *Diaries*, p. 259.

"this happy meeting . . ." Richard Bentley in *Temple Bar*, December 1870, quoted in *Dickens*, p. 101.

357   "Big dinner party . . ." diary, 5 July 1857, *Diaries*, p. 259.

"Wilkie Collins . . ." *The Recollections of Sir Henry Dickens KC*, London 1934, p. 35.

"We are suffering . . ." Charles Dickens to Angela Burdett-Coutts, 10 July 1857, *Dickens*, p. 122.

"Dickens himself . . ." diary, 15 July 1857, *Diaries*, p. 263.

"I travelled alone . . ." HCA to Henriette Wulff, 19 July 1857, *Crawford*, p. 348.

"I'm on the verge . . ." diary, 15 July 1857, *Diaries*, p. 263.

"he was a bony bore . . ." Gladys Storey, *Dickens and Daughter*, London 1939, p. 22.

"Whenever he got to London . . ." Charles Dickens to William Jerdan, 21 July 1857, *Dickens*, p. 122.

358   "None of your friends . . ." HCA to Charles Dickens, September 1857, *Munksgaard*, pp. 46–7.

"sad, very sad . . ." HCA to Henriette Wulff, 19 July 1857, *Crawford*, p. 348.

359   "Baby says . . ." Charles Dickens to HCA, 2 September 1857, *Dickens*, p. 128.

"has a bearing . . ." Claire Tomalin, *The Invisible Woman: The Story of Nelly Ternan and Charles Dickens*, London 1990, p. 94.

"The corn-fields . . ." Charles Dickens to HCA, 2 September 1857, *Dickens*, p. 128.

"Since you last visited . . ." Richard Bentley to HCA, 21 May 1862, ibid. p. 136.

"You ask . . ." Anne Bushby to HCA, 19 December 1862, ibid. p. 137.

"the way in which . . ." *Bentley's Miscellany*, August 1860, quoted in ibid. p. 141.

360   "Done with . . ." *Fairy Tale*, p. 426.

"a beehive . . ." HCA to Carl Alexander, 9 August 1857, *Crawford*, p. 360.

"this rumbling hot town . . ." HCA to Henriette Wulff, 19 July 1857, ibid. p. 348.

"Schiller . . ." HCA to Henriette Wulff, 6 September 1857, ibid. p. 368.

"Like the Nightingale . . ." HCA to Carl Alexander, 9 August 1857, ibid. p. 356.

"I am so little . . ." HCA to Henriette Wulff, 19 July 1857, ibid. pp. 354–5.

"a disease . . ." HCA to Charles Dickens, September 1857, ibid. p. 378.

"over Christmas . . ." HCA to Carl Alexander, 12 January 1858, *Weimar*, p. 219.

20   EXPERIMENTS, 1858–1859

page 363   "The wonder story . . ." *Fairy Tale*, p. 408.

"difficult to rouse . . ." diary, 22 June 1858, *Diaries*, p. 263.

364   "for her it was a necessity . . ." *Fairy Tale*, p. 433.

"That you are . . ." Henriette Wulff to HCA, 9 August 1858, *Wulff*, vol. II, p. 385.

365   "little feeble form . . ." *Fairy Tale*, p. 433.

"Day after day . . ." HCA to Signe Læssøe, 2 November 1858, *Breve* II, vol. II, p. 399.

"In England . . ." *Fairy Tale*, p. 430.

366   "They form some of . . ." HCA to Carl Alexander, 21 March 1859, *Crawford*, p. 395.

369   "how often I live over again . . ." HCA to Carl Alexander, 15 June 1859, ibid. p. 400.

370   "From the immense gulf . . ." *Fairy Tale*, p. 445.

"We drove over pasture-land . . ." ibid.

"barren desert land . . ." HCA to Carl Alexander, 15 June 1859, *Crawford*, p. 399.

"a rich harvest . . ." HCA to Carl Alexander, 16 October 1859, ibid. p. 402.

"was material . . ." diary, 5 July 1859, *Diaries*, p. 266.

"A letter . . ." diary, 4 July 1859, ibid. p. 264.

370   "People will have me . . ." diary, 23 August 1859, *Dagbøger*, vol. IV, p. 357.

371   "The whole description . . ." HCA to Maximilian II of Bavaria, 16 November 1859, *Crawford*, p. 407.

"since your writings . . . I made a note . . ." Maximilian II of Bavaria to HCA, 8 November 1859, ibid. p. 405.

"my dearest wish . . . The last few years . . ." HCA to Maximilian II of Bavaria, 16 November 1859, ibid. pp. 405–409.

21   KISS OF THE MUSE, 1860–1865

page 373   "You are a lucky man . . ." Bernhard Ingemann to HCA, 10 April 1858, quoted in Edvard Collin, *H. C. Andersen og det Collinske Hus*, Copenhagen 1929 (second edition), p. 311.

"a butterfly . . ." diary, 13 November 1865, *Dagbøger*, vol. VI, p. 322.

"is full of life . . ." Auguste Bournonville, *My Theatre Life*, translated by Patricia N. McAndrew, London 1979, p. 169.

374   "Munich has an immense attraction . . ." HCA to Carl Alexander, 23 June 1852, *Crawford*, p. 293.

"I had always feared . . ." HCA to Carl Alexander, 24 July 1860, ibid. p. 417.

"we sat . . ." *Fairy Tale*, p. 454.

"Scharff and Eckhardt came . . . etc." diary, 3, 4, 5, 7 and 8 July 1860, *Dagbøger*, vol. VI, pp. 394–6.

"don't feel at all well . . ." diary, 9 July 1860, ibid. p. 396.

376   "I've never seen . . ." HCA to Henriette Collin, 3 August 1860, *E. Collin*, vol. II, p. 243.

"Andersen's personal appearance . . ." G. W. Griffin, *My Danish Days*, Philadelphia 1875, pp. 207–8.

"Before me stood . . ." John Ross Brown, quoted in "Der Dichter Als Mensch," in Bente Kjolbe, *Hans Christian Andersens Kopenhagen*, Copenhagen 1992, p. 64.

377   "Want to go home . . . etc." diary, 1–7 September 1860, *Diaries*, pp. 269–72.

"I'm drifting . . ." diary, 27 October 1860, *Dagbøger*, vol. IV, p. 455.

378   "went to bed . . ." diary, 14 November 1860, ibid. p. 465.

"Nelly is a strange, cold person . . ." diary, 30 December 1860, *Diaries*, p. 272.

379   "only I myself . . ." diary, 7 September 1860, ibid.

"Dear Scharff . . ." note on back of photograph taken by Rudolph Striegler in Copenhagen, 21–22 January 1861, in the Hans Christian Andersen Hus, Odense, reproduced in Henrik C. Poulsen, *Det Rette Udseende. Fotografernes H. C. Andersen*, Copenhagen 1996, p. 62.

380   "At this moment . . ." Edvard Collin to HCA, 9 May 1861, *E. Collin*, vol. III, p. 15.

"I asked him . . ." diary, 5 May 1861, *Diaries*, p. 273.

"I explained how ill . . ." diary, 9 May 1861, ibid. p. 275.

"Jonas went around . . ." diary, 18 and 19 May 1861, ibid. pp. 282–3.

"he worked on his own development . . ." diary, 14 May 1861, ibid. pp. 279–80.

382   "He was a young man . . ." diary, 8 May 1861, ibid. p. 274.

"I'm not at all pleased . . ." diary, 18 October 1863, ibid. p. 299.

383   "The small people . . ." Henry James, *William Wentmore Story and his Friends*, Edinburgh and London 1903, vol. I, pp. 285–6.

"The North sent therefore . . ." Elizabeth Barrett Browning, "The North and the South," in *Last Poems*, London 1861.

"Andersen (the Dane) . . ." Elizabeth Barrett Browning to Isa Blagden, 17 May 1861, *The Letters of Elizabeth Barrett Browning*, edited by F. G. Kenyon, London 1897, vol. II, p. 448.

384   "was wrought . . ." *Fairy Tale*, p. 464.

386   " 'The Ice Maiden' begins . . ." quoted in ibid. p. 470.

387   "he was surprised . . ." diary, 20 August 1861, *Dagbøger*, vol. V, p. 112.

"Toward evening . . ." diary, 29 August 1861, *Diaries*, p. 284.

"ate at a restaurant . . ." diary, 2 September 1861, ibid. p. 285.

387   "an active participant . . ." quoted in Niels Birger Wamberg, "A Born Achiever: Jonas Collin—
Potentate and Philanthropist," in *The Golden Age of Denmark: Art and Culture 1800–1850*, edited
by Bente Scavenius, Copenhagen 1994, p. 65.
"the high and the lowly . . . a half-opened door . . ." quoted in ibid.
"mighty Collin . . . poor Andersen" Niels Birger Wamberg, "A Born Achiever," in *The Golden
Age of Denmark*, edited by Bente Scavenius, Copenhagen 1994, p. 60.

388   "Scharff bounded up . . ." diary, 2 January 1862, *Dagbøger*, vol. v, p. 141.
"a visit from Scharff . . ." diary, 7 January 1862, ibid. p. 142.
"dinner at Scharff's . . ." diary, 16 January 1862, ibid. p. 143.
"a visit from Scharff . . ." diary, 23 January 1862, ibid. p. 144.
"Scharff" diary, 12 February 1862, ibid. p. 147.
"Yesterday Scharff . . ." diary, 13 February 1862, ibid.
"Theodor put me in a very bad mood . . ." diary, 17 February 1862, ibid. p. 148.

389   "intimate and communicative . . ." diary, 21 February 1862, ibid. p. 149.
"visit from Scharff . . . exchanged . . ." diary, 6 March 1862, ibid. p. 154.
"Scharff very loving . . ." diary, 12 March 1862, ibid. p. 155.
"I told all about my erotic time . . ." diary, 5 March 1862, ibid. p. 154.

391   "Sent letter . . ." diary, 15 September 1862, *Diaries*, p. 290.
"an insolent fool . . ." diary, 15 October 1863, ibid. p. 298.
"to his two dearest friends . . ." diary, 17 June 1863, *Dagbøger*, vol. v, p. 397.
"Scharff's passion for me . . ." diary, 27 August 1863, ibid. p. 413.

392   "I am not satisfied . . ." diary, 16 September 1863, ibid. p. 418.
"Felt old . . ." diary, 5 October 1863, ibid.
"visited Scharff, who gave me . . ." diary, 6 October 1863, ibid.
"Scharff has not . . ." diary, 13 November 1863, ibid. p. 426.

393   "an accident which . . ." Auguste Bournonville, *My Theatre Life*, translated by Patricia N. McAn-
drew, London 1979, p. 371.
"This tragedy . . ." ibid.
"The year is over . . ." diary, 31 December 1863, *Diaries*, p. 301.
"The bloody waves of war . . ." *Fairy Tale*, p. 495.

394   "it was against my heart . . . at present . . ." diary, 14 April 1864, *Diaries*, p. 307.
"Today I've been really . . ." diary, 16 April 1864, ibid. p. 308.
"Every day soldiers left . . ." *Fairy Tale*, p. 498.
"Mrs. Anholm's eldest son . . ." diary, 5 January 1864, *Diaries*, p. 303.

395   "I lost for a moment . . ." *Fairy Tale*, p. 501.
"I feel gloomy . . ." diary, 24 January 1864, *Diaries*, p. 305.
"overwhelmed and bitterly aware . . ." diary, 29 January 1864, ibid. p. 306.
"Now I'm sitting at home . . ." diary, 31 January 1864, ibid.
"the past year . . ." diary, 1 April 1864, ibid. p. 307.
"What a night . . ." diary, 18 April 1864, ibid. p. 309.
"Godless . . ." diary, 30 June 1864, *Dagbøger*, vol. vi, p. 81.
"I am disgruntled . . ." diary, 31 October 1864, ibid. p. 146.
"Last night I again dreamed . . ." diary, 31 October 1864, *Diaries*, p. 310.

396   "the darkest, gloomiest . . ." *Fairy Tale*, p. 503.
"For more than a year . . ." ibid. p. 504.

397   "Especially cheerful . . ." diary, 4 February 1865, *Diaries*, p. 312.

22   ALADDIN'S PALACE OF THE PRESENT, 1865–1869

page 400   "a handsome man . . ." Edmund Gosse, *Two Visits to Denmark*, London 1911, p. 98.
"through the vague land . . ." ibid. p. 96.

400 "May God protect . . ." HCA to Martin Henriques, 25 December 1865, *H. C. Andersens Breve til Thérèse og Martin R. Henriques 1860–75*, edited by H. Topsøe-Jensen, Copenhagen 1932, p. 34.
"a miniature . . ." Edmund Gosse, *Two Visits to Denmark*, London 1911, p. 96.
"showing off . . ." ibid. p. 100.

401 "along with some flowers . . ." diary, 2 April 1868, *Diaries*, p. 339.

403 "A big unpleasant argument . . ." diary, 14 June and 13 June 1870, ibid. p. 359.
"When I consider . . ." Rigmor Stampe, *H. C. Andersen og hans nærmeste omgang*, Copenhagen 1918, p. 265.

404 "How happy you are . . ." HCA to Thérèse Henriques, 27 October 1865, *H. C. Andersens Breve til Thérèse og Martin R. Henriques 1860–75*, edited by H. Topsøe-Jensen, Copenhagen 1932, p. 24.
"Mrs. Henriques . . ." diary, 1 December 1870, *Diaries*, p. 367.
"got an excellent pair . . ." diary, 31 January 1866, ibid. p. 323.
"Felt like an old man . . ." diary, 22 January 1866, ibid. p. 318.
"going-away party . . ." diary, 24 January 1866, ibid. p. 319.

405 "when I went out . . ." diary, 25 January 1866, ibid.
"a perfect faun . . ." Robert Lytton to Wilfrid Blunt, 18 August 1866, quoted in *Bredsdorff*, p. 360.
"like going from the Middle Ages . . ." *Fairy Tale*, p. 530.
"wandered all morning . . ." diary, 21 July 1866, *Diaries*, p. 325.
"during the entire trip . . ." diary, 22 July 1866, ibid. p. 327.
"don't feel quite well . . ." diary, 24 July 1866, ibid.
"Every new sound . . ." diary, 14 August 1866, *Dagbøger*, vol. VII, p. 168.

406 "they were, by the way . . ." diary, 16 January 1866, *Diaries*, p. 316.

407 "I have had to invest . . ." HCA to J. P. E. Hartmann, 16 October 1866, *Breve* II, vol. II, p. 559.
"I think Death . . ." HCA to Henriette Collin, 8 January 1867, *E. Collin*, vol. IV, p. 5.
"Robert Watt told me . . ." diary, 17 April 1867, *Dagbøger*, vol. VII, p. 267.
"with spirit . . ." *Fairy Tale*, p. 548.

408 "Went out to see Watt . . ." diary, 3 May 1867, *Diaries*, p. 330.
"who told about new adventures . . . I wonder . . ." diary, 5 May 1867, ibid. p. 331.

410 "endlessly happy" diary, 12 December 1867, ibid. p. 338.
"near to sinking . . ." *Fairy Tale*, p. 557.
"new screw-propelled ship . . . The passengers . . . the sitting room . . ." diary, 11 December 1867, *Diaries*, pp. 337–8.
"the whole thing . . ." diary, 12 December 1867, ibid. p. 338.
"now ends the year . . ." diary, 31 December 1867, *Dagbøger*, vol. VII, p. 398.
"I however . . ." diary, 17 May 1868, ibid. vol. VIII, p. 69.

413 "I remember . . ." Horace Scudder to HCA, 25 October 1866, *Scudder*, p. 3.
"I consider it . . ." HCA to Horace Scudder, 12 November 1868, *Scudder*, p. 25.
"written so simply . . ." *Spectator*, 14 September 1872.
"I *do* like your fairy tales . . ." Anna Mary Livingstone to HCA, 1 January 1869, *Breve* I, p. 395.
"Don't you think . . . but he was not loved . . ." Annie Wood in *Temple Bar*, 1877, quoted in *Bredsdorff*, p. 294.

414 "All us older folks . . ." diary, 22 February 1872, *Diaries*, p. 373.
"it was extremely interesting . . ." diary, 19 February 1869, *Dagbøger*, vol. VIII, p. 179.
"be ready to have . . ." Georg Brandes to HCA, 10 July 1869, *Breve* I, p. 70.

415 "for true spiritual enrichment . . ." Georg Brandes to HCA, 10 July 1869, *Breve* I, p. 72.
"He who possesses . . ." Georg Brandes, *Eminent Authors of the Nineteenth Century*, New York 1886, p. 61.
"what author . . ." ibid. pp. 64–5.
"the cool, calm . . ." ibid. p. 102.
"I know no poet . . ." ibid.

416 "I am like water . . ." HCA to Edvard Collin, 8 September 1855, *E. Collin*, vol. II, p. 261.

417 "Brandes is a superb character . . ." diary, 9 August 1874, *Diaries*, p. 402.
"he is working for *free love* . . ." diary, 1 August 1874, ibid. p. 399.

417   "Finished the Brandes book . . ." diary, 4 August 1874, ibid. p. 400.
       "With the cleverness . . ." HCA to Georg Brandes, 13 July 1869, *Breve* II, vol. II, p. 598.

23   SO GREAT A LOVE OF LIFE, 1869–1875

page 418   "like an afterglow . . ." HCA to Horace Scudder, 6 September 1869, *Scudder*, p. 55.
       "in spite of all this . . ." HCA to Horace Scudder, 11 January 1870, ibid. p. 66.
       "I have felt myself oppressed . . ." HCA to Horace Scudder, 18 March 1870, ibid. p. 70.

419   "this is an advanced age . . ." HCA to Horace Scudder, 2 April 1870, ibid. p. 75.
       "so we'll never see each other again . . ." diary, 6 June 1870, *Diaries*, p. 358.
       "Thought, as always, of death . . ." diary, 6 June 1870, ibid. p. 357.
       "I'm sitting here . . ." diary, 14 September 1873, ibid. p. xviii.
       "He's now dust . . ." diary, 5 March 1872, ibid. p. 379.
       "the unhealthy despondency . . ." diary, 19 November 1870, ibid. p. 363.

420   "felt depressed . . ." diary, 11 November 1870, ibid. p. 361.
       "It's as if it were written . . ." diary, 18 August 1870, ibid. p. 360.

421   "One goes on living . . ." diary, 4 March 1873, *Dagbøger*, vol. X, p. 41.
       "The Collins have gone . . . In a sensual . . ." 27 November 1870, *Diaries*, p. 365.
       "If I were young and rich . . ." diary, 29 November 1870, ibid. p. 366.
       "I need not hide on these pages . . ." diary, 19 November 1870, ibid. p. 363.

422   "I'll be quickly forgotten . . ." diary, 24 November 1870, ibid. p. 364.
       "I can feel the old man in me . . ." diary, 23 April 1871, ibid. p. 368.
       "God has given me . . ." diary, 2 March 1871, *Dagbøger*, vol. IX, p. 29.
       "in keeping with my mood . . ." diary, 9 March 1871, ibid. p. 35.
       "I happened to push . . ." diary, 12 March 1871, ibid. p. 36.
       "I am living most comfortably" HCA to Horace Scudder, 2 May 1871, *Scudder*, p. 97.
       "his shabby, ungainly, slouching figure . . ." Annie Wood writing anonymously in the *Spectator*, 17 August 1875, quoted in *Bredsdorff*, p. 292.

423   "he liked to walk . . ." Annie Wood in *Temple Bar*, February 1875, quoted in *Bredsdorff*, p. 288.
       "he was perfectly regardless . . ." Annie Wood writing anonymously in the *Spectator*, 17 August 1875, quoted in ibid. p. 292.
       "he became silent . . ." ibid.
       " 'it made And'sen . . .' " ibid.
       "so absurd in their expression . . ." Annie Wood in *Temple Bar*, February 1875, quoted in *Bredsdorff*, p. 289.
       "When the drawing room was full . . ." ibid. p. 289.

424   "by the united influence . . ." ibid. p. 290.
       "Nothing pleases Andersen so truly . . ." ibid. p. 288.
       "a child, according to . . ." Annie Wood writing anonymously in the *Spectator*, 17 August 1875, quoted in *Bredsdorff*, p. 292.
       "At 2 o'clock I drove to my new home . . ." diary, 23 October 1871, *Dagbøger*, vol. VII, p. 345.

425   "We are having . . ." HCA to Horace Scudder, 10 December 1871, *Scudder*, p. 112.
       "grey and wet . . . the fog . . ." HCA to Horace Scudder, 9 February 1872, ibid. p. 118.

426   "felt decrepit . . ." diary, 24 February 1872, *Diaries*, p. 374.
       "feeling old and weary . . ." diary, 30 June 1872, ibid. p. 380.
       "finished and well-rounded" diary, 11 July 1872, ibid. p. 382.
       "quite brilliant" diary, 12 July 1872, ibid. p. 383.
       "in it I have the professor . . ." diary, 19 July 1872, ibid. p. 384.
       "old, feeble . . ." Edmund Gosse, *Two Visits to Denmark*, London 1911, p. 96.
       "there appeared . . ." ibid. pp. 98–101.

427   "decided that the great man . . ." ibid. p. 102.

427   "really fascinated him" diary, 19 July 1872, *Diaries*, p. 384.

430   "received with extraordinary sympathy . . ." HCA to Edmund Gosse, 8 December 1872, *Breds-dorff*, p. 298.

431   "the only carriage . . ." diary, 23 January 1873, *Diaries*, p. 389.
      "Dr. Voss came . . ." diary, 19 January 1873, ibid. p. 386.
      "it seemed to me . . ." diary, 24 January 1873, ibid. p. 390.
      "my recuperation . . ." HCA to Horace Scudder, 26 May 1873, *Scudder*, p. 133.

432   "in a weak and ruined state" HCA to Horace Scudder, 6 November 1873, ibid. p. 138.
      "I am more depressed . . ." HCA to Henriette Collin, 3 September 1873, *E. Collin*, vol. IV, p. 261.
      "it was a great . . ." diary, 6 October 1873, *Diaries*, p. 393.
      "this moved me deeply" diary, 17 April 1873, *Dagbøger*, vol. x, p. 163.
      "I even knew his escort . . ." diary, 1 June 1867, ibid. vol. VII, pp. 297–8.
      "he is cordial . . ." diary, 17 April 1873, ibid. vol. x, p. 163.
      "My convalescence . . ." HCA to Horace Scudder, 27 March 1874, *Scudder*, p. 143.

433   "No fairy tales . . ." HCA to Dorothea Melchior, *Breve* II, vol. II, p. 698, translated in *Hans Christian Andersen: Danish Writer and Citizen of the World*, edited by Sven Hakon Rossel, Amsterdam and Atlanta 1996, p. 119.
      "the scissors move rapidly . . ." Annie Wood writing anonymously in the *Spectator*, 17 August 1875, quoted in *Bredsdorff*, p. 289.

435   "As I entered . . ." Edmund Gosse, *Two Visits to Denmark*, London 1911, pp. 238–9.
      "affectionate . . ." ibid. p. 302.
      "it was thought . . ." ibid.
      "My strength is increasing . . ." HCA to Horace Scudder, 24 July 1874, *Scudder*, p. 147.

436   "Mrs. Melchior is kind . . ." diary, 8 August 1874, *Diaries*, p. 402.
      "Boring out here . . ." diary, 16 August 1874, ibid. p. 406.
      "I don't want to be beholden . . ." diary, 5 August 1874, ibid. p. 401.
      "I got started on my plaint . . ." diary, 6 October 1873, ibid. p. 393.
      "have been on my way . . ." diary, 19 July 1872, ibid. p. 384.
      "there is a strange, febrile resentment . . ." diary, 6 August 1874, ibid. p. 401.
      "the politest man . . ." G. W. Griffin, *My Danish Days*, Philadelphia 1875, p. 223.
      "deep down inside . . ." diary, 13 August 1874, *Diaries*, p. 405.

437   "because it reminds me . . ." diary, 29 May 1875, *Dagbøger*, vol. x, p. 453.
      "Only country quiet . . ." HCA to Carl Alexander von Sachsen-Weimar-Eisenach, 7 May 1875, *Weimar*, p. 258.
      "his arms full of bouquets . . ." George Browning, *A Few Personal Recollections of Hans Christian Andersen*, London 1875, p. 5.
      "*Hans Andersen*, the son of the cobbler . . ." *Daily News*, 5 April 1875.

439   "My birthday . . ." HCA to Carl Alexander von Sachsen-Weimar-Eisenach, 7 May 1875, *Weimar*, p. 258.
      "Lord! Lord! . . ." diary, 14 June 1875, *Diaries*, p. 426.
      "warm, incomparably lovely summer weather" diary, 16 July 1875, ibid. p. 431.
      "a miraculous, lovely sleep . . ." diary, 19 July 1875, ibid.
      "a silk-clad young girl . . ." diary, 21 July 1875, ibid. p. 433.

440   "He felt very tired . . ." diary, 29 July 1875, ibid. p. 436.
      "He says . . ." diary, 31 July 1875, ibid. p. 437.
      "a little smile . . ." diary, 2 August 1875, ibid.
      "I should like to end . . ." Edvard Collin, *H. C. Andersen og det Collinske Hus*, Copenhagen 1929 (second edition), p. 312.

SELECT BIBLIOGRAPHY

Adam International Review, nos. 248–9, 1955.

Albertsen, Leif Ludwig, *On the Threshold of a Golden Age: Denmark Around 1800*, Copenhagen 1979.

Allingham, William, *A Diary*, London 1907.

Hans Christian Andersen Center, *Hans Christian Andersen, A Poet in Time: Papers from the Second International Hans Christian Andersen Conference*, edited by Johan de Mylius, Aage Jørgensen and Viggo Hjornager Pedersen, Odense 1999.

Anderseniana, first series, 1–13 (1933–1946); second series, 1–6 (1947–1969); third series, 1–4 (1970–1986). Published annually since 1987. (Especially useful articles are quoted individually.)

Ashton, Rosemary, *George Eliot: A Life*, London 1996.

Auden, W. H., "Introduction to the Tales of Grimm and Andersen," in *Forewords and Afterwords*, New York 1973.

Bettelheim, Bruno, *The Uses of Enchantment*, London 1978.

Bille, C. S. A., and N. Bøgh (eds.), *Breve til Hans Christian Andersen*, Copenhagen 1877.

Blicher, Steen Steensen, *The Diary of a Parish Clerk and Other Stories*, translated by Paula Hostrup-Jessen, introduced by Margaret Drabble, London 1996.

———. *Memoirs and Letters of Charles Boner*, London 1871.

Bournonville, Auguste, *My Theatre Life*, translated by Patricia N. McAndrew, London 1979.

Boyle, Nicholas, *Goethe: The Poet and the Age*, vol. I, Oxford 1991.

Brandes, Edvard, "H. C. Andersen Personlighed og Værk," in *Litterære Tendenser*, edited by C. Bergstroem-Nielsen, Copenhagen 1968.

Brandes, Georg, *Eminent Authors of the Nineteenth Century*, New York 1886.

Bredsdorff, Elias, *H. C. Andersen og Charles Dickens: Et Venskab og dets Opløsning*, Copenhagen 1951.

———. *H. C. Andersen og England*, Copenhagen 1954.

———. *Hans Christian Andersen: A Biography*, Oxford 1975.

———. "H. C. Andersen og Mathilda Barck," in *Anderseniana*, 3/2, 1975.

———. "Spørg Ottilie om hun kan huske den lille Skomagersøn fra Odense," in *Anderseniana*, 3/4, 1983.

Brix, Hans, *H. C. Andersen og hans Eventyr*, Copenhagen 1907.

Browning, Elizabeth Barrett, *Last Poems*, London 1861.

———. *The Letters of Elizabeth Barrett Browning*, edited by F. G. Kenyon, London 1897.

Browning, George, *A Few Personal Recollections of Hans Christian Andersen*, London 1875.

Bulman, Joan, *Jenny Lind: A Biography*, London 1956.

Cairns, David, *Berlioz*, vol. I: *The Making of an Artist* (second edition), London 1999.

———. *Berlioz*, vol. II: *Servitude and Greatness*, London 1999.

Chesterton, G. K., *The Crimes of England*, London 1915.

Christensen, Jens, *Rural Denmark 1750–1980*, Copenhagen 1983.

Clute, John, and John Grant, *The Encyclopaedia of Fantasy*, London 1997.

Collin, Edvard, *H. C. Andersen og det Collinske Hus* (second edition), Copenhagen 1929.

Dal, Erik, "Research on Hans Christian Andersen: Trends, results and desiderata," in *Orbis Litterarum*, XVII, 3–4, 1962.

———. "Omkring tre nyfundne breve til Ludvig Müller," in *Anderseniana*, 3, 4/5, 1984.

Danish Ministry of Foreign Affairs, *Danish Journal: Hans Christian Andersen* (Centenary Issue), Copenhagen 1975.

Detering, Heinrich, *Intellectual Amphibia*, Odense 1991.

Dickens, Charles, "Frauds on the Fairies," in *Household Words*, London 1853.

Dickens, Henry, *The Recollections of Sir Henry Dickens KC*, London 1934.

Dreyer, Kirsten, and Flemming Hovmann, "Et overset venskab: H. C. Andersens og Otto Müllers brevveksling," in *Anderseniana*, 1993.

Journals and Correspondence of Lady Eastlake, edited by Charles Eastlake Smith, London 1895.

Faaborg, N. L., *Grafiske portrætter af H. C. Andersen*, Copenhagen 1971.

Gay, Peter, *The Naked Heart: The Bourgeois Experience—Victoria to Freud*, vol. IV, London 1996.

Glyn Jones, W., *Denmark: A Modern History*, Beckenham 1986.

Gosse, Edmund, *Two Visits to Denmark*, London 1911.

Griffin, G. W., *My Danish Days*, Philadelphia 1875.

Le Guin, Ursula, *The Language of the Night: Essays on Fantasy and Science Fiction*, London 1979.

Hansen, Albert, "H. C. Andersen. Beweis seiner Homosexualität," in *Jahrbuch für sexuelle Zwischenstufen* III, Leipzig 1901.

Hauch, Carsten, *Slottet ved Rhinen*, Copenhagen 1845.

Heilbut, Anthony, *Thomas Mann: Eros and Literature*, London 1996.

Heltoft, Kjeld, *Hans Christian Andersen as an Artist*, Copenhagen 1977.

Helweg, Hjalmar, *H. C. Andersen: En psykiatrisk Studie*, Copenhagen 1927.

Catalog of the Jean Hersholt Collection of Hans Christian Andersen Manuscripts and First Editions, Washington 1954.

Hoffmann, E. T. A., *Nutcracker*, translated by Ralph Mannheim, London 1984.

———. *Selected Writings of E. T. A. Hoffmann*, translated and edited by Leonard J. Kent and Elizabeth C. Knight, Chicago 1969.

Holland, Henry Scott, and W. S. Rockstro, *Memoir of Madame Jenny Lind Goldschmidt*, London 1891.

Holmes, Richard, *Coleridge: Early Visions*, London 1989.

Howitt, Mary, *An Autobiography*, edited by Margaret Howitt, London 1889.

Hughes, Kathryn, *George Eliot: The Last Victorian*, London 1998.

James, Henry, *William Wentmore Story and his Friends*, Edinburgh and London 1903.

Johnson, Paul, *The Birth of the Modern: World Society 1815–30*, London 1991.

Jurgensen, Knud Arne, *The Bournonville Ballets, a Photographic Record*, London 1987.

Kierkegaard, Søren, *Af en endnu Levendes Papirer*, Copenhagen 1838.

Kjolbe, Bente, *Hans Christian Andersens Kopenhagen*, Copenhagen 1992.

Kleist, Heinrich von, Ludwig Tieck, and E. T. A. Hoffmann, *Six German Romantic Tales*, translated by Ronald Taylor, London 1985.

Kofoed, Niels, "The Red and the Blue Eros: Color Symbols in Hans Christian Andersen's Early Production," in *Anderseniana*, 1980.

———. *H. C. Andersen og B. S. Ingemann Et livsvarigt venskab*, Copenhagen 1992.

———. "The Arabesque and the Grotesque: Hans Christian Andersen Decomposing the World of Poetry," article in preparation for publication.

Edward Lear: Selected Letters, edited by Vivien Noakes, Oxford 1988.

Lederer, Wolfgang, *The Kiss of the Snow Queen: Hans Christian Andersen and Man's Redemption by Women*, Berkeley, Los Angeles, London 1986.

The Lost Letters of Jenny Lind, edited by W. Porter Ware and Thaddeus Lockard Jr., London 1966.

Memoir of Jenny Lind, London 1847.

Lindiana: An Interesting Narrative of the Life of Jenny Lind, London 1847.

Lissmann, Berthold, *Clara Schumann: Ein Kunstlerleben*, Leipzig 1902.

Meyer, Michael, *Ibsen*, London 1992.

Mary Russell Mitford, Correspondence with Charles Boner and John Ruskin, edited by Elizabeth Lee, London 1914.

Molesworth, Robert, *An Account of Denmark As It Was In The Year 1692*, London 1694.

Monrad, Kasper, and Henning Rovsing Olsen, *The Golden Age of Danish Painting*, Copenhagen 1994.

Mortensen, Klaus P., *Svanen og Skyggen—historien om unge Andersen*, Copenhagen 1989.

———. "Demons of the Golden Age: Hans Christian Andersen and Søren Kierkegaard," in *Thorvaldsen's Museum Bulletin*, 1997.

Mylius, Johan de, *The Voice of Nature in Hans Christian Andersen's Fairy Tales*, Odense 1989.

———. *H. C. Andersen—liv og værk En Tidsval*, Copenhagen 1993.

Nielsen, Erling, *Hans Christian Andersen*, Copenhagen 1983.

Nielsen, Kirsten Grau, "Fru Ottilies dagbog, den junge Comediantspiller," in *Anderseniana*, 1991.

Overskou, Thomas, *Af mit Liv og min Tid*, Copenhagen 1868.

Oxenvad, Niels, "H. C. Andersen i Svendborg 1830–og i 1836, Omdatering af et dagbogsfragment," in *Anderseniana*, 1989.

———. *H. C. Andersen Et Liv i Billeder*, Copenhagen 1995.

Poulsen, Henrik C., *Det Rette Udseende. Fotografernes H. C. Andersen*, Copenhagen 1996.

Repholtz, Albert, *Thorvaldsen og Nysø*, Copenhagen 1911.

Robb, Graham, *Balzac*, London 1994.

Rosen, Wilhelm von, "Venskabets Mysterier," in *Anderseniana*, 3, 3, 1980.

Rossel, Sven Hakon, *A History of Danish Literature*, Nebraska 1992.

——— (ed.) *Hans Christian Andersen: Danish Writer and Citizen of the World*, Amsterdam and Atlanta 1996.

Scavenius, Bente (ed.), *The Golden Age of Denmark: Art and Culture 1800–1850*, Copenhagen 1994.

———. *The Golden Age Revisited: Art and Culture in Denmark 1800–1850*, Copenhagen 1996.

Simpson, M. C. M., *Many Memories of Many People*, London 1898.

Smidt, Claus, and Mette Winge, *Strolls in the Golden Age City of Copenhagen*, Copenhagen 1996.

Spink, Reginald, *Hans Christian Andersen and His World*, London 1972.

Stampe, Rigmor, *H. C. Andersen og hans nærmeste omgang*, Copenhagen 1918.

Taylor, D. J., *Thackeray*, London 1999.

Terry, Walter, *The King's Ballet Master: A Biography of Denmark's Auguste Bournonville*, New York 1979.

The Letters and Private Papers of William Makepeace Thackeray, London 1945.

Thiele, J. M., *The Life of Thorvaldsen*, translated by M. R. Barnard, London 1865.

———. *Af Mit Livs Aarbøger 1795–1826*, Copenhagen 1873.

Wollstonecraft, Mary, *Letters written during a short residence in Sweden, Norway and Denmark*, London 1796.

INDEX

Italicized page numbers refer to illustrations.

A NOTE ABOUT THE AUTHOR

Jackie Wullschlager is a writer and critic whose articles and reviews appear regularly in the *Financial Times*. She is the author of one highly praised earlier book, *Inventing Wonderland*, and lives in London with her husband and three small children.

A NOTE ON THE TYPE

This book was set in Caslon, a typeface originally designed by the first William Caslon (1692–1766). This version of the type was designed by Carol Twombley for the Adobe Corporation and released in 1990.

Composed by North Market Street Graphics,
Lancaster, Pennsylvania
Printed and bound by Quebecor World,
Fairfield, Pennsylvania
Designed by Peter A. Andersen